China

From Permanent Revolution to Counter-Revolution

John Peter Roberts

London

China: From Permanent Revolution to Counter-Revolution
by John Peter Roberts

First published by Wellred Books February 2016

Foreword by Fred Weston

Typeset by Wellred Books

Cover design by Nicholas Baldion
We Don't Know What We Are Making Red/ Middle of Tripych, 2015
Oil and Gold Leaf on Board
Private Collection
www.nicholasbaldion.com

Printed by Lightning Source, London, England.

British Library cataloguing in Publication Data

A catalogue record for this book is available from the British Library.

ISBN: 978 1 900 007 63 4

United Kingdom Distribution:

Wellred Books
PO Box 50525
London
E14 6WG

Email: books@wellredbooks.net

Wellred UK online Sales:
www.wellredbooks.net

United States Distribution:

Wellred Books
PO Box 1575
New York
NY 10013

Email: sales@wellredusa.com

Wellred U.S.A. online sales:
www.marxistbooks.com

Dedication

November 12, 1905. St Petersburg Soviet of Workers' Deputies:

> "A middle-aged woman weaver from Maxwell's factory rose to speak. She had a fine, open face; she wore a faded cotton dress although it was late autumn. Her hand trembled with excitement as she nervously fingered her collar. Her voice had a ringing, inspired, unforgettable quality. '... we aren't afraid. We're prepared to die, but we'll get the eight-hour day. We'll fight to the end. Victory or death! Long live the eight-hour day!'" (Leon Trotsky, *1905*, Ch8, www.marxists.org)

Nameless heroine of the international working class, living confirmation of the theory of the permanent revolution, this book is dedicated to you.

Acknowledgements

My thanks to Kimberley Manning and Pun Ngai for their spirit of generosity in sending me copies of their many publications.

Thanks to Niklas and Guy at Wellred for their help in transmuting a manuscript into a finished book.

To Fred Weston for taking the time to read the manuscript and advising, chapter by chapter, on political content and presentation.

Finally, and most important, a big thank you to my wife, Diane, for stimulating discussions on the concepts and ideas contained in this book and then undertaking the enormous task of proofreading and correcting the manuscript.

Contents

Chapter 4

The Rise of the Second Chinese Revolution

Chapter 5

The Defeat of the Second Chinese Revolution

Chapter 6

From the Canton "Commune" to the Jiangxi "Soviet"

Chapter 7

From the Jiangxi "Soviet" to Yenan

Chapter 8

Yenan, the Second United Front, and the War against Japan

Chapter 9

The Final Collapse of the KMT: the CCP Assumes Power

Chapter 10

The New Democracy

Chapter 11

The Unexpectedly Short Life of the New Democracy

Foreword

In 1949 the coming to power in China of the Communist Party under the leadership of Mao Zedong prepared the ground for the liberation of over half a billion workers and peasants from the yolk of landlordism and imperialism. By the mid-1950s not only had the basic task of the bourgeois democratic revolution been carried out – i.e. the abolition of landlordism, the end to colonial rule, genuine national unification and the establishment of the basic conditions for the development of capitalism – but capitalism itself had been snuffed out.

This development reconfirmed the basic idea developed by Leon Trotsky of the Permanent Revolution that the capitalist class in underdeveloped countries, having arrived late on the scene of history, was incapable of carrying out its own, bourgeois, revolution. It remained tied to the feudal landlords on the one hand and subservient to its imperialist masters on the other.

In the Russian Revolution the Menshevik position was that all countries had to pass through a democratic bourgeois stage before they could move towards socialism. This idea stated that a period of capitalist development was first required to build up industry and with it a modern working class. Only after such a period would it be possible to contemplate struggling for socialism. That explains why the Mensheviks sided with the Russian bourgeoisie and ended up in the camp of the counter-revolution.

The weakness in this idea was that it was based on a narrow national view of each country, which ignored the context of the global situation where the rise of powerful imperialist capitalist countries dominated the world market. This changed the conditions in which the fledgling nation al bourgeois classes could develop in the underdeveloped countries into modern capitalist ruling classes.

If Lenin and Trotsky had adhered to this view, they would not have insisted on all power passing to the soviets, i.e. to workers' power, but would have sought an accommodation with a "progressive wing" of the Russian bourgeoisie and would have limited the workers' organisations to being an opposition within a bourgeois-democratic set up.

The reason why Lenin and Trotsky did not go down this road is that they understood full well that in the conditions of Russia in 1917 this would not have been possible. Permanent Revolution, i.e. the revolution beginning as bourgeois-democratic but passing immediately to the socialist tasks under the leadership of the working class is what happened in Russia.

In spite of these essential lessons of the October Revolution, the Communist International under the leadership of Stalin reverted to the Menshevik outlook of "stages"; the first being the bourgeois revolution which would open up the possibility of capitalist development and only years later would this prepare the ground for the second stage, the socialist revolution.

It was this idea that explains the role played by the official Communist Parties in Spain during the Civil War, and in Italy and France at the end of the Second World War. The Communist Parties raised the illusion that a "progressive" bourgeoisie existed, whose task it was to develop society. The defeat of the Spanish workers in the 1930s and of the Italian and French workers at the end of the War is the price the working class paid for this erroneous idea.

By the time the Chinese Communist Party (CCP) took power in 1949 its leadership was steeped in this idea that after taking power the "bourgeois-democratic" stage would begin. That explains why Mao initially did not move towards the abolition of capitalism. He sought sections of the Chinese bourgeoisie with whom the workers and peasants could form an alliance.

This well-researched book by John Roberts provides source material which confirms that this was the perspective that Mao sought to act on post-1949. The problem Mao faced was that the Chinese bourgeoisie was not willing to oblige him in his perspective. The bulk of the Chinese bourgeoisie backed Chiang Kai-shek and fled with him as the Red Army advanced. Those that did remain tried to sabotage any attempt of the CCP to carry out genuine reform.

The key element in understanding how the CCP ended up abolishing capitalism in China is to be found in the fact that it had state power, i.e. the "armed bodies of men" were not the police and soldiers of a bourgeois state, but the "People's Liberation Army", mainly a peasant army under the control of the Communist Party. This meant the old semi-feudal/bourgeois state had been smashed by the advancing forces of Mao.

This state attempted to reach a compromise with the bourgeois elements, but this failed to materialise, not due to any conscious move on the part of the Communist Party leaders towards "socialism" but because the interests of the peasants and workers were irreconcilable with those of the corrupt Chinese national bourgeoisie. Step by step Mao found himself having to take over the whole economy and by the mid-1950s China had become what we would term as a "deformed workers' state". By this is meant a state where the economic base of a workers' state has been established, i.e. the expropriation of the landlords and the capitalists, state ownership of the means of production and centralised planning, but it is "deformed" because the workers do not hold state power directly, do not have control over the system as a whole.

Initially the planned economy proved to be enormously beneficial to the working masses of China. John Roberts highlights throughout this book the immense progress, for example, in the field of women's liberation, a key indicator in any revolution of the progress of working people in general. He also underlines the movements forward and the movements backwards in the winning of women's rights, in line with the general ebbs and flows of the revolution itself.

The abolition of capitalism in China under Mao was achieved in spite of his initial perspectives and not because of them. Mao found that in order to carry out even the most basic of reforms he had to move against the capitalists. But what came into being was a system that was governed and controlled by the bureaucratic caste at the helm of the state. In essence it was the same system that existed under Stalin in the Soviet Union, a tremendously progressive state-owned planned economy, but which was doomed to crisis at some point in its development under the control of the bureaucracy.

The reasons for this can be found in Leon Trotsky's *The Revolution Betrayed*, an analysis of the Soviet Union in the 1930s, in which he raised the perspective of an inevitable crisis of that system, which would either lead to a movement of the working class to gain political power or, failing that, to a collapse of the system and a return to capitalism. With great foresight, Trotsky predicted that the forces of the bourgeois counter-revolution would come from within the "Communist Party" itself.

Trotsky's predictions took several decades before they were proved correct. After the Second World War the Soviet Union was immensely strengthened. Its economy had expanded many times over and it had taken control of Eastern Europe. To its east the Chinese Revolution successfully put in place a system similar to its own. This was followed by the Cuban revolution and then the victory of Vietnam over US imperialism. Not only was the Soviet Union strengthened materially, but its authority within the working class internationally was also enhanced. The workers of the world felt that the Soviet Union was exporting revolution everywhere.

However, all of this only served to hide the real process taking place. The Soviet economy, from the spectacular growth of the 1930s, was beginning to slow down and gradually grind to a halt, and eventually in the 1970s it was close to zero. It was this that determined the eventual collapse and the chaotic return to capitalism post-1991.

In China, the move to abolish capitalism in the 1950s was not a conscious process, but was determined by objective factors. Once that process was in place, however, the rising Chinese bureaucracy became conscious of where they were going. In doing so, they also attempted to remove from the history books their previous positions in an attempt to show that all along Mao knew that his aim was socialist revolution, as John Roberts shows by comparing quotes in later versions of official party texts with previous versions.

The return to capitalism in the recent period also did not start off as a conscious choice but came on the back of the worldwide crisis of Stalinism and the difficulties China was facing internally. Initially, the policy adopted by Deng was similar to the New Economic Policy the Bolsheviks were forced to adopt in the early 1920s. In an isolated backward economy, with international socialist revolution having been defeated in the immediate period after World War One, Lenin understood that some concessions to market methods were necessary, albeit within the context of overall state control of the commanding heights of the economy and with strict control over foreign trade.

However, it is one thing for a relatively healthy workers' state to adopt such policies, it is a completely different scenario when a privileged bureaucratic elite, standing above the working class, adopts the same policy. Trotsky explained that within the privileged bureaucracy eventually the desire would grow, not only to enjoy the fruits of their position within society, but also to be able to pass these onto their offspring, and that would only be possible by ceasing to be merely privileged administrators and becoming owners of the means of production. That is what we see taking place in China today.

This book provides much information on what really happened in the build up to 1949 and the period that followed. It shows how a Stalinist party, whose proclaimed aim was to achieve the "first stage", bourgeois-democratic revolution, was forced in spite of itself to move very quickly to the "second stage" and abolish capitalism. This was a brilliant confirmation in practice of Trotsky's theory of the Permanent Revolution, albeit in a deformed manner. The more recent return to capitalism, i.e. counter-revolution, also confirms

Trotsky's perspectives as developed in his classic *The Revolution Betrayed*. Thus the title, "China: from Permanent Revolution to Counter-Revolution", encapsulates the essence of 90 years of Chinese history and reveals what really happened.

Today China is a very different country to what it was in 1949. Powerful means of production have been developed and with it has come into being the biggest working class ever seen in history. But a capitalist China will inevitably be affected by the contradictions of capitalist production. Then the Chinese workers will seek an alternative and will begin by looking at their own past history. They will need to unbury the truth, which is covered in a mountain of official mythology, to do so. This book is part of that process of unburying.

Fred Weston
London, 26th October 2015

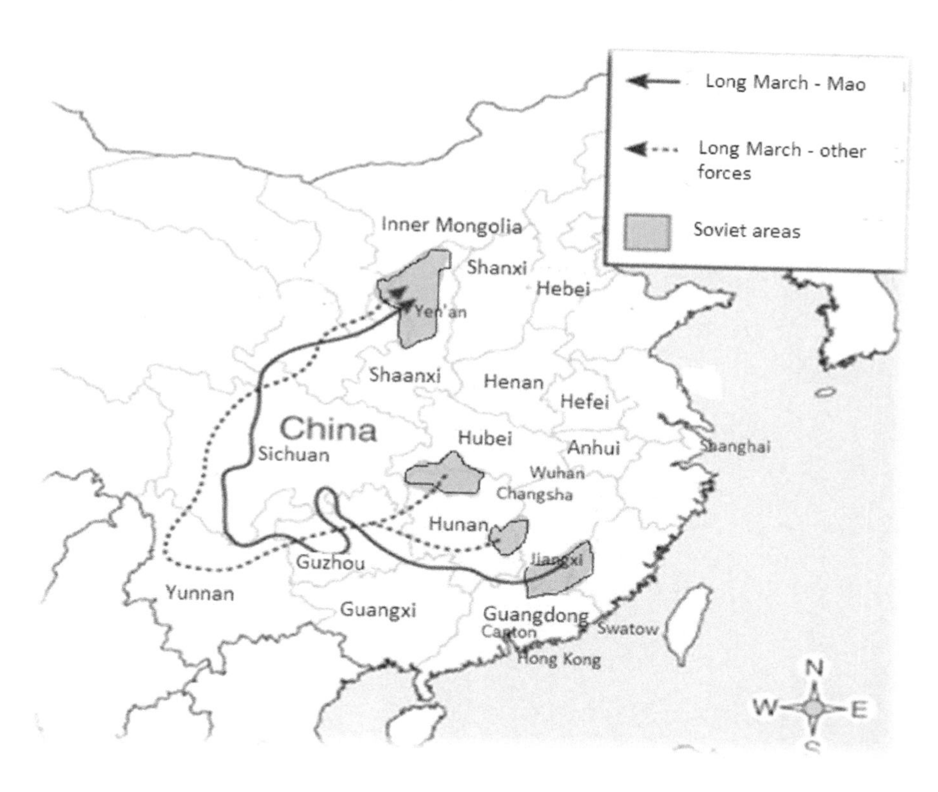

Map of China – showing major Soviet areas remaining after the 4th "bandit extermination campaign", at start of Long March (1934-35)

NOTE: Areas of the Soviets are not to scale

Introduction

Despite its many faults and failings, the Chinese Revolution is second only to the Bolshevik Revolution of 1917 as the greatest event of the 20th century and will have even greater impact on the 21st century. In 1949 the People's Liberation Army (PLA) led by the Chinese Communist Party (CCP), took power and within a short span of time snuffed out capitalism and landlordism. Hundreds of millions of human beings threw off their humiliating and degrading yoke and entered world history as citizens of an independent country. The establishment of the People's Republic of China marked a monumental change in world history.

The sweep to victory of the PLA across the Chinese mainland was due to the collapse of apparently well-trained, well-armed, and well-funded Nationalist armies. The speed of the Communist victory stunned the bourgeoisie in Western Europe and the USA. The victorious Chinese Communist Party emerged as the only real power in the land despite its programme of 'revolution by stages' and its declared aim of a Popular Front government for a prolonged period with no central planning or state ownership of the key sectors of the economy.

Petty-bourgeois politicians, some claiming to be Marxists, were dazzled and hurried to hail Mao success. This book argues that the victory of the Chinese revolution under the leadership of a Stalinist Party was possible due to the conjuncture of specific and unusual circumstances. American and British imperialisms were unable to intervene directly due to the wave of anti-war sentiment at home and, particularly, amongst the very troops that would have been used against the PLA.

Also of enormous importance was the existence of a mighty workers' state, the USSR, bordering China, which gave massive military aid to the PLA at a crucial stage in the military struggle against Chiang Kai-shek and the nationalist Kuo Min Tang (KMT). The bourgeois regime of Chiang was so utterly corrupt and degenerate that it was unable to mobilise any serious resistance to the PLA. At the same time, and possibly most importantly, there was a massive wave of peasant revolts in KMT-controlled territories against starvation, landlordism, and corruption. The Communist Party, as the party of opposition, rode to power on this upsurge.

The Stalinist theory of Socialism in One Country gave the CCP a narrow nationalist outlook. A revolutionary Marxist perspective would have been for China and Russia to have come together in a Socialist Federation with the countries of Eastern Europe to develop an international plan of production using, in a combined and rational manner, the human and material resources of all these countries. Instead the nationalistic outlook of both the Chinese and Soviet bureaucracies eventually brought about the immensely damaging Sino-Soviet conflict as each sought to protect its interests in its own way.

In spite of its shortcomings, the CCP managed to achieve what the effete Chinese bourgeoisie had abysmally failed to do, to create genuine national unity and a modern state. The growth of the Chinese economy after 1949 was spectacular, amply demonstrated by the relative economic development of China and India in the thirty year period after the revolution. In 1950 shortly after India acquired independence, its GDP per person led that of China by 36%. The Indian economy grew by about 7% annually, but by 1980 the GDP per person in China was 12% higher than in India, subsequently bounding even further ahead because China had a centralised, state-owned, planned economy that laid the economic base upon which modern China rests today.

When taking power in 1949, the PLA and CCP were peasant in composition with a petty-bourgeois ideology, and completely isolated from the urban working class. Mao Zedong and the CCP would construct a state in China in the image of Stalinist Russia – a monstrous bureaucratic caricature of a workers' state. A workers' state deformed from birth but a workers' state nevertheless. There were neither Soviets, nor workers' control, nor real labour unions independent of the State, nor an authentic Marxist leadership. The most elementary conditions for workers' democracy were lacking right from its very beginning.

Such an event was a new and serious theoretical challenge for revolutionaries. The CCP had come to power espousing the Stalinist theory of stages, with the declared policy of establishing a bourgeois republic; and as part of that process it attempted, for example, to privatise the state-owned "Big Four" banks. Was this the way forward for the colonial revolution, had stagism trumped Trotsky's theory of permanent revolution?

The Russian Revolution of 1917 had clearly revealed the necessity of taking measures which were objectively socialist to solve the problems of Russia's democratic revolution. Since then the theory of the permanent revolution is often described as the process whereby revolutions in backward countries have a natural tendency to transcend the bourgeois-democratic phase and turn into socialist revolutions.

Is this what happened in China? If so, what was the process, and what was the nature of the regime between 1949 and the formation of a deformed workers' state in 1953? This book investigates and answers these questions.

The victory of the CCP resonated around the world and won many young people to Maoism. Closing their eyes to the lack of workers' democracy in China, they concluded that to be victorious, the Chinese CCP must have broken with Stalinism. Mao was prettified and romanticised, even by sections of the Trotskyist movement: Mao was presented as the Asian version of Fidel Castro, he had freed the CCP from the dominance of Stalin and the Comintern, he was the inspired leader of the Long March, he was responsible for developing the strategy of prolonged rural guerrilla warfare, and he had led the revolution that successfully transformed China. Mao, it seemed, was a new kind of Communist, a poet with an ideology firmly rooted in Chinese history. Was Mao despite his faults, a true revolutionary?

Even leading Marxists behaved as though hypnotised by Mao and serious differences over the causes and significance of Mao's victory resulted in considerable theoretical confusion. Unfortunately, the confusion did not remain in the realm of theory but became a serious practical problem for revolutionaries when determining what attitude to adopt towards the Maoist groups that mushroomed world-wide during the 1960s and 1970s.

If Maoism could actually make a revolution should Marxists give up the fight for a separate, revolutionary Bolshevik party? Was a Communist Party organised on Maoist lines an adequate instrument for achieving socialism? Was it better to act as a pressure group on existing leaderships, perhaps even merge with these forces? The same question is posed today in other forms: the Revolutionary Communist League (LCR), French section of the United Secretariat of the Fourth International have long believed the party that would make the socialist revolution in France would be the result of "recomposition" of the left of the labour movement.That in February 2009 the LCR determined to dissolve itself and launch a New Anti-Capitalist Party is simply this argument taken to its logical conclusion.

Popular Frontism was imposed on the world Communist movement by Stalin in the late 1930s, but its acceptance by Mao and the CCP has meant that it is still seen as a possible route to revolution. Today its legacy threatens to undermine the gains of the Venezuelan Revolution with calls from a section of the Bolivarian leadership for peaceful co-existence with the bourgeoisie, capitalists, bankers, and landowners who still control two thirds of the country's economy. This book assesses whether a Popular Front strategy was necessary for Mao's victory and the establishment of the People's Republic of China, or whether it delayed the establishment of the Chinese workers' state and laid the basis for a later return to capitalism.

The economic growth of China was stupendous but it was from a terribly low level. The outcome of the struggle between Russia, China and the capitalist countries was not determined by the rate of economic growth. Rather, it was determined by the relative total economic power of the two camps as expressed in material accumulation, technique, culture and, above all, the productivity of human labour. From this point of view we see at once the extreme disadvantage of both the Soviet Union and China. Direct military intervention in China in 1949 may have been impossible, but a greater danger remained – the economic pressure of imperialism expressed most clearly in the production of cheap, high quality goods.

The economic achievements in China were made despite the disruption of adventures such as the Great Leap Forward (1959-62), and the Cultural Revolution (1966-68). The Great leap Forward was responsible for a national famine in which as many as 20 million Chinese starved to death. The Cultural Revolution meant a fall of industrial production of about 15% between 1967 and 1968, producing a sharp fall in the living standards of the masses. Nevertheless, the economy recovered swiftly from these two major disruptions thanks to state planning and control.

Initially, although bureaucratic control restricted development, the planned economy rushed ahead. But the more sophisticated the economy became, the more the CCP became a fetter on its development. Within a generation, bureaucratic control had become an absolute brake on the productive forces. With the increasing complexity of the economy it was soon evident that a top-down, bureaucratic command system could not manage every detail. A steady decline in the efficiency of state planning, and a dramatic increase in waste and corruption were observed. This corruption has been a major factor in the internal decay of the CCP, many of whose members had plundered state resources on a vast scale for personal gain.

The CCP leadership twisted and turned, seeking one empiric solution after another to its economic problems. The one consistent feature was the determination of the bureaucracy not to surrender its privileges and positions of power, so one measure they could have taken to solve China's problems was ruled out – there would be no workers' democracy or mass participation in politics. The framework in which the changes took place ensured that each individual measure taken became a step towards capitalism.

This book describes how the CCP enacted a series of key decisions that meant a qualitative change in the nature of Chinese society. In the decade 1980-1989 the CCP ended the state monopoly of foreign trade and currency exchange, abolished state planning of the economy so that production for use was replaced by production for profit, and privatised the great bulk of state-owned enterprises retaining only those with strategic importance for the state. The Chinese Communist Party, while retaining the name "Communist" is, in fact, a bourgeois party. The return of capitalism is an inescapable fact and means the task of revolutionaries is a social revolution.

To be meaningful, any analysis of the Chinese Revolution, and Mao's role in it must face the living facts, whether desirable or undesirable, particularly the decisive influence of the conditions in which a revolution takes place. The specific contribution of Stalinism to the Chinese Revolution, the direction it imposed on events, and the consequences, must be recognised. Events must be seriously evaluated, their causes and effects analysed to obtain a correct understanding of the role of Stalinism in the development of the victorious Third Chinese Revolution, and then the subsequent return of capitalism.

This book addresses important issues for those interested in the processes of revolution and counter-revolution as they happened in China:

- How could how an essentially counter-revolutionary force with an explicitly class collaborationist strategy come to power in a peasant revolution in the era of imperialism?
- What were the motor factors which pushed the Mao regime, against its own predictions and wishes, to take measures which were objectively socialist and to establish the Chinese workers' state?
- The Third Chinese Revolution was a rigorous practical test of Trotsky's theory of permanent revolution and Mao's theory of uninterrupted revolution by stages. Which theory passed the test?
- The degeneration of the Chinese People's Republic to capitalism has been a second rigorous practical test of Trotsky's analyses. Has his prognosis that without a political revolution to overthrow the

regime, a Stalinist bureaucratic state would return to capitalism, been proved correct?

However, in addition to the above this book attempts something else. Before 1949 the peasant woman in China was especially oppressed; isolated in the family home not allowed to speak to any stranger, her feet physically deformed the better to control her, the subject of socially-approved continuous domestic violence, she was often treated no better than a domesticated animal. The Chinese Revolution, to which women made a substantial contribution, made big changes in the lives of Chinese women. This must be recognised and applauded. However, with the return to capitalism many of the gains made by Chinese women have been, and are being, taken away.

The social revolution cannot be achieved without the day-to-day struggle for women's advancement; this the ABC of women's liberation. The book will show that from an excellent start, the more the CCP became enmeshed in Popular Frontism the more ready it was to surrender women's liberation to the interests of the male peasant, who for many centuries considered his wife to be his property and little more than a beast of burden. Today, the CCP, despite its formal declarations, is sacrificing women's interests the better and faster to entrench capitalism in China.

This book advances the thesis that the policies a regime or political party adopts towards women is a direct measure of its revolutionary commitment. How the activities of the CCP impinged upon the mass of Chinese women is used as a measure of its socialist credentials.

Chapter 1

The First Chinese Revolution: Early Years of the Chinese Communist Party

1.1 Introduction

This chapter describes the conditions under which the Chinese peasants had lived for centuries and explains why they were the most rebellious on the planet. It also describes the development of the Chinese working class and how a group of dedicated revolutionaries inspired by the October Revolution and aided by the newly formed Communist International (Comintern, CI) founded the Chinese Communist Party (CCP).

The role of the Comintern is key to the history of the CCP because its representatives determined when and how the CCP was launched and what its structure, programme, strategy and tactics should be. They did this supported by the prestige of the October Revolution, the authority of Lenin, and the provision of substantial funds.

The Executive Committee of the Communist International (ECCI) under Zinoviev's leadership assessed the Kuomintang (KMT) as the most revolutionary of the bourgeois forces struggling against imperialism for national unity and independence. The ECCI accepted at face value, reports from China that the KMT had mass popular support and that the overwhelming majority, nine-tenths of the KMT rank and file, were workers and peasants ready to march hand-in-hand with the CCP. The ECCI concluded that working with the KMT could give the CCP ready access to those masses.

Only under severe pressure from the Communist International did the small group that was the emerging CCP agree to enter the KMT. Lenin had insisted that Communists active in national democratic revolutions must retain their political and organisational independence, but the CCP soon found that to follow the instructions of the ECCI and remain within the KMT, they had to sacrifice their political freedom.

1.2 Conditions for the Chinese Peasants

Typically the traditional Chinese village was dominated by a small number of families. In many villages the major landlord or his agent ('dog leg') was the nominal chief, and an unelected village government had the responsibility for collecting taxes, supplying labour for public works and keeping the peace with the right to arrest, try and punish (even execute) offenders. The rest of the population was kept subservient by the inculcation of Confucianism and a vigilante group (*ming tuan*) comprised of the sons of the gentry and hired thugs, both of which insisted on deference to one's betters. Such an arrangement allowed the rich to evade all responsibilities. The village head would also, naturally, be a merchant and money lender.

Collective punishment and near universal misery was the norm. If a landlord clashed with one of his peasants then the peasant and his family – possibly even his extended family – would be thrown off the land to starve. Thus, only the most severe and life threatening provocation would overcome the peasants' reluctance to act against their landlords. At the same time, the intransigence of the landlords could, under extreme conditions, make revolution the only means of survival.[1]

The absolutist regimes that had existed in China for over a thousand years were inherently corrupt. Tax officials sent Beijing its due and their own incomes came from what they collected over and above that; in 1927/28 in the province of Hupeh 77% of the monies collected were pocketed in this way.[2]

Tawney pointed out a major difference between China and Europe; there was no landed aristocracy in China in the sense it existed in Europe. The laws of inheritance required the land to be divided equally amongst the sons. With the head of the family siring as many sons as possible there were severe practical restrictions on the size of landed estates. It meant the lack of a hereditary land-owning nobility so the land question did not have the characteristic of serf against feudal lord, or nobles standing in opposition to the bourgeoisie as seen in the West. Instead the peasant stood against a coalition of interests that reached from the local landowner and moneylender, via state officials to the capitalist entrepreneur and the international financier. In the specific conditions existing in China, land could not be taken by the peasant without overturning all existing property relations. The native bourgeoisie could not carry thorough the agrarian reform necessary for an 'anti-feudal' revolution since that would be a revolution against itself.[3]

The local bureaucrats ensured their own and their family's continuing privileges by squeezing as much as possible out of the peasants and becoming part of the local gentry. The easiest way was to seize land for non-payment of taxes. This widespread land seizure was important in undermining social order, systematically driving the peasants into violent uprisings to save themselves from starvation. In extreme cases the uprising would succeed in overthrowing a dynasty, the peasants' land rights would be re-established and corrupt, self-seeking mandarins would be replaced by radical officials devoted to the ideals of the new regime – after which the cycle started again.[4]

But oriental despotism had an important characteristic that made the position of the Chinese peasant significantly different from that of the European serf. Due to climate and territorial conditions (especially large deserts), artificial irrigation was the basis of Oriental agriculture. Canal systems were created and maintained by co-ordinated labour on a mass scale. In China these public works required huge armies of labourers organised by the government. Social stability depended on local villages being largely self-sufficient, able to rely on their own agricultural and handicraft production – but as each dynasty decayed, the irrigation projects fell into disrepair causing widespread hunger and famine, with the armies of labourers forming seedbeds of rebellion.[5]

These factors combined to make the Chinese peasants rebellious on a scale dwarfing anything seen in Europe. Peasant armies of hundreds of thousands composed largely of the lowest layers rose in revolt. These rebellions were more successful than any in Europe, violently overthrowing governments and setting up new regimes; two of the great dynasties in China, the Han and Ming, were founded by commoners as the result of peasant uprisings.[6] But the new regimes singularly failed to re-structure the social order because these peasant rebellions were hopeless attempts revert society to an imaginary and idealised past.[7]

Marx described the process in an article on the Teiping rebellion:

> "Oriental empires always show an unchanging social infra-structure coupled with unceasing change in the persons and tribes who manage to ascribe to themselves the political super-structure … The (rebels) are not conscious of any task, except the change of dynasty. They have no … germ of a new formation."[8]

Nevertheless, a collective memory of past rebellions was a living tradition in the minds of the peasants which provided support for example, for the Taiping rebellion and, later, the rural strategy of the CCP.[9]

China remained comparatively untouched by Europe until the Opium Wars (1839-1842 and 1856-1860) when the British bombarded Chinese ports and massacred Chinese people to ensure the continuance of the opium trade, a major source of revenue for the British East India Company. These wars forced China to import opium, imposed vast sums as indemnities and opened up Chinese ports to British trade in perpetuity. The indemnities were paid by borrowing from British banks and increasing taxes on the peasantry to pay off the loans. The drain of silver to pay for opium and the loans, coupled with the progressive ruin of the Chinese handicraft industry by cheap British imports, especially cotton goods, crippled the country and put an end to village self-sufficiency. The closed nature of the communal system which had been the mainstay of Chinese social stability was coming to an end, and the greater the loss of self-sufficiency, the greater the poverty of the peasants and the greater the resulting political unrest.[10]

The Taiping Rebellion that swept through China from about 1849 to 1863 threatened the overthrow of the Qing dynasty thanks to the popularity of its programme which included national integrity in the face of imperialism, radical agrarian reform, suppression of the opium trade and the abolition of foot binding. Its support came from the lowest layers of urban artisans and peasants both devastated by the impact of cheap goods produced in Britain. But for the upper reaches of society this rebellion had a profoundly conservative effect – they discovered they could rely on British cannons to keep them in power and maintain the mutually profitable status quo.[11] Russia, France, Japan, and then America joined the plunder and supplied (at a good rate of interest) the military and financial support needed to prop up the Qing emperor.

The forces of European capitalism neither wanted to, nor could, erase the archaic social relations that existed in China. Just the opposite. The agents of capitalism that arrived in China sought to assimilate pre-capitalist forms and exploit them for their own profits. Direct or indirect, capitalist exploitation gradually extended to the great majority long before capitalist relations were established in Chinese society. In the process, existing social forms were gradually given a different content.

When R H Tawney arrived in China he found a country with less than 56,000 km (35,000 miles) of gravel or tarmac roads. Some provinces (e.g., the south western province of Kweichow [Guizhou]) had no roads at all, not even sufficient for ox carts or any wheeled vehicle (even though the Chinese had invented the chariot), and all goods were transported on human shoulders because their labour was cheaper than that of animals. The recurrence of local famines was inevitable since a surplus in one area could not be transported to offset deficiency in another. Such lack of transport also meant that peasants had no choice where to market their goods, and were tied hand and foot to local dealers who cornered the market and fixed prices. With no financial reserves and loaded with debt, the vast majority had to sell their produce immediately after harvest when prices were at their lowest.[12]

It was common practice for rich peasants to form an important link in the chain of exploitation and engage in commerce, running small stores and peddling farm produce – buying when prices were low and selling when prices were high (Mao's father was one such).[13] Naturally, these activities extended into lending at usurious rates. The rich peasants also made sure they had responsibility for managing common land which thus became yet one more means of exploitation. The adobe castles of the landlords surrounded by the miserable huts of the peasants were a visual representation of the divisions within the villages.

In the late 19th and early 20th centuries it became common practice for land-owners to move to the city for a more pleasant life-style, and their interest in their lands became more exclusively the extraction of rent and debt payments. The nearer to a great city, the higher the proportion of tenant farmers, between 85% and 95% in the case of Canton (Guangzhuo) in Kwantung (Guangdong) province.[14] This did not mean that landlords ignored the possibility of making profit from other sources, but the proportions were low, in Kiangsu 10% of landlords owned small handicraft factories meeting local needs but only about 3% held shares in large modern plants.[15]

Everywhere, population growth and pressure of peasant numbers enhanced land values and made landlordism an ideal form of investment with the small size of the peasant farms an indication of an economy in which the landlords were not concerned with efficient food production but in parcelling out the land to maximise rents.

The well-to-do formed companies to buy up land and sub-let. As the peasants became ever more impoverished, those exploiting them resorted to increasingly brutal techniques. By the 1920s in the rich rice-farming country between Canton and Hong Kong, the peasants were the "landlord's slaves .... Rent was collected with the aid of ropes, chains, whips and other instruments of torture."[16] It was a common sight on rent collection days to see wives and/or children lined-up for sale to offset family debts.

The local gentry sent their sons to participate in the highly lucrative foreign trade using the massive profits to buy additional land and/or lend at usurious rates. The growth and integration of merchant capital with imperialism, the coming together of local gentry with native capitalists, compradors and Western capitalists combined to produce an unholy amalgam which was buying vast tracts of land, renting them out at extortionate rates backed by an extensive system of loans and heavy-handed debt collection. Chinese capitalism as a whole was tied to imperialism and though it would, on occasion, attempt to gain a greater share of the spoils for itself, it was unable to play any independent progressive role in the economic development of China.

Of the Chinese population, roughly 80% were driven by one of the most consistent and powerful of revolutionary forces in all history – the hunger of starving peasants for land.[17] The continuous expropriation of the small peasants due to very high rates of rent, usury and taxes ended in the concentration of property in the hands of the village chiefs, usurers, and merchant-usurer-compradors and it was not rare to find landlords possessing 20,000 *mow* (about 1,500 hectares, nearly 4,000 acres) or more. Ten percent of the agricultural population of China possessed as much as two-thirds of the land. In the province of Shansi, 0.3% of the families possessed one quarter of the land. In Chekiang, 3.3% of the families possessed half the land, while 77% of the poor peasants possessed no more than 20% of the land. And in Kwangtung where 2% of the families possessed over half the land, 74% possessed only 19% of the land. These figures explain why the land hunger of the peasant became transformed into a class hatred of the landlord and all those allied with him.[18]

Those lucky enough to be tenants paid from 25-66% of their crop to the landlord for the use of the land. Given the small land areas involved, this meant perpetual hunger for the great mass of peasants who found it impossible to accumulate any reserve fund. Any natural disaster or poor harvest and the tenant would be unable to pay his rent and taxes, with the consequence he was obliged to borrow money from his landlord or a member of his landlord's family. In fact, tenants were often obliged to borrow to pay for seed for the coming season or even food in order to feed their families a meagre diet of millet. Tenants who had to borrow inevitably lost their land. A good money-lender charged only 25% per annum, but rates of 40-80% were more typical with 150% not unknown. These interest payments to the money-lenders on top of all the other debts were the principal cause of the ruin of peasant families.[19]

Surveys of the livelihood of Chinese peasants,[20,21] found even the more prosperous peasants lived near the margin of subsistence. The families of small peasants could not support themselves on what their farms produced. The gap was made up by working on the lands of rich peasants, or wives and daughters who undertook handicraft manufacture – which traditionally had earned as much, or even more, than labouring but was being hard hit by Western imports giving Chinese peasants one of the lowest per capita incomes in the world.[22] The poverty of the peasant masses was such that an entire strata of the rural population was reduced to the condition of animals, but poorly fed and badly treated animals at that. The result was a life expectancy of about 35 years.[23]

Landless peasants who were about one third the total were in an even worse situation. These semi-slaves were forever hungry and their clothes were rags. A family would have one pair of trousers shared between them, when the father went out he left his wife naked. Belden estimated that in a bad year, a family of seven could expect three or four of its members to starve to death.[24]

The nature of the Asiatic state proved to be a problem for the Russian Stalinist bureaucracy. In the Asiatic state the officials had no inheritance rights to their positions; they were appointed, promoted/demoted and discharged by a 'supreme' authority. Chinese officials, just like Soviet bureaucrats, owed their privileges to their position in the state apparatus and not to their property, and so did not form a possessing class. Analysing and describing this fawning and corrupt bureaucracy was a sensitive issue for the Soviet regime and so it was excised from the analysis of China. In 1931, at a conference held in Leningrad, it was officially denied that Marx had ever recognised a special 'Asiatic mode of production'; and the history of the Orient was explained in Western terms as a development of feudalism.[25]

Hence, the ECCI emphasised that the national democratic revolution in China was a struggle against feudalism. This concept distorted the thinking of the CCP even after its taking power to the extent that the major banking conglomerates were declared feudal because of their links to the leaders of the KMT and their involvement in the practice of usury.

1.2.1 Women in Pre-Revolutionary China

"The degree of emancipation of woman is a natural standard of the general emancipation" and "the changes in a historical epoch can always be inferred from the comparative freedom of women."[26] In China a peasant woman was lucky in the sense she had not been strangled at birth or put on one side to die. The widespread suicides of wives and daughters were convincing proof of the degraded state of women in China.

Women were denied social contact outside their family a position reinforced by physically deforming girls through the practice of foot binding. Women were confined to the home and handicraft work, and over large areas of China women did not work the land. That was done by men only. Folklore reinforced patriarchy and the restriction of women to the home by such sayings as: "potatoes planted by women won't sprout" and "melons planted by women are bitter."[27]

The woman's sense of isolation and vulnerability was enhanced by having the young bride marry outside her natal village after which she might never see her parents or siblings again. The marriages were arranged by family heads and neither groom nor bride had any say. Because women were seen by their birth family as temporary residents who left home as soon as they were productive, they were denied the right to own property and little or nothing was invested in their education; rather daughters (and wives) were sold as cheap labour and/or concubines to meet family debts.

In China the groom's family paid a 'body price' to the bride's family, implying they were paying not for a young woman but a chattel. On entering her husband's home a bride would find herself examined by curious neighbours who pawed her, felt her arm muscles, turned her this way and that, examining her to see if she were worth buying. Peasant women lived in semi-slave conditions, often on a level with the domesticated animals owned by the family.

The practice of wife-beating by the husband and his mother was both accepted and almost universal. Many wives were crippled or died as a result of these beatings. The position of the wife was reinforced at every turn by such customs as the husband's family eating first and the wife eating what little food was left over. Widows were not allowed to re-marry and an 'exemplary wife' committed suicide to show loyalty to her dead husband. In reality, this was a mechanism for killing off older women before they became a burden on family resources.

The inequality of women was deeply reflected in Chinese philosophy and religion in which it was a law of nature that woman should be inferior to man and, before the arrival of the CCP, Chinese society accepted its horrendous treatment of women as natural. Confucianism was the ideological basis of this oppression, as this decreed that a woman should live her life subject to her father's authority, after marriage her husband's, and after the husband's death, her sons. It is said that there is not one line in all that Confucius wrote which praises women.

The lowly position of Chinese women not only had a terrible effect on the women themselves, but also succeeded in degrading all human relations within Chinese society.[28] Little wonder that the reaction of many a woman whose landlord husband was killed by militia or villagers was not grief but joy. So badly were wives treated in the more conservative sectors of society that the death of the perpetrator was an occasion for celebration. One can imagine, then, the impact of the 'scandalous behaviour' of young Communist women who cut their hair short, were able to walk freely, and spoke in public to those who were not members of their immediate family.

The subjugation of women, their misery and degradation, was an essential prop for Chinese society. Jack Belden has described how, in agrarian China, rich peasants with more than one wife and numerous concubines had many sons to act as their *ming tuan*. Belden gives the example of one landlord who used his 68 strong family to control nearly 1,000 small holdings. Any genuine attempt to emancipate women was revolutionary because it threatened the whole rotten social pyramid.[29]

All the more praise, then, to women such as the anarchist HeYin Zheh who helped found *Natural Justice*, a feminist journal which carried the first Chinese translation of the *Communist Manifesto*. It is said that He Yin, who died in her mid-30s, would often claim that feminism brought Marxism to China not the other way round.

1.3 Industrial Development in China

Industrially, China was a country of enormous contradictions. For example, railways had developed rapidly after its defeat in the first Sino-Japanese war, as the military saw their enormous strategic advantage, but as late as 1925 there was still only about 12,300 km (7,500 miles) of track. Nearly all railways were in the eastern half of the country and used for military purposes or by foreign imperialist interests to service industrial and mining complexes. Five provinces had no railways at all and many only a few miles.

Goods produced by the world's most developed technologies flooded into China and pauperised many of the rural population, creating a pool of cheap labour, ideal for exploitation by industry. After 1905, Chinese cities grew rapidly. By 1919 the population of Shanghai had reached over 1.9 million. In the four years from 1919 to 1923 Beijing grew from around 600,000 to over one million. Other cities such as Canton and the Wuhan complex grew into major urban centres.

The new working class was composed largely of peasant immigrants. Industrialisation offered the peasant not only additional income but the chance for an independent existence outside of a large family unit. This separate existence undermined the absolute authority of the head of the family and with it obedience to officialdom, leading to greater receptiveness towards new and revolutionary ideas – a process that had much in common with the growth and radicalisation of the Russian working class some fifty years before.[30]

The Great War of 1914-1918 had an enormous and sudden impact on China; Chinese-owned factories, mills and shipyards based on the latest capitalist technology and methods developed in places like Shanghai and Canton – a modern working class was being created. Nationally, industrial workers grew rapidly to two million in 1922 with another two million miners, railway workers and seamen, and an additional ten million or so handicraft workers. In Shanghai in 1923, 57 factories employed between 500 and 1,000 workers each, and another 49 employed over 1,000 workers each – by 1927 the number of factory workers in Shanghai was estimated to be about a quarter of a million.[31] Of the 12 million non-agricultural workers in China, around three-quarters worked in large enterprises employing more than 500 workers.

Nearly half of Shanghai's workers were women, in silk, yarn, and cigarette factories but at this time the CCP tended to see them as a factor lowering the militancy of the workforce, rather than as an ally in the liberation struggle.[32] In the Shanghai cotton mills women between 14 and 19 years of age made up over half the work force. These women were, if possible, treated worse than the men, gang masters took 40% of their earnings, they slept 30-40 in a room, they could be beaten for errors in their work, they could be locked in cages on public display for infringements of discipline. This was the alternative to forced marriages or being sold into slavery by starving parents. It is understandable that the major complaints of these workers were not about pay but the conditions in which they worked and lived.[33]

The rise of Chinese production brought aspiring Chinese capitalists into collision with entrenched foreign interests. The national bourgeoisie faced serious problems due to the domination of foreign capital made worse by the concession whereby foreign goods paid no duty while Chinese goods did. Foreign capital owned nearly all the railways (either outright or as mortgages), more than half of the shipping in Chinese waters, and almost all merchant shipping. Foreign capitalists had a stranglehold on Chinese industry, sucking it dry. In such a situation the more entrepreneurial sections of the national bourgeoisie were prepared to support anti-imperialist parties which called for revolution.[34]

Once above a certain minimum number, the specific weight of the working class in a social revolution is the dominant factor and there was a general equivalence between Russia in 1917 and China in 1927. Although relatively small proportionally – a few million in a population of over 400 million – these concentrations of proletarians had two qualities that, given the correct political leadership, would be decisive in national democratic and socialist revolutionary struggles; they were located in the cities and they were the only social group which could offer the peasants a solution to the land question.[35]

1.4 The First Chinese Revolution: Sun Yat-sen and Nationalism

From 1840 it was increasingly clear to all sections of Chinese society that something in China was fundamentally wrong and big changes were required. By the beginning of the 20th century, dissatisfaction with the old regime and demand for change were reaching boiling point. It was increasingly apparent that the old regime could not reform itself but was determined to cling to its power and privileges. Organisations with the goal of the revolutionary overthrow of the Qing Dynasty and the establishment of a national bourgeois Chinese republic proliferated, especially in the South and East of the country centred on Canton and Shanghai.[36]

Between 1905 and 1912, Sun Yat-sen built a political movement for the military overthrow of the Qing regime. Sun's prestige came from his successful merging of small revolutionary groups into a single larger party providing a more effective base for the nationalist struggle. Sun was dedicated to the bourgeois democratic revolution, and between 1900 and 1908 he led or organised no fewer than five failed uprisings. In early 1911 another Sun attempt in Canton failed, but on 10 October 1911, soldiers in Hubei province rebelled and proclaimed a republic. This did not ignite any popular response but coming as it did from within the military-bureaucratic apparatus, this 'tap' was sufficient to knock over a thoroughly rotten structure.

Politically, Sun Yat-sen was a petty-bourgeois who presented socialism as a vague state of well-being rather than a social and economic system. His famous Three Principles for the liberation of Chinese society from imperialism specifically exclude the idea that this might require a class struggle; instead the concept of "people" was used to obscure the idea that China might have different classes with different interests.

With the overthrow of the Manchu dynasty, Sun's supporters in Nanjing (capital of Jiangsu province) declared themselves a National Assembly and elected him President of a loosely federated Republic of China. In this capacity he did a deal with the representative of the old dynasty (General Yuan Shikai [Yüan Shih-k'ai] a warlord from the North, with large forces at his disposal), offering him the presidency if he arranged the permanent departure of the Manchus.[37] Rather than mobilise the masses throughout the country on a social programme to overthrow the regime, Sun Yat-sen – in a classic example of the Asiatic mode of rebellion – simply changed the personnel at the top. The party of the liberal bourgeoisie and national democratic revolution entered into a reactionary compromise with the counter-revolution.[38]

After the Taiping rebellion, the authority of the emperor had been more nominal than actual with real power held by the provincial governors. The Republic in 1911 finally severed any remaining loyalties to the emperor and the provincial governors representing themselves alone assumed both military and civil power. These regional warlords corresponded closely to the spheres of interest of the Great Powers, and the incessant civil wars reflected the conflict of interests between those powers. In Manchuria, Japan supported Chang Tso-Lin while Britain supported Wu Pei-Fu in Northern China, and Sung Chan-Fang in Central China.[39] Despite the disintegration of the country, the Beijing government remained the symbol of China's national sovereignty and thus its capture continued to be the goal of Sun Yat-sen and the nationalists.

The failure of the 1911 revolution (known as the First Chinese Revolution) demonstrated the weakness of the national bourgeoisie. Forming a stable national government, creating a national market, and carrying through radical land reform were beyond the capacities of this social group on its own. Sun Yat-sen bowed to reaction with the result that two years after 1911, the party of the revolution found itself outlawed and Sun forced to seek asylum in

Japan. Confusion, disorder and turmoil would now be the order of the day until the CCP victory in 1949.

After the First Chinese Revolution, the situation of the national, middle, and small bourgeoisie became ever worse due to disintegration of the country and continuous civil wars. The previous general hatred of the monarchy was now directed at the warlords and their backers, the imperialists. The energy that had previously gone into peasant revolt now fuelled a nationalist movement of tremendous force for reunification of the country and against imperialism.[40]

1.5 The Communist International 1919-1923

At the 2nd World Congress (19 July-7 Aug 1920), the CI addressed the three major problems faced by Communists in "colonial and backward countries"; how to avoid adopting conciliatory and opportunist positions with respect to the national bourgeoisie, how to avoid ultra-leftism, and what should be their general strategic approach. Lenin published *Left-Wing Communism: An Infantile Disorder*, to guide and educate the young and often ultra-left leaders of the emerging Communist Parties in a non-sectarian approach towards Social Democracy, parliamentary elections, existing trade unions, and nationalist parties in the colonial world.[41]

It was at this Congress that the CI adopted a centralised structure and agreed that the International's strategic line would be binding on its member parties, but the national section would be free to determine its implementation, particularly tactical and day-to-day activities. Lenin may have seen October 1917 as a model for future revolutions but he stressed that concrete events in each specific country had primacy in day-to-day struggles.[42]

1.5.1 The United Front Strategy

A major development in the strategic orientation of the CI was the adoption of a United Front strategy at the 3rd World Congress (June-July, 1921). The concept of the United Front had been advanced by Paul Levi, leader of the German Communist Party (KPD) based on the lessons of the Kapp putsch. On the morning of 13 March 1920, a brigade of soldiers led by Wolfgang Kapp marched into Berlin and declared the German SD government to be overthrown. Not a shot was fired, the government simply fled. The putsch was challenged instead by the workers. Karl Legien a right wing leader of the main trade union federation issued the call for a general strike. At first the KPD vacillated but the great mass of workers threw themselves unhesitatingly into the struggle. By 15 March the strike was solid, and faced with united action by trade unionists, social democrats and communists, the putschists gave up and fled.[43]

We should note that the United Front was not a new concept; it was certainly present in Lenin's writings as early as February 1905.[44] Here Lenin called for a United Front of all revolutionary forces to prepare the uprising, on the basis of the slogan "march separately and strike together" but, as in all his other articles on this topic, he emphasised the absolute necessity of maintaining the complete political independence of the working class party. A well-known and classic example of Lenin's United Front stratagem in action was in September 1917 when General Kornilov at the head of a White Army was advancing on Petrograd. Despite the counter revolutionary and repressive nature of Kerensky's Provisional Government (in July it had attempted to outlaw the Bolsheviks), it was necessary to participate wholeheartedly in the struggle against the open forces of reaction represented by Kornilov. Throughout 1917 Lenin's strategy was to attack the main enemy, the landlords and capitalists, and the reaction, not directly attacking the reformist leaders but outflanking them, demonstrating in practice that the Mensheviks and Socialist Revolutionaries were incapable of acting decisively in the interests of the workers and peasants.[45]

A United Front had defeated reaction both in Russia and Germany, and Levi, supported by the majority of the CC of the KPD, issued an Open Letter on 8 January 1921, proposing a new strategy for winning the mass of workers to communism. The Open Letter called for a United Front, on a limited number of concrete demands (including wage increases and amnesty for political prisoners), with other left parties and the trade unions, and was approved by Lenin.[46]

Zinoviev and Bukharin (both advocates of the theory of the offensive – European capitalism was so weak it needed only a good push to collapse) sharply attacked the Open Letter and without Lenin's intervention the ECCI would have issued a public condemnation.[47] Zinoviev, using the ECCI, sent emissaries to Berlin who by, demanding loyalty to the CI and blocking with the ultra-lefts, removed Levi from the leadership and had the KPD agree to launch an armed revolt.[48]

The first step in the insurrection was for the KPD to call a nationwide general strike. Ill-prepared, the strike was limited to KPD members and close supporters who made the classic ultra-left mistake of attempting to close factories not by gaining a majority vote but by fighting with those workers going to work. The strike was a fiasco which allowed the SD trade union leaders to indignantly denounce the splitting tactics of the KPD. Thousands of militants were thrown in prison, tens of thousands lost their jobs, and the membership of the KPD fell from nearly 400,000 to less than 150,000.[49]

Events in Germany convinced Lenin and Trotsky of the need for a discussion on strategy and tactics as a major topic at the 3rd World Congress of the *CI*. After much heated debate, Lenin and Trotsky obtained a majority for the policy of the United Front but with the supporters of the theory of the offensive unrepentant.[50,51]

This policy signified a new approach toward Social Democrats and nationalists. Common actions should be proposed where it was possible to reach a minimum agreement on practical measures. In this way, communists hoped to demonstrate to the masses that they were in the forefront of the class struggle and stood for the long-term interests of all the working masses. For such a strategy to be successful there had to be in place a leadership sufficiently mature not to succumb to either impatience (ultra-leftism) or to bend to opportunist pressures. Another precondition of any United Front was the independence of the Communist Party. Any agreement which restricted CP freedom of criticism and agitation was "absolutely unacceptable."[52]

1.5.2 Collaboration with National Revolutionary Movements

National liberation struggles in the countries of the east, particularly China, were of major concern to the Communist International, and Lenin spent considerable time and effort in developing a general strategy for Communists participating in anti-imperialist United Fronts in colonial and semi-colonial countries.[53]

In November 1919 and again in June 1920, Lenin described how feudal oppression in Russia was ended **after** the proletarian revolution overthrew the bourgeoisie, **after** the proletariat had demonstrated in practice that as a government they would complete the agrarian revolution.[54,55] The agrarian revolution might be the motor force for the peasants' revolutionary struggle against imperialism but only the dictatorship of the proletariat, supported by the poor peasants, could fully satisfy the peasant's three most heartfelt demands: for land, for cancellation of mortgages and debts, and for an end to feudal oppression as expressed in, e.g. corvee labour.[56]

This analysis was presented to both the CI and Communist Organisations of the East and Lenin meant it to be taken seriously as the strategic basis for the International's orientation towards the peasant masses in the colonial countries and as guide to action in, e.g., China. Despite being a backward semi-feudal country, Russia had a sufficiently strong and politically advanced proletariat to drive the revolution to success under Bolshevik leadership. How could the same perspective be proposed for countries such as China where the proletariat, while growing rapidly, had not reached the social or political weight it had in Russia in 1917?

Lenin's answer was twofold. The national liberation struggles were an integral part of the world proletarian revolution. Each national revolution had to be seen in the international context which had "transformed the present stage of capitalist development into an era of proletarian socialist revolution."[57] The second part of his answer was that it had been demonstrated in the most remote and "backward" of the former Tsarist colonies, that even with no proletariat but with the help of the Soviet Union, peasant Soviets could exist and govern without passing through a capitalist stage.[58] It was the duty of the national CPs to propagandise and organise Soviets suited to local conditions as soon as practicable. Lenin emphasised: "The idea of Soviet organisation is a simple one, and is applicable ... to peasant, feudal and semi-feudal relations."[59]

At the 2nd CI Congress, 11 countries from Asia were represented. The discussions on the agrarian, national and colonial questions were dominated by Lenin's personal interventions. Lenin urged the young communist parties in the colonial countries to actively participate in the emerging national revolutionary movements, but specifically warned of:

> "the need for determined struggle against the attempt to give a communist colouring to bourgeois-democratic liberation trends ... the Communist International must enter into a temporary alliance with bourgeois democracy in colonial and backward countries, but must not merge with it, and should under all circumstances uphold the independence of the proletarian movement even in its most embryonic form."[60]

Maring ('Henk' Sneevliet) expanded on Lenin's report[61] and explained that opposition to imperialism required the "overthrow (of) the rule of the landlords ... Only an agrarian revolution can arouse the vast peasant masses." It was emphasised that the struggle against patriarchy and backwardness was an essential component of the struggle against imperialist domination and such struggles greatly assisted the Soviet Union and the proletarian revolution in the West.[62]

The CI expected that the initial period of revolution in the colonies and semi-colonies (and China was included here) would be nationalist in character. During this initial stage, indigenous Communists could and should enter into temporary alliances but in the process found workers' and peasants' councils to address the aspirations of the broad masses of the peasants. In his report, Maring again emphasised the importance of the demand for the seizure and distribution of the land by the peasants to the peasants. The struggle to carry though these revolutionary measures would mean that, with the help and guidance of the Soviet Union and the CI, the national revolution could "progress to socialism without passing through a capitalist stage."

The Baku Congress of the Peoples of the East held in September 1920 was definite that the poor peasants of the East did not have to pass through bourgeois democracy in order to acquire the capacity for self-government; did not have to pass through a phase of capitalist development before they could go over to a Soviet system. "The masses of peasants of the East should form revolutionary peasant Soviets with the poorest peasants as the leading elements and immediately destroy the system of landlordship."[63] It was accepted that the Russian experience had shown that the middle peasants would support socialist revolution if the resulting regime approved the seizure of the landed estates and their distribution to the peasants by the peasants.

This strategy would never be applied in China but would, instead, be wilfully distorted by subsequent Soviet leaderships to meet the needs of the leading faction in the Russian Party in inner-party struggles.

1.5.3 May 4th Movement, Labour Radicalisation and the Founding of the CCP

In the horse-trading at the peace negotiations after World War I, the victors trampled on China's sovereignty. Popular illusions in Anglo-American democracy were shattered and there was a widespread recognition that whoever won the war, imperialist exploitation of China and other colonial countries would continue. In such a situation the October Revolution became a topic of interest especially after the Soviet government relinquished the territories, rights and privileges that the Tsarist government had taken from China in the past. Such a stark contrast to the Versailles Treaty had a profound impact on Chinese radicals, students, and intellectuals.

The warlords were deeply unpopular, and their supine attitude when they acquiesced to the transfer of German concessions in Shantung province to Japan and the expansion of Japanese control over Manchuria, was the final straw in generating open mass opposition beginning with the May 4th Movement.[64] On 4 May, 1919 in Beijing, some 5,000 university students attacked the residences of those ministers particularly submissive to Japan.

Documents seized by the students revealed that the Versailles decisions were based on prior agreements between the Beijing government and the Japanese. The next day students in Beijing as a whole went on strike, and students across the country followed.

China had sent over 150,000 workers to labour for the allied armies in France, Belgium, Mesopotamia, and Africa and these returned with experience of labour organisation. Radicalised by the May 4th Movement and with experience of trade unions, the returned workers played a key role in early June, when labour leaders declared a strike in Shanghai; it is claimed some 100,000 industrial workers participated.[65] In a few days the Beijing Government was compelled to remove the offending ministers and release those arrested.

The example of the workers in Shanghai was followed by workers throughout the country and was a turning point in the emergence of Chinese labour as an independent political force. The strikes placed the question of class at the centre of post-May 4th political thinking. The older, traditional radicals thought the arrival of the uneducated masses undermined the Chinese national revolution, the left of the KMT sought to integrate the workers' upsurge into a corporatist strategy to render class struggle unnecessary (KMT thinking was, generally, that China's backwardness meant the class struggle was a diversion from the national revolution), but the more radical saw class struggle as a means of freeing Chinese society from imperialism. In September 1919, the Chinese Returned Labourers' Association was set up in Shanghai to fight for better wages, the right to hold meetings, and the right to make public speeches for promoting the welfare of workers, etc. Between 1919 and 1923 Shanghai would have over 450 strikes.[66]

The May 4th Movement was a mass crusade against imperialism, feudalism, and corruption. Its failure astounded and polarised the Movement into the gradualists and the radicals led by Chen Duxiu (Ch'en Tu-hsiu, Dean of the College of Liberal Arts at Beijing University). Chen had a national reputation gained from his founding of the radical quarterly magazine *New Youth* which was published in common speech not classical Chinese. The most politically advanced came to the conclusion that a revolutionary organisation was required to achieve the aspirations of the people, and turned to Leninism and Marxism.[67]

Impressed by the Russian Revolution, Chen decided to devote a special issue of *New Youth* to Marxism; it was published on 1 May 1919, with Li Dazhao (Head Librarian of Beijing University) as acting editor. At the

University, Li had quietly and secretly organised a Marxist Study Society of which Mao Zedong was a member. The collaboration between Chen and Li had a profound effect on Chen who, soon after, declared himself a Marxist.[68] For distributing a leaflet critical of the Chinese president and prime minister, Chen was arrested by the Beijing authorities on 11 June and had to resign his post. He was released in November and moved to Shanghai the following January to become a full-time revolutionary.

In March 1920, Grigori Voitinsky chief of the Far Eastern Bureau of the Comintern met with Li Dazhao to assess the possibility of launching a Communist Party in China. Upon Li's recommendation, Voitinsky proceeded to Shanghai to meet with Chen Duxiu who had already formed a loose political grouping. By the end of May 1920, Voitinsky had persuaded Chen to formally found a Chinese Communist Party, had helped him draft a programme, establish a provisional Central Committee, and construct the first official Communist cell in Shanghai. Voitinsky participated directly in all phases and aspects of party formation and organisation and may, justifiably, be viewed as the architect of the CCP in its initial phase.[69]

The aid provided by the Comintern was essential for creating a disciplined Bolshevik organisation in such a short time. Chen Duxiu was from a family of wealthy government officials. Li Dazhao was from a peasant background. For both of them, the material and theoretical aid of the Comintern in establishing the CCP substituted for decades of theoretical studies, debate and practical party-building. The problems faced by Chen and Li were considerably heightened and the study of Marxism made more difficult because, for example, there was no Chinese equivalent for such terms as proletariat, which made expressing central Marxist concepts doubly problematic. Fairbank makes the point that this confusion in the translation of Marxist terms was given a particular slant by Mao to enhance the appearance of orthodoxy in his writings. For example, Mao translated the word 'proletariat' as 'propertyless class' in which he included landless labourers and very poor peasants who comprised the majority of the Chinese population, and in this way justified his so-called peasant orientation.[70]

China's Communists celebrated May Day 1920 with great fanfare in Shanghai, Beijing, and a number of provincial cities. In August 1920, *World of Labour, Voice of Labour,* and *Labourers* were launched by the Communist groups in Shanghai, Beijing, and Canton respectively to spread Communism among workers, explain the causes of their oppression and exploitation, and urge them to organise labour unions.[71] In November 1920, the Shanghai group made *New Youth* its official organ and established a clandestine monthly, *The Communist*, the first publication in China devoted to the propagation of Communism. Soon, other Communist groups were established in Wuhan, Changsha, and Canton. A Socialist Youth Corps was founded by, amongst others, Peng Shuzhi (P'eng Shu-tse).[72] The CCP did take the decision to launch a daily paper in Beijing (*Far East Daily*) but immediately realised that the Party's strength was insufficient to maintain such an enterprise and instead launched *The Guide Weekly*.[73]

Thirty-eight years of age, Maring had been a leading member of the Indonesian Communist Party (initially the ISDV and later PKI) from its founding, and had been instrumental in persuading it to adopt an entrist strategy into the mass nationalist movement Sarekat Islam. Maring believed this was the root cause of the success achieved in building the ISDV and had vigorously promoted the same strategy for other countries at the 2nd Congress of the CI in July 1920. As Secretary to the Commission on the National and Colonial Questions he worked closely with Lenin, was elected a member of the ECCI and later delegated to represent the ECCI in China arriving in Shanghai on 3 June 1921 where he immediately began to promote the entry strategy.[74]

Maring initially concentrated on organising the 1st National Congress of the CCP. The party was constituted secretly in Shanghai in July 1921 with 12 delegates representing 57 people from seven local Communist groups in China and one in Japan. The Party Secretary was Chen Duxiu and Li Dazhao was head of propaganda. The party programme that was adopted closely followed the Bolshevik programme and called for joining the Communist International.[75] The following month Chen became full-time Party Secretary, a post he would keep until July 1927.

The delegates at the 1st Congress discussed the nature of the Chinese Revolution, predicting it would be national democratic but that it was extremely unlikely that the KMT could carry it through successfully, implying that the CCP would take the lead of the bourgeoise democratic revolution much as had happened in Russia.[76] With his own perspectives in mind, Maring worked hard to tone down the more virulent anti-KMT statements to keep the door open for CCP-KMT co-operation.[77]

Communist nuclei around the country were soon organised into party branches: Beijing, Canton, Hong Kong, Hunan (where Mao Zedong was local leader and created the largest and best organised branch in the CCP), Jinan, Shanghai, Sichuan, Tianjin, and Wuhan. These branches operated at three levels: the illegal 'small group' of party members, the Socialist Youth Corps operating semi-openly, and the open Study Societies.[78] The CCP recognised that women were confronted with specific problems which made them the most oppressed section among the oppressed classes and the battle for women's emancipation was closely tied to the battle for social revolution. The CPC set up a special Women's Department at the 2nd Party Congress held in 1922 to organise and lead women in revolutionary politics. This department was directed by Hsing Ching-yu, one of Mao's fellow student-activists from Hunan and the only woman on the Central Committee of the CPC.

The department produced a list of democratic demands, including: the right to self-determination in marriage, equal husband-wife relations, the right to vote, to hold office and to education, protection for female and child labour, and the abolition of all restrictions on women. With these demands, Hsing drew large numbers of women around the Party. The Women's Department, with its limited resources, concentrated on supporting the industrial activities of women such as the first strike by women workers in the silk factories of Shanghai in 1922 for a 10-hour working day and 5 cents wage-increase per day. The first rally of women, under party leadership, was held on Women's Day (8 March) 1924 in Canton, where a group of female students and women workers raised the slogans: Equal pay for equal work, Protection for child labour and pregnant mothers, Prohibit the buying of girl slaves, Equal education for all, No more child brides, Down with warlords, Down with imperialism.

1.6 Summary

The importance of the disciplined party, with a clear, implacable revolutionary position, was fully grasped by Lenin only as a result of years of experience so it is not surprising that Chen Duxiu, should not instantly come to the same conclusion based purely on his own experiences. The first Bolshevisation of the CCP which introduced the concept and practice of democratic centralism (e.g. accepting the authority of the CI) and which was widely welcomed by the CCP leaders, was carried through under the guidance of Maring.[79]

CCP Central Committee accounts and financial receipts show that before the establishment of the CCP, Chen Duxiu had found the funds needed for the functioning of his radical group from publications, sales and donations, but with the formation of the CCP there was a steep increase in outlay and a major shortage of funds. In 1921 expenditure reached the equivalent of almost 18,000 Chinese silver dollars. The CCP managed to raise only about 1,000 dollars and received 16,650 dollars from the ECCI. In 1922 it is reported that the CCP raised no money at all and expenses were met by 15,000 dollars donated from Moscow.[80] The Kremlin not only funded Chen Duxiu, whose monthly salary was 30 dollars, but also all the regional organisations of the party. Mao is reported to have received 60-70 dollars a month to support himself and his activities in Hunan. Thus, the ECCI representatives not had only the prestige of the October Revolution, the collective experience of the Bolshevik Party and the authority of the CI behind them, they were also the source of material resources which would be a major factor in the ongoing control that the CI exerted over the CCP.

Chapter 2

The Communist International, the Kuomintang and the CCP

2.1 Introduction

Sun Yat-sen returned to China from Japan in 1917 determined to lead the struggle for reunification but with a military not a political perspective. By 1921 he had established himself as a leading member of a regional military government based in the city of Canton in South China. Real power was in the hands of Chen Jiongming (Ch'en Chiung-ming), supposedly the leading KMT general but really the local warlord upon whose tolerance the KMT depended, and who supported the KMT as long as it suited him. Sun was convinced that unifying China required military conquest. This would start in the south but to gain control of Beijing required the overthrow of the northern warlords. At that time Chen was Sun's preferred route to victory.[1] The CI was determined to persuade him to take another route and was prepared to make considerable concessions to win him over.

2.2 The Communist International and Sun Yat-sen

In late December 1921, Maring met with Sun Yat-sen to propose an alliance between the KMT and the CCP. While Sun did not dismiss the proposal outright he was more interested in Maring's suggestion that the KMT could be re-organised along 'Russian' lines as a disciplined, centrally-controlled party, and a KMT military academy be established by the Soviet Army. However, Maring's proposal that that the CCP join the KMT was met by the almost universal opposition of the CCP members.[2]

On 13 January 1922, some 30,000 Hong Kong seamen struck for union recognition and a pay increase to bring their pay more into line with that of Europeans. The Hong Kong seamen held out for eight weeks in a bitter and bloody struggle. The British imperial authorities in Hong Kong were finally forced to raise wages by 20-30%, lift the ban on the Seamen's Union, release arrested workers, and indemnify the families of the martyrs. The crews of the Yangtse steamers went on strike soon afterwards for two weeks and also won victory.[3] This successful strike by seamen in Hong Kong was an inspiration to all those working to unionise labour.

The strike had been led by KMT militants and publicly supported by individual leaders of the KMT. The CCP participated in, and actively aided, the strike and this raised its prestige enormously but the strike demonstrated that the CCP was not yet in the same league as the KMT even within unionised labour.[4] It is claimed that as many as 12,000 sailors from Canton, Hong Kong and Swatow joined the KMT as a result.[5] It was on the basis of this strike that Maring convinced the ECCI that the KMT had serious and important links with working class organisations and understood the need for mass action in support of the anti-imperialist struggle.

This was certainly not true at the top of the KMT but Maring believed that the loose structure of the KMT made it easy for the CCP to enter the KMT, convince its left wing of the need for mass action in support of the nationalist struggle, win a majority and change the composition of the KMT. CCP members within the KMT would educate so-called ideologically independent elements who would eventually be recruited into the CCP, and use KMT contacts to organise caucuses within the trade unions. The discussions within the CCP were over whether, if it entered the KMT, it could maintain its own identity and establish its own independent activity amongst the workers.[6] The majority of the CCP leadership opposed any agreement which did not meet these Leninist conditions.

In March/April 1922, Chen wrote to the ECCI insisting:

> "in any struggle which we may take up or any combination we may make with other parties, we must always show our true face to the masses. Furthermore, we must maintain our complete independence in any arrangement we may make in a United Front."[7]

He would receive short shrift at the 4th World Congress where he would be accused of ultra-leftism.

However, it turned out that Chen Jiongming opposed Sun's scheme, and in 1922 Sun had to flee to Shanghai where he once again sought support from Canada, Germany, Great Britain, the United States, and even Manchurian warlords. They all refused. The Western powers were too attached to their special privileges to support a united independent China. At this critical moment Voitinsky visited Sun. Sun's situation and that of the KMT had changed radically since Maring's visit the previous December and now Sun welcomed collaboration with the Soviet Union even if it meant some form of unity with the CCP.[8]

At the 1st National Congress of the CCP it had been decided to establish a Trade Union Secretariat. This soon became the most important undertaking of the Party. In May 1922, on the back of the Hong Kong strike, it organised the First National Labour Conference in Canton which was attended by 160 delegates claiming to represent 300,000 union members.[9] The CCP was now very active in building trade unions, for example, in September 1922 Li Lisan would lead the Anyuan miners to an important victory; the gains included recognition of the union (it claimed 11,000 members), foremen no longer allowed to physically beat workers, and no withholding of wages as a punishment.[10]

CCP Members approached the 2nd National Congress (16-23 July 1922) with great confidence. Present were nine delegates representing about 123 members.[11] Prominent among the delegates were Communists who had recently returned from participation in the First Congress of the Toilers of the East held in Moscow and Petrograd, and with their support, the CCP Congress adopted a manifesto which endorsed a United Front with the KMT while warning that "workers must not become an appendage of the petty bourgeoisie ... but must fight for their own class interests."[12] This was fully in accord with Lenin's guidance given in his *Draft Theses on the National and Colonial Question.*[13]

At the 2nd World Congress, Maring had heard Lenin define the British Labour Party – a party founded by the trade unions to protect the trade unions and composed largely of workers – as "a thoroughly bourgeois party."[14] Lenin insisted a party had to be judged by the men who led it and its actions. The British Labour Party was an organisation of the bourgeoisie which existed to systematically dupe the workers. By Lenin's criteria, the KMT was a bourgeois party.

However, prior to the 2nd Congress of the CCP, Maring had attended the ECCI meeting of 17 July 1922 and presented a report describing the KMT as a national-revolutionary movement; a bloc of intellectuals, liberal democratic bourgeoisie, petty bourgeoisie, and workers. Maring proposed the CCP enter the KMT even if this meant joining the KMT as individuals; and then find ways of preserving their independence and organisation. Zinoviev and the ECCI endorsed this new strategy and sent a message to the CCP ordering it to move its HQ to Canton and to carry out its work "in contact with" (i.e. under the supervision of) Maring.[15]

Maring took the United Front proposal to Sun Yat-sen who stubbornly insisted that CCP members would be allowed to join the KMT only as individuals who had to abide by its rules; a United Front of equals was out of the question – a condition that Maring and the ECCI had already accepted, but the CCP leaders had not.

Adolph Joffe, later to be a leading Left Oppositionist, was in China heading a Soviet diplomatic mission. After meeting Sun Yat-sen he wrote to Moscow in July 1922:

> "Support the Chinese Communist Party even more than Sun Yat-sen, ... Irrespective of the weakness of this party, regard its complete independence as necessary, and the efforts of certain agents of the ECCI to fuse this organisation with the party of Sun Yat-sen as completely incorrect."[16]

There was stiff and universal opposition to Maring's proposal within the Central Committee of the CCP on the grounds that joining the KMT as individuals would curb the independence of the CCP. The CC argued that any alliance with the KMT should be temporary, based on specific issues, and include the continuing independence of the two parties. Maring called the members of the CC to a meeting on 17 August 1922 at which he strongly argued that the KMT was the "only serious national-revolutionary group" in China, that it was not a party of the bourgeoisie but a "strong national revolutionary political party with members in all strata of Chinese society." Maring argued that the proletarian party should join the KMT in order to advance the revolution; that a small weak party such as the CCP could enormously and quickly expand its membership and influence if it entered the KMT. It took two days of argument and, ultimately, the threat of expulsion from the CI before the CC agreed to accept the ECCI instructions to join the KMT.[17] As a face-saver it was agreed that the matter would be raised again at the next Congress of the CCP.

The discussions between Chen, Maring, and the KMT took place between the 3rd and 4th World Congresses, both of which were concerned with advancing the United Front strategy. Thus, the discussions within the CCP were couched in terms of a United Front, but that was not what was being proposed for China. A United Front was a temporary alliance between independent parties for specific goals, but here was a strategy in which CCP members entered the KMT and worked within it subject to KMT discipline for an unspecified period to achieve goals set by the KMT.[18] For Communists with little experience of any kind of political work the bloc within carried serious dangers. The organisation of the Party had to change to match that of the KMT; there were limits on what the CCP could publicly say or do. The CCP both formally and informally was being tied into relationships with members of the KMT and tempted to make all kinds of concessions to be accepted and, possibly worse of all, the major work being undertaken by many if not most CCP members was to build KMT branches, often from scratch. There was a real danger of these inexperienced and untested CCP members adapting to the KMT, and of alien ideologies finding their way into the CCP.

Maring met Sun on 25 August 1922 in the French concession in Shanghai and the terms of the collaboration were endorsed, i.e. Sun again refused a United Front on equal terms but would accept Soviet and ECCI assistance. Soviet military and financial assistance would begin arriving the following summer.[19]

On 4 September 1922 (coincidentally the day four CCP leaders symbolically joined the KMT as individual members), Sun Yat-sen announced his intention to reorganise the KMT with a tighter discipline. The plans for a new programme and constitution had been drawn up by a committee headed by Maring and Chen Duxiu.[20]

The 4th World Congress of the CI (7 November–3 December 1922) examined the national-revolutionary movements in the Far East, and the United Front strategy was approved as part of the *Theses on the Eastern Question*. The CI gave its support to any genuinely revolutionary national movement against imperialism in the colonial and semi-colonial countries; but before joint actions the Communist Party had to establish itself as an independent factor and only after its complete political autonomy had been secured could it make temporary agreements with revolutionary bourgeois democratic forces. The theses were at pains to point out that in the so-called backward countries, the struggle for the land was a key element in the revolutionary national liberation struggle against imperialism.[21]

The Congress received a report from the Chinese delegate to the effect that the CCP was establishing an anti-imperialist United Front with the revolutionary nationalist party: "The form of the united front is that we enter (the KMT) in our individual names and capacities." Instead of the Congress reminding the CCP that it was "absolutely unacceptable" to enter any arrangement which restricted the freedom of the CCP to criticise and agitate, the Congress was treated to Radek (session leader and supporter of the bloc within) pronouncing that social and economic development in China was so backward that not even a national republic was on the order of the day.[22] The prestige of the Russian leaders was so high that when Radek spouted this nonsense (the Chinese Revolution which had overthrown the emperor and established a republic had taken place eleven years previously, the anti-imperialist May 4th Movement which radicalised an entire generation of workers and students had exploded three years previously), no-one spoke up to contradict him. Instead Chen Duxiu was upbraided for ultra-leftism for arguing for a politically-independent CCP.

At the 4th World Congress, the machinery of the centre was considerably strengthened with an enlarged ECCI scheduled to meet once every four months with a Presidium, on the pattern of the Russian Politburo. Lenin had generally played an important part – in many cases, the decisive part – in the decision-making process[23] but with Lenin increasingly incapacitated, weakness at the centre combined with the weaknesses in the leaderships of the national Communist Parties would prove fatal in Bulgaria, Germany, Estonia and ... China.

Opposition in the CCP remained so strong that in early January 1923, Zinoviev took the matter before the Politburo of the Russian Party where, following Lenin's death, he was in an unholy alliance with Stalin and Kamenev, and gained its approval for the "bloc within" (Trotsky voted against). On that basis he drafted a resolution approved by the ECCI on 12 January 1923 justifying the desirability of "co-operation" between the CCP and the KMT.[24] Zinoviev may have honestly considered the bloc within to be the most appropriate tactic for building the CCP and developing the national democratic revolution but there was a sleight-of-hand in the ECCI resolution which designated the KMT as a "group" and this allowed the authors to emphasise its multi-class membership. The text of the resolution referred to the KMT as a party only in quotation marks and in this way the document avoided having to define the class nature of the KMT as bourgeois. The policy Zinoviev was proposing for China reflected the class-collaboration he had shown in October 1917.

The resolution re-affirmed the central task for China as the national revolution against imperialism, repeating that the KMT was the only serious national revolutionary group so the activities of the KMT and CCP should be co-ordinated. The members of the CCP were to remain within the KMT and avoid conflict with it as long as it maintained an "objectively correct" policy. The CCP was supposed to preserve its own organisation and apparatus and not lose its identity within the KMT, "not furl its own banner". The CCP was instructed to work independently and openly to create trade unions and lay the foundations for a strong mass Communist Party, but how it could do so while its members were limited by KMT discipline was not described.

Implicit in the ECCI resolution was the assumption that the Chinese national revolution would be a self-contained stage in which the national bourgeoisie remained steadfastly anti-imperialist with the CCP playing a supportive role. Ignored was the possibility that the bourgeoisie might have stronger links with the imperialists than the proletariat and peasantry, and align themselves accordingly. In the event, the Chinese national democratic revolution – just as in Russia in 1917 – would have to be carried though against the national bourgeoisie. The CCP would have to choose capitulation or conflict. Pressure from the ECCI ensured it furled its banner.

Inspired by the First National Labour Conference, enthusiastic railway workers attempted to unionise North China. During 1922-23 strikes took place on all the trunk lines with CCP members playing a leading role. On 7 February, the warlord Wu Pei-fu ordered his troops onto the railway stations in Hankou (part of the Wuhan complex) where they opened fire on the strikers. Sixty railwaymen were killed and the strike collapsed. This became known as the February 7th Massacre.[25] This failure of a CCP-led trade union initiative was used by Maring to justify his argument that the CCP was not yet strong enough to go-it-alone and needed the KMT. With the defeat of the strike there was widespread persecution of militants but trade union organisation recovered surprisingly rapidly, and by 1925 the number of unionised workers had reached 570,000, and a year later had risen to 1,023,000.[26]

Mao was an active and able leader. In response to the February 7th Massacre, the Hunan branch of the CCP organised demonstrations, memorial meetings, even an attempt to get the local railroad workers to strike in sympathy. In March, in protest at Japanese territorial demands, the branch organised a protest demonstration of some 60,000 people. However, Mao's policy was towards a radical bourgeois democracy not socialism, In April 1923 he wrote: "If we analyse the influential factions within the country, there are only three: the revolutionary democratic faction, the non-revolutionary democratic faction, and the reactionary faction. The main body of the revolutionary democratic faction is, of course, the Kuomintang; the rising Communist faction is co-operating with it. ... The Communist Party has temporarily abandoned its most radical views in order to co-operate with the relatively radical Kuomintang. ... This [co-operation] is the source of peace and unification, it is the mother of revolution, it is the magic potion of democracy and independence. Everyone must be aware of this."[27]

Convinced the CCP needed further and more comprehensive direction, Maring travelled to Moscow, and largely on the basis of his report the ECCI issued the famous 13 point directive of 24 May 1923 as instructions for the forthcoming 3rd National Congress of the CCP.[28]

The directive repeated that the "Central task for China is the national revolution against the imperialists" and, in the light of the recent strikes declared that the chief demand to be made by the CCP on the KMT was for unreserved support for the labour movement in both north and south China. This would supposedly rally the forces of the working class and enable the CCP to grow into a mass party of the proletariat while it remained within the KMT!

In this directive the ECCI, for the first time, publicly recognised that the success of the national bourgeois democratic revolution depended on the millions of small peasants. It proposed that the CCP urge the KMT to adopt a programme the most important demand of which was seizure of large private estates and church and monastery lands, and their distribution to the peasantry. The KMT responded by agreeing to a token gesture of calling for a 25% reduction in land rent. This minor concession which made little difference to the lives of the peasants was praised to the skies by Borodin and used as a fig leaf to hide his failure.[29]

It would be wrong to draw too close a parallel between Russia and China, but the 1917 Revolution in Russia had demonstrated clearly that peasants do not limit their demands to those acceptable to the landlords. Indeed, Lenin had concluded that the Russian bourgeois-democratic revolution could cross over into the socialist precisely because no party of the national bourgeois (or petty-bourgeoisie) was prepared to satisfy the peasants' hunger for land.[30] The same situation existed in China. The different sectors of the bourgeoisie; comprador, banker, factory owner and, especially, the families of army officers all had large holdings in the rural areas. The CCP was allied with a bourgeois party and if its demands undermined the economic and social position of the entire bourgeois class the KMT would inevitably break that alliance. The ECCI directive sounded great but could not be enacted in any meaningful way without confrontation between the CCP and KMT.[31]

2.3 The 'Bloc Within'

At the 3rd National Congress of the CCP (12-20 June 1923), there was considerable opposition amongst the 40 delegates (representing 432 members of whom only 19 were female and over 100 were in prison) to the bloc within. Two reasons predominated. Firstly, despite the statements calling for the CCP to maintain its independence the actual restrictions being placed on the CCP made 'independence' more an illusion than reality. Secondly, CCP members were having to spend considerable valuable time and effort setting up KMT branches before they could join them.[32] The discipline of the International prevailed but the hostility of the membership to their submergence in the KMT resulted in three quarters of CCP members quitting so that by November 1923, Party membership had fallen to only about one hundred!

The Party manifesto proposed that the:

> "KMT should be the central force of the national revolution and should assume its leadership. ... We hope that all the revolutionary elements in our society will rally to the KMT, speeding the completion of the national revolutionary movement. ... (We also) hope that the KMT will resolutely discard its ... reliance on foreign powers and concentration on military action ... in order to create a true central force for the national welfare and a true leadership for the national revolution."[33]

The qualitative difference from the first manifesto is obvious. From now on as CCP members led the most radical workers' struggles they increasingly did so under the blue and white banner of the KMT and moved towards a class-collaborationist perspective for China.

A five-person Central Bureau was elected at the Congress with Chen Duxiu as chairperson. Mao Zedong was elected to the Central Bureau (CB) and took control of the Organisational Department and so became secretary of the CB, gaining this post because he was one of the few on the CB who personally endorsed the ECCI line. Within the Party, Mao was second only to Chen.

Soon after the 3rd National Congress, Mao wrote an article for *Guide Weekly*. An important passage reads:

> "The current political issue in China is the single question of national revolution: to topple, by our own efforts, the warlords and foreign imperialists .... Due to historical inevitability and current circumstances, the role of merchants in national revolution is more urgent and important than that of others. As we know, semi-colonial China is under the dual political pressure of warlords and

> foreign imperialists who colluded with each other to suppress the people of the whole nation. ... It is, however, the merchants who are most sensitive to such pressure and suffer the most ... The more the merchants unite ... the greater their role in leading the nation, the more chances for the revolution to succeed."[34]

Mao now used his position on the CB to actively promote the formation of KMT branches by CCP members, particularly in Hunan, and in mid-September 1923, he returned to Changsha to help in successfully establishing a KMT branch with three local cells, and by January 1924 claimed a membership of nearly 500, only the branches in Canton and Shanghai were bigger.[35]

Maring returned to Moscow and was replaced by Mikhail Borodin who arrived in China in September 1923. Borodin's primary role was as adviser to the KMT not the CCP, and was responsible to Stalin not the ECCI.[36] Borodin was sent to Canton to work with Sun. Both were fluent in English and so needed no interpreters and this helped in forming a close personal bond between the two men. In due course the Central Executive Committee (CEC) meetings of the KMT would be in English with Borodin an accepted and active member. Borodin was to carry through the reconstruction of the KMT on the 'Russian' lines proposed by Maring and Chen, and turn it into a disciplined, efficient instrument for carrying out Sun's orders. The nature of Borodin's appointment suggests that Moscow saw little or no likelihood of a clash of interests between the CCP and the KMT, which says much about Moscow's perspective for China both in terms of timescales and politics.

Guide Weekly now carried dutiful articles from leading Party members such as Chen Duxiu and newly-elected CC member Ch'u Ch'iu-pai, publicising, embellishing and concretising the new general line: The KMT was the party of the common people (though it had certain negative feudal aspects), the KMT was the centre of power, the KMT could throw off warlord and imperialist oppression and establish a true people's republic. The corollary was "all work should go towards building the KMT" to form a left wing within it which would push and guide the KMT onto a revolutionary path.[37]

Borodin's influence within the KMT was considerable, due not only to his organisational abilities, but also because during 1924 he paid about 35,000 Chinese dollars a month into the KMT. At Borodin's suggestion, and under his direction, the 1st National Congress of the KMT was called for January 1924 in Canton. The entire Congress was stage-managed by Borodin: he convened it, wrote the major documents, ensured Sun was elected leader for life, had the Congress agree formally to take Communists into the party as individuals (who must abide by the rules of the KMT), and arranged for three Communists to be elected as full members and seven as alternate members to the 41-strong CEC. Amongst these ten CCP members were Li Dazhao, Li Lisan, and Mao Zhedong.[38] However, the CCP was excluded from holding positions on the Party Secretariat and in the General Staff of the armed forces.

On Borodin's urging and with the experience of the Hong Kong strike, Sun's Congress speech included the declaration that the nationalist movement in China could not succeed without the support of workers and peasants. But behind the scenes the conservative elements within the KMT were coalescing and increasing their power. To protect their interests, landlords and factory owners raised the demand that KMT members limit their work to purely nationalist goals, i.e. KMT/CCP members could unionise a labour force but not take strike action for better conditions and higher pay!

To present his strategy in the best light, Borodin arbitrarily divided the KMT into a left and a right on the basis of those who approved the entry of the CCP. This, of course, presented a picture of an overwhelmingly left party with a few dissident right wingers. The class basis of the different groupings was deliberately ignored to better disguise the bourgeois nature of the KMT.[39]

From January 1924, all rank and file CCP members were expected to join the KMT on an individual basis subject to KMT discipline. Within the KMT, the CCP members openly organised themselves into fractions, and were acknowledged to be the most energetic party workers and organisers. Even Li Lisan who had been a key and major figure in building the trade unions was re-assigned to help reorganise the KMT. However, from the very outset, the KMT resisted any political suggestions the CCP members made. Sun Yat-sen was of the opinion:

> "Since the Chinese CP has joined the Kuomintang, it should obey the discipline of the Kuomintang and should not openly criticize it. If the Communists do not obey the Kuomintang I shall expel them from it; if Soviet Russia stands on the side of the CCP I shall immediately oppose Soviet Russia."[40]

It was statements such as these and the demand by Sun that he vet all communications from the ECCI to the CCP, which pushed Chen Duxiu into re-assessing CCP policy.

Previously, Sun had manoeuvred between warlords but now with Russian support, he began a determined attempt to build the KMT's very own National Revolutionary Army (NRA) capable of defeating the warlords. The Whampoa Military Academy in Canton – modelled on the military academies of the

Red Army and the basis of Chiang Kai-shek's rise to power – was established and staffed largely by Soviet advisors. In China with its history of mercenary armies, this was an entirely new concept; expecting moral integrity, honesty and loyalty had an effect similar to the introduction of Cromwell's Ironsides into the English Civil War. Chiang became Commander of the Whampoa Military Academy in May 1924, with the Communist Zhou Enlai (Chou En-lai) as his nominal second in command.[41] The majority of the cadets – the future officers in the NRA – came from the families of the landed gentry, a class bias which would erupt as soon as the peasants laid claim to the land.

For the moment, the Communists took as much advantage as possible of their opportunities and continued to organise the proletariat but as the process of reorganising and restructuring the KMT advanced, the CCP found itself more and more constrained by the bloc within. However, in 1924 no-one could have foreseen that the emergence of Stalin as leader would mean the CCP would be ordered to cling to the KMT until hacked away by the swords of NRA officers.

From 1924, the ECCI was empowered to issue directions to national sections that were binding, and to annul resolutions passed at national congresses with which it disagreed. Between the 5th World Congress in 1924 and the 6th World Congress in 1928 most talented and independent minded communist leaders had been replaced by the servile and the "fifth-rate."[42] As a starting point the Congress internationalised Lenin's temporary 1921 ban on factions and raised it to a principle: from then on open dissent was impermissible.

Peng Shuzhi had spent some time in Moscow as a student and then lecturer. He returned with a number of others in August 1924 to help remedy the shortage of trained CCP personnel. They found a Party they considered 'loose' and proposed three actions to the CC: that the returnees take responsibility for renewing Party organisation and discipline, that Li Lisan return to Trade Union work aided by, amongst others Peng Shuzhi, and that a more critical attitude be adopted towards the KMT. This second wave of Bolshevisation was generally welcomed because it was accepted by the CCP that it needed trained and experienced cadres.[43]

However, the contradictions arising due to the fundamental class nature of the KMT abounded and fuelled antagonisms towards the CCP so much so that in 1924, leading members of the CC were again pressing for the CCP to end the bloc within. Peng Shuzhi in December 1924 published an article in the party theoretical journal *New Youth*, of which he had become the editor, emphasising the need for the proletariat to take the lead in the Chinese national revolution.[44] The article was clearly meant to influence delegates to the forthcoming 4th Party Congress, as was the accompanying article by Chen, *The Lessons of the National Movement over the Past Twenty-seven Years*, which concluded that the national revolution could be victorious only if led by the proletariat.[45]

Borodin and the ECCI used the success of a number of joint activities between the CCP and KMT to counteract the arguments of Chen and Peng, to hide the fundamental political differences between the two organisations, and so justify the continuation of the ECCI line. For example, in the summer of 1924, the KMT's rule in Canton was challenged by the Merchant Volunteers, armed and funded by the British and their comprador lackeys. KMT militants (including CCP members) seized a boatload of arms intended for the Volunteers and on 26 August in a short, sharp engagement, defeated and disarmed them. A few months later in February 1925, a local warlord threatened Canton but joint action by KMT forces and peasant militias forced him back. The working class was recovering from the May 7th Massacre of the previous year and strike activity was increasing, particularly in Canton and Shanghai. CCP and KMT militants often worked together to build trade unions, and between May 1924 and May 1925, union membership rose from 220,000 to 540,000, and by May 1926, was over a million.

The 4th National Congress of the CCP (11-22 January 1925) voted to maintain the bloc within, but there was significant criticism of those communists who were considered too subservient to the KMT and who placed the interests of the KMT before those of the CCP. At the same Congress, the CCP (then numbering just under 1,000) on the basis of the rising class struggle, relaxed its membership conditions and attempted to begin the move towards a mass proletarian party rather than remain a mainly intellectual group – within eighteen months the membership would double. This proletarian hegemony line was presented at the 4th Congress by Peng and Chen Duxiu, in stark contrast to the arguments of those such as Ch'u Ch'iu-pai that the CCP should be engaged primarily in recruiting to the KMT. Peng Shuzhi was elected to the Central Committee of the CCP and then became the Politburo member in charge of propaganda activities.[46] It was after the 4th Congress that leading figures such as Li Lisan gave up building the KMT as their primary task and returned to their original activities.

Under pressure of work Mao fell ill, was given sick leave just two weeks before the 4th Congress, and was not re-elected to the Central Committee.

During this time Mao's support for the national as opposed to the socialist revolution was developing and hardening: in the autumn of 1925 he wrote: "I advocate making use of the national revolution … to realize the joint rule of the proletariat, the petty bourgeoisie, and the left wing of the middle bourgeoisie, that is, the rule of the revolutionary popular masses."[47] Mao was developing the idea of a 'bloc of four classes' independently of Stalin but based on the same misconception – that the KMT could be won to revolution.

Sun died suddenly in March 1925. With his death the social tensions within the KMT, which he had kept under control, came into the open. During 1925 membership of the KMT rose to about a quarter of a million, recruited from all sections of society, and was led by two men, the leftist Wang Jingwei (Wang Ching-wei who, at the start of his political career, had favoured distributing the land equally among the people), who held all the nominally important civilian posts and Sun's *protégé*, Chiang Kai-shek, backed by the army and the cadets of the Whampoa Military Academy.[48]

In 1925, workers in enterprises all across Shanghai were striking sporadically against appalling working conditions and low wages and on May Day 1925, the 2nd National Labour Conference opened in Canton with 230 delegates representing over half a million union members.[49] On 15 May 1925, a Japanese foreman in a Shanghai cotton mill, which had been on strike since February, shot and killed a leader of the Chinese workers. On 28 May, the CCP called for co-ordinated protest demonstrations and on 30 May 1925, thousands of workers and students marched in protest and several were arrested. The march went straight to the police station to demand the release of their comrades. There, a British officer ordered the police under his command to open fire, killing nine people and wounding dozens. This May 30th Incident triggered an unprecedented eruption of the working class, more than 100 separate strikes involving 400,000 workers arose directly out of the shootings and culminated in a general strike across Shanghai. "Down with the imperialists", was the slogan of the day but the local government in Shanghai, egged on by foreign imperialism, met demonstrations and meetings by shooting and wounding scores of people. At this time, the CCP branch in Shanghai was led by Chen and Peng and remained sufficiently independent to severely criticise the attempts by the local KMT to compromise with the factory owners.[50] What started as a dispute about wages and a protest against imperialist injustice flashed into a political battle for national liberation.

As the strength of the Shanghai proletariat showed itself, it drew behind it the 'whole people'; the students, the artisans, shop keepers, small traders, merchants and businessmen and, in the special conditions of China as a country struggling for national independence, even sections of the Chinese bourgeoisie. Between the end of May and the middle of September, the class-forces that would struggle for mastery during the coming revolution differentiated themselves. Initially, all the urban classes seemed to support the strike and merchants and businessmen joined the protests. But the workers predominated, the Chinese proletariat was the leading component of the struggle right from its start and, as the strike developed, the necessity of a proletarian party which retained its political and organisational independence was confirmed with startling clarity.[51]

The foreign capitalists who owned the electrical power stations retaliated by shutting off the power to Chinese factories. The Chinese bourgeoisie who had never been very ardent, unable to operate their factories and seeing the growing radicalism of the working class, rapidly ceased to support the strike and began secretly co-operating with the imperialists against the strike movement – a characteristic of the bourgeoisie ever since the revolution of 1848 when the German bourgeoisie had been prepared, even eager, to compromise with the aristocracy.[52]

During July and August 1925, the petty-bourgeoisie and those with an intermediate position in society began to vacillate. Some minor victories were won and Li Lisan was important in organising the end of the strike in such a way that the Shanghai workers returned to work in good order, "with a living, vital experience to help them in the future."[53] In Shanghai itself the strike was over by the end of the summer but the strike wave had reached Hong Kong and Canton via seamen working for British shipping companies, who had walked out on 18 June. A week later, during a demonstration in Canton, over 50 students and workers were killed by Anglo-French military police. A general strike and boycott of British goods followed immediately, and all foreign industrial activity ground to a halt.

To avoid being forced back to work, strikers left Hong Kong for Canton (90 miles up the Pearl River). The movement was well organised through a 13-member Canton-Hong Kong Strike Committee, responsible to a delegate conference which had one representative for every 50 strikers and met twice a week. In a show of workers' power the committees set up a hospital, organised 17 schools and with some 2,000 armed pickets, they captured, tried and imprisoned strike-breakers and other hooligan elements. They organised patrols of pickets (many of these patrols were peasants) along the entire frontier of Kwangsi province to keep out British ships and British goods from Hong-

Kong. The organisation became known as 'government number two' and was the first Chinese Soviet in embryo. Its presence forced the KMT government in Canton to give solid support, legalising trade unions and providing food kitchens for the strikers (earning for itself the label 'left').[54]

The Canton-Hong Kong strike lasted for fifteen months and remains one of the greatest strikes in history. It was anti-imperialist in its demands, proletarian in its methods. It raised the question of who would hold state power if the workers and peasants, guns in hand, seized governmental power – would they voluntarily hold back or would they flood over the limits set by the bourgeoisie?

The main leaders of this tremendous revolutionary movement were Communists. The leaders of the powerful Chinese Seamen's Union joined the CCP. From being a party composed largely of students and intellectuals, the CCP increased its membership ten-fold and of these between half and two-thirds were workers. The CCP moved from being a few intellectuals to a party rooted in the working class, with mass support. During the strike the CCP targeted agitation at specific sections of the population especially women and youth, and helped set up peasant unions in alliance with the urban workers. The CCP was still small numerically compared to the KMT but its leadership of large-scale proletarian actions posed the question of how long it could continue to subordinate itself to the discipline of the bourgeois party.

The radicalism sweeping China had also greatly benefitted the KMT and within two years it had grown into a mass force (in many areas due to the work of Communists); and simultaneously it had been transformed from a loose association into a structured party with an effective army. At the end of June 1925, with Kwangtung province solidly under its control (Chen Jiongming had been driven out), the KMT proclaimed itself to be China's National Government. The KMT now set its eyes on Beijing.

During 1925, the left wing of the KMT had displayed much sympathy for the workers' movement, and had begun to organise peasant leagues to fight against the *ming tuan* and militias of the warlords in the countryside. But, just as the *SRs* in 1917, they vacuously promised the land would be redistributed lawfully in due course, insisting the peasants took no action to seize the land. However, the formation of even reformist peasant leagues caused dissatisfaction among the rightist elements in the KMT. The heart of the KMT (the families of the army officers) were landlords who brooked no challenge to their control over the land. If the Communists supported peasant demands for seizure of the land then that would place the CCP and the KMT on opposite sides of the barricades; the former with the oppressed and the latter with the landlords and imperialists.[55]

The revolution was entering a new phase; the right wing was organising to oppose strike action by workers, oppose organisation of the peasants into peasant leagues and oppose the right of Communists to be in the KMT. At the October 1925 Central Committee (CC) of the CCP, Chen Duxiu argued that the Chinese bourgeoisie was going over to the side of counter-revolution and urged that the CCP should not allow itself to be held hostage by its bloc with the KMT. The CCP should have a public political face and should be ready to withdraw from the KMT at a moment's notice to be able to lead the workers' and peasants' struggles independently. His position was rejected by the Comintern representative, Voitinsky, who won the support of a majority of the Central Committee on the grounds that such a policy would lead to exclusion from the KMT at a time when the benefits of the bloc within were about to be reaped.[56]

Voitinsky pointed out that the KMT CEC was dominated by the left; that the Political Bureau of nine members was also dominated by the left; that Wang Jingwei (a key left figure) was head of the party and of the Canton/Wuhan Government and had supported the Canton-Hong Kong strike; that Borodin was so highly favoured by Wang that he was drafting the resolutions for the forthcoming KMT conference; that CCP members were to be the secretaries of the Peasant Section, Propaganda Section, Women's Section, Workers' Section and Youth Section. To many in the CCP it must have sounded wonderful. Voitinsky also pointed out that the bloc within had assisted the CCP to grow enormously and rapidly. By November 1925 it claimed 10,000 members (and this would triple in the next six months).[57]

However, Voitinsky played down the response of the bourgeoisie to the Shanghai strike and the demands for the expulsion of Communists from the KMT. He closed his eyes to the very sharp differences regarding the policy of land distribution that were exposed during the initial stages of work amongst the peasants; that the peasants were demanding the land but the social composition of the KMT made it impossible for it to carry out land redistribution. He closed his eyes to the fact that sooner or later the CCP would have to choose between supporting the starving Chinese peasantry or the bourgeois KMT.

The theoretical justification for the bloc within and its continuation was provided by Bukharin, who argued that the Chinese national bourgeoisie would play an objectively revolutionary role in the bourgeois revolution against feudalism and imperialism (ignoring the Russian example which demonstrated just the opposite). He presented the KMT not as a bourgeois party but as a neutral academic arena which could objectively discuss and, by a majority vote, determine the best way forward for the national revolution. He used Maring's argument that if the CCP succeeded in recruiting enough workers and peasants into the KMT, it would change its social composition and political nature, and move its centre of gravity leftwards. Even at the strictly organisational level this was untrue – the ECCI (including Bukharin) had only recently provided the model and means for reorganising the KMT into a tightly disciplined organisation controlled from the top down, which effectively blocked such a transformation.[58] An even more fundamental error was the supposition that the Chinese bourgeoisie would accept democratic constraints when its essential interests were threatened.

Bukharin's view was quite the opposite of Lenin's who defined the fundamental task facing Communist Parties:

> "in backward countries (as being) to give special support to the peasant movement against the landowners ... to strive to lend the peasant movement the most revolutionary character ... It is particularly necessary to exert every effort to apply the basic principles of the Soviet system in countries where pre-capitalist relations predominate – by setting up working peoples' Soviets."[59]

Bukharin's scenario failed to recognise that bringing the revolutionary masses into struggle against imperialism was to invite the seizure of the land. It was inevitable that in the end the Chinese bourgeoisie would join with imperialists and militarists to crush the revolution.

Mao was now regarded both in the CCP and the KMT as 'the' expert on the peasantry, and in October 1925, Wang Jingwei personally invited Mao to join the KMT Propaganda Department and edit the KMT weekly paper *Political Weekly*.[60] Here, Mao enthusiastically endorsed the ECCI line dictated by Stalin that Communists should form a bloc with the petty-bourgeoisie, a bloc which would have the form of a single party.[61] Naturally Stalin laid down conditions: no restriction on the freedom of the CCP to conduct agitation and propaganda work, and the bloc must facilitate the CCP taking the actual leadership of the revolutionary movement. However, for Stalin and the ECCI, the collaboration between the CCP and KMT was essential and the conditions optional.

The activism of the rank and file CCP members meant the left and Communists dominated the 2nd Congress of the KMT in January 1926.

This was trumpeted within the CCP as demonstrating the success of the bloc within. The following month at the 6th Plenum of the ECCI, Tan Pingshan, the chief Chinese delegate, claimed that the left and Communists had 166 out of the total of 278 votes and that the Congress had adopted many of the Communist demands for social reforms to the benefit of workers and peasants. This was just what the ECCI wanted to hear and its members took the report as verification of its strategy. However, Tan's parliamentary-style appraisal was self-deception which held great dangers for the CCP as it omitted from consideration the very real power base of the right wing – the armies of the KMT and the warlords – and it over-estimated the strength of the KMT lefts and Communists by omitting the very real differences between them over the key question of land to the peasant. It was this meeting that the ECCI, with only Trotsky voting against, approved the admission of the KMT to the CI as an associate party and elected Chiang Kai-shek as honorary member of the ECCI.[62] In Lenin's time the idea that a bourgeois party would be admitted to the Comintern was something no proletarian revolutionary would have dreamt possible.

Fraternal delegates from the KMT attended the two plenums of the ECCI held in February and November 1926. The KMT associated with the CI to better control the Communists within its ranks and deceive the masses. But this parody of an association meant the ECCI was even more opposed to any suggestion that the CCP leave the bloc within, and it urged the CCP to avoid engaging in class battles in which they would be opposed to the patriotic bourgeoisie of the KMT.

2.4 Summary

The ECCI's advice and material support which ensured the successful launch and initial growth of the CCP would become its antithesis with the coming to power of the Bukharin/Stalin bloc in the Russian Communist Party, after which the ECCI would systematically mis-direct the CCP. The ECCI would go so far as to justify in advance, the failure of the KMT to solve the land question by revolutionary means because its "multi-class composition" meant it could not be expected "to undertake the confiscation of private property."[63] With such an appraisal, the efforts of the young CCP to lead an agricultural revolution were doomed before they began.

In the Second Chinese Revolution, many workers were organised in such groups as the Canton-Hong Kong Strike Committee and the Shanghai General Labour Union (which for a time were functioning practically as Soviets).

The workers were mobilised, and Communists occupied leading positions in a nationwide movement, launching a number of large strikes and giant demonstrations. The coming months would see the working class engaged in several victorious armed revolts as when the worker masses in Hangkow and Chiuchiang seized the British settlements, and in Shanghai where they occupied the entire city with the exception of the foreign concessions.[64]

While the young CCP was weak and composed almost entirely of intellectuals, and while the KMT had the support of large numbers of workers the bloc within was an acceptable tactic. Indeed the entry tactic if treated as an episode on the road to an independent party could have been a magnificent success. Unfortunately, its ongoing application in a distorted form in completely changed conditions would prove disastrous for the Chinese Revolution.[65]

Stalin had a track record of successful manipulation and manoeuvring within the Russian Communist Party (RCP(B))[66] but his successes in Russia had been due to the ebb of the revolution. In China the revolution was on the rise and bureaucratic calculations of who would be voted onto what committee and which resolution would be passed by the KMT Congress were worthless in the face of class war. It would not be the Communists and the left who would eject the right from the KMT, but the right and left of the KMT who would eject and massacre the Communists.

The KMT's 2nd National Congress in January 1926 had, apparently, been for the CCP a huge success. On 13 March, the ECCI declared that the KMT identified ideologically with the CI.[67] Just one week later on 20 March, Chiang Kai-shek carried out his first coup against the Communists.

Chapter 3

Stalin Sets the Pattern for the Chinese Revolution

3.1 Introduction

The advice and material support of the Communist International (CI) was essential to the successful formation of the CCP. At first the CCP received genuine help and guidance but after Lenin's death, with the rise to power of Stalin and his faction first in Russia and then in the CI, a new political line was systematically imposed on the CCP.

As practice proved the new line disastrously wrong, factional interests within the Russian Party became the determining factor and guidance gave way to direct orders. If challenged, the representatives of the CI threatened individuals and even the entire organisation with expulsion from the CI to force acceptance of their proposals. Individuals who attempted to organise opposition were expelled, and dark rumours persist that some in the leadership of the CCP actively betrayed oppositionists to the KMT's secret police. Such actions were quite compatible with the methods used by the Stalin faction in Russia. During the Great Purges, carried out to maintain the Stalin faction in power, more Russian Communists were killed than during the civil war.

From the mid-1920s, until at least the start of the Korean War in 1950, Stalin's wishes were decisive in determining the policies of the CCP on all important matters. The results were major political and military defeats for the CCP, the loss of any significant proletarian support and a twenty year detour during which the Chinese people were subject to horrendous suffering. Knowledge of the development of the Stalin faction within the Bolshevik Party, and how its policies for the Chinese Revolution derived from its own needs not the reality of China, are essential for an understanding of the defeat of the Second Chinese Revolution.

3.2 Russia after the October Revolution

3.2.1 Stalin Becomes General Secretary

The 8th Congress of the Bolshevik Party (March, 1919) agreed to Zinoviev's proposal, made on Lenin's behalf, that the CC should establish a Politburo (also known as the Political Committee) and an Orgburo. The former was intended to be the real leadership in the Party and because of its relatively small membership could decide all issues that mattered quickly and efficiently. The latter would allocate resources to carry out CC decisions. With Lenin's strong support, the 8th Party Congress also endorsed Stalin's appointment as Commissar of the newly created *Rabkrin* (Workers' and Peasants' Inspectorate).[1]

Before 1920 Stalin had played no direct role in leading the party machinery but from now on his attention was on party affairs, and via these three posts Stalin participated in making policy decisions, was responsible for allocating party resources to implement them, and then in charge of the Commissariat which assessed how well he had done.[2] Lenin's promotion of Stalin to such a decisive position may have been the advancement of an efficient functionary but it betrayed a calamitous misappraisal of the man.

By the 10th Congress (March 1921), Stalin was sufficiently powerful to have his supporters elected to the CC and its Secretariat in place of those friendly to Trotsky. The Orgburo was expanded to seven members to give Stalin an in-built majority.[3] The first plenum of the CC two days after the 10th Congress (March 1921) unanimously accepted the proposal of Kamenev naming Stalin as the General Secretary who could direct the work of the Secretariat of the CC. This included the selection and allocation of cadres to Party posts. With this extension of Stalin's power, the office of General Secretary became the *de-facto* control centre of Party activities and the hub for the emerging Party hierarchy.[4]

There is no doubt that Stalin was able to point to a number of successes in streamlining Party organisation and making the Party more effective in carrying out Politburo and CC decisions. However, Stalin began to use the resources of the Party to strengthen a clique personally loyal to him. This unprincipled grouping began as all such groups do, based on gossip and backstabbing, with the principal target Leon Trotsky. Stalin's undoubted organisational abilities were changing from a positive force for building the Party to a destructive force, making the Party apparatus a factor which would eventually destroy the

Bolshevik Party and the Soviet Union. By the 13th Party Conference (16–18 January 1924), Stalin was the real power within the Party.

3.2.2 Ban on Political Parties and War Communism

Prior to October 1917, no leader within the Bolsheviks had ever suggested that after the revolution there would be a one-Party political system, and in the period immediately after the insurrection even the bourgeois Cadet Party remained legal. The only political organisation which was suppressed was the neo-fascist Black Hundreds, infamous for inciting pogroms. This was to be expected since the Bolsheviks had, until 1917, the governmental goal of "a freely convened constituent assembly of the whole people" to which "every class of the population" would turn.[5] In such a schema only die-hard Tsarists and landed aristocrats would seriously oppose the revolution, so the notion of banning political parties had never arisen.

But, contrary to expectations, the October Revolution had been a socialist revolution which meant that the urban middle class allies anticipated by Lenin in 1905[6] now opposed the Bolshevik insurrection. The initial response, on 9 November 1917, was a decree banning hostile newspapers, but the decree specifically stated that the ban was of a temporary nature, and would be rescinded as soon as normal conditions were re-established.[7]

However, under the protection of the Whites who were resourced mainly by England and France, and no fewer than thirteen armies of intervention which included Americans, French, Czech, and Japanese, the Right Socialist Revolutionaries (SRs) and some Mensheviks, with support from Cadets were proclaiming their own governments in a number of places such as Archangel, Omsk, Samara, and Ufa. These people spoke in the name of democracy but, in fact, ceded real power to the counter-revolutionary armies. This made it impossible for these parties to have freedom of propaganda and agitation within Soviet-controlled areas. A sharp polarisation took place in the Soviets. The civil war gave the Bolsheviks no choice but to exclude Right SRs and Mensheviks from the Soviets.

By November 1918, of the 950 delegates at the 6th All-Russian Congress of Soviets, 933 were Communists.[8] But with Party monopoly of power, the separation of Party and state became unrealisable; whatever was determined in a Party caucus was binding on all Party members attending the Soviets. Generally, by 1921, at local level the Party branch secretary had replaced the chairperson of the Soviet as the leading official.[9] This situation posed a serious problem because less and less distinction between Party and state could only lead to a weakening of Soviet democracy and a bureaucratisation of the Party.

The 12th All-Russian Party Conference (4-7 August 1922) formalised the actual situation, and the resolution on *The Registration of Associations and Unions* meant the prohibition of all parties but the Bolsheviks.[10] The ban was necessary because of the counter-revolutionary activities of all the so-called socialist parties, but it was a signal warning of the effects of imperialist pressure on a socialist revolution in a backward country.

During the civil war the Bolsheviks were forced to adopt the policy of War Communism with intense centralisation and Party control of virtually every aspect of society, nationalisation of industries necessary to maintain supplies to the armies, and the removal of decision-making authority from state institutions and non-Party organisations.[11]

War Communism included the forced requisitioning of grain. However, once the Whites were defeated and they considered their land safe, the mass of peasants vigorously resisted requisitioning which they viewed as theft by the state. The peasants responded by planting only what they needed for themselves. This meant there was little or no grain to requisition.[12] The food situation in the towns went from bad to worse, to near starvation. On 1 March 1921, the sailors at the giant Kronstadt naval base rose in revolt – a reflection that the relations between the Soviet state and the peasant masses had reached an all-time low.[13] The mutiny was the final straw in demonstrating War Communism as unsustainable and at the 10th Congress of the All-Russian Communist Party (ARCP(B)) (8–16 March) it was agreed to move towards a New Economic Policy (NEP).[14]

However, War Communism had adverse long-term consequences: the replacement of internal Party democracy by top-down command, and the introduction of a system of appointment rather than election of local Party leaders. That these changes occurred in parallel with the banning of opposition parties meant War Communism brought into existence a hierarchical social system based on the Bolshevik Party which simultaneously became the gateway to a secure job.[15]

3.2.3 The New Economic Policy and Character of the New Members

The NEP meant that the peasants paid a tax on what they produced and sold their surplus on the open market. This move to a market economy satisfied the immediate demands of the peasantry but represented a turn by the Communist Party to the middle peasants and kulaks who were the most efficient and biggest producers of foodstuffs. With the adoption of the NEP by the Soviet regime, the process of equalisation of land-holdings that had taken place after October and intensified during War Communism was reversed.[16]

The NEP with its reliance on the market, strengthened the kulaks and NEPmen (capitalist speculators) to the detriment of the poor peasants and the proletariat. The kulaks had the largest and most fertile farms and the capital necessary for equipment, horses, and fertiliser; they made huge profits. Under the NEP the difference between the rich and poor in the villages began to grow at an alarming rate with the parallel danger of growing political opposition to the workers' state.[17]

The NEP gave the Soviet regime the opportunity to catch its breath, but at the cost of increasing social differentiation. Production of goods and produce for a market economy led to the rapid enrichment not only of petty-bourgeois kulaks, shopkeepers and traders but also a number of sticky-fingered Party officials. Alongside the re-emergence of class divisions, the budding bureaucracies of the state, industry, and Party began to coalesce and flex their muscles.[18]

Material inequalities began to widen rapidly. In 1920, the government ruled that the highest-paid managers should earn no more than four times the minimum wage. With the advent of NEP that ratio was increased to eight times. A survey conducted in 1924 showed that more than 80,000 state officials admitted to earning more than the upper limit, 15,000 were on more than 15 times the minimum – to say nothing of corrupt and illegal earnings, which everyone believed were widespread.[19]

Private trade flourished but state enterprises were constrained by government policy to make good war damage while working without loss, and to fund any wage increases from higher productivity. This imposed considerable pressure on such revolutionary gains as the eight-hour day and women's right to receive paid maternity leave or to take breaks to feed their babies being looked after in the factory nursery.[20] Factories reduced their costs by lay-offs, increasing the number of unemployed industrial workers from about 500,000 to 1,250,000 between autumn 1922 and summer 1923. Women were particularly hard hit.

A wave of strikes and disturbances swept the country sometimes led by stalwart Party members who, as active trade unionists, felt a responsibility to their workmates.[21] The response of the Party machine was to have the secret police (GPU) step in and arrest a number of such activists who were then summarily expelled. Felix Dzerzhinsky, head of the GPU and a devout supporter of Stalin, demanded the members of the Politburo inform the GPU of any known oppositional activity.[22] This was the first time the GPU had been openly used against Party members, though it would soon be normal practice to spy on activists in the factories.[23]

The NEP generated a mood of personal aggrandisement, which often contaminated proletarian Party members returning home from the Red Army. Most of these would be given administrative jobs in the new state apparatus or factory management, cut off from the factory floors from which they had come. During this period, Party functionaries particularly the new influx, were finding their feet and beginning to forge relationships across and within government organisations, industrial management and the state apparatus. In part they were coalescing into an elite that would become the rulers of the Soviet Union.[24]

Over the period of the NEP, the majority of rank and file Party members went from supporting the actions of the factory workers in defence of wages and conditions to – under pressure from the local Party secretaries – siding with the factory managers against the workforce, supporting cuts in pay and working conditions and increased workloads. In many cases this led to disillusion and demoralisation of the rank and file who quit the Party. Those who remained had to develop a tough skin – and all too often these were the most politically backward members.[25]

The continued failure of a revolution to take place in a technologically advanced country left Russia isolated and provided the conditions for the growth of both alien class forces and internal bureaucratic degeneration.

The membership of the Bolshevik Party had been overwhelmingly proletarian in October 1917 and the early days of the civil war when capture by the Whites meant a certain and cruel death. During this period there was an open door policy towards recruitment. However, at the 8th Party Congress it was recognised that many of the enthusiasts who had joined did not have the necessary integrity, honesty, commitment or political understanding.[26] The decision was taken to sift out those who were 'unworthy', and within six months Party membership was reduced from about 250,000 to about 150,000.

However, by the autumn of 1919 the situation had changed again and the regime had its back to the wall, threatened by a ring of White armies. In such a situation the doors were again thrown open and between October and December 1919 nearly 200,000 new recruits entered the Party. By the 9th Congress in March 1920, the membership was over 600,000, and by the 10th Congress in March 1921, almost three-quarters of a million.[27] The large numbers flooding into the Party mean that by the 10th Congress only about 10% of members predated 1917. The new members were in their vast majority honest Communists, prepared to risk life and limb for the revolution, but their political education was more military manual than Marxist text. "It was a Party literally steeled on the fields of battle"[28] where some 200,000 lost their lives.[29]

In the civil war the resolution and solution of problems had to be immediate, with centralisation of decision-making and a non-elected command structure. The very purpose of the Red Army and the central role of the Party within it had enhanced the fusion of state and Party and increased centralisation of decision making within the Party itself. After 1920, the demobilised Communist soldiers who became administrators in the local soviets and the economy everywhere enhanced the trend towards expecting submission to one's superiors and expecting obedience of one's own orders.[30]

The need for Communists in senior positions in government and industry meant that on demobilisation, a large proportion of Party members were directly appointed to administrative posts. Pirani gives figures for the latter half of 1922 when in Moscow alone nearly 2,000 Party members were appointed to local and central state bodies.[31] By the end of 1921 the proportion of members who were still factory workers was no more than 20% while the proportion of members in peasant cells was 30%.[32]

From the Party Congress of 1922 to the Party Congress of 1923, gigantic strides were made in increasing the domination of the Russian Communist Party (RCP) over all aspects of Russian life: the proportion of regional leaders of trade unions who were members of the Party increased from 27% to 57%, the proportion of commanding staffs in the army from 16% to 24%, the proportion of managers of co-operatives from 5% to 50%, and so on in all important institutions of public life.[33] To marshal its forces, the Party Secretariat now had a Personnel Department with branches spread throughout the country and which kept detailed files on all members. It had the power to order members to change their occupation and place of residence at short notice, and this was used not only for promotion but also for maintaining discipline: a shift from the capital to the wilderness of Siberia could be the punishment for voicing dissent.

3.2.4 Ban on Factions and Authority Within the Party

After the civil war a Party card was almost a guarantee of a secure job, and careerists flooded in.[34] Lenin warned again and again against the dangers of careerist, capitalist, white-guard, Menshevik and *SR* infiltration of the Party, and was for their wholesale expulsion. Despite this, one estimate had former Mensheviks and SRs comprising about one quarter of the active higher cadres by 1927.[35]

One cannot properly understand the policies pursued by Lenin, and supported by Trotsky, in this period without remembering the actual situation in Russia: hunger, partial atomisation of the proletariat, economic catastrophe, very low cultural and technological levels of the population, and pressures from the petty-bourgeois peasant masses (which had doubled due to the NEP) – all consequences of the delay of the international revolution. In the face of such stresses how was the Soviet state to be maintained? Lenin was convinced that class enemies who had entered the Party were consciously using the differences raised by genuine Bolsheviks (e.g. the Workers' Opposition) to weaken the Party for counter-revolutionary purposes.[36] Lenin's fear was that with one Party rule, the RCP would begin to reflect the pressures of alien classes, which if allowed to express themselves as factions, would eventually split the Party on class lines. This would mean the overthrow of the workers' state, since it was the Communist Party that held it together and guaranteed its continued existence.

Hence, the 10th Party Congress in early 1921 – with the Kronstadt revolt taking place almost at its door – banned factions within the Party. Lenin made it clear that this was a temporary measure brought in to deal with an exceptional situation and, moreover, favoured a flexible interpretation of this rule, rejecting attempts to make it definitive.[37]

This emergency measure which circumscribed the democratic rights of Party members strengthened the bureaucratic tendencies within the Party. As a 'necessary evil' imposed upon the Party it should have been lifted and full democratic rights restored as soon as conditions eased. But in fact, after Lenin's death this temporary measure was made permanent as part of the manoeuvres by the *Troika* of Kamenev, Stalin, and Zinoviev in their struggle against Trotsky.[38] Ultimately, the ban on factions would be extended internationally and be a major weapon in defeating oppositionists in, e.g., China.

The Party had leapt from the underground to the heights of power and as times changed so too did people. More and more, Stalin was using his increasing domination of the Party organisation to recruit to important posts, people who were personally obligated and loyal to him. In his position of General Secretary as he dispensed favours and fortune, he was losing his moral integrity. The foundations were being laid for an inevitable conflict with Bolshevism.

With the ban on internal factions, power within the Party became progressively centralised in the Politburo and CC. This centralisation inevitably had its organisational form: the Secretariat (under Stalin) increasingly supervised (i.e. controlled) the appointment and allocation of Party personnel. As Kremlin files have become public, much attention has been concentrated on the details of the growth of a centralised system of Party functionaries effectively appointed by, and beholden to, the General Secretary. The wealth of detail now available only confirms the essential analysis made at the time by opposition currents within the RCP. The major difference is that the bureaucracy proved more servile and self-seeking than the Oppositionists ever dreamed.

By the time of the 9th Party Congress of September 1920, the appointment of secretaries of provincial committees was well established, though at that time, local recommendations for the posts were still preferred. Serge described how by the winter of 1920/21, a "state of siege had now entered the Party itself, which was increasingly run from the top, by Secretaries. We were at a loss to find a remedy for this bureaucratization."[39]

Most leading members of the Stalin group were Old Bolsheviks with numerous personal links going back, in many cases, to before 1903. They were efficient capable organisers, hard-working, often patient and prudent, creatures of the apparatus and well aware of their own importance. They shared a common conservative outlook. Stalin, as General Secretary, embodied this new group, united them and brought them together. It was around him that they formed a growing freemasonry. To these 'practical' men, these 'realists', these 'committee men', the time and energy spent reaching a democratic decision was a waste of effort that delayed – even threatened – necessary work.[40]

At the 10th Congress (March 1921) it was reported that the Party Secretariat had been responsible for the transfer and/or appointment of 42,000 members to their posts. It can be argued that from this Congress, Stalin was in such a strong position in the Party that only Lenin's direct opposition could have removed him because of the mechanisms he had in place for controlling who attended the decision-making conferences, ensuring the 'right' people became branch officers, etc.

The 10th Congress had sanctioned a purge of careerists whose behaviour was too gross and blatant to tolerate, but after the 11th Congress (March/April 1922), which placed great emphasis on unity and Party discipline, the purge was also directed at crushing criticism and dissent.[41] The 11th Party Congress was the last Congress in which Lenin participated and the first at which appointment rather than election of Congress delegates was practised on a mass scale.[42] After the 11th Congress, from the summer of 1922 the Secretariat rapidly increased its control over the Party and state apparatuses, and extended the selection and imposition of elements loyal to Stalin.[43]

The practice of appointments had become so widespread by the 12th Congress (April 1923) that Preobrazhensky protested that some 30% of the secretaries of local committees had been recommended for their position by the Secretariat.[44] In fact, Preobrazhensky seriously underestimated the extent of the appointments, recent data shows 94 of the 191 secretaries of provincial committees had been recommended or directly appointed.[45] Soon all secretaries of district and provincial committees would acquire their positions in this way.

Publicly Stalin called for the free election of regional and provincial Party leaders but behind the scenes he was busy ensuring the domination of the centre and appointment from above. Any remaining element of internal democracy in the Party was strangled when the Secretariat appointed unelected provincial bureaux to oversee the work of the elected committees.[46]

The final organisational requirement for the bureaucratisation of the Party was the Secretariat's take-over of the Control Commissions. These bodies, initially composed of independently-minded Party members, could act to protect the rank and file from overbearing and bureaucratic officials. At the 11th Party Congress, however, it was agreed that the Central Control Commission should play a much greater role in guiding the work of local Commissions. Of course, a majority of the seven members elected to the Central Control Commission were strong supporters of Stalin. In this way the Control Commission was made a parallel mechanism to the Party secretaries for control of the members. The function of the Commission was turned on its head; from defending the rights of the membership it became a mechanism for tighter control.[47]

Even the pre-revolution Old Guard was now coming under attack; a 1922 Secretariat report on cadre distribution harangues the 'old boys' as not being sufficiently 'malleable' and argued that post-civil war recruits were much more amenable and therefore preferable:

> "the young, active worker, elected at some All-Russian Congress, meeting or conference, having attended and got the hang of things there, already has a great advantage over an authoritative, respected old cadre."[48]

The dissatisfaction with Old Bolsheviks was precisely because of their independence of mind which inevitably brought them into conflict with the practices of the Stalin faction.

3.2.5 Privileges and Their Enshrinement

In 1920, some tens of thousands of Bolshevik Party members were attempting to bring order to Soviet society. Grossly overworked and with few, if any, material privileges, these Party officials were trying to lay the foundations of Soviet rule. Serge, who was one of these, described the situation:

> "Our salaries were limited to the 'Communist maximum', equal to the average wage of a skilled worker … I would have died of hunger without the sordid manipulation of the black market, where I traded the petty possessions I had brought from France. The eldest son of my friend Yonov, Zinoviev's brother-in-law, an Executive member of the Soviet ... died of hunger before our very eyes. All this while we were looking after considerable stocks and even riches."[49]

After 1921, one-Party rule was assured, and these same Party members together with specialists inherited from the Tsarist regime (industrial managers and technical intelligentsia), now directed the administrative machinery of both state and industry. As this layer exercised its authority it began to accumulate material benefits, first surreptitiously and then legitimised by the Party.

As Lenin talked of the proletarian nature of the Bolshevik Party being determined by the thin layer forming the Old Guard,[50] he was agreeing to take a step that would later be corrupted and used to legitimise material privileges in a way that broke with Bolshevik tradition and advanced the development of the bureaucratic elite. The 11th Congress instructed the CC to examine the material conditions of active comrades and "at all costs ensure them tolerable living conditions."

The CC formed a commission, headed by Mololov (a close ally of Stalin), which reported back to the 12th Party Conference in August 1922 with a resolution providing for about 15,000 senior Party officials to receive: (i) salaries equivalent to middle and senior management grades plus 50%, (ii) guaranteed housing and medical support, and (iii) child care and education for their children. The conference, many of whose delegates would have qualified for the benefits, enthusiastically endorsed the proposals and then called on the CC to work out a similar system for Party officials in rural sub-districts who had not been included.[51]

Before the 12th Conference there was a strong material dis-incentive preventing factory managers from joining the Communist Party, but afterwards membership of the Communist Party provided substantial additional benefits. Carr considered the data for industrial managers who gave their background as non-worker, finding two trends: that the number of such managers almost doubled between 1922 and 1923, and the proportion of such managers who joined the Communist Party increased seven-fold.[52] Managers now saw joining the Communist Party as a means of protecting their material interests.

It is no surprise that at this time there was the gradual abolition of all those activities in and around the Party where free discussion on political matters took place. The first to go were the Party discussion clubs and study circles but later all free discussion, even pre-Congress, would be discouraged and then disappear.[53] In an organisation where votes are cast on the basis of factional loyalty and material interests, an objective, free discussion is not something that can be tolerated. The Party press had to be tightly controlled, *Pravda* and *Izvestia*, became a means of hiding the very sharp struggles taking place inside the Central Committee and the Politburo. The exceptions were those occasions when the Party machine mobilised to launch an attack on an opposition current, as occurred in the *New Course* debate against the Trotskyist opposition's demands for greater internal Party democracy. The CC soon extended such control nationally and after 1925 regularly sent instructions to local newspaper editors about what should and what could not be published.[54]

3.2.6 International Setbacks

The period before and immediately after the 1st Congress of the Communist International was hugely optimistic.[55] A wave of mass strikes and street fighting swept across Europe and many of the sections of the CI transformed themselves into mass organisations – by the end of 1920 the German, Czech, and Italian CPs each claimed membership of over 300,000, the French section had 140,000, and the Bulgarian section over 21,000.

But the revolutionary wave was beaten back. The most decisive defeats were in Germany and Hungary. On 5 January 1919, the German CP (KPD) allowed itself to be provoked into premature armed conflict. The result was a catastrophe, right-wing army units ran riot, killing hundreds of working class militants including Rosa Luxemburg and Karl Liebnicht. In Hungary, a soviet regime existed from 21 March to 1 August 1919 but collapsed in a mix of opportunism (agreeing to share power with the Social Democratic Party, which promptly betrayed the revolution) and ultra-leftism (refusing to distribute the landlords' estates among the peasantry, giving them no reason to defend the Soviet regime).[56] In response to provocation, the Red Army had advanced into Poland generating enormous expectations of revolution in Poland or even Germany, only to retreat in confusion. These events strengthened every conservative and inward-looking trend in the Soviet Union.

By 1923, the situation in Germany was again rapidly approaching revolution due largely to the total collapse of the Deutchmark. In 1923 a barrow load of notes was needed to buy a cup of coffee with the resulting pauperisation of the working class and the ruin of the petty-bourgeoisie but with the export industries making fabulous profits. The trade union apparatus collapsed, belief in the parliamentary system evaporated, mass strikes led by factory committees erupted throughout the country, support for the KPD grew at an enormous rate – particularly amongst factory workers – largely because the Party had adopted a united front strategy.[57]

The ECCI assessed the situation as rapidly heading towards a revolution and approved an overly complex plan for the revolutionary seizure of power. Incredibly, despite the example of Hungary, the plan was based on the premise that the left SD governments of the central German states of 'Red' Saxony and Thuringia could be transformed into bastions of revolution. In many factories the KPD military organisation, the M-Apparat, began openly organising armed defence squads known as the Proletarian Hundreds. The central government moved quickly to demand they surrender their arms within three days. The ultimatum was ignored. On 21 October troops entered Saxony.[58]

In Saxony the left SD government refused to back armed resistance and rather than call for a general strike, abandoned office. The KPD hastily called a trade union conference in the great workers' city of Chemnitz to launch the call for a national general strike. Invited to sit on the platform was SD Minister of Labour Georg Graupe who, when time came to vote for the strike, opposed the proposal on the grounds that it was unconstitutional! A poorly supported general strike simply petered out, the KPD leaders abandoned the plans for an insurrection, and the German October ended not with a bang but a hic-cup.[59]

The consequences had a much bigger impact on the political situation in Russia than in Germany. During the summer and early autumn of 1923, an internationalist, revolutionary fervour had shaken the Party. Meetings, banners and articles celebrated the approach of the German October and the end of the isolation of the Soviet Union. The younger generation responded with revolutionary enthusiasm and under their stimulus the Party temporarily revived. But the shock of the defeat of the German Revolution without a struggle and the disillusion it provoked, reverberated through the discussions in the Russian Party. The disillusionment, all the deeper because the Russian leaders had presented the victory of the revolution as guaranteed, was to weigh heavy on the morale and confidence of the Bolsheviks, strengthening the isolationist and inward-looking tendencies, to the great benefit of Stalin.[60]

3.3 Socialism in One Country

We can date Stalin's adoption of the Theory of Socialism in One Country (TSOC) very precisely. In April-May 1924, *Pravda* published a series of seven lectures by Stalin entitled *Foundations of Leninism* which accurately expressed traditional Bolshevik policy:

> "The overthrow of the power of the bourgeoisie and the establishment of a proletarian government in one country does not yet guarantee the complete victory of socialism. ... For the final victory of socialism, for the organisation of socialist production, *the efforts of one country, particularly of such a peasant country as Russia are insufficient.*"[61]

The lectures were published as a booklet, but a few weeks later in August 1924, the booklet was withdrawn and in October a second edition was produced bearing the same title and date as the first but expressing the opposite view. The first edition does not appear in Stalin's collected works, the second does:

> "But the overthrow of the power of the bourgeoisie and the establishment of the power of the proletariat in one country does not yet mean that the complete victory of socialism has been assured. After consolidating its power and leading the peasantry in its wake *the proletariat of the victorious country can and must build a socialist society.*"[62]

The TSOC is at the heart of Stalinism: it is the justification for the existence of the bureaucracy and its material benefits, it was a doctrine created in response to tiredness and disappointment.[63] It would lead to the return of capitalism, first to Russia and then to China.

Stalin's immediate purpose was to counter what was, to the nascent bureaucracy, the ugly conclusion flowing from Lenin's view expressed many, many times that the final victory of socialism in Russia alone was "impossible"[64] and "inconceivable."[65] Lenin (and Trotsky) argued the Russian Revolution had to spread to Western Europe or it would eventually succumb to capitalist counter-revolution. Stalin now stated that Russia by its own efforts, could achieve socialism because of its vast spaces, riches of raw materials and the advantages of a planned economy.[66]

Stalin had turned Lenin on his head but from now on oppositionists would be presented as lacking confidence in the Russian Revolution, as being faint-hearted and pessimistic. In preparation for the 13th Party Conference Stalin opened an attack on his opponents that was as simple as it was illogical: "(For Trotskyists) … the only choice that remains for the revolution in Russia is: either to rot away or to degenerate into a bourgeois state."[67] The 'either … or' dichotomy was completely false, the historical legitimacy of the Russian Revolution derived not from attempting to create an isolated socialist Russia, but as the start of the world socialist revolution.

The TSOC was to become the nationalist doctrine of the rising bureaucracy, a barrier against socialist internationalism and Marxism.[68] Stalin's theory provided the theoretical basis for the belief of the new masters that nothing (barring a war) would shake their hold on Russia. In its early stages Stalin's theory was posed defensively, claiming to enhance the world revolution by providing a stable base of support, and couched in terms which excluded achieving the "complete and final victory" of socialism in Russia alone.[69] However, the attraction of the theory was plain to all practical people; under the leadership of the RCP, Soviet Russia could move forward from its present misery towards prosperity without having to wait for a revolution elsewhere.[70] It must have sounded like music in the ears of the bureaucrats and officials; we now know it was a siren song.

It is amazing that Stalin was able to progress so far with such an obviously anti-Leninist policy before being challenged. The TSOC was presented at the 14th Party Congress in December 1925 where it was overwhelmingly approved.[71] Stalin then deliberately placed the TSOC as the central issue before the 15th Conference to lance the boil of Opposition criticism. He was eminently successful. The Conference literally howled down Opposition objections that the theory rested on an obvious misinterpretation of Lenin. From now on a loyal Party member would be one who unquestioningly accepted Stalin's interpretations of 'Leninism'.[72]

The TSOC replaced Lenin's requirement for socialist revolutions in "at least several advanced countries" before socialism could be achieved in Russia,[73] with the need to stop imperialist intervention so the Russians could get on with the job on their own. With such a perspective it was just one step to seeing the national sections of the CI as bargaining chips to protect the USSR from imperialist attack.

Today, when we examine the theory of TSOC it is, at first sight, difficult to understand how so many hundreds of thousands of honest communists in the international movement could accept such damaging and reactionary nonsense. But, for a time, this theory appeared to have behind it the authority of the October Revolution and was supported by the material resources of one of the world's superpowers which was prepared to use any methods to silence its opponents.[74]

Mao and the CCP accepted the TSOC unquestioningly and would carry it to the extreme of a short sharp war with the Vietnamese workers' state in early 1979. Mao adhered so strongly to the policy of peaceful co-existence that in February 1972, Nixon, the most despised of all American presidents, was invited to Beijing after which he felt able to take a much stronger line against the Vietnamese war of independence, bombing rail links with China.

3.4 Stalinism and Egalitarianism

The founders of the Bolshevik regime accepted that post-revolutionary society would need a professional bureaucracy, but only for a limited time. It was expected to decline in importance and soon die away. After the defeat of the counter-revolutionary forces, society would have no need for internal state violence.[75] However, the actual development of Soviet society was in the opposite direction. The level of bureaucracy was increasing, material inequalities between citizens were becoming greater not less, repression by the state instead of dying away was increasing by leaps and bounds, real democratic rights were withering not growing; the regime appeared to be heading in exactly the opposite direction to socialism. The goals of the October Revolution had been strongly egalitarian but the reality of Soviet society was a new privileged layer and increasing social stratification and differentiation, creating conflicting social interests.

The Russian bureaucracy was built on a pyramid of privileges and thus Stalin was consistently hostile to egalitarian ideas. After Lenin's death and throughout the thirties, wage and salary differentiation was pushed to extremes. On 5 January 1931, the CC announced an increase in wage differentials and *Pravda* led a press campaign against egalitarianism.[76] The regime used legitimate arguments against petty-bourgeois ideas of egalitarianism during the transition to socialism to justify pay differentials within the workforce. In this way they hoped to gain support amongst the more skilled and better paid workers for the system of pay differentials and privileges of which they were the main beneficiaries. In 1932 Stalin condemned egalitarianism in remuneration as 'anti-socialist' and approved the removal of the *partmaksimum*, which had limited the maximum salaries of Party members to about 250 to 300 rubles a month. This opened the floodgates of privilege.[77, 78]

3.5 Women and the Family

In all major countries in 1917 women not only lacked the vote but were enmeshed in a thick web of discriminatory laws and sexist oppression. The Soviet government of October 1917 took swift action: women in Soviet Russia achieved full legal and political rights, including the right to hold property, act as head of the household, leave the marital home and obtain a divorce on request. Soviet law guaranteed women equal pay for equal work, while also providing on-the-job protection for them. Other laws protected and assisted mothers and assured full rights for children born outside marriage. Abortion became legal in 1920. Women's freedom of choice was also strengthened by the Soviet law, adopted in 1922, legalising homosexual relations among consenting adults. Europe's most backward country achieved more in five years than most advanced capitalist countries would accomplish by the new millennium.[79]

In 1919, the Bolshevik Party created the Zhenotdel (women's department), an organisation that united women in struggle to affirm their newly-acquired legal rights. Thousands of Zhenotdel personnel went to workers' districts and rural villages. They organised women's clubs and through these enabled the election of tens of thousands of women delegates to local soviets and other organisations. For the first time women served as judges and were appointed to important positions in the state apparatus. However, a large proportion of the membership of Zhenotdel were Party members or the wives of Party members and this tended to make it a female auxiliary of the Party.[80]

With the rise of Stalinism, these moves were reversed. The international women's monthly magazine was closed in 1925, the women's secretariat in 1926, and the Zhenotdel in 1930.[81] These were part of a deliberate policy by the Stalinist regime to strengthen conservative attitudes and structures within soviet society; the question of women's rights was pushed off the agenda. The bureaucracy found the traditional family useful, because it provided what the state did not – domestic work and child care – and also because it helped meet the bureaucracy's need for conservative supports throughout society; thus, the regime now trumpeted the sanctity of the family. Marriage and family laws established by the October Revolution were rewritten. In the years immediately following the Revolution the government's priority was the protection of children from "stagnant traditions" including the "natural" authority structure of the family. Now the Soviet regime made a sharp turn, becoming a wife and mother was the goal lauded by the state propaganda machine.[82]

In 1934, homosexuality was made a criminal offence, punishable with up to eight years of imprisonment. An energetic nationwide campaign was launched against sexual promiscuity, quick and easy marriage, and adultery. In 1936, legal abortion was abolished, except where life or health were endangered or a serious disease might be inherited.[83] A campaign was opened against too frequent and easy divorces and in 1935-36 a tax for divorce was introduced: fees of 50, 150 and 300 rubles for the first, second and subsequent divorces.[84]

The massive industrialisation and collectivisation of agriculture, launched in 1929, brought millions of women into the workforce. Employment of women creates conditions for their liberation but it is not necessarily liberation itself. Because improving the lives of women workers was not a political priority for the Stalinist regime, it never really progressed beyond seeing it as an economic problem, a cost on production. Thus, the condition of the social dining halls (e.g. factory canteens) and social laundries continued to be appalling; the better-off workers virtually stopped using them – meaning the return of workers' wives to their pots and pans. The number of *crèches* and kindergartens continued to be much lower than the demand, and quality was dismal.[85]

A clear indication of the conservative attitudes of the bureaucracy and the reaction as regards the family reached its climax with the law of 8 July 1944, which made divorce virtually impossible to obtain and which re-established the legal differences between a child born in wedlock and one born out of wedlock. The latter could no longer claim the surname, the support or the inheritance of his or her father.[86]

3.6 Stalin, Mao, and Theoretical Innovations

Mao is credited with a number of original theoretical contributions to Marxism. However, careful study of his writings confirms the observation that Mao was a premeditated Stalinist and many of his so-called innovations were simply the conscious transfer to China of manoeuvres that Stalin had developed empirically in response to the need to protect the bureaucracy.[87]

In Russia, social inequality was growing with the advance of a "new privileged layer, yearning for power, thirsting for the good things in life, fearful of their positions, mortally fearing the masses and filled with hatred toward any opposition."[88] To defend its material interests this layer was turning the Soviet regime into a bureaucratic tyranny and smothering protest with ever-increasing repression. The Soviet state was becoming a mechanism for the protection of privilege while the ordinary citizen was overworked, under-fed and inadequately housed. The existence of a so-called socialist state which supervised its citizens so closely and was so clearly repressive had to be justified.[89] Stalin's justifications would be taken up, one way or another, and developed and applied by the Mao regime.

Against the expectations of Marx, Engels, and Lenin, Stalin declared the class struggle does not die away but becomes sharper in the period of transition to socialism. In 1933 Stalin argued that the bourgeois elements in the Soviet Union were "weak and impotent", but (somehow) as their social weight declined and society progressed further down the path to socialism they became a bigger problem. This required increased state repression including imprisonment, exile and execution of "class-enemies", suspension of democratic rights and further strengthening of the repressive mechanisms of the state for the common good.[90]

Later Mao would cite the danger of capitalist restoration (i.e. criticism of the excesses of the regime, especially by intellectuals) to justify the Anti-Rightist Campaigns and the Great Proletarian Cultural Revolution. In reality, the degree of repression and the strength of the police state reflected the fear of the bureaucracy of the working class and those remaining revolutionary Communists who might act as sparks in a political crisis.

Stalin prettified the bureaucratic regime by redefining socialism. The successes of the First Five-Year Plan and the steps made in liquidating the kulaks as a class marked "the final and irrevocable victory of Socialism in the Land of the Soviets."[91] Property ownership (e.g. nationalised industries and collectivisation) was deemed of overwhelming importance in defining the stage of development of the Soviet Union. Ignored was the horrendous state of poverty in which the ordinary Soviet citizen lived in order to pay for the Five-Year Plans. Ignored were the millions who had died of hunger due to mis-management, the breakneck speed of industrialisation and forced collectivisation.

Ignored was the low level of productivity and technique relative to the capitalist countries (the Soviet worker produced about one tenth as much as the American worker at this time), the means of distribution (the gross social inequalities which existed) and, most importantly, the lack of any genuine Soviet democracy. Parallel concepts would underpin the CCP definition of Chinese socialism.

On 11 June, 1936, the Central Executive Committee approved the draft of a new Soviet Constitution. The first section, entitled *Social Structure*, concluded with: "The principle applied in the USSR is that of socialism: 'From each according to his ability, to each according to his work.'"[92] This would be a major consideration in the debates within the CCP on just when and how the Chinese workers' state came into existence.

The formula was intended to justify the existing inequalities in the USSR. "From each according to his ability" was the extraction of the maximum labour by any means possible, including the whip of police intimidation; and "to each according to his work" meant the majority of the working population living in general want and on near starvation wages while preserving privileges and luxuries for the tops.[93] Stalin equated socialism in the USSR with the principle "to each according to his work" – a capitalist principle most obviously seen in piecework in factories.

In parallel, in the army, the hierarchy of officers was re-established, from lieutenant to marshal. The changes were not limited to the introduction of titles. There were also substantial material benefits for the officer corps: an accelerated building programme to improve living quarters and hefty increases in salaries (up to about 50%). These reforms had a purely political aim: to give a new social weight to the officers, to differentiate them from the ranks and to bind them closer to the ruling elite.[94]

Zhou Enlai proudly boasted that, in China, the socialist revolution in the ownership of the means of production was fundamentally completed by 1956.[95] How socialism was interpreted by Zhou and his co-thinkers is indicated by their introducing a formal system of ranks into the PLA just one year previously.

Stalin transformed the concept and theory of the revolutionary Party. In a series of iterations, the democratic centralist Leninist combat Party was transformed into a mechanism whereby the General Secretary controlled all aspects of political life within the USSR. From open and frank debate on the most important questions of policy (which took place even when fighting a civil war), through the replacement of free debate with slander and lies, through the use of bully-boy and hooligan tactics, through the anti-Leninist concept that the majority could never be wrong, through the use of the secret police to silence the opposition, Stalin moved step by step to a position where the Secretariat was everything and the Party purely subsidiary. This was also Mao's understanding of the Party save that 'Chairman' replaced 'Secretary'.

Stalin introduced anti-Marxist voluntarist concepts into Party work: he declared to the 17th Party Congress: "... the strength and prestige of our Party and (its) leaders, have grown to an unprecedented degree ... it is their work that now determines everything, or nearly everything. ... the part played by so-called objective conditions has been reduced to a minimum; whereas the part played by our organisations and their leaders has become decisive, exceptional. What does this mean? It means that from now on nine-tenths of the responsibility for the failures and defects in our work rest, not on 'objective' conditions, but on ourselves, and on ourselves alone."[96] This puffed-up, vainglorious and anti-Marxist view was accepted by Mao and taken to extremes in the forcible imposition of Communes and the so-called Great Leap Forward.

3.7 Chinese Students in Moscow 1923–1929

The opening of the Soviet Communist Party and Comintern secret archives has given access to a mass of new information on the training of revolutionary cadres in the USSR.[97] There were a number of important training centres such as the International Lenin School which was for top Party officials, but it is the Sun Yat-sen University (UKT) which is of interest here because for an important period after 1930 this was where many of the key leaders imposed by the Comintern on the CCP were educated and trained.

From 1925, hundreds of young Chinese Communists began to flock to Russia to study at the UKT which attempted to completely mould a student's thinking, starting from philosophical fundamentals and his/her world view, but central was a thorough training in Stalinist concepts of Party organisation and discipline.[98] It is no surprise then, to learn that the most important course was the study of Stalin's *Problems of Leninism*.[99] After 1927 students were also expected to attend courses on 'Trotsky's mistakes'.

In November 1925, Sun Yat-sen University for the Toilers of China was officially opened in Moscow with nearly 300 students. The life span of this university was only five years and at its height it had less than a thousand Chinese students enrolled, but it was a crucial element in the domination of the CCP by the leading faction in the Russian Communist Party. Its students dominated the leadership of the CCP from about 1930 until 1935, and many continued to occupy important posts thereafter. For example, of the ninety-five members of the CC elected by the 8th National Congress of the CCP in 1956, more than a quarter had studied at the UKT.[100]

It is necessary to describe events at UKT to understand what practices these future leaders of the CCP accepted as normal to 'Bolshevism' and how they gained their authority.

Karl Radek was appointed Rector at the founding of the University.[101] However, beginning with Chiang Kai-shek's coup in March 1926, he questioned the CCP policy of entrism and suggested it might be weakening the prospects of revolution. Stalin criticised him personally in *Pravda* of 21 April 1927 and he was removed as Rector.

Radek was replaced by Pavel Mif, a keen Stalin supporter who was first promoted to the directorship of the Chinese Section of the Comintern and then to Rector of the UKT. In two years Mif successfully organised around himself a group of students which would become known as the '28 Bolsheviks' and whom Mif, as the CI representative in China would place into the leadership of the CCP. Mif quit as Rector in the summer of 1929 to go to China, and the University was closed the following year.

When Mif assumed his post as Rector, a student by the name of Wang Ming (Chen Shaoyu) made every effort to become associated with him and win his confidence. Wang Ming had joined the CCP after becoming a student at UKT so he had little or no experience of Communist Party work in China. He had been a member of the first class to graduate (in 1927, aged about 23) but he remained at the University as a translator, occasionally assisting Mif in studying the reports and other documents sent by the CCP to the Comintern. Mif recognised Wang Ming as someone who could be useful to him and from then on Ming acted as Mif's mole reporting on university and Party affairs.

Initially the Chinese Communists in Moscow formed their own Party branch, probably as a matter of expediency as so few spoke Russian. However, in late 1926 the Moscow branch of the CCP was dissolved and its members transferred to the Russian Party, although most were demoted to candidate members with no vote on policy decisions. From this time on all Party meetings within the University were attended by 'Russians' employed or vetted by the secret police, and all key Party posts within the University were held by Russians.[102]

Usually there were twenty or so students in each Party cell, each with a Russian overseer. At meetings every student had to speak on the topic under discussion. No-one was allowed to remain silent – an approach designed to single out and deal with deviant ideas before they developed and ensure everyone adhered to acceptable views.[103]

In February 1927, Krupskaya was invited to speak at the University, and gave a talk, the formal topic of which was "Communist Education". The Party branch had an especially tyrannical attitude towards women students which was codified in its document *A Concrete Guide to the Work of Training*, and from what Krupskaya said it would appear that she had been briefed about what was going on.

Krupskaya was concerned to demolish the *Guide*'s insistence that Party members had no right to individual free will, a common attitude amongst the bureaucracy at that time. In communist organisations there has to be discipline and direction, but it should be the self-discipline generated through carrying out mutually agreed tasks for a common goal. Krupskaya argued that a Communist worked according to Party instructions but beyond that a Communist had his/her own life to live. After all, both joining and leaving the Party were individual acts. It was quite incorrect to see free will as a manifestation of lack of discipline. Party unity could not be achieved by the terroristic imposition of ideas on Party members, rather it required the conscious agreement of Party members on the issue involved. Creating an atmosphere in the Party whereby members were suspicious of each other could seriously damage the Party as a whole. Party unity, she said, should be based on trust and understanding. Such arguments implicitly criticised the Party regime and helped many potential oppositionists make up their minds.

After the hall was cleared of men, she met with the women students of the University. An important topic raised was the heavy criticism of female Party members if they became pregnant. The Party branch had taken the position that Communist women must not bear children. To do so, the branch contended, turned them into mere housewives, who gave a higher priority to raising a family than carrying out revolutionary work. Some students had been intimidated into having abortions. Krupskaya conceded that having a child could make working in the underground difficult, but argued that forced abortions were not the solution. She suggested that the University nursery for the children of female students, located in suburban Moscow, should be extended for this purpose. Krupskaya's visit gave the women students enormous intellectual and emotional support.

The upsurge in spirits felt by the students at the March 1927 seizure of power by the workers in Shanghai made Chiang Kai-shek's subsequent betrayal all the more shocking (see Section 6.3). The students were expected to accept that Chiang's coup was for the best because the slaughter of thousands of Communists represented the KMT getting rid of its right wing. Dutifully the student body followed the Party line and declared its support for the 'truly revolutionary', Left KMT government in Wuhan headed by Wang Ching-wei (Wang Jungwei). However, Stalin's previous policy of cuddling up to Chiang (the Moscow Party had planned to display a huge effigy in honour of Chiang at the May Day demonstration) led inevitably to questions being asked about Comintern Chinese policy.

On 13 May, Stalin attended the University to explain policy on China.[104] Stalin's obvious faith in the Left KMT government in Wuhan as "the centre of the struggle of the Chinese labouring masses *against* imperialism" and his projection that it could become the "organ of a democratic dictatorship of the proletariat and peasantry" would soon be shown to be dangerous nonsense. The Party bureau arranged for all Party cells in the University to hold meetings to discuss the speech. The cell directors were instructed to use the meetings not to defend Stalin's speech but to criticise the opposition. There was to be no attempt to discuss the Chinese Revolution from the standpoint of seeking valid answers to pressing issues, the meetings being solely to support Stalin in the faction struggle taking place within the AUCP(B). This approach did not go down well with the students.[105]

Within two months the killing of Communists began in the area governed by the 'truly revolutionary' Left KMT. The students (now numbering over 550) asked the obvious question: What was wrong with the Comintern policy that it had led to the slaughter of thousands of CCP members, not once but twice? To many students it was incomprehensible that the ECCI had passed a resolution (14 July 1927) instructing the Chinese Communists to remain within the Left KMT at a time when Left KMT generals were killing Communists. They also found it hard to stomach the idea that free discussion of these events and differences within the Party were so severely repressed.[106]

The attitude of the Party branch committee became more repressive, reports at meetings were now largely limited to the 'crimes' of the opposition, reading material to gain an objective view of events was actively discouraged, attempts were made to ensure opposition documents did not enter the University, only material expressing unreserved support for the Central Committee was approved. Such restrictions served only to increase the natural interest of many students to discover what the Opposition was really saying.[107]

Faced with a disaster in China, Stalin moved quickly and decisively. On 11 November 1927, the CC announced that meetings of oppositionists, even in private dwellings would be broken up by force.[108] Three days later a special session of the CC and Control Commission expelled all oppositionists who were members of the CC (Trotsky, Zinoviev, Kamenev, Rakovsky, Smilga, and Yevdokimov). In the days that followed, hundreds of oppositionists were arrested. The 15th Party Congress (2–19 December 1927) opened with not one of the 1,600 delegates from the Opposition, and unanimously declared the programme of the Opposition to be incompatible with Party membership.[109]

To demonstrate to his own followers that his policies on China were correct, Stalin had the CCP organise a stunt to coincide with the Congress. An uprising was to take place in Canton as proof that his political line for China was correct and had enabled the CCP to launch a successful bid for power. The Congress accepted the news at face value and enthusiastically hailed this "victory".

The reality was very different. With little or no preparation, with no support either from the urban masses or the surrounding peasants, and with many thousands of KMT soldiers in and around Canton, the Communist International demanded the CCP seize the city (see Section 6.3 for details). Elleman has described how the dates of Congress and insurrection were juggled so that the insurrection would have greatest impact, and argues that over seven thousand workers paid with their lives to hide Stalin's mistakes in China.[110] By 14 December, the last of the defenders of the Canton Commune had been wiped out and the reign of terror began, although that news was not brought before the Congress.

While formally endorsing all Party resolutions there was a growing mood in the student body that the CI could not be relied upon to correctly guide the revolution in China. Under pressure of events, many students opened their minds and searched for answers to their questions. Many of these would become members of the Trotskyist Opposition. However, those students on the right (e.g. the 28 Bolsheviks) were coming to very different conclusions; that it was the unrealistic demands made by the peasants for freedom and land that had triggered Chiang's two coups.[111]

At the beginning of 1928 a number of veterans of the failed Canton, August Harvest, and Nanchung uprisings together with activists from the women's movement began to arrive at the UKT.[112] The reports and stories these people provided did much to radicalise many independently-minded students and cause them to doubt the official line.

Due to Mif's absence in China (with Wang Ming in attendance), there was a short hiatus between Radek leaving and Mif taking up the post of

Rector. In that short time a bitter struggle for personal authority erupted between two factions: on the one hand the Party Branch faction dominated by the ousted leaders of the Moscow CCP branch ('the survivors') and on the other the Academic Affairs faction led by senior academics supported by a significant number of students. Mif returned and with Wang Ming rallying the uncommitted majority of students, the Rector was soon in charge. In this brief struggle Wang Ming emerged as the Rector's spokesperson and thus a leader in the student body; in this capacity he began to form alliances that would be the basis of the 28 Bolsheviks.

Almost immediately afterwards, the 10th anniversary of the October Revolution took place and during the celebrations students from UKT staged a public demonstration of support for the Opposition. With the help of a member of staff (Bella Epshtein, who would be shot in the spring of 1938), ten or eleven students constructed placards with the slogan "Long live the leaders of the world revolution; Zinoviev, Radek, Preobrazhensky."[113] These students marched with the KUTK contingent and then, when opposite Lenin's mausoleum, unfurled their banner and began to shout slogans in support of the Opposition. A shocked Stalin instructed Mif to conduct a thorough investigation of Trotskyist activities at the UKT and to report his findings promptly to the CC of the AUCP(B).

The subsequent hurried investigation unanimously decided to expel from the Party Epshtein and those students they managed to identify. Staff members found to be Trotskyists or even Trotskyist sympathisers were expelled from the Party and fired.[114] It was during this episode that the political crystallisation of the 28 Bolsheviks took place.

Importantly, the 28 Bolsheviks did not need a separate organisation of their own because with the support of the Russian authorities they now controlled the Party branch. Mif did not create the 28 Bolsheviks; their performance in this, the first anti-Trotskyist struggle at UKT, was a self-selection process whereby they came to Mif's attention as a force which could be useful to him. Once formed, the 28 Bolsheviks determined to root out any potential threats to their dominance, and moved against the remnants of the Academic Affairs faction (now under the name Second Line) which was beginning to re-assert itself.

The charge was that Second Liners – the majority of whom came from Kiangsu and Chekiang provinces – had formed an illegal anti-Party association, the "Jiangsu-Zhejiang Friendly Association", based on provincial loyalties.[115]

Whilst levelling this charge, the 28 Bolsheviks worked hard to hide the fact that nearly every one of them came from the Yangtze River valley.[116]

The 28 Bolsheviks could produce nothing solid and finally the Central Control Commission of the AUCP(B) resolved that there was inadequate evidence to support the anti-Party accusations. As Yueh, one of the 28 Bolsheviks, later admitted:

> "Some slight evidence was uncovered to suggest the vague possibility that such an organisation may have been formed, although at the time I did not believe that it existed formally. But the use of exaggeration as a weapon in power struggles is not an unusual undertaking anywhere, and perhaps this weapon is used within Communist parties more freely than elsewhere."

The tactics of the 28 Bolsheviks went beyond unfounded accusations to include using the GPU against their fellows. This alienated the student body which in its majority now rallied to the Second Line. Such behaviour speaks volumes on the mindset of the 28 Bolsheviks who – to further their positions within the University and Party – were quite prepared to make unfounded accusations that would result in a number of the Second Line leaders being sentenced to years of forced labour in unspeakable conditions. It should be remembered that this was a struggle for positions of personal authority between two Stalinist groups, and that Wang Ming stopped at nothing to achieve his goal of top place, considering any tactic legitimate, no matter how shameful.

Wang Ming now prepared to challenge the authority of the entire Chinese Comintern delegation by tying it to the Second Liners and spicing the charge of provincialism with allegations of 'Trotskyism'. The 28 Bolsheviks now extended the critique to include an attack on Ch'u Ch'iu-pai on the grounds of 'left opportunism'. Ch'u Ch'iu-pai had been elected General Secretary of the CCP on 7 August 1927 and now, as was becoming common practice in the CI, he was being deemed responsible for the recent failures of the CCP.[117] Mif took these criticisms to the ECCI and Ch'u was removed from the post of General Secretary in July 1928 at the 6th Congress of the CCP and kept in Moscow as Chinese delegate to the CI. Zhou Enlai who had been present assessed just how ambitious was the attack made by Wang Ming: "In opposing the Chinese delegation, the Wang Ming faction was in fact opposing the Central Committee of the Chinese Party, asserting that it was no longer competent and its members must be changed."[118] After receiving

Zhou Enlai's report, the CC of the CCP formally accepted the judgement of the Comintern!

By the 6th World Congress of the CI Stalin had concluded that the CC of the CCP did not contain "a single Marxist mind ... capable of understanding ... the events now occurring." In a letter of 9 July 1928, he spelled out his solution:

> "It's time to really busy ourselves with the organisation of a system of Party advisors attached to the CCP Central Committee, the Central Committee departments, regional organisations in each province, the departments of these regional organisations, the Party youth organisation, the peasant department of the Central Committee, the military department of the Central Committee, the central organ [newspaper], the federation of trade unions of China ... The structure has to be set up so that all these Party advisors work together as a whole, directed by the chief advisor to the Central Committee (the Comintern representative). ... The Party advisors will compensate for the enormous shortcomings of the CCP Central Committee and its top regional officials. They will serve (for the time being) as the nails holding the existing conglomerate together as a Party."[119]

This proposal revealed Stalin's approach toward fraternal relations with the CCP, which was to take control of it from top to bottom through his agents. Mif who was Stalin's appointee would be well aware of Stalin's wishes; it is obvious that the 28 Bolsheviks were an important step in that direction.

The 16th Conference of the AUCP(B) of April 1929, initiated a purge within the Russian Party and it was decided to extend this to a vigorous purge of all foreign communists in the Soviet Union.[120] In the autumn of 1929: "iron faced" purge commissars, experienced secret policemen toughened by numerous opposition witch hunts, descended on UKT.[121] A series of meetings was scheduled over which these commissars presided. Wang Ming carefully selected members on whose loyalty he could count and these members were given the task of bombarding 'anti-Party' elements with accusations.

The purge meetings at UKT were shattering experiences, the slightest political or personal blemish was publicly and endlessly questioned until an atmosphere of hysteria prevailed. This witch-hunt resulted in at least one suicide amongst the students. By the end the GPU had the names of some eighty to ninety students. These were arrested as suspected leaders of the opposition and immediately taken to the underground jail beneath the GPU HQ on Lubyanka Square in Moscow. The automatic method of interrogation was sleep deprivation while being forced to stand to attention until a 'confession' was obtained; members of the 28 Bolsheviks participated in these interrogations.[122] The interrogation techniques used on those who did not immediately confess are not described.

The purge increased in intensity and sophistication and by its end the GPU had arrested 171 Chinese as Trotskyists. The fate of most of these is not known, but the overwhelming majority were immediately expelled from the Party, a good proportion was sent to concentration camps such as the forced labour camps of the Altai gold mines in Siberia where it has been reported many were worked to death; few were sent back to China as there was no wish to spread Trotskyism.[123]

Wang Ming returned to China in early 1929. The main force of the 28 Bolsheviks returned by the end of 1930 and made Shanghai their headquarters. In November or December 1930, Mif went to Shanghai where he secretly met with the 28 Bolsheviks to plan a leadership coup within the CCP to overthrow and replace the Party Secretary, Li Lisan, and establish the 'Wang Ming Empire' with Wang appointed General Secretary at the 4th Plenum of the CC in January 1931 at the tender age of 26, with no practical experience of political work in China.[124]

During a key period in the growth and development of the CCP its leadership was largely in the hands of those who had been thoroughly trained in the ideas of the TSOC. But these people had also been trained in the Stalinist methods used during the purges in Russia. They had practical experience of suppressing internal Party democracy, of using outright lies, smears, blackmail, threats, intimidation and even physical violence as acceptable means of settling political disputes within the Party. These people had, in many cases, personally participated in brutal GPU interrogations of Trotskyists and others.[125]

3.8 Summary

The degeneration of the Russian Communist Party began with an unprincipled alliance of Lenin's closest collaborators to prevent the promotion of Trotsky, and ended with the coming to power of the Stalinist bureaucracy. From personal slanders, political lies and suppression of the truth, the Stalin faction descended to organisational and physical intimidation of political opponents, then torture and execution. A witch-hunting hysterical atmosphere was deliberately created to isolate and silence oppositionists; it was in this atmosphere that the Chinese students at Sun Yat-sen University received their training. To their credit it was a magnificent achievement that as many as a third sided with the Trotskyist Opposition. However, from the remainder, who were prepared to stain their hands with the blood of Oppositionists, the Stalinists chose those who were to lead the CCP for the next period.

The course of events in the Soviet Union was determined by historical causes far deeper than the personal qualities of those leading the Bolshevik Party. The mood and orientation of the Russian working class changed in reaction to the enormous effort expended in the civil war. Tired from their heroic efforts, downhearted after the defeats of socialist revolutions internationally, and in a predominantly peasant country where the proletariat maintained close links with the peasants, there was an inevitable revival of petty-bourgeois tendencies in the proletariat itself.

The formation of the *Troika* marked a qualitative change in the nature of the leadership of the Bolshevik Party; previously the differences that arose had been corrected as events proved one side or the other right or wrong, but from now on matters would be decided on a factional basis. It would soon become common practice for loyalty to the majority faction to replace loyalty to the Party, and for those opposing the faction to be treated as opposing the Party. To defeat the opposition became more important than reaching correct conclusions and projecting a line that matched the needs of the situation. Events that gave the lie to the faction line were hidden from the membership. At the very top of the Party, personal considerations replaced political, and this gave the struggle between the *Troika* and Trotsky its bitterness and led to the rapid degeneration of the Party leadership.

Stalin immediately took pole position in developing the cult of Lenin and the Party propaganda machine went into a frenzy of activity; Lenin had always been correct on every issue, every question, every dispute, and the comrade always at his side had been Stalin. In this, the natural affection and esteem, love and respect felt for Lenin by all his old comrades was cleverly used by Stalin to transform Lenin into an icon, to whitewash away all his mistakes and give his political thought a linearity that had never existed in reality. Criticism of Lenin became impossible in the world communist movement.

Completely wiped out was the dynamic of Lenin's political heritage. Importantly, this meant Lenin's change in 1917 from a stagist to a permanentist perspective was erased. Lip service was paid to all Lenin's proposals while moving in the opposite direction. At the end of the 12th Congress, the situation in the RCP was such that Stalin was, *de-facto*, irremovable as General Secretary. His narrowness of outlook, lack of creative imagination, empiricism, personal aggrandisement, and vanity came to the fore and made him the natural leader of the rising bureaucracy.

Chapter 4

The Rise of the Second Chinese Revolution

4.1 Introduction

Stalin's perspective for China was that the national bourgeoisie would lead a successful democratic revolution against feudalism and the imperialist and colonial powers. The leadership residing in the Kuomintang was – despite the personal wishes of those involved – an objectively revolutionary force that would not betray its own revolution.

This perspective was based on the assumption that in China, workers, peasants, artisans, intellectuals and national bourgeoisie (including the officer caste of the NRA) had more in common with each other than the imperialists. It was assumed that this multi-class bloc could become the Revolutionary Democratic Dictatorship of the Proletariat and Peasantry (proposed by Lenin in 1905 but firmly rejected by him in 1917)[1], which would carry through the national revolution and create a bourgeois state friendly to the USSR. Chiang Kai-shek and his generals had a more correct appreciation. They understood that revolutions do not stop when commanded but could flow right over them to a soviet regime. They planned and then acted accordingly.

On 20 March 1926, Chiang Kai-Shek staged his first coup in a clear and unambiguous statement that the bourgeoisie intended to control the Chinese Revolution to protect its interests which were most definitely not the same as those of the proletarians or peasants.

Despite this warning, Stalin continued to argue that a single national revolutionary front was a necessary condition for the successful anti-imperialist revolution and to achieve this, the CCP must sacrifice its organisational and political independence and adopt a subservient role to the KMT. To keep the bourgeoisie in the United Front the CCP should restrain the rebellious peasantry to within bounds acceptable to the KMT, i.e. stop land seizures.

As the national struggle progressed and the KMT armies moved northwards and took control of major industrial centres, the class struggle between the bourgeoisie and sections of the petty-bourgeoisie on the one hand and the proletariat and peasants on the other could no longer be contained within one political party. This problem would be resolved by the KMT, both left and right unleashing a white terror and massacring all the Communists it could. CCP membership had peaked at 60,000 of whom about 12,000 were women[2] by the end of 1927 the vast majority would have dropped their membership or be dead; this would mark the end of the Second Chinese Revolution.

4.2 Chiang Kai-shek's First Coup: 20 March 1926

After Sun's death on 12 March 1925, sections of the Chinese bourgeoisie came out openly for the exclusion of Communists from the KMT and opposed the radical elements in the policy of the Canton Government. The immediate cause of the right wing concern was the mobilisation of the working class in the Canton-Hong Kong strike; the Chinese workers were becoming a powerful and leading force in the democratic revolutionary movement, giving the movement a powerful impulse and greatly strengthening the left in the KMT.

In July, 1925, the first open test between the right wing and the left (including Communists) came in the elections to control the party in Canton. The left won a sweeping victory. Wang Jingwei, who had made a point of being seen to support the Canton-Hong Kong strike, declared a 'National Government' based on Canton with himself as its chairperson.

At once the right wing met separately and demanded the KMT: 1. Expel the Communists, 2. Give power to the military, 3. Dismiss Borodin and his Russian military advisers, and 4. Move the seat of the Central Executive Committee to Shanghai. Tai Chi-t'ao (a member of the Central Executive Committee of the KMT) produced an anti-Communist pamphlet as a rallying call to the right wing. There followed a relentless campaign against Communists and leftists. The campaign was particularly successful amongst the cadets of the Whampoa Military Academy where the anti-Communists (the majority) formed themselves into their own separate 'society'.[3] In response, Peng Shuzhi published the article *Who is the Leader of the Revolution?* in the December 1925 issue of *New Youth*. Here, he openly argued that the Chinese bourgeoisie, including the industrial capitalists were too closely tied to imperialism to lead a successful revolution for national independence.[4]

The leftists and CCP dominated the 2nd KMT Congress in January 1926 and Wang was confirmed as leader. With Communist support, Chiang Kai-shek was elected to the Central Executive Committee (CEC) for the first time. The Congress condemned the behaviour of the right wing and emphasised the need for a KMT-CCP alliance.[5] Borodin and the ECCI took all this as further proof of the success of the bloc within and the weakness of the rightists within the KMT.

The great dream of Sun Yat-sen and Chiang Kai-shek was the Northern Expedition in which the NRA, under Chiang's leadership would march against the northern warlords, defeat them militarily and unite the country. Chiang understood that the Northern Expedition was impossible without massive material support from the Soviet Union. However, the Soviet advisers in China opposed the Expedition, expressing instead a preference for the 'People's Army' of Feng Yu-hsiang (the so-called Christian general). Chiang was worried that the military supplies he needed for his expedition might be diverted. Nor did Chiang wish to go marching off to Beijing and leave behind him a KMT Government under the political influence of Borodin. It was necessary to administer a sharp smack to the Communists and their allies to ensure the military wing of the KMT held the leadership of the Revolution but without provoking too much of a reaction. If handled correctly, such a move could also eliminate his rivals within the KMT.[6]

On the night of 19/20 March Chiang 'discovered' a conspiracy supposedly organised by a Communist naval officer. Chiang's troops surrounded the quarters of the Soviet advisors, all CCP political workers attached to army units under his command were arrested, and in a move that was especially significant and unambiguously showed the motives for his actions – the Canton-Hong Kong strike was at its height – local trade union premises were raided and closed down.[7]

On the morning of 20 March 1926, Chiang was master of Canton. All railway stations were occupied, all telephone communications were cut and martial law declared. Chiang had demonstrated he held the real power within the KMT. His next step was to minimise the incident to ensure the ongoing material (and political) support of the Soviet Union necessary for a victorious march on Beijing. Publicly, Chiang dismissed the incident as a misunderstanding; he apologised to the Soviet advisers (who blamed the CCP for using inappropriately radical propaganda) and withdrew his troops to their barracks.[8]

Chiang's coup was kept secret within the USSR, but news of it slipped out one year later when it was mentioned by Radek in an article that appeared in *Izvestiya*. *Pravda* hurriedly published a reply in the form of a report from Wuhan affirming Chiang's loyalty to the national revolution and proclaiming the absence of any inner party disputes within the KMT.[9]

4.2.1 Outcomes of the Coup

Stalin, confused and confounded, made no public response, but behind the scenes deals were done; the Northern Expedition was unequivocally endorsed, and the coup was minimised or denied.

On 22 March, Solovyev, Councillor of the Soviet Embassy met with Chiang. The next day, Wang Jingwei, pleading illness, left for France. On 24 March many Soviet advisers, including the chief adviser at the Whampoa Academy took their leave of China. Chiang placed his own men in key positions within the KMT. The ECCI instructed the CCP to support the military dictatorship of Chiang Kai-shek and assist the forthcoming Northern Expedition. Action against Chiang or a break with the KMT having been ruled out, the CCP Central Committee passed a resolution pledging its support to Chiang.[10]

Right wing politicians and business men rushed to acclaim the man who had so easily established bourgeois hegemony over the mass movement. But the inaction of the CCP had demonstrated a serious weakness which undermined any possible future alliance with the left within the KMT.

In the face of the coup, Peng Shuzhi and Ch'en Pi-lan (editor of *Chinese Women* and Peng's partner) travelled to Canton to convene a meeting of leading Communists with Borodin to consider whether the CCP should: withdraw from the bloc within and replace it with co-operation of independent organisations, expand the military units under its leadership, and unite its military forces with those of the left wing of the KMT. Borodin won the support of the majority of the meeting by revealing that Stalin had personally ordered that CCP-KMT 'collaboration' be maintained, and the proposals were rejected.[11]

Stalin, Bukharin, and soviet advisors not only closed their eyes to the warning given by the coup, they actively hid it. The international Communist press published deliberately misleading material; when news of the coup appeared in the bourgeois press, the *International Press Correspondence* of 8 April 1926, called it a "lying report", and in the 6 May issue Voitinsky called it "an invention of the imperialists."[12]

Chiang's next step was to camouflage himself as a champion of the masses. On May Day 1926, the 3rd National Labour Conference representing one and a quarter million workers had as its honoured guest, Chiang Kai-shek, now Generalissimo of an army with an efficient, well-trained officer corps. With CCP approval, this representative of the bourgeoisie appeared before the masses as a revolutionary leader. In uniform, Chiang punched the air and shouted "Long Live the World Revolution."[13]

Chiang Kai-Shek took Wang Jingwei's place as head of the KMT, and at a special plenary session of the CEC on 15 May 1926, conditions were laid down for continuation of the bloc within:

1. The CCP press must not criticise the anti-class struggle principles of Sun Yat-sen. 2. The CCP must hand over a list of its members in the KMT. 3. Communists could not control more than one-third of the seats on any of the higher KMT committees. 4. Communists could not serve as heads of departments in the central KMT organisation nor government. 5. Without approval from above, no member of the KMT could call any meeting in its name to discuss party affairs. 6. Without authorisation from a higher body, no member of the KMT could be a member of any other political organisation or engage in any other political activity. 7. If the CCP wanted to send instructions to its members in the KMT, such instructions had first to be submitted for approval to a joint committee of which the majority was non-Communist. 8. Any members of the KMT wishing to join the CCP had to resign and could not rejoin the KMT.[14]

At the very moment when the Revolution needed Bolshevik leadership, the ECCI imposed restrictions on the CCP which constrained it to act as the left-wing within a bourgeois party. In the eyes of Moscow the KMT was "a unique workers' and peasants' party", "a revolutionary bloc of workers, peasants, intellectuals and the urban democracy (i.e. the bourgeoisie) on the basis of a community of class-interests in the struggle against the imperialists and the military-feudal order in general."[15] The ECCI continued to hail the KMT as a friendly, revolutionary party and allowed its delegates to remain on the ECCI with a consultative voice.

After the coup, the activities of the CCP were fatally constrained; it could not issue any public criticism of the KMT, could not form a faction within the KMT to fight to change the official line, it had to publicly subscribe to the capitalist principles of Sun Yat-senism, it was prevented from arming the people, forming Soviets, disarming the bourgeoisie, and it could not work to win over the soldiers of the NRA. Borodin, quoting Bukharin, said openly that the activities of the Communists were restricted to doing coolie service for the KMT.[16]

From this point, the CCP acted as a brake on the Chinese Revolution, a role that would cost many, many Communists their lives. However, for a large proportion of CCP members, recruited on the basis of the bloc within and subjected to continuous bombardment with the idea that a break with the KMT would sabotage the anti-imperialist struggle, these sacrifices appeared worthwhile. Stalinist mis-education which included demanding unquestioning obedience to the CI would end with the collapse of the revolutionary movement.

Landlords took the 20 March coup as a green light to attack peasant associations, and the murder of peasant leaders became widespread. In a tactic that would be used again and again, Communists played a disgraceful role by placing the blame for the killings on individual corrupt officials, avaricious gentry and hooligans rather than the landlord system. In Guangdong province the attacks were particularly severe. On 26 June 1926, Chen Duxiu in his *Appeal* reported that the leadership of the CCP requested that Borodin take 5,000 rifles from those allocated for Chiang Kai-shek, to allow the Guangdong peasants to protect themselves. He refused, on the grounds that the peasants might use the guns to seize the land, and that was quite unacceptable.

In late 1926, Borodin addressed a Peasant Congress in Hankou, central China. The Northern Expedition was to be supported as the first step to unifying China. The warlords and imperialists had to be defeated, after that would come the formation of a national government. This would (1) establish minimum land allocations for peasants, (2) lower rents, and (3) establish popular government at county, provincial, and national level. This was the same 'wait and see' message the Russian SRs had delivered in 1917, and the reason for their obliteration.

4.3 The Northern Expedition: from Guangdong to Shanghai

On 9 July 1926, just over four months after his coup, believing he had made his rear safe from revolution, Chiang began the Northern Expedition for the military unification of China. The NRA was not large, it numbered only about 100,000 soldiers, against over half a million warlord troops. Its successes came from its dynamism and its popular support.[17] The NRA was accompanied by a swarm of agitators, organisers, and propagandists who so well prepared the ground that often the armies needed only to advance on a village or town for the warlord's forces to evaporate. In support of the NRA, railway and telegraph workers attempted to paralyse the warlords' communications, peasants spied on warlord troop movements and made them immediately known to the NRA, and formed guerrilla bands to attack the rear of the warlords' armies. There were even cases where the local peasant association staged an uprising ahead of the NRA.[18]

The NRA proceeded in two columns, the western column headed for Wuhan, strategically placed in the middle of the Yangtze valley, on the river and an administrative, industrial and transport centre, and the eastern column, led by Chiang, headed for Nanchang, capital of Jiangxi province.

As the NRA began its march, the Central Committee of the CCP met in Shanghai (12–18 July 1926). It received and again rejected a motion submitted by Peng Shuzhi, supported by Chen Duxiu, for the withdrawal of Communists from the bloc within and the establishment of a United Front with the left wing of the KMT.[19] The published proceedings of this meeting were permeated with a desire to convince the bourgeoisie that the CCP was no threat to its interests. The resolution on the peasant question was typical, it proposed restricting the CCP policy to what was believed acceptable to the KMT; rent and interest rate reduction, lower taxes and removal of corrupt officials. Such an obsequious approach could only lead to further retreats.

The leadership of the CCP had voted to accept the instructions of the ECCI not only because the latter had behind it the prestige of the October Revolution and provided most of the resources that kept the Party afloat, but also out of loyalty to a body which been a major factor in its foundation, providing essential leadership over its difficult first days. But now the ECCI was proposing a course of action that cut right across Leninist norms. In public, Chen Duxiu, as Secretary of the CCP, followed discipline and declared the KMT one of the pillars of the national-revolutionary movement but within the CCP worked hard to separate the two organisations.

In opposition to Chen and Peng, ECCI representatives made every effort to win the CCP leadership, one obvious method being to promote onto the CC those who agreed with ECCI perspectives. Under Comintern pressure the weaker, the opportunists, those jealous of their positions, and those who genuinely believed in a stagist approach followed Borodin's lead. Incrementally, the character of the Central Committee was changed. Each time Chen and Peng raised the question of breaking the bloc within they received less support and within the Party most new recruits (the vast majority given the rapid growth of the Party) were joining on the basis of support for the Northern Expedition and Chiang.

MN Roy, ECCI representative in China and second only to Borodin, would later claim that by this time the majority of the leadership of the CCP endorsed the Stalinist perspective: "Almost all the Communist leaders believed the stories about the 'excesses' of the peasants and declared that the most effective method of combatting the counter-revolution would be to check them."[20]

Wang Fan-hsi was in Beijing as the NRA progressed northwards. He described how the CCP deliberately mis-educated the membership by fostering the idea that, apart from a few old men, the KMT was solidly on the side of the Revolution; not one word of criticism was voiced against Chiang at CCP meetings. Soon after, Wang moved to Canton where he discovered reality was very different from what he had been told. He found the strength of the so-called left wing of the KMT was largely illusory. The numbers of left-wing individuals within the KMT prepared to stand up for their ideas were so few that they would never constitute a force to be reckoned with. On the other hand, Chiang and the forces of the right had real power, military power in their hands.[21]

As he gained confidence, Chiang suppressed trade unions, peasant leagues and the activities of Communists in the area under the control of the NRA. On 29 July 1926, he declared martial law. All labour disturbances were forbidden for the duration of the Northern campaign. The NRA's triumphant progress continued and by September the Yangtze valley was in Chiang's hands. The ECCI was delirious with joy.

On 9 August 1926, the KMT declared compulsory arbitration in all labour disputes, workers were forbidden to bear arms of any description, to assemble or to parade. Military patrols took possession of the streets. Stalin said: "The withdrawal of the Chinese communists from the Kuomintang at the present time would be a profound mistake. The whole course, character, and prospects of the Chinese revolution undoubtedly testify in favour of the Chinese communists remaining in the Kuomintang and intensifying their work in it." In flagrant opposition to the facts available to him but as a smokescreen to justify his own policies, he presented the advance of Chiang's troops as meaning "freedom of assembly, freedom to strike, freedom to organise for all the revolutionary elements in China in general, and for the workers in particular."[22] The victories of the NRA and the propaganda of their own Party convinced many doubters within the CCP that the curbing of peasant attempts to seize the land was justified.

In Canton the local government had been under the control of the left KMT and initially had been supportive of the Canton-Hong Kong strike, but it soon moved to the right as the consequences of Chiang's coup became clear. The bloc of four classes began to reveal its true face. In May, the Canton Government offered to ensure "the complete cessation of the boycott and of all other anti-British manifestations throughout the territory controlled by the Canton Government" in exchange for a $10,000,000 loan from the British. Squads of soldiers and police patrolled the streets of Canton and the food kitchens were discontinued. The betrayal by the Canton Government broke the back of the strike and on 10 October 1926, the strike and boycott were called off unconditionally. No loan was given.

The strike and boycott had opened the door to an independent working-class perspective and had demonstrated the capacity of the Chinese workers to organise and function in their own interests. The CCP described the abrupt termination of an historic fifteen months' struggle without a single concession as "not a defeat but a great victory".

The CCP had allowed an historic opportunity to slip without even realising it. The workers of Canton would pay dearly for this 'victory'. The gangsters of Canton were mobilised into a Central Labour Union and carried the offensive against the revolutionary workers onto the streets.[23] Against the advice of the CCP, militants defended their organisations, but with the masses disheartened and defeated, this was to no avail.

In early October, the NRA took one of the most important of China's industrial areas, the Wuhan complex comprising the three cities of Wuchang (railroad centre), Hanyang (industrial centre) and Hankou (important commercial port on the Yangtse) each with a substantial industrial population. In November, Chiang took Nanchang which then became the centre for the rightists within the KMT.

Borodin successfully persuaded the remaining left KMT leadership in Canton to move their government to Wuhan to take advantage of the working class base that existed there. No doubt the defeat of the Canton-Hong Kong strike weighed on his mind. The move coincided with the 7th Plenum of the ECCI (22 November–16 December 1926). This was the first Plenum since the counter-revolutionary coup of 20 March and incredible as it might seem, not one word was said about the coup, not one word about the shootings of the workers and peasants carried out by the KMT in a number of provinces, not one word about the withdrawal of support for the Canton-Hong Kong strike, not one word about the efforts made by the Canton government to strangle and denigrate the peasants' movement, to prevent its spread and development. The 7th Plenum passed over in silence the Central Committee of the CCP's public undertaking not to criticise Sun Yat-senism, effectively endorsing the CCP's renunciation of its right to function as an independent workers' party.

The Plenum was guided by a resolution passed at the meeting of the Politburo of the Soviet Communist Party on 26 October 1926 which had decided the CCP should make a significant shift to the right.[24] The Plenum issued a manifesto drafted by Martynov (against whose ideas Lenin wrote *What is to be Done?*) who, by ignoring basic Marxism – that the power of a state was 'bodies of armed men' (e.g. the NRA) – was able to conclude that China was heading towards a multi-class state. On the key question of land to the peasant, the manifesto declared national liberation was impossible without agrarian revolution – nationalisation of the land was fundamental.[25] This sounded wonderful, but the lands and property of KMT leaders and the officers of the NRA were excluded. The heart of the CCP's land programme was reduced to demands acceptable to Chiang Kai-shek.

Martynov proposed that Communists penetrate the new Government and use the state apparatus to confiscate land, reduce taxes and invest real power in peasant committees. But the 20 March coup had been precisely to stop such things happening, to ensure that real power would be kept out of the hands of peasant committees. In such a situation, taking posts within the state apparatus meant Party members punished peasants for revolutionary acts. That CCP members were volunteering to become magistrates to enforce bourgeois laws even before the manifesto arrived, demonstrated the level of mis-education within the CCP and the political level of the people being recruited.[26] The public face of the CCP was class-collaboration and this naturally attracted recruits who favoured such a policy.

Martynov justified the CCP entering the left KMT government by arguing that it would strengthen the 'revolutionary' left wing against the right, that it was possible to change the KMT into a 'real Party of the People'. His classification of 'revolutionary' left was demonstrated by the first on his list of desirable participants – the KMT Government in Canton which was at that moment disarming workers, protecting yellow unions, and attempting to strangle the peasants' movement.[27] Without independent bases in the proletariat and peasantry (which required the clear slogan of "Land to the Peasant"), the CCP did not have sufficient weight within the KMT to counter-balance the right wing which had military support.

The CCP was enmeshed in a net of contradictory requirements, the only way to break out and save the Revolution was to support the peasants' seizure and distribution of the land – and that required Soviets. But by Stalin's direct order Soviets were excluded. Instead the CCP was instructed to use the "apparatus of the National Revolutionary Government", a formula for achieving nothing. In the army, for example, this was interpreted as manoeuvring individual sympathisers into command positions rather than winning the soldiers to a revolutionary position by setting up Communist nuclei of rank and file soldiers.

The Plenum did warn that the bourgeoisie were trying to "smash the revolution", but failed to say who these people were (Stalin personally declared Chiang was loyal), when they would act, under what conditions they would do so, where they would act, and what they would do. The ECCI warning was abstract in the extreme, but the actions it demanded were immediate and concrete – capitulation to the bourgeois KMT.

As the leadership of the CCP tried to square the circle of supporting the peasants without introducing soviets and without offending the officer corps, it became caught up – and partners in – spinning a web of deceit. The CCP had to choose support for the KMT or support for the peasant revolution; rather than risk a break with the KMT it decided to block the revolution.[28] On 13 December 1926 in Hankou, in the presence of Borodin and Voitinsky, Chen Duxiu delivered a report on the current situation to the Party leadership. The published version of the report had the CCP bowing to ECCI discipline: unity with the KMT would be maintained and the disease of "left naivete" eliminated from the body of the CCP. The report argued that the rightists had been "frightened" by the CCP success in mobilising the mass movement, and by the dominance of the CCP at a rank and file level in the KMT. The solution was for CCP members to call for confidence in the KMT leadership but, and in particular, to try to stop the leftward movement of the masses. The political goal was to establish a left civilian government headed by Wang Jingwei.[29]

4.4 Peasants and Workers Self-Mobilise

But the Chinese proletariat and millions of land-hungry peasants were moving into action. The CCP placed itself, the authority of the October Revolution and the Communist International as barriers to this movement. In Hunan, Mao put the party line to a meeting of more than 300 peasant delegates: "The time for us to overthrow the landlords has not come … Now is the time … to reduce rents, to reduce interest and to increase the wages of farm labourers."[30] The response was not reported which in itself is significant.

As the summer progressed and the NRA advanced, it became clear that the Chinese countryside was on the verge of widespread revolt. Behind the NRA the peasants spontaneously organised to demand rent reductions and an end to arbitrary taxation. But such moves have a logic of their own and the peasantry in Hunan and Hopeh, having unilaterally reduced their rents, soon took the obvious next step of paying no rent, and then seizing the land[31]

1926 saw not only a spectacular growth of the peasant movement, but a parallel strike wave of great depth and intensity in all the major industrial centres, with the Canton–Hong Kong strike acting as an example. Well over one million workers were directly involved. In Hunan, trade union membership increased from 60,000 to 150,000, in Wuhan 300,000 workers were organised, and nationally there were 2,800,000 unionised workers, a greater number than in the Russia of October, 1917. Naturally, the great majority of the strikes were fought for wage increases and improvement in working conditions and most were wholly or partially successful. The workers of China were raising their heads as never before. By the end of 1926 – despite the defeat in Canton – the strike wave was stretching beyond economic demands into open political struggle, which demonstrates that individual defeats, even major ones, can be overcome when the mass movement is on the rise.

In a single leap, the workers of Hankou took the lead of the anti-imperialist struggle. On 4 January 1927, a demonstration took place at the boundary of the British Concession in Hankou. Spontaneously the cry went up: "Take it now!" Teams of workers tore down the barbed-wire barricades and joyful crowds stormed the Concession and claimed it for China. This was done without any leadership, either from the KMT or the CCP. When the KMT politicians in Hankou recovered from their fright at the nerve of the workers, the British retreat gave them courage. They stepped in to negotiate and emerged with agreements which returned the Hankou and Kiukiang Concessions to China, a 'diplomatic victory' made possible by the actions of the Hankou workers and their comrades (James, Op. cit).

The reaction of the CCP to these events was a short period of silence and then a statement to the effect that the actions had been incorrect![32] This is an object lesson in the harm a revolutionary organisation can inflict upon itself when it moderates its programme to obtain unity with non-revolutionary forces. In its attempts not to damage the bloc within, the policies of the CCP became less revolutionary, less anti-imperialist than those of the local KMT.

As Chiang's troops swept into new territories the peasants self-mobilised and between November 1926 and March 1927, over ten million peasants joined peasant leagues in the southern provinces of Jiangxi (Kiangsi), Guangdong (Kwangtung), Hunan (the most radical) and Hopeh alone. In Hunan peasant associations grew to over 2,000,000. In a manner similar to Russia in 1905 and early 1917, the peasants organised themselves, with rural agitators eager to push way beyond the limits set by the CCP or KMT.[33]

It was in this context in February of 1927, that Mao wrote his *Report of an Investigation into the Peasant Movement in Hunan*[34] and it was referred to at the 8th Plenary Session of the ECCI (18-30 May, 1927) by Bukharin as 'excellent'. Sections were published in *Communist International.* The *Report* made Mao's name within the CI.[35] Mao presented his *Report* first to the leaders of the CCP in Wuhan and then to the 3rd Enlarged Plenary Session of the CEC of the KMT on 10 March 1927. The *Report*, written as advice to "the revolutionary authorities in Hunan", was first published in a condensed form in the *Weekly Organ of the Central Executive Committee* of the KMT on 15 March.[36]

The writings of Mao Zedong as they appear today are often not the same as when first published. Cohen has demonstrated that many of the claims for the originality of Mao's ideas come from the re-writing of important texts years later when the questions had been decided by actual events, and Mao's *Report* is one such. It contains Mao's supposed innovation that it would be the middle and (particularly) the poor peasants who would be the most important and reliable allies of the proletariat in the democratic revolution. In fact, Lenin had stated this a quarter of a century earlier and had carried through a successful socialist revolution based on just such an analysis. The political content of the original text was in line with the ECCI and CCP decision to designate the KMT not the proletariat as the leader of the national democratic revolution. Thus, the original *Report* makes no mention of the industrial proletariat being the leading force in the Chinese Revolution, nor of a worker-peasant alliance, these concepts were added in 1951.[37]

Importantly, in the original version of the *Report*, Mao avoided discussing the land question as part of the agrarian revolution, no doubt because of the curbs the CCP imposed to maintain the bloc within, but a very significant omission when viewed from post-revolution China. In 1951 Mao added the words in italics – "An economic struggle should also be started immediately in order that *the land problem and other* economic problems of the poor peasants can be completely solved." The lack of any mention in the original version of the CCP as an independent body was another serious omission. Mao had exhorted "all revolutionary parties" to face up to the leadership test presented by the rising peasant movement. In the 1951 version, the Communist Party suddenly appears in numerous places such as "The poor peasants .... are the most responsive to Communist Party leadership."[38]

The language of the *Report* was militant and strident:

> "In a very short time, in China's central, southern and northern provinces, several hundred million peasants will rise like a mighty storm, like a hurricane, a force so swift and violent that no power, however great, will be able to hold it back. ... They will sweep all the imperialists, warlords, corrupt officials, local tyrants and evil gentry into their graves. .... In force and momentum the attack is tempestuous; those who bow before it survive and those who resist perish. As a result, the privileges which the feudal landlords enjoyed for thousands of years are being shattered to pieces."

The form was militant and radical but the content was class collaborationist (private ownership of the land would remain with rich peasants and even some landlords as suitable allies, it was the feudalists who would be swept away), and quite acceptable to Moscow and the left KMT.

Other texts received similar treatment[39] so it is difficult to take current publications as a genuine expression of what was said at the time. Re-writing historic texts is a feature of a regime in ideological crisis, a dishonest regime that cannot face its own past, it is a *de facto* admission that its policies at the time were wrong and it shows a total lack of respect for its own Party members.

Re-writing took other forms; in 1930 a booklet was published in Russia entitled *A Brief History of China's Labour Movement,* written by Deng Zhong-xia, a labour leader executed by the Nationalists. It made no mention of Mao. When the booklet was re-published in Yenan during the rectification campaign in 1943 a passage was inserted: "In 1922, thanks to the leadership of comrade Mao Zedong, the workers' movement in Hunan developed stormily ..."[40] Taking his lead from Stalin, Mao also had the military history of the Long March re-written, every defeat was due to those who did not follow his lead, successes such as the 'Great Victory at Pingxing Guan' against the Japanese army were credited to Mao.

In early 1927, Chiang established himself at Nanchang. Pending the conquest of Shanghai, Chiang Kai-shek attempted to take absolute control of the KMT. He demanded that the seat of Government be moved to Nanchang, but the petty-bourgeois radicals, buoyed up by the victory over the British refused. The 4th January events had stiffened the resolve of the left leaders at Wuhan and demonstrated how important it was for the CCP to have an independent base outside the KMT if the left was to be won to an anti-imperialist position.

In response, Chiang announced his intention to root out the Communists from the KMT:

> "No more differences or tendencies among us! ... every true member of the (KMT) must be just that and nothing else. Whoever goes against the aims and methods indicated by Sun Yat-sen will not be a comrade but an enemy who must not remain among us."[41]

The left KMT held its own Central Executive Committee in Hankou on 10-17 March, its decisions reflecting its buoyant mood. It took back the powers assumed by Chiang Kai-shek just a year before. Resolutions were passed in support of an agricultural policy which reflected Mao's Report in sounding militant in its attacks on local bullies, bad gentry and the feudal landlord class, but in content was mildly reformist. The left was all for 'co-operation' with the CCP, and called upon the latter to send "responsible comrades to join in the Nationalist and Provincial Governments."[42] In open opposition to Lenin's principle that the CCP must retain its freedom of criticism, it was agreed: "the Press organs of the Third International, of the Chinese Communist Party, and of the Kuomintang shall not violate the spirit of co-operation in their reports and criticise one another."

The KMT in March, 1927, launched a Land Commission which began its sessions on 27 April. It was composed of the principal Kuomintang leaders, with Tang Ping-shan representing the Communist Party. This was supposed to find ways of enacting the KMT *Platform for Workers and Peasants* which had been approved the previous October and promised the peasants a 25% reduction in land rent and the 'prohibition' of usury, limiting interest on loans to 20% per annum. Instead of taking the movement forward, this Commission stepped back even from the 25% reduction in land rents by recommending that land rents should not exceed 40% of the harvest.[43] During these discussions the CCP replaced Marxist class-based analysis by moral categories such as 'good' and 'bad' gentry. Unity with the former was essential so their land was inviolate. But it soon turned out that the KMT could find something good to say about every landlord.

The Mensheviks and SRs had got themselves into just such a swamp of inaction in 1917 from which Lenin had deduced that a Bolshevik Government was necessary to complete the bourgeois democratic revolution in Russia. As in Russia, so in China, the Commission proved wholly ineffective and demonstrated to the peasants that partial reforms would not work; the question that had to be addressed was who owned the land.

Even the mild reforms demanded by the left KMT terrified the possessing classes. This fear, supported by the anxious imperialist powers, expressed itself in the murder of workers, peasant agitators, and Communists in the areas controlled by Chiang (Dorland, Op. cit.). The nearer their protector and ally got to Shanghai, the clearer became his intentions on taking power.

On the ground in Jiangxi province strikes were squashed, workers and peasants disarmed, the bourgeoisie was allowed to organise its own forces (gangsters and the *ming tuan* militias) to suppress strikes and kill workers. At the time no reports of these events appeared either in the left KMT or Communist press: both were too anxious to maintain their links with Chiang and the NRA. It would be revealed later that Chiang waged a terror campaign against the peasant unions from at least the beginning of 1927, but these acts were covered up by the CCP on the grounds that at a critical time in the national revolution it was imperative to maintain the united front and this meant "the crimes of those who fight against imperialism" could be "temporarily" overlooked.[44]

The strategy of the bloc of four classes demanded unity with these reactionaries for the success of the anti-imperialist struggle, and this led to the CCP and ECCI deceiving themselves and the world communist movement. Wuhan, simply closed its eyes to Chiang's activities, and declared that the national revolutionary movement was moving forwards unhampered by any suggestion of inner conflict. This fitted well with Chiang's strategy. He would break with the left when he was ready.

What could the left KMT and CCP have done to halt Chiang's counter-revolutionary moves? The best course would have been to launch a campaign among the masses exposing Chiang's actions, to promote the most radical social reforms (above all, land to the peasant) so that if Chiang Kai-shek fought back he would have had to do so from an openly reactionary position and against the mass movement. Instead, with Stalin's praise for Chiang ringing in its ears the CCP took no action and left the way open for him.

Lenin's advice was to get the peasants to form Soviets as soon as practicable. In China there could have been no better time than from the spring of 1926 to the summer of 1927 to form Soviets. In the urban centres the workers were already on the move and in the countryside Soviets could have been based on the peasant leagues around the slogans 'Land to the Peasant' and 'End Debt Repayment'. This would have given structure to the mass opposition to the bourgeois and begun the task of creating a genuinely revolutionary army based on the actual movement unfolding in the liberated areas and in the cities.

4.5 Summary

The ECCI imposed on the CCP the stagist theory that China had to complete the democratic revolution before proceeding to the socialist, and that the appropriate strategy was the bloc within. Maintenance of the KMT-CCP block was deemed essential for a successful anti-imperialist revolution, and as this was a stage that could not be bypassed the CCP had to surrender its own particular interests and submit itself to the nationalist party foregoing an independent, critical voice. The way to hell is paved with good intentions, so it is said, and the attempt to form an unbreakable anti-imperialist front with the national bourgeoisie was one such. The newly-founded CCP, as a member of the CI accepted its discipline and the leadership of Moscow even though the ECCI perspective was increasingly clashing with reality.

The Russian proletariat (and the peasants in the army garrisons) spontaneously created Soviets in February 1917 based on democratic demands. The Soviets were key to destroying the army as a functioning counter-revolutionary force. It was through Soviets that the Bolshevik party was able to make contact with the masses, assess their revolutionary spirit, mobilise them for action and realise the slogan 'Land to the Peasants'. The Soviets mobilised the masses that neither the party, nor trade unions nor even peasant associations could reach, and educated and organisationally prepared them for insurrection. During 1905 and 1917, based on its own experiences and guided by the Bolshevik Party, the Russian proletariat rose from lower to higher levels of understanding. However, in China such a perspective meant a break with the bloc within, with the concept of stages and with the bloc of four classes.

The NRA advance to the Yangtze and the gigantic upsurge of the mass movement had brought the class contradictions in the Nationalist movement to breaking-point. The Communists hid the issues from the masses and, especially, from the Shanghai workers. Unwarned, and unprepared, they would first become Chiang's pawns and then his victims. Chiang Kai-shek, for his part, had concluded that this time the mass movement could be halted only by decapitation.

Chapter 5

The Defeat of the Second Chinese Revolution

5.1 Introduction

As the NRA advanced, the northern warlords were divided into two groups which were waging a war between themselves, a situation which greatly enhanced Chiang's chances of success. Shanghai itself had changed hands twice in the previous three years and was now ruled by Sun Chuanfang whose army had taken the Chinese districts (European districts were, of course, almost untouched) in late 1925. The advance of the NRA inspired the Shanghai workers to action. Despite being under the rule of a warlord, over 200,000 Shanghai workers had bravely engaged in some form of strike action, often successfully, in the nine months after the start of the Northern Expedition. By 18 February 1927, the vanguard of the NRA was within 40 km (25 miles) of Shanghai. The bankers, compradors, national and industrial bourgeoisie in Shanghai saw Chiang not only as a stabilising force but as curbing the mass movement, and prepared to welcome him as their saviour. Only the workers were ignorant of the role Chiang would play.[1]

Chen Duxiu recognised that a successful uprising by the Shanghai workers would pose the problem of the ruling power. At the Central Committee (CC), basing his arguments on the revolutionary upswing amongst the peasants and the militancy of the proletariat, he argued:

> "The Chinese Revolution has two roads: One is led by the proletariat, then we can reach the goal of the revolution; the other is led by the bourgeoisie, and in that case the latter must betray in the course of the revolution. And though we may co-operate with the bourgeoisie at the present, we must nevertheless seize the leading power."[2]

The proposal was, of course, rejected.

The peasant unions and workers' organisations were growing rapidly, and as they grew they made ever more radical demands. Rather than unleash revolution the CCP held the peasants back from taking the land, and workers from political strikes. Stalin's policies of 1917 (unifying the Mensheviks and Bolsheviks into a single party and limiting the Revolution to national bourgeois demands under the banner of the Revolutionary Democratic Dictatorship of the Proletariat and Peasantry) were now being enacted in China. But revolutionary situations do not last forever and with no Bolshevik Party to direct the action, the situation in China changed rapidly, and for the worse.

The Far Eastern Bureau of the Comintern in Shanghai unanimously opposed Chen, arguing that if a Shanghai uprising succeeded, the ruling power should be handed to the bourgeoisie and it was unnecessary to have any participation in the government by workers' delegates. This argument was word for word that used by the Mensheviks in St Petersburg in February 1917.[3]

As KMT armies advanced towards Shanghai, the General Labour Union called a general strike to commence on 19 February 1927. The strike involved practically every worker in Shanghai, a section of the petty-bourgeoisie shut their shops and joined in the strike – between 500,000 and 800,000 people were directly involved. The CCP was taken by surprise and immediately contacted the local KMT to discuss what to do. Spontaneously the strike began to develop into an armed uprising under the slogans: 'Hail the Northern Expedition', 'Hail Chiang Kai-shek'. This first stage of the Shanghai uprising was quickly beaten back by the warlord's troops even as the CCP and KMT discussed their options.[4]

5.2 Chiang Prepares his Second Coup

Chiang understood the threat the uprising posed to the Chinese bourgeoisie and took the political offensive against both the CCP and the left KMT. Co-ordinated gangster attacks on trade unions and peasant associations in the territories controlled by Chiang accelerated. Local union HQs were attacked and smashed up and those defending them beaten and even killed. Peasant associations received the same treatment. In those cases where the pickets successfully defended themselves, police or the NRA would appear and in a neutral capacity disarm and then arrest them, after which the gangsters would take over and 'reorganise' the union. In all cases the unions soon re-appeared as yellow unions. Despite the frequency and widespread occurrence of these attacks, the CCP was so blinded by the desire to keep Chiang on side that they closed their eyes to their co-ordinated nature and limited themselves to resolutions urging the military to protect the workers!

On 21 March 1927, the General Labour Union led the Shanghai workers in a second insurrection that took control from the local warlord and within two days armed workers controlled the city. However, the workers fought under slogans provided by the CCP and local KMT: 'Hail the National Revolutionary Army!', 'Welcome to Chiang Kai-shek!' Internationally the Stalinist press rallied to praise Chiang. *Rote Fahne* in Germany and *L'Humanite* in France went so far as to claim that Chiang's entry into Shanghai would not only be the liberation of Shanghai, not only inaugurate the 'Chinese Commune' but would be the beginning of the liberation for the workers of the world.[5] This complete mis-reading of the situation flowed quite naturally from the anti-Marxism of the bloc of four classes. The ECCI and CCP voluntarily restricted the workers' and peasants' struggles, limited the goals to what was acceptable to the bourgeoisie, and paved the way for Chiang to carry out in Shanghai the destruction of the mass movement, but in a more thorough and determined manner than he had been doing elsewhere.

While the Shanghai proletariat fought, Chiang Kai-Shek delayed his march waiting for the warlord's troops to drain the blood of the workers. However, the workers took the city and held it, spontaneously declaring they did not want Chiang to enter. Despite the CCP, they were prepared to fight to stop him. It was this victory of the Shanghai workers that confirmed to Chiang that he could wait no longer. Simultaneously, the ECCI sent a telegram instructing the CCP "to avoid clashes with the National Army and its leaders in Shanghai at any price", arms were to be surrendered and control of Shanghai given to the NRA.[6,7]

On 26 March Chiang entered the city. On 28 March martial law was declared. Chiang did everything to hide the assault he was planning, a veritable avalanche of statements was produced denying any split with the left KMT or CCP. Chiang even invited Wang Jingwei to return to China and vowed to show 'explicit obedience' to the Wuhan KMT. These devices worked better than he could ever have hoped because the left KMT leaders and ECCI wanted to believe him.[8]

On 31 March 1927, Trotsky, on the basis of a permanentist analysis, wrote to the CC and in complete antithesis to Stalin, he argued that without extending and deepening the agrarian revolution through Soviets there was a real risk of a Chinese Bonapartist coup based on the officer cadre.[9] The ECCI and the majority of the CC of the CCP followed the Stalinist line and insisted that feudal forces not the bourgeoisie were behind the reactionary activities. The result was that they disregarded the main and immediate enemy of the revolution – Chiang and the NRA.[10] Their hopes rested on Wang Jingwei, who returned to China (Shanghai), from France (via Moscow), on 1 April 1927.

On 3 April, in an unpublished article Trotsky, argued that in giving up its political independence and submitting to the discipline of the KMT, the CCP was failing to act as a pole of attraction not only to militant workers and peasants but even to radical petty-bourgeois elements within the KMT. This inaction meant, *de facto*, the strengthening of the power and authority of the bourgeois wing. The consequences of their actions would be just the opposite of what the ECCI expected. At a time when class divisions were accelerating rapidly, the ECCI policy of appeasing Chiang was preparing conditions for a military coup.[11]

Stalin offered the alternative perspective in a speech on 5 April 1927 when he told 3,000 Party members in the Pillar Hall of the Kremlin that "Chiang Kai-Shek cannot do otherwise than lead the army against the imperialists" irrespective of his lack of sympathy for the revolution.[12] Stalin and the ECCI in a major mis-assessment, evaluated the left KMT government in Wuhan as key to the national revolution; events in Shanghai were secondary. Peng Shuzhi and Chen Duxiu pointed out, to no avail, that Chiang Kai-shek had proved in March 1926 that he was the more important factor in the Chinese Revolution and that the Shanghai workers had to defend themselves and their city against the NRA. Chen considered Wang Jingwei the secondary force who would, most likely, fold if tested in action.

To allay the concerns of the workers, the CCP and KMT issued a joint manifesto in Shanghai on 6 April. In all the documents of Stalinism this stands out as one of the most criminal:

> " … counter-revolutionaries both inside and outside China are spreading false reports … that the leaders of the KMT intend to make war on the Communist Party, to suppress the labour unions and to dissolve the workers' defence organisations. … The military authorities in Shanghai have declared their complete allegiance to the Central Committee of the KMT. If differences of opinion exist they can be amicably settled. The Communist Party is striving to maintain order in the freed territories. ... there is no basis whatever for these malicious rumours …"[13]

Wang Jingwei, arrived in Wuhan on 10 April. With full support promised by Borodin, the CCP and the Soviet government, and with Chiang a safe distance away, he sought to re-establish himself as leader of the KMT. Wang called a KMT Central Executive Committee in Hankou at which Chiang (in his absence) was removed from his Party posts but allowed to keep the title of Commander-in-Chief.[14] Chen Duxiu arrived to meet with Wang Jingwei and found him surrounded by known anti-Communists. The weakness of the CCP, demonstrated by its failure to organise opposition to the attacks on workers and peasants in the area controlled by Chiang Kai-shek, pushed Wang and the leaders of the left KMT rapidly to the right, and closer to Chiang.

Until spring 1927, the CCP had a wonderful opportunity before it. If it had followed the proposals of Chen and Peng and assisted the peasants to launch soviets to coincide with and lead the wave of land seizures, there was every likelihood that the CCP could have gained governmental and state power (certainly in southern and central China). The rebellion might initially have had the form of a traditional peasant uprising but with Soviets to act as organising centres, structuring demands on the key and essential agrarian and anti-imperialist questions, the rebellion would soon have become a revolution because only proletarian leadership could ensure the Soviets carried through the agrarian revolution to completion.

5.3 Shanghai Massacre

Amongst the first troops to enter Shanghai (10 April) was a division that sympathised with the workers – the First Division of the Canton army. The commander, Hsueh Yueh proposed to the CC of the CCP that he should remain in Shanghai and fight together with the Shanghai workers against the military overthrow that was in preparation. The CCP leaders, Chen Duxiu included, replied that they knew that an overturn being prepared, but that they did not want a premature conflict with Chiang Kai-shek! The First Division left Shanghai.

At 4.00 am on 12 April 1927 in Shanghai, the NRA, assisted by gangster elements and with the support of foreign authorities, began slaughtering thousands of Communist and CCP sympathisers. Chiang's detachments marched through the streets, executing on the spot any worker who offered resistance. The CCP, trades union movement, and all workers' organisations, were annihilated and made illegal. When Chiang Kai-shek openly betrayed the Revolution it was a signal to the bourgeoisie of the entire country. The defeat in Shanghai was the beginning of a defeat throughout China. The coup in

Shanghai was followed by similar blows against the workers in Amoy, Canton, Foochow, Ningpo, and Swatow (Shantou). Counter-revolution, backed by imperialism, reigned triumphant in the areas under Chiang's control.[15]

The Shanghai events had enormously emboldened the reactionary forces across the country and an undeclared civil war was breaking out in those provinces where the peasants had made the greatest gains, Hunan and Hopeh. So widespread were the killings that women with short hair or unbound feet were executed as Communists!

A young Stalinist functionary (Rafael Chitarov) had been sent as an ECCI representative to China and he later presented a report at the 15th Congress of the AUCP(B) (11 December 1927).[16] From that report it is clear that the situation could have been saved even at the eleventh hour. The workers in Shanghai were in power. They were armed with the possibility of gaining support from at least one division of Chiang Kai-shek's army (there was also the Communist Regiment led by Yeh Ting).[17] But the top of the CCP was paralysed. Rather than prepare for the decisive struggle against Chiang Kai-shek, they proposed to give him a triumphal reception. Chitarov's report made it clear that the CCP ministers had followed the ECCI line and the leadership of the CCP was praised as "devoted to the cause of Communism".

5.4 The Wuhan Debacle

Chitarov confirmed that the Shanghai coup made it "clear to everyone that the bourgeoisie was retreating from the revolution" (even at this stage a Stalinist could not admit that the Chinese bourgeoisie was actively counter-revolutionary, that was the role of the feudalists, the slaughtering of tens of thousands of workers was a 'retreat'). But Stalin and the ECCI still had illusions in the left KMT (Wuhan) government, and this closed their eyes to the preparations of the Wuhan government for its own 'retreat from the revolution'. Following Stalin's lead the majority of the CC of the CCP continued to present the Wuhan government as the democratic dictatorship of the proletariat and peasantry in embryo.[18]

On 17 April, the left KMT expelled Chiang from the KMT, and southern and central China separated into provinces controlled by the Wuhan left KMT supported by the CCP, and those controlled by Chiang. Stalin now adopted the position that Chiang Kai-shek's coup was good riddance to bad rubbish and not a major defeat for the workers. The KMT had divided into a revolutionary centre in Wuhan and a counter-revolutionary centre in Nanjing. The left KMT was now free to lead a decisive struggle against militarism and imperialism.

In close collaboration with the Communists it would eventually transform itself into the revolutionary democratic dictatorship of the proletariat and peasantry.[19] Completely ignored was the fact that the counter-revolution in Shanghai had been carried out not by feudal elements and Northern warlords, but by bourgeois forces which Stalin and Bukharin had proclaimed could not betray the revolution.

In Moscow, Stalin determined that attack was the best form of defence and presented the Shanghai coup as a Communist victory, as evidence of the correctness of his policies. He almost went so far as to present the massacre of the workers in Shanghai as part of a plan by the CC of the AUCP(B) to expose the rightists and remove them from the KMT.[20]

> "As is known, the Central Committee of the CPSU was already at that time of the opinion that the policy of keeping the CCP within the Kuomintang must be maintained, that the withdrawal or the expulsion of the Rights from the Kuomintang must be propagated . . . The events which followed have fully and entirely proved the correctness of this line."[21]

The Comintern and Communist Parties around the world published articles proposing the remarkable argument that the slaughter of the Chinese workers in Shanghai was entirely in accord with the prognoses of the ECCI! Stalin had predicted the 'inevitable' desertion of the bourgeoisie from the united front; he had been proved correct. That Chiang had been personally endorsed by Stalin, the ECCI and the CCP was totally ignored; that the coup had not been against the KMT but represented the direction in which it was travelling. Completely missing was any explanation of why a correct analysis and prognosis had instructed the CCP to politically and militarily disarm the Shanghai working class in the face of the coup, had left the CCP paralysed, had left the largest city in China in the hands of the class enemy without a fight, and had led to the deaths of over 5,000 Communists.

During the following months, Chiang's coup was presented as having cleansed the KMT of the counter-revolutionary elements amongst the bourgeoisie. The official journal of the Comintern went so far as to talk about the "revolutionary government of Wuhan" as nothing less than the "Communist Koumintang".[22] Forgotten was Lenin's warning of "the need for a determined struggle against attempts to give a communist colouring to bourgeois-democratic liberation trends in the backward countries."[23]

Stalin continued to argue that Soviets were a danger to the success of a bourgeois revolution because they would stand in opposition to the Wuhan government.[24] This fundamentally incorrect assessment ignored the experience of Russia in both 1905 and 1917. It also mis-evaluated the actual class relations within the Chinese Revolution. Stalin insisted that the left KMT was the only governmental authority in the region around Wuhan when all that really existed was a small number of self-proclaimed leaders resting on the remains of the old, reactionary and mercenary bureaucracy, temporarily supported by a number of local warlords.[25]

In Wuhan's territory the trade unions were still legal and the workers still enjoyed the opportunity to voice their demands but the Shanghai events gave the employers in Wuhan new heart to resist. They passed over to a counter-offensive; they closed down factories and made every effort to sabotage and paralyse economic life. Peasants were refused loans on any terms meaning they were unable to buy seed and other necessary supplies to tide them over until the next harvest. Speculators drove up the price of rice to unaffordable levels. Foreigners co-operated by closing down their enterprises, curtailing their river-steamer schedules and instituting a virtual blockade of Wuhan. Beginning in May and throughout June and July, the KMT-CCP coalition crumbled under conflicting revolutionary pressures. Not because the CCP was insufficiently subservient, but because the bourgeoisie were no longer prepared to tolerate even the possibility of organised opposition.

This counter-offensive could be defeated only with the unleashing of the mass movement: seizure and operation of the closed factories, shops and ships, the establishment of peasant co-operatives, and support for the peasants' drive to seize the land. But for such measures revolutionary force was needed based on workers', peasants', and soldiers' councils/soviets in both town and country-side. For the left KMT such measures were unthinkable because they violated the existing property relations. For the Communist Party such measures were unthinkable because the bloc within excluded them.

To make matters worse, the workers in Wuhan insisted on struggling for a living wage – between January and April women and children working in the textile mills fought for, and won, increases from 12 to 20 cents a day, dock workers increased their wages from three to seven Chinese dollars a month, and silk factory workers won a reduction in the working day from 17 to 12 hours. The CCP and the General Labour Union issued call after call to the workers not to make "unjust demands"; to make a supreme effort to preserve "the all-class nature of the revolution", to suspend struggles against the Wuhan capitalists because the success of the revolution depended on the support of manufacturers and merchants. In the cause of a revolution that was becoming a counter-revolution, the CCP aligned itself with the exploiters against the exploited.

On reflection it seems unbelievable that the CCP implemented precisely the same policy in Wuhan with respect to Wang Jingwei and his generals as it had in Shanghai with Chiang Kai-shek! The CC of the CCP instructed the workers to be obedient to the left KMT which was presented not as a Kerensky-type regime to be overthrown, but as a potential democratic dictatorship of the workers and peasants that could grow into socialism.

Chitarov described policy during the Wuhan period:

> "... the CC of the Communist Party ... invented the so-called theory of retreat. They declared: We must immediately retreat in order to save the possibility of legal work ... if we defend ourselves or attempt to advance, we will lose everything. ... the Communist Party ... surrendered one position after another without a battle. ... they agreed to subordinate all the trade unions, all the peasant unions and other revolutionary organizations to the KMT; they rejected independent action without the permission of the Central Committee of the KMT; they voluntarily disarmed the workers' pickets .... etc."

The policy of the CCP would help the national bourgeoisie crush the masses and annihilate the best proletarian and peasant fighters.

The 5th CCP Congress opened on 24 April 1927 in Wuhan with Wang Jingwei as guest of honour. About one hundred delegates represented over 50,000 members. The Congress formally blamed Chen Duxiu for the Shanghai disaster but re-elected him as Secretary General. Peng was demoted from the Politburo but remained on the CC, Mao was elected to the CC but removed from leadership of the Peasant Commission.[26] The Comintern was advising bold measures – especially for agrarian revolution – but within the constraints of maintaining the bloc within. Across central China, and especially in Hunan and Hupeh, the peasants were in revolt and seizing the land. Against such a background, the Congress could do no less than call for nationalisation of the land without compensation. However, the seizures were to be of only the largest estates; those of more than about 30 hectares (80 acres), an area so large it certainly excluded the rich peasants, and even most landlords.[27] The estates of the military men upon whom the power of the Wuhan government depended were, no matter what their size, exempted.

The Manifesto of the 5th Congress described the Shanghai massacre in terms of the big bourgeoisie 'seceding' from the revolution, a departure which was supposed to have transformed the left KMT into a revolutionary bloc. This doubly confused the situation because it prevented any realistic analysis of the left KMT while sowing illusions about revolutionary harmony between the left KMT and the CCP. The over-arching slogan for the Congress was "Long Live the Co-operation of Communism with the Three People's Principles (of Sun Yat-sen) to the End."[28] For many of the delegates, their end was rapidly approaching.

The ECCI met (27 April 1927) and Roy reported from China without once referring directly to the massacre in Shanghai! Wang and his Wuhan 'national government' were presented as the new revolutionary leaders despite Wang having consistently avoided introducing any radical policies which would have meant conflict with the KMT conservatives. Not one jot of evidence was presented that the left KMT in Wuhan would wage a determined fight against militarism and imperialism, let alone be converted into the revolutionary democratic dictatorship of the peasantry.[29]

Just as the peasant movement in Hunan and Hupeh was reaching its height the CCP affirmed its support for the new, supposedly better, supposedly more left-wing KMT. The same rules applied: no agrarian revolution, no anti-KMT agitation, no 'excesses', no 'provocations'. Peasants were clearing out the landlords and taking over the land, establishing peasant associations which were embryo Soviets, taking over the local rural administration and organising armed units to battle with the landlords' militia. Many of the soldiers of the NRA under the control of reactionary officers were influenced by the peasants. They needed an organised connection with the peasants and the only practical way of doing this was to form soldier-worker-peasant Soviets and then soldiers' Soviets. With the revolutionary movement on the upswing such a move would have destabilised the Kuomintang armies and halted the reaction.

Instead the CCP accepted the KMT invitation to nominate two Communists to the Government posts of Minister of Labour (Hsu Chao-jen, the Canton trade union leader), and Minister of Agriculture (Tan Pingshan). With this, the CCP formally introduced a class-collaborationist policy in which Communists took governmental responsibility in bourgeois governments. This would become known as the Peoples' Front and be formally adopted at the 7th World Congress of the CI.[30] Cohen has suggested that the idea of People's Democracies that rose in Eastern Europe after WWII and developed in parallel with the New Democracy established in China, originated here.[31]

The KMT paper *People's Tribune,* explained that the offer was made to tighten the bonds tying the workers' party to the bourgeois KMT:

> "The present co-operative plan is important because it signifies greater control by the Kuomintang over all the forces participating in the national revolution. … The Communist Party will have to fulfil its obligations to enable the Party (the KMT) and the Government to exercise full control over the mass movement."[32]

The KMT's plan worked; far from pulling the government to the left, these ministers were used to hold back the Revolution.

Now, at last, Stalin made a call for the arming of the workers and peasants, but this was done in exactly the same way as his warning to beware the bourgeois counter-revolution made before the Shanghai massacre. While sounding like basic common sense, it cut right across everything else he was saying. Arming the workers and peasants was the correct thing to do but it would inevitably have led to the formation of Soviets and that is why it was not done until too late and then in a distorted, bureaucratic and self-defeating manner.

The agrarian question was becoming increasingly pressing for both the left KMT and CCP as the 'excesses' of the peasants were met with forcible repression. As petty-bourgeois radicals, the Wuhan leaders were sensitive to the needs of the masses. But now their earlier, radical, pronouncements on the agrarian revolution needed to be translated into action. It turned out that the bonds binding the left KMT to the landlords – whose sons made up the officer corps of the armed forces – were infinitely stronger than the claims of the peasantry.

On 13 May 1927, Stalin met with students at Sun Yat-sen University to consider the issue: "Should Soviets of workers' and peasants' deputies, in general, be created in China?". Stalin's answer was:

> "Yes, they should, absolutely they should. They will have to be created … after the unfolding of the agrarian revolution, in the transformation of the agrarian revolution, of the bourgeois-democratic revolution into the revolution of the proletariat."[33]

That is, the formation of Soviets would take place at some unspecified time in the future. Historical experience said just the opposite, Soviets had been key in initiating the democratic phase of the revolution in Russia. The problem for Stalin was that if they came into existence in China, no force on earth could stop them posing demands that could be met only by a proletarian regime.

One week after Stalin's visit to the University, generals loyal to the left KMT made their first anti-Communist move. What happened is almost unbelievable. In Changsha (capital of Hunan province, a town of about

250,000 people, 250 miles from Wuhan and served by a railway), the KMT force consisted of 1,700 soldiers, while the armed detachments of peasants around the city numbered about 20,000. When the peasants heard that the counter-revolution had started they gathered round Changsha and prepared to march on the city. This march was set for 21 May. It was clear that the peasants would seize the city without great effort, but at this point a letter came from the CC of the CCP who countermanded the attack and told the peasants to await instructions from the Government in Wuhan. The military command succeeded in seizing power, shooting the leading activists, dispersing the revolutionary organisations and establishing its dictatorship – only because of the irresolute and conciliatory actions of the CCP leaders.

Similar episodes occurred elsewhere – in north-western Hupeh as many as 20,000 people were killed by reactionaries, many of them executed publicly. The dynamic of events in the real world was reducing the situation to its essentials: would the CCP support the workers and peasants, or would it support the KMT landowners and armed forces? News of the countryside killings reached Wuhan: Communist Ministers joined KMT officials in complaining that the peasant unions were not observing 'discipline'. According to Tan Pingshan, the peasants had been making excessive demands, and while these demands were a logical result of their long suppression, "it remains a matter of necessity that they be controlled and checked."[34]

Tan Pingshan would later admit that the CCP, "sacrificed the interests of the workers and peasants ... the government always sided with the landowners ... as a result of our wrong tactics the right wing won the possibility to act."[35] In the reality of the class struggle the 'bloc of four classes' was consistently found to be a mechanism which disarmed the workers and peasants and then handed them over to the generals to be slaughtered.

The 8th Plenum of the ECCI (18-30 May 1927) again rejected 'most determinedly' any suggestion that the CCP leave the KMT. Ignoring the lessons of the Shanghai coup, the ECCI continued to assert that because the revolution was bourgeois and anti-imperialist, those sections of the Chinese bourgeoisie in whose interest it was to overthrow imperialism, could not step aside. This would be ridiculous if it were not so tragic. Stalin ordered the Chinese communists to subordinate themselves to the Wuhan government which, according to Chitarov: "did not even think of leaving the bourgeoisie."

On 24 May 1927 – three days after the crushing of the workers' and peasants' organisations in Changsha and the surrounding areas – Stalin explained to the Plenum why no soviets should be formed in Wuhan:

> "It is clear that whoever calls at present for the immediate creation of soviets of workers' deputies in this [Wuhan] district is attempting to jump over the Kuomintang phase of the Chinese revolution, and he risks putting the Chinese revolution in a most difficult situation ... The Wuhan government is not yet a democratic dictatorship of the proletariat and peasantry. ... It certainly will become a democratic dictatorship if the agrarian revolution develops to the full."[36]

Even as the generals trusted by the left KMT gathered to bury the CCP, Stalin and the ECCI demanded the CCP remain its loyal servant and try and transform it "into a mighty mass organization of the revolutionary petty-bourgeois democracy and the working class." As part of this process it was to deepen the agrarian revolution while halting peasant land seizures! The bloody lesson of Shanghai passed without leaving a trace.

On 1 June 1927, Roy received a telegram from Stalin in response to the Changsha events laying out the course he had in mind for China.[37] Reading the telegram today it is clear that an important function was for it to cover all possibilities so that Stalin could later cite passages from it in defence of whatever actually ensued. This can be seen from the fact that the tasks proposed were mutually exclusive and, in any case, well outside the capacity of the CCP to complete.[38] Fine phrases abounded but the conditions imposed on the CCP by the ECCI robbed them of any real meaning; i.e. the CCP had to "preserve" (sic!) its independence while continuing to be subservient to the left KMT. The comments made here on the contents of the telegram are based on Chen Duxiu's *Appeal to All the Comrades of the Chinese Communist Party* dated 10 December 1929.[39]

- The ECCI was "in favour of the land actually being seized by the masses", but the estates of the KMT officers should not be "disturbed" and "excesses must be combatted". There was not a single major landlord in the Hunan and Hupeh provinces who was not related to army officers and protected by them. If seizing the land of such people was an "excess" how could there be an agrarian revolution?

- It was necessary to stiffen the backs of the KMT leaders or replace them with new leaders. If the CCP could replace the KMT leadership at will then why remain in the subservient position of the bloc within?

- The CCP should mobilise "about 20,000 Communists and about 50,000 revolutionary workers and peasants from Hunan and Hupeh to form a new reliable army before it is too late." How was a new army to be created and armed without coming into immediate and direct confrontation with the left KMT and its generals? If the CCP had the perspective, strength and resources to organise its own army, what was the purpose of continuing the bloc within?
- "… punish officers who maintain contact with Chiang Kai-shek or who set soldiers on the people, the workers and peasants. … The scoundrels must be punished." This was bombastic nonsense intended only for public consumption! The problem was not how to place these officers before tribunals but how to escape their firing squads.

The telegram was revolutionary phrase-mongering which offered no fundamental change to existing policy. To carry out a genuinely left, revolutionary policy, the CCP had to withdraw from the KMT and assert its independence. It had to establish Soviets of workers, peasants, and soldiers, initiate a truly revolutionary agrarian policy and in that way seize the initiative from the KMT. The Political Bureau wired the ECCI: "We accept the instructions and will work according to their directions, but they cannot be realized immediately."[40]

Roy showed Stalin's telegram to Wang Jingwei, apparently in the belief that Wang would take it as confirmation of Russian support for the left and that a joint programme of action could be worked out. Wang had no intention of opposing the generals, and with his closest supporters he began immediate preparations for the expulsion of Communists from the KMT.[41]

On 8 June the leaders of the left KMT left Wuhan for Chengchow the capital city of Honan province to confer with their generals. It was at this conference that the decision was taken to break with the Communists once and for all.[42] The CC met on 20 June to discuss how to respond. Li Lisan's proposal was accepted: a mass demonstration was to be staged to welcome the return of the National leaders. Its slogans would support the reformist demands that the CCP was asking the KMT to adopt.[43] A week later two delegates from Wuhan met with Chiang to strike a deal.

Stalin adamantly continued to present withdrawal from the KMT as "undermining" the revolution, as "playing into the hands of the enemies", demanding that the left KMT in Wuhan must be converted into an organ of "the revolutionary democratic dictatorship of the proletariat and peasantry" which would carry out the agrarian revolution.[44] The ECCI, of course, followed his lead.

The situation in Wuhan quickly deteriorated. Wang Jingwei and his supporters got to work preparing the expulsion of Communists from the KMT, and ever more boldly attacked what they described as the 'excesses' of the peasant movement, and called more and more on the CCP to curb the activity of the Wuhan workers. The Party leadership retreated step by step, there was no political counter-offensive, nor any attempt to organise, even in self-defence.

> "One afternoon, while I was walking down a street in Hankou, I saw a large fleet of rickshaws stacked high with rifles and accompanied by a group of trade union militiamen. ... the trade unions had volunteered to surrender their arms to the commander of the local garrison. ... to avoid misunderstandings and convince the government of our loyalty."[45]

On 23 June, Wang Jingwei was loudly cheered when he appeared on the platform of the 4th National Labour Conference representing three million organised workers.

The leadership of the CCP continued to prostrate itself before the left KMT. On 3 July an emergency meeting of the CC issued a statement re-affirming the KMT's leading position in the National Revolution. Then in a ghastly replay of what happened in Shanghai, ordered the armed labour pickets and other worker and peasant forces under CCP leadership to submit to the KMT; agreed that the workers' and peasants' mass organizations should accept KMT control; ceased all Communist agrarian activities, stopped workers' defence squads patrolling the streets or taking any actions without KMT permission; forbade labour unions to make 'excessive' demands, or to question the right of employers to hire and fire; and then to crown it all emphasised that Communists in the Wuhan government were participating as members of the KMT, and not as Bolsheviks.[46]

Mao's record at this time was not good. Roy remembers "The chairman of the Federation of Peasant Unions, Mao Zedong, in the critical days of 1927, represented the extreme right-wing view in the leadership of the Communist Party."[47] Mao was one of the five members of the KMT's Standing Committee of the Provisional Executive Committee of the All-China Peasant Association and no contemporary records show that he in any way dissented from the policy of keeping the peasants in check while the counter-revolution advanced upon them. Later, Mao would attempt to re-write history as in his interviews with Edgar Snow when he claimed that he had vigorously advocated a radical land policy.[48]

The official assessment of Mao, written during his life-time and with his approval, was that he was a Popular Frontist from the beginning. Mao considered that the Chinese democratic revolution must be carried out to the end. He regarded the opinion then held by the Communist International that the character of the Chinese Revolution remained bourgeois-democratic as completely correct.[49]

Within the Party, Chen and Peng were again arguing for withdrawal from the Kuomintang on the grounds that the left (Wuhan) KMT was following in the footsteps of Chiang Kai-shek and if the CCP did not change its policy they would end up dead. But, as Borodin put it: "I quite agree with your idea but I know that Moscow will never permit it." For the first time Chen stood his ground, he was in a deep depression because his son had just been executed by the KMT, and he tendered his resignation to the CC.[50] Ch'u Ch'iu-pai became acting General Secretary.

Yes, the left KMT did represent the petty-bourgeoisie. But the petty-bourgeoisie was extremely heterogeneous, stretching from the poor peasants barely able to feed themselves and who genuinely supported the Revolution, to petty exploiters whose families were inter-twined with the landlords, and capitalists. Too many of the leaders of the left KMT were the latter. Their differences with the bourgeoisie were of scale not of kind: they would never support the demands of the peasants for land.

The counter-revolution was moving rapidly through the countryside around Wuhan but the ECCI remained in a state of denial. On 3 July 1927 *Pravda* presented a photo of the disarming of Chinese workers by troops under the headline "Fraternisation of the Soldiers with the Workers". On 15 July the left KMT issued an ultimatum to the effect that all CCP members of the KMT and NRA had to resign from the CCP or face punishment; this action ended the bloc within. The military backers of the Wuhan government now began their own murderous coup against the Communists, arresting and killing as many as they could find. Those Stalin had anointed as leaders of the national revolution had metamorphosed from standard bearers to butchers first in Shanghai, then Changsha and now Wuhan. The blame for the disaster was placed on Chen and the CCP.

From the beginning to the end, Stalin and the ECCI had shouted loudly about the Kuomintang as the leadership of the Revolution[51] and this continued until both right and left wings of the KMT became openly reactionary. Now came the most bizarre stage. The ECCI instructed the CCP by telegram: "Only withdraw from the Kuomintang government, not from the Kuomintang."[52] The Communists were to make a big show of resigning from the very Wuhan government that was busy expelling, disarming, arresting and shooting them, and then because Bukharin was still convinced that the left KMT had a mass peasant base (and to save his face), the CCP had to claim the stained and tattered remnants of the KMT banner as its own![53] Somehow, the Communists after being scattered, on the run and hiding from arrest, torture and death, were to obtain a response from the very movement they had betrayed and destroyed. They had to gain the trust of those they had only recently led to the slaughter and they had to do it under the same KMT banner that was flying over the columns of soldiers destroying the peasant unions in the countryside and the trade unions in the towns.

Two new agents were sent to China in July 1927: Besso Lominadze and Heinz Neumann, with instructions to convene an extraordinary conference of the Party, select a new CC, ruthlessly blame the CCP leadership for the disasters resulting from Stalin's policy,[54] and to organise putschist uprisings at Nanchang and Canton.

Without any discussions with those leading the CCP these representatives went directly to the Hunan Provincial Committee which was eager to revenge the killing of peasants around Changsha and began organising an 'uprising' at Nanchang.[55] Remnants of Communist units of the KMT 4th Army in the area were included in the forces brought together for the attack. The Nanchang 'uprising' commenced the night of 31 July and was over by 5 August. It is described in more detail in the next chapter (Section 6.2) as part of the Autumn Harvest Uprisings.

The ECCI representatives then called an extraordinary meeting of the CC on 7 August 1927 in the name of Ch'u Ch'iu-pai (a member of the Politburo only since May and who was prepared to accept the new ultra-left line of the ECCI). The meeting was called in great haste and attended by only twelve or thirteen party members, of whom two were members of the local branch and five were from the CC of the Communist Youth Organisation. Pantsov claims Mao attended this meeting, spoke in support of Lominadze, and used the occasion to argue that political power comes from the barrel of a gun[56] a contribution that the Comintern representative must have welcomed given his perspective of military putsches.

The meeting of 7 August marked a substantial change in the form of the relationship between the ECCI and the CCP. Previously, the CCP had followed the instructions handed down by the CI, but after discussion with the ECCI representatives in which it had been permissible to criticise the application of the line, though never the line itself. It was possible to maintain a semblance of joint agreement. This mask was now discarded and it was clear to all that Moscow intended to crack the whip and expect immediate, complete obedience. The sudden *volte-face* in the policies of the CCP – from class collaboration to putschism – confirmed the degree of CI control over the CCP.

The extent of the decay within the CCP was unmistakable when this rump meeting (subsequently upgraded to a 'Conference' the better to deceive the world Communist movement) blamed the party's failures on Chen Duxiu's and Tan Pingshan's opportunism. Ch'u Ch'iu-pai was confirmed as the new *de facto* General Secretary. Those dropped from the leadership included Mao Zedong. Stalin's prestige had to be maintained and a circular letter from the 'Conference' declared that the new leadership agreed with the criticisms of the CCP made by the ECCI, and that its policy regarding China had been proved entirely correct. Blame lay with the past leadership which had implemented an opportunist, non-revolutionary policy. However, the perspective proposed beggared belief:

> "The Chinese Revolution is not only not on the ebb, but has entered upon a new 'higher' stage. ... the strength of the toiling masses of China … is only now beginning to manifest itself in a new advance of the revolutionary struggle."[57]

In reality, across China in all the territories under KMT control there were mass exterminations of Communists and militants. The defeat of the movement was not simply the huge number of dead (Roy later estimated 25,000 Communists lost their lives), but there was also the psychological and moral demoralisation. The masses had been led to defeat by those they trusted and believed in – who could they trust now? Decimated, dispersed, and demoralised with the masses retreating into passivity, the Communists were told that the Wuhan defeat had propelled the Revolution to a new and higher stage.[58] The ECCI instructed the CCP to launch a series of hopeless putschist actions that would be presented to the world Communist movement as victories to act as a cover for the disastrous decisions of Stalin and the ECCI. Even as CCP members who argued against this new ultra-left line were being expelled, the ECCI sought to protect itself and insure against all eventualities by warning against the tactics of 'skirmishes'. Succeed and the ECCI would take the credit, fail and the CCP would be blamed.

Pravda of 30 September 1927 reported a revolutionary *élan* in the peasant guerrilla movement and in revolutionary elements of the Canton army which were "winning victories with the help of the peasant risings over the oppressors of the Chinese people." This *Pravda* article, confirmed by an ECCI directive on 26 October, marked a change in Comintern policy with respect to peasant insurrections.[59] The CCP now had so little strength left in the towns that the ECCI and CCP leadership were desperately looking for an alternative that they could present to the world Communist movement as a natural extension of the struggles and not have to admit a retreat. Guerrilla warfare was presented as a natural and desirable growth of the struggle of the Chinese peasants. Naturally, to protect itself, the ECCI set conditions: such actions must be integrated into the armed struggle of the masses, and be capable of creating revolutionary base areas which could be expanded.[60] 'Integrated into' and 'capable of' were, of course, value judgements to be made by the leadership of the CCP and thus, whatever it did could be repudiated by the ECCI – unless successful. The result was a noticeable shift in CCP activities away from the city and into the countryside, attempting revolution using peasant guerrilla tactics, peasant risings, and military operations.

Lominadze's (and Ch'u Ch'iu-pai's) perspective was that a revolutionary situation existed in China and would continue for at least some years independent of the mistakes of the CCP. The CC, in November 1927, even passed a resolution to the effect that "by its character it constitutes what Marx called a permanent revolution", the Chinese Revolution was no longer bourgeois-democratic, it was a workers' and peasants' revolution which could and should largely bypass the democratic stage and move to the socialist revolution immediately. This terminology has caused some confusion in the academic world where well-known authorities on China confuse Trotsky's theory of permanent revolution (where the democratic revolution flows over into the socialist because the national bourgeoisie cannot carry through the agrarian revolution) with the ultra-left mis-diagnosis of the ECCI representative in China.[61,62]

The new line decided at the 'Conference' was a dramatic about-face; substituting isolated attempts at violent insurrection for the previous policy of subservience to the KMT. Soviets, inadmissible in May, were now the immediate task – to be created in a period when revolution was in a downturn. Following the ECCI instructions, the CC accepted that the CCP should proceed to take military action against the forces of the KMT while flying the blue-white banner of the KMT!

The new ruling clique was led by Ch'u Ch'iu-pai and supported by, amongst others, Li Lisan and Zhou Enlai. In its turn, the 7 August 'Conference' would take the blame for Stalin's new mistakes and be criticised for the serious error of raising false hopes for the emergence of a left KMT by calling for action under its banner![63]

5.5 Summary

The ECCI imposed on the CCP, the stagist theory that China had to complete the democratic revolution before proceeding to the socialist, and that the appropriate strategy was the bloc within. The newly-founded CCP, as a member of the CI accepted its discipline and the leadership of Moscow. As the ECCI perspective increasingly clashed with reality and the CCP leadership objected, advice gave way to orders and the true relation of the national sections to the centre in a Stalinist organisation was revealed.

Maintenance of the KMT-CCP block was seen as essential for a successful Chinese national revolution, and as the national revolution was a stage that could not be bypassed, the CCP had to surrender its own particular interests and submit itself to the nationalist party foregoing an independent, critical voice. To a degree and to an extent, there will be genuine common interests of the different classes in a colonial country against imperialism, but Marxism starts from concrete reality and by 1925 at the latest, it was clear that the common interests were fracturing.

It was absolutely correct to support the struggle of Chiang Kai-shek against the northern warlords for a united China. But the nature of the support should have been such as to prepare the proletariat to struggle for its own political independence and to overthrow the Chinese bourgeoisie. By the spring of 1927, the NRA had swept north through the provinces of Hunan, Hubei, and Jiangxi to the city of Nanjing. The mass movement exploded and the generals determined that it was necessary to settle accounts as soon as possible in a military manner, and began recruiting as many mercenaries as possible from the defeated warlords. It beggars belief that the CCP assisted in this process.

In China, a Communist Party of nearly 60,000 and a Young Communist League of about 35,000 were thrown into the class war not to take it forward, not to give the mass movement a revolutionary character and direction, but to side with the bourgeoisie against hungry peasants desperate for land, against women and children fighting for a living wage. The result was the almost complete destruction of the party.

The Stalinists insisted on pursuing a policy that resulted in one disaster after another (from Chiang's 20 March Coup to the Wuhan debacle) because the interests of the bureaucracy within the Soviet Union were more important in determining Stalin's policy than the success or failure of the Chinese Revolution. For their own factional interests, the response of the bureaucracy to events in China was to cover up, to lie and finally to blame others for the disasters. The bureaucracy withheld from the CCP any knowledge of Trotsky's proposal to break the bloc within out of fear that the Chinese Communists would compare and weigh the two policies and, in view of their own experiences, might favour what Trotsky proposed. This could have brought victory to the Chinese Revolution, but would have destroyed the Stalinist faction's control of the AUCP(B), an outcome intolerable to the reactionary, privileged Russian bureaucracy. Peng Pi-lan has argued "the second Chinese revolution was sacrificed for the sake of preserving the privileged position of the bureaucrats in Russia."[64]

Finally, in a time of retreat by both workers and peasants Ch'u Ch'iu-pai and Lominadze opposed a united front strategy based on democratic and transitional demands that could mobilise the masses. In a time of reaction, democratic and economic activities such as the call for the right to belong to a union and demands for higher wages were thrown overboard. The result was a rapid decline in worker support of the CCP. This confirmed that the ECCI and the CCP did not understand the importance of the defeats at Shanghai and Wuhan. First the mass of the proletariat recoiled from the policies of the CCP, and then so did the peasantry – though this took a little more time.

Borodin, after the Wuhan debacle, said:

> "The big bourgeoisie can never unify China because they are not really against the imperialists; they are allied with them and profit by them. The small bourgeoisie cannot unify China because they vacillate between the workers and peasants on the one hand and the big bourgeoisie on the other and, in the end, go over to the latter. The workers and peasants did not unify China because they trusted too much to the small bourgeoisie."[65]

Roy offered much the same opinion:

> "Rather than sacrifice the sectional interests of the reactionary landlords and capitalists, the bourgeois nationalist leaders betrayed the revolution. Class solidarity cut across national solidarity."[66]

The Second Chinese Revolution had confirmed Lenin's analysis that in colonial and semi-colonial countries the major tasks of the 'bourgeois' revolution could not be solved under the leadership of the 'national' bourgeoisie. It also demonstrated a basic tenet of the Permanent Revolution, that the interests of the imperialists, compradors, national capitalists and landlords were integrated to a much greater degree than were the interests of the national bourgeoisie, the peasants and the workers.

Chapter 6

From the Canton "Commune" to the Jiangxi "Soviet"

6.1 Introduction

For the Chinese Communist Party the leadership of Ch'u Ch'iu-pai and the ECCI representatives, Lominadze and Neumann, meant objectivity and realism went out of the window. Each set-back was hailed as an advance: Chiang Kai-shek's coup of March 1926 had elevated the revolution to the higher stage of the Shanghai massacre of April 1927, which in turn had raised the revolution to the still higher stage of the Wuhan debacle, and this had advanced the revolution to the insurrectionary plane.[1]

This *Alice in Wonderland* approach was the basis for a series of attempted uprisings each of which proved disastrous, but from which the CC of the CCP deduced that conditions were ripe for an immediate uprising across an entire swathe of China and, in particular, in Canton. It is important to assess the reality of these "uprisings" because, in a truly Stalinist manner, the CCP has prettified these events, re-written history, and today presents them as the start of a new, carefully considered and successful strategy largely due to the efforts of Mao Zedong.[2]

The disasters engendered by its policies did not weaken the ECCI's hold on the CCP; rather they gave it greater control. Almost the only source of support for CCP members (food, clothing, accommodation and travel) was the monies supplied by the Comintern which quite coldly used the situation to advance its control over the Party. Those who demonstrated their pliability obtained material help and thus, to a certain extent, they and their families were protected from the terror. Critics such as Peng Shuzhi found themselves with no job, denied living expenses, and in constant danger of being arrested and shot. Stalinist organisational norms were promoted: as a known oppositionist, even though a member of the CC, Peng was denied access to Party meetings for fear that his criticism of the adventurist actions of the Party would infect others.[3]

Chinese events were a foretaste of Stalinism's "Third Period", which was formally adopted at the 6th World Congress of the CI in the summer of 1928. It was accepted that world capitalism had begun to disintegrate and a revolutionary wave would soon engulf the capitalist world. For Communists active in the trade union movement, for example, this meant establishing separate, radical, so-called red unions under CP control. Even if it had been successful, such a move could only have resulted in splitting the very weak workers' movement that existed in China. Worse, the CI imposed a programme and strategy for these red unions that demanded offensive actions at a time when even being a member of a union could mean being badly beaten or shot.[4]

In China the adventure with the red unions would finally destroy the Party's remaining proletarian base, assisting Pavel Mif, Wang Ming, and the 28 Bolsheviks to take control of the CCP. With the virtual extinction of the Party in the cities, the CC would move from Shanghai to the peasant "Soviet" in Jiangxi in south-central China and the CCP would become overwhelmingly peasant in composition and petty-bourgeois in politics.

6.2 Autumn Harvest Uprisings

Under ECCI direction, the CCP planned a large-scale programme of peasant uprisings for the autumn harvest time when the class struggle would normally be most acute in the rural districts. The term 'uprising' was a complete misnomer. There were no uprisings, armed detachments made a military assault on a town and then invited support from local workers and peasants (those familiar with subsequent Maoist guerrilla activities in Latin America and elsewhere will recognise the tactic).

It was agreed that conditions were not ripe for a nationwide insurrection so the uprisings were limited to the four provinces of Hupeh, Hunan, Jiangxi, and Kwangtung, with particular emphasis on Hunan, where the peasant movement was considered the most radical.[5] Unfortunately, Hunan had been subject to a particularly vicious cleansing and the peasant associations, previously the most radical and effectively organised in the country, had been smashed by white terror. Such armed uprisings as did occur were often initiated by cadres who had been hiding out in the hills and countryside, and generally resulted in their deaths and the deaths of many peasants, for no gain.

However, there were immediate and serious obstacles in the way of such a change in perspective. Events in Shanghai had had a debilitating effect on Party members, workers and peasants generally. CCP members had been miseducated for years into accepting opportunist methods and perspectives, and were now expected to make a sudden and abrupt *volte-face* and lead armed insurrections. The CCP would discover, too late, that its own personnel were not up to the task of engineering insurrection.[6] CCP members themselves had been continuously dampening the revolutionary sentiment of the masses and Communists were widely distrusted as opponents of peasant seizure of the land. This distrust surfaced when orders to begin the uprisings arrived, and the support promised by the peasant associations evaporated.

Attempting uprisings in such unsuitable conditions would only weaken the Party and increase its isolation from the masses. However, the CC believed, like so many ultra-lefts before and since, that they were administering a shock treatment that would immediately correct the opportunism of the past.

The first uprising under the new policy took place on 1 August 1927 at Nanchang, capital of Jiangxi province, about 250 km (160 miles) south-west of Wuhan, under the overall direction of Lominadze but with Ch'u Ch'iu-pai and Li Lisan in command on the ground. The attack was a purely military affair by a force of up to 20,000 soldiers drawn predominantly from mutinous KMT units, many of which had been commanded by Communist officers. The town was taken easily as the garrison was heavily outnumbered.[7]

Once taken, the town was placed under a Revolutionary Committee of twenty-five members which included both KMT and Communists. The nonsense of an uprising against the KMT made under the KMT banner was demonstrated by the inclusion on the Committee of the General (Chang Fah-kwei) who at that very moment was rushing to crush the uprising.[8] The town was evacuated by 5 August to avoid any serious engagement with KMT troops.

What was quite clear was that no uprising occurred either in Nanchang or in the surrounding areas despite the CCP announcing that "Agrarian reform shall be carried out." Only estates of more than three hectares (about eight acres) which did not belong to the families of NRA officers were to be seized, meaning it was unlikely that many local landlords were affected.[9] But the lack of support amongst the peasants had deeper roots – the track record of the CCP.

During the remaining months of 1927 the Communists were to stage two more equally unsuccessful insurrections: an ineffective attack on

Changsha (Mao Zedong arrived too late to participate) and an attack made by the remnants from the Nanchang uprising on the treaty port of Swatow (Shantou) which was defeated.[10] During this period the Communist Party continued to march under the blue and white banner of the Left KMT, further mis-educating CCP members in the principles and organisation of a Leninist party. Worst, it presented to the peasant masses the appearance that the fighting was limited to a fight between the left and right of the KMT.[11]

In all areas the uprisings were defeated after a day or two of 'success'. The uprisings were little short of fiascos, a series of military mis-adventures with little or no peasant support. The few CCP military forces that remained after the defeat of the Second Chinese Revolution were being destroyed by blind adventurism. When it became clear that these putsches had failed to spark a revolution, responsibility was pinned not on Stalin, the ECCI or its agents or even Ch'u Ch'iu-pai, but on Tan Pingshan who was denounced and expelled for promoting illusions in the Left KMT.[12] On 19 September 1927, the Politburo of the CCP finally announced: "uprisings can under no circumstances take place under the Kuomintang banner", and formally laid to rest the stinking corpse that had been the bloc within.

Otto Braun describes how individuals and small groups of rank and file troops who survived these adventures fled to isolated rural areas such the Chingkan mountains on the border between Hunan and Jiangxi, often taking up a semi-bandit existence in order to stay alive.[13]

6.3 The Canton Uprising and its Aftermath

Pravda of 30 September 1927 reported: "After the southern revolutionary army had achieved important successes, it became perfectly clear that there would be a new revolutionary *élan* in China." The Communist-led troops which had occupied Nanchang and marched on Swatow were routed the very night the *Pravda* article was published. The original plan had been for these forces to proceed from a Communist-controlled Swatow to Canton to participate in a major urban uprising. This warning of the strength of the reactionary forces was, of course, ignored.

In one last attempt to correct the ultra-left policy and abandon the proposed Canton uprising, Peng Shuzhi and Chen Duxiu wrote to the CC on 26 October 1927 arguing that the situation in China was no longer revolutionary and that the correct and key slogans for drawing the masses into action were democratic demands such as the eight-hour-day, the confiscation of land, with the governmental slogan "Convoke a National Assembly". Such slogans would bring the broad masses into activity again and prepare the ground for raising revolutionary slogans, in particular to establish Soviets.[14] The proposal was summarily rejected. Later Liu Shaoqi (Liu Shao-ch'i) when making an overall assessment of the work of the CCP, would conclude that the question of government had, indeed, been the "central practical question among the masses" and (indirectly) admitted that democratic slogans were what had been required. He explained that the CCP had condemned the use of legal means as "rightist" and had done its best to encourage adventurist activities ... "the losses we have suffered on this account are countless."[15]

The CC of the CCP met in enlarged session 7-14 November 1927 to assess the outcomes of the programme approved at the August Conference. However, as Li Ang, the corresponding secretary of the Party would later admit, "The Comintern sent telegrams daily urging the CCP to bring about uprisings in Canton and other large cities. These telegrams were all extremely emphatic in tone and allowed no room for argument."[16] Obediently Ch'u Ch'iu-pai (and Lominadze) blindly accepted that the rising revolutionary wave was continuing and demanded more dramatic actions by the CCP. Scorning the evidence that China had entered a counter-revolutionary period, the sequence of bloody failures was taken not to be the result of an erroneous political line but due to the personal inadequacies of those involved. For example, Mao's late arrival and consequent non-participation in the attack on Changsha resulted in his being kicked off the Politburo.

Without any sign of a peasant rising, with the urban masses still reeling from the Shanghai massacre, with thousands of Kuomintang soldiers in and near Canton, the Communist International insisted that the CCP lead the workers in an attempt to seize the city. The insurrection (11-14 December 1927) was timed to coincide with the 15th Congress of the Russian Party, and its primary purpose was to allow Stalin to claim a victory in China, the better to denounce the Russian Oppositionists. Elleman has described how the dates of insurrection and Congress were juggled so that the Canton insurrection would have greatest impact in Moscow. To enable the uprising to meet the timetable set by the ECCI, the call for a general strike, an essential prerequisite of any communist insurrection if the urban masses are to be roused to action, was omitted. Over 7,000 workers paid with their lives to provide a smokescreen to hide Stalin's mistakes.[17]

The Canton uprising was heroic in the conduct of Party members, criminal in the adventurism of the leadership. It was immediately clear that the revolt had little mass support. Yeh Ting, the Communist officer in *de facto* charge of the insurrection later said:

> "The masses took no part in the insurrection. ... The workers of the power plant cut off the light, and we had to work in the dark. ... The river sailors placed themselves shamefully at the service of the Whites. The railway workers of the Hong Kong and Canton-Hankou line transmitted the telegrams of the enemy and transported their soldiers. The peasants did not help us by destroying the tracks and did not try to prevent the enemy from attacking Canton. The workers of Hong Kong did not display the least sympathy for the insurrection."

By 14 December, the last of the defenders of the Canton Commune had been wiped out and the reign of terror had begun. This latter news, of course, never reached the Russian Congress.

During the four days in which the Communists controlled the city, *Pravda* did indeed claim that "a Soviet government had been established in Canton." But this "Soviet" was a handful of unelected individuals (Blick claims 16 persons in a city of millions), each of whom had been handpicked by the ECCI representative acting under Stalin's direct instructions. The workers of Canton knew nothing of its existence until the uprising was well under way.[18] The 'Canton Soviet' or 'Canton Commune' was a Stalinist fiction, a smokescreen to conceal a failed putsch.

During the Wuhan debacle the concept of the Soviet had been distorted to avoid its implementation. Now in this perverse application it was being mangled further and turned into a tool of the bureaucracy instead of organiser and expression of the exploited. A Soviet is above all, a body elected by the widest franchise from workers, peasants, and soldiers. In times of tremendous revolutionary upheavals, Soviets emerge organically from the mass movement: from strike committees, action committees, peasant leagues and other representative bodies. Soviets bring into action the broadest sections of the masses and directly express their will. The self-activities of the Soviets educate the masses by direct action, providing a training ground that can carry the masses through revolution to the capture of governmental and state power. This concept of the Soviets disappears under Stalin and the CCP. Instead, Soviets appear by bureaucratic decree only on the very threshold of the capture of power.

The educational dimension and representative nature of the Soviet were entirely excluded. The confidence of the masses in the Soviet gained by testing it out over a period of time (both when advancing and retreating), was missing. The CCP put on the uniform of the Soviet after the insurrection had begun but its role was that of spectator watching a doomed adventure. The sad fact was that by the time of the Canton insurrection, the movement was in a downturn, too debilitated both politically and numerically to launch Soviets.

The ECCI and CCP had a stagist perspective for China, which was to first complete the bourgeois democratic revolution against imperialism and feudalism, and then at some later date to carry through the socialist. This made it necessary to distort the concept of the Soviet to make it a tool of the party rather than have it as the most democratic mass organisation possible. If, during 1926-27, Soviets had genuinely existed to represent the wish of the majority then those Soviets would have demanded seizure of the land. But this could only have been effected against those the CCP had designated the leaders of the revolution, and would have inevitably have posed the question of the dictatorship of the proletariat.

Lominadze was in China between July and December 1927, faithfully following Stalin's orders and being largely responsible for the Canton disaster – which he reported to the 15th Party Congress of the RCP as a victory confirming Stalin's analysis and inaugurating an era in which the Chinese workers and peasants would struggle directly for state power. For that he was elected a candidate member of the CC. Later, Lominadze was bitterly assailed by Pavel Mif, Stalin's new man in China, who inherited the mess he had left behind. Lominadze soon fell out of favour and committed suicide in 1935 rather than be a defendant in the forthcoming show trials. Mif was executed three years later.

The Political Bureau of the Chinese Communist Party, in its resolution *The Significance and Lessons of the Canton Uprising*, adopted on 3 January 1928 declared:

> "Only cowardly opportunists can call such an uprising a premature act, a putsch ... The Canton uprising in mid-December was an inevitable outgrowth of the development of the class struggle as a whole and the conjuncture of the objective conditions ... This analysis was completely in accord with the facts."[19]

In flagrant contradiction of every fact before them, it was declared that the revolutionary forces had not diminished but were uninterruptedly growing and that the question of armed insurrection was still "directly on the order of the day." The general situation, it was claimed, made Soviet power a practical and immediate question.

As the CCP was pushed ever harder to adopt an increasingly unrealistic assessment of the situation in China, Moscow's domination became ever more obvious. But, of course, Stalin could not be associated with the disasters that followed. A smokescreen of lies was published in the international Communist press. On 7 February 1928, *Pravda* wrote:

> "The Chinese Communist Party is heading toward an armed insurrection. The whole situation in China speaks for the fact that this is the correct course. ... Experience proves that the Chinese Communist Party must concentrate all its efforts on the task of the day-to-day and widespread careful preparation of the armed insurrection."

The Communist, March 1928, carried an article by British Communist Ralph Fox[20] which described an immense (but entirely fictitious) wave of peasant insurrections following on from Canton, that had established "Soviet Governments" in

> "eastern Kwantung, between Canton and Swatow, the districts of Hai Fong, Lu Fong, Pulin, Hoyuan … the island of Hainang … in Hunan province the Tsalin, Kwitong and Lincheng districts have Soviets; in western Kiangsi, in Tsuichuan and Hailing districts; … and in eastern Hupeh."

The 9th Enlarged Plenum of the ECCI (9-25 February 1928) foresaw the imminent approach of a new revolutionary upsurge which posed before the CCP the "practical task of organizing and carrying out the armed uprisings of the masses … (and) the overthrow of the present power. … The Party must consider as its principal task the preparation of general and combined actions in the cities and in the countryside in several adjoining provinces." The ECCI approved a policy of irresponsible adventurism which meant the destruction of the best revolutionary elements in new adventures, further separating the CCP from the masses, and further weakening the Party.

The same 7 February issue of *Pravda* had the effrontery to write:

> "The provincial armies fought undivided against Red Canton and this proved to be the greatest and oldest shortcoming of the Chinese Communist Party, insufficient political work decomposing the reactionary armies."

But one year previously, just a month and a half before the Shanghai massacre, the *Communist International*, central organ of the Comintern had written:

> "The Chinese Communist Party and the conscious Chinese workers must not under any circumstances pursue a tactic that would disorganise the revolutionary armies …."[21]

Chiang Kai-shek was, of course, already actively planning the Shanghai massacre; we now know that given the weaknesses in his forces, to have 'disorganised' the NRA (as proposed by the Opposition) would have placed the Shanghai workers in a much stronger position, and with Hsueh Yueh's and Yeh Ting's troops, would almost certainly have tipped the balance in their favour.

Two months after the Shanghai massacre the same journal would state:

> "The best illustration of the nonsense of the arch-left line of the Opposition is in the slogan for soldiers' deputies as one of the forms of the dual power. … To proclaim it now for the army fighting for the Wuhan Government would be consciously to seek to decompose this army."[22]

As it turned out, decomposing this army was just what had been required. Instead, the CCP paid little or no attention to the concerns of the rank and file soldiers nor made any attempts to form links between the soldiers, workers, and peasants. Now these armies crushed the Canton insurrection.

6.4 The 6th Congress of the CCP

The 6th Congress of the CCP (18 June-10 July 1928) was held in Moscow not only because the situation in China was so dangerous, but also to allow the ECCI to better stage-manage the proceedings for public consumption. The Congress took place on the back of a series of policy failures of disastrous proportions and of major changes in international policy.

Internationally the Third Period line had been adopted at the 9th Enlarged Plenum of the ECCI (February 1928) and confirmed at the 6th World Congress (17 July-1 September 1928) which decreed that a revolutionary mass armed uprising was imminent in China, and outlined a revolutionary programme based on urban revolts similar to the abortive Canton insurrection of the preceding December.[23] These ideas naturally flowed into the 6th Congress of the CCP and meant the CCP placed an anathema on democratic demands and rejected any meaningful united front activities. The CCP had to immediately and consistently advocate seizure of state power, organise Soviets as organs of insurrection (*à la* Canton), expropriate landlords and big property owners, and expel the foreign imperialists.

There were two serious problems with this perspective. The first was that the movement was in a severe downturn and proposals of this nature simply alienated any remaining support amongst the urban masses. The second was that the goal of the armed insurrection was given as the overthrow of the Kuomintang and its replacement by … the democratic dictatorship of the proletariat and peasantry. Another cycle of betrayal was in the making.

In political terms, and for the healthy development of the CCP, the Congress was a disaster. The Congress resembled a bear pit with accusations flying in all directions (except at Stalin!) as the different trends vied for Moscow's support.

The defeats suffered had been the result of the policies accepted and enacted by the CCP itself. But the Congress did not attempt to come to grips with the fundamental errors underlying the defeats – the mistaken assessment of the revolutionary role of the national bourgeoisie in China, and the need for a truly independent Communist Party. From these had flowed the mistakes of failing to support the formation of workers' and peasants' Soviets, and of submitting to the discipline of the bourgeois and petty-bourgeois politicians of the KMT.

At the Congress, Bukharin's nine hour speech heaped the blame for the Party's defeats on those who had implemented Moscow's instructions, Chen Duxiu and Ch'u Ch'iu-pai (appointed less than a year before).[24] Within the Party those who attempted to objectively review events were expelled.

The new style 'Bolshevisation' which had begun with the 7 August Conference advanced significantly during the 6th Congress when the delegates accepted Stalinist-style self-criticism as acceptable behaviour. Lenin's democratic centralism meant the minority was required to accept the decisions of the majority and then allow the test of events to determine who was right. Such a procedure could not be tolerated under the bureaucracy because the desired outcome was not a political line best matching events but a policy that best protected the bureaucracy. Indeed, a political line matching reality would have meant the end of the bureaucracy. The new style Bolshevisation meant any minority had not only to enact the majority line, it had to publicly confess and repent its 'errors', promise to expunge its 'erroneous' thoughts and swear unquestioning loyalty to the majority (bureaucratic) line. This self-flagellation became accepted procedure within the CCP and would grow into the rectification campaigns extensively used in Yenan and later.

Having to defend Stalin's line and cover up the mistakes of the recent past meant the CCP sank into a self-contradictory mess: it formally condemned putschism, but endorsed the continuation of the policy of isolated uprisings; it formally endorsed the need for a democratic programme for China while its ultra-left activities prevented united actions. It condemned the call for a national assembly as an opportunist error and so lacked a central focus for democratic demands. By default the call to establish Soviets, intended as a propaganda slogan to be actioned at some indeterminate time in the future, became the governmental slogan of the Party at just the time when the proletariat needed defensive slogans.[25]

The Congress defended the policy which produced the Canton tragedy. A resolution declared that "the Nanchang insurrection, the Autumn Harvest uprising, and especially the Canton Commune, did not constitute adventurism"; rather "the Canton Commune opened the Soviet period" in the Chinese Revolution while simultaneously (and contradictorily) being a "heroic rear-guard action". The CCP formally accepted Stalin's view that Soviets should only appear "when the solid victory of the uprising is assured" but warned that allowing elections in these Soviets would give a voice to "petty bourgeois democratism" which would be dangerous (for the leadership of the Party).[26] Given the history of the CCP, free discussion was anathema and so was classified as petty-bourgeois and a threat to the revolution. That the CCP believed it had the authority to decide when and how to launch Soviets and who would be elected, starkly revealed how far its bureaucratic and anti-democratic views had developed, and was an open warning of how Soviets in the base areas being set up by the Red Army would be managed.

The 6th Congress chose a forty-year old labourer, Hsiang Chung-fa as new General Secretary because of his proletarian background, a dedicated but not overly clever man. The real authority within the Party would soon lie with Li Lisan as head of the Propaganda Bureau aided by Zhou Enlai as head of the Organisational Bureau. During the 6th Congress, Li Lisan was called to the Kremlin to be interviewed by Stalin and it was on that basis that he was given the leadership.[27] We can be confident that Stalin assessed how loyal Li Lisan would be to him personally and the new ultra-left Third Period line.

The Congress agreed that work amongst the peasantry was essential but its general outline was determined by events in the Soviet Union not what was happening in China. Over the summer of 1928 the struggle between Bukharin's Right Opposition and the Stalinists had not been finally resolved; thus the 6th World Congress of the CI and the 6th Congress of the CCP agreed that the Party should "unite with the petty-bourgeoisie and rich peasants (kulaks) to oppose all reactionary forces." In June 1929 the struggle against the Right Opposition was over and the political line of the CI changed to one of resolute struggle against the kulaks for leadership of the peasant masses.[28] These changes were transmitted into the CCP and caused considerable friction between those such as Mao who favoured the softer line, and others who would try to force the adoption of the more radical.

The Congress, with ECCI guidance, adopted a long resolution *On the Organisation of Soviet Political Power*,[29] which declared the central issue in the peasant movement was the need for an amalgam of the CCP, peasant Soviets, and the Red Army to establish military-style bases in the countryside which would grow to encircle the cities and give an impulse to the rising tide of revolution. Interpretation of this resolution would lead to differences between those who emphasised the building of bases in the countryside (Mao) against those (Li Lisan) who wanted to use the Red Army to attack urban centres sparking an urban, proletarian revolution. Mao's defining strategy, which would later be paraphrased as 'from the periphery to the centre', originated with the ECCI and was, to a degree, a desperate attempt to hide the failure of the CI and CCP to win the urban proletariat.

The CCP was in disarray everywhere, communications between groups, cells and individuals was difficult and slow. Mao, thus largely freed of central direction, took advantage of the situation to push his own perspective. In April 1927 he persuaded Zhu De to join forces with him to set up a Communist-controlled area in the border region between Jiangxi and Hunan. Subsequently, Mao would claim that nearly 20,000 'fighters' had joined him. This move was approved by the local Party committee and, later, by the 6th CCP Congress. In his absence, the Congress elected Mao Zedong a full member of the CC as a "representative of the tendency that demanded the prompt carrying out of an agrarian revolution."[30]

Certainly up until the end of 1928, the Red Armies generally did not remain in one place for long enough to be able to carry out the CCP's agrarian policy. Mao had attempted it in the Jiangxi/Hunan border area but had been driven out and moved south to the even more remote area of the Jiangxi/Fujian border. However, during 1929 the CCP was able to begin effecting land distribution in a number of areas, thereby gaining a social significance that it had lacked previously. In line with the resolution passed at the 6th Congress, the land confiscated was limited to that of the larger landlords and public land. It will be shown that the benefits of this distribution often went to the better-off peasants who rushed to join the Red Army and staff the administrative apparatus in the territories controlled by the CCP.[31]

Mao's land programme sounded radical and revolutionary; the old tax offices were destroyed and many tax collectors, KMT officials, military men, gentry and missionaries were killed. The policies of 'No rent (to the landlords), no taxes (to the KMT authorities), and no debts (to the usurers)' were implemented. All deeds, land titles, debt registers, tax rolls of the old regime were completely destroyed.[32] By allocating ownership of the land to the peasants who had previously farmed it, the policies remained within bourgeois democratic limits. We should not, however, belittle the progressive nature of these measures as far as the individual peasants were concerned. For many it represented a significant improvement in their lives and the basis of their support for the CCP.

In the meantime, Chiang had captured Nanjing, boastfully declared it the capital of a unified China, announced an all-China government had been established, the aims of the revolution achieved, and an end to military rule!

6.5 The Li Lisan Line

Li Lisan had a genuine base within the Party because of his heroic role in a number of workers' struggles,[33] and with the support of Moscow came the support of the ECCI representatives and those such as Zhou Enlai who followed every twist and turn of the Moscow line. It cannot be stressed too strongly that the so-called Li Lisan Line was the Chinese version of Third Period Stalinism. Ultra-left and adventurist policies were pursued which further isolated the Party from the proletariat and effectively destroyed the CCP in the major urban centres.

Shanghai had brought to an end the period of rapid Party growth. With the Wuhan and Canton massacres, the prestige of the Party plummeted and workers turned their backs on it. The exodus of Party members turned into a flood with the policy of putschism, launched not to match Chinese circumstances, but to maintain Stalin's prestige in Russia.[34]

On 8 February 1929, the ECCI sent a letter to the CC of the CCP claiming that a new revolutionary wave was clearly detectable in China. The June 1929 plenary session of the CC of the CCP formally endorsed Stalin's line of the collapse of capitalism and confirmed Li Lisan's leadership.[35] On 26 October 1929, the ECCI sent another letter to the CC, announcing "the beginning of the revolutionary wave" in China. The Party was to take over the leadership of this new revolutionary wave by overcoming its "petty bourgeois waverings". The Comintern reinforced this view by declaring that "rightism" was the most dangerous trend internationally and in the CCP.

The CCP responded by adopting resolutions on 20 December 1929 and 11 January 1930 that fully accepted the Comintern's position and hailed the arrival of a "fresh revolutionary upsurge" in China.[36] Li Lisan affirmed that China was in an immediately revolutionary situation and that insurrection by any means at any cost was the order of the day. Preparatory work organising and mobilising the masses was not considered necessary, a mistake that proved fatal for many CCP members in the urban areas.[37]

Opposition to Li Lisan's overly optimistic estimation of the "revolutionary high-tide" was led by members of the Party Committee for Jiangsu Province and the Shanghai-based National Labour Federation, both of which had their headquarters in Shanghai. This opposition was overcome only when the June 1929 Second Plenum of the CC reformed the Jiangsu committee and expelled several "Trotskyites" including Peng Shuzhi.[38]

One of the first victims of the attack on rightism was Chen Duxiu who was expelled from the party in late 1929. He was denounced viciously for his "Trotskyite", "liquidationist" and "rightist" tendencies. Given his enormous prestige his conversion to Trotskyism had created a crisis in the Party and – in true Stalinist fashion – a major purge was launched. Chen Duxiu had been a staunch defender of internal democracy and he warned Party members that the suppression of dissident views would lead to a regime of bureaucratic centralism. He was proved correct immediately as the Party marked his expulsion by formally implementing the resolution banning factions, (i.e. democratic discussion and debate) passed at the 6th Comintern Congress. Chen himself was finally excluded from the party on 15 November 1929, after which the leadership then expelled hundreds of members who supported him. This was a great purge 'in the Russian manner'. Oppositionists were cleared out. Every week the Party newspaper, *The Red Flag*, published a long list of the latest to be excluded.[39]

Strike figures for 1928 and 1929 reported to the 16th Congress of the AUCP(B) by the Chinese delegate, made it clear that there was an upsurge in union activity largely due to an economic upturn. The CCP, with the correct tactics, could have made contact with these workers and re-established itself amongst the proletariat. But the Party had abjured democratic slogans such as "For the eight hour working day" when posed as part of a defensive programme. Instead the CCP attempted to set up red trade unions, actively dividing the working class, just as was being done in Germany in the face of the Nazis. Party members in the urban areas worked hard, intervening in every labour dispute, e.g., on 13 May in Shanghai about 300 strikers urged on by Party militants, attacked and disabled trams on Ferry Road – but a total of about 100 were arrested, most of whom were badly beaten.

At the end of 1929 and the start of 1930, there were numerous small-scale violent skirmishes between groups of workers and the police, for example police in the French concession had openly attacked striking women mill workers who fought back (and went on to win their strike). The ultra-left Li Lisan saw enough activity to justify his belief in an approaching revolutionary situation. Li had a very simple plan: the objective situation was directly revolutionary so the Party would increase agitation from May Day up to the glorious anniversary of 30 May when a CCP-initiated general strike would start the revolution.

> "At that time, in order to co-ordinate and if possible hasten the 'imminent nation-wide high tide of revolution', we frantically searched everywhere for the slightest sign of a struggle. Sometimes top-level conferences would be called, with members of the CC, the District Committee and the Provincial Committee, to discuss some trifling altercation between shop owner and employees. ... From early morning to late at night we searched high and low for 'the spark to light a prairie fire', keeping ourselves in a state of artificially induced tension. ... We would get up at the crack of dawn and hurry down to talk to the shop workers before business started. Then we would hold a meeting, rush around making contacts, and so on until the early hours of the following morning."[40]

The public actions taken by CCP members required a high degree of heroism, some historians have described such displays as "suicidal" and put the fall in membership in Shanghai, in particular, down to the resulting arrests and executions.[41] The outcome of this frenetic activity was not the expected general strike but the wholesale arrest and imprisonment of CCP members and, in many cases, their immediate execution in the Longhua barracks.[42] Despite the setback experienced in May, which clearly demonstrated that the workers were not in in a revolutionary mood, Li continued to push the line that world capitalism was on the brink of collapse ... and that any incident could start "the great fight".[43] How could Li Lisan have been so blind to the results of his policies? Probably because, as with so many ultra-lefts, he knew his analysis was right, the membership just wasn't trying hard enough.[44]

Looking for ways to recapture its influence in the cities, the leadership decided to use the undoubted (relative) successes of the Party in the countryside. This was spelled out in the Politburo resolution of 11 June 1930 entitled *The New Revolutionary High Tide and an Initial Victory in One or More Provinces*, which proposed Wuhan be seized as a part of a military take-over which was predicted to grow rapidly into the Chinese socialist revolution.[45]

The revolutionary years had trained quite a few rural local leaders, and the counter-revolution had not succeeded in eliminating them all. Also, a significant number of revolutionary workers hid in the countryside from the militarists. Quantities of small arms had been obtained by the peasants, and guerrilla bands (calling themselves "Red Army units") had been organised by soldiers who deserted to the side of the peasants, individually, in groups, and sometimes in whole companies. Thus, even after the defeat of the revolution, peasant rebellion continued in a number of areas often with Communists at the head, to the extent that in isolated areas, armed peasant bands drove out local landlords, usurers and rich peasants. For example, the remnants of the troops defeated at Swatow formed the very first Chinese Soviet in Hailufeng in Guangdong province.[46] Li Lisan believed these forces could be combined to spark the proletariat into activity.

To implement his scheme Li determined to take more direct central control of the armed struggle. To counteract this threat to his position Mao called his own conference of Red Army delegates in December 1929 which approved the building of rural bases and made substantial (though implicit) criticisms of Li Lisan. This undermining of Li was couched in terms that appeared in complete harmony with the declared aims of the CC: against egalitarianism, for tighter organisational discipline, for correcting mistaken ideas in the Party, and for the subordination of personal interests to the political needs of the Party.[47] Mao's pamphlets at this time made great show of endorsing the decisions of the 6th Congress of the CCP and claimed to enact ECCI directives. Without naming Li, Mao criticised his strategy by emphasising the positive gains to be made from establishing base areas in the countryside and the risks of attacking urban centres.[48]

Mao had already made a name for himself as a military strategist and was well known for his four tactical principles:

i. When the enemy advances, we retreat.

ii. When the enemy halts and encamps, we harass him.

iii. When the enemy wants to avoid battle, we attack him.

iv. When the enemy withdraws, we pursue him.

Braun insists that these principles represented Mao's interpretation of the *Treatise of the Art of War* by Sun Tzu, a Chinese general of antiquity. Braun also pointed out that Mao's famous eight rules for the good behaviour of Red Army troops, which won them so much support from a peasantry used to mercenary troops that pillaged and raped as a matter of course, were an updated version of the rules of the T'ai-p'ing Rebellion of the nineteenth century.[49]

To counteract Mao's manoeuvres, to establish better central control over the disparate groups that made up the Red Armies, and to present his strategy for implementing the Politburo resolution *The New Revolutionary High Tide and an Initial Victory in One or More Provinces*, Li Lisan called a conference of delegates from the Red Armies in Shanghai in May 1930. Despite difficulties of terrain and distances, Li wanted the disparate forces of the Red Army to prepare for the new strategy by combining into four Armies, and to be prepared to move from guerrilla and bandit tactics to mobile warfare and capturing of urban centres.[50] Mao Zedong and Zhu De showed their opposition by failing to attend.

In June 1930 the Political Secretariat of the ECCI wrote to the CCP appraising Li's proposals.[51] There was no suggestion that Li Lisan was deviating from either ECCI general policy or practical strategy and the letter was taken as an endorsement of the Li Lisan Line. With the apparent support of the ECCI, Li now called a National Conference of the CCP and its front organisations in Shanghai on 18 July and informed them that the immediate task was armed uprisings to seize political power.

The initial focus was the Wuhan complex. As the Red Armies converged on Wuhan it was expected that there would be urban uprisings in the central Yangtze area which would spark a nationwide series of revolutionary strikes which would turn into a civil war and link the Chinese and world revolutions. Accordingly, after victory at Wuhan, uprisings would take place in Beijing, Canton, Hong Kong, Nanching, Shanghai, and numerous other cities.[52]

International Press Correspondence reported "that in all the big towns, such as Shanghai, Hankou and Hong Kong, workers' defence corps were being founded in preparation for an armed revolt." "The preparation of the 'Fourth Insurrection in Shanghai' has become the general slogan of the workers of the town."[53] This nonsense was used to deceive workers all round the world as to the success of Stalin's Third Period line. Li Lisan knew there were only 200 Party members and 150 members of the Red Trade Union in the Wuhan area on which to base any military organisation of armed workers in the three cities. The baselessness of the Li Lisan strategy was emphasised when the call: "The time for insurrection has come! Organise yourselves!" was issued; in all of Shanghai, for example, only 125 persons came forward to enlist in the Red Guard.[54]

The 5th Red Army Corps was given major military responsibility for carrying out the attack on Wuhan. This was a small but experienced army of about 10,000 men of whom possibly 7,000 were armed. It left its bases in the Hunan-Jiangxi-Hupeh border region and seized the small town of Yochow on

5 July, after which it marched to take Changsha (capital of Hunan) prior to moving on Wuhan.[55]

On 28 July 1930, Changsha was captured. The gains made were magnified totally out of proportion to justify the strategy. The *International Press Correspondence* boasted:

> "Changsha, the capital of the province of Hunan, one of the most important provinces in the heart of China, was captured on the 28th of July by the victorious Fifth Red Army of the Chinese Soviet territories. Supported by insurgent workers and peasants in town and country and by the mutiny of some of the government soldiers, ... the red workers' and peasants' army was able, after heroic fighting, to achieve a tremendous victory ... In a surprisingly short time the whole of Changsha was covered with a sea of red flags ... The Soviet Power, the power of the workers, peasants and soldiers was proclaimed ... The capture of the three sister towns (Hankou, Wuchang and Hanyang), the largest industrial towns of Central China, is the aim of the Red Army . . . All around Wuhan there already exist Soviet districts. The Red Army is endeavouring, with the aid of the insurgent peasants, to extend its field of operations more and more to the centre and to encircle Wuhan ..."[56]

Initial reports completely divorced from reality boasted of the largest mass meeting ever held in Changsha with 100,000 of its half million inhabitants attending. It was later admitted by Li Lisan that only about 3,000 had attended; the masses had not rallied to support the Red Army or CCP. Similarly, the claim that within three days 50,000 workers were organised into trade unions was fiction. The CC of the CCP on 30 September 1930, would admit: "there was insufficient connection between the attack of the Red Army and the mass struggle in Changsha." This was especially damaging because the reception given to the Red Army and CCP was fundamental to the success of the Li Lisan Line. Without active popular support, the campaigns could never be more than military adventures. The passivity of the urban population had again demonstrated unambiguously that 'the line' would not succeed, but Li Lisan blindly stuck to his predictions that, given a proper chance, his adventures would rally the masses to the revolution.[57]

The 5th Red Army (now joined by Mao's 4th Army to form the 1st Front Army) withdrew from Changsha on 3 August to avoid being surrounded by KMT forces which, on entering the city, killed some 5,000 of the local inhabitants for being too friendly with the Reds. Moscow strongly condemned the withdrawal but not the attack and ordered Li Lisan to instruct the Red Army to attack Changsha again, but it was unable to retake the city and that was the end of the adventure. At no time did Red Army forces come close enough to pose a threat to Wuhan. The Changsha episode bared the fatal weakness of the whole project: the military forces had no connection with the workers in the cities. The attack on Changsha was such a disaster it was the end of Li Lisan as leader of the CCP, the only question was how and when to deal the *coup de grace*.[58]

The ECCI had Ch'u Ch'iu-pai and Zhou Enlai investigate the reasons for the defeat. But Ch'u and Zhou found that Li Lisan had made only tactical mistakes in the application of Comintern policies in the attack on Changsha. They did not ask the CC to remove him, but merely to criticise him for having "overestimated the tempo" of the revolution. They stated his general line was "in complete harmony with the Comintern"[59]

Such a conclusion was unacceptable because it linked Stalin too directly to failure. Ch'u Ch'iu-pai and Zhou Enlai were side-lined, and in the spring of 1930 Pavel Mif was delegated to be ECCI representative to the CCP.[60]

Pavel Mif prepared to remove Li Lisan and enthrone Wang Ming and the 'returned students' group. This group, the 28 Bolsheviks, would be significantly different from all previous appointments; they had no independent base within the CCP and relied totally on Mif for their positions, they were completely Moscow's creatures. Steeped in Stalinist methods and ideology, they had proved themselves loyal to the Stalinist bureaucracy by being prepared to spill the blood of fellow Chinese students for personal advancement. Wang Ming's opposition to Li Lisan had little to do with politics. Prior to arriving in China, Wang Ming's publications showed no significant differences from Li Lisan and, after assuming leadership, the line proposed by this group differed in few, if any, significant ways from that of Li Lisan.[61]

In October 1930, the ECCI made a devastating attack on Li Lisan raising the stakes by labelling him "anti-Comintern" and a "semi-Trotskyite". The CCP Politburo declared its solidarity with the Comintern on 25 November and Li Lisan resigned in disgrace. Mif arrived in China in mid-December and proposed that the CC be convened as soon as possible so the leadership of the CCP could be re-organised.

The Plenum was held in Shanghai on 7 January 1931 and was dominated by Mif and Wang Ming who harshly condemned Li Lisan for betraying the correct instructions of the Comintern and bringing havoc to the party.[62] Wang was elected to the Politburo and two of the 28 Bolsheviks were elected as alternates to the CC. The nominal head of the Party continued to be the innocuous but esteemed Hsiang Chung-fa (until he was captured and executed in Shanghai in June), Zhou Enlai recanted his views, degraded himself in a way that was now a feature of Stalinist Party methods but, due to his organisational skills, vast experience and 'knowing everyone', managed to retain a top position. Mao was seen by Moscow as a rising star and the Far Eastern Bureau of the ECCI wrote to the Politburo of the CCP complaining that Mao was confined to military matters and suggesting that he be given a greater political role.[63]

Li was summoned to Moscow (where he remained in exile for some 15 years) leaving the field open for Wang Ming.[64]

6.6 Red Unions

In 1926 almost two-thirds of CCP members had been proletarian with only 5% peasants and 2% soldiers, but by the early months of 1930 the proletarian element had dropped to less than about 5%. After the Communists in Shanghai had handed power to Chiang Kai-shek, the Party suffered continual repression. Party membership in Shanghai had been around 8,000 in April 1927, no more than 2,000 in 1930, about 500 in 1932 and a mere handful in 1934. The errors of adventurism in a time when reaction was triumphant meant members deserted just to stay alive.

By 1930 the pressure on Li Lisan to correct this deficiency was compelling both because of his personal background of union work and because the CI was warning of the dangers of a "peasant mentality" and urging the Party to strengthen its work in the cities.[65] The organised labour movement was a shadow of its former self and the overwhelming majority of China's industrial workers had no organisation of any kind. In the areas controlled by the Kuomintang "yellow" unions were grudgingly permitted. The Wang Jingwei group was in the leadership of most of these and was moderately successful in channelling and containing the democratic demands of a significant stratum of the petty-bourgeoisie and workers.

Li Lisan was assuming a Herculean task in seeking to rebuild a Communist base in the trade union movement. He was determined to successfully apply the Third Period policy of the CCP building its own red unions and was confident his own experience would be invaluable. However Li attempted this ultra-left policy at a time when the great mass of the workers had already turned their backs on the Party. In the end the red unions consisted of CCP members and a few close collaborators. In conditions of white terror, frightened workers turned away. The yellow unions preached class collaboration, compromise and submission but by disdaining to enter them and conduct a struggle from within, the CCP left the field clear to the Wang Jingwei group.

In 1928 a brief economic revival helped restore confidence and workers fought a number of battles for better wages and shorter hours. Strikers were arrested, beaten up and shot as a matter of course. They would have responded readily and positively to agitation for elementary democratic rights – freedom of assembly, of organisation, of speech – slogans flowing from their immediate needs and reinforced by every economic conflict. The slogan for a National Assembly, elected by universal suffrage, was a focus for such a programme and offered common ground to every section of the population oppressed and terrorised by the KMT military dictatorship.[66]

But the CCP failed to gain any ground either among the thousands organised in unions or among the millions of the unorganised. The Communists remained impotent because the Third Period method was "to transplant, in a wholesale fashion, our Party's entire programme and basic slogans" into each and every leaflet effectively turning the small groups around the red unions into a second party. Abstract calls for "a general strike," "support for the Red Army" and "Soviet power" fell on deaf ears.[67] On 8 November 1928, the CC received a report which stated: "The party does not have a single healthy party nucleus among the industrial workers."[68]

So antagonistic were the workers to the CCP that Communist cadres often concealed news of an impending strike from the Party! "The work and influence of the red unions shrank to almost nothing and the masses were left under yellow union influence."[69]

In the Stalinist Communist International it was quite impossible to accept that the Third Period line had been a disaster. For self-protection, Communist Party leaders made extravagant and preposterous claims in public as to their successes. It was standard practice to blame scapegoats for the failures; the ECCI blamed the Central Committees, the Central Committees blamed the Provincial Committees, the Provincial Committees would blame the local organisations and the local organisations would blame ….. and so on. As each new leadership was appointed it revealed the false claims of its predecessors. This went on year after year, the leaders continuously complaining that their followers were failing to carry out the 'Party line'. It was never suggested that the 'Party line' was itself responsible for the stubborn unwillingness of the workers to follow the Party.

In February 1929, a letter from the Comintern stated "in most cities, even in great working-class centres like Wuhan, Tientsin, and Canton, no work has been done at all. . . . In the big and important enterprises there are no nuclei whatever." The letter went on to say there were only 4,000 workers in the whole Party, 1,300 of them in Shanghai and the rest scattered elsewhere. In November 1929, the 5th National Labour Conference was held. It claimed to represent a mere 30,000 workers, about one hundredth of the number represented at the 4th Labour Conference in Hankou two years earlier. In September 1930, Zhou Enlai told the CC that the Party could claim only 2,000 factory workers.

The workers had turned their backs on the CCP which never re-established a foothold of any consequence in any of the great urban centres until after the end of the civil war. While the workers departed from the political arena, peasant revolt, which had burned brightly during 1925-27, continued to flare episodically. Putschist methods found more response in the countryside in areas where peasants were taking up arms or where mutinous soldiers were breaking from the armies of the KMT. The remnants of the Communist Party re-emerged from the 1927 debacle at the head of a scattered, diverse insurgent peasant movement largely confined to the least advanced areas of Central China. In just such an area it would establish the so-called Chinese Soviet Republic.

6.7 Wang Ming and the 28 Bolsheviks

The policies of both Li Lisan and Wang Ming were variations of the same ultra-left Third Period strategy. Li Lisan was an experienced militant while Wang Ming was a self-serving bureaucrat; Li Lisan had the courage to actively participate in carrying out his policies, whereas Wang Ming did it by telephone, telegram or radio. Despite all the name-calling and heat generated, the political policies of the two men were no different in matters of principle or ideology; the differences were who would carry the can for past mistakes and who was the more subservient to Moscow. In the eyes of the ECCI, a major crime of Li Lisan had been his "dangerous spirit" – he had dared to suggest that the Chinese were better placed to understand the local situation in China than those in Moscow.[70]

The appointment of Wang Ming and his adjutant Po Ku (Qin Bangxian) was part of the worldwide trend within the CI to have lap dogs leading the national CPs because, as their authority came from their Moscow links, they were quite prepared to act as tools of Soviet diplomacy. This 'Bolshevisation' was a classic Stalinist intervention intended to transform the Party and would have a lasting impact on its politics and internal regime. With Wang

Ming's accession, the CCP was no jot different in principle from the Stalinist Communist Parties of Italy, France, or Spain.

Wang Ming and the 28 Bolsheviks were not to supplement the existing leadership but to replace it. Wang was particularly grovelling; Li Lisan had spoken of China as the weakest link in world imperialism stating that a revolution in China would spark a world-wide class war. Wang's criticism was that such an analysis made China the "centre of the world, denying the Soviet Union as that centre" and thus was in opposition to Stalin and the theory of "Socialism First in One Country".[71] Could there be a clearer statement of abject submission to Moscow?

Either directly or through Po Ku (acting General Secretary between 1932 and January 1935), Wang Ming held power within the CCP for four years and, in accord with the analysis of the CI and with its approval, would take the CCP leadership from the cities to the relative safety of rural areas controlled by the Red Army.

Wang possessed all the necessary qualities for a Stalinist policeman, being personally ambitious, strong-willed and intelligent, but also narrow-minded and conformist and with a talent for manoeuvring. His ideological rigidity expressed itself as an absolute intolerance of the slightest stirring of intellectual curiosity or innovation, enforced by a regime of ruthless purges and absolute regimentation.[72]

In January 1931, the CC approved Wang Ming's document *The Struggle for the CCP's Further Bolshevisation*, also known as the *Two Lines*. This document, which extolled the Comintern's direct intervention in CCP affairs, was a joint enterprise with Mif and had as a central feature, the replacement of experienced cadres with those loyal to Wang Ming (hence, so much opposition within the Party).[73] Pavel Mif and Wang Ming completely dominated the January plenum so it is interesting that Mao was elected a candidate member of the Politburo, and Zhu De as candidate member of the CC, at that meeting. Mao and Zhu obtained these positions largely because of Stalin's support. Both had been extensively praised in the Russian press as "heroes" and the Far Eastern Bureau of the ECCI in Shanghai had recommended Mao for membership of the new CC and Chair of the Revolutionary Military Committee.[74]

After the CC meeting, a group drawn from the remnants of the trade union leaderships formed to oppose Wang Ming, calling his policies an extension of the Li Lisan Line. For this action they were expelled from the Party. On 17 January, the leaders of this group met in the International Settlement in Shanghai where it was raided by British police and over 20 executed. After these deaths the CCP "could be said to have lost its last concrete link of any consequence with the urban proletariat."[75] Rumours persist that Wang Ming informed on the dissident trade unionists to remove a potentially embarrassing opposition, rumours that were strengthened when Wang Ming called for the death penalty for Chen Duxiu after his arrest by the KMT.[76] At that time all manner of vile slanders and provocations against Trotskyists were being put about by the CCP press to rob them of support, create confusion, and provide a cover should a Russian agent kill Chen or Peng.[77]

Within the Party the 28 Bolsheviks implemented what they had learned in Moscow. To ideologically remould the membership and eliminate dissent they began a Rectification Campaign of criticism and self-criticism which bore a striking similarity to the purge meetings at Sun Yat-sen University. This was accompanied by expulsions of dissident Party members. However, the effectiveness of these measures was greatly hampered by the hostility to the new leaders generated by their preoccupation with hierarchy and rank, bossing subordinates around, making others do their chores and refusing to take responsibility for the consequences of their own directives.[78]

In the Party there was considerable bitterness over the manner of the removal of Chen Duxiu, Li Lisan, and the trade union group, and it is reported that opposition to Wang Ming was so strong that as many as a quarter of the members were expelled on the pretext that those who opposed the Comintern's representative opposed the Party, and those who opposed the Party should be expelled.[79] These expulsions were at the heart of Wang Ming's 'Bolshevisation', after which the Party was as good an example of monolithic centralism as any.[80]

6.8 Peasant Soviets

The failures of the CCP in the urban areas and the relative successes of the Red Army (the 28 July attack on Changsha was highly influential), had their effect on the ECCI. The *Resolution on the Chinese Question* by the Political Secretariat of the ECCI (June 1930) again recommended the CCP to concentrate its efforts on the Red Army and Soviet government but now placed this as a "top priority".[81] Any idea of immediate insurrection in the towns (as envisaged by Li Lisan) was abandoned. Trotsky's statement to the 8th Plenum of the ECCI that the Chinese revolution would go forward in form of Soviets or not at all was being proved correct but as the antithesis of what he had intended.[82]

By the early 1930s, most of the cadres of the CCP were corralled in these Soviets which had a high degree of autonomy due to their isolated locations and the lack of an effective central leadership after the dismissal of Li Lisan. There were three Soviet areas in the Wuhan area of central China; the E-Yu-Wan Soviet to the north, the Xiang-Exi Soviet to the west and the largest and most important, the Jiangxi central Soviet, to the south of Wuhan. These soviets existed where the borders of two or more provinces came together, where administrative responsibility was unclear, where the KMT presence was weak or non-existent, in hilly or mountainous areas which were economically backward, considered not important and thus left alone.[83]

An ECCI letter of 16 November 1930 confirmed earlier instructions to concentrate the best forces of the Party into building the Red Army and establishing a Soviet government which, given the defeats in the cities, meant a peasant Soviet. The most important task for the CCP was to muster support for the Red Armies, in particular to recruit fresh troops. When Wang Ming and his allies followed these ECCI instructions they adopted a policy even more destructive than the red unions. Instead of seeking to build Party cells in the factories they transferred working class militants to the Soviet Areas in an attempt to proletarianise the Red Army. Industrial activities were used not to build the labour movement but to act as recruiting drives for the Soviet districts.[84]

The 28 Bolsheviks refused to shoulder any responsibility for the policies they proposed, and passed the buck by accusing Party members of abandoning, especially in the heavy industries, attempts to organise the red unions. In February 1931, the CCP admitted that "now there are no real red unions ... They have been wiped out. All work has been abandoned."[85] 1931 was the year of the Japanese invasion and there was a wave of protest strikes in factories with close ties with Japan, but the Party had to admit: "We have not succeeded in organizing a single anti-imperialist strike."

For a short period (1932-33) after the Japanese invasion there was increased militancy amongst workers and a small but significant boost to Party membership. However, Wang Ming and his allies threw this opportunity away when they followed ECCI instructions and continued to call on working class militants to leave industry and move to the Soviet Areas.

The Politburo, CC, and Secretariat remained in Shanghai as long as possible but were forced to transfer to the central Soviet, a move that was complete by the spring of 1933. Many of the 28 Bolsheviks and all of the CC were elected to the Central Executive Committee of the new Jiangxi Soviet government.

In 1934 the Young Communist League noted:

> "Our comrades are unaware of impending struggles in the factories. ... As a result of this isolation we not only cannot lead the mass struggles but we cannot even grasp them by the tail!"[86]

Six years of red unions and Red Army recruitment had been six years of urban impotence. This policy so weakened the CCP in the cities that when the KMT made a series of arrests in March 1934 and again the following year, CCP activity in major cities such as Shanghai virtually ended.[87]

6.9 Summary

Peasant rebellion and partisan warfare has a long tradition in China and these traditions were alive in south and central China in the aborted revolution of 1925-7. The millions who stood up and made an effort to take the land for themselves were in direct line with those who had founded the Han and Ming dynasties and marched in the footsteps of the Long-Haired Taipings.

Yet the peasants who rose in 1926-7 could have succeeded where all their ancestors had failed. Out of a society dissolving under imperialist penetration, the elements of a new solution were taking form. The peasants, backward, scattered and socially-stratified could supply the motor force of change but play no independent role. The Chinese bourgeoisie was bound into the system by rent and usury. The new class of urban workers seeking to change society in its own interests could, by linking its fortunes to those of the agrarian workers and poor peasants, break through the vicious historical circle by leading the struggle for seizure of the land and its re-distribution to the peasants by the peasants.

Shortly after its founding, the CCP was confronted by great revolutionary questions. The immaturity of the leadership, the lack of grounding in Marxist theory or practice, combined with the speed of development of events, meant there was little possibility of it developing its own independent policy. The leadership of the CCP sincerely believed their only hope of avoiding very grave errors was the guidance of the Communist International. They subordinated themselves to the policies of the ECCI and in so doing surrendered the independence of the Party to the bourgeoisie.[88]

As a result of ECCI advice and instructions, the second Chinese Revolution (1925-27) was crushed in three distinct stages: Shanghai, Wuhan, and Canton. The completely opportunist line of the Comintern which was accepted by the majority of the CC of the CCP was expressed in five issues:

- *The question of the Party.* An absolutely independent party of the proletariat is a first and decisive condition for communist politics. The CCP entered a bourgeois party and became subservient to it depriving the working class of its own party at the most critical period of the class struggle. Stalin and the ECCI considered the KMT to be a multi-class party, but no matter what the proportion of workers and poor peasants within the KMT, it was a party of the bourgeoisie because of its leadership and its actions.
- *The question of imperialism.* It was quite correct for the CI to state that the agrarian feudal remnants in China were inextricably linked with imperialism, but the CI refused to accept that the fundamental interests of feudal elements, compradors, landlords, bankers, factory owners and business men were all linked together in a network based on usury and rent.
- Of course the Chinese bourgeoisie conflicted with the most reactionary feudal militarists and occasionally with imperialism but such conflicts always took second place at the decisive moment to its irreconcilable antagonism towards the workers and poor peasants. The only hope for the success of the anti-imperialist revolution was for the proletariat supported by the poor and middle peasants to crush the bourgeoisie's attempts to compromise with imperialism.
- *The question of the KMT.* The Comintern leadership mistook the petty-bourgeois intellectuals at the top of the KMT for allies in the class struggle. However, these people were more closely linked to the bourgeoisie than the rural and urban poor, selling them out at the decisive moment to the big bourgeoisie. It was not a question of alliance with Wang Jingwei against Chiang Kai-shek, but of an alliance of the toiling masses against Wang Jingwei and Chiang Kai-shek.
- *The question of Soviets.* Soviets can and must be created from the very first stage of a broad revolutionary upsurge. Soviets can arise from strike committees or peasant associations and then grow and extend their functions and increase their authority in the eyes of the masses. Finally, they become the organisations of a revolutionary

uprising and, if victorious, they become the organs of revolutionary power.

- When the revolution was on the rise, the Stalinists denied any place for Soviets in the democratic struggle and the CCP actively opposed their formation. Then, with the revolution in retreat, in a sudden and complete about-face, the CCP declared Soviets to be the immediate task of the Chinese Revolution and launched them, bureaucratically deformed and short-lived.
- The Stalinists were completely out of phase with reality. An international smokescreen of lies and deception was used to conceal the fact that Stalin's policies, especially regarding Soviets, had resulted in defeat for the Chinese Revolution.
- *What strategy to adopt in a counter-revolutionary situation?* Trotsky proposed a defensive policy of democratic demands to preserve the revolutionary forces, unite and re-energise the masses. These would have been along the lines of demands for an eight hour day, freedom of speech and assembly, the right to strike, capped by the demand for a National Constituent Assembly elected by universal suffrage. Instead Stalin proposed as an "immediate practical task the preparation for and carrying through of armed insurrection as the sole path to the completion of the bourgeois-democratic revolution and to the overthrow … of the Kuomintang."[89] Millions of peasants would die as a result of this directive (about a million in one encirclement campaign alone) not to mention the many millions of peasants left to the tender mercies of vengeful landlords.

The defeat of the revolution placed Chiang Kai-shek in power, and ushered in a period of counter-revolutionary terror, economic disintegration, impotence in the face of imperialism, and military invasion by the Imperial Japanese Army. In these circumstances the bourgeoisie were unable to develop democratic institutions, and could hold onto power only through brutal military dictatorship. Chiang Kai-shek adopted a policy of 'non-resistance' to the Japanese invasion but there was no policy of 'non-resistance' towards the Chinese masses; for them it would mean ruthless suppression of any attempt to organise resistance to the invasion, it meant extermination of whole sections of rebellious peasantry in central China, and it meant handing over large sections of the country to the Japanese imperialists. These were fruits of the defeat of the revolution of 1925-27.

Chapter 7

From the Jiangxi "Soviet" to Yenan

7.1 Introduction

This chapter describes the so-called peasant Soviets created by the CCP as it retreated from the cities. The Stalinist nature of the CCP dominated the character of these Soviets from their start. The political and organisational structures supposedly for the self-rule of the peasants by the peasants were, in fact, forced on the local populations by a Communist Party which was, in effect, an invading and occupying force, although a benign one. These so-called Soviets were set up in the most backward and isolated areas and had little or no basis in the experiences of the peasants involved.[1]

At all times the needs of the Red Army and the CCP overrode the wishes of the indigenous peasants and ultimately the Red Army would march out leaving them to the tender mercies of Chiang Kai-shek. Nevertheless, the Soviets did become popular with the middle and poor peasants and even amongst many rich peasants.

The KMT bandit extermination campaigns are presented in so far as they reflected the balance of power in China between Chiang Kai-shek and the CCP, forced the Communists to quit their major base in Jiangxi, and commence the Long March. The destruction of the Jiangxi 'Soviet Republic' and the flight of the Communists was both a military and political defeat for the CCP. It was the end of the first attempt to establish a revolutionary power based exclusively upon peasant rebellion. However, the idea that Soviet power could be transported in the baggage train of the Red Army from Jiangxi to Yenan was totally bureaucratic and one further step in dissolving the socialist revolution into peasant revolt.

The CCP, in true Stalinist manner, has re-written its history to iron out the wrinkles, give it linearity and continuity, and place an omniscient Mao in the lead role. As the bureaucracy became more established as an independent factor and gathered to itself more power over the organisation, it increasingly required its own 'pope' to resolve disputes that arose from the inevitable conflict of interest between individuals and groups within the bureaucracy. The very nature of bureaucracy means it cannot submit such disputes to the democratic process of discussion and action by the masses without endangering its own existence.

The official history presents Mao taking the helm at the Tsunyi conference (15-17 January 1935, soon after the start of the Long March) at which the brilliance of his military strategy won the day, and after which he was always right and the undisputed leader of the CCP, ousting the 28 Bolsheviks who had led the Party almost to extinction. This re-writing began in 1945 when Mao Zedong presented the *Resolution on Some Questions in the History of Our Party* to the CC. This document re-wrote Party history to present the defeats of the CCP as due to the opportunism of Chen Duxiu, and the left adventurism of Ch'u Ch'iu-pai, Li Lisan, and Wang Ming.[2] Nowhere does Mao rebuke the architect of CCP policies, Joseph Stalin, because Mao accepted Socialism in One Country, the theory of stages, the bloc of four classes, and the bureaucratic structure that allowed Stalin to force his strategies onto the CCP.

At the end of the Long March, the Communists would arrive in Shensi province, an area which many considered to be outside China proper. The final stages of the Long March coincided with the 7th World Congress of the CI and the launch of the Popular Front strategy. This meant an about turn for the CCP, leaving ultra-leftism behind and returning to class collaborationist policies. The CCP's base area would be declared a special administrative region of the KMT and not a Soviet, and its social policies would be limited accordingly.

7.2 Soviets and Land Reform

The move to peasant Soviets was a public admission that by the end of 1930 the CCP's adventurist course had converted it into an overwhelmingly peasant party with few roots in, and little or no influence among, the urban workers. These Soviets could exist only in areas where the central state authority was virtually non-existent, far removed from any military centre, isolated with few roads, no railways, and of little interest to the National government.

These Soviets were formed, at least initially, by the remnants of Communist military units, local CCP members, impoverished peasants who had fled their debts, mutinous NRA units and peasant organisers known to the secret police and on their death list. They were islands in the sea of Nationalist China and, of necessity, had to be as self-sufficient as possible. However, given the nature of China in the late 1920s and 1930s they could be large. Braun claims that the Jiangxi Soviet was a contiguous area which varied between 40,000 and 60,000 square km (15,000 to 20,000 square miles) with a population of up to four million peasants, significantly greater than that of Albania (in total throughout China up to 10 million people were in Soviets).[3]

The Communist International had published considerable material on the "invincible" Soviet revolution that was supposed to have been advancing across the whole of China as a result of Stalin's policies.[4] It continued to present the events in China in this light. Communists outside the highest levels of the Comintern were denied accurate information on what was actually happening in China. The Communist International needed victories to continue to boost Stalin, so the Soviets in China – where it was almost impossible to confirm or contradict reports – were hailed as a great success. This means that the public record was overly positive about the achievements of, for example, the Jiangxi Soviet. The myth of glorious Soviets glamourised the reality and prettified those associated with them – particularly Mao Zedong.

The first Chinese Revolution of 1925-7 had been a genuine proletarian revolution but the isolated and backward areas in which Soviets would be formed were the traditional hunting grounds of bandits. In Jiangxi, attempts were made to incorporate many thousands of armed bandits into the revolutionary ranks. However, bandit gangs were not Robin Hood-like figures standing in opposition to the local power structure; more often the gangs were tied to the local landlords and judiciary who accepted bribes to turn a blind eye and even fenced the stolen goods.[5] Few of the gangs made the transition from bandits to Communists.

Thus, when Mao arrived in Jiangxi in 1929 and began concentrating local power into his own hands, he had to fight on three fronts: physically battling reactionary forces and local bandits, fending off the centralising efforts of national Party leaders in Shanghai, and overcoming the resistance of local CP leaders to his taking over their base area.[6] By the time of the founding of the Jiangxi Soviet, Zhu De and Mao Zedong were the leaders of probably the most powerful armed force in the Chinese Communist movement (Zhu was commander and Mao was political commissar), and articles praising them and their actions were appearing in the journals of the Communist International.[7]

The decision to form Soviets was taken while the Party was passing through its Third Period phase and that determined initial policies implemented within the Soviets. For example, enforced land confiscation and its re-distribution which greatly appealed to the poorest peasants.[8] Generally, the judicial and social measures taken were hugely progressive but it must be remembered that the most basic requirement for a Soviet was missing from their very inception; there was no real democracy. The Soviets were the artificial, bureaucratic creations of the CCP, and in all important matters decisions were determined in advance by the Party. With the Soviet Union as their example, this was seen as a quite natural and correct way of proceeding.

Everybody over the age of 16 was supposed to participate but there was neither experience nor understanding of the processes of democratic decision-making and administration was constantly hampered by the almost universal illiteracy of all but the rich peasants and landlords. The Soviet areas were not fertile and the peasants had a hard time feeding themselves so there was considerable pressure to maximise food production to feed the occupying Red Army and the high work load on most peasants left them too tired to participate in lengthy communal meetings.[9]

Nevertheless, the Jiangxi Soviet was an important testing ground for administrative structures and methods of governance, tax collecting, child care, judiciary, etc., which would serve as the foundations for later Soviet governments.

During the 1926-27 peasant upsurge, the real authority in much of the countryside resided with the peasant associations which maintained peace and order, settling disputes between peasants. In Hunan Province "people's justice" made its appearance when the peasant associations adopted a series of measures to enforce land redistribution, reduce interest rates, abolish exorbitant levies, advance women's rights, prohibit gambling and opium-smoking and eradicate corrupt officials and landlords.[10]

In the initial stages of the Soviets, the remnants of these peasant associations, many containing CCP cadres, provided important experience, and a number of radical measures were taken that gradually won for the Soviets the support of the great majority of the peasants. Land deeds were destroyed, taxes on poor peasants abolished, official corruption, foot-binding, child slavery and infanticide were made illegal. Much good work was done in bringing the peasant masses into action and the measures taken formed a natural basis for the legal codes introduced by the CCP. It was made plain that people's justice was to be administered from a class viewpoint. Account had to be taken of the class of the offenders and their accomplices; counter-revolutionary elements with capitalist backgrounds, landlords and rich peasants were to be punished severely (including death), while all those from the ranks of workers, peasants and the toiling masses were to be treated relatively leniently.[11]

For fifteen hundred years, ever since the middle of the Tang Dynasty, peasant uprisings had been characterised by the determination of the insurgents to fight the landlords for the land.[12] Thus when, for example, in November 1927 the first Soviet was formed (the Hailufeng Soviet) under pressure from the peasant associations, particularly the poor and landless peasants, it immediately committed itself to the policy of land seizure. As many as 1,800 landlords were executed within a few months and the seized land distributed at village meetings.

The earliest land law promulgated by the Jiangxi soviet government was the Land Law of December 1928, prior to Mao's arrival. This called for the seizure of all land and stated "all men and women, old and young, shall be entitled to equal redistribution" provided they were able-bodied and could work the land. An important element was a move towards communalisation, land ownership was turned over to the local Soviet government.[13] Later Mao would call these actions "left extremism."[14]

However, the seizure and redistribution of the land was not welcomed by all peasants. Not only landlords and rich peasants lost land, some of the better-off middle peasants had also suffered and were worse off. After his arrival, Mao had the Land Law modified to give greater protection to rich and middle peasants, citing the Political Resolution adopted at the 6th Congress of the Party of not forcing the struggle against the rich peasants because to do so "would confuse the fundamental contradiction between the peasant and landlord class."[15]

This fitted well with the need to feed the Soviet population, particularly the Red Army troops. Re-division of the land for the benefit of the poor peasants was effectively abandoned in order not to unsettle crop production, and the land of rich peasants was often left intact. By the end of 1931, confiscation of land without compensation was limited to public land, and the lands of the gentry, militarists and big private landowners. The lands seized were to be distributed equally irrespective of sex, but now the tenant, not the Soviet, was confirmed as owner of the land previously rented. Such a policy meant there was little land available to allocate to the semi-proletarian agricultural labourers and village craftsmen.[16]

Initially, the wives and children of the landlords were allocated land as individuals, but as the family remained the unit of production and because the richer peasants tended to have larger families, they benefited relative to the poor peasants. It was also true that the landlord's wives shared the land they were allocated with their husbands so this aspect of re-allocation was soon curtailed and landlords' wives, sons, daughters and daughters-in-law were formally denied any share of the seized lands.[17]

However, in many places the rich peasants adopted a radical face, speaking loudly about non-payment of rent and taxes, and in this way – with their experience of public speaking – became the village spokespersons. With their better education and ability to write they often became the office personnel in the very organs created to execute the land reforms and were often able to direct their efforts in ways that preserved much of their former positions, frequently acquiring the best land for themselves and retaining their farming implements and draft animals. This process was greatly helped by the composition of the Party in Jiangxi in early 1931, "from first to last intellectuals, and of these the children of rich peasants and landlords constitute an important component."[18]

Isolated in purely rural and economically backward pockets, the Communists gradually became integrated into the rural hierarchy in the districts under Red Army control. Despite all its pious resolutions and exhortations to the contrary, the CCP had to lean upon the merchants whose contact with the external market was indispensable to the maintenance of even a minimal existence in the Soviet areas. In this way, the CCP leaders did largely succeed in keeping the base area economies functioning.[19]

Propaganda was made against the rich peasants but day-to-day the CCP leadership surrendered to their economic interests because they were the major producers of surplus food. Some rich peasants did lose land but retained as much land as they and their family could productively farm, and because they were allowed to keep their implements they were allocated relatively more land per person than the poor or middle peasants.

From 1931 the pattern of land reform, supported by rent and interest rate reductions and debt cancellation, was settled and remained in place in Communist-controlled areas until after 1945. Notwithstanding the *Land Law of the Soviet Republic* of November 1931 these reforms tended in practice to favour the middle peasants. These held some land to begin with, were often allocated additional land and, very importantly, were freed from debt.[20] It was the agricultural labourers who benefited least.[21] Despite its limitations, the policy was hugely popular with the vast mass of peasants.

This approach was due to the economic realities of rural life. The food surplus needed to feed the Red Army could not be disrupted so the CCP had to tread carefully around the most productive peasants (the rich and middle peasants). Collaboration with the merchants had to be maintained because anything manufactured had to be imported, from salt to kerosene, and only the merchants supplied these. The goal of the CCP was a democratic dictatorship (not a proletarian revolution) and for this to be achieved the rich peasants and the merchants had to be kept on-side. Already in western Fukian by 1930, the CCP had compromised with local merchants to resolve difficulties with the import and export of supplies. The merchants were exempted from taxation while the peasants paid a 15% land tax. Price rises by the merchant were ignored and sometimes the economic struggles of shop employees and workers were restrained.

Even after the experience of Wuhan, the theory of the democratic dictatorship which had been so thoroughly tested in 1925-1927 remained the CCP's major ideological weapon. In 1925-7 this perspective had led them to dependence on the bourgeoisie with disastrous results. Now it provided justification for leading a purely peasant movement, relying, as before, on class interests which were separate from those of the proletariat.

To the peasantry with its internal divisions and conflicting interests, the Communist Party claimed that it brought proletarian leadership. It based its claims on the abstract proposition that because the Communist Party was, by definition, the 'Party of the proletariat' its presence guaranteed working-class hegemony in the peasant revolt. It strengthened this illusion by importing a trickle of workers from the cities and giving them positions in the Red Army and governmental committees that had been established. The net effect of its policies was to deprive the workers in the cities of their most advanced representatives. Removed from their factories, working within a Stalinised Party and in an overwhelmingly peasant milieu, these workers soon succumbed to petty-bourgeois ways of thinking and working. If KMT terror did not cut militants off from the labour movement, the CCP did.

7.3 Women's Liberation and the Jiangxi Soviet

In 1928, the 6th CCP Congress resolution on the Peasant Movement accepted that failure to win over the women in the villages would result in the failure of the agrarian revolution. Communist progress was everywhere affected by its attitude to women, by their social status, by their relationship to men and by their symbol as an object of property.

The Jiangxi Soviet set up a Women's Department with specific responsibility to care for the interests of women. This progressive step was reflected in the many reforms undertaken in the Jiangxi Soviet to improve the position of women. Often these measures were the results of personal efforts by Mao Zedong, "fervent fighter for the liberty of love since the era of the May Fourth Movement."[22] The conservatism he had to struggle against within the Party can be seen in the editing of Mao's *Collected Works*. In the original version of his *Report on an Investigation into the Peasant Movement in Hunan*, Mao made the point: "From the sexual point of view, the poor peasants dispose of a fair amount of liberty. In the villages, triangular and multi-lateral relationships are almost universal among poor peasants." This was cut out of the official version.[23]

However, the life of peasant women was such that any measure enacted by the CCP meant little or nothing while they were confined to the home and forbidden to speak to any male other than a relative. The CCP established Women's Associations (WA) which attempted to meet and co-ordinate women in the villages. The first and immediate concern of these associations was to put a stop to the almost universal habit of wife beating – both by husbands and by mothers-in-law – because any woman who attended an association meeting would receive a thrashing when she got home.

The organisers found a practical solution that worked wonders. A violent husband was selected; he would be stopped in public by a group of association members and asked to mend his ways. Invariably the man's reaction was arrogant disbelief that such a thing could be happening and his reaction would arouse a furious protest from the women surrounding him. Within moments he would be knocked to the ground and given his very own drubbing which did not stop until he promised to cease beating his wife. Soon a visit from a WA representative was enough to bring most erring husbands into line. However, Hinton reports that the first secretary of the WA in Long Bow village was made to resign because her husband, a CCP cadre, demanded she spend more time at home.[24]

In August 1930, the Soviet government of Jiangxi issued a decree that said simply: "Let those men who do not have wives be free to find themselves wives as rapidly as possible, and let those women who do not have husbands be free to find themselves husbands as rapidly as possible." To the delight of both sexes the CCP, at a stroke, had removed the exorbitant cost of getting married. Immediately, there was a frenzy of activity throughout the entire Soviet zone; within two months nearly all the middle, poor peasants and artisans who had not previously taken wives had done so. As for labourers, the proportion of those married leapt from about 1% to nearly 50%.

The Regulations on Marriage enacted by the Chinese Soviet Republic was a good example of the rapid transformation of a feudal-patriarchal matrimonial system based on a superstitious belief in predestination. Isaac Deutscher looked at this as an application of the Law of Combined and Uneven Development; China, possibly the most archaic of nations, avidly assimilated the latest doctrines and translated them into action before more industrially advanced countries.[25] The Regulations were preceded by a preamble which outlined what could be called the three principles of marriage: (1) In the Soviet areas, the economic independence of men and women being assured, marriage must be concluded according to the principle of free choice. (2) Attention must be paid to the protection of children. (3) The suffering of women under feudalism which included deliberately subjecting them to physical abuse such as having their feet bound, meant that they had not yet succeeded in acquiring complete economic independence. Thus, in the matter of divorce, women's interests must be protected.

Measured against traditional Chinese morality, these principles were revolutionary. But an even greater innovation is found in the Regulations concerning divorce. There are only two clauses: (1) Divorce is granted if both parties desire it, but it is equally granted when only one of the two parties insists. (This would later be curtailed so that the wives of serving soldiers could obtain a divorce only with the consent of their husbands.) and (2) All divorces must be registered with the authorities of the Soviet zone. There is absolutely no question of having to obtain previous authorisation for marriage or divorce from the local CCP or the local Soviet.

The 1931 Constitution of the Jiangxi Soviet Republic expressly stated that one purpose of the government was "to guarantee the thorough emancipation of women." During the Jiangxi period the Party formally enacted the Marriage Laws described above but Johnson claims that there was stiff opposition from many local cadres and only when the Party leaders from Shanghai arrived was there any effective attempt to implement the Law. Even then, cadre behaviour was not uniform and some abused their position: in the north zone the local Party men insisted that marriages had to have the prior approval of Party or the local Soviet, and in certain counties women were forbidden to ask for divorce.[26] Official CCP policies regarding women were undoubtedly immensely progressive but their implementation depended on the balance of forces locally and so was neither uniform nor consistent. Thus, there were ongoing simmering differences between Party needs, the conservatism of the male peasants (particularly the richer male peasants), and the drive for greater liberation by peasant women and young CCP cadres.

In practice, a peasant-based strategy made the promotion of women's rights difficult because the many male peasants who felt their patriarchal rights threatened, vigorously resisted such policies, fearing the loss of their 'property'. Their conservatism and their material interests made it very difficult for them to tolerate free-choice marriage, divorce, female equality, and women's roles outside the home. The CCP backed off from implementation of much of the Marriage Law in the face of this male hostility because it needed the support of these people since they produced most of the food for the Red Army and Party officials.[27]

The CCP land reform heroically granted women important property and economic rights for the first time. But in a peasant economy with traditions going back a thousand years and with the traditional family structure largely intact, if a parcel of land was to be redistributed and a woman was to receive a share, the deeds for her share would be ceremonially handed to the (male) head of the household, accepting that the woman's land *de facto* belonged to her husband.

Within the CCP a quota system was established in response to the instruction that, "every local party should do its best to reach the goal set up by the Central Committee which requires that women comrades in the movement should occupy one-third to two-thirds of the party positions", unfortunately even the lower target was rarely met.

Nevertheless, the continual drive to meet the manpower needs of the Red Army meant a shortage of men to work the land and women stepped into the breach. Women who did not have bound feet came out of the home, worked on the land and performed tasks that had previously been for men only. True, the women were expected to surrender these newly-gained positions when the men returned but they demonstrated abilities that culture and tradition said they could not possess.

The move to the countryside and the setting up of peasant Soviets had serious long-term adverse effects on Party ideology, policies, and practices. Despite its initial good efforts, in the end the Jiangxi period imposed a move away from commitment to gender equality. Many Party members felt that in the countryside women's participation in the revolution was marginalised and that their liberation was restricted in order not to impinge adversely on other Party policies.[28] By the time the Party left Jiangxi in 1934, in conflicts between issues concerning women's rights and the demands of male peasants, the Party was openly supporting the latter.[29]

Cheng analysed the dynamic of land reform in the Jiangxi Soviet and concluded:

> "despite the efforts ... of the CCP, the household-based economy and the remnants of patriarchal ideology combined to allow husbands and fathers to manipulate women both to improve their own situations and to subvert the Party's stated goal to transform the basis of women's class status. ... It seems clear that women cannot have an independent class status within a household-based economy under patriarchy."[30]

The CCP was, of course, a very long way from challenging patriarchy.

7.4 The Futian Incident

By the time he arrived in Jiangxi, Mao had been singled out for public praise and advancement by the ECCI and Pavel Mif. In its letter of October 1929, the ECCI called on the CCP to " ... strengthen and expand guerrilla warfare, especially .... where Mao Zedong (has) been active. We must fight firmly against the tendency in the party to overlook the revolutionary significance of the peasant struggle (particularly guerrilla warfare), emphasise the importance of military work, ... and build up the soviet base areas in the places where the peasant revolutionary struggle is active and well developed."[31]

Mao had taken care that his opposition to the Li Lisan Line was always within the limits of what was acceptable, but the "Mao machine" is reported to have eliminated a "long list" of local leaders as part of his take-over of the Jiangxi Soviet. Eventually, Mao was able to impose his side-kick and manager of his machine (Tseng Shan) as Chair, and other members of his entourage (including his two brothers Mao Zetan and Mao Zemin) as leaders of the Soviet.[32,33]

It was here that Mao demonstrated definitively that the Jiangxi Soviet was not a Soviet in any meaningful sense. He determined that it was quite acceptable to use physical violence against Soviet members when his personal interests were at stake. Mao introduced the Stalinist concept only recently adopted in the Soviet Union, that loyal Party members who honestly differed in their opinions could be 'objectively counter-revolutionary' and be imprisoned or executed.[34]

While Mao was at Changsha (July-August 1930) those previously ousted by Mao, encouraged by his absence, formed an anti-Mao group, rallied support and removed his appointees from office. There are no claims that they did this by violent means. This anti-Mao group showed there were political differences when they proposed a more radical land policy. They raised the slogans: "Oppose the practice of dividing land on the basis of the possession of tools and labour power!" "Oppose the rich peasants!", "Divide the land equally!", "Oppose the capture of the government by landlords and rich peasants!". The basis of the anti-Mao forces was for land allocation on the more egalitarian basis of the number of persons in a family.[35]

It was this that led to the infamous Futian incident. In the words of Mao, "... the fate of the revolution depended on the outcome of this struggle" (i.e. his own prestige and position).[36] On his return from Changsha (with the army) Mao set about removing his opponents. First he claimed they were following the Li Lisan Line which allowed him to appear as supporting the new Wang Ming leadership while in fact strengthening his own position. On 7 December 1930, Mao had some seventy members of the Jiangxi Soviet arrested. The Twentieth Corps of the Red Army was so incensed by this mass arrest that some four hundred men attacked Futian prison and liberated more than twenty of the accused. During this attack a number of Mao's supporters were killed.[37]

Mao now falsely accused his opponents of being members of a secret nationalist organisation, the Anti-Bolshevik League (ABL) and began purging them using the methods of the Stalinist witch hunt vigorously and extensively.

Active oppositionists were arrested and "the most merciless torture" authorised to obtain confessions and the names of others, who were tortured in their turn, and so on. "The number of killings rose steeply, as each confession produced a new clutch of victims, and each victim a new confession." The tortured confessed to all kinds of wild schemes not least of which was that they were planning an uprising against the CCP. It is claimed that in the First Front Army more than 2,000 were summarily shot.[38] Next Mao turned his attention to the Jiangxi Communist Party. The details of this witch hunt make horrific reading and are as bad as anything done in Soviet Russia – however, unlike in Russia, the torture was often carried out in public.[39] The revolt was finally quelled to Mao's satisfaction.

Depending on whose version is accepted, the total number executed in this purge – which was aimed at suppressing the egalitarians and the left in the Party – ranges up to 10,000. In principle Mao was repeating what the 28 Bolsheviks had done in Moscow, but on a larger scale, more ferociously and with fewer constraints.[40] At the Plenum of the CC in January 1931 the execution of the Futian rebels was explained as a move against Li Lisan supporters with explicit parallels being made to the anti-Li Lisan measures being taken in Shanghai.[41]

An investigation by the Central Committee (led by Zhou Enlai) which was completed by mid-1931 did not condemn the witch hunt, the methods used, nor the deaths which resulted. It did contain the mild rebuke that too many ABL suspects had been summarily executed – they should have been 'interrogated' first.[42] By such means the local leadership of all three Soviets in Jiangxi was brought under much tighter central control with those in charge owing their immediate loyalties to Mao.

7.5 The KMT Bandit Extermination Campaigns

Chiang and the KMT classified the Communists as bandits, so the campaigns to destroy them and their bases were known as bandit extermination campaigns. At the start of these campaigns multiple Soviets and their corresponding Red Armies existed, of which Jiangxi was the most significant. Five campaigns later it would be claimed that only one Soviet stronghold remained, in the wilds of Shensi in northern China.[43] This annihilation, as much as anything else, enabled Mao to climb to the top of the CCP.

In November 1930, the KMT, in response to the capture of Changsha the previous July, launched the first of five bandit extermination campaigns. At Jiangxi this was beaten back relatively easily using tactics developed by Zhu De and Mao, of retreating to lure nationalist forces deep into the Red area and striking when they were exhausted and isolated. When these very tactics would be used by others, Mao would condemn them as "flight before the enemy", emphasising their inherent weakness of surrendering the peasants to the tender mercies of NRA troops.[44]

Zhu's and Mao's tactics were greatly helped by intelligence information provided by Russian intelligence who had more than a hundred moles in the KMT, some in very senior positions, and a smaller but very effective network of agents at the top of the KMT security services recruited by Zhou Enlai.[45] The Russians had broken the cypher codes used for the transmissions from the KMT General Staff to operational units which allowed details of troop movements on the ground to be fed to Mao. All this information helped the Red Army to avoid superior Nationalist forces and, when it chose to engage, to do so with numerical superiority. It would take Chiang Kai-shek five extermination campaigns before he developed a strategy and tactics which offset these intelligence advantages.

However, the radio set in Jiangxi was not sufficiently powerful to transmit directly to Russia and messages had to be sent to Shanghai and forwarded to Moscow and vice versa. The office also acted as a centre for distribution of ECCI and CC instructions and Party information, thus giving Wang Ming a high degree of control and authority over the Red Army.

In early and late 1931, the second and third extermination campaigns were beaten back and Mao's success in leading the fight against the KMT forces gained him enormous prestige in the Red Army and in the Party. His prestige was now sufficient to make him a natural contender for the leadership and protect him from accusations of brutality against those who opposed him.[46]

In September 1931, the Japanese invaded Manchuria and established a puppet regime. The Japanese invasion of Manchuria caused Chiang Kai-shek to momentarily digress from the encirclement campaigns and this allowed the Red Army to re-form. More scared of the masses than the invaders, the KMT regime did not dare mobilise for a popular war of self-defence. Instead it took the course of 'non-resistance', conceding ground and hoping Japan would be content with Manchuria, or, at most, with Manchuria and North China.

In response, the Party decided to re-designate the Soviet areas as a state power without waiting for the capture of a major city. On 7 November 1931 (the anniversary of the Russian Revolution), the small town of Juichin – badly damaged by bombing raids – was designated the Soviet capital and hosted the First All-China Conference of Soviets to formally declare a Provisional Central Government of the Chinese Soviet Republic – officially designated "a democratic dictatorship of the proletariat and peasantry" despite there being no democracy nor any proletariat.[47]

To maintain its control, Moscow insisted that its chosen people be the leadership of the Chinese Soviet Republic so the CC of the CCP, many in their absence, were elected *en masse* onto the Central Executive Committee of the new government. This was a contradictory situation, the CC formally, had Soviet authority in its hands but now CC members sat with previously obscure Party members who held the real power, had their own local loyalties, and no interest in accepting control from arrogant, ill-informed booksellers from Shanghai. With the external pressure of the NRA forcing them together, confrontation between the different groups would be postponed until the CCP and Red Armies fled Jiangxi to escape extermination.

A Central Government gave a uniform structure to the Communist controlled areas. It approved a number of radical laws already in operation;

Land (1931), Labour (1931), Marriage Regulations (1931), and enacted new laws such as the Regulations for Punishing Counter-revolutionaries (1934). It also formally introduced a system of people's courts to administer these laws.[48]

The laws on Labour were the first to be breached in the interest of the bloc of four classes. Agricultural labourers and other rural workers working singly or in twos or threes, were scattered over the land and occupied a subsidiary position in the peasant economy. They lived by selling their labour power for wages and in that sense were proletarians. But unlike factory workers, they played no independent role in production and so tended to be part of the general petty-bourgeois mass of the peasantry. The capitalist cannot exist without the factory worker, but the peasant can get along without a hired hand. Operating on the slimmest of margins, the peasant resisted when his labourers demanded shorter hours or an increase in wages, usually by firing them. Similarly, in the shops and small enterprises, the merchants countered employees' demands by the simple threat to close down altogether. This would have meant slow suffocation of trade and the merchants knew they held the whip hand.

Thus it was, that the admirable Labour law adopted by the newly established Provisional Soviet Government was never enforced and was quietly abandoned. Its limits on working hours, its requirements for improved working conditions and wages were widely publicised by the Comintern for propaganda purposes but never enacted in the face of merchant-peasant opposition. Lo Fu (Chang Wen-t'ien, one of the 28 Bolsheviks) writing in the Party journal *Struggle* in June 1933 would explain that the workers must understand that while they were the "masters of the state" they had to consent to remain the "exploited class" and refrain from making "excessive demands" or conducting strikes whose only effect was "to wreck the worker-peasant alliance."[49] This was the real essence of the democratic dictatorship within the Soviet areas. The Party called upon the peasant poor, the rural workers, the artisans, and handicraftsmen to sacrifice their own interests in order not to alienate the rich peasants and the merchants.

Across China at this time, in response to Japanese actions there was a spontaneous boycott of Japanese goods and a great wave of student unrest in opposition to appeasement. This began in Shanghai (November-December 1931) and soon spread to all the major cities of China. Japan responded by attacking and capturing Shanghai in January 1932. Rather than retaliate, the KMT actively suppressed the boycott and protest campaigns, and subsequently crushed every manifestation of an independent anti-Japanese movement.

The huge resentment against Japanese imperialism grew as the KMT concluded a succession of deals with Japan. But this popular feeling had no organised expression not least because the CCP failed to propose an effective programme.[50] The isolation and impotence of the CCP can be seen from the near zero response it got in working class areas to its ultra-left proposals for the defeat of the Japanese invasion: the immediate setting up of Soviets, and for workers to leave the urban centres to join the Red Army. The CCP could not rally the masses against Japanese imperialism because it had no programme that voiced their aspirations, but by this time neither did it have the forces to take the slogans into the proletariat.

The mass boycott of Japanese goods temporarily made the wheels of Chinese factories turn faster which stimulated greater self-confidence amongst the workers. Strikes began to take place, but most workers had no organisation and those that did were in the yellow unions. The strikers were soon clubbed into submission.[51] It was just such circumstances where the great mass of the Chinese people were sincerely demanding opposition to the Japanese attacks that the political call for a Constituent Assembly (supported, of course, by slogans for freedom of association, freedom of speech and assembly, an end to usurious loans and land to the peasant) would have given the CCP a good chance of regaining leadership of the proletariat.

However, Moscow was seriously worried about Japan's advances and in response to the invasion of Manchuria, the ECCI called for China to launch a national revolutionary war against the Japanese imperialists. Trapped within the ultra-left policies of the Third Period, the leadership of the CCP interpreted this to mean the CCP should launch a military programme and on 9 January 1932 passed the resolution; *Winning an Initial Revolutionary Success in One or More Provinces.*[52] In no significant aspect was this different from the Li Lisan Line, except that Ganzhou in southern Jiangxi stood in for Wuhan. The results were even worse. Ganzhou was poorly defended and a numerically much stronger Red Army was soundly beaten. Mao was an adept military commander and had assessed that the attack would be a failure. His lack of enthusiasm was noted and he was severely criticised by the CC.

This attack was taken by Chiang as confirmation that the Communists were a greater menace to Chinese capitalism than the Japanese invasion. Under the slogan "First internal pacification, then external resistance" he organised the fourth extermination campaign which began in the summer of 1932 and succeeding in destroying the E-Yu-Wan Soviet and forcing the Fourth Front Army to leave and flee to safety in north Szechuan. The Soviet at Xiang-Exi was destroyed and the Third Front Army just survived, reduced to less than 3,000 soldiers it barely existed as a disciplined force until it re-united with the Sixth Army corps in October 1934.[53]

The 12th Plenum of the ECCI (September 1932) again called for strengthening the Red Army and the Soviets; it also called for linking of the Soviet government with the urban masses through the tactic of the so-called "United Front From Below" – this ultra-left strategy was the continuation of the very one that had separated the CCP from the urban proletariat in the first place (and in Germany was a major factor in the Nazi victory).[54] As Stalin's grip on the world Communist movement tightened, Po Ku followed Moscow's dictat ever more closely without reference to the realities of China. Thus, his politics became increasingly unaccountable which inevitably meant the Party was plagued by factionalism with the leaders using the methods learned in Moscow to crush criticism.[55] The new leaders depended solely upon Stalin and the ECCI for their positions in the Party whereas Mao had a solid and extensive base within the Jiangxi Soviet; hence, he was both feared and mistrusted by Wang Ming.

As the NRA advanced, the party leaders discussed the how best the Jiangxi Soviet could defend itself. Official policy was to defend the peasants in the Jiangxi Soviet against the incursions of Chiang's forces, but Mao argued that the Red Army should stick to tried and tested tactics and avoid large defensive battles, which meant the sacrifice of entire villages. Such policies were, of course, extremely unpopular with the peasants, and the Party leaders took the opportunity to attempt to reduce Mao's influence and remove him from his military and political posts.

In October 1932, a Conference of eight top CCP members was held at Ningdu to discuss military affairs. Mao was heavily criticised for his guerilla mentality and it was agreed he take sick leave. This meant retirement from military matters which would last until after the beginning of the Long March.[56] Mao received a second slap when he was not re-elected to the CC but appointed Chairperson of the Central Executive Committee of the Soviet government.[57] In this post he would remove collectivisation from the land programme, and liberalise the land laws to permit the buying and selling of land.

On hearing of Mao's removal, the Political Secretariat of the ECCI sent a telegram "With respect to Mao Zedong it is necessary to employ maximum patience and comradely influence, providing him full opportunity to engage in responsible work." The ECCI representative in China (Arthur Ewert) added

"We ask you work closely with Mao Zedong."[58] The reasons why they sent these messages were obvious: a new and bigger extermination campaign was on the way and the new leadership lacked Mao's experience on the battlefield, also there had been a hostile reaction by Red Army personnel and local CCP members to the incomers' moves against Mao.

During the fourth extermination campaign which lasted through the winter of 1932-1933, Po Ku, Lo Fu, and the remaining CC members moved from the Shanghai headquarters to Juichin, while Wang Ming left for Moscow, where he served from 1932 to 1938 as Chinese representative. He was replaced as Secretary General by Po Ku, who, with Zhou Enlai's support and under Wang Ming's direction, remained in control of the party until the Long March.[59]

Intelligence information and greater resourcefulness enabled the Red Army defending Jiangxi to ambush and destroy two KMT divisions which forced an end to the fourth extermination campaign. Po Ku and the Party Centre moved quickly to claim the credit for this victory and consolidate its leadership within the Soviet by accusing a number of middle and second-rank CCP members who were known Mao supporters of "indecision" and "factional activities", and replacing them with their own people.[60] The 28 Bolsheviks now took three (including Wang Ming) of the six seats on the Standing Committee of the Politburo, and with Zhou Enlai's support had control of this key body.[61]

However, the heroic efforts and victories of the Red Army in defeating Chiang Kai-shek's fourth extermination campaign were the beginning of the end. It was clear that it was only a question of time before the superior strength of the Kuomintang prevailed.

Within the Jiangxi Soviet, the pressure of the KMT economic blockade was leading to an ever more conciliatory attitude to the richer peasants and to the merchants who maintained trade with the nearby towns. As the KMT blockade of Jiangxi became ever tighter and food scarcer, Wang Ming would prohibit further re-division of the land because this practice had become "one of the most serious obstacles to an improvement in peasant agriculture." By the end of 1933 a Soviet government official is reported to have said that of the three million inhabitants of the central Soviet district, two million were oppressed by rich peasants and landlords and the Soviets themselves had become instruments for oppressing the poor.[62]

> "The land was divided, but the landlords and rich peasants also received land and better land at that. ... Not a few of them are in control of Party and Government

> institutions and use them to carry out their own class interests. … In many places the land problem seems to be fully solved, but upon close scrutiny it appears that even landlords are found to have received land and the rich peasants still retain their superior land."[63]

For Chiang, the military success of the Jiangxi Soviet in defeating the extermination campaigns made its elimination a priority. For the 5th campaign which began in September 1933, Chiang's bombers devastated whole districts while his troops moved inexorably down the province, building impenetrable fortifications as they advanced. Chiang abandoned the previous strategy of sending columns deep into Red territory, where they were cut off and annihilated. No units were allowed to advance without strong support. Blockhouses were built to control and defend an area, after which the army moved forward to the next position. His army of more than 500,000 men, schooled by the German General von Seeckt, supported by some 300 American, British and Italian bombers and armed with the latest weapons from the munitions factories of Europe and the United States, closed in on the Jiangxi Soviet like a fine-mesh steel net. The philosophy of the attacking forces was that it was impossible to draw a line between a good citizen and a Red partisan. As many as one million people died during this final campaign, by bomb, gun or starvation.

7.6 The Tsunyi Conference and the Long March

In response to the gradual encroachment of the KMT block-houses, the Soviet adopted a more defensive strategy proposed by Zhou Enlai of so-called protracted war which meant defending the territory of the Soviet and protecting its inhabitants from the ravages of KMT troops. This strategy required the construction of static fortifications. The key fort was at Guangchang, blocking the approach to Juichin.

The alternative strategy was proposed by Otto Braun who arrived in Juichin in October 1933, fresh from military academy and appointed by the ECCI to be military advisor to the Red Army. Braun wrote under the alias Hua Fu and advanced the strategy of 'short, swift thrusts' that laid stress on the mobility of the Red Army which would choose a target and strike with all its energy in one blow, and then retreat, not giving the KMT forces time to prepare or respond. In the background but no longer a serious contender, was Zhu De's strategy so successfully used by Mao to defeat the first three campaigns, now deemed inappropriate because it offered no defence of the civilian population.[64]

In January 1934, seeing the seriousness of the situation, the Comintern intervened directly and insisted Mao be a full member of the Politburo. However, not receiving an offer of a return to military command, Mao chose to remain a sick man. Po Ku was the faithful servant of the ECCI but his limitations were recognised by the Comintern, and Mao's abilities and experience sufficiently valued that Stalin intervened to ensure Mao's presence in the CCP's leadership structure. The popular view that Mao was a dissident communist who defied Stalin and defeated Wang Ming, the proxy of the Comintern, and thereby saved the Chinese revolution should have been buried long ago.[65]

A major assault with extensive use of heavy artillery destroyed Guangchang which fell to the KMT on 28 April. As it became clear that Guangchang would fall, Zhou distanced himself from the defence strategy by moving to Juichin while Otto Braun went to the front, took command and directed military operations, thus associating himself with the defeat. The fall of Guangchang was not decisive militarily but was a major psychological blow and led directly to the decision by a three-man committee of Po Ku, Zhou Enlai, and Otto Braun, that Juichin was no longer defendable, and the Soviet should be evacuated. The CC was informed in late August 1934 and agreed to the "strategic transfer" or the famous and heroic Long March as it would be known.[66]

In August, 1934, the 6th Red Army of about 10,000 men, led by Hsiao Keh, broke through the KMT cordon and escaped westward as one of a series of diversions which successfully deceived Chiang's troops. In November the main force moved out from Yutu some hundred kilometres (about 60 miles) west of Juichin, virtually unopposed. Nym Wales reported that it took the more than 86,000 marchers (the majority teenagers, some as young as 13) three days to evacuate, but that only thirty women were allowed to join the march, an observation confirmed by Agnes Smedley.[67,68] That so few women were officially included (though many tagged on) is a clear and damning observation on how significant the CCP leadership saw women comrades in the revolutionary struggle.

The intention was for a relatively short march to join with Hsiao Keh who was active in north west Hunan and that is why they took everything that they could carry – including an X-ray machine.

With the fall of Guangchang and the decision to evacuate, Moscow built Mao up as a heroic figure clearly indicating who it wanted leading the Red Army during the evacuation. Mao's name appeared in Comintern publications being praised as "the leader of the Chinese soviet movement," and the "pre-eminent young politician and military strategist of the Chinese Soviet Republic." The Comintern even published a volume of his selected works, probably the first of its kind, then the journal *Abroad* carried an approving sketch of Mao and Zhu De (the linking of the two was an unmistakable nudge), and finally in September 1934 the ECCI advised the CC of the CCP "to follow the example of Zhu De and Mao Zedong and work directly in the guerrilla detachments."[69]

On 10 November 1934, almost exactly three years after the proclamation of the Chinese "Soviet Republic", Chiang Kai-shek's troops triumphantly entered Juichin, the Soviet capital. Chiang had failed to exterminate the Communists as he had promised, but he had succeeded in winning Jiangxi back for the landlords. Stalinists worldwide needed victories to demonstrate the successes of the Comintern, and because events in China were virtually unverifiable, Moscow reported the desperate flight of the Red Army as a series of victories and successes.

To escape the encirclement, the Red Army, still under the command of Otto Braun, had to break through four lines of block-houses. The first three were easy but at the fourth, on the banks of the river Xiang (where it crossed the Hunan-Kiangsi border), the column was ambushed after one half had crossed, and by 1 December 1934 only about 45,000 marchers were left to flee towards the west. Such figures are estimates because few records were kept and fewer survive. What can be said is that over half of those who started the Long March were killed or deserted in the initial stages.

The top CCP military leaders met in a series of meetings beginning on 12 December 1934 to discuss how to proceed. Mao was invited due to his relevant experience and pressure from the Comintern. He sensibly proposed that the Red Army not bang its head against entrenched KMT forces to the north but march west to Guizhou (Kweichow) province. His proposal was supported first by one of the 28 Bolsheviks, Wang Jiaxiang, and then by a second, Zhang Wentian, and then by Zhou Enlai.[70] Mao had won the day.

The Red Army moved into Guizhou, attacked but failed to capture Kweiyang (Guiyang) and moved towards Tsunyi, capturing that town on 14 January 1935.[71] The available Politburo members met with the chief military officers and Otto Braun from 15-17 January in the Tsunyi Conference to determine military strategy for the remainder of the Long March (at that time destination unknown). The extent of the military disaster, defeat of the Jiangxi Soviet and the terrible losses sustained in the initial stage of the Long March, badly damaged the standing of Zhou Enlai and Otto Braun and created an authority crisis in the CCP.

At Tsunyi, Mao blamed Braun for the disasters to the Red Army and in his contribution amalgamated the short, sharp thrust and protracted war strategies putting the blame for the defeat at Guangchang on Braun, letting Zhou Enlai off the hook. Zhou, as ever, shifted his support to the likely winner. The direct results were that Braun's proposals were rejected, Mao's accepted, the three-man group of Zhou Enlai, Otto Braun, and Po Ku abolished, and the total loss of military influence by Braun. How did Mao have the courage to place the blame on the ECCI representative? Two reasons spring to mind: Mao stressed that he was making military, not political, criticisms so there was no challenge to the authority of the ECCI. And he had been consistently praised by the ECCI and CI, and this gave him the necessary confidence.

The Tsunyi Conference resulted in Mao being promoted to membership of the Standing Committee of the Politburo. Mao would not take the Party throne for some time but emerged from the Tsunyi Conference with the reputation as a man who could lead the revolution to victory.[72] By mid-March, Mao had been appointed political commissar to the Front Commanding Headquarters (with Zhu De Commander in Chief), and as the lead figure on a three-person standing committee (with Zhou Enlai and Wang Jiaxiang) in which capacity he handled all crucial military matters.[73]

Mao was now *primus inter pares* in the leadership of the Party, but he was not undisputed leader. He did not control the whole Party and the army, because individuals such as Zhang Guotao (Chang Kuo-t'ao) who had established the E-Yu-Wan Soviet and was commander of the Fourth Front Army, and followers of Wang Ming such as Xiang Ying (commander of the rear guard remaining behind in Jiangxi, Anhwei, and Chekiang), were not ready to accept Mao's leadership. It would not be until the 7th Congress of the CCP in 1945 that Mao would gain complete supremacy over the Party.[74]

The defeat in Jiangxi did not terminate the peasant war, but it dealt a stunning blow to the insurgent peasant movement and consequently to the labour movement in the cities, then at its lowest ebb. New waves of terror, of capitulation and betrayals destroyed most of the small groups of Communists remaining in the principal cities. Events laid the ghosts of a thousand Comintern propaganda myths. In the months after the Tsunyi Conference, the

Red Army continued to roam Guizhou, northeastern Yunnan, and southern Szechuan provinces. Red forces marched and counter-marched across Hunan, Kweichow, Yunnan, and Szechwan into Shensi, suffering incredible hardships, and performing incredible feats of valour and cunning. The "Long March" has been recorded as a most remarkable military exploit, but it carried the Red Army ever farther from the political and economic centres of the country. The Communists marched into the sparse desert land of the Chinese northwest toward a new impasse.

Chiang Kai-shek had his own agenda for the march. Chiang's intentions were to force the Red Army to march into provinces which he did not control, and offer his assistance to the local warlord and soon the guest would become the master. He also intended the Red Army should move away from the Chinese heartland while gradually depleting the Red Army until it had served its purpose after which he would deliver the *coup de grace*. Chiang could be pleased with himself. By the end of the Long March, he had increased his area of control by a million square kilometres with a population of 100 million; the Soviet areas had been largely eliminated save for an isolated and poverty-stricken area controlled by the CCP so far north that Chiang could claim the Reds had been chased out of China proper.[75] But he had failed to deliver the hoped for *coup de grace*.

7.7 The Red Army Arrives in Yenan

The First Front Army left Tsunyi in mid-January, and headed south for a short while before Mao and Zhou Enlai disrupted Chiang's plan somewhat by marching north into Shensi rather than west into Szechuan.[76] Shensi was close to the border with the province of Gansu, outside the area controlled by Chiang Kai-shek, and contained the only remaining secure Soviet in China. Marching in the general direction of the Japanese army allowed Mao to rename the march as *The Anti-Japanese March* and claim that this had been his aim all along.

The Long March ended when Mao led between 4,000 and 7,000 troops into Paoan in the province of Shensi in October 1935. Mao had reached the Shensi Soviet led by Lui Chih-tan, with about the same number of troops as he had in his very first days at Jiangxi. Paoan would be the Communists' capital until December 1936 when they seized Yenan.

So backward was this region that there were no major roads, railways or navigable rivers to carry relief supplies during the Great Northwest famine of 1928-33 when about one-third of the population starved to death.[77] During the famine peasants had borrowed to stay alive and by 1934-36, in a typical village in the eastern part of the county of some 85 households, three small landlords, 11 rich peasants, 39 middle peasants, 28 poor peasants, three farmhands and one tenant farmer, all had their land and property sequestered by creditors, and the land had passed into the hands of a finance company. This was fertile ground for the CCP.[78]

Jiangxi had been poor enough but this area of Shensi was absolutely impoverished with poor soil and low levels of productivity. The area of the Soviet fluctuated but did at various times extend into the three adjoining provinces of Shensi, Kansu and Ningsia. It was inhabited by scattered tribes that numbered less than one million; most villages consisted of no more than four or five farms. Only Yenan, a town with a population of less than four thousand people, could be reached by lorries and these travelled along a dirt track.[79]

Outside of the towns most people (and this includes Red Army troops) lived in caves or, even, just holes dug in the ground into which the water from melting snow ran. Food was barely adequate, the soldiers' clothes were threadbare and their straw sandals falling to pieces. With winter coming on, Chiang corralled the Communists in these appalling conditions making sure they could proceed no further north, thus cutting them off from any possible supplies from Soviet Russia.

Mao sent Chun Yun as courier to Moscow to report on his success in reaching Shensi and on 13 December 1935, *Pravda* carried an edited version of the report as a major article headed; *Leader of the Chinese People, Mao Zedong.*[80] By June 1936, the radio link with Moscow had been restored but now Mao controlled the Chinese end with a consequent increase in his authority and prestige within the Party. The first telegram sent to Moscow from the Party Centre was dated 16 June 1936, and the first one from Moscow was received by the Party Centre on 2 July. The restoration of CCP-Moscow communication immediately strengthened Mao's position. In the telegrams which the Centre sent to the Fourth Front Army under Zhang's control, Mao often used phrases such as "according to the Comintern telegram" which forced Zhang to accept his authority. There are many cases of Mao going to great lengths to maintain radio contact with Moscow – for example, organising complex and dangerous missions to get kerosene to run the generators. It is inconceivable that if Mao was opposed to Moscow's policy he would have made such persistent efforts.[81]

When the Communists settled in Shensi they again faced the problems of securing political support and maximising economic output. Two-thirds of peasants formally owned their land but nearly all were drained by usury. The CCP gained mass support with its radical policies of lowering rents, taxes and interest rates and negating debts to the landlords and usurers.[82]

There was little capital for agricultural development. Mao recognised this and stressed that in such a poverty-stricken region, increases of revenue could only come from increased production; and that the support of the population would depend on their gains in income being greater than the increase in taxes to support the Red Army and local administration. The solution was to require all Party members and troops to work in the villages to help produce the food and goods they consumed, and co-operate with villagers to mobilise labour for land reclamation, mutual aid in farming, and marketing co-operatives. Returns from these activities over and above the food taken by the Communists went back to the villages, to the surprise and delight of the peasants who, previously, had only been robbed by any troops stationed with them.[83]

Once again, under pressure from Mao, the CCP took the very positive step of introducing the same Marriage Law as in Jiangxi and, once again, backed off when faced with the hostility of the local male population: introducing restrictions on a woman's ability to get a divorce which, of course, reduced her social position and the value of the formal right to own land.[84]

7.8 Summary

Soviets were founded in China as the result of a series of defeats of the working class and peasantry, resulting from a class collaborationist policy that gave the interests of the bourgeoisie priority in order to maintain a "United Front" with them. Nevertheless, the Soviets introduced a number of vital reforms: abolition of debt to usurers and large landowners; reductions in interest rates, rents, taxes and mortgages. Land re-distribution also improved the lives of most middle and poor peasants, and some landless labourers. These changes ensured peasant support for, and loyalty to, the CCP.

The CCP also introduced progressive legislation regarding women including; marriage reform, abolition of foot binding, and the right to own land and property. Reforms which were essential for improving the lives of women.

These reforms and all other progressive measures taken by the CCP were wholeheartedly supported by Chinese Trotskyists. But who also pointed out that the "Soviets" were not islands of socialism, they were part of a class-collaborationist strategy with the goal of a so-called democratic dictatorship of the proletariat and peasantry which would be, in fact, a national bourgeois-democratic, capitalist state. Trotskyists also pointed out that these so-called Soviets lacked an essential pre-requisite, being completely undemocratic. In the Leninist sense they were not Soviets at all.

Despite strong peasant support the armed strength of the KMT armies overwhelmed the early Soviets and forced the Red Army onto the Long March. The defeats suffered allowed Mao Zedong to successfully challenge the existing leaders and, with Stalin's support, to re-enter the Politburo as its most authoritative figure.

By the time of Mao's arrival in Shensi province, Third Period Stalinism was dead and had been replaced by the Popular Front strategy which, in China, was interpreted as political subordination of the CCP to the KMT in a way that mirrored the tragedy of 1925-27. Mao welcomed this strategy of right opportunism as his own. Lenin, it should be remembered, had considered such coalitions a betrayal and fought against them the whole of his political life. To him it was the epitome of revisionism and upon his return to Russia in April 1917, he had threatened to split with those Bolsheviks (who, incidentally, included Stalin) who favoured merging with the Mensheviks and supporting the coalition government established after the February Revolution.

Chapter 8

Yenan, the Second United Front, and the War against Japan

8.1 Introduction

The Long March was a major factor in consolidating the peasant/soldier brand of Maoism with its authoritarian and privileged command structure, and confirmed the lack of any genuine orientation by the CCP towards the urban working class.

This chapter shows how the so-called Second United Front in China was the Chinese version of the Popular or People's Fronts being implemented in Europe, America, and elsewhere under the direction of the Comintern. It describes the abrupt about-face from adventurism to social patriotism, and the abasement of the CCP before Chiang Kai-shek in order to achieve a temporary and false unity with the KMT against the Japanese invasion. Mao's *New Democracy* synthesised this class collaborationist doctrine, would threaten the creation of a Chinese workers' state, and would eventually form part of the conceptual basis for capitalist restoration.

After arriving in northern Shensi in 1935/6, the Chinese Communists under the direction of the Communist International made a strategic shift climaxing in the formation of a so-called United Front with the Nationalists. In a parallel move intended to bolster Chiang against the Japanese, the USSR signed a non-aggression pact with the KMT on 21 August 1937, and began delivering military supplies to it.

Under the terms of the agreement with the KMT, the Chinese Soviet government was renamed and notionally replaced by a Border Regions' Authority, nominally under the Nationalist regime. The CCP continued to promulgate its own laws and regulations, but now these were based on the Nationalist codes and in many cases simply adopted relevant and useful Nationalist laws, such as those against opium and banditry. During the Yenan period, the primary task of the people's courts in the border regions was to defend the anti-Japanese Popular Front and the Party bureaucracy; to punish traitors, criminals and other harmful elements.[1]

The agreement with the KMT required the CCP to halt the seizure of landlords' lands (which caused many peasants to fear that the land that had been distributed might be taken back), backtrack on women's rights (which was strongly opposed by the more radical elements in the Party), and propose an alliance with the NRA (which was seen by many soldiers as a shameful betrayal of the sacrifices they had made in ten years of civil war). To overcome this opposition the CCP would launch a rectification programme of structured political indoctrination that sought to "unify the thinking of the entire membership" and give the leadership a degree of control much greater than Stalin had exerted in the Soviet Union.[2]

8.2 The Second United Front

The ultra-left policies of Third Period Stalinism had split the German working class in the face of the Nazis and allowed Hitler to come to power "without breaking a pane of glass". A frightened Stalin turned to diplomacy to protect the Soviet Union from the results of his own policies. The Soviet leadership cynically manipulated the national Communist Parties in its own interests to relieve the twin pressures of Germany in the west and Japan in the east. The national Communist Parties would seek to control the class struggle using so-called Popular Fronts; in return their own bourgeoisie would extend goodwill towards the Soviet Union.

Thus, the 7th World Congress of the CI (25 July–21 August 1935) advocated a Popular Front policy for a number of countries of which China was one.[3] The CCP was to reach a detente with Nationalist China to protect the Soviet Union's eastern seaboard.[4] The CCP itself almost never used the term Popular Front preferring instead "United Front". In this way it hoped to demonstrate the similarity in political and social content with the so-called United Front of 1925-27, and to preserve the fiction that this venture was a continuation of the 'unity' of 1925-27!

The 7th World Congress had Wang Ming announce that the anti-imperialist peoples' United Front was the only "means for the general mobilisation of the entire Chinese nation for the sacred national revolutionary war against Japanese imperialism."[5] Only eighteen months previously the same Wang Ming had, at the 13th Plenum of the ECCI, boldly affirmed that no improvement in the condition of the Chinese masses was possible without completion of the agrarian revolution, without the overthrow of the Kuomintang and its replacement by a Communist government.

Many Marxists in Western Europe have made strenuous efforts to differentiate Mao from Stalin. The adoption of the United Front strategy is one example. While the 7th World Congress was in session, the Red Army was resting in the town of Maoerhkai from which it issued the *Maoerhkai Appeal* on 1 August 1935 calling on all classes and armies in China to form a political and military alliance against Japan. It promised the CCP would co-operate with the KMT if it stopped attacking its own people and fought the Japanese invaders. The *Maoerhkai Appeal* thus appeared to anticipate the Comintern's own Popular Front appeal made the very next day. For some time, radicals in Europe and the USA argued this was an independent CCP initiative not only because it pre-dated the appeal of the 7th World Congress (if only by a day) but also because the Congress cited China as a prime example of how to proceed. However, with the opening of Soviet and CCP records it is now clear that the *Maoerhkai Appeal* was drafted by Wang Ming in Moscow, and an integral part of the Comintern move towards the Popular Front strategy.[6]

Naturally, at this stage the appeal was not directly to Chiang or the KMT. How could it be? KMT armies were at that very moment attempting to annihilate the Red Army and the CCP. It would take a little time before Chiang would be claimed as the ally of the CCP and saviour of China.

The call was largely ignored by Chiang Kai-shek; the Red Army had been defeated at Jiangxi and had been reduced to a small rump, there had been a bumper crop in 1935, there was an economic upturn as world trade revived, and an accompanying political stabilisation. Still hoping a compromise could be reached with Japanese imperialism, the Chinese bourgeoisie conducted a purely defensive struggle which slowed down the Japanese advance but could not withstand a determined imperialist attack nor ever achieve Chinese national liberation.

With moves towards Popular Frontism under way, the Chinese contingent to the 7th Congress led by Wang Ming approved a series of proposed changes to CCP policies that would make them more acceptable to the KMT; these included making landlords who actively supported the resistance to Japan, exempt from expropriation. This, if effected, would end land redistribution and the land revolution. The changes were considered sufficiently important for an envoy carrying details of the 7th Congress decisions and Wang's proposals, to be airlifted into North Shensi.[7]

Moscow now called for the CCP to enter an alliance with the Nationalists and for a joint military struggle against the Japanese to protect the Soviet Union from attack. With such a strategy the natural choice of leader for the CCP was Mao, and at the 7th Congress he was singled out for praise as an "outstanding and valiant standard-bearer" of the Communist movement. In Moscow's exhibition hall of CCP history, the only personal portrayals of CCP leaders were Mao and Zhu De. In the *Communist International*, No. 33-34, 1935, Mao was praised as the "legendary leader of the Chinese people."[8] The myth of 'Mao-versus-Wang' with Wang the red comprador, was spread later by Maoist historians to absolve Mao from responsibility for mistakes in Party policy. Unfortunately, many young militants in the West were deceived by this into believing that Mao was politically opposed to Wang, and that Mao had adopted an anti-Stalin stance.

The last stages of the Long March had been named *The Anti-Japanese March* and the Red Army was supposedly 'in preparation' for fighting the Japanese, but in its day-to-day activities it had to defend itself from the immediate enemy, the 'troops of the Chinese traitors'. This was reflected in a continuation of its policy of "resist Japan and oppose Chiang."[9] We can safely assume that this policy was a pretty faithful reflection of the hatred of Chiang felt by most of the Red Army troops.

At the end of March 1936, the ECCI intervened to accelerate the process of forming an anti-Japanese front with the KMT.[10] On 5 May 1936, Mao Zedong, as Chairperson of the Soviet Government of China, and Zhu De, commander-in-chief of the Red armies, made the first formal overtures in an appeal addressed to the Nanjing government and the Military Affairs Commission (of which Chiang Kai-shek was chair). This appeal called for cessation of hostilities between the Red Army and the Nanjing troops and called for a "peace conference in order to realize our common aim of resisting the Japanese."[11]

Chiang felt he had nothing to gain from discussing terms with a vanquished adversary. His position was enormously strengthened when, on 24 June, *Pravda* condemned as a Japanese plot, an attempt by local authorities in Guangdong and Guangxi to force Chiang into fighting the Japanese! The Chinese Stalinists would have to do a lot more belly-crawling before they would shake Chiang's blood-stained hand.

In public, the ECCI declared its sympathy with the internal difficulties faced by the CCP in making a complete about-face: from defending the Soviets against the attacks of KMT armies to transforming and restructuring those same Soviets to be subordinate to the National government and placing the Red Army under the command of Chiang Kai-shek.[12] In private, in his notes made during a meeting with Stalin, Dimitrov was more obdurate: the CCP must take a leading role in the war against Japan and for that the confiscation of land must stop; there was to be only one slogan "For a free China against Japanese war-mongers", no further fighting against Chiang Kai-shek until victory in the war against Japan; it was "not advisable" for the CCP "to engage in theoretical discussions" they could leave such discussion until after the war.[13] It can be understood why even in such an obedient Party as the Chinese, there was a delay in adjusting to the Moscow line.

However, the CCP's move towards a Second United Front was by no means exclusively the result of pressure from Moscow, it also had its Chinese line of descent. After all, Mao had been an active protector of the rich peasants in Jiangxi and before that had been strongly in favour of alliance with the KMT. But now there were two big differences; the KMT and CCP had been at war since 1927 and it was clear that even if Chiang were forced into an alliance, he would turn on the Communists as soon as he felt able, secondly Mao was within grasp of Party leadership and this would be a factor in his decisions – and as we know the struggle for leadership in undemocratic Stalinist parties could be a matter of life or death for hundreds, even thousands of comrades. These considerations led to a difference in emphasis – but not in political line – between Moscow and Mao, which would later be presented by some as a fight for the independence of the CCP from Moscow.[14]

With direct CCP-Moscow radio contact re-established, July-August 1936 formed a watershed in the CCP's transition towards the Popular Front. On 22 July, the Party endorsed Wang's land policy and began a campaign in its press to convince the KMT that it offered no threat to essential bourgeois interests. To do this Wang Ming reminded the bourgeoisie how the CCP had renounced the agrarian revolution and attempted to keep the peasants in check during the peasant upsurges of 1925-1927.[15]

Mao Zedong outstripped even this, offering the Chinese bourgeoisie the same renunciation of revolutionary struggle as in 1927. He then went one step further, offering guarantees that should the forces of the revolution raise their heads, should rank and file militants speak of "class against class", the CCP stood ready to play the role of executioner.[16]

The Politburo meeting on 10 August formally endorsed Zhou Enlai's statement that "the old slogan 'to resist Japan one must oppose Chiang first' is no longer suitable."[17] The government was renamed the "People's Soviet

Government" and the Chinese Workers' and Peasants' Red Army became the "People's Red Army", later to be re-named "People's Liberation Army". The name "Communist Party" was ordered to be removed from all governmental institutions and replaced by "Anti-Japanese Salvation Association". The omnipresent red star was replaced by the Chinese sun on a blue field, the symbol of the Anti-Japanese United Front. All previous laws in the Soviet districts limiting the civil rights of the bourgeoisie were repealed and a decision made not to confiscate the land of rich peasants. The CCP would protect the property and the factories of the big and small merchants and capitalists. In an echo of the worst decisions of 1925-27, the CCP pledged to limit itself to demanding a bourgeois democratic republic and declared the estates of serving officers and anti-Japanese big landowners were no longer subject to confiscation.[18]

An ECCI directive of 15 August advised the CCP to negotiate with Chiang directly and to immediately announce that the CCP was prepared to send a delegation to Chiang, or welcome a KMT delegation in the Soviet area. However, the directive contained several warnings: the establishment of a Japanese national united front should not be used to reduce soviet power, nor should the Red Army be integrated into the KMT armies.[19]

This might sound a big step forward in the thinking of the ECCI but no such luck. The Russian bureaucracy had observed Chiang's dealings with the Japanese and appreciated that Chiang would be only too keen to accept a face-saving deal with Japan that left the Imperial Army free to attack the Soviet Union. It was a necessary defensive measure to preserve an armed force loyal to the CCP because that might become the only barrier between the advancing Japanese army and the USSR. The Red Army had to be maintained independent of the bourgeoisie, under the exclusive leadership of the CCP. Submerging the Red Army into the NRA could lead to its destruction. What was being suggested was still the same old goal of a national bourgeois democratic regime, but now the Red Army would fight for it in parallel with, rather than as part of, the Nationalist armies. The degree of separation and subordination would depend on circumstances. The struggle for socialism would, as previously, take place at some unspecified time in the future.

As a result the CCP sent an open letter to the KMT on 25 August, appealing for KMT-CCP unity against Japan. The *Open Letter to the KMT*, drafted by Mao followed ECCI advice:

> "We are prepared to form a strong revolutionary united front with you as was the case during the … great Chinese Revolution of 1925-7, when there existed

> a broad united front for struggle against national and feudal oppression, for that is the only proper way to save our country to-day. You ... have not yet forgotten the glorious history of collaboration between the Communist Party and the Kuomintang. ... It was precisely thanks to this collaboration that all the national and feudal oppressors shook before us. At that time our national oppressors and Japanese imperialism in particular, were very much afraid that our collaboration might lead to final victory and the complete emancipation of China. Therefore they sowed the seeds of strife between us and set in motion all possible means, threats, and temptations as a result of which one side gave up its collaboration and buried the united front. Do you feel no pricks of conscience when you recall this to-day?."[20]

Such a blatant falsification of events was not meant to deceive the leadership of the KMT (who, after all, were still intent on destroying the CCP and killing every Chinese Communist), it was meant to counter the very real mistrust felt by the majority of the Party.

On 1 September, the Party Centre directed Party organisations to formally relinquish the old slogans of "Resist Japan and oppose Chiang" and "Down with Chiang Kai-shek."[21] The directive stated that political and military agreement with the KMT would require the Soviets and Red Army to be placed under the unified command of the national defence government and allied anti-Japanese armed forces. But added, "the independence of the soviets and the Red Army in their organisations and leadership shall not be abolished." KMT officers and administrators would not be allowed to join the Red Army or Soviet area government. The CCP would continue to enlarge and consolidate its own political and military forces to assure a thorough victory in the anti-Japanese war and the creation of a bourgeois democratic republic.[22]

But in 1927 the CCP could have led a mighty mass movement of many millions in a revolutionary situation; in 1937 it stood at the head of 100,000 badly equipped, poorly disciplined peasant soldiers without the faintest concept of the working-class movement. In 1927 the CCP had stood in opposition to the peasant struggle and had suppressed its demands; now ten years later it was promising to repeat its mistakes.

Before the call for the Popular Front, the CCP had repeatedly addressed itself to the front line units of the KMT offering a fighting alliance against the Japanese army setting only the elementary conditions: an end to the offensive against the Soviet districts, democratic rights for the people and the right for volunteers to organise and arm themselves into anti-Japanese fighting units. Appeals of this kind were designed to tear the supports from under the Kuomintang, thereby relieving the pressure on the Soviet districts, promoting the anti-Japanese struggle, and preparing for the defeat of Chiang Kai-shek's regime. This was accompanied by a propaganda campaign along the lines that Chiang Kai-shek and the whole KMT had been unmasked as preparing to partition China in the face of the Japanese advance. To aid this process, prisoners taken by the Red Army, after first aid treatment were subject to intensive political instruction and released. All this good work was now found to have been an error and was summarily ended: the anti-imperialist front was to be promoted 'in a new manner'.

The arguments used in 1926-27 were dusted off and brought out to justify the Second United Front but on their own, were clearly inadequate. Three new reasons were produced. The first was the universal indignation of the Chinese people at the expansionist policies of Japan (in fact popular opposition with mass boycott and student actions was greatest in 1931-32 when Japan seized Manchuria); the second was the increased strength of the Red Army which had grown to a "mighty military factor throughout China" (in fact the Red Army having been defeated at Jiangxi, had arrived in Shensi on the outskirts of China a shadow of its former self); the third reason was that the national bourgeoisie were freeing themselves from their illusions in the KMT and were turning towards the toiling masses (in fact the national bourgeoisie had opted to support the KMT in 1926-27 and were still clinging to it).

Anyone who stated the elementary truth, only recently promulgated by the CCP, that the overthrow of the KMT was the condition of a successful national-revolutionary war was branded an "enemy of the Chinese people" and an "agent of Japanese imperialism". The policies of class struggle and agrarian revolution were publicly jettisoned. The theme of Stalinist propaganda welcomed the "People's Anti-Japanese United Front" embracing "all parties and groups" (in practice the CP and KMT), leading to the establishment of an "All-Chinese Government of National Defence". Care was taken to remove any suggestion that the CCP was even hinting at the overthrow of the KMT regime, even as a distant aim. Wang Ming declared any such suggestion to be "an absolutely false and unfounded legend spread by pro-Japanese elements ... It is slander, provocation!"[23]

8.3 The Sian Incident

During 1936 Chiang was under pressure to resist the Japanese advances from Nationalist troops, particularly those in the north east who were most threatened. These troops had engaged the Japanese forces on a number of occasions, and were vigorously opposed to Chiang's continuous retreat and his refusal to fight. By the end of 1936 a *de facto* truce existed between local generals and the Red Army to the extent that the Red Army was given uniforms and weapons and the CCP allowed access via Yenan to Communist groups in Nationalist China.[24] On 12 December 1936, Chiang flew to Sian (Xi'an, capital of Shensi province) to personally remonstrate with General Chang Hsueh-liang the local commander, and induce him to begin an offensive against the Soviet area. In an astounding turn of events, the younger officers seized Chiang and refused to release him unless he agreed to a bold anti-Japanese programme. The rank and file soldiers threatened a 'people's trial' and there is no doubt that initially Mao also supported this proposal.

Moscow intervened strongly; on 14 December a *Pravda* editorial, and on 15 December an article in *Investia*, condemned the action, calling the rebellious generals Japanese puppets. Within days, Dimitrov dispatched a telegram to the CCP calling for it to effect Chiang's release. Mao is said to have stamped his feet in rage at this proposal but it was confirmation that he was not the undisputed leader of the CCP when Po Ku and Zhou Enlai immediately accepted the ECCI's directive, and Zhou Enlai stepped in to meet with Chiang, to save his life, reinstate him as leader of the KMT, and send him back as national leader to Nanjing. With his life on the line, Chiang agreed to Zhou's proposals which were so mild they were not so difficult to swallow.[25]

One reason for the CCP's sensitivity to Stalin's wishes was the material aid being received from Moscow. In 1936 the Comintern subsidy to the CCP was about US$2,000,000 (about half the annual budget of the Yenan Soviet).[26,27] This level of support would continue until the defeat of Japan in 1945.

It was at this time that the HQ of the Red Army moved into the walled town of Yenan which contained some hundreds of decent enough houses, some even with small gardens. Agnes Smedley who was in Sian at the time and reached Yenan shortly after the take-over, describes how the Red Army entered Yenan without a fight, extended the area controlled by the Soviet by many thousands of square kilometres and about one million people without firing a shot because the local troops were fed up with offering no resistance to the Japanese.[28] By the end of 1938, Yenan was reduced largely to rubble by Japanese bombing raids and the population moved to the surrounding hills where they again lived in caves.

A short time after his return to Nanjing, Chiang called a meeting of the CEC of the KMT to consider the CCP proposals for a Popular Front. During February 1937, Zhou negotiated with the KMT. The CEC insisted that it remained determined to uproot Chinese Communism but would accept the CCP proposal subject to four conditions: (1) Suspension of the class struggle, (2) Cessation of all Communist propaganda, (3) Dissolution of the Soviet Republic and the appointment of KMT officials to take charge of the local areas, and (4) Abolition of the Red Army and its incorporation into the Government armies under the direct control of the Military Affairs Commission – but it must not number more than 3,000 and officers above division commander must go abroad.[29]

The CCP replied on 15 March 1937, and declared that it had already voluntarily met the first two conditions; confiscation of the land of the landlords had ceased and the Communist Party would no longer promote class struggle. To show goodwill a Communist youth congress held in Yenan in April elected Chiang Kai-shek to its presidium alongside Mao Zedong. These actions by the CCP helped save Chiang who was facing an officer corps on the verge of revolt.

In May 1937, the CCP called a National Conference to assess its work, address the confusion within its ranks, approve the line proposed by the ECCI and discuss its practical implementation. The conference was a rubber stamp and, just as in the USSR, attendees were appointed. In Yenan no elections were ever held for delegates to CCP conferences.[30]

Lo Fu described as "Secretary of the CC of the CCP" was interviewed by Nym Wales (wife of Edgar Snow) on 14 July 1937.[31] Lo gave a very positive picture of the block within, maintaining it had been "a united front against imperialism and feudal forces" and that "in July 1927 the CCP and the KMT finally split." After a decade the Stalinists still refused to admit that the Chinese bourgeoisie had massacred peasants, workers and Communists in a bloody counter-revolution. Lo dated the Soviet programme of the CCP as continuing up to the Sian incident after which "it continued only pending completion of negotiations with the KMT" and Lo referred to Yenan as the "ex-Soviet capital". Lo maintained, "To continue with the Soviet slogan would be to demand the overthrow of the KMT, which would mean civil war and make it impossible to realise the anti-Japanese struggle."

On 15 July 1937, the CC of the CCP announced the basis of its co-operation with the KMT.[32]

- "The CCP CC finds it necessary to proclaim its sincere devotion to the cause of national liberation. Therefore, it once again solemnly declares to the whole nation:
- that since Dr Sun Yat-sen's *Three Principles of the People* are what China needs today, our party is ready to fight for their complete realization;
- that we shall give up our policy of encouraging insurrection to overthrow the KMT regime, call off the sovietization movement, and discontinue the policy of forcible confiscation of the land of the landlords;
- that we shall abolish the present soviet governments and call for the practice of democracy in the hope that state power will be unified throughout the country; and
- that the Red Army will give up its present name and designation, that it will be reorganized as part of the National Revolutionary Army and placed under the Military Council of the national government, and that it will be ready for orders to march to the anti-Japanese front and do its duty."

From here on, Yenan surrendered the designation of Soviet becoming a special administrative region, the Shensi-Gansu-Ningxia Border Region, of the Chinese Republic, and renounced all revolutionary claims. However, the only noticeable change (apart from the name changes and disappearance of the red stars from buildings) was the discontinuation of circulation of the CCP's own currency; post offices, schools and all local services remained very strictly under local control.

However, against KMT demands, the CCP insisted that the old Soviet area would not be divided and there would not be new local government elections. The CCP did agree that the Red Army would be nominally integrated into the NRA as the 8th Route Army (the New 4th Army was added in October 1937), re-organised into three divisions and placed under nominal KMT control. However, against KMT demands, the CCP insisted its command personnel would not change and each division would number 15,000.

Discussions failed to resolve the differences. What decided the matter for Chiang was that the Japanese army marched into the Beijing-Tienjin area in July 1937 and Japanese gunships shelled Shanghai in August. Chiang had no choice but to accept the status quo *vis a vis* the CCP and no doubt, the promise of arms from the Soviet Union sweetened the pill.

The Japanese were determined to take all of north China and every important port on the coast. After crawling for six years before the Japanese, the KMT was finally compelled to offer resistance because Japanese aggression now threatened to extinguish the Chinese bourgeoisie altogether. Chiang could retreat no further without widespread revolt amongst his own troops. Within a year the invading Japanese armies held all the main centres of the north, almost all the principal seaports, and all but two of the principal railways. "Patriotism throughout history has been inseparably bound up with power and property. In the face of danger the ruling classes (the so-called 'national' bourgeoisie) have never stopped short of dismembering their own country so long as they could preserve their own power over part of it,"[33] but that was no longer an option in China.

As part of Stalin's Popular Front strategy, Communist Parties worldwide pressurised their governments to form an alliance with Russia against Germany and/or Japan, in return for which the CP would attempt to suspend the class struggle. The CCP occupied a key place in these machinations as a pawn of Russian diplomacy with the goal of preventing the KMT Government from joining Japan in an anti-Soviet pact. The Red Army and the Communist Party insisted that they no longer struggled for either an agrarian or proletarian revolution, but for bourgeois democracy.

8.4 Wang Ming Returns

When Wang Ming returned to China in November 1937, his importance was demonstrated by his being airlifted to Yenan. Wang was accompanied by two other Politburo members, Kang Sheng and Chen Yun, and these three made a substantial difference to the Politburo. With support from Zhou Enlai, these three were in a majority against Mao, Zhang Wentian, and Rem Bishi. Wang was a member of the Presidium of the Comintern and had received personal instructions from Stalin. When he addressed meetings his "speech resembled that of an imperial envoy transmitting an imperial decree."[34]

Despite there being no obvious or major political, policy or strategic differences between Mao and Wang whatever topic was discussed at the Politburo the meeting ended in heated deadlock. It was agreed that the Comintern should adjudicate. The ECCI appreciated that the major element in the disagreements was the jockeying for leadership of the CCP between Wang and Mao. Dimitrov pulled no punches:

> "You must tell everyone that it is necessary to support Mao Zedong as the leader of the CCP. He has been tempered in practical struggle. Such persons as Wang Ming should no longer fight for the leadership."[35]

To get him out of the way, Wang Ming was assigned to liaise with the KMT. In this role he continued to push an extreme version of the Popular Front; e.g. that any struggle for democratic reforms should have prior KMT approval. When in December, 1937, the KMT decreed the death penalty for workers who went on strike or even agitated for strikes while the war was in progress, Wang Ming told an interviewer that the CCP was "fully satisfied" with the Kuomintang's conduct of the war. From 1937-45 "The Communists opposed strikes as detrimental to the war effort, and undertook no independent organization of labour (or the peasants) in Kuomintang administered areas."[36]

In February 1938, Mao spelled out the CCP's perspective in answer to the question: "Will the CCP-KMT co-operation last long?" He replied:

> "The CCP has never wanted to break away from the KMT. In the past 10 years of split both parties and the people have suffered enough. This painful experience will serve to reinforce our co-operation, the aims of which are joint resistance at the present and joint reconstruction in the future."[37]

On 2 July 1938, Mao explained to a visiting student delegation, his view of China after victory over Japan; a free and equal democratic nation with agriculture, industry, and commerce jointly operated by the state and the people. Workers would benefit from an 8-hour day and peasants would own their land. The bourgeoisie would have complete freedom of speech, publication, meeting and association. Such a nation would not be a socialist state, nor its government a Soviet government, but a state and a government that practised democracy under the principle of respecting private ownership. To achieve this goal the CCP desired to unite with the KMT and other revolutionary parties and factions as well as with the people of the entire nation.[38] What reformist, social democratic politician has not painted the same picture?

At the 6th (enlarged) plenum of the CC of October 1938 Mao presented his analysis of the then current situation in China in *The New Stage*.[39] The tone of his report is represented by the sub-heading *The Kuomintang Has a Brilliant Future* and, let it be noted, also "a glorious history"! Chiang is referred to as a "great leader" waging a courageous war of resistance: "In its 50-year history the KMT whenever it encountered a great revolutionary struggle always transformed itself into an alliance of national revolution."

The massacres of 1927 and the subsequent extermination campaigns are airbrushed from history.

Pierre Rousset, a spokesperson for the former Ligue Communiste Révolutionnaire and a founding member of the Nouveau Parti Anticapitaliste, has claimed that during the Sino-Japanese war, the CCP made "major efforts" to reforge its links with the urban working class, and cites the work led by Liu Shaoqi as proof.[40] In fact, Mao's speeches at the October 1938 plenum polemicised against the proposals of Liu Shaoqi that greater emphasis be placed on mobilising the urban workers. His alternative was that the "fulcrum of Party activity" must lie "in the front zones and in the enemy's hinterland."[41] It is quite true that there was considerable underground work by the CCP within KMT areas but there are no records of substantial or effective work in the factories.

Belden, who was present at the time, reported conversations with local CCP leaders in the liberated areas:

> "There was little or no connection between the Central Committee of the party and its underground workers, but messengers and orderlies were dispatched to the large towns to post slogans, distribute handbills and spread the word as best they could. General instructions were for workers, students and farmers to unite, to evacuate the cities immediately and to help organize guerrilla warfare... Their nuclei among the workers in Chiang's areas was almost nil."[42]

It is true that as the CCP took on the mantle of the party of national resistance its support amongst university students grew. During 1947 and 1948 the KMT regime launched a campaign against the universities and middle schools in an effort to root out any traces of Communism. Thousands of students were beaten up, arrested, imprisoned and tortured. So deep was the hostility these moves engendered that many non-socialist democrats and intellectuals saw their only hope of ending the civil war was to support the CCP. However, the emphasis of the CCP was not to encourage the students to link their demands with those of the workers but for them leave the cities and travel to the liberated areas to help administer the Border Regions' Authority. In one month alone, October 1948, over 4,500 students are said to have moved to the Communist areas.[43]

To justify the united front and bloc of four classes, Mao's writings of 1937-40 developed the idea that the Russian Revolution was qualitatively different from the Chinese because the Russian bourgeoisie, although military-feudal, had carried out imperialist aggression against other countries and so entirely lacked any revolutionary quality. The Chinese bourgeoisie was the victim of imperialist aggression and so retained some revolutionary quality.[44] Mao's views were coloured by the needs of the moment so, for example, the successes of the Northern Expedition were described as due to Chiang Kai-shek's brilliance, not mass peasant mobilisation. Mao did realise that the relative weakness of the Chinese bourgeoisie meant the democratic revolution would have to be carried forward on the backs of the urban workers and peasants, but instead of following Lenin and recognising that this opened the way to a socialist revolution, he intended that the peasants and workers of China would act in the service of the bourgeoisie and stop the revolution half-way. Mao not only closed his eyes to the lessons of history, he re-wrote history to match his own class-collaborationist perspective.

The ECCI had determined that Mao was the most suitable leader for the CCP both because of his military abilities and skills and for his natural inclination towards an alliance with the KMT. In 1939 the Moscow publishing house Ogiz-Izogiz produced a monograph which was a shortened version of Edgar Snow's *Red Star Over China*, with all the critical comments on Mao removed. At the same time a brochure entitled *Mao Zedong and Zhu De: Leaders of the Chinese People* appeared describing Mao as a model leader of the Chinese Communists.[45] In early 1940 Dimitrov made a series of comments on the membership of the Politburo. Mao is described as "truly the most outstanding political figure in the CCP. He knows China better than the other CCP leaders, knows the people, correctly interprets political events and basically frames problems correctly."[46]

The KMT was fighting a progressive war, representing an oppressed semi-colonial country against Japanese imperialism. The progressive nature of the war was not negated by the fact that the struggle was led by Chiang Kai-shek, hangman of the Chinese Revolution. Surely it was the duty of all revolutionists to support him? Were the Stalinists not right, then, in making a united front with Chiang Kai-shek and the Kuomintang?

It was the duty of revolutionists to support China's struggle by all means possible, including agreements of a strictly practical nature with Chiang Kai-shek and the Kuomintang – but not to abandon their own programme, to dissolve themselves in a People's Front, to relinquish the right to criticise and condemn the Kuomintang's conduct of the war. The Stalinists, spurning the Leninist United Front tactic, did just this latter, thereby aiding and becoming party to the betrayal of China's struggle. The Bolsheviks under Lenin's leadership 'supported' Kerensky against the white Russian General Kornilov, while simultaneously preparing to overthrow Kerensky and establish workers' power. The Chinese Stalinists, however, accorded Chiang Kai-shek unconditional *political* support, thereby betraying the revolution and the national struggle which was indissolubly bound up with it.

Just as in 1925-1927, KMT-CCP unity meant the political subordination of the Communists to the KMT, so in 1937 it was directed against any signs of revolutionary activity. Wang Ming wrote:

> "The Chinese people ... will judge of the degree of determination and readiness of the KMT ... to undertake the armed struggle against the Japanese aggressors, by (the KMT's) attitude to Japanese agents and national traitors and, in particular, to the Japano-Trotskyist-fascist agents. The government and peoples of the U.S.S.R. are setting us an example of how to ... purge the state, military and party apparatus of these vipers."[47]

On 25 September 1937, the 8th Route Army ambushed and defeated two Japanese divisions at Pingxingguan in eastern Shanxi, a much needed victory in time of general defeat. Because of this and the supply of arms and munitions from the USSR, the Nationalist government agreed through 1938, 1939 and 1940, to provide the 8th Route Army with a cash subsidy (on the basis of a strength of 45,000) and a small supply of ammunition.[48]

However, the KMT was demonstrating not its ability to defend China, but its complete rottenness. The key battle to defend Wuhan and hold the Yangtse valley, began in June 1938 and ended at the end of October with the victory of the Imperial Japanese Army. This was the longest, largest and most significant battle of the Second Sino-Japanese War, and one of the largest battles in all of history. More than one million NRA troops under Chiang Kai-shek's personal command gathered to defend Wuhan. However, corruption was so rampant at the top of the NRA that Japanese General Iwane Matsui could boast to the New York Times correspondent that for $80,000 in silver dollars he had bought safe passage and landing for his troops. The key defences for Wuhan were the forts at Matow, which fell almost without a fight because the commander was in a brothel in a town several miles away. All supplies to treat wounded soldiers had been sold to privateers, and wounded Chinese soldiers were left to crawl as best they could – the Japanese army took no prisoners.[49] The loss of Wuhan was the loss of the most important transport hub of inland China, and the only remaining major military and economic centre.

As the war continued, units of the Red Army (8th Route Army) infiltrated behind the Japanese lines and advanced into the northern provinces of Hopei (Hebei), Chahar (Inner Mongolia), and Shanxi. The Japanese army usually sent no more than advance scouts into the villages, the sight of which caused the KMT troops to flee. The local villagers freed from KMT domination and not under direct Japanese control, spontaneously formed their own militias and elected underground administrations, which were nuclei of anti-imperialist resistance. When the 8th Route Army arrived it inherited these organisations. The militia units were soon co-ordinated and integrated into the anti-Japanese resistance. The local government organisations were also co-ordinated through the CCP but, given the general chaos that existed, retained a high degree of autonomy.[50]

By 1939 the CCP had set up six liberated zones in regions far from Japanese garrisons which tended to confine their activities to control over the economically important areas. Each zone extended over many thousands of square kilometres, with a total population of as many as 20 million. In January 1939, a conference of 500 delegates from these zones declared themselves the Shanxi-Hopei-Shantung-Honan Border Government. This became the pattern, wherever Communist forces won control they set up a border region government. Based on the three-thirds principle (see Section 8.5) representatives were elected by secret universal ballot, but the presence of the 8th Route Army was decisive in all important decision-making. The mass of peasants, observed the new government to be the first which had not acted against the people and welcomed its policies on rents and interest rates. They were ready to grant it their support.

To the delight of the poor and middle peasants, the lands and properties of those considered to be traitors were seized and shared out. In this way some 15% of agricultural land was redistributed. Rents were cut, eviction of tenants was prohibited, and a three-year moratorium imposed on all debts. The grain tax which had fallen most heavily on the poor peasants was reformed so that the richer the peasant the more he paid. Initially about one quarter of the poorest peasants were made exempt, but as the demands of the war increased so did the burden of the tax. The maximum legal interest rate was reduced to 10% annually. Payments were rigorously enforced, but there was a degree of laxity regarding the enforcement of rates which remained well above the 10% target. To prevent Japan from using the area's resources, wheat was grown instead of cotton and, after an initial dislocation this change had the beneficial effect of increasing the food supply. It was significant that, despite the land and tax reforms, numerous wealthy citizens (merchants and landlords) who had fled at the approach of the People's Red Army, now returned. Communist Party policy was, it appears, acceptable to them.[51]

Despite having a common enemy in the Imperial Japanese Army, tension was always present between the Communist and Nationalist forces. This grew with the relative success of the Communists in establishing extensive areas of control, initially within the limits set by the KMT but gradually extending outwards. As Chiang manoeuvred his armies to fight the Japanese, vast areas adjoining those controlled by the Communists were stripped of troops and the Red Army moved in, displaced KMT officials and established new local government bodies. In this way the Shen-Kan-Ning administrative area expanded considerably. The New 4th Army operated across Japanese lines in the provinces of Anhwei and Kiangsu outside areas previously agreed with the KMT and in close proximity to some of the most reactionary generals in the NRA.

In January 1940, the puppet government of Wang Jingwei was launched in Nanjing and simultaneously both the KMT and Japanese began to prioritise the cleaning up of their hinterlands.[52] In January 1941, Mao accepted Chiang's request to send 10,000 troops from the 4th Army across the Yangtse river. They were surrounded and attacked by more than 80,000 KMT troops. Some 5,000-6,000 Communist troops were killed or wounded compared to 20,000 on the Nationalist side. This was known as the Southern Anhwei Incident.[53] From this time onwards the Nationalists spent as much or more of their resources on attacking Communists as fighting the Japanese army. American Intelligence analysis made at the time claims that with the Japanese attack on Pearl Harbour (7 December 1941), the best of the Nationalist forces were re-allocated to blockade Communist areas because Chiang realised that the US and Britain could be left to defeat Japan.[54]

8.5 Women in Yenan

Shensi had been largely under warlord control so the CCP was bringing law and order for the first time, and this was widely welcomed. For local administration, Mao introduced his own variation of the bloc of four classes, dubbed the three-thirds:

> "The system whereby the Communists (representing the workers and the poor peasants), and progressive elements (representing the petty bourgeoisie), and the intermediate elements (representing the middle bourgeoisie and enlightened gentry) each contributed one-third of the leading personnel of the government administration, was introduced in all the Liberated Areas."[55]

CCP members were told to sincerely co-operate with, and genuinely listen to the views of, non-Communists.

From February 1937, Yenan was the seat of government of the Shensi-Gansu-Ningxia Border Region. In this Communist-controlled enclave, the CCP continued to work to win the support of the population by implementing programmes that would benefit the majority of people. However, the ways these were formulated and carried out were constrained by the move towards the Popular Front e.g. an end to radical land reform programmes. Particularly affected was the policy to raise the status of women.[56]

The Communists were under siege, and in the arid land of Shensi which provided little material comfort, the CCP depended for its survival on Party discipline and, more importantly, a community spirit that was the opposite of the corrupt, decadent and self-seeking KMT. The CCP was eager to show the world that Yenan was organised in accordance with a fair and just social ideal, a model society where everybody, regardless of position and power, worked for the common good. However, those in Yenan who had to battle with the harsh realities day to day saw a different picture, where uneven access to resources and privileges left many feeling disgruntled.

From its earliest days, the CCP paid particular attention to the problems of women because women were a vast reservoir of support for the Revolution as they were among those who could benefit most from it. Belden quotes from a school book he came across in the liberated area, headed *On women's equality:*

> "The old society is too dark; men and women are treated differently. The man goes to an office, the woman stays within the compound. The man wears new clothes, the woman dresses in rags. The man eats white flour, the woman, husks and chaff. The man can scold until heaven bursts, the woman seldom opens her mouth. The man reads books, the woman stands at the side of the cauldron. The man three times changes his temperament, the woman swallows into her stomach the words she has to say. In the (liberated areas), a great revolution has taken place. People are free, male and female have equal rights, men and women jointly apply themselves to production, and men and women together enjoy better times."[57]

Formally the administrative programmes of the Border Region ensured "that women enjoyed an equal position in society", including "equal pay for equal work" and "five weeks paid maternity leave."[58] With the drive for a Popular Front with the KMT, the Party re-assessed its goals and big changes took place in its policies.

The first and major shift was a change in emphasis, criticisms of traditional family values (the extreme subjugation of women in the family home) were downplayed and instead it was argued that women would reach equality simply by joining men in production. Of course, the CCP leadership presented their policy in Marxist terms. Great emphasis was placed on Frederick Engels' argument that: "The emancipation of woman will only be possible when woman can take part in production on a large social scale and domestic work no longer claims anything but an insignificant part of her time."[59] But this one sided, economic, approach relegated the importance of social elements such as equality in marriage and divorce. It also omitted the important consideration that the end result of all these efforts would be a liberal bourgeois, capitalist society in which women would remain second-class citizens.

The main concern of the leadership was maximising the war effort, and the emphasis in Party literature was for women to become spinners and weavers to produce their own clothing and clothing for the troops. This had a certain resonance locally in Shanxi where women tended to dominate in handicrafts, but it bowed to patriarchy by preserving the tradition that women remained at home and did not participate in agricultural work.

The responsibilities and goals of women's groups during the Popular Front were outlined in a pamphlet entitled *The Mass Movement of the Shanxi-Gansu-Ningxia Border Region* published in 1938. Party policy was that the movement to liberate women was secondary to building unity to resist Japan. Rather than risk upsetting their allies in the Popular Front, Party leaders called for the utmost caution when implementing any moves to emancipate women. Activities to eradicate traditional feudal practices (e.g. arranged marriages, foot-binding, and demanding protection of human rights) had previously been pushed with vigour but now these were put on the back burner and it was declared that male-female equality would be achieved by women voting in local elections, participating in production, and joining in defence work. Local cadres were to tell women that by contributing to the war effort, they could break away from the traditional system that had oppressed them for centuries. In principle this was correct, but little guidance or evidence was presented on how these activities would help achieve social equality within the foreseeable future.[60]

A similar response had occurred in the Soviet Union when the Stalin-Bukharin leadership of the Party had bowed to the conservative social demands of the kulak to restrict the rights of women. Take the question of divorce. The CCP cadres arrived in Yenan with the example of Jiangxi fresh in their minds, and women cadres actively promoted divorce as a means of breaking up the traditional family structure. The result was a significant improvement in the treatment of women, but at the expense of disruption of the traditional family unit which had a negative effect on the local economy. The CCP leadership, susceptible to pressure from the rich peasants and "patriotic" landlords, shifted its position to one of asking women to avoid drastic action and to try and find liberation within the family! *Liberation Daily*, the CCP's daily newspaper in the border region, now published articles arguing that the wife of even a violent and extremely abusive husband should stay with him and work to reform him rather than get a divorce.[61]

Women's associations were tasked to solidify the family unit by making them more harmonious; women were to achieve a sense of fulfilment from the knowledge that increased production contributed to Japan's defeat. Women comrades were instructed to form study groups within the associations to raise their cultural level and political understanding, a move meant to overcome the objections of members and bring them into line with the new policy.

The theme of the *Liberation Daily* articles was that women's liberation would be achieved if the women's movement participated in resistance work against the Japanese, but singularly failed to explain how. Nor were women given any direction on how they could obtain the skills and training needed to enter production on an equal basis with the men. In practice, in many cases, when women took more skilled positions they were of men called away, and the woman had to relinquish that position when the man returned. While women's associations still encouraged women to participate in village politics, their main emphasis changed to the co-ordination of child care and other efforts to increase production.

At the same time the conservatism of certain leading cadres could be seen in reports on party work where it was claimed that "promiscuous women" inspired "disgust" and "fear" in "ordinary peasants."[62] These were the women Mao had referred to (without prejudice) in his *Report on an Investigation into the Peasant Movement in Hunan* as having "triangular and multi-lateral relationships."[63] Conservative attitudes were gaining ground with the growth of the Popular Front.

In an attempt to head-off criticisms of the leadership, male comrades were taken to task for dominating their female partners and limiting their activities to household chores. However, the consequence of the political perspective of a democratic dictatorship meant that women's associations downplayed the importance of the fight for equality within the family. Equality was presented as one aspect of the liberation struggle, but one which could have the undesirable consequence of women blaming men not society for their plight.[64]

The extent to which Party officials sacrificed the cause of female emancipation to political and wartime objectives, can be seen in marriage reform. Traditionally the woman was effectively imprisoned in the family house with her labour supporting the status quo; thus the right of women to divorce ran counter to the interests of the middle peasants, an essential support for the Party. Faced with the KMT blockade and the increasing demands of the war with Japan, the Yenan government determined not to alienate peasants by disrupting the social system. The Party claimed there was no alternative but to subordinate radical reform of marriage to the immediate need to survive. Soon marriage reform was only a propaganda slogan.[65]

8.6 Yenan, the CCP and "Wild Lillies"

The bulk of the Kuomintang troops who surrendered to the Japanese became puppet troops. The CCP in its official history claims Chiang Kai-shek secretly ordered many of his troops to surrender to the Japanese invaders and then, under the command of the Japanese, to attack the 8th Route Army and New 4th Army. Because of Chiang's orders the Japanese were able to mobilise over 90% of those who surrendered.[66]

The KMT – as a result of the Southern Anhwei Incident – imposed a tight blockade on the entire area controlled by the CCP and withdrew its subsidies to the 8th Route Army (worth about 10 million silver dollars in 1940). In Yenan, prices of everything rocketed and there were substantial tax increases on all sections including the formerly-exempt poor peasants. October 1940 saw the Red Army launch a surprise attack on Japanese forces causing significant losses of Japanese troops. In response by January 1941, the Japanese army had concentrated nearly two-thirds of its forces on the Liberated Areas located behind Japanese lines, and a large-scale campaign was launched based on the policy of 'Burn-all, Kill-all and Loot-all'. The essence of this policy was to surround a given area, kill all young men, kill or steal all livestock, destroy everything possible, all the houses, furniture, farming implements and tools, so that the area would be uninhabitable for the foreseeable future.[67]

When rallying support in the face of these adversities and attempting to make the Border Region economically self-sufficient, the CCP found serious divisions opening up in the Party. There was conflict between the largely illiterate peasant layers recruited as a result of the land revolution (mild though it was), and who formed the great majority of the rank and file, and the more recent incomers who were invariably literate had joined the Party on the basis of its Popular Front and reformist policies, and formed the majority of the administrators. The taxes imposed on one group supported the other and the self-sufficiency campaign threatened to generate a division of potentially disastrous proportions. There was also grave concern about the quality of the cadres. Party membership had risen from 40,000 to nearly 800,000 between 1937 and 1940 but with the exception of the leading cadres and some intellectuals there had been virtually no education in Marxist-Leninist ideas (or any other kind of education or training).[68]

An added complication was that for the local population, Party membership had become a route to upward social movement. Selden has provided data which shows that in at least one area, over half those who joined the Party locally did so as poor peasants or landless labourers but within a year the majority had gained sufficient land to be classed as middle peasants: "Party members ... had been major beneficiaries in the land revolution."[69] This had a conservatising effect, promoting opposition within the CCP itself to the new higher taxes, a large part of which were spent in supporting the newcomers.

The answer was a Rectification Campaign that sought to educate Party members in the CCP version of Marxism, motivate them to adopt the radical measures necessary for self-sufficiency and to accept Party discipline. In 1941, the CCP began a series of training programmes to overcome the deficiencies in Party cadres that had appeared. Possibly in preparation for this campaign Mao, in early 1938, had made a study of the works of Stalin to determine which should be translated into Chinese.

The character of this initial Rectification Campaign can be seen from material which participants were expected to read, study and make notes on prior to discussing them: Stalin, *On Bolshevisation of the Party*; Stalin, *Problems of Organisational Leadership*; Dimitrov, *Cadre Policy and Cadre Education Policy*; a selection of Stalin's writings on Party Discipline, Party Democracy and Equalitarianism; the Conclusions from the *History of the Communist Party of the Soviet Union*.[70] To emphasise Mao's pre-eminence within the CCP six of his pamphlets were on the list to be studied.

Within the Party there was a group of intellectuals, writers and artists who were becoming increasingly dissatisfied and had come to believe the rich peasant elements within the Popular Front were putting a brake on social progress, particularly with respect to the liberation of women. This group coalesced around Ding Ling, the Party's most outspoken and free-thinking woman, and took the opportunity of the Rectification Campaign to publish material unmasking the CCP's hypocrisy by pointing out instances of inequality in Yenan.

Ding had toured the Border Regions as part of a propaganda group performing plays for the peasants and had been given the job of leading the development of women's organisations in Yenan, which put her at the focus of the contradictions between mobilising women but limiting their activities to those not deemed divisive. She edited the Literature Section of *Liberation Daily*, which appeared several times a week. Based on her wide experience of the actual life of peasant women and women within the Party, she wrote an article *Thoughts on 8 March, Womens' Day*, which appeared in the 9 March 1942 issue of the paper.[71]

The article only hinted at some issues (those seeking abortions risked punishment; some babies were wrapped in soft wool and looked after by governesses while others were wrapped in soiled cloth and left crying on their parents' beds), its main emphasis was to blame the Party for its contradictory attitude of promoting the role of wife and mother and then when the "woman's skin was wrinkled, her hair thin, and fatigue had robbed her of the last traces of attractiveness, she was blamed for her political backwardness" which was then used as a reason to get a divorce. The article was condemned as "narrowly feminist", Ding Ling was removed from her post on *Liberation Daily*, and she and others were successfully pressured to repent and disown their criticisms.[72]

Ding's accusation that Party leaders married at their convenience and divorced their wives when it suited them with little regard for the principles of equality, is supported by Hua Chang-Ming.[73] In a situation where men outnumbered women by as many as 18:1 this behaviour of the leaders must have seemed particularly reprehensible and a clear abuse of position. In Yenan the bureaucracy was increasingly becoming aware of itself and defence of the family as an institution took on the character of defence of a conservative element in society which would act as a prop for the Party elite. This was very similar to the defence of the family taking place in the Soviet Union at about this time. Zhou Enlai took the lead to emphasise the importance of motherhood, to argue that women had a "natural" pre-disposition to look after the welfare of the home within the context of family life.[74] He laid down ground rules that the Party would faithfully follow. Mao, in 1958, would return to this theme and claim that not only did Chinese society need the family but that the family needed a head.[75]

Ding Ling's article was the first of several that criticised the ruling Party elite. The most damaging came from Wang Shiwei (Wang Shih-wei), a young writer and translator who had been to study in Moscow in the late 1920s and early 1930s. He had associated with a Trotskyist group in Shanghai for which he translated a number of Trotsky's works. In 1936 he travelled to Yenan to become a research officer in the translation department of the Academy for Marxist-Leninist Studies. In this post he enjoyed privileges of cadre clothing and extra food, and was close to the Party elite.[76]

Wang was also employed on the *Liberation Daily* and specialised in the short essay (*zawen*), traditionally used in China to expose social ills and often used by Communist writers in political debates. Wang Shiwei was by no means the only one who spoke out against the CCP's leadership, but he was unique in that he refused to recant and remained unrepentant. His *Wild Lilies* which criticised the hierarchical structure and privileges of the Party bureaucracy appeared in two parts in the Literature section of the paper on 13 and 23 March 1942.[77]

The title *Wild Lilies* was itself a barb against Mao's taste for women, especially young actresses from Shanghai, which was common gossip. Mao had married one such actress, Lan Ping (Jiang Qing), in 1939. Ostensibly *Wild Lilies* is a story about 26 year old Li Fen a student comrade who was handed over to the authorities by her uncle because she was a Communist. "Before going to her death, she put on all her three sets of underclothes and sewed them tightly together at the top and the bottom. This was because the troops in Pao-ch'ing often incited riff-raff to debauch the corpses of young girl Communists they had shot." Li Fen is presented as a model of sexual reticence and self-sacrifice which stood in stark contradiction to the activities of the Party elite who were well known for their parties, dances and drinking, and which were a clear symbol of the social stratification that existed. Readers could well contrast the woman – Li Fen – to whom the article was dedicated, with Mao's taste for dramatic beauty. In case the lessons were missed, Wang wrote the articles in a parody of Mao Zedong's renowned colloquial style and salty peasant language.[78]

More importantly for the bureaucracy, was the criticism of the hierarchical system of ranks maintained by the Party, and justified by attacks on petty-bourgeois egalitarianism. Rank and file Communists had little or no money with which to buy food or clothes on the open market and so depended on the food and clothing allocated by the local Soviet administration. Wang made his often-quoted criticism of the five levels for food:

> "At present there is no noodle soup for sick comrades to eat and young students only get two meals of thin congee (a type of rice porridge) a day – when they're asked whether they have had enough to eat, Party members are expected to lead the rest in a chorus of 'Yes, we're full!'. What is more, relatively healthy 'big shots' get far more than they need or than is reasonable to eat and drink, with the result that their subordinates look upon them as a race apart."[79]

Wang also attacked the three levels of clothing whereby the higher the Party rank, the better the clothing provided.

The bureaucracy had been challenged where it was weakest, on its privileges. The CCP machinery swung into action and pressured Wang Shiwei to retract his criticisms. Wang refused, the CCP's initial attacks only made him more intransigent and popular amongst his supporters. Wang was put on trial for disrupting party unity, slandering party leaders, espousing Trotskyist ideas, and being a member of a group of subversive Trotskyists within the CCP. The trial took the form of a series of public struggle sessions in May and June of 1942, and on 10 June Wang was found guilty of absolute egalitarianism, being hostile to democratic centralism and Party discipline and hence, anti-Party.

The *Liberation Daily*, produced a day-by-day diary of the anti-Wang meetings including his public cross-examination. This diary was to act as a guide for future public meetings in CPC rectification campaigns. Its purpose was to popularise the Party's view and guide the readers to accept the leadership's rationale for the social differentiation that existed, and the predetermined verdict of the trial.

Mao and the Party leadership broadened the scope of the Rectification Campaign to include all critical writers; first in Mao's *Yenan Talks* in May 1942, and then in the campaign against Wang Shiwei. The Yenan Forum on Literature and Art was held in relative secrecy and was not reported in the *Liberation Daily*. Mao published his *Talks at the Yenan Forum on Literature and Art* about one year later.[80] His themes sound familiar – literature, especially, must serve the workers, peasants and soldiers, content should be Party-directed and form should suit the needs of the Chinese peasants and workers. All the Party's newspapers were re-organised to fit with the Party's rectification movement, i.e. no dissident writers allowed. Mao side-stepped the content of the criticisms and counter-attacked along true Stalinist lines: "There are a few people who speak from an incorrect standpoint, that is, the concept of absolute egalitarianism and the methods of covert attacks."

Mao was simply repeating in a Chinese context the arguments for proletarian (or socialist) art given a decade earlier in the Soviet Union.

Despite the propaganda, the arguments that sought to reduce literature to an expression of the immediate political and practical needs of the Chinese workers and peasants were, in reality, arguments to protect the interests of the bureaucracy. Since the bureaucracy equated its interests with those of the socialist revolution it interpreted any attack on itself as counter-revolutionary.

After Mao's Yenan talks, the Rectification Programme to "correct unorthodox tendencies" took on a much darker character and was extended and deepened to eradicate all independent criticism within the Party. The thought-reform movement which was carried out in Yenan during 1941-44 would become a well-established part of CCP cadre training. As with the Futian incident, to both stimulate and justify the excesses of the campaign, it was suddenly announced that as many as 10% of CCP members were KMT agents who had to be rooted out.

Benton has described Mao's intensive purging of the Party from 1942-1944 as the fourth Bolshevisation of the CCP, and has claimed that it was even more effective than when Stalin mastered the Comintern after 1924.[81] The 1942 Rectification Campaign did not use the term Bolshevisation largely because it sounded too foreign for a movement that was purporting to unite Marxism-Leninism with the concrete reality of the Chinese Revolution. The purpose was to root out and destroy all remaining leftist opposition to the leadership of the Party, especially those influenced by the Trotskyists who opposed the Popular Front. It also had the aim of extending the rule of the Mao group into the subsidiary bases established outside the main Shanxi base and to politically homogenise the new raw recruits.

What made this campaign uniquely sinister and effective was the extent it extended into the lives of ordinary Party members. In Yenan the same comrades tended to sleep and socialise in their work groups. One of the first instructions by the leadership was to limit contact between different groups to trusted Party cadres. These semi-isolated groups then became the basis for the campaign, which was managed so that the personal ties and links that had formed within a group became a weapon against the individual members. Group criticisms isolated individuals and subjected them to the rebukes and admonishments of all others present, which was intended to shake their self-confidence. These meetings, which could be daily and last for three or four hours, could result in demotion and additional work that placed the offender in a humiliating position. It is claimed that all members of the CCP had their activities reviewed and if sufficient ground were found (a chance remark, even cracking a joke), they were made to provide additional information on themselves and their life experiences sufficient for their peer group to subject them to extensive criticism.

Individuals who were believed to require thought reform were reported to a Party committee and the next step, if necessary, was one or more public struggle meetings where the individuals were publicly accused and humiliated before a large and usually jeering audience, allegedly representing the community. In Chinese society where great emphasis was, and is, placed on group esteem, these were powerful and effective methods of obtaining obedience to authority.

Mao did not exempt the top of the Party if he sensed any weaknesses. In the case of Peng De-huai (deputy commander of the 8th Route Army) who took equality and fraternity too seriously, these sessions are said to have lasted forty days, while for Zhou Enlai who had been too close to Wang Ming, five days was deemed enough.[82]

The combination of one's workmates, colleagues, comrades, friends, and companions exerted an almost irresistible pressure to conform. As the pressure increased and individuals found no escape from the denigration of their old selves, they were made to write and re-write confessions of their evil conduct, analysing the reasons why and asserting their desire to change. Pressure was often increased by a period in jail, possibly in solitary confinement but more likely in a cell with others. This prepared them for the final stages of recantation and reconciliation. When the confession was finally accepted and the Party welcomed them back into the fold, the accused naturally experienced a tremendous relief and elation and willingly accepted Party guidance. Whether this psychological experience did change personalities is less certain than the fact that it was a highly unpleasant experience to be avoided in future. One way or the other, the result was conformity to the Party line.[83]

The Rectification Campaign, which lasted from 1942 to 1944, was largely successful in eliminating the last vestiges of democracy, free speech and open criticism of the leadership within the CCP. How many were driven mad, to nervous breakdowns or to mental disorder will never be known but it is certainly in the thousands. Sad to say, the main way of protest was suicide, with some desperate individuals killing their families first.

During the upsurge of Maoism in the West, during the sixties and seventies it was often claimed that Mao had shown a qualitative difference from Stalin in that the rectification programme had not massacred dissidents but had re-educated them. This, it was argued even by certain leading Trotskyists, was a qualitative difference between Mao and Stalin.

The outcomes of the purges in the Soviet Union and of the Rectification Campaign in the CCP were the same: complete domination by the leader. Mao had shown in the Futian incident that he was prepared to kill thousands of Party members and Red Army troops to secure his position. In Yenan he used a different approach for many reasons, including:

- The CCP was part of a Popular Front and promoting unity. It would have been very difficult to launch a mass extermination campaign simultaneously.
- Stalin purged the Bolshevik Party, a party which had led a successful revolution and had a history of internal democracy. To ensure bureaucratic rule he had to remove all those whose activities extended back to 1917 and before. No such situation existed in China. The CCP had been thoroughly Stalinised by the time of the defeats of 1927, party membership did not pose the same threat to the leadership as in the USSR.
- Mao, unlike Stalin, was not yet in total control of the Party. Any moves to physically eliminate dissidents were likely to have been seen as a threat to his opponents (such as the 28 Bolsheviks) who would – to save their skins – have had to fight back, and they still held a large number of leadership positions within the Party.
- Stalin was seeking to eliminate any possible threat to the bureaucracy's hold on state power after a successful revolution. The CCP was still in the stage of making a revolution, Mao had time to achieve his domination of the Party by other means.
- By the time Mao launched the Rectification Campaign it was clear that the Great Purge in the USSR had resulted in widespread chaos in government departments, an atmosphere in which no-one would make a decision and there had been a sharp drop in recruitment to the Party. From Mao's viewpoint the Great Purge had been a wasteful and disruptive process. The Rectification Campaign could achieve the same goals much more efficiently and without the disruption.
- Unlike Stalin, Mao had played a leading role in the development of the CCP and PLA and could honestly lay claim to the leading

> position; to be accepted as Lenin's Lieutenant, Stalin had to imprison or kill those who knew the real history of 1917.

It was openly argued that in the Yenan period, Mao emphasised magnanimity towards his opponents. This was part of the so-called 'Yenan spirit'.[84] However, the scientific truism that the exception tests the rule, is applicable here. Acceptance of the Rectification Campaign in the West was because Mao appeared relatively benevolent to those whom he considered a political threat. Wang Shiwei spent five years in prison making matchboxes, and was allowed to meet a number of outside visitors to demonstrate the nobility of the CCP. In 1947, when Yenan once again came under KMT attack, the Communists were forced to quickly retreat. Wang Shiwei was summarily executed during the evacuation from Yenan. Sources differ, but all agree he was killed: either shot or hacked to pieces with an axe, most likely on the direct orders of Mao, confirmed by Kang Sheng, head of security of the Communist Party.[85] While Wang Shiwei was imprisoned and then murdered for revealing the layers of bureaucratic privileges that existed in Yenan, eminent socialists such as Isaac Deutscher could write that Mao "had lived all those years amongst the poorest peasants, … had allowed no differences in food rations and uniforms and no social estrangement between officers and men."[86]

At the start of 1942, as the Rectification Campaign swung into its stride, the CCP abandoned any attempt to mobilise women behind appeals to emancipation and gender equality. A meeting of senior cadres agreed that raising women's political consciousness was generally permitted but that cadres should ensure it took second place to economic mobilisation, because of both war needs and concerns about potential resentment from male peasants. For the next period the CCP would continue to emphasise women's participation in production as opposed to a wider general equality, and moved decisively to shore up the patriarchy of its civilian and military forces on the grounds that to make the border region self-sufficient required avoiding inter-social conflict.[87]

On 26 February 1943, the CC issued a statement apparently criticising itself for the lack of progress towards equality for women. In reality it was a re-orientation of Party work away from women's self-organisation, women-specific projects and slogans. These were now considered a waste of labour power and material resources. Now the Party emphasised "the need to overthrow feudalism gradually" and called on women to achieve liberation through "working harmoniously within the (patriarchal) family towards common economic goals." There followed a stream of articles in *Liberation Daily* explaining that work in production and the economic freedom it brought was the way for women to gradually liberate themselves from feudal discipline.[88] In fact, the CCP needed to revive the old handicrafts that had been destroyed by the influx of Western machine-made goods because these articles could no longer be obtained due to the KMT blockade. To supply the cloth for uniforms, weaving and spinning were re-introduced.

The drive to get women into production resulted in major successes such as the development of the textile industry, in which the Women's Federation took a leading role. The CCP used local technical knowledge to develop cotton and hemp production, based almost completely on women's labour and expertise. Much of the raw product was grown through women's work teams, with virtually all the spinning and further processing out-sourced to co-operatives of women working at home. The articles carried by *Liberation Daily* now focused almost exclusively on promoting such activities and praising the women involved for their contributions.

However, the Yenan women were too successful at organising themselves, and by 1945, lack of co-ordination and planning by the Party tops led to serious supply and distribution problems. Bureaucratic direction and lack of involvement of the women concerned in overall planning soon became apparent; there was no work plan to match production with need, there was little or no matching of training and personnel with equipment available, the places where cotton was grown were too far from where the spinning was done, the Party cadres had emphasised spinning so that a village could be without weaving facilities, and there were no plans on how to train women to effect repairs, etc.[89]

Goodman has pointed out that in words, the CCP formally remained committed to gender equality but this was not supported by practical activity. The previous encouragement for women to participate in politics now gradually disappeared whilst their mobilisation for production was highly praised. The emphasis on social issues was placed on the rights of the male. Despite constant pressure from the Women's Federation, the traditional practice whereby widows were forbidden to remarry was repeatedly upheld. It was only under the pressure of food shortages that this finally changed in 1944, resulting in the marriage of 300 bachelors and widows. However, the same logic – that a lower number of households should be generally encouraged because they required less food – had also led a year earlier to divorce being banned.[90] Of course occasionally, in some places, outstanding women did take the lead and create opportunities for genuine participation in social and political activities but these were exceptions to the general rule.

Despite the Popular Front, progress was made in women's liberation up to about 1945 particularly in taking women out of the home and into production because this required eliminating such feudal customs as foot-binding and the isolation of women. However, radical social measures could only be enacted if 'self-financing', so the Party developed a system, for example, whereby women suing for divorce, besides supporting themselves took on the additional burden of paying their husbands grain or money to compensate for the loss of a worker.[91]

8.7 Summary

The KMT united all reactionary influences, including the feudal remnants, to resist the masses and to suppress them. It was consequently unable to fulfill any of the bourgeois-democratic tasks, not even such a slight reform as a 25% reduction in rents. It was mainly characterised by consummate Asiatic despotism, corruption, and inefficiency. These characteristics were completely revealed during the 'War of Resistance'.

Following the twists and turns of Moscow and the ECCI, the CCP returned to the class-collaborationist policies that had ended in white counter-revolution and the massacres of tens of thousands of Communists and millions of peasants. The so-called United Front was revived and the political direction of the CCP was determined not by the needs of Chinese workers and peasants, but by Stalin. The political programme adopted by the CCP – in particular its land programme – was limited so as not to offend the KMT. This unity had other consequences such as undermining the gains made by women in society by backtracking on freedoms gained in marriage and divorce.

The CCP presented to the world the rose-tinted picture of a Yenan as a fair, just and equitable society where everybody worked for the common good and enjoyed a common standard of living. However, within the Soviet areas and within the Party, the bureaucracy was quietly acquiring for itself material and social privileges that set it apart from the rank and file. This behaviour was corrupting the party and many Shanxi peasants who joined did so in the hope of acquiring land and/or stock to rise from being a landless labourer or poor peasant to a middle peasant.

Mao, the major figure in the Party, was determined to silence criticism of the bureaucracy and, if necessary, was quite prepared to kill the individuals concerned. Within the Party, extreme methods were used in rectification campaigns to ensure unquestioning obedience by the mass of Party members. This approach to Party discipline and democracy was Stalinist through and through.

The CCP was a Stalinised organisation: it accepted the theories of socialism in one country and of stages, was part of the Stalinist International, and had the corresponding bureaucratic centralist party structure and norms. Party democracy was stifled and the cult of the individual promoted – first Stalin and then Mao. As would be expected, the general direction of the CCP programme was towards class-collaboration; occasionally in specific circumstances it would zig to the left to strengthen peasant support before zagging to the right and returning to its natural path: thus land expropriation and re-distribution policies varied with date and location.

The fable that Mao had fought against Stalin and put the interests of the Chinese before those of the Russian bureaucracy has been debunked by documents released in Moscow and Beijing. Before and during the Yenan period the ECCI and Moscow consistently promoted Mao's interests and finally in 1938 the General Secretary made it plain that Mao Zedong was his choice for leader of the CCP.

Chapter 9

The Final Collapse of the KMT: the CCP Assumes Power

9.1 Introduction

In 1934, as a coherent and co-ordinated force, well-funded, well-armed and supported by imperialist bombers, the Nationalist armies drove the Communists from the Jiangxi Soviet and hounded them to the border with Manchuria. The Japanese invasion of China in 1937 saved the Communist stronghold in Shensi from its own bandit extermination campaign and subsequently the People's Liberation Army (PLA) was able to extend its control to large areas behind Japanese lines. In purely military terms the PLA could not match the Nationalist armies, but in a civil war politics are decisive and here the PLA had key advantages.

During the Sino-Japanese War, the forces tearing Chinese society apart (famine and the peasant hunger for land), accelerated rapidly and riding on the crest of a wave of peasant rebellion, the PLA was able to destroy Chiang Kai-shek's armies. This occurred in the short period after WWII when "Bring the Troops Home" movements made it impossible for the imperialists to intervene directly in China. The CCP took the leadership of the Third Chinese Revolution, secured national independence and united mainland China.

Broadly speaking, Mao's thought boiled down to the strategy of peasant war for an extended period on a national scale, and the application in China of the theory of revolution by stages (whether expressed in adventurist or opportunistic terms). This class collaborationist approach was the ideological and political expression of Mao's Stalinism and showed itself in Mao's attempts to slow the disintegration and collapse of the Kuomintang regime with the offer of coalition government. This was a crime, not only against the Chinese masses and the Chinese revolution, but against the world proletariat and the world socialist revolution.[1]

9.2 Mao Becomes Supreme Leader

The Politburo meeting of March 1943 appointed Mao its Chairman, with the authority to single-handedly settle disputes. On 8 July 1943, the *Liberation Daily* used the phrase "Mao Zedong Thought" for the first time, after which it began to be widely used within the Party. By the end of the 1942-44 Rectification Campaign, "Long Live Chairman Mao" had become an acceptable slogan within the CCP. *Liberation Daily* began to carry headlines such as: "Comrade Mao Zedong is the Saviour of the Chinese People!".[2] All bureaucracies require a supreme leader to arbitrate between conflicting groups. Mao was on the point of achieving that position within the CCP.

Having completed the Rectification Campaign, Mao convened the 7th Party Congress in Yenan, from 23 April-11 June 1945. Germany had surrendered in May and it was certain that Japan would soon be defeated. Mao's ideas and theories would guide the Party on the major task of how to deal with KMT regime. Mao delivered the main report *On Coalition Government* and dominated all the sessions.

The CC meeting immediately prior to the Congress adopted a *Resolution on Certain Historical Questions* which re-wrote CCP history and elevated Mao to omniscience. The catastrophes suffered by the CCP prior to the Tsunyi Conference became a chain of deviations from Mao's correct line. Chen Duxiu was blamed for the defeat of the 1925-27 revolution; Ch'u Ch'iu-pai and Li Lisan were blamed for the defeats during the adventurist Third Period; Wang Ming was held responsible for the defeat of the Red Army in Jiangxi which made the Long March necessary. Stalin and the Comintern received no rebuke whatsoever.[3]

A new Party constitution was adopted at the Congress. This was proposed by Liu Shaoqi in a fawning report exalting Mao and naming Mao Zedong Thought as the ideological foundation of the CCP. The preamble of the constitution read "The CCP takes the theories of Marxism-Leninism and the combined principles derived from the practical experience of the Chinese revolution – Mao Zedong Thought – as the guiding principles of all its work."[4] By 1948 at the start of village and CCP meetings all those present would stand, face a portrait of Mao and bow their heads three times exactly as had been done with the emperors.[5] In the primary schools the children were taught to sing: "Mao Zedong is like the sun; He is brighter than the sun; Little brother, little sister; Everyone clap hands, come and sing."[6]

At the First Plenum of the Central Committee of the CCP following the 7th Congress, Mao was elected chairman of the CC, of the Politburo, and of the Secretariat. At the end of August 1945, he finally and formally concentrated all power in his hands when he was elected chairman of the newly reorganised Military Council of the Central Committee.[7] Stalin rose to leadership over the bodies of Lenin's Central Committee and the bureaucracy sustained itself only with a police state and by burying an entire generation of Bolsheviks. The major achievement of Stalin's policies was the rise to power of Hitler in Germany; no wonder then that free discussion and dissent were impermissible in the CC of the AUCP(B). This was not the situation for Mao. True he had been favoured by Stalin and the ECCI, but he had genuinely played a leading role in the activities of the CCP. This gave a very different character to CCP Politburo and CC meetings; there could be genuine discussion and dissenting opinions tolerated (within a Stalinist framework) – at least for a time.

We should note that over this period the CCP was making every attempt to show the political lines of Stalin and Mao as being essentially the same:

> "Comrade Mao Zedong's views on the nature and tactics of the Chinese revolution were based on the teachings of Stalin and were identical with the views of Stalin. ... Comrade Mao Zedong is Stalin's ... outstanding disciple and has been able to lead China's revolution to victory because his method of work and his way of reasoning are those of Stalin."[8]

Po-ta also quotes Mao on Stalin:

> "Stalin is the leader of world revolution. This is of paramount importance. It is a great event that mankind is blessed with Stalin. Since we have him, things can go well. As you all know, Marx is dead and so are Engels and Lenin. Had there been no Stalin, who would be there to give directions? But having him – this is really a blessing. Now there exist in the world a Soviet Union, a Communist Party and also a Stalin. Thus, the affairs of the world can go well."[9]

In the spring of 1950, Stalin sent Academician Pavel Yudin, Rector of the Institute of Red Professors, part of the Department for Agitation and Propaganda, to edit a new version of Mao's Selected Works to be published in Russian. Yudin was charged with checking the ideological content, and after two years in Beijing during which time he had a number of nocturnal meetings with Mao to thrash out doctrinal issues, he reported to a private meeting of the Russian Politburo: "They are Marxists, Comrade Stalin."[10]

Stalin died 5 March 1953, and in his funeral oration, Mao said: "All the writings of Comrade Stalin are immortal Marxist documents. His works,

The Foundations of Leninism, The History of the CPSU (Bolsheviks), and his last great work, *The Economic Problems of Socialism in the USSR,* are an encyclopaedia of Marxism-Leninism, the summation of the experience of the world Communist movement in the past hundred years."[11] The list embodies Stalin's betrayal of Leninism, his falsification of the history of the Bolshevik Party and the Theory of Socialism in One Country. It was these texts that CCP members, the cadres of every organisation (teachers, students, trade unionists, women's groups, etc.) were instructed to study as the ideological underpinnings of Mao's leadership.

9.3 Mao Attempts Compromise with Chiang

In July 1945, the Red Army was entrenched in the economically primitive Shanxi-Gansu-Ningxia Border Region covering thirty counties and eighteen large liberated zones primarily in the north-east and east of China. The total combined area was about the size of France with a population of tens of millions and a militia of nearly half a million. In Russia in 1917, the dual power took the form of Soviets of workers, peasants and soldiers on one side against the provisional government on the other. In China it would take the form of opposing armies. This situation was encouraged by the CCP because it gave them greater control of the revolutionary dynamic and enabled agrarian reform, for example, to be presented as a gift from above for which the peasants should be grateful and which maximised their political passivity.[12]

Stalin declared war on Japan on 9 August 1945, the same day the second atomic bomb was dropped on Nagasaki. The Soviet armies launched an offensive into Manchuria on a front extending over a thousand miles. In the space of a few weeks 700,000 Japanese troops surrendered, and the Soviet army occupied Manchuria, Inner Mongolia, and North Korea. With the removal of Japan as a military threat there was a short honeymoon period during which Stalin mistakenly believed he could peacefully co-exist with the imperialists who had been his war-time allies. Stalin urged Mao to meet Chiang Kai-shek, do a deal, and enter the KMT government as a junior partner.

Behind enemy lines in the liberated zones of north China, most of which the Japanese did not consider worth occupying, the Stalinist authorities – within the constraints imposed by the war and their class-collaborationist perspective – had considerably improved the lives of the peasants under their control. In these regions, the big landlords were prevented from expanding their holdings so the independent middle peasants remained predominant, and the poor peasants were able to maintain themselves.

The same was not true in KMT areas. Traditionally it had taken tax collectors generations to rob the peasants of their land and leave them so impoverished that they rose in rebellion. The degree of corruption of the KMT regime meant a race as local officials got as rich as they could before the regime collapsed totally. Taxes were heaped on the poorest peasants until in aggregate they were greater than the crop value. For the first time in Chinese history, land was left idle. In Honan province taxes were so high that the peasants not only lost all their grain, they lost their land, clothing, farming implements and had to sell their children as slaves, and their wives and daughters as servants and concubines. Belden claims that this phenomenon was observable as early as 1941 and contributed substantially to the great war time famines – as Belden put it: "They were taxed to death."[13]

Starvation in KMT areas was rampant, the peasants were being forced into conditions that were intolerable, conditions that had traditionally meant widespread rebellion; the great masses of peasants were making their own 'forcible entrance' onto the stage of history. The peasants flocked to a party which was actually fighting the hated KMT regime, stood for lower taxes and interest payments, offered order and democratic reforms and, in the liberated areas, ensured peasants were not starving.

In August 1945, Chiang under pressure from the Americans, invited Mao Zedong to Chongqing (Chungking, the KMT capital 1937-45) for peace negotiations. American imperialism had accepted that the CCP could not be eliminated using only military means and so long as civil war raged in China it was difficult, if not impossible, for it to cash in on the victory over Japan. A country torn by armed strife is hardly a safe field for profitable investment. Nor, under such circumstances, could it proceed with its plans for converting China into a base for military operations against the Soviet Union. Thus the United States urged Chiang Kai-shek to compromise with the CCP, democratise his regime, and broaden the base of the Nationalist government.[14] The US ambassador to China, Patrick J Hurley, visited Mao in Yenan and was successful in persuading him to meet Chiang in Chongqing on 28 August and to order the 8th Route Army to halt its progress in the liberated areas.

Stalin was delivering on his promises made at Yalta and elsewhere to US and British imperialism, and on 14 August 1945, the Soviet Union signed a Sino-Soviet Treaty of Friendship and Alliance with Chiang, so that when the hand-over of Manchuria took place it was KMT forces that moved into the cities. However, the situation internationally was changing and from October

1945 the Red Army began quietly supplying the PLA with munitions seized from the Japanese, the first signs of the cold war were emerging and Stalin wanted to keep all his options open.[15]

Negotiations with Chiang lasted forty-three days. On 10 October 1945, an agreement between the KMT and CCP announced that it accepted Chiang as leader of China and on 30 January 1946 a truce was formally signed between the KMT and CCP. During the negotiations, US marines occupied key railroads and the two main cities in northern China, Tianjin and Beijing, holding them while Chiang organised his armies.[16] In keeping with the alleged end of class war, the 8th Route Army and the New 4th Army were merged and renamed the People's Liberation Army.

With Japan's surrender, Chiang Kai-shek (with American approval) ordered the 400,000 Japanese puppet troops to remain at their posts and to act as his garrison until Nationalist troops arrived. During the negotiations at Chongqing the US transported to north China three Kuomintang armies of half a million troops. In accord with the CCP agreement to recognise Chiang's regime as the official government, the PLA halted its attacks on the cities and industrial complexes. However the PLA retained control of the countryside.[17]

From September 1945 to the end of 1946, there was a considerable revival and growth of the mass movement in China. The students and working masses in the great cities, particularly Shanghai, protested against civil war and called for a coalition government including the Communists. Workers demanded the right to organise trade unions and there were more than 2,000 strikes in Shanghai alone over this period. These struggles were limited to democratic and economic demands and did not reach a nationwide level, but did show that the masses were confident enough to raise their heads and fight to improve their living conditions. The CCP made no attempt to link the factory workers' struggles to either those of the peasants or the students, nor to transform the strikes into political struggles. Instead it attempted – as it had done so many times before – to persuade the working masses not to go to extremes, and not to hinder the united front with the national bourgeoisie; and it worked closely with the leaders of the yellow trade unions to check 'excessive' demands.[18]

In the liberated areas, those peasant militias least controlled by the CCP were carrying through their own land grab, killing landlords, expelling rich peasants and sharing out the seized lands at village meetings. Initially, many lower rank CCP cadres were carried along by these initiatives and in some areas there was a significant transfer of land to the poor and middle peasants.

The PLA was instructed to step in and to contain this upsurge within the official policy of "double reduction" of rent and debt. Nevertheless, many poor peasants accrued sufficient land to feed their families and so graduated to being middle peasants with the added bonus that their debts and rent repayments were either greatly reduced or abolished.[19]

During the negotiations in Chongqing, the CCP and the Kuomintang convened a Political Consultative Conference to determine the basic organisation of a new government. The conference began on 10 January 1946 and was attended by representatives of the KMT, the CCP and – as window dressing – the Democratic League (which would be banned on 13 October 1947), the Youth Party, and notable public figures. A military truce was declared on the first day of the conference in the names of Generalissimo Chiang Kai-shek and Chairman Mao Zedong. The major documents agreed at the conference were the *Resolution on Government Organization* and the *Resolution on Military Problems*.

It was widely expected that the military question would be the make-or-break issue because the CCP was at the conference only because of the existence and strength of the PLA. However, in 1946 Chiang was confident of victory on the battlefield and this mis-assessment led to his intransigence on every question. Even the composition of the 40-strong State Council (the supreme organ of the Government) became an irreconcilable difference.[20]

The State Council was to decide matters by a simple majority vote, except in those cases where the decision involved changes in administrative policy when a two-thirds vote of the State Councillors was required. Chiang quite deliberately provoked the Communists by destroying the effectiveness of this safety measure. Against the advice of the American ambassador he demanded the CCP be restricted to only 13 delegates, one short of being able to exercise a veto. Simultaneously, he demanded the CCP immediately withdraw the PLA to designated areas and begin decommissioning.

Mao drew back from political suicide but otherwise did everything to maintain the agreement – even appealing to US imperialism to intervene on his behalf (which it did!) – but the Generalissimo insisted on unconditional surrender. As the Sino-Japanese war had progressed the KMT had retreated inland and had been cut off from the industrial centres with the result that the specific weight of the conservative and backward sections of the big landlords increased substantially.

The big landlords were convinced that the freedoms enjoyed by the peasants in the Communist-occupied regions would spark widespread peasant uprisings and seizure of the land. To avoid this catastrophe, the rapid re-conquest of these regions was needed. These landlords were Chiang's strongest support in his military adventure against the CCP. They urged immediate action while the balance of military forces appeared favourable to the KMT.[21]

To convince the KMT it was prepared to make real concessions to be accepted into a coalition, the CCP issued a decree on 4 May 1946 permitting landlords to own 50% more acreage than middle peasants, and 100% more if they had been active in the war against Japan. Any 'excess' land was to be *purchased*; sold to peasants with the funds to buy it. Reductions in rent and interest were presented as "solving the land problem."[22] This policy did not reflect the wishes of the peasant masses; what they wanted was agrarian revolution.

Middle and poor peasants, and land labourers comprised over 90% of the peasant population, and events in the liberated areas had shown they were prepared for revolutionary seizure of the land.[23] If the CCP had called on the peasants to seize the land and merged that with the demands of the urban workers, the Chiang Kai-shek government would have collapsed like the house of cards that it was. Such a call would have transformed the pre-revolutionary situation that existed into insurrection and power could have been taken in the most propitious way for the Chinese people. But that was not Mao's goal.

All parties to the Chongqing conference agreed that an independent PLA controlled by the CCP was quite impossible within a unified bourgeois democratic China. Thus the *Resolution on Military Problems* laid down the fundamental principle: "Separation of army and party. .... All political parties shall be forbidden to carry on party activities, whether open or secret, in the army." The *Resolution* also covered practical methods for creating a new army for the new democratic Republic of China.

Washington made strenuous efforts to effect this compromise between the KMT and the Stalinists because the alternative was massive intervention by its own armed forces, taking over the Chinese government and overseeing its economic, military and governmental affairs. This was excluded. The "Bring the Boys Home" campaign within the US armed forces and public opinion at home made large-scale intervention impossible.[24]

9.4 Chiang Breaks off Negotiations

To work out how to implement the *Resolution on Military Problems*, a three-person committee was convened, consisting of General Chan Chih Chun

(National Government), Zhou Enlai (CCP), and US General George C Marshall, (chairman and 'advisor'). Only unanimous decisions were to be implemented. Naturally, the Committee was paralysed. Nationalist forces were moving into the towns, major industrial complexes, and communication routes in Manchuria, while PLA units were extending the liberated areas as fast as they could. Clashes were inevitable. In June 1946, the Generalissimo unilaterally called a 15-day halt to activities in Manchuria and demanded that the PLA withdraw within that period or suffer the consequences. The ultimatum was condemned by the CCP as a violation of the January agreement. At this, on 30 June, Chiang launched a general offensive against the PLA.[25] The disparity in weaponry and troop numbers meant that initially the Nationalist forces scored important victories, forcing the PLA to retreat, leaving the Nationalist armies in control of all the major and strategically important towns and the railway lines

Up to this point no-one has suggested differences in policy between Mao and Stalin. Mao had faithfully adhered to Stalin's post-war Popular Front coalition strategy. However, in China there was now a resumption of hostilities between the Nationalists and Communists which was leading to full-scale civil war. It was this escalation which led many to believe there was a break between Mao and Stalin on the grounds that Stalin still wanted a coalition government in China.

But it was just at this time that Winston Churchill announced the cold war in his 'Iron Curtain' speech on 5 March 1946. This had given Chiang the confidence to harden his position, convinced Washington would bail him out. On 15 November 1946, Chiang convened a hand-picked National Assembly and the CCP was excluded. From now on, the question of governmental authority (let alone state power) would be resolved by force of arms. Still enmeshed in the theory of stages, the CCP now pressed for a coalition government of liberals, democrats, independent groups and organisations, and 'social luminaries' but without Chiang Kai-shek and KMT reactionaries (shades of Wuhan!).

There were strong similarities to the trajectory followed by Stalin in Eastern Europe. Stalin had initially declared that the USSR intended only to replace fascist collaborators by governments friendly to the USSR; there was no intention of altering the social system of these countries. They were to be bourgeois democracies in which the Communist Parties would play an important but not decisive role, and there was no question of the dictatorship of the proletariat as the state form.[26] Of course, in Eastern Europe the factor determining the course of events was the presence of the Red Army, but the political direction pursued by Stalin and Mao was parallel.

Meanwhile, the cold war continued to escalate, and rather quickly. On 12 March 1947, Truman laid down the Truman Doctrine: Washington would defend the 'Free World' against Communist aggression. It seemed that once again war against the Soviet Union was high on imperialism's agenda. The coalition governments in Eastern Europe artificially imposed by the Soviet Army were unceremoniously thrown into the dustbin and replaced by People's Democracies in which the leading and decisive role was given to the national Communist Parties loyal and subservient to Stalin. Soon Eastern Europe would become a buffer zone protecting the Soviet Union, and with a matching economic system.

A Nationalist or even a coalition regime in which the CCP was stripped of the PLA, would have meant China becoming a puppet of American imperialism, placing US air and naval bases at Stalin's back door. Stalin had launched the Second United (Popular) Front between the CCP and KMT to protect the Soviet regime from a war on two fronts. Now, precisely the same considerations pushed him in exactly the opposite direction. The Soviet Union needed an ally on its eastern frontier and the only real chance of getting one was for the PLA to win the civil war. Stalin had no reason from either a political or military viewpoint, to break with Mao; instead the Soviet Army rushed to assist the PLA in its preparations for a counter-offensive.[27]

Initially, the Nationalists had an estimated five-to-one advantage in troops and a virtual monopoly of heavy equipment, transport, and air power. The PLA, on the other hand, enjoyed the advantage of already holding liberated zones not only across the crucially important area of Manchuria but also across much of China that had been behind Japanese lines and was now in the rear of the Nationalist armies.[28]

The total amount of American aid given to the KMT was considerable. It is a flagrant lie when reactionary circles in the United States and the world try to explain the victory of Mao Zedong by the insufficient support Washington gave Chiang. After the end of the war against Japan, strictly *military aid*, besides numerous American advisors in China and the transport of soldiers and materiel in American ships and planes, amounted to nearly US$30 billion in today's money. Additional economic aid amounted to a further US$30 billion. In fact, no amount of US dollars paid to Chiang Kai-shek would have held back the mounting flood of the Third Chinese Revolution.[29]

The Nationalist army swept westwards and reached the peak of its military successes when it seized Yenan in March 1947. The greater number and fire power of the Nationalists pushed the PLA back to the Russian/Manchurian border where Stalin gave it sanctuary and allowed it to recuperate, re-arm, and re-train. Despite the Soviet bureaucracy's desire for a compromise with American imperialism on a world scale; in its own immediate interests it had to offer help to Mao. The Soviet Army provided the PLA with huge amounts of light and heavy weapons taken from the Japanese army and supplied numerous Soviet technicians and advisors. Modernised, well-armed, well led, well-motivated and determined, the PLA soon occupied villages, smaller cities and towns and laid siege to the great cities where Chiang's huge armies with the best American equipment were stationed.

Despite the massive US aid, the war was turning against the Nationalists. The PLA used the same tactics as during the bandit extermination campaigns – cutting communications and destroying bodies of troops – but now it was advancing on the cities. Defending the cities of Manchuria fragmented Chiang's armies and finally they would become death-traps.[30]

The peasant armies under CCP leadership differed greatly from any former peasant armies. Here was a force systematically organised and trained, equipped with modern techniques, endowed with a national and up-to-date programme of democratic reform even though of an opportunist nature. In the face of the KMT armies the CCP needed the active support of the peasants and so carried through its reformist programme of rent and interest rate reductions and cancellation of debts in a much more vigorous manner. However, to remain within the limits of the New Democracy no revolutionary land seizures were called for even in CCP-controlled areas such as the provinces of Jiangsu, Hopeh, and Hunan.[31]

Nationalist morale was rapidly ebbing away. The military structure was demoralised and permeated from top to bottom by a general feeling of helplessness. The Communist forces they were facing now had weapons as good as their own, a better sense of solidarity and a fighting spirit. Nationalist soldiers were isolated and besieged with little hope of reinforcements, their generals had gained their positions through being cronies of Chiang not ability, their officers abused the soldiers under their command, were openly corrupt and using the war to enrich themselves, and they faced a hostile population.[32]

9.5 CCP Land Policy: 1945-49

During the initial period of the Jiangxi Soviet, the CCP enacted its most radical land programmes when it began seizing the land of the landlords and rich peasants and distributing it to the middle and poor peasants. But maximising food production in an isolated community imposed limits on seizure and redivision of the land, and the lands of the rich peasants were soon protected.

In Yenan between 1937 and 1945, for the sake of the Anti-Japanese United Front with Chiang Kai-shek, the Stalinists renounced the revolutionary content in their agrarian programme and proclaimed themselves defenders of private property both in land and in industry. They declared their opposition to the expropriation of landlords (save those that had collaborated with the Japanese) and limited the peasant struggle to the reformist demands of lower rents (reduced by 25% but to be no more than 37.5% of the crop) and lower interest rates (less than 15% annually).[33] These reforms were important and their implementation greatly improved the lives of the peasantry, saving many from starvation, but the Stalinists did not use them as a means to build a revolutionary movement, rather to put a brake on it.[34]

After Japan's surrender, cadres in the liberated areas found it difficult to square Party policy with the demands of the peasants who wanted revolutionary seizure of the land. In many villages where the 8th Route Army had only a notional presence, even the rich peasants rose spontaneously against the landlords and those who had collaborated with the Japanese. The peasants demanded a settlement of scores and in many cases this meant killing the landlords, but it always meant seizing their land.[35] So fierce was this movement that CCP cadres hid as peasants settled accounts and took revenge. Where they could, the landlords fought back, relying on thousand-year-old traditions and strong arm tactics. Some succeeded in forcing the peasants to momentarily take a step back, but new peasant leaders invariably stepped up to replace those who had been murdered, and led the masses forward.

With the breakdown of the truce and the advance of the Nationalist army during 1946-47, the CCP re-appraised and radicalised its agrarian programme, and acknowledged that the peasants were not satisfied with the reformist People's Front policy. Under attack from KMT armies and pressured by the peasants, the CCP effected a left turn in its agrarian policy. During late 1946 a great show would be made of bringing landlords and rich peasants who had collaborated with the Japanese before village meetings where they would be judged, and if found guilty their lands seized and divided.[36] The CCP put on a radical face by seizing landlords' "excess" land, holdings more than twice that of a middle peasant. Hinton has described in some detail how in individual villages, inexperienced cadre could be swept along by the general mood and take measures popular with the peasants – all landlords would have all their lands re-distributed. But official CCP policy still stopped well short of general land reform and these actions would later be condemned by the CCP leadership as "extreme leftism."[37]

The CCP was on the horns of a dilemma, Mao had to explain why the Party had to balance between opposing forces and how to control dissent. Reforms were needed to arouse enthusiasm for the war effort which was good, but cadres had to ensure that the enthusiasm did not spill over into land expropriation, which was bad. To avoid this, the reforms must be modest: "this is not the time for a thorough agrarian revolution ... our present policy should stipulate that the landlords shall reduce rent and interest, for this serves to arouse enthusiasm of the basic peasant masses ..., but the reductions should not be too great."[38] The hope of a Popular Front alliance with the KMT was more important to Mao than the demands of the peasant masses for land.

"Land to the Tiller" and the expropriation of pre-capitalist landholders has been the core demand of bourgeois revolutions, beginning with the French Revolution of 1789. In China, official CCP policy was that the distributed land was personal property with title deeds supplied by the government and its re-sale was permitted. Thus, the seizure and distribution of land was not the end of class divisions in the countryside, merely a new starting point. Richer peasants were allowed to buy land confiscated from the landowners, and hence take the first step to being a landlord, perpetuating the very practices that were supposedly being abolished.

The measures deliberately provided landlords with ways to evade the worst effects of land reform. For example, Mao insisted that the rich peasants and landlords who co-operated (i.e. by donating the least fertile part of their lands to the peasants' association as a token of co-operation) should be treated leniently, could retain their moveable property, and should be left enough land to cultivate with family labour (just the policy which caused the Futian incident). The families of communist soldiers and cadres were allowed to retain 50-100% more land than the standard holding. This meant in practice that many landlords could retain most, if not all, their best land by sending one son to serve in the PLA. As land reform progressed it became increasingly clear that the most needy were benefitting least.[39]

In April 1947, Liu Shaoqi carried out a survey and found that in the Chin-Sui Border Region after two years of land reform, re-distribution had been fully satisfactory in only 200 of 1,500 villages. Many poor peasants remained without land. As part of its Popular Front policies the CCP had encouraged rich peasants in the rural base areas to join the Party, and Liu concluded that landlord and rich peasant elements had infiltrated into village Party branches, peasants' associations, and local militias, and had successfully limited the land reform measures.[40] This was due not only to the limited nature of the land expropriations but also because many of those in authority, having acquired the best land and larger areas of land for themselves by underhand and/or dishonest methods, had little interest in continuing the process.

The CCP attempted to solve the problem with a 'Wash Your Face' campaign, the major aims being for higher cadres to persuade local cadres to give up some or all of their illicit gains, to restore party discipline and correct the errant behaviour of hooligan elements within the Party and militias.

In northern China the fluid nature of the fighting first against the Japanese army and then against the KMT and the *ming tuan*, meant that despite any official truces, a guerrilla war continued unabated with local militias the first line of defence of many villages. In the first stage of liberation there was a justified gratitude towards the militias which expressed itself, for example, as the provision of free meals. Unfortunately, given the political level of the militias and the Stalinist nature of many of these groups, in numerous villages this became the start of a creeping corruption.

One of the first tasks of the militiamen was to question landlords to identify who were KMT personnel and *agents-provocateurs*. The nature of the relationship between landlord and peasant, its intimacy, its casual cruelty and violence meant that the questioning sessions had a revenge element and often degenerated into beating the suspects, many of whom died as a result. Many landlords and their sons fled leaving their wives and daughters. Very rapidly rape became common practice. Soon it was being used against middle and poor peasant families who raised objections or awkward questions. All too often the militia moved from being a scourge of the gentry to being a scourge of the peasants. Too often the militia commanders were CCP members who closed their eyes to what was going on. Hinton explained that the Wash Your Face Campaign was an attempt to clear out these local despots.

As part of the campaign the conduct of all CCP cadres was to be reviewed at village meetings where the peasants were allowed to raise what criticisms they wanted with the promise that those cadres whose behaviour was unacceptable would be ejected from the Party. Initially, the process appeared to be working well and many cadres were suspended from the CCP, some even being held in jail. However, the criticisms of the CCP rapidly escalated to an extent that the leadership hurriedly intervened to bring the process to an end.[41] Simultaneously, the CCP understood it would soon be the national government and feared the Wash Your Face Campaign could undermine Party cohesion and discipline. Soon, most of the cadres who had been criticised and even those jailed were re-integrated into the Party. The first part of the Wash Your Face campaign was widely trumpeted to further establish Mao's populist credentials, the final outcome kept quiet.

On 10 October 1947, soon after the Nationalists had seized Yenan and in a move to the Left to firm up its peasant support, the CCP adopted the *Outline Land Law*. This law was to be uniformly and rigorously enforced in those areas controlled by the PLA. This law formally sanctioned "Land to the Tiller" (Article 1), and provided for expropriation of landlords' and rich peasants' properties without compensation (Article 3). However, sequestered land was to be distributed so that each person in the village would own an equivalent area. It was intended that poor peasants would benefit, middle peasants would remain much the same but rich peasants and landlords would lose. Importantly the Land Law cancelled **all** prior debts (Article 4), but expressly permitted the unhindered transfer of money to invest in commercial or industrial enterprises (Article 12).[42]

Landlords and their family members would each receive an equal share, KMT soldiers would receive an equal share, even the family members of collaborators.[43] Party cadres in the village peasants' associations were empowered and entrusted to implement the agrarian reform. They did this mainly though *ad hoc* "people's tribunals" which were meetings of the entire village (Article 13).

Stalinism is an inherently corrupt system based on privilege, so the new land reform programme was often distorted to the benefit of Party members just as the previous land reforms had been. The many Party members from landowning families who had penetrated the ranks of the Party over the past decade were now joined by cadres who had become middle or even rich peasants. The *Open Letter to the Members of the Party*, published in January 1948 by the Central Committee of the Shansi-Shantung-Hunan region, described the situation: "...a section of the party membership ... is composed of landowners and rich peasants who are protecting the property of their families and relatives" and in some areas "these elements occupy most of the positions in our party ... (our) agrarian reform ... policy appears to reflect the views of the landowners and the rich peasants."[44]

During the war with Japan, outside of the CCP-controlled areas, concentration of land ownership advanced at a greatly accelerated rate. At the start of the war the Chinese village was already facing destitution; within KMT areas it emerged from the war completely ruined. Small, middle and even some rich peasants had to borrow to feed their families and as a result were largely bankrupted. Huge tracts of land fell into the hands of the big landlords, village usurers, officers of the Nationalist army, and local KMT officials, all of whom had close ties with the banking capitalists.[45]

At the end of the war with Japan, land ownership took a new and dramatic turn. The leading circles of the murderous and foully corrupt Kuomintang government were determined to enrich themselves no matter what the social cost. Using state-owned companies the government began to nationalise the land of collaborators in territories previously occupied by Japan, dispossessing large numbers of peasants and creating a new layer of speculators and parasitic owners. The breakdown of civil society due to the complete disorganisation of the KMT regime was completed by the severe drought of the summer of 1945. Villages in KMT areas were virtually depopulated as millions of peasants died of hunger. The situation was rapidly escalating towards the classic conditions for widespread peasant rebellion.

As the Nationalist armies collapsed it became clear that the CCP would soon form a government. The blueprint for the economy was to be Mao's *New Democracy* which meant the nationalisation of only:

> "the big banks and the big industrial and commercial enterprises ... the republic will neither confiscate capitalist private property in general nor forbid the development of such capitalist production as does not 'dominate the livelihood of the people'.... A rich peasant economy will be allowed in the rural areas. Such is the policy of 'equalisation of land ownership'."[46]

The official Party line was further elaborated in a speech by Jen Pi-shih on 12 January 1948 opposing hostile treatment of landlords because it might "adversely affect the productive labour force in the countryside."[47]

With governmental power near at hand, the party leadership swung hard to the Right. Only three months after the introduction of the *Outline Land Law,* Jen Pi-shih demanded an end to land re-distribution until the peasants had been properly educated. Six days later, Mao himself weighed in against "left excesses", urging that "newly rich peasants" in the liberated areas should be treated as "middle peasants", that former landlords and rich peasants could be reclassified as middle or poor peasants, that no one should pursue landlords into the towns, that poor peasant associations should be compelled to admit rich peasants, landlords and the enlightened gentry:

> "there has been an erroneous emphasis on 'doing everything as the masses want it done' ... one-sidedly propagating a poor peasant-farm labourer line ... the democratic government should listen (to) the middle peasants, the independent craftsmen, the national bourgeoisie and the intellectuals."[48]

This change in line was ideologically driven. The combined strength of the PLA, over 90% of the peasants, students and workers was more than sufficient to take power against KMT forces that were dissolving. But the CCP had the perspective of revolution by stages and this schema was now artificially imposed on the actual revolution.

The turn in land policy required local cadre conferences to explain the new line. There was great confusion in the ranks of the Party and a substantial degree of hostility. To sweeten the pill the leadership instructed that henceforth the families of cadres would receive the same support as those of soldiers fighting at the front. Cadres would now be released from a substantial burden and freed to concentrate on Party work. Those who had been found to have stolen goods during the land re-distribution would face no charges if they returned the goods. Those cadres still being held in jail on, e.g. rape charges, would be freed on making an apology.[49]

As the PLA moved into the southern provinces, the limitations of the new policy conflicted with the wishes of the peasants. The most serious problems were in Hunan where, before Party cadres could intervene to stop them, the peasants' associations expropriated the landlords' lands and the people's tribunals handed down death penalties. Here class war was labelled a "left deviation" and Communist leaders called for moderation, but seizure and redistribution of land and harsh treatment of the landlords and rich peasants continued in many liberated areas.[50]

In the spring of 1948, Mao insisted that in the areas which had newly come under PLA control there was no urgency in introducing agrarian reforms which should, in any case, be carried through only on condition that the "Party cadres were adequate both in numbers and quality to grasp the work of land reform and must not leave it to the spontaneous activity of the masses."[51] On 24 August 1948, the *New China News Agency* officially announced that the existing agrarian reform programme was ending and from then on the peasants would have to be satisfied with a reduction of rent, taxes and interest to usurers (Chao Kuo-chun, Op. cit.). The cut back in land reform derived directly from the class collaborationist approach of *New Democracy*.

Officially, policy returned to reducing rents and interest rates and the Stalinists showed the other side of their political face. As in Yenan, rents and interest rates were reduced so as not to exceed 37.5% of the crop and less than 15% respectively, but now the CCP and PLA enforced payment to the landlords and village usurers. By these means, the Communists attempted to prove to the landlords and capitalists that they were better and more efficient defenders of private property than the KMT, in the hope this would enable an alliance with the 'national' section of the bourgeoisie.[52]

9.6 The PLA Cruises to Victory

The most effective weapon in the hands of the CCP was propaganda with the most decisive element its land policy. It shattered the apparent inertia of the peasants by linking their aspirations to a means of achieving them. The promise of land reform brought the hitherto crushed masses into open revolt against the KMT regime.

By 1948, Chiang Kai-shek and the KMT were maintaining themselves in power by bribery and terror. The KMT was controlled by a clique so utterly corrupt that ministers lined their pockets by selling war materials supplied by the United States to the PLA.[53] Mayors of villages responsible for sending young recruits to the army organised a system whereby families able to pay an exorbitant fee could keep their sons at home. The missing soldiers were listed in the regimental books so that the officers could put their pay in their own pockets. The result was that many armed formations had no more than 60% of their listed strength.[54]

The PLA successfully transformed guerrilla warfare into positional warfare in a very short time. In the autumn of 1948, the PLA launched an all-out counter-offensive. In Manchuria, the big cities, one after another, were occupied without a fight as a result of the capitulation or disintegration of Chiang's armies. The key battle was for Mukden (Shenyang, largest city in Manchuria). Its defenders, five well-equipped and well-trained armies, took their weapons and equipment and defected to the Communists. The city was occupied by the PLA on 1 November 1948.[55]

Thereafter, Communist victories tumbled one upon another. By the end of 1948 the PLA had captured all the cities of Manchuria including the capital, Changchun, and the big mining districts of Anshan and Fuhsun, where the

Japanese had built a miniature Pittsburgh which, at its height, had mined 20,000 tons of coal a day. The Communist occupation of Manchuria was a mortal blow to Chiang's government, giving the CCP a solid economic base bordering the Soviet Union and from which they would be almost impossible to dislodge.[56]

The advance of the PLA had a sympathetic resonance amongst the workers and the students, and gave them the confidence to challenge the KMT. There was a new wave of strikes, e.g. in Shanghai, protesting the banning of the sliding wage scale. The students played a notable role, representing the petty-bourgeoisie in general. Large-scale protests and demonstrations took place in the big cities: Chongqing, Nanjing, Shanghai, Canton, Beijing, etc. The slogans demanded democracy and peace, against KMT dictatorship, and against the persecutions conducted by the KMT. The CCP played a divisive role, keeping the workers and students as far apart as possible and using both separately to exert pressure on the KMT to accept peace talks. If the CCP had been responsive to mass pressure, it would have called on the workers and the masses in the big cities to join with the peasantry and students and rise in rebellion to overthrow the regime, it would have been as easy as knocking down rotten wood. But Mao called on the people to wait quietly for their liberation by the PLA.[57] His objective was to restrict the struggle as much as possible to the military plane and he was largely successful. The deliberate discouragement of workers' struggles and the rapid advance of the PLA brought a period of quiescence in the labour movement.

In every village under PLA control, Communists were instructed to retain plots of land ready for any soldiers who deserted from Chiang Kai-shek's army and joined the PLA. Coupled with the obvious fact that the KMT was rapidly losing the war, this proved to be highly effective, seen in the fact that Chiang's army had probably the highest rate of desertion of any army in history. Evidence of this was clear in the great cities and important military bases north of the Yangtze River: at Tsinan the KMT troops rebelled against their own officers and surrendered to the Communists on 24 September 1948, at Tientsin (Tianjin) the KMT troops simply melted away and the city fell on 15 January 1949, Beijing surrendered later that month without a fight, and at Kaifeng the KMT army evaporated and the PLA entered on 19 June 1949.

The American Intelligence Services were unanimous that the Nationalist government was in its "death throes". "The process of disintegration and fragmentation is so far advanced as to render almost impossible the establishment of a functioning government or even (one) capable of offering resistance to the Communists."[58] Respect for the civil population and abstinence from plunder which distinguished the PLA from all KMT armies contributed greatly to winning the support of the population.[59] In its report the CIA mentioned this as a major factor in the welcome the PLA received from the peasants:

> "the following major policies benefit the peasantry ... (3) recruitment on a voluntary basis rather than conscription .... ; (4) close cooperation between the armed forces and the peasantry; (5) a high degree of economic self-sufficiency (on the part of the PLA)."[60]

Many of the bourgeois who had previously supported Chiang were in a state of despair. Anti-Chiang sentiment was disorganising the army and paralysing the government. Inflation was impoverishing the great mass of the population, including lower level government functionaries who, to stave off hunger, were forced to demand bribes and actively participate in the corruption of a regime that was rotten from top to bottom and decomposing. Commerce and industry was coming to a halt and the living conditions of the middle and lower classes (including the middle and lower functionaries in the government institutions) cast them into the pit of despair. Its only prop was US imperialism and when that was removed the regime collapsed.

As the PLA prepared to cross the Yangtse, an important political and psychological incident occurred which demonstrated decisively the end of imperialist gunboat diplomacy in China. On 19 April, HMS Amethyst was dispatched from Shanghai to sail up the Yangtse to Nanjing, ostensibly to relieve the destroyer Consort, but in reality as a threat to the PLA to leave British interests alone. After a shoot-out with PLA shore batteries, the Amethyst turned tail and made good her escape. From then on, foreign companies in China had to abide by the rules of the New Democracy. The *Liberation Daily* announced:

> "foreign interests ... under the jurisdiction of the People's Government ... have been deprived of their special privileges which they enjoyed in the past ... if they can dutifully obey all ordinances and rulings of the People's Government and engage in business which is beneficial to the livelihood of the people and the livelihood of our country, they will be permitted to exist and will be protected."[61]

On 21 April 1949, the PLA crossed the Yangtze River and proceeded on a triumphal march southwards. Nanjing surrendered without a fight on 23 April. With complete victory in sight, to allay the fears of the most affluent peasants, the CCP took steps to reorient their policies even more towards moderation and class compromise. On 25 April 1949, Mao Zedong as Chairman of the People's Revolutionary Military Committee, and Zhu De as Commander in Chief of the PLA, declared the new government to be a democratic (i.e. bourgeois) dictatorship and promised protection of property for every individual and of all privately-owned factories, stores, banks, warehouses, vessels, wharves, etc., except those controlled by "war criminals" and "bureaucratic capital."[62] When Lenin addressed the Petrograd Soviet immediately after the October Revolution he ended his short speech with the words: "We must now set about building a proletarian socialist state in Russia. Long live the world socialist revolution!."[63] One searches in vain for a similar sentiment in Mao's pronouncement.

A seven point proclamation on land reform was also issued: "reduction of rent and interest should be carried out first and land distribution later ... after the PLA has arrived and work (organisation and indoctrination) carried on for a comparatively long time." The CCP was certainly not going to bow to mass pressure and allow China to follow the Russian model where peasants took the land and the Bolshevik Party legitimised the seizure after coming to power. Instead, the party would exercise a tight control and limit any changes. Bourgeois commentators praised Mao for his "cautious approach" and reported the "confusion" and "bewilderment" of the poor peasants when they did not receive the hoped-for land after liberation. Another cause of bewilderment was that in Article 4 of the 1947 Land Law, all debts had been cancelled but now only rent debt was cancelled, though interest on the remaining debts was supposedly limited to a maximum of 15%.[64]

Hangchow fell without a fight on 3 May, and Fuchow on 20 May. On 7 July, (birthday of the CCP), Lin Piao, top commissar in Central China, issued a directive to the Party membership, drawing attention to a serious situation in the countryside. Being an army man, Lin was blunt: peasants in the villages were being neglected and were taking the law into their own hands. Too many Party cadres believed they had earned the right to a comfortable urban life and were resisting being assigned to the countryside. These expectations were natural in a party based on privilege, and represented the conflict between cadres wanting to enjoy their privileges and the need to participate in the agrarian struggle to maintain Party control.[65]

On 20 August 1949, the *New China News Agency* reported that peasants across Hunan and Jiangxi provinces were again up in arms against the limits set by the CCP's class-collaborationist land policy. The response of the CCP is very informative; naturally there was no error in the political line – the fault lay with local cadres who had been either insufficiently alert to head off the rebellion or not firm enough when carrying out punitive raids against the rebels. This bureaucratic response was in accord with the time-honoured practice of Mao's mentor in Moscow.[66]

The question Lin did not address was why did the peasants in areas which were supposed to have been liberated, feel neglected? This occurred because once national power was within their grasp, the CCP moved from a policy of reliance on the middle and poor peasants, to actively courting the exploiting classes. Collaboration with the capitalists necessarily meant collaboration with the landlords too, for the two were entwined in innumerable economic and social activities. When Mao returned to his native province, it was not as a pioneer leader of peasant uprisings, but as a long-lost son of the landowners!

Shanghai offered token resistance but surrendered on 26 May. Mao Zedong proclaimed the People's Republic of China (PRC) on 1 October 1949.[67] Article 1, which defined the nature of the state, was careful to describe the People's Republic of China as a New Democracy or People's Democracy with no mention of socialism. Article 3 made it clear that the new regime would protect the economic interests of the petty-bourgeoisie and the national bourgeoisie.

Canton (Nationalist capital for the previous six months) surrendered on 15 October. Chiang Kai-shek fled to Taiwan (Formosa).

The complete collapse of the Chinese Nationalists and the speed at which the CCP took over southern China astounded even them. The PLA did not conquer but rather was handed the cities. Here was a situation in which the objective conditions for revolution had become rotten ripe. The exceptional historic, national and international circumstances which prevailed at the time enabled a peasant army isolated from the urban working class, to take power from the bourgeois-landlord rule of Chiang Kai-shek.[68]

With its entrance into the big cities, the peasant PLA squashed all attempts by the urban workers to participate in the overthrow of the KMT regime and promised protection of private property, Chinese and foreign.[69] Only 'bureaucratic capital', i.e., only enterprises directly controlled by members of the Kuomintang government were affected; and even in these cases the investments of independent private capitalists were left intact.

The strategy of the PLA in north China had been to establish deep roots amongst the peasants in the liberated areas before taking the towns. The speed of its advance meant that in the south the situation was reversed. The PLA first took the towns and then extended out into the countryside. There were two consequences: substantial armed resistance by KMT units continued for some time, and the local power structure of gentry, landlords, rich peasants, merchants, and usurers remained in place, and land reform had to start from scratch.

The victory of the PLA was a magnificent military achievement but it was possible only because of the complete blind alley of landlordism and capitalism in China; all the propertied classes were inter-twined with each other and entangled with imperialism, forming a bloc so reactionary it was opposed to even the minimum changes which might have saved itself from the coming revolution.

In southern China, where landlordism was most developed, the CCP adopted the policy of forming *Committees of Poor Peasants* to mobilise mass support for agrarian reform. These committees unified the landless and poor peasants and were supposed to be tightly controlled by Party cadres but began to force the pace of agrarian reform in ways unacceptable to the Party. In a short time the *Committees of Poor Peasants* were replaced with *Peasant Committees* which middle and rich peasants could join and which were much more restricted in their functions. It is no surprise to discover the CCP complained that these Committees often did not include a sufficient number of rich and medium-rich peasants. There was also a constant stream of complaints by cadres that the poor and landless peasants "always want to control everything" and "violated the property of the medium-rich peasants." The next step was for the *Peasant Committees* to delegate authority to the *Village Congress of People's Delegates* which Mao demanded should "embrace all democratic classes, including workers, peasants, artisans, the free professions, intellectuals, entrepreneurs and enlightened landowners."[70] An organisation based on class collaboration replaced the authority of the poor peasants.

The Stalinists pursued a conservative, reformist policy in a situation pregnant with the greatest revolutionary possibilities. For twenty years and more, since the defeat of the Chinese Revolution in 1927, the Stalinists had based their activity and then their programme almost exclusively on the peasantry. The peasantry, for all its revolutionary actions against the landlords, is a conservative social formation: the worker wants to socialise industry, but the peasant wants to own the land. The conservatism of the peasant was fed by almost universal illiteracy, by isolation and by the economic backwardness of rural villages, and by patriarchy and medieval social traditions and customs.

The Stalinists directed their attack at feudalism – not capitalism – in the belief that the feudal remnants had an independent social and political significance and the destruction of feudalism was necessary to clear a path for capitalist development. The conclusion that the main fight in China was against feudalism (and imperialism) led naturally to the CCP seeking to establish its political rule on the social base of the peasantry.[71] Such a perspective had a conservatising effect on the CCP itself because it drew it away from the proletariat, a process accelerated by the failure of the ultra-left policy of red unions.

Only after the flowering of capitalism would it be time to talk of the socialist revolution. This was a classic Menshevik conception of the historical process, using a schema in which history was chopped into arbitrary, predetermined stages which ignored actual class relations. Despite weighty feudal remains, the world market held sway over the Chinese economy. Property relations in China, even in the countryside were *bourgeois* property relations. To treat feudalism as the main enemy was to throw the class struggle in China off its true course and this was a core weakness at the heart of the CCP's programme.

Despite the huge preponderance of the peasants and the great weight of agriculture in the economy, the agrarian problem could not be solved separately from China's economic problems as a whole. Even after expropriation of the landlords' excess land, a small plot remained a small plot, inefficient and primitive. This kept open the door to the village usurer and even the return of landlordism as richer peasants bought up the land of bankrupted peasants under Article 12 of the Land Law.

In 1950, the Regulation on Urban and Urban Fringe Land Reform stipulated that urban land was to become state land and would be managed by city governments. We shall see that the Stalinist nature of the CCP would mean this became a source of extensive corruption within local and national government.

9.7 Summary

The Chinese Revolution took place in a society so diseased that it was disintegrating. There was universal, bitter hostility to a ruling regime rooted in all that was rotten, that had again and again demonstrated it had neither the will nor the capacity to get China out of its blind alley. The great mass of the population was facing hunger and starvation, driven to despair and willing to make almost any sacrifice to save themselves and their families. This combination of exceptional conditions broke the fetters of conservatism and brought the masses to insurrection. The upsurge of the peasantry was of seismic proportions. The CCP rode this wave to power.

With imperialist support, the strength of the Nationalist forces was sufficient to crush the Jiangxi Soviet. With the internal collapse of the KMT, brought about by corruption and the loss of imperialist support, "Land to the Tiller" became a realistic option for KMT soldiers, undermined the loyalty of Chiang's troops, and substantially aided the victory over the Nationalists.

The mass upsurge of the peasantry against hunger, starvation and KMT corruption was victorious due to specific and exceptional conditions. American imperialism was unable to intervene directly to support Chiang; Russia had invaded Manchuria and Mao gained an impregnable base and huge quantities of arms; the PLA was present to provide structure and the focus for that rebellion.[72]

However, while revolutionary peasant armies had a thousand-year-old tradition, in 1949 they were confronted by a quite different world from their forefathers; a world dominated by two super powers, one of which had given them much needed support at a critical time in the civil war, and the other which backed their enemy. The result of the victory of the peasant armies was bound to be shaped in fundamental ways by this international context.

The government that began wielding power in Beijing in 1949 would establish a workers' state in China despite Mao's declared goal of maintaining capitalism for a prolonged period. Of course, if Stalin and Mao had been Leninists they would have proposed the creation of a Socialist Federation of the Soviet Union and China in 1949. Instead, the Mao regime tried every which way to construct a stable bourgeois state until faced by the Korean War and the aggression of American imperialism. To protect itself it took measures that were socialist in principle.

Chapter 10

The New Democracy

10.1 Introduction

The New Democracy was Mao's interpretation of the Revolutionary (bourgeois) Democratic Dictatorship of the Proletariat and Peasantry introduced by Lenin in 1905, and firmly rejected by him in April 1917.[1]

Despite the experience of the civil war, Mao and Stalin still argued that China was not a capitalist country but a semi-colonial, semi-feudal country which would require a lengthy transitional period before a workers' state could be achieved. According to this stagist theory, the national democratic revolution in colonial and semi-colonial countries was one in which the national bourgeoisie was a revolutionary force opposed to imperialism and feudalism.

With the collapse of Chiang's armies, this theory hypothesised a united front of workers, peasants, petty-bourgeoisie and national bourgeoisie – the bloc of four classes – building a prosperous, independent China. This coalition government would have its own specific New Democratic economy which would achieve national independence and carry out agrarian reform but with no suggestion of overthrowing the whole bourgeoisie or expropriating private property, rather the national bourgeoisie was essential for re-building the economy.[2]

10.2 The New Democracy

That Mao's natural politics and personal ambitions fitted him well for the Popular Front perspective, is testified to by Chen Po-ta in his pamphlet *Mao Tse-tung on the Chinese Revolution,* written in 1951 and published in a revised edition by FLPH, Peking, in 1963[3]:

> "After 1927, Mao Tse-tung repeatedly refuted the erroneous 'Leftist' ideological trend in relation to the question of the character of the revolution. He considered that the Chinese democratic revolution must be carried through to the end … Mao Tse-tung regarded the opinion then held by the Communist International that the character of the Chinese revolution remained bourgeois-democratic as completely correct. He said, 'The struggle which we have gone through verifies the truth of the opinion of the Communist International'."

The action programme flowing from Mao's New Democracy was contained in his report to the 7th National Congress: *On Coalition Government.*[4] This was a clear and systematic expression of class-collaboration. To preserve Mao's omnipotence it was re-written subsequently to match actual events. The official version published in Peking in 1955 was significantly different from the original. We know this because the American Communist Party published Mao's original speech as a pamphlet, *The Fight for a New China*, in 1945.[5]

> "It is a law of Marxism that socialism can be attained only via the stage of democracy. And in China the fight for democracy is a protracted one. It would be a sheer illusion to try to build a socialist society on the ruins of the colonial, semi-colonial and semi-feudal order without a united new-democratic state, without the development *of the state sector of the new-democratic economy and* of the private capitalist and co-operative sectors."[6]

The phrase in italics was added in 1955 and liberally sprinkled throughout the document.

Liu Shaoqi elaborated:

> "The immediate policy of the Communist Party is to realise completely its minimum programme …. it is known that the Communist Party of China has in addition to its minimum programme, its maximum programme which is not included in the common programme …. In the course of consultation, some delegates proposed to write the future socialism of China into the common programme, but we deem this to be out of place, because the taking of serious socialist steps in China is a thing of the rather far future."[7]

Mao expected the bourgeois-democratic stage to last for generations. The original 1945 version of the report says: "In the entire bourgeois democratic revolution stage, over scores of years, our new democratic general program is unchanged", and "The carrying out of (the CCP) program will not advance China to socialism. This is not a question of the subjective willingness or unwillingness of certain individuals to do the advancing; it is due to the fact that the objective political and social conditions in China do not permit the advance." The 1955 version contains neither passage because the laws of Marxism contradicted Mao, the workers' state was created rather rapidly, not after a protracted time, not after 'scores of years'.

The theory of revolution in stages leads inevitably to coalition government and class collaboration. Thus, even after the overthrow of the Chiang regime, Mao persisted in maintaining unity with the section of the bourgeoisie which had separated from Chiang and the doomed KMT regime, as one step in realising his New Democracy. This unity was embodied in the Political Consultative Conference, composed of representatives of the CCP, various bourgeois and petty-bourgeois parties, leading figures from the KMT who had deserted Chiang at the last moment, trade unions and peasant organisations and numerous individuals who represented no-one but themselves. This People's Government of four classes which defined the general policy of the state was appointed, there was no room in the New Democracy for direct elections by workers' and peasants' committees – that smacked too much of Soviets.[8]

In 1945, Mao had been supported by US imperialism when he attempted to achieve a *modus vivendi* with Chiang, and *On Coalition Government* reflected this:

> "We are also grateful to Britain and the United States, particularly the latter, for their immense contribution to the common cause – the defeat of the Japanese aggressors. We are grateful to the governments and the peoples of both countries for their sympathy with the Chinese people and their help. ... Large amounts of capital will be needed for the development of our industries. ... Enterprises profitable to both the Chinese people and foreigners are swiftly expanding large-scale light and heavy industries and modernizing agriculture, which can become a reality when there is a firm internal and international peace, and when political and agrarian reforms are thoroughly carried out. On this basis, we shall be able to absorb vast amounts of foreign investments. A politically retrogressive and economically impoverished China will be unprofitable not only to the Chinese people, but also to foreigners."

After the onset of the Korean War these paragraphs were removed. With American diplomats, Mao was less reserved:

> "China must industrialize. This can be done – in China – only by free enterprise and with the aid of foreign capital. Chinese and American interests are correlated and similar. They fit together, economically and politically ... The United States would find us more cooperative than the Kuomintang. We will not be afraid of democratic American influence – we will welcome it."[9]

The New Democracy was to be a coalition, but the bourgeoisie in its great majority stuck with the KMT despite its being so decrepit and degenerate and so obviously losing the civil war. On 1 May 1948, the CCP issued an open appeal for allies in a broad united front against the Chiang regime:

> "Labouring people of the entire country, unite; ally with the intelligentsia, liberal bourgeoisie, all democratic parties and groups, social luminaries and other patriotic elements; consolidate and expand the united front against imperialist, feudal, and bureaucratic capitalist forces; fight together to destroy Kuomintang reactionaries and build a new China. All democratic parties and groups, people's organizations, and social luminaries, speedily convene a Political Consultative Conference, discuss and carry out the convoking of a People's Representative Assembly to establish a Democratic Coalition Government!."[10]

The response from mainland China was almost zero! But from Hong Kong came a cheer. Individuals who had once been leading figures in the KMT but were now refugees saw a chance to re-gain lost prestige and importance, and half a dozen grouplets (mostly no more than a few dozen strong) grasped at the offer. However, there were two small but significant organisations; the Kuomintang Revolutionary Committee (led by Li Chi-sen, the KMT general who gained notoriety as the butcher of the Canton Commune in December, 1927 and which had Song Qingling [Mme Sun Yat-sen] as a member), and the Democratic League (representing the cultured middle classes of the cities with support from about 50,000 teachers, professionals and petty-bourgeois intellectuals). Within eighteen months these would provide the staff for many important positions in the New Democracy. The multi-millioned CCP was forming an alliance, not with the Chinese bourgeoisie but with its ghost. These opportunists represented little but themselves, their politics did not differ in any substantial way from Chiang's; they were attempting to board the gravy train.[11]

Traditionally, the leaderships of Chinese peasant rebellions had compromised with the existing regime. Mao was no different. His call for a bourgeois democratic dictatorship of the proletariat and peasantry was an offer to collaborate with the Chinese bourgeoisie. This had been Mao's stated aim almost from the day he joined the CCP, it was a clear thread through his actions and writings. Supporting the bloc of four classes, Mao was consistently reluctant to use class terms when analysing Chinese society. In March 1926 he classified society in terms of 'our friends' (which, naturally, included the left wing of the bourgeoisie), later he would talk in terms of 'good' and 'bad gentry' and now the CCP attempted to divide the ruling bourgeoisie into two mutually antagonistic sections: 'bureaucratic, feudal and reactionary', and 'national, democratic and progressive'.

After the surrender of Japanese imperialism, KMT tyranny and corruption reached a climax. Four families, the Chiang Kai-sheks, the Soongs, the Kungs, and the Chen brothers, who dominated the KMT, expropriated properties of those they designated enemies and traitors, and with low interest government loans soon came to dominate mining, heavy industry (metallurgical, machine tools, electrical, chemical), textiles, sugar, transportation and, of course, banking and overseas trade. Using their political positions they treated these nationalised enterprises as their private domains ensuring they were virtual monopolies, and amassed fabulous fortunes.[12]

The enterprises owned by these four families and their closest associates were designated bureaucratic capital. Bureaucratic capitalists were those who had acquired dominating positions in the economy by exploiting public office or purchased important posts in government using the enormous profits wrung from the economy. The so-called 'national' bourgeoisie were those relatively smaller capitalists who, despite their efforts, had been unable to gain a place in the big financial oligarchies. While the four families were certainly oligarchical and reactionary, to designate them as feudal meant concealing the true character of the ruling summit of the entire Chinese bourgeoisie.

Naturally, the four families were up to their ears in all aspects of usury, attracted by its astronomical profits. As finance-capitalists they had close ties with Wall Street and using the four Chinese government banks they gripped the economy by the throat and indulged in a mad orgy of speculation to extract the maximum from the masses in the time left before their inevitable downfall. These bureaucratic capitalists provided capital to the village heads and landlords to loan to the peasants at ruinous rates of interest.[13]

Yes, the national bourgeoisie were dissatisfied with the unbridled domination and corruption of the four families. Yes, they complained about the arbitrariness and unfairness of the government. Yes, they talked about democracy. But they were progressive only to the extent that they would support the New Democracy while it allowed them to retain their property and guaranteed them their profits. As soon as the opportunity presented itself, these democratic national capitalists would reveal their reactionary face and their essential class solidarity with world imperialism. On 1 October 1949, Mao formally proclaimed the Chinese People's Democratic Republic. The new government was a People's Front coalition in which the Stalinists joined hands with the national bourgeoisie and petty-bourgeoisie. Part of the price

Mao Zedong paid for securing the co-operation of these elements was to abandon the more radical elements of land reform in south China.

However, the character of Mao Zedong and the lessons he learned from the defeats of 1925-27 and the Jiangxi Soviet are important. It is clear that Mao, while genuinely committed to an economy in which the national bourgeoisie had a more or less free hand and there was no monopoly of foreign trade, was even more determined to be the leading figure in the New Democracy. Mao balanced between the bourgeoisie and the workers and peasants during the New Democracy period while concentrating power into his hands, and to achieve this he crushed all signs of an independent workers' movement.[14]

When the Mao team assumed government of China they had a huge advantage over the Bolsheviks of 1917, having accumulated some 20 years of invaluable experience of administering local government covering many millions of people (taxes, public works, police force, judiciary, armed forces, etc.) under the difficult conditions of a civil war. Thus, when the PLA arrived in south China the CCP had a good understanding of the implications of the decision to retain two million KMT officials in post to continue performing their functions.[15] However, the major difference with the Bolsheviks was not governmental experience nor the relatively large number of trained CCP cadres (Fairbank estimated over half a million) to do this kind of work; rather it was the political perspective of the two parties. The Bolsheviks understood that the personnel inherited from the previous regime were an alien class force that had to be overcome. The CCP saw the personnel they inherited as part of the New Democracy, as collaborators in creating a bourgeois democratic state. The membership of the CCP rose from 2.7 million in 1947 to 5.8 million in 1958, many of the recruits were existing officials, and as they were welcomed into the regime to positions of authority they brought their own methods and perspectives with them.

During this time the Party made a determined attempt to recruit students and intellectuals because their ability to read and write was needed for effective administration. Their skills put these people into relatively senior positions even though they had little or no experience and lacked any formal training in Party ideology. There was considerable tension between these so-called upstarts and their new ways and the domineering attitudes of old cadres, which was one factor motivating Mao to take such an interest in the activities of Chinese intellectuals.[16]

It must not be assumed that the coalition government was stage scenery used to hoodwink the public. Real power remained with the PLA but an important and substantial partner in the governmental coalition was the Revolutionary Committee of the Kuomintang. Li Chi-sen had gathered around himself important elements representing the interests of a section of the Chinese bourgeoisie from south China, bourgeoisie who had deserted Chiang Kai-shek's sinking ship of state at the last moment. The Revolutionary Committee was the gateway through which they hoped to make their way into the safe haven of the new People's Republic, hoped to retain their fortunes and, in due time, get back into the political saddle. Li Chi-sen now sat alongside Mao Zedong as one of the six vice-chairmen of the People's Government.[17]

The initial priority of the New Democracy (October 1949 to June 1950) was clearing away the military remnants of the KMT and suppressing independent activities of the workers and peasants. On the political plane, the CCP assiduously courted the bourgeoisie, landlords and rich peasants, military men and top Kuomintang bureaucrats in an attempt to create the bloc of four classes and reinforce its own power. But simultaneously it had to cover its costs and to do this the government extorted food and money from the only people who had them. They levied severe taxes on all of industry and commerce, forced the bourgeoisie, landlords and rich peasants to buy Victory Bonds, Patriotic Bonds, etc., and appropriated 'voluntary contributions' of foodstuffs from the countryside.[18] It has been claimed that even with rent lowered to 37.5% of the crop, the taxes levied by the CCP (and collected much more efficiently) were not much less than paid under the KMT, but were, of course, more evenly distributed.

The reality was that the CCP held the final decision-making power in its hands through complete control of the armed forces, despite having a majority of ministries headed by non-CCP personnel. The bourgeois democratic parties existed only so far as the CCP allowed them to, they were able to influence the policies of the People's Government only because the CCP wished to maintain bourgeois property relations. Bourgeois representatives were given important positions in the People's Government on a whole number of levels: vice-presidents, ministers and vice-ministers in the central government, presidents of provincial governments, etc. In contradiction, the working class and poor peasants had to be content with CCP-nominated delegates from trade unions and peasant associations. The number of such delegates was far fewer than those allocated to the so-called democratic parties. Soviets were, of course, not countenanced. Workers were further constrained by being deprived of the right to strike; indeed one of the first activities of the PRC was strike-breaking in the interests of the national bourgeoisie.[19]

As an aside it should be noted that as the PLA swept southward it was particularly rigorous in arresting all known revolutionaries, especially Trotskyists, together with their spouses, siblings, relatives and friends. These people simply disappeared. Many were killed immediately, the remainder imprisoned for decades without trial or public notification.

Formally, the elections to the People's Congress were based on universal suffrage but the representatives were determined beforehand by the CCP in agreement with the various bourgeois and petty-bourgeois parties or groups. In view of the composition of the new regime and its political line it was certainly no bourgeois dictatorship. But it could not be characterised as a proletarian dictatorship either. Rather, it was a distorted form in transition between bourgeois and proletarian dictatorships, but without any certainty that it would actually complete the transition. It has become common practice to designate such a contradictory and transitional form as a Workers' and Peasants' Government. This is used in the same sense as it was by the early Communist International – to indicate a regime that had taken anti-capitalist measures but had not broken definitively either politically or economically from the capitalist system.

Mao considered the New Democracy as the Chinese version of Lenin's Revolutionary Democratic Dictatorship of the Proletariat and Peasantry (RDDPP). However, the New Democracy was Lenin's 1905 concept filtered through Stalinism and so the revolutionary content was removed. Indeed, three essential components of the RDDPP were actively suppressed by the CCP: Soviets as the free and democratic expression of the proletariat, peasants and soldiers; proletarian activities in support of the overthrow of the Chiang regime; and independent peasant activities to seize the land.

If a revolutionary Marxist party had gained governmental power in China under the impulse of a proletarian revolution, as happened with Lenin in Russia, then there would have been no doubt about the subsequent dynamics of the regime. Even though the Bolsheviks held power for a short initial period based on a capitalist economy and a capitalist state structure with a petty-bourgeois minority party in the government, it would be correct to say the state form was a dictatorship of the proletariat from October 1917. This was Lenin's consistent view from 1917 until his death.[20]

But in China the party which had come to power was non-Leninist, class-collaborationist, bureaucratised, had betrayed the revolution in 1927, and had achieved power based on peasant armies with the declared aim of creating a bourgeois democratic state. It had no real base amongst the workers and had no intention of allowing them free trade unions or introducing any direct democracy, certainly not through Soviets. Ted Grant, an eminent Marxist, added three additional important points: a) Mao was a premeditated Stalinist who had consciously incorporated into his ideas and strategy many of the manoeuvres that Stalin had developed empirically in response to the needs of the bureaucracy; b) The "simple and austere life" of the leaders in Yenan (it has since become known that even there the bureaucracy had its privileges) would disappear and those with the power would soon surround themselves with pomp and honours; and c) The state machine developed and controlled by the CCP would be separate from the masses and tower over them as a means of repression, not least to protect the bureaucracy from criticism.[21]

It did not take long for the top bureaucrats to acquire the same trappings as their Russian mentors. A leading member of the Democratic League who was a delegate to the People's Congress from 1949 to 1956 fled to Hong Kong where he published his memoirs and blew the whistle.[22] The top Party men took the best villas belonging to the richest capitalists, imported luxury furniture and carpets, hired servants and the best chefs, had luxury clothing for private use. There were exclusive cinemas, and dance parties. How the CCP provided cars to Party cadres is an excellent example of the hierarchical system that existed; at the top were a select few who used the same luxury limousines as the Russian Politburo, next came ministers who were supplied with less sumptuous vehicles, and so on down to the departmental bus and individual bicycles. Special residential complexes were built for provincial and municipal Party leaders from which middle and lower ranking Party members were excluded. Similarly with "kitchens", the food supplied to party personnel; a number of the very top restaurants in Beijing, Shanghai, Tientsin, etc., were reserved for officials such as Zhou Enlai, Zhu De, Liu Shaoqi and their immediate entourages, and then there was a descending order matching rank to restaurant. Extra rations (and the best at that) were sent to the residences of party officials. Naturally, the enormous cost for all this was met by the state – as were summer and seaside holidays.

In the same way that the CCP imported the privilege structure of the USSR so it also copied an ever-present police system. Thousands of Russian experts arrived in China to train agents to implement a network which kept records on all citizens, their work activities, their travel, their visitors, their views, their earnings, what letters and/or parcels they received, and so on.

The working class were hailed as the masters of society while the CCP used its new dominance in the trade unions to establish a general system of compulsory arbitration which enforced the policy that in private industry increased production came first, better conditions might come later. The Party recognised that there could be legitimate conflicts of interest between management and workers and they should be resolved amicably but the factory manager had the final say, whilst those elected by the workers had only a consultative voice. As in the Soviet Union, the Chinese Stalinists made the trade union "a school of production which encourages the productive and positive characteristics of the proletariat." Defending the interests of the workers was dubbed "leftist adventurism."[23]

A series of Labour and Capital Consultative Conferences was held to determine how to revive industry and commerce. With government support these consultations accepted the proposals of the industrialists and merchants and concluded that workers and employees in factories and shops should accept lower wages and undertake voluntary unpaid overtime or else return to work on the land in their native provinces. These decisions were then approved by the Political Consultative Conference in May 1950, rubber-stamped by the government, and passed into law.[24]

The bourgeoisie, were the main beneficiaries of this turn, whilst the working class, especially the workers in the private enterprises, were its victims. But all workers were subjected to methods used in the Soviet Union to extract maximum value from their labour: tight control of real wages, longer working hours, and increased exploitation through piece-work and Stakhanovism.

The American Secret Services appraised these CCP policies as having gained wide support amongst Shanghai and Nanjing businessmen who were won over by promises that taxes would not be confiscatory, that governmental enterprises harmful to private enterprises would not be permitted, that workers would not demand excessively high wages, and generally that all means would be used to encourage private industrial production. Among the middle classes, the CCP gained support by paying technical and managerial specialists twice the salary of government officials and giving them more authority within the workplace than they had enjoyed under the KMT.[25]

In early 1950, the Party was forced to recognise serious unrest amongst the peasants in south China. The limits placed on land reform meant the broad mass of peasants believed they were being forced to contribute endless taxes and food for no gain. The situation was made worse because the peasants were well aware of the land re-distribution that had occurred in the north and liberated areas. There was general confusion and sabotage of production, social order was becoming increasingly unsettled. So-called 'lawless' landlords were exploiting the uncertainty in the situation to unload their taxes onto their tenants who were being rendered so destitute of food and seed that they could hardly proceed with the spring sowing. Some became so desperate they plundered public stores of foodstuffs. The outbreak of the Korean War gave a boost to the confidence of reactionary elements and KMT agents were able to successfully exploit the situation to kill unpopular CCP cadres.[26]

The regime was failing to meet its agricultural targets and was obliged to change the emphasis of its policy beginning with the *Land Reform Law* of June 1950. The Act strictly forbade all violence – arrest, beating and/or killing of landlords and rich peasants – but so explosive were conditions in the south that a safety valve had to be introduced to defuse the situation. Under strict Party control, peasants were permitted to struggle against individual 'vicious autocrats' whose land could be expropriated.[27] To further appease the peasants the regime did relax its food appropriation measures, and reduced the overall tax burden, but the main policy emphasis remained firmly on the enforcement of reductions in rents and interest rates.

Prior to the Korean War, and despite the increasingly hostile atmosphere, most landlords and rich peasants survived with at least some of their holdings intact and many with most of their land and holdings intact.[28]

10.3 The New Democracy and Industry

The CCP had very few concrete plans for the operation of industry and what they did have came from the Soviet Union. Mao and the CCP accepted and enacted a version of the Soviet Union's 4th Five-Year Plan (FYP) of 1946-1950. The Soviet plans were copied because of the lack of relevant experience within the CCP, because the Soviet Union had suffered almost as much in the war as had China and was demonstrating a rapid recovery, and because there was no other source of such help.

The PRC's industrial management model, primarily used in heavy industry, was taken lock, stock, and barrel from the Soviet Union. The essential features of the plan were: (1) Linking economic goals and patriotism (Party members and activists would paste the factory walls with slogans and distribute leaflets urging co-workers to ever greater exertions); (2) Involving the work force in campaigns to increase production and reduce waste through work unit and factory meetings; (3) Trades unions to educate and motivate workers in how to improve their working methods; (4) Meticulous attention paid to plan fulfilment; and (5) Authority within the factory resting with the local CCP cell which had responsibility for increasing labour productivity.[29]

In private enterprises, the capitalists retained their power. In nationalised factories power was nominally invested in a Control Committee consisting of representatives of the former owners, representatives of the supervisory personnel and representatives of the workers, and chaired by the factory manager. The *Regulations for the Conduct of Factory Committees* stated[30] that if a decision passed by a majority of the Committee was judged by the manager to be in "conflict with the factory's best interests" or "in conflict with the instructions of higher authority", the manager was empowered to prohibit its implementation.

The petty-bourgeois and bureaucratic nature of the CCP, through its overwhelmingly peasant membership and its Stalinist politics, soon became obvious as was admitted in the *North East Daily News*;

> "members of the party working in the factories lacking an understanding of the point of view of the masses, believe that the manager should take responsibility for all important decisions without asking for the opinion of the Party and the trade union, and believe that the Control Committee is superfluous and the trade unions are only meddlers."[31]

The basic policy of the PRC was "mutual consideration for both state and private property, equal benefits for both labour and capital." In practice this meant the property of the bureaucratic bourgeoisie was confiscated by the state while the private property of the national bourgeoisie was protected and allowed to secure 'legal profits' subject only to the condition of working in 'coordination' with the nationalised industries.

The contradictions in Mao's programme were becoming ever more apparent. The CCP wished to construct a democratic capitalist economy, but in seizing bureaucratic capital it had taken ownership and control of virtually all heavy industry and a sizeable chunk of light industry. It wished to industrialise China, particularly the hinterland, but the magnitude of the task meant that quite spontaneously planning was being adopted as the rational way forward. It wished to leave the road of capital accumulation open to the rich peasants, landlords and national bourgeoisie but the agrarian struggle in the south kept on bursting out.[32] Mao's *New Democracy* called for a mixed economy and protection of private capital but the actual direction being taken to solve Chinese capitalism's problems was all too clearly towards state planning and control.

On 6 June 1950, Mao addressed the Central Committee and sounded the alarm, calling for a re-adjustment of relations between the state and private sectors of the economy. He endorsed moves towards a new economic policy for China. Private (light) industry was to be encouraged by the state handing out huge orders and granting generous credits. The number of state retail shops was to be substantially reduced and the number of products they could sell was to be limited. There would be a big reduction in the "tax burden" through large scale demobilisations of PLA troops. In the countryside there would be "a change from the policy of requisitioning surplus land and property to one of maintaining a rich peasant economy." He concluded "The view ... that it is possible to eliminate capitalism and realize socialism at an early date is wrong, it does not tally with our national conditions", and to put a lid on such thoughts "the whole Party must carry out a large-scale rectification movement."[33]

The regime attempted to proceed according to Mao's wishes but the Korean War intervened. By the autumn of 1950, US troops led by General MacArthur and fighting under the banner of the United Nations, had pushed the North Korean army until its back was against the Chinese border. This greatly revived the KMT anti-communist guerrillas who drew around them dissident peasants. With the Korean War (China entered October 1950) the regime was compelled to mobilise broad mass support, and to modify its policies accordingly, making yet another turn in its policy towards industry and agriculture and sharpening the struggle against the urban and village bourgeoisie.[34]

10.4 The New Democracy and Women

The CCP came to power with a reformist programme that promised much. Fairbank described the situation: "After 1949 public sentiment in the cities was one of euphoria, ... Here was a conquering army which was strictly self-disciplined, polite and helpful, at the opposite pole from the looting and raping of warlord troops and departing Nationalists." Women's liberation is a good example of progress made under the regime and the limits imposed. The new marriage law made wives equal to husbands: "All marriages are to be based on the free consent of men and women." It was a new day for women, divorce which had been all but impossible under the old regime was now available. Polygamy, the sale of women into prostitution, and the killing of female babies were all banned with severe punishment for those who broke these laws.[35] The liberation of more than 200 million Chinese women from the yoke of feudal custom represented an historical 1,000 year jump in the course of a single year.

On 18 February 1946, *Liberation Daily* had opened a discussion to prepare for the launch of a revised Party policy for women. Given the difficulties of holding such a wide-ranging discussion with the poor communications that existed within Communist-controlled areas (telephones were almost unknown, it took a day to travel twenty miles and a letter carried by the Post Office Bureau could take a month to travel a couple of hundred miles)[36], it is little short of a farce that two weeks later on 3 March 1946, the *Liberation Daily* could conclude the discussion and list eighteen points that had been agreed. These were codified in an editorial in the *Liberation Daily* of 8 March 1946; not surprisingly it was reported that women supported CCP policy that the demands of the peasants be limited to reducing rents and interest rates but not land seizures. Nor is it surprising that equal rights for women came well down the list, the top demands called for "a peaceful solution to China's post-war problems" and committed women to working with other groups to solve them.[37] Women, it appeared, fully endorsed Party policy.

The Party next launched a woman's Political Consultative Conference. This was an effort to mobilise women throughout China behind Party policy on the grounds that reduced rents and interest rates would allow women greater participation in mass struggles. Women were mobilised behind slogans proclaiming political freedom and equal rights for women, but peace, (bourgeois) democracy and national unity were the proclaimed goals for the women's organisations. In *Liberation Daily*, the dominant theme of all articles regarding women was building a (bourgeois) democratic China.[38]

By the end of 1946, civil war was the order of the day and the CCP was using language similar to that of the late 1930s urging women to join the war effort. There was no doubt about what the role of women was to be. On 8 November, 1946, *Liberation Daily* urged women to expand their movement in response to the war crisis and listed their responsibilities: improve textile production to guarantee each family had clothing; give moral support to men away fighting; encourage husbands and sons to join the army; and promote healthy habits. A week later an editorial added: women should undertake agricultural work in the fields to replace those men who enlisted. The CCP clearly saw women's liberation as an important but subsidiary goal.

Nevertheless, the New Democracy represented a major step forward for women. *Article 6* of the Common Programme stated:

> "The People's Republic of China shall abolish the feudal system which holds women in bondage. Women shall enjoy equal rights with men in political,

> economic, cultural, educational and social life. Freedom of marriage for men and women shall be put into effect."

The All-China Women's Federation was established on 24 March 1949 as China's first country-wide women's organisation with a watching brief to protect the interests of women and promote gender equality within the prescribed goal of building a democratic China.

However, the proof of the pudding is in the eating, and while enormous gains were made, a Stalinist bureaucracy will always put its own interests first. Just as in Jiangxi and Yenan, the CCP would bow to the pressure of the male peasants and actively restrict the democratic rights of Chinese women. CCP cadres almost without exception saw women's right to work, to own land and property as sufficient conditions for women's liberation. Too often however, the latter condition was not enacted. For example, under the new laws a wife inherited the land of a husband, but all too frequently the local village association (invariably under CCP leadership) seize the land on the grounds that women are unable to tend their own fields, and re-allocate it to one of her dead husband's male relatives, leaving the wife to cope as best she can.[39] In 2011, some 80% of rural land was exclusively in a man's name, and the proportion is increasing.

10.5 "Under the leadership of the proletariat"?

Bourgeois academics have long argued that Mao's New Democracy was a master strategy for the CCP to take power: that the New Democracy was a façade, a sugar coating behind which Mao hid his true intentions. The New Democracy was intended to deceive the national bourgeoisie, landowners and rich peasants, neutralising them while the CCP prepared to transform China into a workers' state. All the manoeuvres and confusions generated by the New Democracy have been lauded as contributions to the final victory of the Chinese Revolution while, in reality, victory was actually achieved in spite of them.

It is, of course, axiomatic that revolutionaries should maximise the forces arrayed against imperialism, but if this is done at the cost of principle then the unity achieved becomes self-defeating. Unfortunately, within the world Trotskyist movement there has long been a current with a 'get rich quick' mentality that has consistently looked for ways to short-circuit the arduous task of building a Leninist Party. Their siren song is that the socialist revolution could be better and sooner accomplished by joining with other forces. These people greeted Maoism as a genuine revolutionary force and accommodated their politics to it. In Italy, for example, under the leadership of Livio Maitan (prominent member of the United Secretariat of the 4th International) the formation of Maoist groups was welcomed and no serious political fight put up against Maoist ideas with the result that in the late 1960s the majority of the Maitan group broke away from Trotskyism and joined the Maoists, possibly the only time in history that such a thing has happened.

Maitan and Ernest Mandel (Secretary of the United Secretariat of the 4th International) were sufficiently impressed to support a Maoist strategy of peasant guerilla warfare for an extended period, looked for a suitable environment and hit on Latin America as an appropriate location "on account of technical and military considerations."[40] What followed was scandalous, the good name of Trotsky was appended to ultra-left, rural, sectarian Maoist guerrilla groups, leading an entire generation of revolutionary youth down a blind alley and contributing to the needless deaths of numerous young revolutionaries. There was even a discussion within the Ligue Communiste (largest and most prestigious of the sections of the USec) as to whether the rural (sic!) guerrilla tactics used in Latin America should be applied in France on the grounds that power comes from the barrel of a gun!

Mandel and Maitan were the most prominent representatives of an international mood. Michael Lowy, a respected academic, whose book *Combined and Uneven Development* was widely promoted as a defence of Trotsky's ideas was not immune. The manner in which he introduced Mao in this book showed where his emotions lay. Mao is presented as a "young and unknown Communist leader", who "largely in defiance of Comintern directives" was the organiser of the 1927 radical peasant movement in Hunan which was actively seizing the land and killing landlords, supported apparently, by no lesser person than Trotsky. It turns out on investigation, that Mao was already an established leader in both the CCP and the KMT and a firm supporter of the policies of the Comintern, and that Trotsky was praising the independent peasant movement in Hunan and Hupeh which was acting against the wishes of the CCP and, especially, Mao Zedong.[41]

Maitan, Lowy and others saw Mao as having led a successful revolution and, taking appearances for reality, accepted him as a genuine revolutionary. Marxist analysis and the history of Stalinism was thrown aside by these people because they wanted to believe that Mao would make the revolution for them. Lowy makes it clear that he did not consider the CCP either Stalinist or petty-bourgeois, rather he suggests that large sections of the Red Army and CCP had attained a socialist consciousness.[42] It could be argued that the facts were not known, that Mao had led a revolution and that he appeared a genuine revolutionary. But such an approach is impressionism, taking the appearance for the reality. These people wanted to believe in Mao and this desire trumped Marxist analysis and the counter-revolutionary history of Stalinism.

In the UK, publications which considered themselves both left and intellectual, such as the *New Left Review*, swung behind Mao and the CCP with many on the editorial board appearing to believe there was no real difference between Mao and Trotsky.[43] As the revolutionary mask of Maoism slipped, the *NLR* failed to produce an in-depth critique of either Mao's record or its own analysis, probably because that would have threatened a split in its own ranks. Instead it adopted at local level a policy of ideological peaceful co-existence. This was all the more scandalous because leading editorial board member Robin Blackburn had only recently been feted as a new recruit to Mandel's Fourth International.

In France, Pierre Rousset considered that despite his avowed Stalinism, Mao adhered in practice to revolutionary Marxism. Rousset's confusion may be due to a selective reading of Mao's writings such as *The Chinese Revolution and the Chinese Communist Party* where the "new-democratic revolution" is described as

> "part of the world proletarian-socialist revolution ... Politically, it means the joint revolutionary-democratic dictatorship of several revolutionary classes over the imperialists and reactionary traitors, and opposition to the transformation of Chinese society into a society under bourgeois dictatorship ... This kind of new-democratic revolution ... results in the dictatorship of the united front of all revolutionary classes *under the leadership of the proletariat,* not in the dictatorship of the bourgeoisie."[44]

In 1939, in the original text which had the bloc of four classes in mind, the phrase in italics did not appear.

Possibly Rousset was unaware of the original text; perhaps like Lowy, he took Mao's additions as a "self-criticism" rather than Stalinist face-saving.[45] However, for revolutionary Marxists "under the leadership of the proletariat" can be guaranteed only by mobilising the broad masses of the urban proletariat through Soviets or similar democratic organisations. For the CCP, "under the leadership of the proletariat" meant its own continuing domination, Soviets remained anathema.

Dazzled by appearances, this political current failed to appreciate that Mao gained power due to a special conjuncture of world events. Instead it was proposed that Mao's actual political practice "was flatly in contradiction to Stalin's policies."[46]

10.6 Summary

With the victory of the CCP in 1949, national unity was achieved – except for Tibet and Taiwan – which gave the new regime legitimacy and mass support. This was the most important single achievement needed to overcome the economic chaos which sapped what little strength remained in the nation. Without effective central administration, there could be no standardisation of money, no genuine struggle against inflation and no co-ordinated and fair system for the collection of taxes. Without a unified national transport system, there could be no effective measures against local famines. The new central government devoted major efforts to the realisation of national unity and achieved rapid and remarkable successes.

Viewed in this way the Chinese Revolution appears as a phenomenon of combined development on an enormous scale. The military-bureaucratic victory was achieved because the bourgeoisie was without any mass base, deserted by its imperialist protectors and with the peasant masses rising in rebellion and following the Communist Party. The victory of the CCP was predominantly the result of the conjuncture of specific conditions created by the Second World War: the entire capitalist world was in a state of unparalleled decline and disarray, the disintegration of the KMT regime was only the most extreme manifestation of the deterioration of the whole capitalist system. American imperialism was obliged to abandon its aid to Chiang just as the peasant masses in China were rising in rebellion against impossible living conditions.[47]

The conservative and petty-bourgeois nature of the CCP was immediately demonstrated when the PLA entered the big cities – it has been claimed that amongst the Shanghai proletariat, CCP cadres numbered a mere 800.[48] The Stalinists immediately demonstrated that what was important to them was winning the confidence of the bourgeoisie and not that of the working class. The efforts of the urban workers to create independent organisations were stifled, the right to strike was taken away and compulsory arbitration instituted on 19 August 1949, when provisional regulations for the adjustment of labour-management disputes were promulgated in Shanghai. Capitalists alone had the right to hire and fire, and all labour conflicts had to be settled by negotiations during which the workers had to "maintain discipline."[49]

Irresolvable differences were settled by the PLA. However, the PLA soldiers were almost entirely peasants, the officers were, approximately, 70% peasant with a leavening of workers, students and the sons of merchants and small landowners.[50] When the workers struck in support of demands for wage increases or against oppressive conditions, the PLA was brutal in its repression. At a large textile factory in Shanghai in early 1949, eight strikers were shot. In factories in Tientsin, striking workers were arrested and executed. The workers of Shen Hsin Factory Number 9 were machine-gunned, resulting in more than 300 casualties. In May 1950, in the Ching Hsing coal mines in Hopeh Province, when the workers went on strike against the cruelty and arrogance of the Soviet advisers the PLA killed or wounded 200. Such events confirmed the CCP's petty-bourgeois character and its distrust, even hostility, toward the working class.[51]

However, in the three decades between the announcement of the People's Republic on 1 October 1949 and Mao's death 9 September 1976, many academics and commentators in Europe and the USA, with the strength of the Stalinist state behind them, idealised his achievements. They argued, in one way or another, that if he achieved power, his general strategy must have been correct. China experts such as John Fairbank, Alexander Pantsov and Steven Levine have presented Mao's New Democracy strategy as the master plan for the CCP to take power. Arthur Cohen has claimed that Mao made a unique contribution to Marxist theory when he included bourgeois parties in the government which took the final steps to a workers' state. Patricia Stranahan argues that Mao's masterstroke was accommodation with the landlords and rich peasants and that was key to his successes. These commentators mistake the appearance for the reality.

Mao wished to confine the revolution to within China but the imperialists understood that revolution cannot be contained by bureaucratic decree and acted accordingly. Despite Mao's intention that the New Democracy would follow a path different from that of Russia in 1917, the Korean War and imperialist blockade would force the regime to extend state ownership into all sectors of the economy, not to loosen the state monopoly of foreign trade but take an even tighter grip, not to reduce state planning but extend its scale to all sections of the economy, not to give the national and petty-bourgeoisie ever greater weight in society but instead to mobilise the masses to save the new regime. Lenin had already explained the reasons for this a generation earlier: "The extremely high level of development which world capitalism in general has attained .... (has) transformed the present stage of capitalist development into an era of proletarian socialist revolution."[52] To carry through the bourgeois democratic tasks China would have to take measures which would leave her with one foot in ... socialism.

The PLA and CCP had taken power in China not because of the application of correct theory but because the mass of peasants in China could no longer go on living in the old way and rose up in rebellion in a time-honoured manner. The CCP were the beneficiaries and their peasant armies were able to defeat those of the KMT because the World War had weakened imperialism to the extent that Chiang was left to his own devices. Mao's class-collaborationist ideology and method were fundamentally flawed and when applied under less favourable conditions in Indonesia in 1965, led to the deaths of as many as a million workers and Communists. The Indonesian Communist Party (PKI), the largest in the world outside China and the Soviet Union, followed the Maoist strategy of advocating a united national front of four classes and taking ministerial posts within a bourgeois government. Events followed all too closely what had happened in China in 1927 even to the PKI handing over lists of names and addresses of Party members; the biggest difference was the scale of the resulting slaughter.

Chapter 11
The Unexpectedly Short Life of the New Democracy

11.1 Introduction

For Marxists the Chinese Revolution is second only to the Bolshevik Revolution of 1917 as one of the greatest events in human history. In 1949 the People's Liberation Army (PLA) took power and within a short span of time snuffed out capitalism and landlordism.

However, Mao talked the language of bourgeois democracy, and on assuming power had the PLA stamp on any signs of independent activity by the workers. But the bourgoisie had fled *en masse* with Chiang Kai-shek, and to maintain his perspective, Mao was forced to form a united front with rag tag remnants of the bourgeoisie. Notwithstanding Mao's declared goals, the Third Chinese Revolution progressed rapidly from the New Democracy – a regime which had the defined goal of a capitalist economy with an extensive nationalised sector, protected the national bourgeoisie, and postponed the transition to socialism to many decades in the future – to the threshold of a workers' state. In this transition the leading members of the CCP, immersed in their Stalinist, petty bourgeois ideology stood in opposition to the press of events.

It will be argued that the establishment of a workers' state in China is striking confirmation of the general tendency for revolutions in backward countries to transcend the bourgeois-democratic phase and turn into socialist revolutions. The situation after World War II may have had specific characteristics, such as imperialism being temporarily impotent and the leadership of the mass uprising being in the hands of Stalinists, which gave the Chinese Revolution particular features, but the trend was, inevitably, towards the establishment of a (deformed) workers' state, or as some describe it "proletarian Bonapartism."[1]

At the time, those analysing Chinese events had to paint in broad strokes; details available today were unobtainable then. This chapter attempts to fill in those details. It describes and analyses the processes and forces which acted over the transitional period between announcing the PRC and achieving a workers' state. The nature of the state is at the heart of Marxism and transitional regimes test our ability to apply Marxist theory to contradictory and dynamic phenomena which are important for the analysis of future events and the development of the revolutionary movement.

11.2 The First Stage of the New Democratic Regime (1949-51)

The absence of a mass revolutionary Marxist party meant a petty-bourgeois, Stalinist party was carried to power in China on a mass upsurge so extensive that it swept away the bourgeois government and disintegrated its armed forces. The period immediately following 1949 was a transitional period during which the CCP attempted to form a viable state with the shades of the bourgeoisie, and with the declared aim of maintaining capitalism in China. The New Democracy encouraged capitalists to remain in charge of their factories, apparently secure in their positions. Overseas Chinese businessmen were encouraged to return to help build a capitalist China.

11.2.1 New Democracy and Bureaucratic Capital

In 1947 Mao estimated that the four families had accumulated assets worth US$ twenty thousand million and that under their rule, China had reached a condition of state-monopoly capitalism.[2] This turned out to be a gross under-estimation of the extent of bureaucratic capital.

When the new regime seized bureaucratic capital it found, to its surprise and consternation, that it had four-fifths of the country's heavy industry (90% of the metallurgical industries, 90% of power generation and electrical equipment, 75% of chemicals and 70% of machine building), about one third of light industry, and control of the transport and communication systems. After seizing Japanese-owned industry it acquired 83% of all foreign capital in China. The New Democratic government found itself employing about half of all factory workers, far more than it had expected or wanted.[3] The CCP was dismayed to inherit such a great share of the economy because it demonstrated just how weak was the national bourgeoisie.

The four families had also been entrenched in the banking system. On capturing Shanghai, the Military Control Committee immediately seized the banks owned by "comprador-feudal state monopoly capitalism" which included the two most important, the Farmers' Bank of China, and the Central Bank. The regime was again taken by surprise, now being in *de facto* control of the banking system with no perspective or plan. As a stop-gap measure and to strengthen the national bourgeoisie, the regime attempted to rationalise the banking system by forcing small and medium-sized banks to merge. These banks had to register with the government but were encouraged to continue operating privately.[4]

State ownership of the banks was absolutely essential if the intention was for China to break with capitalism. The banks are an essential instrument of economic policy because control of the allocation of resources must be in the hands of the state in a planned economy. This would be a decisive issue regarding the future of the Chinese revolution. The CCP did appoint cadres to sit on the decision-making bodies in the banks but the government was happy to see the joint state-private banks and the private banks that had existed under the KMT to continue to function for the benefit of the national bourgeoisie.

The banks belonging to the four families were amalgamated into a newly-formed People's Bank of China with the mergers negotiated jointly with the former senior managers who mostly remained in post. By and large, personnel simply transferred to the People's Bank. In some cases prominent bankers who had fled China were personally invited by Zhou Enlai to return and take leading positions in the People's Bank.[5] To attract these people, and other Chinese business men abroad, the CCP hinted at privatising at least some of these banks to strengthen the national bourgeoisie. At first, the New Democracy worked hard to support the private banks, but the need to bring inflation under control required a degree of centralisation that knocked privatisation off the agenda.

Inflation was so bad that the economy was collapsing, many factories and shops were unable to sustain themselves, and those which did, did so by not paying the wages of their employees. Trade was reduced to barter and workers demanded to be paid in kind, usually rice. The corrective measures had to be on a grand scale, co-ordinated and draconian to be effective.

The need to bring inflation under control required the People's Bank of China to tightly regulate credit and foreign currency exchange. During 1951-52, private banks were progressively rationalised, combined into a small number of joint state-private enterprises and then nationalised. By the third anniversary of the founding of the PRC, banking had become the first sector of the economy to be completely socialised. This extremely important development was not in the direction predicted by Mao, and at odds with the expectations of the New Democracy.

To minimise the effects of inflation and the resulting chaos, representatives of state industries began meeting to draft plans for future development. This was the first step to an integrated plan for the whole economy. For example, to avoid widespread hunger and profiteering, it was found necessary to set up state trading companies which monopolised both retail and wholesale trade in such basic essentials as food and farm produce. These functioned through fixed price state stores and co-operatives which, by August 1950, had 20 million members.[6]

The Party had promised to boost the growth of private capitalism and at first was as good as its word, but it had relatively few native capitalists to work with because businesses of any size had either been taken over by one or other of the four families or had fled with Chiang. Bourgeois property generally was left untouched, given protection, and its growth artificially bolstered. During this phase private businesses could depend on the state for raw materials, distribution channels, and a ready market. Representatives of the bourgeoisie were placed in prestigious and public positions, and even though they may have had no real power they were able to influence the regime because the state wanted their opinions and listened to them. The strength and importance of the national bourgeoisie was artificially and deliberately exaggerated.[7]

Because the national bourgeoisie were so weak on the ground, the New Democracy made a feature of encouraging over seven million small retailers and self-employed artisans to continue their operations. The forcible confiscation of the property of the self-employed taken by the Stalinist regime in Russia was a bureaucratic and short-sighted course of action. Forcing such people into state-controlled co-operatives was not an indication of a workers' state but the action of a bureaucratic regime. Both Lenin and Trotsky had been against compulsory confiscation of the property of artisans and shopkeepers.

11.2.2 New Democracy and Workers' Democracy

For the proletariat, political rights such as freedom of assembly, association, speech, and to strike, were strictly limited. Free, democratic workers' Soviets, or factory councils, are the mechanism by which the masses assess and impose their will on the parties that claim to represent them, and so were completely forbidden. To justify this approach Lo Fu developed the novel argument that the Bolsheviks came to power against the Soviets – any other interpretation was deemed 'Trotskyist'.[8]

A handful of workers held governmental posts (very few in senior positions) but these were appointed – the working masses had no right to freely elect their own representatives. Workers were hailed as the masters by this regime, but in reality they were as disenfranchised as workers in the Soviet Union under Stalin. Workers' democracy is a key issue for revolutionary Marxists because without genuine workers' democracy it is impossible to create a healthy workers' state "under the leadership of the proletariat."[9]

Nevertheless, the New Democracy did give workers significant protection from the worst excesses of exploitation. This was of real substance in the treaty ports where the imperialists had carried out their business with little concern for the laws of China or their Chinese employees. The PLA took control in quick succession of Nanjing, Hangchow, Wuhan, and then Shanghai. Foreign companies now had to abide by Chinese employment law and regulations; firms had to hire as permanent, their casual and temporary staff, and pay their workers in rice to beat inflation. However, while foreign companies now faced the same financial burden as Chinese companies, "there was little that was specifically socialist in the policies pursued by the CCP in the early years of the PRC."[10]

As late as August 1950, the *Liberation Daily* was promising foreign companies that they could continue operations in China and would be protected. However, without their privileges the foreign firms found it hard to compete and gradually they reduced their levels of activity. The UN embargo imposed during the Korean War reduced foreign trade to barter and meant it was closely controlled by the state. With the Three-Antis and Five-Antis Campaigns (see below), foreign firms effectively withdrew from China.

Far from smashing the old KMT state machine, the New Democracy absorbed important sections of it. Later, in 1952 – three years after the assumption of power, the PRC ruefully reported: "the People's government adopted a policy of taking over all the personnel in the former Kuomintang government offices and educational institutions when the reactionary rule of the Kuomintang collapsed."[11] This degree of presence in the state structure meant that the measures taken by the New Democracy to support capitalist initiatives struck a natural resonance and became amplified.

During the three years of recovery the number of private industrial enterprises increased from 123,000 to 150,000; most of these were small businesses employing fewer than 10 persons but a number of larger factories producing consumer goods did thrive. The size of the private industrial labour force grew from 1.6 to 2.2 million workers. The number of businessmen in major cities had increased by a quarter by the end of 1951 and in that year the average rate of profit was a remarkable 29%.[12] One Hong Kong business journal concluded: "The new regime has so far brought prosperous living conditions to all and sundry; the bankers and traders have no reason to complain, and, in fact, no substantial complaints are ever heard. Private trade is doing well and profits are high."[13] These developments had little independent substance and depended on the goodwill of the CCP, but with hindsight, it is clear that with continuing support from the CCP leadership, these small forces could have quickly grown into a real power within the state.

11.2.3 The New Democracy and Agrarian Reform

The Land Reform Law, published in June 1950, soon after the CCP became the new government, was historic in eradicating feudal remnants such, as mentioned above, that women were entitled to own land. But all activities were carried out under tight Party control, were constrained by the CCP's bureaucratic methods, and did not violate capitalist property relations and the principle of private ownership. The intention was to have 75% of China's farmland in private small holdings.[14] The CCP permitted the sale, purchase and renting of land and allowed rich peasants to keep their property and use hired labour.

The Bolsheviks had nationalised the land to create an agrarian system which was the most flexible for taking the socialist revolution into the countryside. In doing so, they had demonstrated that a contradiction can exist for some time between a peasant rural economy and state superstructure during a transitional period, that private production on the land (like private ownership of retail trade) was not a decisive factor in determining the class nature of the regime.

However, the huge preponderance of peasants in Chinese society made the changes in land policy good indicators of the direction in which the regime wanted to travel. Not nationalising the land was an important signpost for the direction in which the Mao regime intended to proceed. "Land to the Tiller" was not anti-capitalist and the New Democracy promised a "rich peasant economy" based on the private ownership of land and the continuing, if limited, presence of landlordism.[15] Simultaneously the CCP and PLA were ready to put down independent actions by peasants who wanted a revolutionary policy.

During the civil war (1947) the land policies of the CCP had been formulated to win peasant support against the KMT armies; immediately after the civil war (1950) the CCP was attempting to re-assure the national bourgeoisie that the New Democracy was no serious threat to its existence, and with the Korean War (see below) it was to increase support for the regime and to protect it from bourgeois sabotage.

There is thus, a chronology to the land policy of the CCP, but there are also geographic considerations: (a) the liberated areas and Soviets with over 100 million people where agrarian reform was completed before 1948, according to the Agrarian Reform Law of October 1947; (b) the Yangtse valley and surrounding regions with over 150 million people where land was distributed during 1950-51 according to the Agrarian Reform Law of June 1950; (c) the south-central region of China and the coastal region of eastern China where land reform was completed only at the end of 1952. This latter area contained nearly 100 million people. Given the considerable differences between areas, the implementation and monitoring of the Agrarian Reform Laws was delegated to regional administrations.[16]

In 1949 the advance of the PLA was so rapid that only partial and incomplete peasant associations could be formed before the PLA arrived and took control. There were some attempts at organising non-payment of rent which were tolerated but the CCP emphasis was on not disrupting the harvest, and thus the start of land redistribution was postponed until the autumn of 1950. In the plan for agrarian reform adopted in May 1950, excessive actions by the poor peasants and landless labourers against the landed proprietors and rich peasants were prohibited and special emphasis was given to 'the gradual execution of land reform'. As stated above, the immediate actions taken by the CCP were to limit rent to no more than 37.5% of the harvest and to lower interest rates to 15% though, as previously, the latter proved almost impossible to enforce.

The Land Law of 1947 had decreed the expropriation of all property of the landlords and the surplus land of the rich peasants (the area of land they owned above that of the typical local middle peasant). The 1950 Law declared that the land of the rich peasants, whether cultivated by members of the family or hired hands or rented out to poor peasants, had to be protected and must not be distributed. This, naturally, led to an outcry from the majority of peasants who saw their peers in the north being given land while they had to wait.

To give the CCP greater control, the land distribution programme was implemented in a specified order: first combat bad gentry, then reduce rent and interest rates, and finally expropriate land. The process took place sequentially village by village so the process was completed in one area before commencing in another. Since, in any given village the process could last many months, land distribution was slow.

The CCP's policy of protecting rich peasants, often giving them the best and the largest share of the land on the grounds of maximising food production, placed the rich peasants in a superior position in the rural economy. Rich peasants were in the business of loaning money to poor peasants; these activities could now flourish and rapidly did so. Many poor peasants who had been given their share of land were again sinking into poverty often due to debt repayment and a lack of the tools needed for farming. The land reform allowed the buying and selling of land on the open market and poor peasants were selling their land in order to maintain themselves. The rich peasants soon re-emerged as the dominant social factor (e.g. as head of the local Peasants' Association) controlling increasing areas of land.[17]

11.2.4 The New Democracy and Marriage Reform

In April 1949, the CCP founded the All-China Women's Federation (ACWF) and on 1 May 1950, the PRC enacted a New Marriage Law announced by Mao Zedong personally: "All marriages are to be based on the free consent of men and women." The Law raised the minimum marriageable age for males to 20 years and for females to 18, it banned marriage by proxy and both parties had to consent to a marriage. Under the slogan "Smash feudal marriage", Chinese law for the first time granted women the right to divorce their husbands and a right to a share of family property. This represented a dramatic step-change in the position of women and became an important part of land reform.

However, these changes were incomprehensible concepts to many peasants, certainly in the south of China where the CCP had no traditional base and women were considered as less than human, more like a sheep or a cow.[18] Women were encouraged to attend village mass meetings, convened under CCP guidance to decide how to share out confiscated lands. The form was preserved, but the reality was that almost all these women, most of whom had not been outside their homes for years, were terrified of speaking in public and had little effect on the outcomes.

Where cadres of the Women's Federation persuaded young women to attend and speak out they were usually ignored and occasionally physically assaulted. However, unlike in Jiangxi where the Women's Associations took direct action to end the physical intimidation, the Federation trod very softly.

Within three years the CCP, bowing to patriarchal pressures and fearful of a bad harvest, had dropped any co-ordinated effort to implement the land rights elements within the Marriage Law. It was argued that giving land to women was unproductive because: women lacked agricultural skills, a large number of women could not work the land because they were crippled having had their feet bound, women had to look after their children so could not spend enough time on the land, and the patriarchal family structure meant many women were unable to turn their legal rights into actual control of the land.[19]

Leader is clear that CCP cadres – at least in southern China – were sympathetic to peasant views which considered women the property of their husbands, and saw the attempts to liberate women as little more than legalised theft.[20] Leader points out that even though the number of divorces under the new law was minimal (less than one twentieth of one percent of marriages) the threat of divorce became a very real weapon for the emancipation of women. This was not presented positively by CCP cadres as a weapon to be used to obtain better treatment within the family but as a serious and severe threat to social stability; as "high treason against the natural order". It appears that cadres covered up, or even led, criminal activities to terrorise young women who threatened divorce using such slogans as: "A good woman hangs herself, a bad woman seeks divorce."[21]

By 1953 it is estimated that as many as a quarter of a million women (mostly aged under 25) had committed suicide or been murdered as a result. It can be argued that these women were paying the price for a bureaucratic approach to an age-old problem with very deep roots. The bureaucratic mentality sees issuing an order as resolving the problem, but here substantial preparatory educational work was needed and then strong support for the women affected.

Engels in *The Origin of the Family, Private Property, and the State*, had predicted that as women became increasingly economically independent, they would be able to abandon the institution of marriage and engage freely in sexual unions based on love.[21] The CCP, however, was vehemently opposed to women engaging in non-marital sexual unions and attempted to ensure that women fulfilled their biological destiny within the family. Party leaders did make public statements encouraging men to share in the division of household chores but at the same time made it clear that the primary responsibility for the well-being of the family, including cooking, making clothes, economising, cleaning and minding children, was that of women:

> "Participating in agricultural production is the right and duty of rural women. Taking care of children and dealing with housework, however, is also a responsibility that women cannot reject. This is the special way in which women and men are different."[22]

The CCP leadership had considered the Marriage Law for at least two years before enacting it and with their experience of similar laws in the liberated areas must have expected a hostile reaction. However, what they had not expected was the outbreak of the Korean War and to avoid any undermining of the support of the peasantry, the Marriage Law was soft-pedalled from at least 1950 and by March 1953 had been effectively abandoned. The bureaucracy undermined the value of the Marriage Law because it needed the family as a prop to the regime, just as had Stalin.

The official statement issued by Zhou Enlai and entitled "Thorough Enforcement of the Marriage Law" was notable because the content was the opposite of the title. Zhou ordered restricting the grounds for divorce and, with the 1st Five Year Plan (FYP) just around the corner, placed responsibility for smashing the feudal family on women's organisations within a framework of united, reconciled and harmonious families engaged in gainful production.[23]

The 1st FYP would be a contradictory experience for women in China. Official propaganda called on Chinese women to turn to industry, emphasising that joining the paid labour force was essential for their emancipation. But the plan did not specifically address jobs for women, and women tended to be confined to low skilled jobs (on the co-operatives for example, women planted rice seedlings while men drove tractors); despite official policies female unemployment was high and women were often paid less for work of equal value (women formed over half the agricultural labour force but got only 35% of total pay), and on getting home, women were stuck with housework and childcare.

By 1955 it was clear that with the influx of peasant men into the towns there were few jobs for women, and the CCP proposed a new mass line: women were to stay at home, encourage their husbands to work hard, and to manage their homes with "industry and thrift."[24] The proportion of women in employment fell sharply and those who continued in work were required to perform the same physical labour as men with dramatic consequences for their health and for their children's care.[25]

11.3 The Korean War

North Korea was a satellite of the USSR and the evidence available indicates Beijing was not informed of, not prepared for, and had little or no part in the decision to launch the attack on South Korea in June 1950. The Korean War was most unwelcome to the PRC: its hold upon China was still not fully secure and it needed peace to carry through its policies for economic reconstruction. The CC meeting in May 1950 had decided upon large-scale demobilisation of the PLA (1.4 million troops) in order to reduce government expenditure and help provide the resources to accelerate the re-building of the country. The war imposed crippling defence costs of between 15% and 18% of the national budget and seriously delayed the advance of the country by taking scarce resources from civil investment and skilled labour from the civil workforce.

When the war broke out, the Chinese had only one army, the 42nd Army of the Fourth Field Corps, stationed along the Yalu river border area but it was there primarily to assist with harvesting. The nearest troops ready for military action were the 9th and 10th Field Corps about 1,000 km away on the eastern coast preparing for the liberation of Taiwan.[26] Initially, the Chinese leaders limited their support to sending, at Kim Il Sung's request, 14,000 Korean Chinese then serving in the PLA but, at Stalin's insistence, became progressively more involved.[27]

On 27 June 1950, the United States President, Harry S Truman, ordered direct American air and naval support for South Korea and re-intervened in the Chinese civil war by positioning the 7th Fleet between the Chinese mainland and Taiwan to defend Chiang Kai-shek.

By August 1950, it had become clear that the objective of United Nations' action was the extinction of the North Korean regime and the forceful reunification of the country under the direct control of American imperialism. Even if Washington did not plan to attack China immediately, it intended to establish and protect a hostile regime on the Korean Peninsula and deploy its troops along the Sino-Korean border to exert military pressure, which would constitute a very grave threat to north-eastern China, the industrial heartland of the country. CCP statements and propaganda made it clear that such a scenario was unacceptable not least because it feared that the South Korean 'strong man' Syngman Rhee (supported by General MacArthur), might attempt to annexe parts of South Manchuria with its large Korean population.[28]

Zhou Enlai warned the US that the crossing of the 38th parallel by UN troops "would encounter Chinese resistance."[29] The Chinese leaders took this course of action with extreme reluctance and only as a last resort, deciding to send in 'volunteers' only after US troops had crossed into North Korea and were approaching the Chinese border. The initial Chinese intervention was cautious and limited and not until major engagements in November 1950, was China irrevocably involved in the war.

After the PLA had crossed the Yangtze river in 1949, the US government put China on an export control list. A license was required to export goods for direct military use (always refused) or multipurpose capital goods (approved only when no military use was possible). Immediately after the outbreak of the Korean War, the US required oil companies to stop shipment to China of petroleum products (even today every oil tanker docking in a Chinese port is shadowed by a US Navy warship). Soon after Chinese volunteers entered Korea, on 16 December 1950, the US government froze Chinese assets in American banks and formally prohibited all trade with China. In retaliation the CCP regime seized all American banks and enterprises, including all schools, hospitals, and similar institutions. By the end of 1950, US-China trade, both imports and exports, had virtually stopped.[30] On 15 May 1951, the United Nations imposed its own sanctions on China.

The significance of these events was that they were just the opposite of what Mao had been seeking when he had promised to be a better partner for US imperialism than had the KMT, offering better and more secure investment opportunities for Wall Street.[31] Mao's regime now became the government most hated by the American imperialists and the hoped-for compromise was postponed to the far distant future.[32]

With the outbreak of the Korean War, the regime undertook a broad mass mobilisation campaign – "Aid Korea, Resist America" – to increase its popularity. The wages of workers in state enterprises were increased and managements were instructed to be more sensitive to workers' opinions. That said, the executive power over production remained in the hands of the manager appointed by higher echelons. In the private sector, the regime showed greater tolerance towards workers' struggles and permitted trade unions to engage in 'legal struggle' with capitalists to improve living conditions, and oppose wage cuts and the arbitrary firing of workers, on the condition of not fundamentally hampering production.

The number of women recruited into industry jumped, and particularly in light industry; for example, 70% of the workforce in the Peking No. 3 Cotton mill and 80% in the Wusih State Silk Factory were women, though men still formed the overwhelming proportion in heavy industry. There was, generally speaking, a noticeable improvement in the life of the working masses. At the same time demands for increased production as part of the war effort were intensified. The essential rights of the working class in politics – democratic participation and control of government – remained anathema.

To successfully conduct a war, the state must be able to direct the economy according to its needs. The Korean War obliged the Chinese state to extend the public sector control of industry so that by the end of 1952, the state's total share of national industrial output was two-thirds. The war also imposed much greater centralisation of the economy. Just as imperialist intervention in Russia had accelerated nationalisation of basic industries, so the Korean War increased the pressures pushing China towards a workers' state.

The PLA, armed, trained and advised by soldiers of the Soviet Army, had defeated a KMT army funded and supported by US imperialism, the very people who were now threatening a back-door invasion of China via the Korean Peninsula. Against the model of economic planning which had lifted Russia out of poverty and backwardness were the threats and fury of the USA. The natural momentum of events was inexorably pushing China in the direction of a workers' state while Mao, guided by his Stalinist theories, attempted to delay or even reverse the process.

The direction which the regime was actually taking meant an increasing proportion of the national bourgeoisie saw the victory of US imperialism as their last hope and they started to act accordingly. The regime launched a campaign to suppress war criminals, traitors, bureaucratic capitalists, and counter-revolutionaries. Thousands of "vicious local autocrats", the most reactionary of the landlords and rich peasants, the most corrupt of the KMT bureaucrats inherited from the old regime, and captured KMT agents, were imprisoned and publicly executed, usually after party-sponsored trials attended by huge numbers of people.

This anti-counter revolutionary campaign was widened to include the universities and artistic communities. It began as a discussion of the film *The Life of Wu Xun*, (an historical figure who considered charitable works more effective than revolutionary activity in bettering the lives of the poor) after a critical editorial was published in the *People's Daily* on 20 May 1951. The discussion was soon transformed into a widely publicised ideological reform campaign requiring self-criticisms and public confessions by faculty members, film-makers, artists, writers, and scientists. All were criticised for failing to heed Mao's dictum that culture and literature must reflect the class interest of the working people (i.e. avoid any criticisms of the Party).

The campaign was extended to include parties represented in the government. As a signal of what was soon to come, a number of rank and file members of the Democratic League were arrested. The Kuomintang Revolutionary Committee was unscathed because it contained Song Qingling. Under the same pretext of suppressing 'counter-revolutionaries', the more advanced and discontented elements among the workers and peasants, especially the Trotskyists, were repressed, imprisoned and killed, demonstrating the regime still carried its anti-democratic, Stalinist baggage.[33]

11.4 The Three-Antis and Five-Antis Campaigns (1951-54)

As a result of campaigns carried out between 1951 and 1954, over half a million members would be expelled from the CCP for accepting bribes, being 'tainted by the class enemies', lacking commitment or not being up to the job.[34] The campaigns would begin by rooting out elements corrupted by the bourgeoisie but by their end, would be against the bourgeoisie as a class. Those foreign firms remaining in China after the US and UN embargoes would be subject to Three-Antis and Five-Antis Campaigns and, by early 1952, almost all foreign firms had ceased operations and withdrawn from China.[35]

11.4.1 The Three-Antis Campaign

Before the anti-counter revolutionary campaign was over, Mao had launched two new major campaigns. The first was at the end of 1951; the Three-Antis Campaign (anti-corruption, anti-waste, and anti-bureaucratism) was meant to identify corruption of urban cadres, particularly those in business administration dealing with private enterprise. This began as the Chinese advance in Korea was halted and the war settled down to a bloody slog. The CCP could no longer close its eyes to an extremely serious situation that was causing enormous financial and economic losses to the various state institutions and was arousing widespread discontent, especially amongst industrial workers in the ranks of the Party. Weeding out corruption and inefficiency in the government apparatus had become an urgent task.[36]

A news report in August 1950 had claimed that corrupt cadres had misappropriated 450,000 tons of grain and then flaunted their ill-gotten gains in shows of 'arrogance and vanity'. A subsequent series of articles in the *New China Press* and *Peoples' Journal* in early 1951, revealed that the level and extent of corruption was stupendous. In central government alone the corruption was valued at 73 billion yuan at a time when the annual salary of a civil servant could be as little as 1,000 yuan.[37] The situation in the regions was, apparently, much worse! If this level of corruption was attained within just two years, what did the future hold?

Corrupt cadres fattened themselves by pilfering state funds and spending public monies on luxurious lifestyles. They were selling state resources, such as raw materials at cut prices, rubber stamping increased production costs to assure additional profits to the capitalists. The capitalists, it appears, did not hesitate to repay the favours. Corruption, waste, and bureaucracy were becoming entrenched in the state apparatus, the army, mass organisations and, in particular, in the industrial and commercial sectors. A general malaise was appearing within the CCP. In some rural districts, CCP members had become the foci of commerce, land purchase, and usury to the extent that they were asking to be allowed to quit the Party to pursue careers as capitalist entrepreneurs. It was claimed that in some areas these same CCP members had bought up as much as 20% of the land allocated to poor peasants.[38]

The anti-corruption campaign began in the north east of China where CCP control over society was most established but also because in Manchuria the Korean War had provided the greatest opportunities for the generation of a new layer of capitalists and the brazen bribery of administrative officials. Capitalist influences undermined the behaviour of cadres and were amplified because those cadres were not freely elected, not subject to criticism from the workers and peasants, and not subject to democratic control and recall. Used to abusing their authority, receiving higher wages, special treatment and privileges, they considered it their right to surround themselves with ever greater luxury; they were easily corrupted and debased because the bureaucratic state apparatus already had a culture of privileges and perks.

For the millions of KMT bureaucrats with their sleazy practices, corruption had long been a way of life. These people were now well-placed to take advantage of the opportunist policy of class collaboration which feted and praised the national bourgeoisie as partners in the New Democratic economy, just as the shortages created by the Korean War generated ideal conditions for crooked dealings. What the Three-Antis Campaign demonstrated was that the protected capitalist sector had an effect out of all proportion to its size.

To effectively eliminate such practices required workers' democracy. This was not possible under the Mao regime, but the CCP did have extensive experience of initiating and overseeing mass campaigns which used women's and youth organisations, professional bodies, and trade unions to mobilise the population in support of issues the government deemed worthy. These techniques were used with the Three-Antis Campaign with the addition that public criticisms of local officials who had blatantly taken bribes or openly used their positions for personal aggrandisement, were encouraged. In this way the campaign had the beneficial effect of appeasing discontent in the Party ranks.

This campaign was not intended to change the bureaucratic nature of the CCP and so could not eliminate opportunism, corruption or waste as was demonstrated when the excesses of the party tops were left untouched.[39] The CCP leadership was obliged to expel obviously rotten cadres and to attack certain bourgeois elements because, embroiled in a war with US imperialism it could not tolerate incompetent and politically unreliable public officials and an inefficient, ill-disciplined, and unresponsive bureaucratic system.

The rapid corruption and moral degeneration of the CCP revealed the bankruptcy of the New Democracy. Representatives of a world system that was much more technologically advanced, the national bourgeoisie were much more corrosive than either their numbers or the value of their products would imply. The CCP simply failed to understand the nature of the national bourgeoisie, failed to understand why the national bourgeoisie turned their backs on what was so obviously the rational way forward for China. On 15 January 1952, the editorial of the *Tientsin Journal* plaintively pleaded: "The orientation of the popular democratic front has not changed … we still hope the bourgeoisie will conscientiously accomplish their own reform to conduct themselves peacefully in the new democracy." The Maoist regime was increasingly being faced with having to end the New Democracy or move to the full restoration of the bourgeoisie.

11.4.2 The Five-Antis Campaign

During 1951, it became clear that the output in many sectors of the economy would soon reach the pre-1949 peak. This gave the Chinese bourgeoisie greater confidence and they became bolder in defending their interests against the state and in intervening in the state machine through bribery and corruption. As the economy began to expand, private business based in the light industries expanded most rapidly and attempted to acquire a larger share of scarce raw materials, legally (by paying up to 40% more than the state) or through the black market (bribery). Skilled labour moved from the state sector to private firms able to pay more because of their high profits. These boom conditions for the private sector undermined government control of the economy.

No sooner was the Three-Antis Campaign underway than Mao launched the Five-Antis Campaign (anti-bribery, anti-tax evasion, anti-fraud, anti-embezzlement, and anti-leakage of state secrets) in January 1952. This programme complemented the Three-Antis Campaign and was aimed at eliminating corrupt practices by businessmen and industrialists. In reality, the Mao regime could not allow a class whose objective interests lay in the victory of the US to retain control over light industry and much of agriculture. Wholesale expropriation – in whatever form it took – would be an inevitable result of the Korean War.

In Shanghai alone, 15,000 inspectors were trained to investigate their employers' business affairs for tax evasion and other corrupt practices. The CCP encouraged business people to confess or denounce one another (some big companies made thousands of voluntary confessions to try to protect themselves); citizens were invited to write letters denouncing businesses (about 200,000 letters a month were received); friends and family were encouraged to join in. The campaign had loudspeakers on every street corner broadcasting denunciations of local recalcitrants, wall newspapers carried reports of the misconduct and offences of businessmen, in the streets there were demonstrations by the employees of companies denouncing the crimes of their employers, and factory owners would be continuously besieged in their offices by workers demanding they admit and recant their crimes.

The intention was that the business leaders identified by the Five-Antis Campaign should be humiliated and intimidated, should go through public criticism sessions, be made to confess their crimes, and forced to pay large fines (the owner of Dahua copper company confessed to having illegally obtained 50 million yuan but his employees continued to criticise him until he re-confessed to having obtained 2 billion yuan). Fines were heavy and some offenders were sent to labour camps.

In its early stages, the campaign was limited to an assertion of CCP control of society from bottom to the top. To save face, official statements presented the struggle as being against individual 'mangy sheep' of the bourgeoisie. However, in the course of this campaign the Party uncovered well-organised attempts by important businessmen and industrialists to corrupt Party and government officials. Before it ended the Five-Antis Campaign would become an all-out war against the bourgeoisie as a whole.[40]

The *People's China* editorial of 15 March 1952 complained: "as (the capitalist) enterprises have developed and begun to flourish the bourgeoisie has become less inclined to conform to the Common Programme and obey governmental regulations." Capitalists were reported as having set up secret monopolies to control supplies to the state or to state enterprises; the Chinese bourgeoisie were using "the same lamentable methods as are habitually used by big capitalists in the capitalist states." It was becoming clear that the national capitalists collaborated with the New Democracy only out of immediate necessity and not out of idealism or belief in the Common Programme. The greater the success of Mao's policy of stabilising and enriching private enterprise, the bolder and more determined it became in defence of its own interests against those of the state. The regime was having its eyes opened by the Korean War and realising that the national bourgeoisie were not willing allies in the New Democracy, and could become a fifth column.

Chen Po-ta (CC member) presented an in-depth analysis of the situation in *Pravda* (23 April 1952):

> "Spurred by their hunger for profit ... (the capitalists) placed their agents in our state institutions and our public organizations ... hired employees of the state and public bodies as their agents ... did not give up their hope of conquering power bit by bit in the PRC ... the bourgeoisie is striving to push China onto the road to capitalism."[41]

During 1952 the CC, in its majority, became convinced of the need to push the private sector into mixed public-private enterprises with the government having the determining role. Private operations had accounted for three quarters of wholesale trade in 1950, but by 1953 their share had shrunk to less than a third. As a result of the Five-Antis Campaign there was a considerable state presence in the remaining private sector through joint companies.[42]

Once the civil war was over the New Democracy was supposed to provide a peaceful (even if slow) transition to socialism. The reality, as found in the Five-Antis Campaign was that the national bourgeoisie were sabotaging the regime and the use of force was widely used to compel the largest private corporations to convert into joint private-state enterprises, and the smallest factory owners and merchants to give up their capital assets. Many were grateful to have escaped with their lives, some did not.[43]

It has long been accepted by Marxists that the destruction of capitalism, e.g. the ending of private property in the means of production and the introduction of state-owned property, can take place only as a result of the revolutionary mobilisation of the masses. Here the mass mobilisations deviated markedly from the ideal norms and occurred under the watchful eye of the PLA, under the guidance of a Stalinist Party. The similarities with Eastern Europe are obvious.[44] In China, to maintain technical continuity, and to gain a degree of assent, the previous owners were often offered managerial positions in the joint private-state enterprises so they could continue to contribute to the state economy, and previous shareholders were compensated with a pension guaranteed for seven years at 5% per annum of their share of the business. Such arrangements are matters of convenience not of principle, but the net effect was a dramatic contraction in the private sector.

The presentation of these events was a problem for Mao and the CCP. Officially the New Democracy was a lengthy preparatory stage during which Chinese society would be made ready for launching socialism. In true Orwellian manner, the texts were re-written to match actual events; this is why so many of Mao's works were re-published in 1951. Now, New Democracy was presented as a rapid transition to socialism. Cohen gives an interesting but disturbing picture of the public self-rectification that had to be undertaken by many, particularly academics and students, who had studied *On New Democracy*, thought they had understood it well, had even been given responsibility for lecturing on it, but now found they had not understood it at all.[45]

It is to be expected that the CCP presents the Third Chinese Revolution as having followed the course outlined by Mao. The expectation was that the New Democracy would last for scores of years, but the laws of historic development meant there were only two years between October 1949 and the first moves against the national bourgeoisie in the Three-Antis and Five-Antis Campaigns. In reality it would have been difficult to move against the national bourgeoisie any sooner. Being a bureaucracy, the CCP over-reacted and even small retailers were herded into co-operatives under Party control. Lenin, of course, had argued that such small enterprises should be taken over by the state only when the individual retailers themselves wanted it.

11.4.3 Agricultural Policy and the Korean War

With the outbreak of the Korean War the activities of all reactionary elements revived, and anti-communist guerrillas re-appeared across southern China. These successfully incited not only landlords but also many poor peasants and landless labourers (angry at receiving little or nothing from the land reforms) to acts of open rebellion such as refusal to pay taxes, forming groups to plunder public food banks, harassing local officials, etc. So bad did the situation become in some counties that the *Yangtze Daily* (published in Hankou) concluded there was a danger of the peasants following KMT agents and country autocrats rather than the CCP and the People's Government. Mandel claimed that in many counties in the south a veritable civil war was raging between thousands of bandits mobilised by KMT agents and supported by local landlords against poor peasant associations organised by the CCP.[46]

The CCP was forced to adopt a more conciliatory line towards the poor peasants and a less conciliatory attitude towards the remaining landlords who were – of course – closely inter-linked with the national bourgeoisie. The "Aid Korea, Resist America" campaign (1951-52) won considerable support from the peasant masses because re-distribution of landlords' excess lands was accelerated and extended southwards and throughout China, until by the end of 1952 it had been largely completed. In parallel with Party policy in the urban areas, there was increased emphasis on the mobilisation of poor peasants and landless labourers to root out landlordism and right-opportunist deviations in the land reform movement. These activities were meant to be closely supervised by Party cadres but the poor peasants and landless labourers often took the law into their own hands to effect a fuller and fairer distribution. In the face of the Korean War, the CCP leadership generally acquiesced to, and even allowed cadres to lead a number of these actions but without formally changing regime policy.[47]

The CCP skilfully used this situation to initiate the first step towards co-operativisation, and towards the state taking greater control of agriculture to provide the necessary resources for industrialisation. But the requirement not to disturb food production imposed a major constraint on the rate of rural change. In December 1951, the CC of the CCP, in a move that was justified as helping poor peasants and improving production, proposed voluntary mutual-aid teams. This was a form of basic co-operation where individual farmers worked together on the separate land holdings and then shared the produce according to the amount of labour and farming tools they contributed. This meant the rich peasants who possessed tools such as hoes and carts got the larger portion of the crops, but the scheme increased overall production so everyone benefited. Such teams had been tested in the liberated areas during and after the Sino-Japanese War and found to significantly increase production. The intention was to have 80-90% of all peasants organised in mutual aid teams by 1955.[48]

11.5 The End of the New Democracy

The dynamic of class contradictions on an international scale revealed the core weakness in the theory of socialism in one country, forcing Mao to abandon his New Democracy step by step. An economic blockade had obliged the CCP to carry out the seizure of US property in China, and destroyed the hoped-for collaboration. The Korean War and direct threat of imperialist invasion together with their growing strength in the economy had given sections of the national bourgeoisie sufficient confidence to mount a campaign of economic sabotage, to corrupt CCP members, and to launch other anti-revolutionary activities. In the countryside, the rich peasants were feeling their strength and demanding to be allowed to get on with the job of food production, i.e. to grow into landlords.

Industrial output had grown rapidly after 1949, by roughly a fifth to a quarter each year and it soon became clear that a major factor limiting expansion was the disparity in growth between the different sectors of the economy; insufficient raw materials, and inadequate power supplies and transport facilities. This on its own pointed to the need for greater co-ordination and planning. Under these pressures and threats, the CCP was forced to take a big step forward by abandoning the reactionary illusions of New Democracy and adopting a series of objectively revolutionary measures. These were reactions, taken for self-preservation without any real understanding of the motor forces driving events.

In the exceptional circumstances following WWII the class-collaborationist stance of the CCP had not stopped Mao coming to power. But once in power the official line of the CCP meant that the New Democracy was at odds with what was actually happening. The national bourgeoisie was not rationally assessing what was best for China and acting accordingly; it was acting in its own interests. Even though it represented the smaller part of the economy it was successfully corrupting the CCP and the state machine. In only three years it had shown it could soon grow into a real threat to the interests of the bureaucracy. Determined to protect their newfound privileges and power, the bureaucracy made a series of empirical adaptations to events before accepting that the New Democracy was irreversibly breaking down.

At the beginning of 1953, the CCP proclaimed that the bourgeois-democratic phase of the revolution was passing and its socialist phase was beginning. With its 1st FYP (1953-1957) for economic construction and industrialisation, the CCP abandoned the New Democracy and replaced it with the policy of state and private co-operation, which aimed at the abolition of bourgeois property and the beginning of socialist construction. On 1 October 1953, the fourth anniversary of the founding of the People's Republic, the government proclaimed "the general line for the transition to socialism" and finally buried the New Democracy. Despite the prominence of the New Democracy in formal Maoist theory, and its promise of a lengthy stage of capitalist development, the bourgeois phase of China's post-revolutionary history was abruptly terminated after just four years.[49]

Cohen describes the abruptness of the change in Party line that took place in mid-1953 when suddenly the "transition to socialism" was at hand in China. He says that in a four-month period (July to October), the perspective that the New Democracy was an economy in which the private sector could flourish, was ditched and replaced by the perspective that capitalism could and should be crowded out quickly. Then in October 1953, an intense national campaign was launched. This lasted about two and half years until by 1955/6 there had been a complete transformation with even small businesses becoming state enterprises.[50]

By 1956, approximately two-thirds of all modern industrial enterprises were directly state-owned, and the remaining one-third was under joint public-private ownership. No privately-owned firms remained. In true Stalinist fashion the change was all-encompassing, even micro-scale industries were organised into co-operatives which accounted for just over 90% of all handicraft workers.

In 1954 there was widespread discussion on the new state constitution to supersede the Common Programme and which would bring the New Democracy phase of China's development to a formal end. The constitution proposed was based on the Soviet constitution established by Stalin in 1936 with integration of party and state and a highly centralised structure.[51] Naturally, the discussion about and around the constitution, and the nature of the regime, was taken up by intellectuals who tended to favour more freedoms rather than less. The CCP moved quickly to curb dissent by launching an attack on the well-known author and Party member Hu Feng for criticising the harsher aspects of Party control of art and literature. Hu Feng was arrested in 1955 and imprisoned as a counter-revolutionary. The campaign soon extended its scope and over 190,000 individuals made 'voluntary' confessions to avoid public humiliation or worse. This can be seen as setting the stage for the Party's dealings with intellectuals and would lead to the Hundred Flowers in May-June 1957 (see Chapter 13).

11.6 Can the Petty-Bourgeois be Revolutionary?

Here is the place to answer the challenge posed by Pierre Rousset who has written extensively on political developments in Asia, that a party which takes power in a revolution that leads to a workers' state cannot be Stalinist.[52] Rousset is not defending Marxism, quite the opposite! Rousset had previously made an overly positive assessment of the strength and prospects of Stalinism. He saw Mao as a genuine revolutionary who had been able to drag the CCP behind him and create a Chinese workers' state. Thus, he was determined to paint a revolutionary face on Mao and prettify Maoism.

The source of the Chinese Revolution did not lie in the personality of Mao Zedong but in the very deep crisis of capitalism that occurred on a world scale at the end of WWII, and the contradictory character of petty-bourgeois political parties. It is one thing to say the theory of permanent revolution had found confirmation in China where the CCP was compelled to undertake socialist measures to resolve the bourgeois tasks of national independence and freedom from landlordism; it was quite another to suggest Mao Zedong was acting as a Trotskyist, even if as an 'unconscious Trotskyist'.[53]

Rousset suggests that to argue that a non-socialist, petty-bourgeois party can, under certain exceptional circumstances, overturn capitalism revises Marxism. Rousset might appear to be on strong ground since in 1922, the 4th World Congress of the Communist International had considered the case of a petty-bourgeois government brought to power by a revolutionary upsurge and decided that it would be unlikely to progress to the dictatorship of the proletariat. However, very different conditions existed in 1949 than in 1922. Imperialism had been seriously weakened and China was rotten ripe for revolution.

Marx described and explained that even though a petty-bourgeois party was a contradictory phenomenon it could still be revolutionary, for example in his analysis of the Paris Commune, Marx reported that the *Alliance Républicaine des Départements* – a political association of petty-bourgeois representatives – called on the people throughout the country to fight against the Versailles government and the monarchist National Assembly and to support the Commune.[54] Petty-bourgeois formations were, and are, quite prepared to use revolutionary means but the contradictory nature of their goals (to harmonise the interests of capital and labour) meant that in the era of the growth of capitalism, such groups invariably ended on the side of the bourgeoisie.

But they are also pulled in the opposite direction, especially in the era of the decay of capitalism. Could a petty-bourgois grouping having taken power move towards a workers' state? Based on his experiences in Russia and his analysis of unfolding events, Trotsky concluded:

> "one cannot categorically deny in advance the theoretical possibility that, under the influence of completely exceptional circumstances (war, defeat, financial crash, mass revolutionary pressure, etc.), the petty bourgeois parties, including the Stalinists, may go further than they wish along the road to a break with the bourgeoisie. .... one thing is not to be doubted: even if this highly improbable variant somewhere at some time becomes a reality ... it would represent merely a short episode on the road to the actual dictatorship of the proletariat."[55]

In China the pre-conditions for such a petty-bourgeois group coming to power was a mass upheaval so extensive that the bourgeois government and its armies were swept away. It would be expected that the resulting petty-bourgeois government, even in a Stalinist form, would carry through substantial reforms of the system but, at a crucial point, would have to choose between deepening the revolution or conceding power to the bourgeoisie.

What were the exceptional circumstances that pushed the Mao regime to make the final decision to become a workers' state? Ten reasons spring to mind, though there may be more.

- Capitalist development in China had reached an *impasse*. China was over-ripe for revolution and this had been confirmed by the implosion of the KMT and the collapse of its armies.
- The initial impetus for the course of events lay not with Mao but with Chiang Kai-shek's refusal to accept the advice of US imperialism or listen to the pleas of the CCP, and his decision to launch his armies against the PLA in a fight to the death.
- Imperialism was temporarily paralysed.
- There was no credible governmental alternative to the Mao regime and this political vacuum permitted the entrenchment of a petty-bourgeois Stalinist government.
- The CCP was determined to seize bureaucratic capital, but the assets of the four families were so huge that the state took effective control of heavy industry, the banks, communications, and transport. The CCP was unable to privatise these holdings because the collapse of

society had been so severe that to end famine, bring inflation under control and get the economy moving again, required extensive state intervention and economic measures that were socialist in principle.

- The capitalist elements in the New Democratic government had little independent weight, no mass support, and could be tolerated. When these bourgeois elements became a hindrance they were rapidly and easily eliminated, although to preserve the appearance of continuity these parties remain in government even today!
- The historic links between the Chinese and Russian Communist Parties, the Soviet Union's incredible economic progress, and the aid supplied by the Soviet Union meant that most Party members in China saw a Soviet style, planned economy as the natural outcome of their efforts.
- The entire membership of the CCP from Mao down genuinely wanted social reform for the betterment of the lives of peasants and workers. This would have been complemented by pressure from the peasant masses (including many in the PLA) to carry through the land reform rapidly and in a revolutionary way. Because of the links between the landlords and the national bourgeoisie this mass pressure pushed the regime in the direction of a workers' state.
- Under pressure from imperialism (the Marshall Plan), Stalin had swung left and overthrown the coalition regimes in Eastern Europe. This short-lived left turn meant that the 'highly improbable variant' of transition to workers' states under petty-bourgeois leadership, actually took place in a number of countries after WWII. China was part of this international development.
- The CCP had a twenty-year history of being the sole governing body in extensive areas of China (notwithstanding the three-threes arrangement). In October 1949, the business of running a government was not a new venture for the Maoists; rather it was the continuation of what they had been practising for years. When considering annexation of territories by the USSR Trotsky wrote: "… the Moscow government will carry through the expropriation of the large land-owners and stratification of the means of production … not because the bureaucracy remains true to the socialist program but because it is neither desirous nor capable of sharing

> the power, and the privileges the latter entails, with the old ruling classes ….."[56] While prepared to give the appearance of sharing power with an enfeebled national bourgeoisie, the Maoists were not prepared to accept counter-revolutionary activities that could lead to the end of their power and privileges.

The debate concerning whether the petty-bourgeois can be revolutionary was decided once and for all by the Cuban Revolution. This was made by a party that at first did not even claim to be socialist and finally dissipated any mystification on the character of these revolutionary upheavals. The key is in the contradictory character of petty-bourgeois political groups and the degree of decay and corruption of capitalism.

Even while making the final moves towards a workers' state in China the Stalinist framework of class-collaboration (epitomised in the slogan "Peaceful coexistence"), the theory of socialism in one country, revolution by stages, bureaucratic party structure and administrative methods, the systematic denial of Soviet democracy, and limitation of workers' rights remained constant factors in the Mao regime.

11.7 Summary

In China in 1949 a Stalinist petty-bourgois party was the sole effective force in the government, and the power of the state (bodies of armed men, etc.) was in its hands. It had reached this position not because of a principled conscious decision to fight its own bourgeoisie, but because its own bourgeoisie (the KMT) collapsed, rotten to the core. Only when threatened by imperialism did Mao end his attempt to balance between the national bourgeoisie and the masses. Mao broke with his stated programme and accepted the overturn of capitalist property relations but not to the extent of allowing the emergence of independent organisations of workers' democracy. The privileged bureaucratic caste that had consolidated in the CCP continued to exclude the masses from political decision-making.

The CCP had taken power through peasant armies rather than a proletarian uprising. Its declared policy was to delay forming a proletarian dictatorship because such a development clashed with the theory of stages and the New Democracy. Mao artificially delayed the revolutionary progress, stifled the initiatives of the masses, and for a time, made the CCP a prop for the national bourgeoisie.

The pressures on the PRC to solve its immediate problems – inflation, feeding and housing the population, replacing industries destroyed or stolen during the war, launching new industries, making good dams, canals and irrigation systems on a mass scale – all pushed the regime in the direction of measures which were socialist in principle. By 1951, within government ministries, planning and collaboration were taking place spontaneously as the only realistic means of achieving the stated goals of the regime.

Initially Mao did his best to resist the trend but the Korean War and the imperialist embargo on trade with China finally resolved the contradictions between the declared aims of the government and what was actually happening. The CCP was forced to face up to the corrosive effect of bourgeois control of light industry and medium and small banks. Bourgeois corruption of the state and Party reached an intolerable level and there was active sabotage of economic plans as the factory owners formed their own, secret cartels to manipulate supplies and prices. The regime responded with two mass campaigns – the Three-Antis and the Five-Antis – which effectively ended the national bourgeoisie as significant factors in industry or finance.

The central tasks of the revolution in colonial and semi-colonial countries are national unification and independence (overthrow the imperialist yoke) and the agrarian revolution (liquidation of feudal heritages). These two tasks are interlinked and the theory of the permanent revolution predicts that in the era of imperialism they can be fully realised only with the dictatorship of the proletariat.[57]

Chapter 12

Establishing the Chinese Workers' State

12.1 Introduction

The abnormal and contradictory conditions in which the PRC found itself after the civil war were the product of exceptional historical circumstances. It was not possible to find a previous regime in history analogous to it. To Marxists, right from the start, it was clear that the New Democracy contained huge contradictions and would be short-lived. It was a highly precarious regime and at the time only the most farsighted were convinced it could move forward to a clean sweep of capitalism's remnants and not find itself, willy-nilly on the path of capitulation to imperialism.

12.2 First Five Year Plan (1953-57)

In its early years, for historic, political and geographic reasons, the New Democracy was economically heavily dependent on the Soviet Union and its East European allies who gave very real support in the form of US$300 million in credit over five years at 1% interest, 12,300 technical experts to work in China, and taking some 14,000 Chinese students and 38,000 apprentices for training. Volumes of technical information that would have cost billions of US$ on the world market were freely given, and joint design teams worked on all major and important projects.

Those at the work face across many different Government Ministries exerted huge pressure for a comprehensive, planned, state-controlled economy as the best and most rational way forward for China to overcome her mind-boggling problems. An important goal for the First Five Year Plan (1st FYP) was to expand and integrate the separate economies that had developed in China largely due to the Sino-Japanese War: the heavy industries of Manchuria, the light industries, textiles and consumer goods of the coastal regions, and the huge agrarian areas of inland China. For the latter a special effort was needed to repair canals and drainage systems destroyed by the Imperial Japanese and KMT armies.[1]

After the outbreak of the Korean War, the new regime's economic and military dependence on the Soviet Union deepened. Over 1952-53 the Soviet Union continued to work closely with the PRC especially in detailing the final drafts of the 1st FYP, which had a Russian-style emphasis on heavy industry. The increased control over society and the economy required to wage the Korean War successfully had created a dynamic which inevitably led first to the Party agreeing a "general line for transition to socialism" in June 1953, and then to its public pronouncement.

The signing of the Korean Armistice in 1953 meant a big reduction in military expenditure and the release of resources for accelerated economic expansion. A State Planning Commission determined production targets and material allocation. The distribution of key commodities was controlled according to a central plan, not market forces. Products were distributed to achieve state planning objectives, not private profit.

The introduction of the 1st FYP eliminated the contradiction between the declared and actual policies of the CCP, it extended state control to all significant areas of the economy and meant the co-ordination of the different sectors within an overall plan. As part of the "high tide of socialist transformation", joint private-state enterprises were, in essence, nationalised, private retailers were merged into co-operative teams, and private markets in rural areas were banned. It is from the launch of the 1st FYP in October 1953, that revolutionary Marxists date the bureaucratically-deformed workers' state in China.

The private sector of the Chinese economy was marginalised, eliminated as a significant source of production or employment, and by the end of 1956 all private industry had been nationalised or absorbed into joint enterprises. Importantly, by the end of 1956, foreign trade was fully under state control.[2]

In 1954, Zhou Enlai declared that the 1st FYP was not only to "free the productive forces of our country from the oppression of imperialism, feudalism, bureaucratic capitalism ... and the shackles of capitalism" but also to remove "the limitations of small-scale production."[3] The 1st FYP emulated the Soviet model with high rates of investment in capital intensive, large-scale industrial projects to lay the primary foundations for China's socialist industrialisation, with agriculture providing the major source of funds.

Surprisingly, the 1st FYP was not formally approved by the National People's Congress until 30 July 1955. This was followed in September 1955 by the publication of a report on the fulfilment of the annual plan for 1954.[4] The two-year delay in publication was due to the unexpectedly poor performance of agriculture and the need to come to a decision on how to deal with it.

In terms of overall economic growth, the 1st FYP was a stunning success. Despite the best efforts of imperialism to sabotage the plan, wages rose by a third in real terms, life expectancy rose from about 36 years in 1949 to 57 years in 1957, the proportion of children attending primary school doubled to 50%, the quality and quantity of urban housing improved significantly, and the rights of women were extended and protected in law, exemplified by the abolition of the binding of women's feet. Famine appeared to be a thing of the past.[5]

Discussions began on the tasks to be undertaken in the 2nd FYP. Mao argued for an increase in the rate at which the state was acquiring privately-owned small-scale handicraft establishments and an even higher rate of industrial development. There followed a coded exchange of views in the press (e.g. *People's Daily*) in which the State Planning Commission countered Mao by arguing for a 2nd FYP which avoided excessive investment in heavy industry and attempted a more balanced development including light industry and agriculture. The Chairman of the State Planning Commission, Kao Kang, committed suicide in August 1954 after having been purged, apparently for daring to voice his opposition to Mao. However, Kang must have had considerable support on the CC because the debate was not resolved until Mao by-passed the CC and launched the Great Leap Forward (GLF) in the spring of 1958.[6]

In September 1956, at its Eighth Party Congress, in a report given by Liu Shaoqi, the CCP declared the People's Republic of China to be a proletarian dictatorship. There had been esoteric discussions by CCP theoreticians on 'bourgeois rights': whether distribution on the basis of to each according to his work was a socialist or capitalist principle. The very same topic had been discussed in the Soviet Union when in 1936, the draft of a new Soviet Constitution had been published, see Section 3.6, above. In Russia the formula had been intended to justify the extraction of the maximum labour from the workers and peasants while preserving privileges and luxuries for the Party tops. The Chinese Stalinists came to the same conclusion as their predecessors, and for the same reasons, convincing themselves that this undoubted capitalist principle was socialist, and the CCP declared China a workers' state.[7]

One reason the CCP had delayed declaring the PRC a proletarian dictatorship was to avoid embarrassing itself. One of Mao's supposed original and major contributions to Marxism had been the theory of the New Democracy which would last for decades and flow painlessly through to socialism. Instead, it had lasted just four years, and was consigned to the dustbin of history under the watchful eye of the PLA and an aggressive mass movement. The changes in CCP policy clearly showed that under the pressure of objective events it had been forced to take "practical measures" that when carried out, left China "standing with one foot in socialism."[8]

12.2.1 The Peasants and the Five Year Plan

During preparatory discussions of the 1st FYP it was soon realised that the necessary investment to expand heavy industry would require an increase in agricultural production, prevention of hoarding of raw materials and an end to leakages into private consumption. There was also the need to take control of foodstuffs to ensure an adequate supply of food to the towns to feed the huge influx of peasants who would be the new industrial workers. In 1949 the city population had been 49 million, by 1956 it was nearly 100 million, and by 1961 had reached 130 million. This would necessitate urban rationing of grain and a state monopoly of trade in agricultural commodities.

As the need for agricultural produce increased, the relatively well-off farmers (the major producers of food) began to flex their political muscles, demanding greater economic autonomy. But the government was now looking in a different direction and responded by replacing the all-inclusive Village Associations with committees of selected poor and middle peasants, a reversal of the processes carried out in the liberated areas, particularly in south China, in 1947-48.[9]

It was understood by all Party tops that the 1st FYP would require wide-ranging changes for the peasantry but differences were emerging on what they should be. The division had first surfaced in July 1951 when the Party leadership in Shanxi proposed an accelerated pace towards co-operatives. This was openly criticised by Liu Shaoqi at Party meetings where Liu emphasised the "four big freedoms": freedom for peasants to engage in trade, to hire labour, to rent land, and to make loans and charge interest. Mao had the more radical approach and by January 1953 was proposing the elimination of private ownership of the land as part of the general move against bourgeois property. However, Liu supported by Zhou Enlai, fought a rear guard action for a more gradual approach to industrialisation and a slower rate of change in the countryside.[10] The differences within the CC reached such a level that Mao sent a letter to the State Council in which he mounted (without naming names) a concentrated attack on efforts to maintain private property in the countryside.[11]

Measures to extract as much surplus as possible to fund industrialisation were announced. In August 1953, grain rationing was introduced in an attempt to limit personal consumption and ration cards (or 'coupons') were issued by local authorities, the smallest being for only 5 grams of rice or wheat. More importantly, the government moved to take control of the grain trade from the village level upwards which meant peasants would no longer buy or sell grain on the open market, but only from and to the state. Publically, these moves were promoted as necessary to obtain food to feed the poorest peasants and those in areas hit by natural disasters but were, in effect, an increase in agricultural tax. This monopoly was soon extended to include cotton and cotton cloth, and oil-bearing crops.[12]

To improve the efficiency of farming, and increase government access to agricultural products, the CCP encouraged peasants to organise themselves into 'state guided' Agricultural Producers' Cooperatives (APCs). The peasantry had experienced the benefits of mutual-aid teams which had gone well with little recorded dissent because any extra work produced more for the peasants themselves. A directive was issued by the CC of the CCP in October 1953 proposing a move from mutual aid teams to village level co-operatives (Lower Stage APCs), in which the peasants pooled not only equipment but also their land and received a return in proportion to their input. Mao may have described these as "semi-socialist", but they were based firmly on private ownership of the land and piecework payments. The CC proposed 20% of all peasant households be incorporated into APCs by the end of 1957.

The CC saw co-operatives as a cure-all for its agrarian problems: the poorest would be better off, there would be a greater surplus to be taken for industrial investment, and the resurgence of landholding and growth of usury would be ended. By the end of 1953 some 4,000 viable co-operatives existed.[13] A typical size was 30-50 households with small fruit and vegetable plots allowed for private use. At first most peasants really did join voluntarily because regulated co-operation meant that all team members had to carry out their fair share of the work and, in the end, this benefitted everyone. Once the projects reached a certain size or the co-operation was sufficiently complex it became the norm to hire "an intellectual" to keep records.[14]

With recovery from the devastation of the civil war there had been big increases in agricultural output during 1951 and 1952. This was a once-and-for-all increase and could not be sustained but it led to over-optimistic targets being introduced. Even with the introduction of co-operatives, the rate of increase in grain production was a modest 2% for 1953 and 1954, compared to a target of 9%. This was a serious problem for the industrial development of China. Agriculture directly supplied about 80% of raw materials for the manufacture of light industrial products, and taxes on agricultural produce supplied much of the investment for heavy industry.[15] It was clear that an agricultural economy based on near-subsistence farming produced too little surplus to fund the desired industrial development.

By the end of 1954 over 50,000 Lower Stage APCs were operating and by the end of 1955 the claimed number of such co-operatives was nearly two million, containing more than 70 million rural households.[16]

By 31 July 1955, Mao Zedong was strongly advocating an acceleration in agricultural policy and in his report to the CC, he enthusiastically called for a "high tide of social transformation in the countryside", and ridiculed the conservatives as "women with bound feet". After painting a picture of the masses "running" to form co-operatives he called for the inclusion of the whole of the peasantry in Higher Stage APCs by 1960; land was to be owned by the village and not individuals, all peasants worked for wages with no additional return from their input of property, tools or land. Mao saw this development as being "of a socialist nature", because agricultural production was part of a state plan in which the great majority of industry was nationalised and there was a state monopoly of key agricultural produce.[17]

Liu Shaoqi, Deng Xioping, and Deng Zihui (Minister of Agriculture) argued for a more prudent policy, based on genuinely voluntary membership, to be completed by 1967, and may even have had the support of a majority on the Politburo.[18] Mao simply by-passed their objections and over the head of the Politburo, called an enlarged plenum of the CC for October 1955 and packed it with lower ranking Party officials; municipal, provincial, and regional secretaries who had previously declared themselves supporters of his line, and who outnumbered full members by about 10 to 1. The plenum strongly endorsed Mao's proposals and agreed that co-operativisation be effectively completed in 1957.[19]

The speed at which co-operatives were created reflected not the wishes of the peasants but the desire of party cadres to please their superiors. Mao's target was met; by the end of 1957 nearly 95% of peasant households were enrolled in Higher Stage APCs. However, in too many cases the cadres with responsibility for establishing the co-operatives behaved in rude, arbitrary, harsh and even violent ways to meet and surpass their targets. As the number of co-operatives expanded, and to accelerate the pace, some peasants were coerced: join or lose your fishpond or fruit trees or have credit withheld. This was possible because the peasants remembered the Three-Antis and Five-Antis Campaigns and the moves took place during yet another campaign to suppress traitors and counter-revolutionaries.[20]

The Lower Stage APCs had generally been welcomed but middle and rich peasants often opposed the transition to the Higher Stage because it meant they received a smaller share of the crops. In many areas the changes required coercion through mass struggle actions to force so-called counter-revolutionary peasants into acceptance. The result was a serious decline in grain production by up to one third in some co-operatives. Local cadres, who owed their positions to Beijing, saved face by not reporting the real situation. This meant state procurement levels were not reduced to match the actual harvest, and peasants went hungry. Inevitably there was resentment, general unrest and even riots in some rural areas which were suppressed under the campaign against counter-revolutionaries. Many who voiced dissent were sent to border regions for hard labour to reform their thinking.[21]

Numerous peasants sought to solve their problems by fleeing to the towns which meant fewer hands to plant and harvest the crops and an increase in the food needed for the cities. The regime responded by introducing residence permits and movement passes, making it difficult for peasants to leave their villages. Factory managers were prevented from hiring rural workers, 'non-productive' workers were sent into the countryside to increase the labour available for the rural 'production front'. The government fixed the volume of output of firms, the number of workers, and the total wage bill, while banks were instructed to exercise tighter controls over each firm's finances. Just after defining itself as the dictatorship of the proletariat, the government introduced severe wage controls which kept the lowest urban wage rate close to rural earnings to reduce costs but also, and more importantly, to dissuade peasants from moving to the cities.

On 9 August 1957, the CC of the CCP, concerned at the low level of rural productivity and the threat this posed to industrialisation, issued a directive calling for CCP cadres to go into the countryside, take part in the peasants' daily work, and mobilise them for greater productivity. This movement, coupled with extremely good weather, produced an exceptional harvest in

1958. On Mao's insistence, the grain harvest was reported as a record 375 million metric tons. The CC was aware that this figure was due as much to cadres exaggerating performance to curry favour, as good weather and hard work. So much exaggeration went on that the announcement of a record harvest was a political decision not a statistical measure, but one which would have catastrophic consequences.[22]

12.3 The New Democracy – a Chinese Workers' and Peasants' Government?

The date usually chosen to mark China's transition to a deformed workers' state is the launch of the 1st FYP in 1953. So what was the nature of the transitional regime between 1949 and 1953? The reality of the Chinese Revolution was that the proletariat did not play a leading role as a class. Instead, this role was assumed by the peasantry. A Stalinist party stood at the head of the revolutionary forces. Not only that, but Stalinism was quite consciously cultivated by the new regime. How to explain these contradictions and determine what lessons should be drawn, and what they might mean for the future?

In Russia, the October Revolution broke the power of the bourgeoisie with a mass rising of the urban proletariat supported by the peasantry. Leading the revolution was the revolutionary Marxist party of Lenin and Trotsky which had gained majority support for its policies in virtually every urban Soviet. The power of the state after the Revolution was in the hands of the proletariat in the form of the factory-based Red Guards, in their great majority loyal to the Bolsheviks, and the direction and dynamic of events were such that the regime was clearly a proletarian dictatorship, though it was popularly known as a "workers' and peasants' government".

From October 1917, Lenin consistently referred to the October Revolution as a socialist revolution with a workers' and peasants' government resting on the dictatorship of the proletariat even though there had not, at that stage, been a fundamental change in property relations.[23] The short duration of the transitional regime between the October Revolution (when the proletariat took power) and the workers' state (when the industry was extensively nationalised, in the summer of 1918) was imposed on the Bolsheviks by the need to defend the new state against imperialist threats. Left to their own devices, the Bolsheviks would have delayed the nationalisations. For Russia, the workers' state was nationalised property, monopoly of foreign trade, state planning, destruction of the Tsarist state machine (though Lenin recognised that would take a long time to fully root out), and the dictatorship of the proletariat (since the power of the state must remain with the proletariat until the state withers away).

During and after the Russian Revolution, the term workers' and peasants' government was widely used by the Bolsheviks in two mutually exclusive ways.

Case 1: "This formula, 'workers' and peasants' government', first appeared in the agitation of the Bolsheviks in 1917 and was definitely accepted after the October Revolution. In the final instance it represented nothing more than the popular designation for the already established dictatorship of the proletariat. The significance of this designation comes mainly from the fact that it underscored the idea of an alliance between the proletariat and the peasantry upon which the Soviet power rests."[24] In this sense the workers' and peasants' government represented the transitional regime between the proletarian revolution and the resulting workers' state.

Case 2: "From April to September 1917, the Bolsheviks demanded that the SRs and the Mensheviks break with the liberal bourgeoisie and take power into their own hands ... If the Mensheviks and the SRs had actually broken with the Cadets (liberals) and with foreign imperialism, then the workers' and peasants' government created by them could only have hastened and facilitated the establishment of the dictatorship of the proletariat."[25]

In the latter case the workers' and peasants' government was definitely not the dictatorship of the proletariat. It would have been a petty-bourgeois government led by reformist parties. But the call for the SRs and Mensheviks to form a workers' and peasants' government, the call for the Mensheviks and SRs to take power, was intended to expose their reluctance to do so before the masses. This had tremendous educational value and was a significant contribution in assisting the creation of a Bolshevik government – a workers' and peasants' government that would have simultaneously been the dictatorship of the proletariat.

In 1922 at the last World Congress which Lenin attended, the *Thesis on Tactics* accepted the possibility that as the result of class struggles the power of the state could pass into the hands of a workers' and peasants' government, but declared that such a government did not represent the dictatorship of the proletariat, was not an inevitable transitional stage, but could become an important launch pad for the fight for that dictatorship. However, under the conditions that existed in 1922, it would not establish a genuine workers' state; only a revolutionary Communist party, rooted in the working class on a mass scale could achieve that.[26]

That is where matters rested until the *Transitional Programme* founding document of the Fourth International was published. We have presented the following quote earlier, but it is the key to understanding the process that took place in China and deserves a second reading:

> "... one cannot categorically deny in advance the theoretical possibility that, under the influence of completely exceptional circumstances (war, defeat, financial crash, mass revolutionary pressure, etc.), the petty bourgeois parties, including the Stalinists, may go further than they wish along the road to a break with the bourgeoisie. In any case one thing is not to be doubted: even if this highly improbable variant somewhere at some time becomes a reality and the 'workers' and farmers' government' in the above-mentioned sense is established in fact, it would represent merely a short episode on the road to the actual dictatorship of the proletariat."[27]

It has been claimed that Joe Hansen, one of Trotsky's aides, was responsible for suggesting this form of words for the Transitional Programme. True or not, after WWII Hansen studied the process which Lenin and Trotsky had only touched on, petty-bourgeois parties coming to power in revolutionary situations and overthrowing bourgeois political and economic power. However, Hansen took account of a new feature, also observed by Ted Grant: that with imperialism temporarily "impotent" the process could be carried through to the creation of a workers' state, as happened in China.

Hansen married the theoretical considerations of the 4th Congress, a petty-bourgeois party taking power in a revolutionary struggle, with the observed fact that such regimes did progress to a workers' state (e.g. China and Cuba), though some could regress (e.g. Algeria). All real processes take time so there would be an interval between the overthrow of bourgeois military and political power, and the decisive expropriation of bourgeois economic power. This period which could last for months or even years, was not the dictatorship of the proletariat it was a transitional regime; a form of workers' and farmers' government.[28]

Lenin and Trotsky had both emphasised the necessity of the mobilisation of the masses to break the power of the bourgeoisie.[29] Without the revolutionary mobilisation of the masses there can be no anti-capitalist revolution. The mass mobilisations which break the power of the bourgeoisie can force, in completely exceptional circumstances such as occurred at the end of World War II, even petty-bourgeois leaderships to accomplish the transition to a workers' state. That is, in the so-called backward countries of Asia, Africa, and South America a leadership determined to better the conditions of the working masses could break with the bourgeoisie. The creation of the deformed workers' state in China showed that real life rarely conforms to the ideal; instead distortions and variants are the norm.[30]

In Cuba it took some eighteen months from January 1959 before Cuba became a workers' state with the sweeping nationalisations that took place in the autumn of 1960. This was a process in which the 26 July Movement progressively shed its links with the bourgeoisie, took control of foreign trade, introduced a planned economy, expropriated the lands of the US sugar companies, and established friendly relations with the then Soviet bloc. All this took place in the public domain.

In China the matter was not so clear cut because as the regime stumbled from one empiric response to the next, being bureaucratic it attempted to save face by covering up the differences between its stated goals and actual events. The original aim of the Mao regime had been to preserve capitalism but as with Cuba, this goal gradually evaporated under the pressure of events.

In China there was no Bolshevik Party to lead the revolution. Instead a petty-bourgeois Stalinist Party was carried to power. The most obvious place to start any Marxist analysis was the 4th World Congress of the Communist International which had classified such a regime as a workers' and peasants' government not a dictatorship of the proletariat. However, the norms set out in 1922 would have to be adapted to meet the very different circumstances applying after WWII.

The New Democracy claimed to be a coalition government of four classes (workers, peasants, the petty-bourgeoisie, and the national bourgeoisie) and it was clear that the social basis of the regime was the petty-bourgeoisie, in its majority, the peasantry. While the national bourgeoisie did not have a decisive role in government, the constitution and the laws of the regime protected private ownership of production and sought to develop a non-socialist, New Democratic economy.

The first consideration must be that a revolutionary mass mobilisation had destroyed the power of the bourgeoisie, and the establishment of a workers' and peasants' government was a clear and striking confirmation of the Theory of the Permanent Revolution; that in colonial and semi-colonial countries there is a natural tendency to transcend the bourgeois democratic phase and progress more or less directly to a workers' state, even if deformed.

However, in China the new government did not accept such an analysis, stood in the way of such a development, and called instead for an ongoing alliance with the national bourgeoisie, giving it an economic weight its social position did not deserve. The PRC proclaimed protected status for private industry including imperialist interests, and equal benefits for labour and capital.

Nonetheless, the New Democracy began life with direct control over a far greater proportion of the economy than the Bolsheviks had, even in 1918. Its initial measures were to assist the construction of a national capitalism with key sectors of the economy such as banking, largely under the control of the same people who had served the KMT (despite the liberated areas having established their own central, Chinan, bank). Reality negated these moves; to solve the most pressing and immediate problems, the direction in which CCP cadres were moving was towards greater state control and a national plan. But this process took time, for example it would take three years (end of 1952) before the CCP leadership reluctantly issued instructions to bring all important banks formally under the central control of the People's Bank of China.

After WWII many advanced countries, e.g. Britain, brought key basic industries such as coal mining, steel, and the railways under state control to provide the investment and co-ordination necessary to modernise them and keep British capitalism competitive in the world market. Nationalisation by itself does not make a country a workers' state. However, the problems facing China were on a qualitatively greater scale both in extent (a population twenty times that of the UK) and depth (the Chinese were starting with a country shattered by war, its most advanced industries destroyed and essential irrigation systems devastated). From overcoming hunger and starvation to establishing national unity, from controlling hyper-inflation to re-creating industry, the tasks were so overwhelming and so inter-related that they could be accomplished only through co-ordinated state planning and directed investment. These pressures pushed the CCP to take measures which were socialist in principle, in the direction of developing a state with one foot firmly in socialism.

What was in question was the outcome of the conflict between the stated programme of the CCP and the natural progression of events which everywhere were flowing past the limits set by Mao. In 1927 such a conflict had been resolved in favour of the bourgeoisie; what would be the outcome this time?

From the Marxist point of view, it is not possible to have a party in which two (or more) classes have equal weight: in 1925-27 the KMT had been hailed as a multi-class party but its true nature soon emerged. Nor is it possible to have a two-class state – though it is possible to have two-class governments. In China the so-called People's Democratic Dictatorship was a military dictatorship with the peasantry as its main base. Peng Shuzi, veteran Chinese Trotskyist, argued that "in the last analysis, in view of its fundamental stand for the preservation of bourgeois property relations, it was a bourgeois regime."[31] In reaching this conclusion, Peng had failed to follow his own advice to take actual property relations as more decisive than the statements of party leaders.

12.4 Proletarian Peasantry and Revolutionary Stalinism?

This book has shown how the specific circumstances existing on an international and national scale enabled the Stalinist CCP to take power – both state and governmental power – at the head of a peasant army. Today we have access to material which allows us to plot the course of events and demonstrate that the pressures on the CCP hierarchy to create a nation state, to feed the Chinese people and to maintain its authority and privileges, pushed it in the direction of a (deformed) workers' state.

Citing the events in their historical context allows us, today, to readily answer the apparent contradictions between certain long-held theoretical postulates and the actual course of events. Before about 1949 there had never been any serious dispute over the following:

- The peasantry as a class could not lead a social revolution through to a successful conclusion; this could be achieved only by the proletariat.
- The proletariat could do this only with the leadership of a revolutionary Marxist Party.
- Stalinism does not represent revolutionary Marxism; in essence it was, and is, counter-revolutionary.

At the time, the clash between these postulates and actual events posed serious questions for socialists. Unfortunately, the bizarre answers provided by many, even within the world Trotskyist movement, were based on *a-priori* schema, impressions and wishful thinking which substituted for a Marxist analysis. However, all had the same aim, to prettify Maoism and present it as a genuinely revolutionary force – desperately cuddling up to the Maoists and trying to shortcut the hard work necessary to build the revolutionary Marxist Party. The political vitality of the CCP and PLA was often overestimated and the degree of disintegration of the KMT underestimated. Failing to recognise that the CCP had filled a vacuum left by the collapse of the KMT too often led to the conclusion that the CCP was truly revolutionary and that, possibly, the Chinese peasantry could have acquired a proletarian consciousness.

The latter point was posed as a two-part question; How was it possible for petty-bourgeoisie forces to undertake an armed struggle of over twenty years duration? This argument, advanced by leading figures on the left, showed an ignorance of the history of the Chinese peasantry and their remarkable ability to form huge armies which overthrew governments and set up new regimes. The Taiping rebellion lasted fourteen years (1850-1864), established control over some 30 million people in southern China and was overthrown only when imperialist armies intervened. The simultaneous Nien rebellion lasted 17 years and conquered substantial areas in northern China. We have already quoted Marx on this and seen that he never suggested a socialist or working-class content in these rebellions or doubted that a petty-bourgeois leadership could mount such impressive and lengthy struggles. The duration of the struggle and the taking of power by a peasant army posed no challenge for Marxists.

This led to the second part of the question: If a deformed workers' state existed in China after October 1953 and the regime was based on the peasantry, did that mean the class nature of the peasant armies which had fought a long civil war under Stalinist leadership had undergone a qualitative change? Had the character of the Chinese peasantry been mis-judged? Perhaps Chinese peasants had achieved a proletarian or even socialist consciousness because the armed struggle they had fought was against not only the KMT but its imperialist backers.

The position of the CCP was clear and simple, peasants and intellectuals who joined the Party changed their original class character and became "Marxist-Leninist fighters of the proletariat."[32] After the creation of a (deformed) workers' state many on the left toyed with the idea that there may be something in this claptrap.

Lenin considered the existence of a democratic, centralist, Marxist party an essential requirement for a revolutionary victory. If that were true, some argued, could the CCP really have degenerated into a peasant party in the 1930s? Was the flow of workers from the towns into the Soviets sufficient to maintain the CCP's revolutionary and proletarian character? Others posed the alternative that the CCP could have changed back into a proletarian organisation after taking power in 1949.

After the defeat of the second Chinese Revolution, from about 1930, the CCP gave up building an urban workers' movement and turned its face toward the countryside. It threw its whole strength into creating peasant Soviets and as it absorbed ever greater numbers of peasants its composition became almost exclusively peasant. The tiny stream of workers from the cities was not enough to maintain either the party's working class composition or outlook. Living with peasants, working with peasants, fighting alongside peasants with the perspective of peasant guerrilla warfare for an extended period, Party cadres even those from the factories, assimilated a peasant, that is petty-bourgeois, outlook.

More importantly, the ideology and actions of the CCP were petty-bourgeois; the logical extension and continuation of the political line contained in Mao's 1927 *Report on the Peasant Movement in Hunan*. The key elements in the CCP programme, the bloc of four classes and the New Democracy were petty-bourgeois, class collaborationist strategies. The Three People's Principles in the CCP programme, of which Mao appeared very proud, were taken directly from the programme of the KMT and were written by Sun Yat-sen.[33] In this way Mao Zedong confirmed the CCP as a petty-bourgeois party not only because of its peasant composition but also because of its petty-bourgeois programme.

An important factor in confirming the petty-bourgeois nature of the CCP was that it did not attempt to mobilise the urban masses into revolutionary action during the PLA's rapid advance southwards, choosing instead to rely solely on peasant armies to conquer power.[34]

At the time it took power, the CCP claimed about 3.5 million members of which not more than 5% were workers. It is true that from June 1950, after entering the cities and taking power, the Party temporarily suspended its recruitment of peasants and made a big effort to recruit workers. But a political party cannot change its composition in 24 hours, especially when, as in the case of the CCP, it had an almost exclusively peasant base. By 1951, 6.3% of CCP members were workers; in 1952, 7.2%; in 1956, 14% – that is 1.5 million workers out of 11 million members.[35]

It can be pondered whether these membership figures are a serious indicator of the re-proletarianisation of the CCP. We are talking of one member in seven who, as new recruits, would have had little or no weight at

Party meetings. Grant pointed out that even when the CCP prioritised the recruitment of workers they did so in a Bonapartist manner, workers were recruited and unionised not to give them control over their working lives and Party policy, but the better to control them.[36]

Another line of argument was that Stalinism was the dominant ideology of the Russian workers state so could the Stalinist nature of the CCP have given it a proletarian character? The argument that the CCP could not be Stalinist and petty-bourgeois at the same time identifies Stalinism with the workers' state. But Trotskyists have always argued that Stalinism stood in contradiction to the workers' state, that it was a cancerous counter-revolutionary growth.

In the Russian Revolution only the bourgeoisie and the big landholders were expropriated. The peasantry, sectors of the urban petty-bourgeoisie and even some of the technical intelligentsia remained property holders. The Soviet proletariat existed as a class quite distinct from these elements. As the Stalinist regime progressed, the Soviet bureaucracy became ever more petty-bourgeois in its composition and almost entirely petty-bourgeois in its spirit, a parasitic growth concerned primarily with its own privileges.[37] The ideology and methods which this bureaucratic caste generated to preserve itself and its privileges were in essence counter-revolutionary and were fully absorbed by the CCP so that by 1949 they were an integral part of its practices and ideology.

Of course, capitalist restoration in Russia (of which Trotsky had warned in 1936 – that as the Stalinist bureaucrats in the USSR increasingly adopted bourgeois norms of distribution for their own benefit they were preparing a capitalist restoration) brought this discussion to an end and buried any idea that Stalinism was revolutionary. Yes, the bureaucracy had defended the nationalized property relations but in its own peculiar way – its privileged position came first. It was a considerable error not to see that the privileges of the bureaucracy must eventually conflict with nationalised property relations.[38]

To avoid mistaking the appearance for reality it is necessary to analyse the development of the Third Chinese Revolution via historical materialism which sees the process in China as part of the developments that brought the second generation of workers states into the world in its historical and international context (in addition to China there was North Korea, North Vietnam, and Eastern Europe). Any consideration of the events in China must always bear in mind four major consequences of WWII: (a) the weakening of world capitalism both as a whole and in its constituent parts (though this was short-lived), (b) the victory of the Soviet Union, (c) the resulting temporary strengthening of Stalinism, and (d) an upsurge of revolutionary struggles on a colossal scale in both the imperialist centres and the colonial areas.

12.5 Summary

In China, October 1953 was a defining moment; the CCP introduced the 1st FYP for economic construction and industrialisation and proclaimed the beginning of the transition to socialism. The CCP finally rejected the concept of the New Democracy in favour of a policy of what was euphemistically termed state and private co-operation – the final seizure of bourgeois property and the creation of the Chinese (deformed) workers' state.

If we were to distil the revolutionary experience of China it could be expressed in the following passage from the *Transitional Program*:

> "Colonial and semi-colonial countries are backward countries by their very essence. But backward countries are part of a world dominated by imperialism. Their development, therefore, has a *combined* character: the most primitive economic forms are combined with the last word in capitalist technique and culture. In like manner are defined the political strivings of the proletariat of backward countries: the struggle for the most elementary achievements of national independence and bourgeois democracy is combined with the socialist struggle against world imperialism. Democratic slogans, transitional demands and the problems of the socialist revolution are not divided into separate historical epochs in this struggle, but stem directly from one another."[39]

Chapter 13

China under Mao: The Great Leap Forward

13.1 Introduction

The question mark placed over the nature of the Chinese Communist Party after the success of the Chinese Revolution – was it a political obstacle to the independent mobilisation of the working class or an alternative instrument for realising socialism – was fully removed by subsequent events. This Chapter presents an analysis of the Great Leap Forward (GLF), Mao's disastrous attempt at collectivisation of the peasantry which unambiguously confirmed the Stalinist core of the CCP.

Two factors gave Mao's leadership very different characteristics from those of Stalin's. In Russia, Stalin was a usurper, he had been a "grey shadow" playing a minor role in the October Revolution, his faction had gained power by deceit and deception, and retained it only by murder on a mass scale. Mao's situation was very different. He was accepted within the CCP as a natural leader, though Moscow's backing had been important in accelerating his promotion. The second major difference was that the CCP came to power when the world revolution was on the rise, whereas the Stalin regime was a reflection of the defeats of the proletarian masses in the 1920s and 30s.

With the revolution moving forward, Mao as undisputed leader, could allow genuine discussion on practical issues in both the Politburo and Central Committee of the CCP. If Mao did lose a vote on a matter he considered important, then with the powers vested in him as Chairman, he could call an enlarged meeting of the CC and pack it with his supporters. Such an arrangement had numerous very positive advantages for Mao, not least was his being kept aware of alternative lines of thought developing within the Party. However, it was not until the regime ran into severe difficulties as a result of obvious mis-assessments on Mao's part that serious differences arose within the Politburo.

13.2 Let One Hundred Flowers Bloom

Communist parties throughout the world were strongly affected when, in 1956, Khrushchev exposed and denounced many of Stalin's crimes. The impact on the CCP was particularly severe and at the 8th Congress, held in September 1956, a resolution from the Politburo, moved by Liu Shaoqi (ranked second in the political hierarchy) proposed revising the Party constitution to remove the sentence, "The CCP takes the theories of Marxism-Leninism and the combined principles derived from the practical experience of the Chinese revolution – the ideas of Mao Zedong – as the guiding principles of all its work." In its place the Congress stressed collective leadership.[1] It is not known whether Liu took pleasure in this announcement, given that Mao, the previous October, had squashed the more prudent policy towards co-operativisation advocated by Liu and most of the Politburo, using his authority as Chairman to call an enlarged plenum of the CC and pack it with his supporters (see Section 12.2.1).

Whatever its declared intention, the resolution was a criticism of Mao, but the groundswell against the cult of the individual was sufficiently strong for Mao not to openly resist the revision of the Party statutes. For this downgrading of Mao, Liu would be hounded to his death during the Great Proletarian Cultural Revolution.

A succession of revolts in Eastern Europe, particularly East Germany in 1953, and Hungary in 1956, had an echo within the CCP and, especially, amongst the radical youth. Against the advice of Liu and others, Mao attempted to spike the development of a critical current by encouraging dissidents to speak out, and in February 1957 he announced to the Supreme State Conference: "Let a hundred flowers bloom, let a hundred schools of thought contend." The ferocity and extent of the flood of revelations and criticisms of the privileges of the bureaucracy and its arbitrary behaviour was a severe jolt. By the end of the summer the Hundred Flowers Movement had been brought to an end. Some 50,000 leftists were thrown out of the Party, expelled from schools and colleges, sacked, arrested, sent to labour camps, and forced to recant. The masses assessed the Hundred Flowers Movement as a cruel trick, a trap to identify and eliminate dissidents.[2]

The bureaucracy interpreted the criticisms not as a call for it to change its ways but as a reflection of the strength of the hold which capitalist ideas still had on intellectuals and students. The episode was viewed as a mis-assessment by Mao, weakened confidence in his judgment, gave greater confidence to the more cautious members of the Politburo and made them more wary of his decisions.

A Stalinist regime is inherently dictatorial and does not self-reform, at least not in a democratic direction. Faced with the possibility of a threat to Party rule, Mao did an about-face formally launching a counter-attack in the summer of 1958 as an Anti-Rightist Campaign with the declared aim of refuting the criticisms made of the Party. Over the next period there was a vociferous anti-rightist, anti-intellectual drive which some see as marking Mao's abandonment of intellectuals, experts and professionals on the grounds of their having insufficient revolutionary consciousness. This fed into the programme for economic development as "politics in command"; loyalty to the Party, not professional competence determined the outcome of technical discussions.[3] In the coming period this idealistic, non-materialist approach would grow and be immensely damaging for the Chinese people.

13.3 The Great Leap Forward and the People's Communes 1958-1962

The PRC was a Bonapartist regime, a bureaucratic dictatorship based on the Chinese Communist Party and the People's Liberation Army that denied democratic rights to the worker-peasant masses. Stalin had demonstrated with his U-turn from pandering to the rich peasants to enforced collectivisation, that such regimes can change from opportunism to adventurism very quickly. This would be confirmed in China with Mao's compulsory collectivisation of the peasantry.

Special attention is given here to the agricultural communes because many on the political left, especially certain petty-bourgeois circles and intellectuals, naively accepted the communes at face value and praised them extravagantly as a major step towards socialism, the emancipation of women, and industrialisation of China. Livio Maitan (see Section 10.5) was one such. Swept along on an impressionist tide, Maitan listed among the successes of the commune movement: "real possibilities for people at lower levels to make democratic choices."[4]

As the 1st FYP drew to a close, disagreements arose within the Politburo over the speed and direction of economic development. Capital investment in heavy industry was seen as key to developing a modern society, and the produce from agriculture as providing the necessary funds. But little was being invested to improve agricultural productivity and it was clear that if things continued as they were, the rate of growth of heavy industry would have to slow considerably. One side argued that peasants would not produce more without material incentives, an approach which meant at least temporarily, reducing the rate of investment in heavy industry. This was in line with the promises made by the regime that collectivisation of agriculture would be delayed until there was a powerful industrial sector which would provide the tens of thousands of tractors, harvesters, and other necessary machines. However, Mao idealistically argued that the peasants could be persuaded to increase output to fund industrialisation through exhortation, mass mobilisations, and communalisation under the direction of the Party.[5]

Forced collectivisation in the USSR had been an anti-Marxist programme carried out against the wishes of the peasantry. Stalinist officials plunged into collectivisation to put an end to the threat to the regime posed by the rich peasants' stranglehold on food production. There was no preparation and little thought on how to minimise peasant opposition and smooth the transition. Administrative incompetence linked to an undemocratic and fundamentally hostile stance toward the peasants magnified the consequences of the severe drought of the spring and summer of 1931 and resulted in the 1932-33 famine and the death from starvation of 3% of the population.

The GLF of 1958 was just such a Stalinist adventure – an attempt to fund an over-ambitious industrial programme. It aimed to overcome the limitations imposed by backwardness through the forced mobilisation of tens of millions of peasants. It was believed that this would be sufficient to overcome the technical, engineering, economic, social and political problems faced by Chinese society. This anti-Marxist voluntarism was the basis of the communes.

The GLF called for increased extraction of resources from the peasants and, as in Stalin's case, the amount extracted by the state was based on a refusal by the centre to accept that a serious shortfall in production had occurred, and also on fear at the periphery of reporting the disastrous conditions that actually existed. The extraordinary mismanagement of the GLF and the famine that resulted was an outcome for which Mao Zedong and his associates were responsible. When the dust had settled it turned out that much the same proportion of the population had died of hunger in China 1960-62 as in the USSR between 1931-33.[6] Then, just as in 1933 Stalin had retreated and re-introduced private plots for the peasants at the expense of the collective farms, so the Chinese leaders retreated from the policies of the GLF and re-introduced private plots. In both cases private farming and hostility to the regime would make a significant contribution to capitalist restoration.

Mao launched a course of action whereby a campaigning spirit was supposed to be enough to conquer objective reality. Mao's approach to the communes was, as the CCP itself would later put it: "a subjectivist misinterpretation of the historical dialectic ... not founded on an accurate perception of material reality or on sufficient synthesis of revolutionary experience."[7]

At the time Mao, imbued with the petty bourgeois theory of socialism in one country, expressed his perception of material reality as:

> "Why can't 600 million 'paupers' create a prosperous and strong socialist country ... by their own efforts? ... Provided they take their destiny into their own hands ... and energetically tackle problems instead of evading them, they can overcome any difficulty on earth."[8]

Intellectuals were expected to perform in a similar manner: the eminent writer Pa Chin was pledged to write one long novel, three medium length novels and complete a number of translations per year – and all in a manner to arouse enthusiasm for Party policies.

Let us remind ourselves of Marxist method and theory as expressed by Engels and Lenin in regard to the peasantry. It is an axiom of Marxist political economy that large-scale production is superior to small scale production. Marxists have always maintained that individual peasant farming must give way to agricultural collectives. Only as individual, scattered, small-scale peasant economy is superseded by co-operative ownership can the peasant become part of an integrated highly productive socialist economy. The superiority of large-scale farming was undoubtedly the most powerful objective argument in favour of the communes and this had been stated by Li Fuchun, Chairman of the State Planning Commission in July 1955: "Socialism cannot be built on a small peasant economy; it must have ... large scale collective farming."[9]

But this economic principle must be considered in a political context: the participation of the peasants in large-scale units or collectives must be voluntary. If the 'political principle' is ignored, then collectivisation can do more damage, much more damage than good to the work of socialist construction.

Engels combined these economic and political principles when he wrote:

> "... when we are in possession of state power we shall not even think of forcibly expropriating the small peasants (regardless of whether with or without

compensation), as we shall have to do in the case of the big landowners. Our task relative to the small peasant consists, in the first place, in effecting a transition of his private enterprise and private possession to co-operative ones, not forcibly but by dint of example and the offer of social assistance for this purpose. And then of course we shall have ample means of showing to the small peasant prospective advantages that must be obvious to him ...."[10]

Lenin took Engels' strategy and applied it to the reality of the Russian Revolution. He was clear that only after re-organising the whole of industry on large-scale collective lines and on a modern technological basis would the towns be able to provide sufficient technical and social assistance to the backward and scattered rural populations to enable them to raise the productivity of agricultural and of farm labour so that in their own interests they would adopt large-scale collective mechanised agriculture.[11]

Lenin repeatedly stated very clearly that it was absolutely forbidden to use compulsive measures against the peasants; they had to be convinced by practical example.[12] He did not limit this policy to predominantly rural countries but also considered them applicable to the advanced capitalist countries.[13]

Trotsky summarised Engels' and Lenin's principles for collectivisation in the *Transitional Programme* of the Fourth International:

> "The program for the nationalisation of the land, the collectivisation of agriculture, should be so drawn that from its very basis it should exclude the possibility of expropriation of small farmers and their compulsory collectivisation. The farmer will remain owner of his plot of land as long as he himself believes it possible or necessary."[14]

The relationship between the Chinese Communists and the peasants was supposed to be one of mutual support and co-operation; after all, the Chinese Revolution was based on the peasantry. During the civil war, and before, the Communists had secured the mass support of the peasants and had established extensive rural organisations. The Party leaders were committed to improving peasant well-being, and until at least 1957 the CCP's economic policies were relatively restrained when procuring agricultural resources to feed industry.[15]

However, resources for investment in industry could only come from agriculture but small scale agriculture provided very little surplus. The Politburo agreed a plan to merge Higher Stage co-operatives into much larger units, and in April 1958 the name "people's commune" was adopted for these giant complexes.

Such a proposal had many benefits in the eyes of the Politburo. In a period of transition, greater Party control was required and with a large number of small co-operatives this was difficult. By combining them into larger, more centralised units, the local cadres were better able to exert their authority. Large communes made it easier to collect taxes, to control the price paid for agricultural products, and to force the peasants to pay the high prices demanded for industrial products. The cadres would be better placed to stop the hoarding of grain, impose stricter rationing, and expropriate more produce for the state.

The communes were seen as a convenient instrument for maximising the surplus labour extracted from the peasants. By optimising the division of labour by, for example, establishing communal dining halls and nurseries to free women from the drudgery of home life to work in the fields, it was claimed that the number of working hands would be increased by one-third. Supposedly this would free large numbers of peasants to be shifted from area to area and from job to job, according to needs and requirements.

However, there was growing tension within the Politburo between Mao and those who argued for more gradual progress. Mao's public statements became increasingly adventurist, following Stalin who, at the 17th Congress of the Russian Party, had declared the part played by objective conditions had been reduced to a minimum while the role of the Party had become decisive; that failures rested "not on 'objective' conditions, but on ourselves, and on ourselves alone."[16]

In China the greater part of farming was done by extremely primitive means, most of it relying on human labour alone. But the communes were to be on a grand scale – averaging about 4,000 hectares (10,000 acres) with 5,000 households. There was an obvious contradiction between such extraordinarily large farms and the low technique used to work them.

Contrary to popular belief, the Chinese peasants had a high level of productivity fine-tuned over centuries to match the given conditions including the planting of specialised crops suited to local ground and climate.[17] Productivity could be improved only by the general application of modern techniques (tractors, chemical fertilisers, electrification, etc.). Without these resources there would be no increase in productivity; however, production could be increased by lengthened working hours and increasing the number of peasants labouring in the fields. But such measures would not overcome the backwardness of the agrarian techniques; they would simply make more peasants work longer and harder.

Such an approach could only increase peasant opposition to the communes, and ran the risk of reducing their productivity. The CCP's policy toward the communes thus had a much greater compulsory element than its policy toward the co-operatives. CCP propaganda had it that the Chinese communes were formed with the enthusiastic support of the peasant masses; the mass exodus of peasants into the towns gave the lie to that.

The first of the people's communes was set up in Weixing, southern Hunan in April 1958. This project which combined 27 co-operatives with 43,000 people was announced as an experiment. However, had it really been an experiment, its performance would have been monitored and assessed before launching communes nationwide; that such an assessment was not made demonstrates beyond any doubt the adventurist and bureaucratic character of the programme.

At the beginning of August 1958, Mao visited the commune and, without consulting the Politburo, launched a national campaign mobilising the CCP rank and file to establish people's communes everywhere. The communes were described as self-supporting units "for the all-round development of agriculture, forestry, animal husbandry, handicrafts and fishery, as well as for the all-round combination of economic, political, cultural and military affairs where industry, agriculture, trade, education and military affairs merge into one."[18] Even in the largest communes such a perspective was nonsense. In the era of the international division of labour, commune production would only be weakened if the workforce were dissipated into unnecessary and uneconomic activities that were a drain on the main business of agricultural production.

The communes were formed on the basis of geographic proximity by amalgamating adjoining co-operatives, and so tended to be traditional marketing areas surrounding the village or market town containing the local administrative centre. The commune subsumed the functions of local government, with the result that the local CCP cadres naturally stepped into the leading roles within the communes.

Within about two months, 500 million peasants were organised into communes! How, in such a short time, could the peasants be fully appraised as to what was being proposed let alone give their informed consent? Everything was decided by decree and the commune movement as a whole was compulsory in character with Party cadres, who had full control over local economic, social and political matters, acting more to intimidate the peasants than convince them.[19] The agricultural work cycle being years, prompts the question of how in two months could a commune demonstrate its superiority over the co-operatives it replaced either as a means of increasing production or of improving living standards?

Red Flag, the monthly theoretical journal of the CCP, painted a rosy picture of the benefits to be gained from the commune system. The August 1958 issue stated: "The People's Communes are the best form for the transition from collective ownership to ownership by the people as a whole. It contains the first shoots of communism ... such as the communal kitchens, nurseries and sewing facilities to emancipate women from the household." Unfortunately, these first shoots of communism were rooted in the very essence of capitalism – the piecework wage system.[20] Members were promised food, clothing, housing, child-birth care, education, medical treatment, weddings, funerals and even, in some places, haircuts, though nowhere was the quality mentioned.[21]

Such a picture may have convinced the Young Communist League members posted to areas where the communes were to be formed, but to believe that the vast majority of peasants were convinced to hand over their land, tools, animals and even personal property such as pots and pans in just eight weeks is ridiculous.

The weather in 1958 had been good, and the harvest of near record proportions. For their own reasons, Mao and the CCP leaders ascribed the marvellous harvest as due to the communes as a superior form of socio-economic organisation. In fact, the great increase in farm production in 1958 was not an achievement of the communes. The communes only began to spread in the early autumn of 1958. Wheat had been harvested in the middle of June, the early rice crop between July and August, while cotton, raised in the summer, was ripe for harvest by the time the communes were established. Thus the communes, at best, harvested crops planted and tended by the co-operatives.

13.3.1 Back-yard Steel Production

The continuing US trade embargo (it did not end until 1971) meant that iron and steel for construction and other purposes was in very short supply; it was difficult, if not impossible, to obtain iron and steel for anything but the most important projects. Mao, refusing to slow down the development of heavy industry, called on the communes to set up various kinds of industry, including the production of iron and steel for local use using micro-scale blast furnaces. With responsibility for the construction and operation of blast furnaces, CCP cadres were given tasks for which they had neither experience nor knowledge.[22]

Up until 1957, the strategy of the Ministry for the Metallurgical Industries had been for a network of 14 modern small and medium-sized metallurgical plants that would be quick to build, take advantage of local occurrences of raw materials, and reduce the pressure on China's weak transport system. This strategy was assessed by western experts as having serious environmental drawbacks (smoke emissions) but would have attained the declared production targets.

During 1957 the Anti-Rightist Campaign, an integral part of which was criticism of intellectuals and experts became strident. With "politics in command", engineers and economists who warned of likely problems resulting from Party policies were demoted or fired. Expert advice was rejected and the building and operating of micro-scale open-hearth blast furnaces became an additional burden on the communes, imposing on the peasants much back-breaking labour over and above that spent in the fields.

Some regions of China such as Sichuan and Hunan had long experience in blast furnace operation which had traditionally supplied local needs, but these were few and far between. In September 1958, Mao Zedong visited a small traditional style steelworks in Anhui and was greatly impressed, calling for a mass campaign for steel production. "Everyone, *everyone*, should produce iron and steel."[23]

By the end of 1958 as many as 600,000 micro steelworks are said to have been built, involving up to 90 million people. Most of these were blast furnaces of traditional design hurriedly built and operated by inexperienced local craftspeople such as the village blacksmiths. Nothing was spared in the drive for building materials; even the stone marking the spot where Mao's parents were buried was taken. However, traditional blast furnaces are not simple. Efficient operation required experience which could be gained only through a long apprenticeship.[24]

The planning of communes had been hurried and considerations of economic geography had been largely omitted. Thus, for example, a commune in Fukien province was expected to construct an iron smelting plant with an annual capacity of 2,000 tons but the area had neither iron ore nor limestone. This particular commune had only 1,700 hectares (about 4,000 acres) of farm land, and intensive farming of rice and vegetables was needed to feed the population of over 40,000, but the commune was instructed to set aside nearly 70 hectares of arable land for cotton to meet the clothing needs of the commune members despite never having grown cotton because the natural conditions were unfavourable.[25]

In such circumstances pots and pans were seized as a valuable source of raw material for the commune furnaces. Cadres argued that families would no longer need cooking utensils since they were to eat in mess halls. Richard Crossman, Labour Minister for Health and Social Services 1968-70, toured China at this time and witnessed the absurdities:

> "In a corner I spotted five old ladies sitting in a circle and asked what they were doing. 'That,' I was told, 'is the ball-bearing section'. Sure enough, a thin iron rod had been cut into slices a centimetre thick, and each old lady was rounding a slice with a pestle and mortar, while a couple of boys were polishing the finished article."[26]

This was happening across China, the drive to diversify but simultaneously increase production meant the quality of products was generally quite appalling. For example, it is reported that to meet targets, coal miners were loading their trucks with rubble.

By the end of the year it was claimed that over 11 million tons of steel had been produced. Mao, safeguarded from reality by the bureaucracy he had done so much to create, was delighted. In truth, the small blast furnaces which he had urged the peasants to build were a massive failure; almost all of the steel produced was of such poor quality as to be useless. The Chinese propaganda magazines of the time were wildly enthusiastic about the mass campaign, but the photographs which accompanied the glowing reports told a very different story; in the West only the technically illiterate were convinced.

As the utter failure of the commune blast furnaces became apparent and the consequential serious imbalances were being felt across the economy, the steel target for 1959 was progressively reduced from 30 million tonnes, to 20 million, to 13 million and eventually to 12 million. An editorial in the *Peking Daily* (20 January 1959) instructed that where "it is too costly to carry out steel and iron production communes should quickly discontinue operations and divert their labour power to other fields of work." The waste of human and material resources had been colossal and just at a time when they were most needed elsewhere.

Many millions of peasants had been dispatched to work on steel production at the expense of the harvest. Fortunately, the weather was good and the harvest was excellent, but the harvesting had to be undertaken mainly by old people and children with consequent delays and shortcomings. Because cadres seized produce to meet the state procurement quotas as a priority, food shortages and queues appeared in the cities despite the spectacular harvest.[27]

The bureaucracy was convinced that the grain harvest for 1958 had been exceptionally good due to communalisation so the improvement could be expected to be maintained. One consequence was that the land allocated to grain crops was substantially reduced for the 1959 harvest, and other crops such as cotton increased. This was done despite the need to feed the big increase in the non-rural workforce resulting from the huge expansion of coal mining, electricity generating, chemical, and metallurgical plants.

13.4 Lushan Conference and the 1959 Campaign against Rightist Opportunism

In July 1959, the CC met for the now-famous Lushan Conference. There was a sharp debate following criticisms of the GLF made by Peng Dehuai (Peng Te-huai) who reflected the criticisms of the people's communes made by the peasants, describing them as "the result of the subjective wishes of a few people and did not reflect the desires of the peasant masses", in effect challenging the very basis of the GLF. Mao categorised this as a "programme of right opportunism". Peng Dehuai was immediately replaced as defence minister by Lin Piao (a Mao protégé) and those who had supported him were dismissed from their posts and disappeared from public life.[28]

After Lushan, in the autumn and winter of 1959, the Party leadership launched an extremely harsh Anti-Rightist Campaign led by Liu Shaoqi, Deng Xiaoping (Teng Hsiao-p'ing, General Secretary of the Party) and Peng Zhen (mayor of Beijing). This campaign, which Mao relentlessly promoted into the spring of 1960, was unleashed to defend the communes and silence their critics.[29] A carrot and stick approach was used: those who expressed doubts about the GLF were weeded out of the Party and cadres who favoured a more cautious approach were publicly condemned. But minor concessions were made; communes were instructed to assure adequate food rations to everyone and members were to receive cash wages for the work they had performed. These concessions were calculated as being sufficient to mollify the peasants so that the expansion of the communes could continue. The underlying assumption was that the communes would accelerate the increase in agricultural production.[30]

The supremacy of the commune system appeared unassailable. However, in 1959 China was hit by a series of natural calamities but given the Campaign against Rightist Opportunism, local cadres dared not report reality, and almost without exception they reported that agricultural targets were exceeded. In fact, the harvest would be little short of a disaster with much effort still being wasted on the useless blast furnaces.[31]

During 1959 a drought gripped northwest China while torrential rains caused severe flooding in the south. Famine threatened Anhui, Gansu, and Sichuan provinces and by early 1960 there was no hiding the fact that the poor harvest was reaching the proportions of a national disaster. The weather in 1960 was even worse. First a terrible drought gripped the entire country. This was followed by extensive floods and typhoons. The grain harvest shrank to less than 150 million tonnes. The resulting famine was possibly the worst in China's long history. Just as Moscow had refused to accept the extent of the 1931-33 catastrophe and pressed forward with its procurement plans, so too did Beijing. Terrible distortions can be produced when everything depends on a bureaucratic central command, and this famine – in which as many as 20 million people died – was an extreme form.

The harvest of 1960 was a disaster but the consequences were greatly exacerbated by attempting to maintain industrial growth through levels of state procurement that were based on grossly exaggerated reports. The government showed beyond any doubt that it was not only the weather which was responsible for the increasing difficulties in agriculture; organisational and technical problems were also to blame and may have played a more significant role.[32]

In the communes, hungry and starving peasants were making their own criticisms, directing them not just at unspecified 'higher levels' but at Mao Zedong himself. The leadership of the CCP could no longer cover up the scope of the disaster, reality had caught up. The communes, instead of overcoming grain shortages, compelled China to import massive quantities of grain from Canada and Australia between 1960 and 1963. In July 1960, Zhou Enlai attempted to place the blame for the problems encountered onto local cadres, who it now appeared, had acted without authorisation and exceeded their authority.

In self-defence, Mao Zedong promoted the Anti-Rightist Campaign: "at present the main danger comes from right deviationist thinking, which has been growing among some cadres", and Party committees "at all levels must resolutely criticize and overcome such thinking."[33]

Mao took the Anti-Rightist Campaign into the communes on the grounds that most of the problems would be resolved if Party members provided a more direct and firmer leadership. Party cadres were instructed "to go deep among the masses", i.e. to spend less time in their offices and re-integrate with the work teams of the communes to provide more direct supervision, supress dissent, and increase agricultural production.[33] This was an attempt by Beijing to re-affirm its control over a Party apparatus badly damaged and disoriented by the extent of the failure of the GLF.

However, after the disastrous harvest it was necessary to restore food supplies as soon as possible. The basis for this was a return to greater material incentives for the peasants. In November 1960, the Politburo through Zhou Enlai, drafted emergency measures for restructuring agricultural policy: the *Twelve Articles on People's Communes.* Appearances would be maintained, but in all important respects there was a return to the Higher Stage APCs. The authority of the central commune administration was severely curtailed: production units were given the right to plant and work according to the soil conditions of their land, and draft animals and farm implements were now owned, kept and used by production brigades as and how they saw fit.

As had happened in the USSR, there was restoration of personal ownership of land and livestock and the revival of free markets. A contract system was introduced whereby individual households were given land on the promise they delivered a set quota of the harvest to the state and paid certain charges to the commune (limited to about 10%). It was the death knell of the commune system. Peasants were free to sell the produce from their private plots (pigs, sheep, chickens, ducks and other livestock) and resuscitate family handicrafts (household weaving, bee keeping, fishing, hunting and foraging). The detested communal kitchens and nurseries were mostly abolished.

The very basis of the GLF had imploded and the daily life of the peasants returned to previous patterns of agricultural activity. By midsummer 1961, about 5% of land was being farmed privately. One year later between 20% and 30% had been returned to the peasants – sufficient to overcome the food crisis.[34] In March, 1962, with private markets and private cultivation close to full restoration, Zhou Enlai announced that the Party expected private handicrafts to continue for a long time. Obscure phrases were found to suggest that these changes were foreseen and planned.

By the end of 1962, the private harvests in some provinces were greater than those of the communes, by the beginning of 1963 agricultural production was restored almost to the level before the launch of the communes, and by 1964 in at least Kweichow and Szechuan, there was more private than communal land. Mao's standing was so badly damaged by the catastrophic failure of his voluntarist approach that he was forced to stay silent until early July 1962 when he called a meeting of loyalists intending to put a stop to the contract system which he saw as restoring private ownership of the land, and halt once and for all the activities of Liu Shaoqi and Deng Xiaoping.[35]

In a series of meetings between mid-July and the end of August 1962, Mao raged against the Liu-Deng current and labelled the contract system "bourgeois" giving rise to corruption, speculation, thievery, and the return of usury. Lui and Deng were, in effect, being accused of counter-revolutionary activities. Mao was gathering his forces and preparing to purge them.

13.5 Working, Living, and Dying on the Communes

The purpose of the communes was to increase production to accumulate as rapidly as possible the capital needed for China's industrialisation and, of course, to meet the cost of the huge bureaucratic apparatus. Living conditions for the majority of peasants deteriorated. Working hours and intensity of labour were increased; wages were continually in arrears; women released from family duties were put to work with the same intensity as men (a twelve to fourteen-hour day in the fields) while retaining responsibility for housework and child care; food supplied in the communal kitchens was neither sufficient nor of good quality; under such conditions the health of the peasants deteriorated and they were frequently ill while medicines were in extremely short supply. While as many as 75% of women participated in agricultural production, there were approved child care places for only 5% of children.[36]

Generally, commune managers simply transmitted instructions from above. People who had one kind of skill were often sent to jobs requiring an entirely different kind of skill – peasants who spent a lifetime in farming were assigned to smelt iron. Those who were familiar with the lay of the land and soil conditions in one area were sent to work in other areas where they were strangers both to the area and to the agricultural conditions. Peasant teams could be freely transferred to other duties, even to other communes, a practice which allowed for huge irrigation and construction projects but could detract from the harvests. Too often when a production brigade was sent to a different place to work – sometimes for up to six months – their payment and/or compensation for the time expended would be lost in some bureaucratic muddle. For many young women, however, these absences from the claustrophobic discipline of the home were welcomed and living side-by-side with young men, much preferred.

Peasants were further demotivated because too many orders were given which flew in the face of reality, such as the setting of wholly unrealistic production targets compelling peasants to do exhausting labour after which the grain would be seized and taken from them. Finally, there were the special privileges given to cadres who, for example, received extra food during the periods of severe shortage.[37]

The intensification and exploitation of the peasants to the utmost inevitably aroused resentment and resistance and contributed significantly to the magnitude of agricultural failures of 1959 and 1960. Constant supervision and tight control became absolute necessities, which was why the communes were from the start organised with a militia style discipline euphemistically called "living the collective way" or more exactly "working as if fighting a battle."[38]

13.5.1 Famine in the Communes

Famine was a hallmark of the GLF, rural death rates leapt from 11 to more than 28 per 1,000 people/year in 1960.[39] Population growth rate in Henan, for example, went into reverse and dropped from +22.8% in 1958 to – 4.3% in 1961.[40] Only in 1980 did the CCP admit that at least 20 million people had starved to death during the great famine.[41]

The famine was due to the combination of severe natural disaster and, possibly more importantly, the bureaucratic system itself. The bureaucracy had reduced the area of land sown with grain and insisted that a vast amount of unnecessary work be carried out on the blast furnaces, but a third and important factor was the Anti-Rightist Campaign which scared lower level bureaucrats into exaggerating the harvest to please their superiors. In late August and September, Mao himself, uncritically accepted boastful provincial reports that state grain purchases had been fully met and accomplished in record time. Mao ordered the publication and distribution of these falsehoods with his accompanying observations containing a blistering attack on 'rightists', further increasing the pressure on lower rank cadres. Grain procurement by the state based on these false figures played a major causal role in the famine.[42]

The "Wind of Exaggeration" was a hallmark of the GLF and was due to the intense pressures exerted by the higher echelons on rural cadres. The Anti-Rightist Campaign vehemently criticised rightist, conservative, and 'capitalist' thinking, and pressurised cadres into competitive target-setting. Commune leaders vied with one another to promise incredible yields. The targets could escalate into the ridiculous – thousands and ten thousands of catties per mu (1000 catties/mu = 2500 kg/hectare).[43]

Bernstein quotes the following exchange from a post-Mao short story, *The Black Flag* which claimed to report actual events when a Commune Party secretary refused to go along with promises by neighbouring communes to attain impossible yields of between 30,000 and 60,000 kg/hectare:

> "Secretary Mi [the county party secretary] bellowed over the loudspeaker, 'Well, Ding Jingzhong [the commune secretary], have you lost your tongue? You haven't said anything'. Everybody turned to Ding who, flushed and tense, was fidgeting, tearing up bits of paper ... Ding spoke calmly into the microphone: 'Our commune has discussed our plan. We'll try to produce 800 catties per mu (2000 kg/hectare) this year'. To achieve this would require a lot of hard work from everyone. But it seemed as if no one understood this. The loudspeaker went dead. After a long while, Secretary Mi said at last, 'Attention. Have you all heard him?' Angry voices screeched out from the loudspeaker, 'Yes. We did'. Secretary Mi again. 'What shall we do? Are they leaping forward or going backward? Are they sabotaging us on purpose?' There was more clamour. 'They are sabotaging us. We'll have it out with them. We'll give them hell!' When one of Ding's supporters backs him up, Sun, the commune secretary's assistant, exclaims: 'That man isn't one of the masses. He is a big rightist, an extreme rightist!'. In the end, just as debased coins drive out the good, the stalwart hero was purged."

Despite initial evidence of famine in parts of the country the government persisted through 1960 in trying to maintain industrial growth. But agricultural output in 1960 was considerably less than that for 1959, and industry's efforts collapsed due to the shortage of raw materials and lack of foodstuffs. In the middle of the year the sudden withdrawal of Soviet assistance greatly exacerbated the problems.[44] The government was forced to curb the expansion of heavy industry and increase its assistance to light industry, handicrafts, family commercial activities, and agriculture. Mao called for the bureaucracy to moderate its pressures on the peasants but despite the scale of the disasters resulting from the GLF, he never accepted the underlying problems as systemic, and never renounced the voluntarist, anti-Marxist ideas that underlay the GLF.[45]

13.5.2 Women in the Communes

Prior to the GLF, the CCP had allowed traditional, patriarchal relations to continue in the villages and even developed institutions that reinforced them. The land reforms undertaken by the PRC had given the poor and middle peasants redistributed land, and reduced rents and taxes so that with the continuation of a patriarchal family structure they became, *de facto*, the patriarchs of their own family small-holdings. When these farms were combined into mutual aid teams, Lower and Higher Stage APCs, in the mid-1950s, the process was on the basis of existing structures and pre-existing male kinship groups (women married out of their natal villages and so tended to be isolated individuals), which enabled the traditional family and patriarchal structures to persist. Women's participation in agricultural labour may have expanded considerably, but they were brought into the production process under conditions that increased their value as chattels but did not give them greater control over their own lives or even over the fruits of their labour.[46]

We find in the propaganda supporting the Communes, statements to the effect that: "The communes have ploughed up and pulverized the crust of outworn social and family relations" and the communes "have accelerated the liberation of women from domestic slavery (and) opened up new avenues of cultural development." These claims refer to the liberation of women from the bonds of the feudal or patriarchal family. The question is "Did the communes actually achieve either kind of liberation for women"?

We must not forget the hugely positive and progressive moves introduced by the CCP which benefitted Chinese women. From 1927 in the Soviets and liberated areas, and after 1949 in the entire country, women were recognised as: having equal status in law with men, the right of inheritance, equal rights in education, freedom to participate in social and political spheres, equal pay for equal work, and freedom in marriage and divorce (except for the wives of soldiers). There is no doubt that the PRC made an important contribution towards the liberation of Chinese women even though this legal equality was far from being realised in the rural areas. Did the communes add anything of significance?

A great many women participated in political activities both through the CCP and in women's organisations such as the All-China Women's Federation (ACWF), and in all kinds of social movements such as land reform and agricultural co-operatives. All this was accomplished a few years before the establishment of the Communes and was not the result of them.

For women, the first year of the GLF was full of promise. In the spring there was a literacy drive amongst both women and men and, it is claimed, practically all women between the ages of 16-25 had learned to read and write. Importantly, they were also talking to people outside their immediate family and outside the home. It was claimed that immense opportunities had opened for women in steel making (true) and driving tractors (highly unlikely), but at the cost of a dramatically increased daily workload for most women.[47] The ACWF and Party leadership did instruct rural cadres to provide special care to women who were pregnant by, for example, allocating them lighter work. Communes were also warned to restrict the kinds of work performed and the number of days worked by pregnant, postnatal, and menstruating women, but these tended to be more honoured in the breach than the observance.[48] In some particularly active communes, lower rank women cadres organised sewing and washing circles, and organised women to staff homes for the elderly and the newly-established reproductive health centres.

At the launch of the communes, it was announced that a major goal was to free women for productive labour and so housework would, supposedly, be socialised through mess halls, nurseries, and communal laundries. In 1959, *People's Daily* claimed that nearly 100% of rural women were engaged in agriculture or other productive labour in the communes. At the same time, women's participation in public and political affairs was to be encouraged: women's federations were to assist in training women so that a woman director or deputy could be appointed in every co-operative, and a woman chief or deputy chief found in every production squad. Women members, women deputy chiefs, women technicians, and women book-keepers were to be increased and promoted every year in the management committees and control committees of the co-operatives.[49]

An important innovation was that the commune paid wages directly to people who had earned them (regardless of age or sex). This broke with the tradition of giving the money to the head of the family, or a woman's husband, and struck a blow at the patriarchal system even if the woman immediately handed her wages to the head of the household. The number of women gainfully employed increased but when the women joined the labour force they found that they were allocated labour intensive, less-skilled jobs, and that pay rates were higher for the jobs done by men on the basis of: 'From each according to his ability, to each according to his work'. It is now claimed that Party cadres deliberately set pay rates for 'women's work' (no matter what its character, how demanding intellectually or physically) at lower levels than 'men's work'.

Cadre abuse of villagers was well-known in the Maoist era and collectivisation of land, labour, and tools in the mid-1950s had substantially increased the power of the local cadres. The Anti-Rightist Campaign following the 1957 Hundred Flowers Movement, enabled some over-zealous cadres to act as local tyrants during the initial phase of the GLF. To maximise participation of women in the workforce, dining halls and nurseries were built and villagers were pressurised into giving up cooking at home and placing their children in the nursery. But the cafeterias and child care were often inadequate with the result that women had to work long hours in the fields and then again at home just to keep up with their allotted tasks.[50]

The CCP forcibly replaced family life with collective life under unfavourable material and cultural conditions in a way that brought misery to many peasant women. The commune movement became a compulsory forced march and this was reflected in the commune kitchens. Cadres compelled everybody to eat in the canteens and, in extreme cases the peasants were forced to dismantle the stoves in their homes so there was no hot water or warmth for the children, the aged and the sick. No rations were issued to individuals, but the canteens were of poor quality and the food was inadequate. In many cases there were no covered canteens and the peasants ate in the open or took meals home on rainy and cold days. But quite shamelessly the cadres ate in their own small, separate mess halls![51]

The situation in the nurseries was, if anything, worse. Little thought had been given to the cost of establishing and running the nurseries. Soon after the Sandinistas took power in Nicaragua they attempted to introduce nurseries but found "the cost of construction, equipment and maintenance very high" which had seriously limited the number of nurseries they could provide.[52] In China it meant many children were crowded into makeshift small rooms with no nursery equipment under the charge of old people, invariably illiterate or women whose feet had been bound. How could such children be well cared for? Mothers labouring in fields some distance from their homes were unable to breastfeed their babies and came home to a distraught, dirty and famished child. We can only imagine the mental anguish of these women; the common saying was: "mothers may be in the field, but their minds are back home."[53]

What was the situation of the women liberated from domestic slavery to participate in social production? In many communes 'equality with men' meant 12 and 14 hour shifts on farms, dams, highways, mines and factories. Many pregnant women suffered from sleep deprivation, miscarriages and illnesses, certainly in late 1957 and 1958. Children also were injured and even died during the busiest periods of the year because adequate supervision was unavailable.[54] The main aim of the communes was not the thoroughgoing liberation of women but the mobilisation of maximum labour power for agriculture, and it was this that pushed women in the rural areas out of their homes to supply needed labour. From domestic slavery, women were thrown into social slavery, often driven by women cadres.

By 1960 it was clear that the commune was not going to be the road to equality for women. During the GLF, the Anti-Rightist Campaign had meant expertise had been down-graded, often in favour of brute strength and the latter was rewarded by higher pay grades. The social labour most often performed by women – such as in the commune kitchens – was further degraded by being used as a punishment for 'bad elements' who had broken some rule or other. Party theoreticians explained this by saying gender equality was postponed until women could perform the same labour as men, i.e., when physical labour was replaced by machinery. The struggle for gender equality was seen as enabling women to do men's work, rather than questioning the supposed superiority of men's work and gender stereotyping.[55]

The commune was presented as a massive attack on the feudal family, as offering women new roles of greater status and income (but still lower than those of men), with socialisation of certain aspects of housework. However, by 1960 the Chinese press was filled with articles aimed not at promoting socialised housework but at allaying fears that family life was being destroyed. A torrent of theoretical works on the necessity of the family even in a communist society was produced to allay popular (male) apprehension and resentment of women's progress.[56]

The retreat from the GLF, and increasing unemployment levels, meant a new and extremely conservative line concerning women. Once again women were exhorted to return to keep home for their menfolk and children. The model woman was no longer a Stakhanovite worker but the housewife who patched clothes to make them last a decade, and Party journals contained articles such as "How to Choose a Husband". The result was a massive resurgence in arranged marriages, bride prices, and wedding feasts.

With the failure of the Hundred Flowers Movement and the growth of anti-intellectualism, the focus of women's policy shifted from achieving equality and liberation from patriarchal oppression to an acceptance that women's emancipation would be achieved only through loyalty to the regime's scheme for building a socialist China. Accordingly, it was claimed that the groundwork for liberation already existed in law and so women were told to turn their energies to work to build a socialist China. The Chinese leadership now encouraged women to balance housework and productive labour, with the emphasis on the former.

The communes did give rise to great hopes for the liberation of women, and initially there were important, progressive moves such as the literacy campaign, such as the shift to more individual rights within the communes (e.g. wage payments to individuals). And these did raise the status of women in rural China. But the bureaucratic and adventurist nature of the project meant it was bound to fail and in the end took women backwards. The subsequent shift to the contract system returned power to the household and enhanced the authority of fathers and husbands over daughters and wives. The canteens and nurseries may have been hated but their disappearance was a symbol of the increase in women's domestic duties. The contract system has remained in place up to today though there have been a number of modifications and adjustments, most of which have further reduced the authority of women as landowners. For example, the Chinese government since 2009 has been re-interpreting the Marriage and Divorce Laws so that a woman who cannot produce a land deed in her own name, loses everything on divorce. The problem for the woman is that the deed was likely handed to her husband and remained in the possession of his family, to disappear when she needed it most. Because China has no central land registry the deeds to a property are crucially important. In many cases the women found themselves robbed of the land that should have been theirs.

Subsequently, this practice crept into the cities, and due to family and social pressures it is now customary, even when the woman makes the major contribution, for a dwelling to be registered in the man's name alone. The 1950 Marriage Law gave the woman equal rights but in 2011 the Supreme Court ruled that the property belonged to the person named on the deeds. Even in those 25% of (urban) cases where the couple share the cost and both names appear on the deeds, the man's name comes first, he being considered the "primary loan recipient" with the greater stake in the property.[57]

13.5.3 Democracy in the Communes

The CCP's view of Party democracy was derived from Russia of the 1930s so that outside of the Politburo and CC, Mao was projected as the undisputed leader. In 1962, possibly reflecting the situation within the Politburo, Mao defined democratic centralism as the Party carrying out his instructions whether correct or incorrect except in the exceptional circumstances where "everyone disagrees with me."[58]

Outside the leadership, the best that Party members could hope for was that when an issue arose, the leaders consulted the cadres and listened to their views before reaching a decision. The same applied to the relationship between Party members and non-members. The latter were to be encouraged to attend commune meetings and give their views, but only to ensure that oppositionists were exposed and to fine-tune 'the line' so that it was carried through more effectively. At no level were the officials of the Party or state freely elected, subject to recall, or paid an average wage. The bureaucracy of the Chinese state was appointed, worked in secret, and was privileged by income and status.

The election of the Commune Councils followed the same general pattern. The village head or Commune Party Secretary (often these would be the same person who would have been selected by the Party hierarchy and, at best, approved by the branch) would propose a list of candidates, invariably dominated by Party cadres. The peasants, having gone through the procedure many times were familiar with this kind of election and knew full well that their only right was to approve, not oppose, the list of candidates.[59] The administration of the communes was a violation of democracy, everything being decided by bureaucratic edict with the consequence that the peasants became ever more alienated and politically passive. Manning, in her visit to Chinese villages, appears to confirm that posts of, e.g., team leaders were preferentially allocated to relatives of local Party leaders[60] and that many of these people recalled the GLF as a "happy" time! Manning also reveals that ordinary peasants were still bitter forty years later, charging these leaders with stealing rice from the village store during the famine, for abusing and beating peasants to maintain a discipline that ensured privileges for the local Party tops (which included interest free loans from the Commune which were never paid back).

The cadres had to faithfully implement Party directives (whether popular or not, feasible or otherwise) and take the blame if Party policies failed. The dilemma for cadres and a genuine test of their innovative skills, was their ability to follow the instructions given in the *People's Daily* that cadres could "neither alter the resolutions of the Party committee without asking for instructions" nor "observe the rules to the letter without regard to the actual situation". Creative, flexible, resourceful bureaucrats were required; rigid, inflexible bureaucrats could be ejected from the Party.

Assigned to their posts rather than elected by commune members, secure on the state payroll rather than receiving wages agreed with the peasants, cadres had little personal or material interest in peasant attitudes and concerns or in optimising the use of local resources. As state employees, their rewards came from faithfully executing central policy. In such circumstances the ethic of serving the people and genuine popular supervision of Commune personnel could not be sustained and serious distortions in Commune performance resulted.[61]

13.6 Summary

The reality of the GLF and the communes offered incontrovertible evidence of the bureaucratic and Stalinist nature of the CCP. But there are none so blind as those that will not see: Rousset, after the event when he had the facts to hand, continued to offer a half-hearted defence of the communes – they were initiated with the best of intentions but the CCP had bitten off more than it could chew and after "an initial success" intolerable burdens on the administration resulted in chaos and failure.[62]

The real lessons of the communes are very different, the most important being that workers' democracy was needed in China not least because it could have saved the Chinese people from the waste, suffering and famine caused by the GLF and the communes. A centralised bureaucracy cannot determine *every* aspect of production, terrible distortions and inefficiencies are inevitably produced. A centrally planned economy can only work efficiently if there are checks at every level by the workers involved. Workers' democracy, workers' control, and workers' management are essential for determining the optimum goals and the efficient functioning of any proletarian regime. The workers, who are also the consumers, have a material interest in making sure that the plan works efficiently at all levels. Bureaucrats are only interested in meeting their quotas regardless of quality of output – so that they will get their bonuses and retain their positions.[63]

The GLF and the communes had demonstrated that the bureaucracy was not a necessary social layer in the development of the Chinese economy and it soon became a hindrance. This was clear confirmation of Leon Trotsky's analysis of the bureaucracy published as *In Defence of Marxism* written in October 1939. Trotsky explained that the Soviet bureaucracy had no historical purpose. It was born out of the degeneration of the Soviet Union under conditions of extreme backwardness and isolation. He argued that the idea that the Stalinist regime in Russia would eventually reach socialism was mistaken and that without a political revolution to remove the bureaucracy a backslide to capitalism was quite possible, and the longer the bureaucracy lasted the more likely that would be.

Chapter 14

China under Mao: The Great Proletarian Cultural Revolution

14.1 Introduction

The Stalinist nature of the Chinese Communist Party and Mao was further confirmed by a second major event that sent a shockwave through the political left worldwide, the Great Proletarian Cultural Revolution (GPCR). This was widely presented as a rebellion of youth against the Party diehards, and if those old diehards were proud to call themselves Stalinist how could the youth (and their Maoist sponsors) who were struggling against them not be a genuine revolutionary force?

However, the GPCR cannot be understood unless it is appreciated that the Red Guards were a top-down phenomenon, launched, supported, guided, and eventually ended by the Maoist faction. This was quite the opposite of the revolutionary upsurge of students who erected barricades in Paris in May-June 1968, who inspired workers across France to strike and very nearly brought down the General de Gaulle government.

The CCP was a Stalinised Party and in the final resort when opposition to Mao's adventurist policies hardened into a concerted attempt to remove him from power, the democratic façade was dropped and the Mao faction launched the GPCR to physically annihilate the capitalist roaders such as "the renegade, traitor and scab Liu Shaoqi."[1]

This chapter will show that the GPCR was a demonstration of the lack of proletarian democracy within the CCP; that deep divisions on how to take China forward were settled, as in Russia, by the physical subjugation of the losing faction. However, Mao would be forced to launch his attacks to annihilate his fellow veteran Communists before he had made full preparations. The result was that his opponents were strong enough, at least in some areas, to organise their defence and the struggle sometimes took on the appearance of a civil war. Various estimates exist for the number of people killed during the GPCR; these vary from 750,000 to three million. With Mao's death in 1976 his opponents staged a semi-military coup to remove his designated heirs, the 'Gang of Four', and consign them to lengthy prison terms. When the dust finally settled it would be Mao's opponents who had won the struggle.

14.2 The Great Proletarian Cultural Revolution

14.2.1 Mao Prepares the Cultural Revolution

The debacle of the communes and the GLF was such a terrible blow to Mao's standing within the CC that his opponents considered the time had come to openly criticise his policies. The enlarged CC of 22 February 1962, heard Peng Zhen call for Mao to make a self-criticism, and Liu Shaoqi claimed that the economic difficulties being experienced were 30% due to natural disasters and 70% due to the serious errors and mistakes in Party work. Liu and Peng supported by Deng Xiaoping, were openly attempting to kick Mao upstairs into a symbolic figurehead stripped of all real power.

So severe was his loss of prestige, that Mao was forced to bow to the majority, but he was not ready to retire and immediately began to re-build his base within the Party, preparing his counter-attack to destroy the Liu/Peng grouping. This was possible because although Mao was temporarily removed from frontline politics, he remained the figurehead of the regime with considerable formal authority within the Party and a base within the army. Lin Piao, a Mao loyalist and Defence Minister, would play a central role in Mao's bid to regain his authority. His response to the disaster of the GLF was the opposite of that taken by Liu and Peng, and he began a campaign intended to turn the army into a Maoist bastion. He had Mao glorified; the first issue of the Little Red Book was published. The battle lines were being drawn for what became within a few years, the GPCR.[2]

Liu Shaoqi and the Politburo introduced a period of economic relaxation: in the communes, private plots were allowed, trade in private services such as mending and repairs was encouraged. However, during this period when Liu and his co-thinkers held supremacy within the Party, their practices remained firmly Stalinist and quite indistinguishable from those of the previous period. Thus, when intellectuals were told they could widen their studies to include even politics and the class struggle – but with the clear proviso that the authority of the Party must not be challenged – they remained too cowed by the experience of the Hundred Flowers Movement to respond. It was intellectuals in the higher echelons of the Party, who, better understanding the intentions and limits of the new policy, took the opportunity to publish between-the-lines criticisms of Mao's GLF adventure.

A group around Teng T'o (editor *People's Daily*, 1952-1957, member of the Beijing Party Committee) which included Wu Han (vice-mayor of Beijing and a leading historian), and Liao Ma-sha (member of the Secretariat of the Beijing Party), supported by Peng Zhen, published a number of articles critical of Mao's leadership over the period 1961-1965. Criticisms were oblique and hidden in stories and plays concerning historical characters and incidents: one such was the play by Wu Han, *Hai Jui Dismissed from Office*. The honest official Hai Jui was dismissed from his post by the emperor for criticising bureaucratic misdeeds – a reference to Mao's dismissal of Peng Dehuai for his criticisms of the GLF made at the Lushan Conference. It was still not possible to openly or directly criticise Mao in the press so, for example, to make an assessment of Mao's voluntarism, Teng T'o wrote an article analysing the works of Ernst Mach, an influential German physicist and philosopher, an anti-materialist who denounced natural-scientific materialism. Teng would become increasingly bold in his criticisms, culminating in his declaration that Mao's famous slogan "The East wind will prevail over the West wind" was … "hot air."[3]

How did such a group arise in Beijing? In May 1961, as a Politburo member, Peng Zhen had initiated a research project to determine what lessons could be learned from the GLF. The emphasis was on what instructions and guidance was given in central directives written by Mao personally. Teng T'o was given responsibility for leading the investigation. His findings placed the blame for the disaster directly on the GLF strategy itself. The centre had accepted unquestioningly too many false reports, had issued too many conflicting directives, and had ignored the few who had attempted to report the reality. The blame for the GLF disaster was laid at the door of the Politburo and Mao.[4] Biting though these criticisms were, they were of Mao and his voluntarist policies not the Stalinist system that gave rise to them.

At the CC meeting of September 1962, it was agreed that a rectification campaign was needed to address the errors and excesses of rank and file cadres committed during the GLF. Such a campaign would have been, and was intended to be, immensely damaging for Mao. However, to maximise the impact of the campaign the leadership needed to make an assessment of the situation at rank and file level within the Party. It was felt that little confidence could be placed in reports received from Party personnel submitted through the usual bureaucratic channels, so trusted individuals were sent to work incognito in the provinces to draw up reports based on their experiences.

During the interim period while the testimonies were being compiled, Mao declared support for the rectification campaign and, in December 1963, launched a pre-emptive broadside saying art and culture was a serious problem, promoting feudal and capitalist aims. Mao picked an issue on which he could appear to agree with the Liu group who also wanted control of intellectual criticism of the regime. However, Mao widened the attack in February 1964 when he disparaged the role of intellectuals in China's history, emphasising that the only two Ming emperors of any worth were barely literate and that "to read too many books is harmful."[5]

At the same time Mao also began an attack on Tung Pien, editor of *Women in China*, and ally of Liu Shaoqi, for being a feminist and for her editorial policies. The specific charges against her were that she emphasised interests such as love, marriage, and the family, while neglecting the class struggle. Mao's standing in the Party meant she was dismissed from her post. The attack on Tung Pien was the beginning of an open attack on the Party faction that had ordered the retreat from the GLF. This should be seen as significant an event as the later and better known attack on Wu Han in auguring the GPCR.

The reports received from the countryside were deeply worrying; corruption was again widespread involving many lower and middle cadres, and the Party was widely viewed with distrust and even hatred. The CC agreed, in late 1964, to launch a Socialist Education Campaign (to be known as The Four Cleans Movement – to clean the Party economically, organisationally, politically, and ideologically), the emphasis of which would be to combat corruption within the Party and re-impose discipline. However, in January 1965, Mao seized the initiative by unilaterally publishing his own programme for the Socialist Education Campaign that turned it into a general campaign against revisionism within the Party. The chosen target was CC member Yang Hsien-chen (President of the Higher Party School of the Central Committee), who, after a visit to the countryside in 1958, had written an article that claimed the GLF had represented the theory of obedience to the will and abandonment of objective laws. Yang was a carefully chosen target, he was a close associate of Liu Shaoqi, and an attack on Yang for the reasons given, effectively silenced criticism of the communes and the GLF.

However, events at the international level would force Mao to launch his counter-offensive sooner than he had planned. The Indonesian Communist

Party was the largest in the capitalist world, with three million members and ten million sympathisers. Mao had invited the leader of the Indonesian Communist Party, D N Aidit, to Beijing many times and had convinced Aidit to adopt a policy of co-operation with the Sukarno government, modelled on CCP-KMT collaboration during the second Chinese Revolution. The result was to disarm the Indonesian CP in the face of a military coup which took place in October 1965, and during which as many as one million Communists and militants were slaughtered, including Aidit. The policies advocated by Mao had produced exactly the same outcome as they had in China during 1925-27.

This horrific tragedy dealt a further heavy blow to Mao's credibility. Liu and, particularly, Peng Zhen, voiced their dissatisfaction with Mao's policies at a special meeting of the CCP called to discuss the Indonesian events. At the meeting, Peng Zhen, went so far as to say: "Everyone is equal before the truth", and if Chairman Mao had made mistakes he should be criticized.[6] Following on from the catastrophe of the GLF, the annihilation of the Indonesian Communist Party, because it had followed advice given by Mao personally, fatally undermined Mao's standing with many of the intelligentsia. These were the people most vociferous in demanding an honest and open discussion on Party history, so it is no wonder that Mao chose them as his initial target.

Mao left Beijing for Shanghai to regroup his forces, among them Yao Wenyuan, literary critic and editor of the important Chinese newspaper, *Literary News* published in Shanghai. Under Mao's guidance, Yao wrote and published a criticism of the play *Hai Jui Dismissed from Office,* (Jiang Qing appeared as co-author). This article is widely considered the first shot of the Great Proletarian Cultural Revolution.

14.2.2 The PLA is Made Ready and the Cultural Revolution Begins

The support of the PLA was crucial to Mao but officers in army units in the different regions often had considerable loyalty to local party cadres because these were the people they had fought beside during the civil war. These officers were usually the senior ranks, and Mao and Lin moved quickly to neutralise their influence.

It was widely reported at the time, May 1965, that the PLA had abolished all military ranks. The abolition of distinctions and symbols of rank was described as a reversion to the army's revolutionary practice intended to promote closer relations between officers and men, and between soldiers and civilians. Many impressionable people on the left greeted this at face value as a move towards greater democracy and as evidence of the radical nature of the Maoists. In fact the command structure was not abolished but simply re-defined in such a way as to give Lin Piao and Mao greater control of the PLA.

The 8th Route Army, for example, did not have ranks but it had a clearly defined command structure which enforced a strict discipline. Officers were in post and had titles such as Squad Commander or Company Commander, etc. The uniforms of the officers were identical with those of other ranks, but officers could be identified in numerous ways: they carried pistols, they had orderlies, they issued orders and were obeyed, Divisional Commanders rode a horse or a mule, and so on.

The reforms maintained the field command structure more or less intact. The big change was that the number of troops directly commanded now determined status within the military establishment. Top ranking officers, those more likely to ally with Liu Shoaqi and Deng Xioping, tended to have desk jobs, directly commanded few if any soldiers, and so lost rank and the status it conferred. On 5 April 1966, the *Liberation Army Daily* gave the game away when it warned previously high ranking officers they now had no rank to protect them, they were completely at the mercy of Lin Piao. To safeguard themselves they were urged to

remould their world outlook and completely subordinate themselves to the thinking of Mao Zedong.[7]

Lin Piao stepped up the campaign to propagandise Mao's thought and the *Liberation Army Daily* carried slogans such as: "Mao's thought is the beacon of revolution for the world's people."[8] An editorial on 1 January 1966, stated:

> "Every word of Chairman Mao is truth ...We must firmly support and carry out everything conforming to Mao Zedong's thought and we must firmly resist and oppose everything which does not conform to Mao's thought."

This message was a direct challenge to Liu Shaoqi and the CC.[9]

By April 1966, the ongoing criticisms of Wu Han and his play *Hai Jui Dismissed from Office* had taken on a very dark tone and moved from Wu being mistaken in his thinking to being anti-Party and possibly a counter-revolutionary. The attacks spread outwards and soon included Peng Zhen. Liu and Deng Xiaoping called an emergency meeting of the CC in an attempt to block Mao. Mao refused to attend. In an open declaration of factional war and a clear indication of how far he would go to preserve his authority, Mao had Piao send troops to occupy the offices of the Beijing local government. In a public display of his approval for this action Mao returned to Beijing and proclaimed the "Great Proletarian Cultural Revolution". The Beijing municipal government, headed by Peng Zhen, would be formally dismissed in early June along with Lu Ting-i, head of the Party's propaganda department, Chou Yang, vice-minister of culture, and many other high-ranking cadres in cultural institutions.[10]

Mao launched the Great Leap Forward in the Ideological Field to eliminate all those within the Party who did not toe the Maoist line, with Peng Zhen, Liu Shoaqi, and Deng Xioping at the front. However, Mao had been forced to launch this inter-bureaucratic struggle to regain his authority before he had the chance to fully mobilise his support within the Party. The disaster in Indonesia and the moves by the CC for a rectification campaign that might reveal the truth about his role in the GLF forced his hand. An important consequence of not having a sufficient base within the Party hierarchy, was that Mao was compelled to seek support from outside the Party. In this he took the unprecedented step of by-passing the monopoly of authority of the local Party cadres and mobilising students to act outside the Party structure.[11] Mao chose middle and high school students to be his battering ram and on 16 May 1966, he launched a frontal attack on meritocratic education policies and educators generally.

Education was a natural battlefield between the two factions. Mao's stress on voluntarism made him over-emphasise the importance of the remnants of bourgeois ideas in education. This led him to favour opening the doors of education preferentially to the children of CCP cadres, while the Liu/Deng group favoured a more meritocratic approach and in this were supported by most of the existing educational establishment.[12]

Liu and Deng responded quickly to head-off Mao's initiative and on 3 June, directed the Party to send 'work teams' of experienced cadres into the universities, major colleges, and schools to 'guide' the formation and development of Red Guard groups. The children of higher Party cadres took the leading role in founding the Red Guards under the slogan: "The father's a revolutionary, the son's a hero." In many Beijing schools the first Red Guard organisations were composed almost exclusively of the children of Party cadres.[13] The work teams presented the GPCR as an extension of the Anti-Rightist Campaign and their efforts were concentrated on restraining those students who showed any independent initiative.

Mao's reaction to this latest attempt to block him was immediate, by mid-June 1966 he had ordered the closure of all schools, from elementary to university level in the name of the GPCR. Next he convened a special, enlarged plenum of the CC, 1-12 August. The character of the plenum can be deduced from it being the first for four years, included a large number of representatives from the Red Guards, and was held in Beijing under the watchful eyes of PLA troops who had just been instrumental in overthrowing the local government. The plenum lasted for twelve days and adopted an official programme for the GPCR, commonly known as the *16-Points Decision.*[14]

The *16-Points* was a clearly factional document with its major goal: "to struggle against and crush those persons in authority taking the capitalist road." To this end it sought to re-assure the great bulk of Party members ("95%") that they had nothing to fear because only a "handful" had taken the capitalist road. This was a deliberate smokescreen to minimise opposition. The army as part of Mao's power base was, naturally, to be excluded from the factional struggle (*Point 15*).

Mao fully appreciated that the Party cadres were, in reality largely loyal to the capitalist roaders, and to be successful his scheme required some form of parallel organisation to balance "those in authority" in the Party. The *16-Points* contained in *Point 9* a call for the establishment of Cultural Revolutionary Groups, the "organs of power" of the Cultural Revolution. These would institute a system of elections, "like that of the Paris Commune" whereby delegates would be elected by the masses and subject to recall.

Immediately following the CC meeting, the Party's theoretical organ *Red Flag* published an article entitled "*The General Election System of the Paris Commune"* which aimed to mobilise the masses in support of Mao. It was very clearly intended that these new organisational forms of would be under the control of the Maoist faction of the CCP. There was no intention that the GPCR would introduce workers' democracy.

However, there is many a slip between cup and lip, and in Shanghai a "People's Commune" was set up and existed for 20 days before being put back into the Maoist straightjacket. The so-called Shanghai Commune became a genuine inspiration for large numbers of Chinese students and workers who threatened to break free of Party control. For revolutionaries this can be said to be the highest point of the GPCR.

The *16-Points* called on students "to criticize and repudiate the reactionary bourgeois academic 'authorities' and the ideology of the bourgeoisie and all other exploiting classes and to transform education" opposing "reactionary bourgeois scholar despots". After 1949, the schools contained an increasing proportion of peasant and working class pupils who often came into conflict with the traditional teaching methods and attitudes of the staff who had been inherited from the KMT regime. Many of these students were alienated by their treatment and hostile to the educational establishment. It was this pent-up animosity that Mao would tap into for his counter-attack. Tutors were an easy first target.

Almost all presidents and principals of universities and middle schools, as well as many teachers and professors were removed from office, publicly humiliated and, sometimes, beaten to death for "intellectual elitism", having "bourgeois tendencies" and being "counter revolutionaries."[15] Under the general direction of Ch'en Po-ta, the Red Guard "heroes" were egged on to commit horrible acts – the *Beijing News* reported a total of 1,772 people killed in Beijing alone during August and September 1966.[16] After this trial run, in the autumn of 1966, Mao instructed the Red Guards to "take Beijing to the rest of the country".

Andreas claims that about this time there began an increasing differentiation within the Red Guard groups. An opposition to those groups led by the children of higher cadres, which had increasingly become mouthpieces for one or the other Party factions, was starting to form based on the children of workers, peasants, and lower cadres who wanted increased independence and freedom of criticism. This separation was much more clear-cut in the universities where, to gain entry, the children of peasants and workers had scored high marks in tough entrance examinations and so had greater self-confidence.

14.3 The Shanghai People's Commune

Much of the factual material on the Shanghai Commune comes from a Doctoral thesis entitled *The Paris Commune in Shanghai*, written by Hongsheng Jiang, in 2010. Readers can access a copy on http://dukespace.lib.duke.edu.

Shanghai was (and is) China's biggest city, its commercial and industrial centre. A study of how the GPCR came to Shanghai and took hold there showcases the artificiality of the Cultural Revolution, how it was directed from Beijing and controlled by Mao and his faction. But the lessons of Shanghai are important in demonstrating that the Maoist faction and the 'capitalist roaders' each saw proletarian democracy as the greatest threat. As soon as the workers and students in Shanghai began to demand some basic democratic rights, the forces driving the cultural revolution and their targets the 'capitalist roaders' joined forces to block a development that would have meant the end for both of them. Soon after, the GPCR was brought to a finish.

Wang Hongwen was security chief at Shanghai's No. 17 Textile Mill, an enterprise employing about 8,400 workers. After meeting with Zhang Chunqiao (a top person in the Shanghai Provincial Committee, a commissar in the Central Group in Beijing assigned overall control of the Cultural Revolution (CCRG), and who would later be one of the Gang of Four), Wang set up a Red Guard cell of about 30 workers and posted a big-character poster criticising the factory authorities on or about 12 June 1966. On 20 June local party leaders sent in a work team led by Shi Huizhen, a female veteran revolutionary and at that time the vice-chairperson of the Shanghai General Workers' Union, to take control of the situation. The work team formed an official Red Guard group, invited Wang to stand for election to the committee, and then ensured he was not elected. For a time, Wang and the rebels were successfully isolated.

14.3.1 The Red Guards Arrive

With Mao's public endorsement, large numbers of Red Guard students from Beijing travelled to Shanghai (travel and subsistence paid by the state) intending to launch an all-Shanghai Red Guard organisation. The students toured the Shanghai schools, colleges, universities, and factories encouraging the formation of Red Guard groups, but on 2 September a number were beaten up by factory workers. The next day, groups of students converged on the mayor's office at city hall to protest and, so it is said, physically threatened top Party officials who responded by calling on Shanghai workers for protection – a fight broke out with the Beijing Red Guards getting the worst of it.

Wang Hongwen now made a trip to Beijing where Zhang ensured he met Mao – which was publicised as an endorsement of Wang's Red Guard activities – and on his return he was able to attract the support of over 1,000 employees at his own mill. On 6 November with strong student support, Wang convened a meeting of workers from seventeen Shanghai factories which agreed to establish an all-city alliance known as the Workers' Revolutionary Rebel General Headquarters (WGH).[17] The hostile reaction of the local Party leaders enabled Wang and the WGH to provoke a number of public disturbances including selected strikes. This gave Beijing the excuse to send in Zhang Chunqiao to investigate events for which he had a significant responsibility, and empower him to make suitable recommendations.

In what had all the signs of a pre-arranged deal, Wang got the strikers back to work and Zhang agreed to recognise the Shanghai WGH as a revolutionary and legitimate organisation which would be allowed to criticise the Party tops in Shanghai. In response to this stitch-up, the local Party launched its own 'Scarlet Guards', organised through the Shanghai General Workers' Union. The majority of the Scarlet Guards (notionally over 100,000 strong) were CCP and Communist Youth League members, model workers who occupied most of the management and administrative posts in enterprises and had the support, overtly or covertly, from the local authorities at most levels.

However, the strikes initiated by Wang had an unintended consequence. Workers dissatisfied with pay and conditions began to voice their own demands. The local Party tops may have been concerned at signs of independent activity by the proletariat but at that moment considered they could contain it and, more importantly, could use it as a weapon against the Red Guards. To win the support of these workers they began a programme of improving pay and conditions, enhancing welfare, pensions and health insurance in the factories. To embarrass Zhang they allowed workers time off to travel to Red Guard rallies and justified this as "not standing in the way of the masses", claiming to follow the guidance laid out in the editorial of the *People's Daily*; *Welcome the Upsurge of the Great CR in the Factories and Mines.*[18] Naturally, there was a snowball effect with more and more workers making demands.

The Maoists shouted loudly that if these moves by established Party cadres continued for any length of time they would bankrupt China's biggest city and seriously disrupt international trade. Using this as a cover, Beijing encouraged the Shanghai Red Guards to seize power. On 23 December 1966 the WGH called a meeting of worker activists and it was agreed to attempt to replace the local Party tops in Shanghai. In protest, the local Party instigated and promoted a one-day general strike. The Scarlet Guards went on strike and effectively closed down the railway, and the post office, and severely hampered production, bringing many important factories to a standstill. The Shanghai Port, was one example when, at the wharves alone, nearly 6,000 workers went on strike.[19]

The Maoists now threw their forces into ending the strikes.[20] The WGH and a number of student Red Guard organisations operating in Shanghai united to "take firm hold of the revolution and promote production". For example, the Shanghai Glass Machinery Factory was a joint public-private enterprise that employed over 1,200 workers. Here production was halted when about half the workforce joined the general strike. Pushed by Red Guard students from Shanghai Kongjiang Middle School, about 100 workers who had turned up for work agreed to form a "Workers' Committee of Production

Management" and to take responsibility for running the factory. Ten workers were elected by secret ballot to the Committee; it was agreed these were subject to recall if their work mates were dissatisfied with their performance. Jiang explains that this was considered a revolutionary development because it abolished the practice of having a vertical hierarchy of Party bureaucrats who stood above, and divorced from, the workforce and the production processes.[21] This system was proposed by the Red Guards to win the support of the workers for strikebreaking, but such democracy carried great danger for the CCP. News of events at the Shanghai Glass Factory spread and other factories attempted to follow suit.

On 4 January, Zhang Chunqiao returned to Shanghai to meet with the leaders of the WGH and plan a response to the strike actions. On 6 January 1967, the Red Guards within the offices of the *Shanghai Liberation Daily* seized the paper and had it distribute the WGH statement; *Message to All Shanghai People,*[22] which was a call to maintain production and which fiercely attacked the strikes. Because this take-over was backed by the authority of Beijing, it was a crucial step in the Red Guards taking charge in Shanghai.

On 7 January, a number of other Red Guard groups including the WGH visited the Shanghai branch of the People's Bank of China. Together with Red Guards working within the bank, they persuaded the manager not to provide further funding to anyone without WGH approval, effectively freezing the accounts of local government, factories and other workplaces. This meant that despite deals made with the local Party tops, from now on strikers would receive no pay. On 8 January, the WGH and Red Guard student organisations held a joint emergency meeting and formed the "Frontline Headquarters" composed of seven workers, two cadres, and 35 Red Guards. The initial task of this organisation was to mobilise Red Guards to enter the factories as model workers who would work for no pay and ensure the factories of Shanghai maintained production. Because of their lack of skills the students tended to replace manual labourers who had walked off the job.

On 9 January, the "*Message to All Shanghai People*" was reprinted in the *People's Daily* and broadcast to the whole country, providing a clear demonstration that Beijing approved of the actions of the WGH and its allies. Beijing also approved an *Urgent Notice* published in Shanghai which, in effort to win support, made it clear to the workers that the new arrangements regarding wage increases, back payment of wages and other material benefits would stand but could, in principle, be re-considered at a later date. As further indication of its support, Beijing sent a *Message of Greetings to Revolutionary*

Rebel Organizations in Shanghai, From the Central Committee of the Chinese Communist Party, the State Council, the Military Commission of the Party's Central Committee and the Cultural Revolution Group under the Party's Central Committee.[23]

On 9 January, the WGH and students from Shanghai Tongji University seized the general control rooms of the Shanghai Railway Bureau, and between 11-14 January, groups of Red Guards took over district and county level units of the Shanghai government, factories, docks, and other units. In most cases the take-overs were led by the WGH and student Red Guards with the assistance of employees though, naturally, the most publicised incidents were the few cases where the seizure was by employees alone.

Now the Red Guards (invariably students under the guidance of strike-breaking workers), by Stakhanovite efforts got the trains, factories, etc., functioning again, claiming that in many cases the original production figures were exceeded. By this time the Scarlet Guards had more or less totally disintegrated and many joined one or other of the Red Guard groups. This acceptance of Beijing's authority was greeted with a congratulatory telegram *Message of Greetings to Revolutionary Rebel Organizations in Shanghai.* On 12 January, in celebration of the telegram, the Shanghai rebels held a mammoth rally at which workers volunteered to take on extra work and overtime without extra pay, as organised by the *Committee for Grasping Revolution and Promoting Production.* A resolution was agreed to replace the Shanghai Party Committee with a new organisational form, as specified in the *16-Points.* As a sign of official approval, the New China's News Agency released the complete text of this proposal the next day.[24]

14.3.2 The Red Guards Organise to Take Over Shanghai

On 14 January, the *People's Daily* published an article applauding the formation of the *Committee for Grasping Revolution and Promoting Production* in Shanghai. This article was followed by two more that further glorified the Committee, demonstrating that Mao was firmly behind this initiative. Claiming to have Mao's personal support, the WGH attempted to co-ordinate and organise the numerous Red Guard groups in Shanghai. On or about 16 January 1967, it launched the *Shanghai Revolutionary Rebel Workers' Liaison Department* in conjunction with 15 other Red Guard organisations. Attempts were made to include all the Red Guard factions in Shanghai but these had not been successful because some Red Guards were beginning to question whether strike-breaking really was a revolutionary activity.

On 16 January, *Red Flag* published an assessment of events in Shanghai under the title *Proletarian Revolutionaries, Unite!*, which many took as the Maoist leadership encouraging the Red Guards, under the guidance of Zhang, to take over local government wholesale. However, this was not entirely correct. Beijing was beginning to have serious reservations about events in Shanghai. Mao's general strategy was for the Red Guards to remove the "capitalist roaders" but their activities would be kept within safe limits by the presence of PLA units which would be controlled by Lin Piao and the Maoist faction. In Shanghai, PLA units had not so far been included in the process. The dangers were brought into sharp focus when, on 18 January, a group of Fudan University students put up the wall poster: "Carry forward the proletarian spirit of doubting everything."

Beijing hurried to specify the limits on Red Guard activities: "In the Great Cultural Revolution, it is correct to doubt everyone. But you cannot doubt Chairman Mao…"[25]

In Beijing on 19/20 January, Premier Zhou Enlai chaired a meeting of the Military Commission of the Central Committee. Naturally, Marshall Ye Jianying the principal leader this Commission was present. Later, he would be a key figure in organising the overthrow of the Gang of Four. Ye had the support of the majority of the meeting in successfully rejecting a proposal by Jiang Qing that Red Guard groups be formed within the PLA: instead the meeting determined that "the great CR movement in the military regions … should be postponed."[26] The meeting did pass a resolution directing the PLA to be more aggressive in its support of Red Guard activities, but its refusal to endorse Jiang Qing's proposal and the subsequent resignation of the officer in charge of the All-Army Cultural Revolution Group showed that the PLA, despite Lin Piao's efforts, was not solidly behind the Mao faction.

On 22/23 January, a joint meeting of the WGH and leaders from the major Red Guard organisations in Shanghai was held to discuss the formation of a city-wide liaison centre based on the broadest unity of all so-called proletarian factions. It was unanimously agreed that the time was right for this alliance to take over the administration of Shanghai. The name *Shanghai People's Commune* was finally agreed, possibly on the advice of Zhang Chunqiao to suggest continuity with the agricultural communes.

It must be remembered that the Red Guard groups were inexperienced, their political and organisational training had been gained through watching a Stalinised Party at work, in the main they were students not workers, and at the same time they were largely motivated by Maoist politics. But in the circumstances all kinds of ideas were bubbling to the surface and being discussed. Some of the groups were raising criticisms that objectively challenged the Maoist leadership. Fudan University's Red Guards began to openly criticise Zhang as part of their campaign to dismiss and bring down 'all cadres'.

Simultaneously, the largest Red Guard group (Red Revolutionaries with about 40,000 members, mostly students) also began voicing criticisms of Zhang, though the basis of these has not been determined. A group of Red Revolutionaries took Zhang hostage and placed him before a tribunal, making him stand for six hours while bombarding him with questions. They decided to parade him through the streets the following day and hold a mass rally for his public humiliation. A major and violent clash with the WGH and its allies was avoided only when Beijing telegrammed on 29 January to demand the Red Revolutionaries release Zhang and apologise to him. Such activities posed a problem for both the Maoists and their opponents in the CCP bureaucracy. Daring to criticise Zhang suggested the Red Revolutionaries were seeking a level of democracy which threatened the existence of all the bureaucracy. The Red Revolutionaries, as an organisation, was excluded from membership of the Shanghai Commune.

On 31 January, the *People's Daily* contained an editorial; *On the Proletarian Revolutionaries' Struggle to Seize Power*. This had been drafted by the CCRG and revised by Mao himself:

> "Proletarian revolutionaries are uniting to seize power from the handful of persons within the Party who are in authority and taking the capitalist road. This is … the decisive battle between the proletariat and the masses of working people on the one hand and the bourgeoisie and its agents in the Party on the other. This mighty revolutionary storm started in Shanghai. The revolutionary masses in Shanghai have called it the great 'January Revolution'. Our great leader Chairman Mao immediately expressed resolute support for it. He called on the workers, peasants, revolutionary students, revolutionary intellectuals and revolutionary cadres to study the experience of the revolutionary rebels of Shanghai and he called on the People's Liberation Army to actively support and assist the proletarian revolutionaries in their struggle to seize power."

The editorial was taken as a signal by the Red Guards nationally to attack the local Party tops everywhere. Only military units and elements of central government in Beijing were exempt. The editorial had been careful to call for the establishment of provisional organs of power of the triple alliance, combining representatives of the Red Guards as the local revolutionary mass organisations, of local People's Liberation Army units, and of revolutionary leading cadres from the Party and government organisations. The former was to purge Mao's opponents, the latter two to stop them going too far, either organisationally or politically.

14.3.3 The Shanghai Commune is Proposed

At the end of January a sub-committee of the "Frontline Headquarters" submitted a draft *Manifesto of the Shanghai People's Commune* to Zhang. Attempting to emulate the Paris Commune it called for "smashing the old state machinery" stating that "all committee members would be elected as the servants of the people." Zhang advised delaying the launch of the Commune to allow him to take advice from Beijing. The Red Guards insisted on moving ahead immediately and the inauguration was set for 5 February 1967.

Zhang changed the title of the Manifesto to: *Long Live the Victory of the January Revolution!* and edited the document so that the final form made every effort to promote the supremacy of Chairman Mao and give precedence to Mao Zedong Thought. The edited document faithfully reflected Mao's policy of the triple alliance and called for the leadership of the Commune to be composed of revolutionary mass organisations, the responsible officers from the PLA units stationed in Shanghai, and CCP cadres in Shanghai who had faithfully followed Chairman Mao's revolutionary line. It retained the promises of extensive democracy.

A representative Provisional Committee was agreed: Zhang Chunqiao and Yao Wenyuan (both representing the CCRG), three responsible persons from the armed forces stationed in Shanghai, three from the WGH, one peasant, one student, one from the Revolutionary Rebel Liaison Centre of Organisations of the Shanghai Municipal Party Committee. The committee also contained those Red Guards appointed to lead the seven departments that would be administering Shanghai, e.g. the *Grasping Revolution and Promoting Production Team*, in charge of industry. Zhang – whose authority came primarily from his association with Mao – was to be head of the Commune. The Red Guard representatives were mostly chosen by their own mass organisations (and subject to recall) so the Commune as a whole adopted a system that combined delegates and appointees. Accepting assurances that Shanghai was under Zhang's control, Mao endorsed the arrangement.[27]

However, it proved difficult to form a triple alliance because the Red Guards and rebel workers groups excluded very nearly all the old Party tops from the Commune and were refusing to appoint experienced Party cadres to any responsible post. This not only made it difficult for the CCP to exercise effective leadership but posed a potentially serious problem for the Maoist faction; how could it hope to win Party support if, in practice, its line meant that the very cadres it was appealing to would be thrown out of office?

A further difficulty in imposing the triple alliance on Shanghai was that many local Party tops had close links and friendships with the local army officers that sometimes dated back to the revolutionary war. Chairman Mao was insisting that any new power structure must include the military to act as a stabilising factor and a power base for his faction if needed, but the rank and file founders of the Commune feared that the Shanghai garrison would be loyal to its old friends on the Party committee. As a result, the three persons from the military were able to participate only marginally.[28]

Many Shanghai Red Guard and rebel leaders were not CCP members and it soon became clear that if the presence of Party tops and army officers was restricted it would be quite possible for the Commune to have an administration in which Party members were in the minority. Terrified Maoists raised the objection that in such a situation the masses might not follow the CCP, which could lose its legitimacy and authority in consequence.

The Maoist faction breathed a sigh of relief when, on 31 January 1967 (six days prior to the inauguration of the Shanghai Commune), in the far north east of China, in Heilongjiang Province, the Red Guard successfully formed a triple alliance with leading members of the PLA and the Provincial Party Committee, and set up the *Red Rebel Revolutionary Committee of Heilongjiang*. The editorial in the *People's Daily* of 10 February hailed the Heilongjiang RRRC:

> "The revolutionary rebels, ... carrying out the Party's policy in a clear-cut manner, have united with the principal leading members in the Provincial Party Committee who have carried out Chairman Mao's correct line and with the principal leading members of the People's Liberation Army units in the area to weld all three into one in the seizure of power."[29]

Mao had intended the targets of the GPCR should be the Party tops taking the capitalist road, not middle cadres and Party rank and file, but the Shanghai events demonstrated that slogans such as "down with the diehard elements who uphold the bourgeois reactionary line" were interpreted by Red Guards and rebel workers as license to attack bureaucrats, whatever their factional loyalty.

Mao saw the writing on the wall, mass democracy even in the distorted form of the Shanghai People's Commune threatened bureaucratic control. He pleaded: "If everything were changed into communes, then what about the party? Where would we place the party? Among commune committee members are both party members and non-party members. Where would we place the party committee? There must be a party somehow! There must be a nucleus, no matter what we call it. … can the commune replace the party?."[30] The *Red Flag*, the official paper of the Red Guards, waded into the debate backing the triple alliance and proposing that in Shanghai, the Commune be replaced by a Revolutionary Committee.

14.3.4 …and Deposed

It was true that as part of the GPCR, Mao had publicly advocated that "the working class must exercise leadership in everything." But as can be seen from his reaction to the Shanghai People's Commune, this was a smokescreen. The congratulations sent to the Heilongjiang RRRC, and the lack of official acknowledgement of what was happening in Shanghai were taken by both the Commune leaders and opponents as a rebuke. The degree of control by the CCP over the Commune was considerable through, e.g. Zhang Chunqiao, Yao Wenyuan and Wang Hongwen, but the principle of popular elections and the right to recall had been raised and were in limited operation. It was only a matter of time before these would be taken up by other Red Guard groups.

Mao proposed changing the name of the Commune. How unnerved he was at developments can be seen from the farcical reasons he gave: it would mean his title as Chairman would no longer stand, he would have to adopt an alternative title such as 'director'; the country could no longer be the PRC – it would have to become the Chinese People's Commune! At a serious level he was terrified that the democratic elements in the Shanghai Commune would be a signal to other cities to follow suit and that would mean the end of his Bonapartist rule. On 19 February, the CC of the CCP, united from Mao to Marshall Ye, agreed to issue a circular to all Party committees: "the name of people's commune shall, as a rule, not be adopted."[31]

The emphasis was now placed on the triple alliance of CCP cadres, PLA and domesticated Red Guards, as the model to be followed. These triple alliances would have to be approved by the higher levels of the Party (i.e. CCRG), and army representatives would be appointed by the army subject to the approval of higher commanders. On the 24th February, in a televised speech to the people of Shanghai, Zhang announced the end of the Shanghai

People's Commune and in the following weeks the *Revolutionary Committee of the Municipality of Shanghai* (Shanghai Municipality RC) was established. The Shanghai People's Commune had lasted a mere twenty days.

The Commune had had an elected element with some mass participation but the triple alliance in Shanghai was restricted to unelected representatives of the Red Guards, army, and party cadres. If Mao had genuinely wanted to eliminate the "capitalist roaders" then the Commune would have been much more effective than the triple alliance, which opened the door to "rightist, revisionist, bureaucratic, and elitist elements" on condition they pretended that they were in favour of Mao Zedong's line. Mao's triple alliance put the elitist managerial and governmental apparatus back in positions of authority.[32]

The Party leadership claimed that the major difference between the Commune and the Shanghai Municipality RC was the inclusion of many old Party cadres who had rectified their errors and returned to Mao's line.[33] All seven departments of the Commune directly linked to the masses were abolished in a move that was supposed to strengthen the administrative functions of the Shanghai Municipality RC. The mass organisations were dismantled. On 28 August 1969, the armed conflicts between Chinese and Soviet troops in the border areas were used by the CC of the CCP to order all mass organisations to disband and to make it illegal to form any new ones. This left the remaining Red Guard representatives on local RCs isolated and they were gradually replaced by military or Party personnel.

During February 1967, the army took the initiative across China, and Red Guards who challenged Maoist directives were beaten up, arrested, imprisoned and even shot. Jiang[34] reports how Marshall Ye Jianying approved a request from General Gan Weihan in Sichuan province (Chengdu Military District) for permission to arrest and detain over 30,000 rebels. Allegedly, all the prisons in Sichuan province were filled with rebel Red Guards and the authorities had to convert at least one Buddhist temple into a temporary prison. The most shocking slaughter was in Qinghai Province on the Tibetan border on 23 February. Troops dispatched by the vice-commander of the Qinghai Military District, seized several thousand rebel Red Guards staying in the *Qinghai Daily* building, more than 300 were killed, many more were wounded by gun fire and the rest imprisoned.

The situation was greatly complicated because not only were rebel Red Guards being hounded by the PLA, but there was open warfare between different Red Guard factions; between Maoist Red Guards and Red Guards loyal to established Party tops. The *People's Daily* reported that in Yunnan province alone between 80,000 and 160,000 people were killed. In Wuhan the established leadership successfully resisted the (Maoist) Red Guards' attempt to take power, and with the support of local army units, arrested over 500 and attempted to disband their organisation. During June and July 1967 there was virtual civil war between the two factions and in one encounter 250 were killed and at least 1,500 wounded.[35]

Two envoys from Beijing arrived in Wuhan to adjudicate and, of course, decided in favour of the Red Guards. The local CCP stormed the hotel where the envoys were staying and took one of them hostage. Lin Piao moved an airborne division and a naval squadron to surround Wuhan and the envoy was released. The Wuhan incident was the beginning of the end for the GPCR: the constant changes in instructions from Beijing undermined its authority with the radical elements amongst the Red Guards; the different balance of forces within the triple alliance in different areas meant national, effective leadership was impossible; Mao Zedong Thought was interpreted according to which group or coalition dominated the local triple alliance.

In a last desperate attempt to gain national dominance, the CCRG called for a more radical policy towards the conservative elements in the Party and PLA. Some Red Guard publications were demanding *The Proletariat Must Take Hold of the Gun* and advocated internal revolt within the PLA. By the spring of 1968, the most extreme of the Red Guard groups (in Kwangsi) had seized weapons from trains bound for Vietnam and were skirmishing with PLA forces and conservatives to take control of the local Revolutionary Committee.[36] Other Red Guard groups having analysed the situation for themselves, began to present an analysis that was not in support of Mao. Students in Hunan issued a proclamation labelling Zhou Enlai and other supporters of Mao the "new bourgeoisie" and calling for "genuine" Communes. By early 1968 radical student elements in Shanghai and Beijing were proposing a national conference in defiance of orders from the CCRG.[37] It was developments such as these which threatened the bureaucracy root and branch, that were important in bringing the GPCR to an end.

The activist phase of the GPCR was formally terminated at the CCP's 9th National Party Congress in April 1969. As would be expected with the Party still reeling from the GPCR, this Congress was dominated by the Maoist faction: Mao was confirmed as the supreme leader and others who had been active in the GPCR were allocated positions on the Political Bureau. Lin Piao became CPC Vice Chairman and was designated constitutionally as Mao's successor, and Mao Zedong thought was reinserted into the Party

Constitution. Jiang Qing and Yeh Chun, the wives of Mao and Lin Piao respectively, became the first ever female members of the Politburo (they were formally elected to the 170-member CC which lasted until 1973, but which held only two plenary meetings). Due to Lin's poor health Yeh Chun was already in the habit of attending Party meetings on his behalf![38]

However, these victories were all sound and fury, Liu Shaoqi and Deng Xiaoping may have been labelled "traitorous scabs and renegades", but the "capitalist roaders" in the Party had, by and large, retained their positions. In this respect Mao's weakness was obvious; over 40% of the CC were serving military officers, but in China the PLA was the creature of the Party, not the other way round. Mao's victory was superficial and temporary. The Red Guards were soon instructed to return to their localities; otherwise they would be expelled from the schools and would not be assigned to work after graduation.[39]

After 1969 the CCP placed its emphasis on reconstruction: rebuilding the party, re-vitalising, and stabilising the economy. The Maoists, led now by Madame Mao (Jiang Qing) attempted to retain their decisive role but they were now swimming against the stream. Factional tensions persisted, so that it was not until the start of 1971 that Party committees were re-established at the provincial level, but practical solutions to current problems was the central theme of the Party, and inexorably the Maoists were increasingly side-lined.

The only institution with a relatively undamaged structure and real power was the PLA, but this was divided in its politics. On one side was the Lin Piao faction, which continued to exhort the need for "politics in command" and for an ongoing struggle against Soviet revisionism. On the other side was a majority of the regional military commanders who looked to Marshall Ye Jianying, and whose views generally were in tune with the "capitalist roaders". The matter was decided in a most decisive and surprising manner. Lin Piao died in a plane crash on 13 September 1971, the circumstances surrounding his death are still shrouded in mystery but soon after, Lin Piao's closest supporters were rapidly purged and there was an immediate and precipitate drop in the influence of the Maoist faction. The Party and state now attempted to depoliticise and promote professionalism within the PLA, accompanied by the rehabilitation of many persons who had been persecuted or fallen into disgrace in 1966-68.

The political tide in China swung decisively towards the "capitalist roaders" who spoke for more material incentives for the peasantry, and efficient economic planning. They also advocated improved relations with the West in general and the US in particular. That they held the reins of power was clearly demonstrated in February 1972 when President Richard M. Nixon made a formal state visit. (It should be noted that at these talks the Chinese leadership gave the nod to the US extending its bombing of Vietnam to include important economic targets in the North.)

The most prominent of those rehabilitated was Deng Xiaoping, who was reinstated as a Vice Premier in April 1973 and came to exert a strong influence favouring an approach based on the New Economic Policy used in Russia in the early 1920s. At the 10th National Party Congress in August 1973 Deng Xiaoping was again made a member of the CC (but not the Politburo) with sufficiently seniority to be in charge of the negotiations with the UK government on the return of Hong Kong to China.[40]

In January 1975, at the 4th National People's Congress, Deng Xiaoping was elected a Vice Chairman of the CCP, a member of the Politburo and its Standing Committee, and installed as China's first civilian chief of the PLA. At the same Congress the policy of the "Four Modernisations" was agreed for the four sectors of agriculture, industry, national defence, and science and technology. This would be affirmed as an action programme at the 11th National Party Congress, held in August 1977, after Mao's death. Deng did suffer one further indignity, however, after Zhou Enlai's death in January 1976 Madame Mao was able to rally sufficient support to remove Deng from his most important posts. Mao died in September that year and the Gang of Four were arrested in the October. The role played by Deng in their downfall is not known but within weeks he had openly returned to the leadership team.

The CCP was a party deeply rooted in Stalinism. Neither before coming to power, nor in the process of taking power, nor in its turn to the "general line of socialist construction" after it was in power, was there ever any purge of Stalinist ideology. However, significant currents in the Marxist movement took Mao's verbal statements on the GPCR and the Shanghai Commune as good coin, as representing a genuine attempt to curb the Chinese Party bureaucracy rather than as a factional move by Mao to regain undisputed leadership of the CCP. Ernest Mandel and Pierre Frank, one of Trotsky's secretaries on the island of Prinkipo, took to calling Mao's policies bureaucratic centrist rather than Stalinist. The use of the term bureaucratic centrist was highly significant since it was a term used by Trotsky to describe the Stalin faction in the USSR before 1933, before it was judged as wholly counter-revolutionary.[41] The lessons of thirty years were thrown out of the window, a movement unleashed by one wing of the Chinese bureaucracy against another was confused with a genuine attempt at workers' democracy.

14.4 Summary

After 1949, with access to state resources, the tops of the CCP went on a spending spree (see Section 10.2). The Chinese bureaucracy did not view privileges and salary differentials as temporary, imposed by the isolation of the Revolution and the underdeveloped nature of the economy as the Bolsheviks had done, but as their natural reward for running the country. Inherent in such a situation was the possible restoration of capitalism at some stage. Trotsky had warned that if the bureaucracy was not overthrown in a political revolution, the bourgeois norms of distribution would inevitably become a key factor in determining the class nature of the state: "Privileges have only half their worth, if they cannot be transmitted to one's children ... The victory of the bureaucracy in this decisive area would mean its conversion into a new possessing class."[42] As would later be found out in the scandal around the murder of Neil Haywood in a Chongqing hotel in 2011, tops in the CCP were sending their sons to English public schools such as Harrow.[43]

The bureaucracy defended the state's economic plans in order to defend their own interests, their own privileges. As Trotsky explained in *In Defence of Marxism*:

> "The bureaucracy is first and foremost concerned with its power, its prestige, its revenues. It defends itself much better than it defends the USSR. It defends itself at the expense of the USSR and at the expense of the world proletariat."

However, Mao failed to identify these material and socio-economic conditions, rooted in the Stalinist nature of the CCP as a chief cause of capitalist restoration. Instead he blamed the strength of bourgeois ideas in art, literature, and science. He maintained his belief that incessant appeals to the spirit of sacrifice and idealism as demonstrated by the CCP cadres during the darkest days of the civil war, were enough to overcome the material backwardness of the productive forces in China. Instead of motivating the Chinese people by moving towards greater workers' democracy, Mao revived Stalin's anti-Marxist theory that in the transition from socialism to capitalism the class struggle intensifies, and added the flourish that this could endure for hundreds of years. Just like Stalin, Mao erected and then justified a repressive state apparatus to protect the bureaucracy.

It is true that to an extent, the GPCR was an attack on the excesses of a section of the bureaucracy that was threatening the interests of the entire bureaucratic caste. Mao was following Stalin who had individual, excessively corrupt bureaucrats shot to better preserve the bureaucracy as a whole. Mao combined the attack on the capitalist roaders (to consolidate his own position) with the curbing of the more extreme forms of corruption (to maintain the bureaucracy as a whole). For the privileged bureaucracy, the GPCR was three-years of chaos that had done nothing to halt the growing irreconcilable contradictions between them and the disfranchised and abused worker-peasant masses.

The Cultural Revolution is important in understanding the later progress of the CCP under Deng who inherited the problem of developing the economy. The majority of the bureaucracy breathed a sigh of relief when the Cultural Revolution was brought to an end – they wanted to return to stability and enjoy their privileges within the system. Deng and his supporters drew the conclusion that mass action was a threat to their privileged existence and began their economic and social analyses with the clear condition of involving the Chinese masses as little as possible in decision-making. Introducing genuine workers' democracy was the last thing these bureaucrats would do.

Despite claims to the contrary, the GPCR was never widely supported by the proletariat because of two key factors: the Red Guard took the voluntarism of the GLF into the factories and other work places and demanded the ending of bonus schemes and pay differentials, and a lowering of safety standards. The workers were to increase production by working harder and undertaking unpaid overtime for no other reason than their love of Chairman Mao. Another important factor was that the GPCR was taken into the factories largely by factory chiefs and party bureaucrats anxious to preserve their privileged positions or by students who, for all their good intentions, knew little or nothing about factory work.

The Cultural Revolution did impact on the factories but not in the way the Maoists had hoped. Factory workers took advantage of the situation to protest at the appalling conditions in which they worked; demanding a safer, healthier environment, higher wages and an end to the privileges of the managers and their replacement by elected persons. As the industrial workers began to voice their own demands and take independent action, Mao drew back and in 1969 put the genie of the GPCR back into the bottle of bureaucratic control. The main slogan, "The masses are right, what the people say is right," became, "What is right is what is in the mind of Chairman Mao."

One cannot fight the bureaucracy with bureaucratic means. This explains why both the Great Leap Forward and the Cultural Revolution failed, ultimately adding to the social and economic disruption caused by the bureaucracy. The Maoist wing of the bureaucracy could not go so far as to give power to the workers because to do so would mean turning their own world upside down. This meant the outcome of the struggle between the Maoists and their opponents would be determined within the Party, but the GPCR had been launched precisely to avoid such an outcome. Party and state officials at all levels had been given an object lesson that to eagerly implement present policies made one a hostage to fortune and future shifts in policy. The result was excessive bureaucratic timidity.

The CCP leadership and the Party itself had suffered a severe loss of legitimacy. Millions of urban Chinese had recognised the GPCR as an obvious power play between competing factions that had taken place in the name of political principle resulting in a steep decline in living standards. The scarcity of goods created by the GPCR meant a leap in corruption within the CCP and the government, as people fell back on personal relationships and bribery to get things done.

Mao's strategies of the GLF and the GPCR had meant a near collapse of agricultural production, the closure of all the schools and universities and finally, severe disruption of industrial production. The wing of the CCP led by Deng Xiaoping (the majority of middle and higher level cadres) was horrified at what had happened and began drawing its own conclusions from these experiences, a process which was accelerated by the collapse of the Stalinist regimes in Russia and Eastern Europe.

Chapter 15
China Marches Back to Capitalism

15.1 Introduction

This chapter will explain the process whereby, in order to protect its privileges, a hardened, Stalinist caste took the Chinese workers' state back to capitalism. The defining point in the process was the bloody crushing of protests that took place on a national scale but centred in Beijing at Tien An Men Square. After this watershed, the dominant section of the CCP increasingly came to see capitalism as its salvation.

The alternate solution to the social and economic problems besetting China was Soviet democracy, but the bureaucracy knew this would mean the end of its privileges and preferred capitalism. This chapter concentrates on the bones of the process. How and when the CCP relinquished the three key pillars of a workers' state: a national economic plan, monopoly of foreign trade, nationalisation of the key industries including wholesale food distribution and, especially, the banks. The process of the so-called reforms was piecemeal due, not least, to the very real powers of the provincial authorities each with its own interests, but also due to the CCP acting cautiously and testing each step as the process progressed.

15.2 A Cold Transition?

Trotsky had argued that the Soviet Union could not be "reformed" into capitalism, without some form of violent counter-revolution.[1] But Eastern Europe, Russia and China have all made the transition back to capitalism without armed counter-revolution, without even major confrontations between the different wings of the bureaucracy.

This observation confirms that we should not take from Trotsky single sentences isolated from their historical context. Trotsky's argument rested on Russia as it was in 1933, where the traditions of the revolution were still alive. The Russian working class had played the key role in the October Revolution, they had suffered dreadfully in the imperialist war and fought heroically to defeat the White Armies. Despite the severe hardships imposed by the bureaucracy they would have resisted capitalist restoration. The purges had not yet physically removed the Bolshevik heritage of the Communist Party and, despite the growing bureaucracy, Party members were committed to maintaining the Soviet regime.

Trotsky was writing a few months after Hitler had come to power in Germany, but before finally concluding that the bureaucracy was irrevocably counter-revolutionary. It was nearly two years later, in August 1935, that he issued his open letter calling for the formation of the Fourth International and the removal of the bureaucracy by a political revolution.

However, the Stalinist regime survived in the USSR for far longer than Trotsky could have anticipated, for more than 60 years in fact. In that period the revolutionary traditions were eradicated from the consciousness of the workers. The generation that had experienced the revolution was gone. The new generations witnessed a gluttonous bureaucracy hoisting itself further and further above the masses. They saw only mismanagement, waste and corruption at every level, and towards the end all that was left facing them was a system which was grinding to a halt.

However, we should remember that Stalin did, in fact, carry out a civil war against Bolshevism. Vadim Rogovin in his detailed and authoritative history of the purges[2] concluded that the number of political prisoners during the Stalin period reached approximately four million, and between 700,000 and 800,000 were actually executed. Three times as many Party members were killed in the Siberian slave camps as in the Civil War against the Whites. The purges were the logical response of the bureaucratic caste as it sought to protect itself by eliminating actual and potential opposition in the communist movement, both within the USSR and internationally.

During Trotsky's life the Stalinist bureaucracy retarded the development of the Soviet economy which, because of its planned nature, nevertheless surged ahead. But, as industry and commerce became increasingly advanced, until in its final stages the bureaucracy became an unqualified brake on economic development. The bureaucrats protection of their own interests had higher priority than the performance of soviet industry, so they never considered introducing the one measure, the most effective measure, for solving the problems of the Soviet economy – workers' democracy.

However, Trotsky did warn that as the bureaucracy developed, the more senior the bureaucrat the more they would want to pass their privileges on to their children. And this was best done through private ownership. He predicted that the bureaucracy could and would adapt very easily to capitalist restoration.

Transforming the workers' state into a bourgeois regime would be realised largely by the bureaucrats themselves, who would become the captains of capitalist industry or its favoured servants. Few bureaucrats would have to be purged. On the other hand, a political revolution would impose on those bureaucrats a worker's wage and remove their privileges. For most bureaucrats there was a bigger conflict with workers' democracy than capitalism! Trotsky's prognosis of capitalist restoration was almost a blueprint for the actions of the Chinese Stalinists:

> "... The chief task of the new (bourgeois) power would be to restore private property in the means of production. First of all, it would be necessary to create conditions for the development of strong farmers from the weak collective farms .... In the sphere of industry, denationalization would begin with the light industries and those producing food. The planning principle would be converted for the transitional period into a series of compromises between state power and individual 'corporations' – potential proprietors, that is, among the Soviet captains of industry ... and foreign capitalists."[3]

It must also be remembered that the 1949 Chinese Revolution was not made by a Leninist Party. The CCP was a Stalinist organisation long before it came to power, so in China there was never a period of workers' or soviet democracy and it was natural for the leaders of the CCP to see China's future in terms of their own wellbeing.

The collapse of the Soviet Union and the resulting chaos was a very powerful factor in the thinking of the Chinese bureaucrats. The leadership of the CCP, in its majority concluded that in order to prevent the same thing happening in China market methods must be introduced, but under tight CCP control. They began a series of steps each of which was an attempt to increase the rate of development of the economy. It is now generally accepted that the Chinese bureaucracy staggered from one support to the next to avoid the collapse that had taken place in Russia. Three factors slowed the process: lack of understanding of a market economy, important special interest groups that opposed the reforms and – most important of all – fear of how the masses would respond. But the process had a logic of its own and empiric step by empiric step eventually ended in the restoration of capitalism.

While generally peaceful, and often welcomed. it would not be correct to say there were no protests against the bureaucracy and the measures it was taking. In 1989 there were demonstrations of protest across China but centred on Tien An Men Square in Beijing. These were crushed by the PLA under the direction of the hard line Stalinists within the Party. These people took the protests as a sign that reform needed to gather pace, and within five years the CCP had ended the monopoly of foreign trade, allowed unfettered foreign currency exchange, ended state planning of the economy, and were using the giant State Owned Enterprises (SOEs) to support private industry at the expense of the Chinese workers. When these measures were carried through China ceased to be a workers' state. However, important sections of industry and the banks remain in state hands, the better to support privatisation and the growth of Chinese capitalism.

Among the top layers of the bureaucracy there is no evidence that any group wanted to retain the old state-owned, centrally planned economy. From the viewpoint of the Party tops the present system is working. For them it is doing very well, because now the bureaucrats are successfully passing their privileges on to their offspring. Many of the sons and daughters of the bureaucrats have been transformed into owners of the means of production and amongst this layer there is no desire to return to a nationalised planned economy. There is no material basis for them to wish to do so. They would resist any attempt to turn the clock back, and they would have the backing of the CCP and the state.

It is also worth noting that the tops of the army have also been transformed into owners of property. In fact, for a period the PLA was spearheading the creation of private enterprises. In 1996, for example, the South China Construction Company, possibly the largest in China, was just completing the Diwang Building, one of the tallest buildings in Asia. But the South China Construction Company was an off-shoot of the PLA. Its senior personnel alternated between wearing their army uniforms and business suits. The officer caste within the "armed bodies of men" forming the power of the state, has been integrated into the new property relations that have been established.

15.3 A New Economic Policy

1976 to 1978 was a period of intense political activity in China. Mao Zedong died in September 1976 and on 6 October 1976, Madame Mao and her three principal associates (the infamous Gang of Four) were arrested on the orders of Marshal Ye Jianying, Minister of National Defence. They would be subjects of a show trial in 1981 and all would receive lengthy prison sentences.

By the CC meeting of December 1978, after a period of bitter infighting, Deng emerged as the key figure within the Party and it was this meeting that repudiated the "two whatevers" policy – whatever Mao said must be correct, and whatever policy Mao proposed must be adopted. This was replaced with a new Party line, the "Four Modernizations". To overcome the inheritance of the GPCR there would be a period of huge investment and rapid development of Chinese science and technology which would then be applied to agriculture, industry, and national defence. At the time the proposed programme stressed economic self-reliance but had as its target China becoming one of the world's major economic powers in the early part of the 21st Century. On 5 December 1978 in Beijing, a former red guard, Wei Jingsheng, posted on the Democracy Wall calling for a Fifth Modernization: "democracy". He was arrested a few months later and jailed for 15 years.[4]

The CCP was a thoroughly Stalinised Party but claimed the Bolshevik revolution as part of its heritage. It was only natural that Deng should look to the history of the USSR to see what lessons could be learned on how to re-vitalise the Chinese economy and, especially, increase food production. The obvious lesson was the introduction of the New Economic Policy in 1921. This had been tremendously successful in restoring food supplies to Russian towns and had generated a boom in light industry. The main points of the NEP had been: Once the peasants had paid their taxes they were free to sell their surplus at free farmers' markets in urban areas; Private merchants were allowed to buy and sell produce in a market environment; light industry was left in private hands while state-owned large-scale industry had to be self-funding. Increased wage differentials were allowed so that productivity and level of responsibility could be rewarded; foreign capitalists were offered concessions.

On 4 February 1919, Lenin presented a resolution to the Council of People's Commissars along the lines, that one way of securing the investment necessary to develop the productive forces of the weak and underdeveloped economy of the young workers' state was to grant short-term concessions to foreign capital for the long-term benefit of the revolution. It was the delay of the world revolution that forced the Bolsheviks to propose this compromise with capitalism. At that time, however, the foreign capitalists, far from wanting to reach economic deals with Soviet Russia wanted to crush it; first by armed intervention and then by economic blockade. With China, by the late 1970s, it was quite a different matter. The imperialists were perfectly willing to make deals with the bureaucratic, privileged caste running the state. Even the arch-reactionary Nixon had no problems in reaching agreements with Mao.

In the conditions which prevailed in China in the late 1970s some form of NEP was eminently sensible, subject to certain conditions. The Deng wing coined the phrase "market socialism" in which the main levers of the economy remained under state control guided by the state plan including a monopoly of foreign trade. These proposals were acceptable as a means of stimulating and developing the Chinese economy. Deng and his co-thinkers drew the conclusion that the attempts to make China self-sufficient had failed and, correctly, recognised that China could not develop in isolation from the world market. Socialism in One Country, while remaining official ideology was finally, though quietly, buried.

Lenin perceived the NEP as a temporary retreat, but Deng saw it as an advance. The difference was that Lenin's Russia was a relatively healthy workers' state, which the NEP would be used to *strengthen*, whereas Deng's China was a Stalinist, bureaucratised deformed workers' state which the introduction of a NEP would *weaken*.

Deng and his co-thinkers argued that, despite 25 years of almost continuous growth, the Mao era had left the economy in a mess. The GLF and the GPCR had caused serious shortfalls in agricultural and industrial production but, more importantly, as the economy became increasingly sophisticated the centralised, bureaucratic command system was proving so inept, corrupt and wasteful that future growth was threatened. Industrial productivity was declining, the quality of the finished products was very poor, there were inflationary tendencies, and scarcity of consumer goods. Workers and peasants were becoming restless and threatening to take their demands onto the streets.

When Deng came to power in 1978 he had no intention of restoring capitalism. He, and the wing of the bureaucracy he represented, understood the need to introduce the most advanced techniques into the Chinese economy, but the bureaucracy's inherent conservatism meant that it moved empirically, responding to the needs of the moment. Having accepted a market-led approach, it was only a matter of time before China would open up to foreign investment and participate wholeheartedly in the world market.

15.4 Deng's 1978 Turn

At the CC meeting of December 1978, Deng presented his version of the New Economic Policy. Central planning would remain dominant, but it was proposed to introduce elements of decentralisation and encourage private initiatives. The concept was that market forces would be introduced at the periphery to ensure the targets of the planned economy were met.

The Beijing leadership began warily, communal ownership of agricultural land would remain, but private use of that land would be permitted. Simultaneously, it launched a small number of special economic zones (SEZs) subject to severe controls.

The basic points of the 1978 reforms were:

- Peasants were offered the opportunity to lease the land they farmed. To ensure profitability the government would allow the prices of agricultural produce to rise by more than 20% in 1979.
- Local rural organisations would be permitted to launch collective and/or private business enterprises: these would be known as Town and Village Enterprises (TVEs).
- Foreign investors were invited to invest in China, subject to strict conditions.
- Market forces would play a much bigger role in determining prices. More investment was to be channelled from capital investment to consumer goods.

The country began the process of lurching towards the world market.

15.4.1 Agriculture, Land and the TVEs

The disaster that was the Communes has been described in Chapter 13, following the deaths of as many as 20 million through starvation there had been a de facto restoration of personal responsibility for land and livestock. This was achieved by allocating land to individual households on the promise they delivered a certain quota of their harvest to the state. There was a tolerance of a free market in farm produce, peasants were free to sell their surplus produce as they wished. Individual enterprise in the form of the revival of handicrafts was encouraged, after having virtually disappeared during the GPCR: cobblers, tailors, tinkers and vendors became common sights in the cities.

Constitutionally in China urban land was owned by the state and in rural areas by collectives, but these new measures allowed land to be treated as private property. Chinese agriculture was returning to traditional patterns under the slogan of "collective land ownership but individual land use". There was a massive growth in a free market in agricultural produce. This was accompanied by the removal of state control of prices to help ensure the profitability of the more efficient farms.

In terms of increased production of agricultural produce, Deng's moves were eminently successful. By the end of the 1980s those who leased land were permitted to sell the lease or even leave it as an inheritance. Just as with the NEP in Russia this led to a differentiation within the peasantry with some peasants growing rich and expanding their holdings at the expense of others. Layers of Chinese peasants lost their lands, were impoverished and were forced to migrate to the cities, providing an inflow of cheap labour for the development of the SEZs. But in China the scale of what happened was unprecedented both in terms of the scope and the speed of the process.

During the period 1978-84 the reforms were predominantly rural with great emphasis on decentralisation and with greater autonomy given to provincial governments.[5] Private enterprise in the countryside was encouraged in the form of the Town and Village Enterprises (TVEs). These usually originated from commune workshops so there were hundreds of thousands of them. With the demise of the communes, the workshops extended their repair of agricultural implements to include manufacturing light machinery for farm use. These TVEs were notionally under the control of local municipalities, but with the effective privatisation of agriculture were in an anomalous position being notionally communal enterprises run for the benefit of the local peasants while becoming increasingly self-funding and self-sufficient.[6]

Because the TVEs were largely independent they were very flexible in terms of organization and ownership, and significantly enhanced economic and infrastructure growth in rural areas. TVEs would all commence as communal ventures but would pass through every shape and form, some retaining their communal nature, some adopting mixed communal and private ownership, and some rapidly became private property. They were a glimpse of what might have been achieved if the creative powers of the peasants and villagers had been unleashed within a planned economy.

However, the TVEs were launched by a Stalinist bureaucracy to better preserve themselves and their privileges. Within this framework the TVEs served the valuable purpose of employing and training many middle and lower level CCP cadres in the smaller towns and villages who were in danger of being left behind by the moves to a market economy, and who could have become a focus for opposition to regime policies. In 1994 the government produced an "honour list" of successful TVE "Peasant Entrepreneurs"; it was noticeable that being a Party member gave one a head start in being successful.[7]

TVEs were market-oriented from the outset and so became a pressure for institutional change at a time when the place of privately-owned companies in the economy and society had not been established; they were a mechanism whereby the managers and local CCP tops accumulated the necessary experience and knowledge to run private enterprises and the capital to eventually acquire them.[8] Initially, only TVEs with fewer than ten workers could become a private firm (within the European Union enterprises with fewer than ten employees were classified as 'micro'), but in 1987 this limit was abolished which opened the door to the privatisation of all TVEs. In practice, even the supposedly collective TVEs responsible to the local authority were soon operating as private enterprises.

In many townships and villages local officials began a rapid sell off of TVEs (to themselves) for a small fraction of what they were worth. By the time of these sell-offs the Party tops managing the TVEs had a decade of experience of running what were in practice private enterprises, and were well versed in capitalist management techniques. By the year 2000 all TVEs were openly functioning as capitalist firms. Helped by generous state loans and economic decentralisation, the TVEs grew rapidly and in 1996, at their peak, accounted for 30% of GDP and employed 135 million people.[9] However, after 1996 the number of TVEs decreased sharply as the state privatised small SOEs many of which were light engineering companies, which then began to compete with the TVEs.

The TVEs are a good example of how an economic form generated with one goal in mind, to assist economic regeneration in the countryside within a deformed workers' state, became an important transitional element in the development of capitalism. In supporting the TVEs the state sector nurtured and supported nascent bourgeois elements until they assumed ownership directly.

15.4.2 Foreign Investment, Trade and Market Forces

In 1979 Deng announced the creation of the first four Special Economic Zones (SEZs) open to foreign investment, these being on the borders of Hong Kong and Macao, and in the Guangdong and Fujian provinces on the southern coast. These were to be a means of modernising the productive forces within a centrally-planned and state-controlled economy, and at this stage the bureaucracy was very cautious and made only limited concessions.

In preparation for attracting foreign investment, the Chinese regime introduced a series of reforms which allowed managers of selected SOEs (those designated to be part of joint-enterprises in the SEZs) to end "lifetime" jobs for workers. This was a break with previous policy in which a worker was a state employee and had a job for life (the so-called "iron rice bowl"). For workers in these enterprises job security was replaced by fixed-term contracts. At the time these measures did not affect the great majority of Chinese workers who were employed in heavy industry in the inland, giant SOEs. Nevertheless, to spike workers' opposition, the right to strike was dropped from the 1982 Constitution; instead a worker had to observe labour discipline and public order. In effect strikes were outlawed.

However, the SEZs were not as successful as expected. For capitalists to invest the bureaucracy had to create more favourable conditions, requiring a compromise with market forces. In 1983 certain of the restrictions were lifted: the necessity for investment to be in a joint enterprise with a Chinese company was removed and wholly foreign-owned companies were allowed to operate; the area covered by the SEZs was expanded to open up almost all of China's long coastline to foreign investment. The bureaucracy may have been proceeding empirically, but how many compromises and of what kind would be made?

Soon the government was actively encouraging foreign-owned and operated enterprises to establish factories in China as a means of absorbing unemployed young people, especially peasants migrating to the towns, and at the same time helping to increase supplies of consumer goods. On 20 October 1984, the CC adopted a series of measures which marked the beginning of the end for the state monopoly of foreign trade. An important initial difference between Lenin and Trotsky as against Stalin and Bukharin was that they considered a workers' state in a capitalist world must have a state monopoly of foreign trade. First loosening and then abandoning this control was a key move towards developing capitalism in China.

Controls on foreign trade were greatly eased, allowing individual enterprises to engage in direct trading with foreign firms outside the control of the Ministry of Foreign Trade (which was re-named the Ministry of Foreign Economic Relations and Trade). Subsequently, the government introduced another tranche of legislation in 1986 to further facilitate Chinese businesses entering the mainstream of international trade: in particular access to foreign exchange and credit, and reform of the wages system to allow much greater bonuses to be paid to managers.[10]

Beginning in 1979 and throughout the 1980s, the Chinese government was preoccupied with incentivising state enterprises most of which were characterised by gross inefficiency. The Party appreciated the benefits being realised from TVEs and expected that extending the same reforms to the urban industrial sector would have the same effect. It was agreed to introduce market mechanisms such as allowing greater autonomy for management, and permitting horizontal relations between enterprises (previously characterised by a rigorously enforced top-down structure).

At the 12th Congress of the CCP in September 1982, Deng Xiaoping announced the building of socialism with Chinese characteristics; of a so-called "planned commodity economy" which, in effect, was a significant move away from a planned economy. The managers of small (and medium) SOEs were given much greater autonomy, encouraged to produce goods outside the state plan for sale on the market, and permitted to introduce individual bonuses. From this time on the planning element of the economy was applied only to major projects. However, the official position of the Party was that the state sector of the economy was, and would remain, dominant.[11] In the mid-1980s, in total, the state sector employed about 70% of the urban workforce and throughout that period the giant SOEs dominated the overall economic processes in China.

The government also tested a change in financial procedures for selected small and medium SOEs (SMSOEs)[12]: rather than remitting all of their profits to the state, as previously, they were allowed to pay a tax on their profits and retain the balance for reinvestment and distribution as bonuses. Here we have the bureaucracy of a deformed workers' state, using capitalistic methods to revitalise part of the state sector.[13] However, these measures on their own proved insufficient to change the basic economics of SMSOEs, many of which continued to lose money. Nonetheless, a significant step had been taken in downgrading the importance of the national economic plan.

Determined to reduce the financial burden imposed by the SMSOEs, and to simultaneously increase the number of private companies in China, the government encouraged management buy-outs. These were to be sold off as going concerns or broken up into separate companies, with the more profitable sectors being privatised and the less efficient being closed or remaining under state control. Managers were encouraged to rationalise their companies to make them profitable. Millions of workers faced dismissal. However, SOEs in China were not simply for generating government revenues, they also served many other purposes, including the provision of social welfare.[14] The measures imposed left many of those who managed to keep their jobs with no health care, no sickness payments, and even no pension scheme. Those sacked were left with nothing.

One group of managers of SOEs (those more familiar with Western practices) were busy asset-stripping. The most modern machines in the factory were sold to friends in the private sector at knock-down prices. When the time came to privatise these companies their managers bought them cheaply because they had few worthwhile assets, and then in partnership with their friends re-stocked them with the machines previously removed. Another group of managers, especially senior CCP members with links to the local Party organisation which controlled the local town councils, entered into partnerships whereby the councils designated companies as collective ventures but then ran them for private profit which went to the local Party tops. This latter strategy was Beijing's preferred option since it gave jobs to Party officials who would otherwise have been unemployed. The number of private companies rose from 1.83 million in 1981, to 11.71 million in 1985.

In 1987 there was a classic "scissors crisis", too few industrial products to satisfy the demands of the newly-enriched peasants. The peasants responded characteristically and, despite an excellent harvest, there was a shortfall in basic food products (rice, corn) in the shops. In consequence, inflationary pressures exploded. The two years 1988 and 1989 saw the annual inflation rate hit 18%, the real purchasing power of working class families was hard hit, and social unrest ensued. The rationalisation and privatisation of state-controlled companies had led to a marked rise in unemployment, pushing the official unemployment rate above 5% (a real unemployment rate of more than 10%). Workers took strike action and laid-off workers rioted.

In response, in 1988, the regime put a brake on the so-called "reforms" and in an attempt to control inflation tightened the money supply. This provoked a new phenomenon for the Chinese economy, the recession of 1989. This economic crisis was transformed into a political crisis inside the CCP and the General Secretary, Hu Yaobang, was forced to resign for failing to take action against students protesting against the government measures. All this led to growing social unrest and a wave of strikes. This was the context of the protest movement in and around Tien An Men Square in Beijing.

15.5 Tien An Men Square

Initially, its reforms made the Deng Xiaoping regime the most popular since 1949, but the transition to a market-based pricing system and the lifting of price controls, meant prices of goods rose faster than wages, and those living in the Beijing area were particularly penalised. Between 1987 and 1989 an increase of over a third in consumer prices caused workers and students to fear that soon they would no longer be able to afford staple goods; many took to the streets in protest.[15] The government rescinded the price reforms in less than two weeks, but inflation continued to soar.

Oppositionists, many of whom were CCP members and/or ex-Red Guards, put up posters on Democracy Wall in Beijing and began to produce magazines to sell to the crowds who flocked there.[16] The youth on the streets sang the *Internationale*, as if to say to the regime and to world opinion, "Look we are not in favour of capitalism, we are not counter-revolutionaries." There was no co-ordinated list of agreed demands but reports concur that that right from the start there were calls for greater democracy (free speech and a free press, removal of restrictions on street demonstrations); and anti-bureaucratic demands such as the call to publish the assets of the CCP tops and their families and – given the nature of the protestors – an increase in funding for education and an increase in teachers' salaries.[17]

However, what had started as a student and youth protest began to spread to workers. The privatisation of SMSOEs, and the drive for profit meant workers were laid off to cut costs and many who still had a job had suffered a significant fall in living standards. The protestors, initially students but subsequently joined by workers, occupied Tien An Men Square in central Beijing for seven weeks. All around were placards and meetings protesting against poor living conditions, rising unemployment, poor career prospects, and the lack of democracy in China. At its peak, over one million supporters of the Tien An Men Square protest marched in demonstrations in 24 cities across China. The elements of a political revolution were appearing.

Certainly, there were many rank and file CCP members who sympathised with the demonstrators but they had no organisation or structure to make their opinions felt, and they had no theory which allowed them to reach a correct appraisal of events.

At first, a section of the CCP tops were prepared to tolerate the student protests, but having workers join in was far too dangerous for the regime to tolerate. Workers in the Capital Steel Corporation, one of the Beijing steel plants, went on strike, as did small groups of postal workers and bus drivers, and the number of workers involved was growing rapidly. The Beijing Workers' Autonomous Federation (BWAF) was founded; it existed for only a short time but was the only independent Chinese workers' organisation in the PRC since 1949. An independent observer present in China at the time claims that similar independent workers' groups came into existence in Shanghai, Xian, Hangzhou and Guangzhou.[18] This, of course, made the initiative quite intolerable to the Party tops. Those who were prepared to adopt a more relaxed policy towards the protesters were swept aside, and the movement was crushed.

The central demands of the BWAF were published on May 21, a month after the students started their struggle, and it can be seen immediately how the initiatives of the students had sparked an important development amongst the workers.

Firstly, the BWAF demanded total independence, it would not be under the control of any other organisation, and it would be a democratic organisation in which workers would participate of their own free will. It requested that it be recognised by employers as having equal status with other mass organisations.

Secondly, the basic aim of the BWAF was to put forward the majority views of the workers on economic and political questions and never be a simple welfare organisation, as were existing state unions.

Thirdly, the BWAF demanded the authority to monitor the activities of the CCP and other workers' representatives in firms and businesses that were the property of the state (collectively owned) to ensure that the workers really were genuinely the masters of those firms.[19]

The BWAF challenged the CCP on a crucial issue, calling for the workers to be the real masters of the collective factories. In the context of the direction being taken by the CCP towards capitalist restoration this was clearly a revolutionary socialist demand and one the CCP could not tolerate. The regime had to respond quickly, which it did with a mailed fist. On 4 June 1989, the Chinese army moved into the square killing several hundred demonstrators. It is claimed that the troops entered the square at the point where the BWAF had its headquarters in a tent, and made their first targets the core leaders of the BWAF.[20] The BWAF was declared an illegal organization and disbanded.[21] Through its brutal clampdown, the regime made certain it retained a tight grip on society. The massacre at Tien An Men square marked a definitive victory of the hard-liners in the CCP.

The movement around Tien An Men Square raised the hopes of many workers and youth, and had the potential to topple the Deng regime, but the lack of a coherent leadership and disciplined organisation meant it was never able to realise that promise. The masses were defeated. After Tien An Men the regime sought out all the key leaders many of whom disappeared or spent many years in prison. Indeed at the millennium some 50 protesters from Tien An Men Square remained in jail, nearly all were workers. At the same time the bureaucracy temporarily slowed down the process of market reform to restabilise the situation. The crushing of the Tien An Men protests meant a swing to the right in the political pendulum and once equilibrium was restored, the movement in the direction of capitalism intensified.

In 1989, the Stalinist regimes of Eastern Europe collapsed one after another. The Russian bureaucracy had lost control of the situation and a chaotic transition to capitalism opened up. The Soviet Union resisted a little longer, but it too eventually succumbed to the same process, with the regime collapsing in 1991. These Stalinist regimes were so rotten that they fell with hardly any resistance on the part of the bureaucracy. The system they represented had passed its limits and had decayed from the head down.

Undoubtedly, these events had an impact on the Chinese Stalinists. Up until then they had been introducing market reforms, opening up whole areas of China to capitalist investment, but with the state-owned sector still dominant, and the process could still have been reversed. However, the CCP leadership was united in its determination to accelerate the process of "market reform" as a means of stoking-up the economy and so dampening social unrest. After Tien An Men and the collapse of the Soviet Union a growing proportion of the bureaucracy saw capitalist restoration as the solution to their own crisis, but were determined that the process would take place under their firm control.[22]

15.6 "Socialist market economy with Chinese characteristics"

In 1989/90 the Japanese economic bubble burst and precipitated a market crash across South-East Asia. China assumed the dominant role within the region. Convinced that its privatisation policies had underpinned its success, the CCP accelerated the process. In common with neo-liberals everywhere the CCP hierarchy firmly believed that private firms were more efficient than state-operated ones. Their Stalinist approach meant that the only kind of state-owned industries they could imagine were those that existed under a state bureaucracy, with all the mismanagement that this involved. They could not envisage efficient state-owned industries under workers' control.

By 1991, China had become the second-largest recipient of foreign capital investment after the US, and by 2012 it would beat the USA into second place with an inflow of US$258 billion against US$193 billion.[23] The amount of direct foreign investment in China is a clear indication of the confidence of imperialists in the new capitalist relations.[24]

The direction in which China was now moving was very clear. In January 1992, old and half-paralysed, Deng Xiaoping visited the Shenzhen SEZ, presenting it as an exemplar of the economic reforms that should be undertaken in all China and launched the slogans by which he is best remembered: "Enrich yourselves!" and "As long as it makes money it is good for China."[25]

At 14th Congress of the CCP in October 1992 a tough economic programme was agreed with advice from the IMF and the World Bank; the market economy and the law of value as operated in the SEZs were to be applied across the entire economy. The central state economic plan was downgraded in priority to below those of the provincial authorities, each of whom was to develop its own markets in competition with other provinces. The public sector was to gear itself for commodity production. From now on the market would decide prices.

The 14th Congress officially abandoned the idea that a national state plan should dominate the economy. From now on the federal umbrella would guarantee the free flows of goods, capital and labour nationally, while the autonomy of the provinces and major cities such as Shanghai meant close cooperation between local government and business in pursuit of regional development. The Chinese provinces would enthusiastically promote economic growth using their powers over local banks, infrastructure, wage rates, the application of labour law, the unions and police.

The 14th Congress also officially decided to substantially shrink the size of the state sector and privatise all remaining SMSOEs under the slogan of introducing the so-called Modern Enterprise System (MES). The government's slogan now became "the state retreats and the private sector moves forward". The MES introduced many Western practices such as boards of directors and shareholders and it is no coincidence that in this period there was a marked trend for top Chinese managers to have been educated in capitalist universities.[26]

Many of the sell-offs were for a song. Chan cites the case of one general manager who is now receiving about US$3 million a year in dividends, more than he paid for the business.[27] Within a decade, the World Bank analysed data from a sample of six cities and concluded that if these were typical of the rest of the country then the privatisation process had gone further in China than in many East European and former Soviet countries.[28]

Finally, the 14th Congress agreed in principle to end the state monopoly of foreign trade, though it would take another two years before this had been fully implemented.[29]

In 1997, under the slogan "Grasp the large, let go of the small", the state adopted a policy of retaining control of the 1,000 largest SOEs which held 38% of the industrial assets of the entire country, employed many millions of people, some of which provided large revenues for the state, but to let go (privatise) all other SOEs.[30] Thus, in July 2000, the Beijing City Council, for example, determined that state and collective ownership would be phased out in all SMSOEs within three years. Through such privatisations state controlled industry progressively diminished; in 1988 the state controlled sector produced 41% of GDP, by 2003 it had declined to 34% and by 2011 was 26%.[31]

At the same time large SOEs were given a qualitatively greater degree of management autonomy and told to shift their emphasis from meeting production targets set as part of the central national plan to making profits.[32] This was accompanied by a process of rationalisation which, when completed nationally, meant the proportion of the national urban workforce employed in SOEs had dropped from three-quarters to only one third.[33]

1997 was the year of the Asian Financial Crisis. Dr Kai who was a participant in the events revealed how a mix of short-sighted desperation and conservatism, not planning, were the major determinants of the actions of the Chinese leadership. One result of the crisis was that China desperately needed to boost its foreign exchange reserves. Hurried meetings were called of the top level advisors – including Morgan Stanley – and it was agreed that the least controversial action would be to launch a new company, China Telecom on the Hong Kong stock exchange. Those taking the decision did so on the basis of their belief that mobile phones were a peripheral consideration and their actions would have no major consequences! The company was launched for US$4.2 billion. Today that company is China Mobile, one of the largest companies in the world.[34]

By the late-1990s, market determination of commodity prices had become the norm. Although government intervention remained common, it was market forces that determined the pricing and distribution of commodities.[35]

The bulk of the Chinese economy was now functioning on a capitalist basis with only one quarter of GDP being produced by the state sector. However, restoring capitalism is not simply the process of selling state enterprises, and whilst property relations are the decisive factor in social transformations, the relative percentages of state and private ownership are not the only features to be considered, since questions concerning how the various sectors are functioning, and with what aims are relevant. After the Second World War, the UK Labour Government extensively nationalised key industries and introduced several major social reforms – not to introduce socialism, but rather to assist the British capitalist class. Hence, it is necessary to look at the overall direction of the process, and in China this was inexorably towards capitalism.

At the moment there appears to be a consensus amongst the Party tops: the rationalisation process whereby the 1000 largest remaining SOEs under state control was reduced to only 112 will be continued until only about 40 are left. The reduction will likely be achieved through mergers and rationalisations not sell-offs. Most of these SOEs have been partially floated on the stock exchange so that their shares are traded, but the proportion of their capital in private hands is always less than 50%. These companies attempt to operate according to the laws of the market but have to fall in line with government requirements when so ordered. Shares in SOEs are considered blue chip since they are 100% safe, but return on capital invested is as low as half that in the private sector. These SOEs are largely confined to banking where the government must retain the Big Four banks because of all the bad debts they have accrued, and a mix of telecommunications (security reasons), energy (to guarantee supply) and heavy industry (debt laden).[36]

As the newly privatised enterprises were streamlined for greater efficiency, the workers paid dearly, with the loss of millions of jobs; with women over 43 and men over 48 being the initial targets. Indeed, during the decade 1994-2003, as many as 60 million workers were made redundant.[37] These have generally found alternative employment in the expanding capitalist sectors but usually with lower pay, with no job security and the accompanying loss of important benefits. Likewise, the flow of rural workers who poured into the cities has been largely absorbed, and although they generally took the lowest paid jobs, they still earned at least twice what was paid in the rural areas.

The 20th People's National Assembly met in Beijing in March 2003 to confirm Hu Jintao as General Secretary and approve changes in the leadership of the executive bodies of the People's Republic of China. This was accompanied by the dissolution of the State Commission for Planning and Development, responsible for the five year plans. The content had disappeared ten years previously but now even the symbol of a planned economy was eradicated, and with it the market was publicly installed as the regulatory mechanism of the Chinese economy. "Guidelines" were introduced in 2006 after the tenth, and final plan.

The scale and speed of economic development was phenomenal. In 2004 China consumed half of the concrete used in the world. It was possible to drive from Hong Kong to Shenzhen, through the SEZ, along a modern eight lane motorway and as far as the eye could see on either side was an unbroken gigantic construction site where factories, warehouses, offices, shops and blocks of flats for workers were being constructed in their thousands and millions.

Until the present time, there has been no national bourgeoisie capable of managing the major manufacturing corporations on the scale of, for example, Pfizers or GlaxoSmithKline (both of which now operate in China), without the help of the state. However, in 2013 the PRC announced that many of the large SOEs that are profitable, such as the China National Pharmaceutical Corporation which appears on the *Fortune* 500 list, are to be privatised. These companies are already stock exchange listed because they have minority shareholders, but private shareholders will now become the majority and company structures will be radically changed by the profitability imperative.[38] This move suggests, that while investment in certain strategic areas will remain tightly controlled, the CCP believes it is on the last lap of creating a Chinese bourgeoisie that can adequately support itself without state assistance. By 2014 the 112 remaining SOEs employed about 20% of the national workforce.

The service industries, however, are outstripping their western counterparts. In 2014, Alibaba which handles 80% of all online commerce in China, is bigger than Amazon and EBay combined and claims annual profits of over US$1 billion, was floated on the US stock exchange.

In principle the capitalist transformation of China is complete, there is no longer either monopoly of foreign trade or a central economic plan, and those nationalised industries that can are being progressively privatised.[39]

15.7 Integration into the World Economy

In Chinese schools great emphasis is placed on the opium wars, the prostration of China before British and French colonialism and the terrible suffering of the Chinese people that resulted. The bureaucracy in China has no intention of becoming prey to imperialist domination. However, this goal is achievable only if a strong Chinese capitalist sector is created, and this is being done by building up and strengthening key companies, such as Sinopec (oil and gas), China Mobile (telecommunications), China State Construction Engineering (construction) and SAIC (automobiles). These companies have access to huge amounts of capital from the government's trade surpluses with the US and the rest of the world, which the bureaucracy is ready to pump into these corporations.

According to Nicholas Lardy,[40] of the *Fortune* 500 list of the world's biggest firms, 95 are Chinese companies, giant corporations and conglomerates that are competing successfully in the international market. These huge companies have achieved this success by laying off millions of employees to cut costs and streamline their businesses. They compete with the Americans, Japanese, and other imperialists on a capitalist basis. Without doubt, a strong bourgeoisie has been created in China, but as yet it lacks the experience of its competitors.

Property relations have changed qualitatively and much has already been done to bring the legal structure into line. However, there is never perfect matching and the development of new property relations will always lead and, at times, conflict with the old legal forms. That said, sooner or later, the "superstructure" must come into line with the economic base. As Karl Marx pointed out in 1859 in his preface to *A Contribution to the Critique of Political Economy:* "The changes in the economic foundation lead sooner or later to the transformation of the whole immense superstructure."

In China we are not dealing with a social revolution, but rather a counter-revolution. Nonetheless the point Marx made remains valid. If one looks at the legal structure in China it is readily apparent that changes have been made to bring the legal framework into line with the new property relations. Initially, the new employment laws were introduced in a piecemeal fashion, but the 1994/95 *Labour Law* attempted to consolidate the scattered workplace regulations and adapt them for a market economy.[41] To obtain worker support the government attempted to curb the excesses existing in many industries where it had become (and still is) routine for workers (especially on construction sites) to have to wait until the end of the year for their pay, with the inevitable result that many workers received no pay whatsoever.

In 2004 important changes were made to the Constitution, stressing the role of the non-state sector in supporting economic activity in the country and protecting private property from arbitrary seizure. A year later (2005), the laws which regulated or prevented private companies from entering such sectors as the public utilities and the finance services were abolished.

On 1 January 2008, the *Labour Contract Law of the People's Republic of China* (LCL) was implemented. Previously in China managers would, as a matter of course, call on the CCP to resolve industrial disputes. But with the moves towards a capitalist economy the government has determined that, using Western capitalism as the model, courts are to be the final arbiters and companies must rely on the legal system not the state. Such a move will take a considerable time to implement not only because of the conservatism of the bureaucracy and the close family and political ties between local Party tops and the new companies but also because such a system requires a legal agreement between employer and employee, the written contract.

The LCL had the goal of bringing all workers within this contract system, that is to say, within a capitalist relationship, and offers sweeteners to get them to accept the contract system. All workers are supposed to have a written contract and any employer that does not sign a contract with an employee is supposed to pay that employee double his or her wages for every month worked without a contract; any employee who has worked for an employer more than ten years or who has already signed two successive fixed-term contracts should be being taken on the permanent staff (a non-fixed-term contract).

Today the percentage of workers with a contract can be as high as 95% in some local government offices and the average nationally is nearly 60%. However, for migrant workers, in their majority women, only about a third have signed contracts.[42] Despite the right to strike being outlawed it is precisely these female migrant workers who are leading the fight for better pay and conditions in the huge factories owned by or servicing foreign companies.

15.7.1 Entry into the WTO

Before 1978, the combined value of Chinese imports and exports had seldom exceeded 10% of GDP, in 1986 it reached 35%, in 2007 it was 40%, and today it is nearly 50%.[43] The present Chinese economy can exist only if it is tightly linked to the world economy. It depends heavily on exports and must have international agreements on trade and participate fully in the world economy. On 11 December 2001 it joined the World Trade Organisation (WTO) as its 143rd member.

Marx and Engels wrote in the Communist Manifesto: "The cheap prices of commodities are the heavy artillery with which it (the bourgeoisie) batters down all Chinese walls ... " now the Chinese themselves describe joining the WTO as "opening the door to the world", no doubt in the hope it will be their cheap products that batter down the walls of the older imperialist countries.[44]

By joining the WTO China formally committed itself to abandoning state control over foreign trade by 2007. As would be expected, despite the permissive legal framework the bureaucracy has proceeded cautiously and has placed severe practical limits on, for example, foreign banks wishing to become established in China. Thus the approval process is made painfully slow, the banks must provide large capital sums to ensure ongoing solvency, there are restrictions on how much and to whom monies can be lent, there are constraints on where the banks can be located, and so on. The People's Bank of China (PBOC) is still promising to relax restrictions in preparation for enhanced integration into the world's financial markets, but is slowing the process until the new generation of Chinese banks have a head start.[45]

The PBOC recognises that bad debts renders the Big Four banks unprivatisable and has approached bank privatisation from another angle. From the commencement of the so-called reforms the PBOC encouraged provincial and city governments to set up local banks and, since around 2000, the PBOC has encouraged these banks to increase their services to the private sector and now is proposing that the route to bank privatisation is for these local banks, e.g. Bank of Shanghai, to be sold off as private companies. This has the added advantages of ensuring that the finance industry servicing China is largely in Chinese hands and puts local governments in control of the privatisation process.

It has also determined that the Bank of Shanghai will be the focus for the free, international movement of capital, the capacity to settle payments and trade freely in China's currency on world financial markets. This financial free-trade zone will be a significant move in China's march to a fully neo-liberal capitalist economy and further confirms the plans the CCP has for China as a whole.

15.8 China Now World's Second Largest Economic Power

In the three decades since Deng Xiaoping began to introduce free-market reforms China has bounded up the world league of economic powers. It outstripped Britain and France in 2005 and Germany in 2007, and at the end of 2010 overtook Japan's faltering economy to become the world's second-largest.[46]

China sales across the world are prodigious because it has very cheap labour and, in some industries, very modern means of production.[47] In 2014 the US trade deficit with China exceeded US$300 billion and is expected to exceed even that in 2015. The European trade deficit with China is about US$125 billion. The imperialists are of one voice: China is exporting too much, to the USA, to Europe, to the whole world.

China's highly competitive industry is in direct conflict with US imperialism but the relationship between the two powers is deeply contradictory. Major US companies and most large internationals have invested heavily in China, are producing cheaply and selling their goods in the USA (and elsewhere) at prices determined by the world market. This is highly profitable for them. At the same time the US is one of China's biggest export markets and because of the US trade deficit, China is the biggest holder of US Treasury bonds, and thus, for the moment, has an interest in maintaining the American dollar buoyant.

The CCP bureaucrats would prefer this cosy relationship to be ongoing, but that is out of the question. With the huge development of its productive forces and the consolidation of capitalist relations, it is logical that China behaves like an imperialist power. It imports raw materials and capital, and exports manufactured goods and capital in direct competition with the old imperialist powers.

The flooding of America and Europe with Chinese goods is likely to continue while China continues to be a major pillar supporting the profitability of US and European companies, and those countries are prepared to run up ever higher debts. However, the essential relationship between the US and China is conflict over world markets and resources, especially in Latin America. Already voices are being raised on Wall Street, Congress and the Senate that "unfair" Chinese competition must be curbed.

In 2003 the Bush Administration claimed that the Beijing trade surplus with the United States (about US$120 billion at that time) caused the loss of more than 1 million American jobs. The opposition of the USA to China's expansionist aims were seen in August 2005 when Washington blocked a takeover of the American oil firm Unocal (which has extensive interests in Asia) by Sinopec, China's largest oil refining company. That skirmish symbolises the growing trade and political tensions between China and the USA.

Nearly half of China's foreign investments are in Latin America and the Caribbean, mostly through joint infrastructure products. In January 2015, the *South China Post* reported that China was planning to invest US$250 billion in Latin America over the next five years and increase bilateral trade to over US$500 billion in ten years. Specifically, in Venezuela, China concluded two large oil investment deals which were announced during the Venezuelan President's visit to China in September 2013. China has agreed to invest a total of US$42 billion in two oilfields in Venezuela's Orinoco Belt. Additionally, it is in the process of establishing a "strategic alliance" with Mexico in mining and energy projects.[48]

US Congressmen worried about the growing level of Chinese involvement in Latin America are invoking the "Monroe doctrine" that no foreign power should have more influence than the USA in Latin America. In response, China is building a large navy because it is clear that in the future it will need to control sea-lanes in the Pacific and elsewhere. This will inevitably bring China into increasing conflict with the USA. There can be little doubt that whichever of the Republicans or Democrats are in power, there exists the potential for a trade war which could plunge the world into economic chaos.

China might seem hugely successful but its very success is its Achilles heel. Exporting so much makes China highly dependent on the state of the world market. But there are signs of overproduction on a world scale – in large part due to Chinese growth – and any significant decline in world markets would drastically and adversely affect the Chinese economy. The reverse is also true, any slowing down of China's rate of expansion would have a serious knock-on effect on national economies around the world.

This is causing alarm because already, many Chinese industries including, coal, iron ore, steel, heavy machinery and ship-building have problems of over-capacity. The result is falling prices and decreased demand on a global scale. In the UK, for example, the Thai owners of the Redcar steel plant (sited in the north-east of England and the second largest in Europe) placed it in liquidation in October 2015 as no longer commercially viable. In an area already hard-hit by recession the remaining major employer fell victim to the anarchy of the world capitalist market. The *Guardian* of 25 July 2015, estimated that some 12,000 workers in the South African mining industry would be laid off as a result of the fall in demand for raw materials. These are symptomatic of the problems that China and the world is increasingly going to continue to face in the future.[49]

Currently China's rate of economic growth (7.3% for 2014) means it is doubling its productive capacity every decade, a rate of growth that in a capitalist economy will, inevitably, lead to a an even more massive crisis of overproduction. However, every indication is that the CPR's solution is to wade even deeper into market reforms because with a capitalist economy it needs a rate of increase of at least 7% to maintain present levels of employment.

15.9 The Chinese Communist Party and Chinese Capitalism

At the moment the Communist Party dominates and controls China. But what kind of Communist Party is this? The CCP has over 85 million members.[50] Since at least 1949 the Party has been a haven for opportunists looking for a career in the state bureaucracy, and has a long history of corruption. In 2001 the Party launched a campaign to co-opt so-called "red capitalists" drawn mainly from larger enterprises. At the time this was not considered a major decision because these people were, in their vast majority, Communist Party members, state officials and their relatives. But this group of entrepreneurs has taken on a life of its own within the CCP, and become a powerful force representing the non-state sector of the economy.[51]

The 16th Congress of the CCP (8-14 Nov. 2002) carried out a major reform of the Central Committee and Politburo, strengthening the Party's pro-capitalist representation. A number of prominent capitalists were elected to the CC, further consolidating the weight of the bourgeois within the Party. For ordinary Chinese, joining the CCP is a lengthy, bureaucratic and formal process involving having a sponsor who is already a Party member, having a track record of supporting the Party's policies, and attending an interview that includes questions on which approved texts have been read. After that there is a probationary period. Nevertheless, 6% of the population are members of the CCP, but by 2004 the Party included as many as one third of all private entrepreneurs.[52]

Large numbers of these were already CCP cadres, senior managers of privatised SOEs, who, by definition, became entrepreneurs on privatisation. It is this group that has been favoured for membership of local people's congresses and other bodies with responsibility for leading local privatisation measures, for health and safety policies in the factories, etc. The CCP's strategy appears to have been to provide political advancement for so-called "crony communists" as a means of controlling the rate of economic change and to prevent non-CCP elements from using official institutions to pursue any alternative political agenda.

The efforts made by the CCP to build a market economy are the means by which it justifies and sustains its rule and protects the privileges and properties of its members. Hu cites the so-called 'Prince Party', a grouping within the CCP consisting of the offspring of the older generation of leaders who have been appointed to occupy top political positions to protect the vested interests of Party members.[53] About half of China's most senior leaders fall into this category.[54] Today, the CCP is being used by those at the top, who have state power in their hands, to defend the interests of the bourgeoisie, because they, themselves, belong to that category.

The CCP has demonstrated an astonishing tolerance at the bribes Party members have been given by the business sector. Bribery is widespread, offered as payment of tuition fees at overseas schools for children, stocks and bonds allocated to family members, etc. The rise of TVEs in rural China and the privatisation of SOEs in the mid-1990s, allowed many Party cadres to benefit personally, and sowed the seeds of the tolerance that prevails today.[55]

In 2002 there were three, as late as 2005 only ten, but in 2014 China had over 150 US$ billionaires, second only to the United States. The familial ties linking Party tops to these super rich are often very direct. In 2005, the richest of all was Larry Rong Zhijian – son of a former Vice President of the PRC and leading "red capitalist" Rong Yiren, who did a great deal to open China to the global market.

A *New York Times* investigation found that the close family of Wen Jiabao, China's Prime Minister until November 2012, had wealth amounting to around US$2.7 billion. The family of the new President and anti-corruption hero, Xi Jinping, has interests including investments in companies with total assets of US$376 million; an 18% indirect stake in a rare-earths company with US$1.73 billion in assets; and a US$20.2 million holding in a publicly traded technology company. Control of the communications industry and state censorship ensures information such as this is not available in China.

Because in China there is no significant divide between Party and state there are few, if any, effective checks and/or balances on top officials so corruption is absolutely rampant. It is true that the government has a policy of "killing the chicken to frighten the monkey" and occasionally demotes, imprisons or even executes an official as a warning to others, but the money to be made is so fantastic and the chances of being caught so small that these measures are generally ineffective. An accidentally leaked PBOC report revealed that between 16-18,000 CCP officials that have fled China in the last 20 years, took a total of about US$160 billion with them!

Given that most, if not all, state officials are considered corrupt, corruption charges are a means of dealing with one's opponents. Two recent and major trials fall into this category. Zhou Yongkang had been a member of the 17th Politburo Standing Committee (PSC), China's highest decision-making body, and Minister for Public Security with responsibility for overseeing China's security apparatus. At the 18th Congress of the CCP in November 2012 Zhou was removed from the PSC.

Zhou, it appears, was an opponent of Xi Jinping who attempted to build a power base in the CCP to challenge Xi's election to leader. He also opposed moves to further reduce state support to the remaining SOEs, many of which are controlled by the Party elite. Zhou lost the faction fight and with his removal from the PSC, there was a purge of those he had placed in senior positions, particularly in the oil and gas industry.[56] However, as Minister of Security, Zhou had gathered a lot of dirt on senior Party officials and there was a fear of what he might do with it. Xi took on this "tiger" to consolidate his own authority, safeguard the reputations of his colleagues, gain respect within the CCP and break the opposition to his economic policy. Officially, Xi was "scrubbing the party clean", but really he was purging his political enemies.

Zhou was convicted of abuse of power, accepting bribes and revealing state secrets, the last being a certain indication that more then corruption was involved. He was sentenced to life in prison.

At the same time Bo Xilai, (ex-Minster of Commerce) a fast-rising protege of Zhou was waging a controversial war against organized crime in Chongqing, a major city in south west China. Bo introduced a comprehensive surveillance system that monitored all phone calls and internet communications, but overstepped the mark by tapping into phone calls to and from President Hu Jintao, and using information gained against fellow Party members. The Party tops rallied and in a short time Bo Xilai was brought to trial for having taken bribes in the form of, amongst other things, a luxury villa in France. He was sentenced to life in prison.[57,58]

Of course smaller "flies" get caught up in the anti-corruption measures. Wei Pengyuan, Deputy Chief of the National Energy Commission, had generated a local scandal when he publicly threatened to kill his mistress. A police raid on his home followed in October 2014, and found the equivalent of US$30 million in cash at a time when the average salary in China is less than US$5,000.[59] Wei was subsequently charged with corruption, found guilty and jailed for life.

How serious President Xi is in tackling corruption can be seen by the arrest of three **anti**-corruption campaigners: Liu Ping, Wei Zhongping and Li Sihua, who dared to ask for China's top 200 officials to disclose their assets. They were initially arrested on charges of subversion, later changed to illegal assembly. The court in which they first appeared was surrounded by lines of police and independent observers denied access. Just to make clear the position of the government their lawyer was subsequently harassed by the police, including being detained for questioning.[60] In June 2014, Liu Ping and Wei Zhongping were each sentenced to six and a half years in prison and Li Sihua to three years.[61]

The stench of sleaze and vice hangs over the super rich leaders of the Chinese bourgeoisie, an all-pervasive corruption flourishes at every level, an inevitable consequence of a bureaucratic and totalitarian regime that is founded on the consumption an undue share of the wealth created by the working class. The super rich are supported by a stratum of wealthy Party and state bureaucrats, their corporate partners. Private entrepreneurs and compradors serve multinational corporations some, such as Foxconn, are economic giants in their own right. Next comes the "new middle class" of cadres, business people, managers, professionals, and academics, large in absolute numbers – estimated at 100-200 million – though still proportionately quite small. It is these well-to-do strata who are the most enthusiastic about the new capitalist economy.[62]

As long as the economy continues to develop at a sufficiently fast rate, the Party leadership will be able to contain the situation and maintain a certain stability within society and within the Party. However, the CCP is not a political party as usually understood, it has been an integral part of a state apparatus since the 1930s and contains within itself representatives of all the political currents within government and the state. Any major economic crisis would be accompanied by major class, national and social conflicts which would be reflected within the Party which, in turn, would be subject to strong centrifugal tendencies. Groups who felt their vital interests were threatened would surface as factions threatening the unity of the Party, and its grip on the state could be broken. In the case of the Russian bureaucracy this happened in a convulsive way. The old, monolithic, Stalinist party shattered into numerous parties representing different interest groups. For the moment the Chinese Party remains in control.

China is a huge country and the different provinces and even different regions within provinces have significant leeway in the interpretation of Beijing's directives. Chinese history shows that the bureaucracies of the different provinces inevitably have different views and interests. There are divisions within the Party hierarchy over proposed anti-corruption measures and in proposed changes in the laws governing property rights, both of which would impact on the more acquisitive wing of the Party. Xi Jinping and the majority of the bureaucracy appreciate the dangers of an accelerating class polarisation and call for a clamp down on the most flagrant examples of corruption, for social reforms and increased social spending to soften the blows being experienced by the masses and give the appearance that the regime is listening to the masses and can self-correct.

Present conflicts within the CCP are not between those who want to "go back" and those who want capitalism, but rather about how best to maintain the stability and continuation of the present system. Capitalist relations have been established and, inevitably, this process has been accompanied by differentiation between wage labour and capital. The bureaucracy of the CCP in its overwhelming majority stands on the side of capital. The irony is that in the long run this process will tear the CCP apart. The key element in such a situation is that the link to the state could be broken.

Of course there will be elements within the CCP that genuinely wish to serve the people, but the fact such elements exist does not alter the real nature of the CCP. It is highly likely that opposition to the current leadership of the Party will dress its ideas in Maoist rhetoric, harking back to a period when the masses had job security, better welfare coverage etc. Thus, striking miners in the coastal province of Shandong protesting wage arrears placed a large picture of Mao at the front of their demonstration on 22 March 2015.[63]

In 1995 direct foreign investment was about 5% of national total investment, by 2002 it was about 12% and by 2012 the level of was about 20%. It is important to realise that over 80% of investment in China's capitalist industries came from within China, from primitive capitalist accumulation.[64] The monies invested by these entrepreneurs was from the high rate of surplus value extracted from the workers because of state enforced low wages, high rents paid by urban workers and robbing workers of their pensions, medical and housing schemes.

Many wealthy Party members began to acquire fortunes when they gained control of successful TVEs. The ownership of nominally collective enterprises was gradually consolidated in the hands of their managers or local Party officials, often the same person.[65] In towns, many Party and government officials were able to translate their managerial positions into ownership of privatised SMSOEs. Party cadres, generally, found the property sector a particularly fertile ground for amassing quick riches. Permission for construction projects valued at billions of dollars depended on the say-so of local Party tops who, not surprisingly, soon acquired extensive property holdings. On 12 September 2014, CNBC News claimed the number of dollar millionaires in China had reached more than 1 million. Many of these, if not the majority, are CCP members who use the loophole of a lack of central land records to salt away their ill-gotten gains from bribery and corruption, buying the leases of prime city-centre apartments under pseudonyms.

Outside of the Party many capitalists emerged in private retail and business services, beginning as small tradesmen or professionals. A good example of how crony capitalism and the end of central planning combined to enable the meteoric rise of those with good Party connections is Liu Yongxing. In the early 2000s, the China Aluminium Corporation (Chinalco, an SOE), had a 98% share of the aluminium market in China. The central government gave Chinalco exclusive rights over all national bauxite deposits. Yet, by 2008, the market share of Chinalco had dropped to less than 50%, due to the entry of large private firms into the aluminium market.

Liu Yongxing, the moving spirit of the East Hope Group understood the Achilles heel of Chinalco; that its exclusive right to purchase Chinese bauxite was given by central government and not the local governments that had actual physical control over the minerals. With the end of central planning, the East Hope Group went to the local government of Sanmenxia, a mid-size city in Henan Province with large deposits of bauxite, and effected a deal with the local Party secretary who had strong links with Li Keqiang, Chinese Premier. The East Hope Group started to produce aluminium in 2005 and today Liu claims to be worth US$5 billion.[66]

15.10 Summary

The question of the class nature of China had been a key question for the Marxist movement and it is not possible to grasp the processes that took place in China from the point of view of formal logic and abstract definitions. There is no simple litmus test that can be applied here, complex historical processes do not admit such an elementary approach. Only a method, which takes the process as a whole and concretely analyses its contradictory tendencies as they unfolded, stage by stage, can shed a clear light on the situation.

The Stalinist bureaucratic counter-revolution in Russia in the period 1923-36 was by no means a preordained event determined in advance. Trotsky followed the process through all its stages, showing concretely the relation between the balance of class forces in Russia, the different tendencies in the Communist Party and their relationship to the classes, the evolution of the world situation, the economy, and the subjective factor. As the situation developed and the different factors changed their specific weights, Trotsky's position developed accordingly, finally concluding a new regime existed in the Soviet Union, which he termed Soviet or Proletarian Bonapartism.[67] Such a development did not reflect vacillation on Trotsky's part, but rather the way his analysis followed the process of bureaucratic degeneration as it unfolded.

In *In Defence of Marxism*, Trotsky outlined the way in which a Marxist should pose the question of the class nature of the Russian state:

> "(1) What is the historical origin of the USSR? (2) What changes has this state suffered during its existence? (3) Did these changes pass from the quantitative stage to the qualitative? That is, did they create a historically necessary domination by a new exploiting class?."[68]

The method of our analysis of recent and present events in China is in no way different from that of Trotsky. The demand for an immediate answer to the question "workers' state or capitalism" reveals, not intellectual rigour, but a formalistic "either ... or" approach. However, the situation in China has now developed to such a stage that we can give a definite answer.

The return of capitalism was an ongoing and complex process but it is possible to date the process by the Central Committee meetings at which key decisions were made. We can see that the transition lasted from 1982, when selected SOEs began to produce outside the state plan according to market forces, to October 1992 when the 14th CCP Congress finally buried state planning and the monopoly of foreign trade and agreed to begin wholesale privatisation of SMSOEs with the perspective of selling-off the larger companies as soon as suitable arrangements could be made.

The fear of chaos has always been central theme in Chinese history. The PRC itself emerged following a long period of war and chaos and the events of that period were still alive in the memories of the CCP leadership during 1991/92 when the Soviet regimes in eastern Europe and the Soviet Union collapsed. The Chinese Party tops saw the resulting chaos, the break away of the different national republics, the collapse in production, the rise of the Russian mafia and they were appalled and terrified. But at the same time they came to an understanding and agreement between themselves, no doubt spurred on by the recent events in Tien An Men Square, that they had to remain in control of the situation even if that meant adopting capitalist measures.

The restoration of capitalism slowed and accelerated as the different groups within the CCP leadership argued out their differences. Added unevenness occurred in the process due to the specific conditions in the different regions of this enormous country and in the different sectors of the economy. China has a long history of dispersed power, with considerable provincial, county and even city autonomy. In fact, an integral part of the transition to capitalism was encouragement and greater decentralization of state powers.[69]

To accelerate the process it was determined, at an early stage, to delegate substantial responsibility for enacting the reforms to Party tops in the provinces and the four great cities of China (Beijing, Shanghai, Chongqing and Tianjin). To further accelerate the process, the revenues of local governments throughout China were made dependant on local business taxes and taxes on sales. The promotion of Party cadres came to depend on their ability to deliver economic growth, employment and foreign investment.[70] Many local Party members served as brokers and deal-makers between the public and private sectors, others greased the wheels through black-market deals, bribes and informal networking. It was only natural that these came to have stakes in private businesses or took posts as advisors on company boards or senior management positions in private companies.

However, for Marxists, this does not exhaust the problem. Have the new property relations have established themselves unequivocally and irreversibly? Or, on the contrary, is it possible that the return to capitalism can be reversed? It is necessary to analyse the process as a whole and lay bare the relations between the different class forces involved. These factors are discussed in the next chapter.

Chapter 16
A New Chinese Working Class

16.1 Introduction

In 2014 the number of mobile phones in use exceeded the world's population, and about half of them were produced in the Chinese coastal province of Guangdong. This 'Made in China' phenomenon is based on the highest level of human migration in history, the movement of hundreds of millions of poor peasants from the interior of China to the coastal regions to work in ultra-modern factories catering for a multinational market.[1]

The Chinese economic miracle was created by the sweat and sacrifice of peasants and workers, but average real wages, compared to the 1950s when the giant SOEs dominated the economy, have fallen considerably. Tens of millions of jobs have been lost in the SOEs, jobs which had been seen as secure for life and carried pensions, health care and housing allowances. A so-called "rust belt" has appeared across the traditional industrial areas, such as the North East, the heartland of China's old state plan as many loss-making SOEs, both factories and mines, were rationalised for privatisation – an ongoing process.

The majority of Chinese workers are now predominantly low-paid, short-term migrants working in giant high-tech factories. They have little or no job security, and do not receive the welfare benefits that their predecessors in heavy industry had enjoyed. Since the mid-1990s company retirement pensions have largely disappeared, health services have been privatised and moved out of the reach of many, housing has been privatised and the rents being extracted from the workers are a major source of capital for financing factory expansion. Many of the gains of the 1949 revolution have simply evaporated.

16.2 The Making of a New Working Class

In China, a vast working class has been assembled with startling rapidity, most visibly in the three great regions of industrialisation: the Pearl River delta

(Guangdong), the Yangtze River delta (Shanghai region), and the Yellow River valley (Beijing–Tianjin). There has been a feminisation of the workforce; female labour plays a leading, even dominant, role in the new proletariat, forming 60 to 70% of factory workers, many of whom are housed in on-site company dormitories. These women are better educated than their mothers and grandmothers. They are more aware of their rights and in the labour-intensive factories of the SEZs, stereotypes of female passivity are breaking down.

China's cities are growing at an unprecedented rate. In 2013 it was estimated that for the first time, over half of China's 1.4 billion people lived in towns and cities.[2] By 2030 it is estimated that there could be as many as 1 billion urban dwellers; over 200 cities with populations of more than 1 million, compared with 35 such cities in Europe. To meet this projected growth there are 40,000,000 construction workers.

This degree of urbanisation is unprecedented and it has brought into existence the largest and most powerful proletariat in history. With the massive development of the productive forces comes an enormous strengthening of the working class. The economic development raised living standards for many, incoming peasants were prepared to do the worst jobs and live in terrible conditions because they received an income of at least twice what they would be paid working the land, and were able to remit some money to their dependents. This improvement in living standards for hundreds of millions of people was the major factor in the easy victory of the pro-capitalist wing in the CCP.[3]

We are witnessing the creation of millions of the 'gravediggers' of capitalism, a new mass proletariat. What has been happening in China has some striking similarities with the early development of capitalism in Russia over one hundred years ago, but on a much larger scale. Then, the growth of industry brought into being a fresh proletariat made up of peasants who had abandoned the land. Although a terrible price was paid, a mass proletariat was created that would lead the October Revolution. Today the conditions are being created in China for future class conflicts that will inevitably lead to a revolutionary upheaval.

The storm clouds are gathering. China faces serious and inter-linked problems. Firstly, as a UK Government report[4] on the Chinese economy points out, the total number of migrant workers may be at its highest level ever, about 274 million, but the rate of growth has been declining such that today it is virtually zero. There has been a marked change in the destinations of these migrants, more and more are looking for work in smaller cities closer to home because of the discrimination they experience in the larger cities under the infamous *hukou* system (see Section 16.3 below). It is to overcome this problem and tap into new sources of labour power that huge investment is now being poured into creating factories in inland China.

Secondly, China's economic growth for 2014 was 7.4%, and the IMF projects a growth rate of 6.8% for 2015 and 6.5% in 2016.[5] This is serious because to successfully maintain present standards of living and employment levels, to sustain social stability, a continued economic growth of 7-10% for the next decade or two is a necessity.[6] Thirdly, this decline is taking place when global economic growth for 2015 will be the lowest since the recession year of 2009, and prospects for 2016 do not appear much better – due to China's own slowdown.

The first generation of migrant workers moved from the countryside to work in the new SEZs of south China in the 1980s and 1990s. These were mostly female workers who came to work in electronic and toy factories in the first SEZ, the Shekou Industrial Zone of Shenzhen. The second generation of peasants arrived in the late 1990s and 2000s. These included children of the first generation who, benefitting from the experience gained by their parents, were much more prepared to take collective action to improve job safety and increase pay rates.

Now the first of the third generation are entering the production process and bring with them a much greater awareness of workers' rights and ways to protest. They have a sense of self-worth and are beginning to demand respect with a consequent dramatic increase in the number of actions by shop-floor workers. A constant theme throughout the history of capitalism is that self-awareness by the working class usually takes place in the second and third generations who come to work in industrial centres.[7]

The Chinese government does not publish statistics on strikes (officially strikes do not exist, strikes and accompanying activities such as go-slows, street demonstrations, etc., are designated 'collective actions') but all available evidence shows they are on the increase. Workers whose parents emigrated to one employer are returning to work for another but they bring with them the knowledge that short, sharp strikes are an effective way of redressing grievances. As the confidence of the workers grows, strikes and picket lines are becoming normalised.[8]

16.3 Distinctive Features of the Chinese Proletariat

However, the PRC is determined to minimise the capacity of its proletariat to fight national and international capitalism, and this gives the process of proletarianisation in China certain specific characteristics.[9]

After 1949 the Chinese state played the determining role in shaping industrial relations, primarily through the Five Year Plans and the All China Federation of Trade Unions (ACFTU). With the transition to capitalism the core of that intervention moved to collaboration with the largest employers to provide a recruitment-work-residence pattern that produces an exceptionally profitable and productive labour force.[10]

In China, the state plays a major role in the labour markets by regulating the movement of labour from rural to urban industrial areas. This is done through local governments and inter-province co-ordination and co-operation for the provision of labour directly to local factories, to the SEZs and the cities. For example, the inner provinces of Hunan and Guangxi have long-standing undertakings to systematically provide labour through their own recruiting offices for the construction sites and factories of Guangdong at a rate which attempts to ensure that labour costs remains at one fortieth those in the USA.[11]

The provision of cheap labour, for every kind of work, has become an important activity for the governments of inland provinces because they benefit directly from the fees paid by the companies to which they supply labour, and indirectly from the monies remitted home. The local governments are ideally placed to be the recruiting agents, to co-ordinate supply and demand, screen and recruit (predominantly) single females aged between 17 and 22, supply all necessary documents (no fewer than six separate visas might be required for the major cities), and arrange transportation from village to factory.[12] The recruits would invariably be eager to leave their villages where there is an oppressive patriarchal system, little or no schooling after the age of 16 due to cut-backs in education, few job opportunities and, possibly, to flee an unwanted arranged marriage.

By the end of the 1990s, these government agencies were complicit in widespread illegal practices such as covering up the failure by the hiring company to provide work contracts as required by the Labour Laws of 1995 (and 2008). Without a contract it is impossible to claim such entitlements as paid maternity leave or for a worker to take an employer to court for compensation for occupational injury. To cut costs, migrant workers are deliberately kept in ignorance of their entitlements.[13]

However, for the Chinese working class industrialisation and urbanisation are two different processes. The peasants come to the cities to work but have no right to live in those cities and must return to the village in which they are registered at the end of their contract. From this arrangement arises the extraordinary situation that, for example, only 30% of Shenzhen's population are categorised as permanent residents.[14] This system has its origins in ancient China and applies even to the children of migrant workers born in the cities because status is passed on through the mother. The *hukou* system is now a hereditary system for ensuring a generous supply of low-cost rural labour for the SEZs. It saves urban governments which co-operate so willingly with the capitalist enterprises from having to meet medical costs for these migrants and their children who are not entitled to attend the local urban state school. In fact there is an entire range of benefits and rights which are denied the migrant labourers, including the right to vote.

The migrant worker is a temporary resident, tolerated in the towns only so long as s/he is employed. Any action of which the employer disapproves could mean not only dismissal but removal of the residence permit and forced return to the home village. Because the migrant worker has no right to stay in the city, residence permits are a means by which the state attempts to control both labour mobility and worker dissent. The benefits for employers are immediately obvious, they have access to an abundant supply of cheap labour to hold down costs, and there is substantially less likelihood of organised labour solidarity to fight for better wages and working conditions.

Richer elements from the countryside, however, can obtain an urban residence permit provided they are married, purchase a residence within the city limits, and hold down a post for a prescribed period of time, typically a year. Given the prohibitive cost of apartments in China, migrant workers are excluded from this arrangement.

The dormitory-labour regime is an integral and important part of the system for the control of migrant workers to maintain China's status as the global workplace. Workers' dormitories are temporary residences for single workers (the great majority) for one or two years. Usually they are close to or within the grounds of the factory they serve, integrating working and non-working life so that the company exerts exceptionally close control over the workers' activities. Such dormitories are communal multi-storey buildings, housing hundreds or even thousands of workers. Generally, between eight and twenty workers share a room with communal washing and toilet facilities. Living space is intensely collective, only the area within the closed curtains of the worker's bunk is private space. To cut costs there is always pressure to overcrowd the dormitories which can make them dirty and unhygienic.

Work teams receive pay based on collective performance; hence, the sharing of rooms can increase pressure to conform and perform. However, many companies have a policy of assigning dormitory places at random. This means that there is frequent disruption of sleep because of different working hours, there may even be nightshift and day-shift workers mixed into the same dormitory. The purpose is to break up any existing social networks, and hinder communication and interaction between workers on the same shift. It is believed that this reduces the self-organisation of the workers. At the same time, it also makes the factory a solitary place for newcomers, who, having forfeited their personal and social lives, encounter great loneliness and anxiety, and the resulting alienation and can lead to acts of desperation. Suicide is the extreme manifestation of the migrant work experience.

Dormitories are ideal for the Just-in-Time production system, so favoured by international companies. Confined to the factory compound, workers can be asked at a moment's notice to work overtime or to work during their rest day to ensure the company meets its delivery deadlines. Living in company-supplied dormitories with extended work hours ties the worker to one employer because it is almost impossible for workers to look for another job.

In total, the pressures on these young women are unlike anything previously experienced by the working classes. Apple made the world's largest ever recorded profit in the last quarter of 2014, nearly US$18 billion, mostly from sales of 74.5 million iPhones made by second generation female migrant workers in China. Apple supplier Foxconn, employs over one million workers across China[15] and its working conditions were the subject of an investigation by Pun Ngai and Jenny Chan after 14 young migrant workers committed suicide, and another four attempted suicide during 2010. All were between 17 and 25 years old. This section draws on the investigation of working conditions at Foxconn by Pun and Chan.[16]

Foxconn moved its production base from Taiwan to mainland China in the late 1980s to benefit from state support and cheap labour. This support has enabled Foxconn to grow rapidly and now it dominates the global market by producing half of the world's electronic products. Initially confined to the Shenzhen SEZ, its thirty factories are now dotted all over China with the smallest factory employing some 20,000 and the largest over 400,000.

This geographical expansion has enabled Foxconn to continue to tap into the lower cost labour available in northern, central, and western China. With the encouragement of the central government, these local governments are creating a business friendly environment by promising to provide access to land, roads, railways, bank loans and labour. Naturally, the local governments are in competition, each fighting the others for Foxconn investment.

For example, after the Sichuan government won a US$2 billion Foxconn investment project a total of 14 villages were demolished to create space for a 15 km^2 Foxconn "Living Zone". It is reported that the Sichuan leaders waived a "significant" amount of rent and tax and provided land "far below the market rate". In addition the Sichuan government provided a free labour recruitment service, with local government officials being given a recruitment quota, setting up stalls at the sides of roads and escorting recruits to the factory gates. It is claimed that over-eager officials told villagers that if no-one from a family went to work at Foxconn, then that family would be fined 1,000 yuan.[17]

Foxconn's largest factory complex is in Longhua, Shenzhen, and has more than 430,000 workers. Within the walls of Foxconn, most of the employees are young women migrants who work and live there with an average age of about 21 years. Such women are preferred for their supposed docility, nimble fingers, lack of experience of worker self-organisation and preparedness to pay attention to the monotonous, detailed, and mind-numbing work undertaken.

Company managers refer to it as the 'Foxconn campus' and it is the model factory presented to visitors from media organisations and other inspection units. This 'campus' includes the factories themselves, twelve storey dormitories, warehouses, an employee care centre including a counselling clinic and hospital facilities, a library and bookstores, a post office, a small fire brigade, an exclusive television network, an educational institute, numerous sports facilities, supermarkets, cafeterias and restaurants, and even a wedding dress shop.

In designing its production lines, Foxconn was able to draw on lessons learned around the world ever since Henry Ford first introduced mass production of automobiles. Thus, notwithstanding its facilities, Longhua is a dormitory-labour regime which seeks to organise workers' activities 24 hours a day to maximise profit. Terry Gou, the CEO and founder of Foxconn has made clear the philosophy which underpins the 'campus': "Leadership is a righteous dictatorship."[18]

Production lines have two properties: minimise human qualities in order to standardise production and eliminate errors, and a division of labour so precise and detailed that workers become cogs in the machine. Today, Foxconn production operators in general are engaged in endless, mechanical repetition of movements made as fast and as simple as possible.

Work is timed to the second and must meet targets set by time and motion studies, at the limit of what workers can produce: "I take a motherboard from the line, scan the logo, put it in an antistatic-electricity bag, stick on a label, and place it on the line. ... Every ten seconds I finish five tasks" reported one young woman. In a typical day she might repeat this operation more than 15,000 times, little wonder that so many of these workers claim they feel worthless. It is soul destroying.

If one worker commits an infringement of the rules the entire shift – possibly a hundred or more workers – must remain after work. The woman (80% of these workers are women) is forced to stand and read aloud a statement of self-criticism. She must be loud enough to be heard. The line leader drives home this lesson in humiliation by asking if the worker at the far end of the workshop clearly heard the mistake made. This process forms part of a policy used to penalize workers for petty offences and so enhance shop-floor discipline. A worker can "lose points for having long nails, being late, yawning, eating, or sitting on the floor" and such loss of points jeopardises the monthly bonus. Production workers who stand during work are supposed to receive a ten-minute break every two hours but this only applies if they meet the hourly production target. After a 12-hour shift, factory-floor managers and supervisors can lecture production workers for as long as half an hour, evaluating the shift's output and listing those areas where performance needs to be improved.

The hours worked and the wage rates paid at Foxconn appear to fit the national pattern and Foxconn likes to point out that workers sign written "agreements" before working overtime. However, since workers have no effective trade union representation or protection, such agreements are meaningless, and whilst Chinese Labour Law specifies a maximum of 36 hours overtime per month, Foxconn workers can work 80 hours of overtime a month. Effectively, the working day is 12 hours, leaving the workers exhausted to the point of tears, for as little as US$300 a month. Workers are lucky to get one rest day a week.

However, despite the near total domination of workers' lives, the close confinement means that if an issue of common interest arises – e.g. the local government decides not to raise minimum rates – the workers are in a position to discuss and take immediate action. Hence, once action is agreed, the dormitory arrangement can greatly strengthen the workers' unity.[19]

It has also been found that workers use proximity to form study groups and that they listen to educational programmes on the radio, particularly on labour law to help them in formulating demands on employers: e.g. that in law each worker must have a contract, that the rates paid must be equal to or greater than the local legal minimum wage, that the company must pay social insurance premiums, and so on.[20]

Clearly, the Foxconn management exercises as much control as possible over the workers, yet despite these efforts, Pun and Chan found the workers resisted in many ways, including go slows, stoppages, small-scale strikes, and sometimes even sabotage. As reported by Foxconn workers, on one particular occasion they deliberately failed to meet targets in order to have senior management remove a rude and harsh line leader, and on another occasion everybody stopped working when there was a rush order in order to gain specific concessions.[21] The lessons learned at grandmother's knee are paying dividends.

16.4 Working Conditions

In 2014 the Hong Kong based China Labour Bulletin carried out a survey of the causes of labour disputes in China.[22] Of course, each dispute is specific and, apparently, has its own particular causes. However, the CLB is concerned to point out that each of the three major factors it identified have been greatly exacerbated by the year-on-year decline in China's industrial output.

The most common factor is employers seeking to move their factory to take advantage of cheaper labour elsewhere – moving to inland China or, even, Bangladesh – some of them attempted to sell off equipment and flee the scene, not only leaving Chinese workers with no job but attempting to avoid payment of wages owed, statutory redundancy and other obligations. Claims for compensation give rise to about one third of all disputes.

The second most common factor is attempts to reduce labour costs by, for example, re-classifying Saturday and Sunday working as 'normal hours' so as to avoid paying double time for weekend work, or ending weekend working and forcing workers to work extra overtime during the week which is paid at a lower rate. Many workers get a pay raise only when the local government increases the minimum wage, but employers are, more and more, attempting to claw back any such increase in pay by reducing, or even eliminating, housing and other allowances, or by cutting bonuses. Another technique is to delay the payment of workers so that they work not a week, but a month in arrears. Problems with wage arrears and overtime payments account for about a quarter of all strikes.

The third most common cause are straightforward claims for an increase in wages to compensate for increases in the prices of consumer goods, rent, etc. Claims for wage increases account for about one fifth of all disputes.

The above ratios refer to factory workers and the experience of other sectors will be different. For example, teachers in the smaller cities and villages are often poorly paid, especially when compared with civil servants and other public employees with the same experience and qualifications. It is not unusual for teachers to go several months without being paid at all. CLB recorded 69 teacher strikes over the period of its report the great majority for payment of wage arrears and increases in pay.

In most factories the actual working day is at least ten hours (including compulsory overtime) and rest days are provided only if there is a break in production, such as during the low season. In the event of a rush order, employees are required to work 12 hours/day in sequential shifts. The situation in many factories is that employees work at least 72 hours each week, far more than the total allowed by Chinese law (40 hours each week, and 36 hours overtime work per month).

It is to be expected that under such conditions, accidents at work are commonplace. Indeed, the International Labour Organisation has stated that, officially, about 380,000 Chinese workers die annually in industrial accidents, but industry is characterised by gross under-reporting:

> "... (T)here were more than 20,000 industrial and mining enterprises with occupational hazards problems in Dongguan (a major export centre on the Pearl River Delta in Guangdong Province). They employ more than 5.5 million workers, but only 6,000 enterprises report occupational hazards to the related government offices. The State Administration of Work Safety only monitored 280 of these ..."[23]

Possibly the most extreme conditions are to be found in the construction industry which, in 2010, employed about one-third of all migrant labourers. Safety standards are appallingly low. Even in Hong Kong, scaffolding for high rise buildings can be no more than lengths of bamboo tied together with what looks like string. A major reason for the transient nature of the construction workforce is that, in 1984, the government introduced new regulations which made it an offence for construction companies (especially those under state-ownership) to retain permanent on-site staff. From then on the norm has been for workers to be hired by sub-contractors who recruit teams of cheap, unskilled migrant workers from rural areas.

It is normal for workers employed by sub-contractors to work on subsistence wages, expecting to receive their pay as a lump sum at the end of the year. The big problem, especially in the construction industry, is that many sub-contractors simply disappear at the last moment leaving the workers without even the means of returning home. This scandal of unpaid wages is the cause of over half of all China's strikes, many of which have resulted in violent clashes between furious workers and police.

The PRC has begun to recognise the unsustainability of this situation and in 2008 enacted the Labour Contract Law which accords some workers the right to challenge their employers in the courts. However, those worse hit are effectively excluded from this process because the worker must have a contract before his/her case can be heard, and in some SEZs – and in the construction industry – nearly two-thirds of the workers do not have one.

A second barrier is the obvious anti-worker bias of the great majority of court decisions. Local government finances depend heavily on the success of local enterprises. Hence, the resulting intense competition between localities for outside investment has sensitised local courts to the needs of employers, such that enforcement of labour laws is patchy. However, there is every likelihood that a higher court (or the CCP) will overturn any judgement in the workers' favour: "Under these circumstances, workers' rights often end at the courtroom door."[24]

Many barriers have been erected to prevent workers ever reaching that courtroom door. Before a case can be presented to a court, workers must first go through a mandatory arbitration process, and for the few who possess a contract, that process is complex and lengthy.

It can take a journey of several hours to reach the relevant Ministry building, and having done that it can take days of petitioning, and being sent from one department to another before the correct bureau is found, invariably crowded with other workers seeking redress. If more than five of the applicants appear at any one time they are guilty of an illegal gathering and can be arrested (as the Artigas workers found, see Section 16.3) and, if migrant labourers, stripped of their residence permits and returned to their villages. The workers must argue their own case against professional lawyers and whatever the court decision, there is invariably a lack of will by the local government to enforce it and the workers often end up worse off.[25]

The same obstacles are placed in the paths of any women who seek legal redress for breaches of China's anti-discrimination laws, with the addition that lawyers screen their cases to avoid this type of dispute because of their low fee potential and limited access to legal aid.[26]

The traditional 'labour aristocracy' of the Chinese working class was in heavy industry and mining, and it is these workers who have suffered most under the so-called reforms. The means used to carry through the privatisation of the giant SOEs included such promises as being kept fully informed of all relevant plans, substantial redundancy payments, of being found new jobs and of payment of large sums of money obtained from the sale of the enterprise.

Many, if not most, workers received none of these things. Instead local officials, enterprise managers and privateers proceeded to plunder the state assets for personal gain. According to official estimates, since China first began restructuring the SOEs, state assets valued at between 80 and 100 billion yuan have been embezzled annually.[27]

In March 2007, the vice-chairman of the ACFTU, Xu Deming, stated unpaid wages owed by SOEs which had been 'restructured' amounted to over two billion yuan, together with a total of as much as one billion yuan in unpaid compensation. He further noted that in enterprises that had been privatised, 25% of the laid-off workers were not receiving any form of social security benefit.[28]

To redress their grievances the workers were encouraged to use the so-called petitioning process whereby citizens, either individually or collectively, can appeal to the authorities over specific grievances. In China this is a well-established procedure. But it is a system that serves as a buffer protecting government officials, absorbing the petitioners' anger but without any meaningful outcome. For laid-off SOE workers it was a bureaucratic trap, with complainants being sent off on an endless paper chase as bureaucrats passed the buck and covered each other's backs. When the wrongdoing was by a government department the accused person was a high-level official or business associate of the government, cases were quietly shelved.

Worse, the system generally meant petitions ended up in the hands of the organizations and officials being complained about, and who might be the employers of the complainants. Thus, petitioners could be putting themselves at risk of retaliatory action by those targeted in the complaint.

In parallel with petitioning, workers were taking their cases to the courts. But all too often the case would include government officials and government departments who were also often direct beneficiaries of the privatisation. As the number of privatization dispute cases rose rapidly China's senior judicial authorities instructed the courts to stop hearing such cases. On 26 March 2006 the All-China Lawyers' Association directed its members that if they took on a collective case then they had a responsibility to "*actively assist the judicial authorities*", that is to collaborate with the accused against their clients.[29]

When they discovered that the system served to shield the corrupt and, possibly, expose complainants to the risk of retaliation, the workers soon lost all faith in it. As a result, many workers proceeded with their own actions, just about every SOE restructuring/ privatisation programme led to some kind of dispute with the laid-off workers demanding payment of wages owed, payment of a pension, medical insurance and social security benefits, along with assistance promised in securing re-employment.

Left with little alternative the workers were forced to demonstrate on the streets to make their demands heard. However, many of the local government officials and Party tops were personally involved in the privatisation deals and saw these worker demonstrations as a threat their own positions which, of course, they presented publicly as a criminal threat to "political stability". Using their influence with the police and judiciary they attempted to have the demonstrations broken up and banned and the activities of the protest leaders arbitrarily punished. Under Chinese legal procedures the police can hold protestors charged with criminal offences for an extended period of time, weeks, months and even years without trial.

Between 1998 and 2001, workers at the Ferro-Alloy Factory submitted numerous petitions to a wide range of government bodies accusing plant manager Fan Yicheng and others of embezzlement, but received no response from any of them. Fan was only investigated after more than 10,000 workers took to the streets in March 2002 and publicly pressured the government to take action. The strike leaders attempted to spread their strike to neighbouring factories and for this were arrested, beaten up and jailed for subversion and terrorism.[30]

Disputes arising from the privatization of SOEs have typically dragged on for many years, as local governments, the courts and the ACFTU failed to address the widespread injustices committed against workers in the course of restructuring. Indeed, these long-running collective labour disputes amount to a festering sore. Leaders in the fight for workers' rights have been silenced, persecuted and imprisoned, while the grievances of those they represented have been ignored by those in authority and laid-off workers have been left to fend for themselves.

So great and obvious was the divergence between the promises and reality that it brought the officially-recognised trade unions and the labour laws into disrepute. And there is ample evidence that Chinese workers, especially women migrant workers, are increasingly prepared to by-pass these laws and self-organise: to go on strike, demonstrate in public, and take direct action such as blocking major roads, even wrecking offices or work completed.[31]

The then President and Party Secretary Hu Jintao and Premier Wen Jiabao, concerned that such hard line measures were not reducing the number of independent labour actions, introduced a softer approach and launched a campaign calling for a "harmonious society".

Now, it is not uncommon to see court staff racing to a flashpoint where workers are publicly protesting, in desperate attempts to defuse the situation and restore social stability by giving free advice on how to take the dispute through the courts. For the time being the police are being reined in and while strike leaders are still being arrested and demonstrations broken up, any deaths are seen as a 'mishandling' of the situation and a blot on the career of the Party top responsible.[32]

Harmony as a social ideal has roots in the paternalistic and hierarchical ethics of Confucius. Efforts have even been made to harmonise Confucius with Marx, but this is something that can be achieved only by entirely eliminating Marx's concepts of class struggle and revolution. The appeal to Confucianism is intended to give modern concepts a veneer of Chinese exceptionality and promulgate the idea that the PRC is following a uniquely Chinese path for the good of the country as a whole.[33]

The appeal to "social harmony" has meant that the regime has had to offer concessions to peasants and workers. In respect of the peasants, the government has reduced taxes, raised prices for farm products and provided subsidies; whereas for city workers, it introduced a substantial increase in the minimum wage in May 2015. Simultaneously, in both rural and urban areas the regime promises the expansion of educational provision and healthcare services. The government is also pledging a significant improvement in pensions provision – no doubt hoping to enlarge the internal market. Great publicity is being given to bringing the most openly corrupt of the CCP cadres to justice and there have been some high profile trials. The need to appeal for social harmony is a façade to convince workers, especially, to trust the CCP leaders and do nothing to threaten the present system.[34]

The state also excuses itself to the working class by presenting its current economic problems as being shared worldwide, that the solutions proposed are common to all workers internationally. For example, Britain's 'Workfare' programme was used as an example to support China's own plan to deny benefits to workers who do not join re-training schemes.[35]

16.5 The Official Trade Union

The fundamental right of all workers – the right to strike – was deleted from China's Constitution in 1982. The state, however, makes a point of never arresting workers for strike actions, the charges are invariably damage to property, public disorder or assault, but these are widely used. Despite the law regarding Trades Unions being amended twice since then, once in 1992 and again in 2001, workers remain denied their basic democratic rights of free association, free collective bargaining and strike action. The ultimate strength of the working class comes from collective action, to deny the class that right is to hamstring it in the face of the employers and their state.

The ACFTU is the only legally-permitted trade union in China and has a very close structural relationship with the CCP, with considerable overlap in membership and with key ACFTU personnel, even at a local level, appointed on CCP advice.[36] The ACFTU was (and is) not a union as understood in the West, but rather a branch of government staffed by careerists whose primary role is to ensure the workers accept government policy. Just like union leaders in capitalist countries these people ensure union power at the point of production is paralysed. To date, the reality has been that if workers take industrial action they find themselves confronting a bloc consisting of the employers, the state (police), and the ACFTU – which has, on occasion, hired thugs to break picket lines and beat up strikers.

Union officials will visit trade union members who are sick or injured and ensure they receive their due payments, arrange New Year parties, works' outings, sports days and, a speciality of China, matchmaking events, but their key tasks are to maximise productivity and minimise work stoppages whether due to accidents or industrial actions.

However, the form of the official trades union has changed and developed under the pressure of events and government directions. Traditionally, the ACFTU had the bulk of its membership in the huge SOEs of the north east and in government departments. It received its income not from the dues paid by workers but by direct payment from the government, typically 2% of the payroll. The post of trade union branch chairperson carried with it the salary and benefits of a deputy director of the relevant enterprise, and this was a post for life if the activities of the workers were kept within limits acceptable to the enterprise.[37]

A collapse in ACFTU membership and income occurred during the 1990s as the SOEs shed staff in preparation for privatisation. In a decade, membership fell from about 40% of the country's workforce to just over a quarter. However, with the explosive growth in the number of workers in the SEZs and outbreaks of wildcat strikes and other actions, the government decided the ACFTU should make a determined attempt to establish itself in the private sector as a mechanism for controlling the militancy of the workforce, and increasing the profitability of the enterprises. Over the next five years the ACFTU increased its membership massively and, in an echo of its Stalinist past, professed to have recruited 110% of the workforce in some areas.

These recruitment drives were largely paper exercises whereby the ACFTU, working through the regional or town Trade Union Council, contacted all those companies in a given area with more than 25 employees and reminded them they were legally obliged to have a union and, in many cases, guaranteed no collective actions. The employers signed up with the ACFTU, usually without mentioning it to the workers and were allowed to appoint the company's union representative, typically the Head of the Personnel Department.

It must be understood that the workers themselves played little or no part in this recruitment drive. In many, possibly most, cases the workers were unaware that they had become members of the ACFTU, which negotiated directly with the employer for the block recruitment of all workers (and managers) in the company. Union dues would be paid by the company as a percentage of the payroll in a direct continuation of arrangements made in the SOEs.[38] Ching Kwan Lee carried out a study of trade union structure in the SEZs and she found that in most cases, enterprise managers were the union officials. Of 250 enterprises examined, senior managers were the branch chairmen in 144 cases, and middle managers in most of the remainder; in only very few cases did shop-floor workers hold even the most minor union posts.[39]

Typically, the owners of a company establish the shell of a union, appoint managers as the required officers and register the union with the ACFTU, paying all the necessary monies. Once recognised, and there are no recordings of such submissions being rejected, any attempt by the workers to organise outside of this company union is illegal and any activists are open to arrest, to be stripped of their residence permit and returned to their villages.

For example, NCW, a Taiwanese-owned enterprise in Shilou Town, Guangdong, employed 550 (mainly) migrant workers who had not been given contracts. As part of the ACFTU recruitment drive the Shilou Town Trade Union Council (STTUC) urged NCW to set up a "grassroots union". Under pressure from the local Party committee, NCW completed the required paperwork, paid membership fees to the STTUC, and received an official document declaring the establishment of a NCW union, but took no further action. The workers were kept completely ignorant of this process.

Subsequently, a group of migrant workers with some previous experience of factory work arrived at NCW and challenged the company's illegal labour practices. In the belief that a trade union would help them they approached the STTUC only to be told they were already in a union and must cease their efforts of self-organisation because Chinese Trade Union Law prescribes that only one union can exist in an enterprise. In the meantime, the employer acted quickly, called all the managers (who were, of course, union members) to a meeting and activated the union by appointing the HR manager to the post of union branch chairperson. Naturally, the workers refused to participate but its existence meant that no genuine trade union could be legally established.[40]

A second example is Foxconn. Eight years after its founding (2006), the management of the Longhua plant set up a trade union. This was done at this time because of the double pressure of adverse media publicity about working conditions in Foxconn factories, and the Shenzhen Federation of Trade Unions. The Foxconn union chairwoman is a special assistant to the CEO with corresponding pay and conditions.[41] However, it appears that participation in the union is not encouraged, and a survey found that about 90% of Foxconn workers claim to have never heard of elections for union officials.

A variant of these recruitment processes is where the ACFTU establishes a regional union which attempts to organise all the workers in a particular trade across a number of small factories, and may have been introduced because the ACFTU leadership wanted to head off and prevent a movement similar to Solidarity in Poland. These unions are independent of any one employer but remain highly dependent on the CCP and state policies. The process of recruitment is the same but because the union branch covers a number of small firms there is a tendency for wages to rise to the level of the highest, which is popular with the workers. This system is accepted by the employers because it is backed by the state, acts to control worker militancy and, in the final resort, is of net benefit to the enterprise.

This then, was the policy of the ACFTU during the growth of the SEZs. However, there were three serious problems with it. Firstly, workers were generally unaware that they had become members of the ACFTU, so it had little direct effect on employee-employer relations. Secondly, the ACFTU had, in the main, negotiated with the larger employers but, at that time, it was workers in the medium and small private companies (less than 1,000 employees) who were walking off the job, demonstrating, threatening to commit suicide in public, besieging plants, setting fire to facilities, and even holding bosses captive. The third problem was that few ACFTU officers had any experience of dealing with workers who were in conflict with management, and even fewer had any sympathy with the workers.

However, the impact of second and third generation migrants is having its effect on the workplace. From a very small start, and despite being a very contradictory process, genuinely elected workers' representatives are beginning to appear. In many cases they emerge during (unofficial) strike action, actively representing the strikers and continue in this role when the strikes are over. At one Shenzhen toy factory, the workers elected five representatives, three of whom were women who had led a recent strike and organised the picket lines, blocking police action. However, such shop stewards are often fired on some pretext once the industrial action is over and the situation defused.

At the same time, the lowest levels of the ACFTU bureaucracy are increasingly having to face angry workers who are taking industrial action and try to get them to end their protests and return to work. This can be very uncomfortable for them. In such a situation the full-time union officials can find it beneficial have the staff approve (but not choose) the leadership (officers) of the local branch. To date, the one and only time an ACFTU branch has opposed a company's actions, it was led by such a branch officer.[42] As the class struggle develops the lower echelons of the bureaucracy, those in daily contact with the workers at the point of production, are subject to pressures that make it very difficult for them to behave in an openly dictatorial and class collaborationist manner. Once class struggle is in the air it is quite possible that a number of bureaucrats will side with the workers. Experience shows that a small number of union bureaucrats will give up the gravy train and side with the workers, but only so long as the latter remain steadfast.

As a general rule, Walmart is opposed to the unionisation of its workforce. China is an exception. No doubt the decision was made easier by the ACFTU's history of subverting effective collective bargaining.

The creation of the Walmart workers union for more than 100,000 workers in the company's 400 stores followed the usual pattern, being little more than an exchange of correspondence, completion of forms followed by the payment of union dues by Walmart. The process was undertaken quietly, on a store-by-store basis which kept workforce awareness and unity to a minimum. Once the local Walmart store manager received notice that the store was being unionised, the union officers were selected from the store's managers.

Early in 2014, as part of its response to the slowdown in China's economy, Walmart suddenly announced the closure of its store in Changde, Hunan province. To everyone's surprise, Huang Xingguo chairperson of the store's ACFTU branch, led over 75 workers in a strike against the closure, throwing a 24-hour picket line around the delivery depot to prevent the company from removing goods from its shuttered building.

Despite the company and the local authorities joining forces and the police being sent in to clear the site of pickets, the workers' determination and the publicity surrounding the event meant the detained workers were released and the pickets were able to return the next day. The outcome was that Walmart was forced to go to arbitration, to negotiate with the strikers, and significantly increase the severance deal.[43]

It was at this time that the ACFTU had launched its so-called 'grassroots' initiative so that in a small number of enterprises the branch chairperson was subject to election by, or approval of, the workforce. Huang was one such. Huang says he was motivated by a sense of the injustice being suffered by his fellow workers: "I knew I needed to help the workers, … I knew that if I didn't, I would not be able to forgive myself."[44]

The Walmart strike has been widely hailed as small but symbolic. Huang's participation as chair of the ACFTU branch made a tremendous difference to the combativity and level of organisation of the workers. The case of Huang Xingguo has been hailed as of enormous significance, for reactionaries it is a warning of the dangers of democratisation of the ACFTU, and for militants it is a pointer to the advantages that can be gained by working within the official trade union movement.[45]

16.6 The 2015 Labour Regulations

The measures taken by the government and the ACFTU have been largely ineffective in halting the rise in worker militancy and the rapid increase in the number of strikes. In the five years from 2011 to 2015 inclusive, there has been a sevenfold increase in the number of strikes. Furthermore, strikes are taking place in sectors previously immune, such as the state-owned power company (State Grid) which, in reply to workers' demands for a pay increase and equal pay for equal work, has sought to push through an unpopular wage structure which would seriously disadvantage the lowest paid.

Of course, the government would love to continue its collaboration with the employers, ignoring labour law violations by companies, harassing activists and sending police with dogs to restrain any action by the workers. But such a policy is of decreasing effectiveness because, despite increased police activity, there are objective factors making the workers more militant.

The bourgeoisie themselves, recognise a number of factors for the increasing unrest on the factory floors[46]:

i. The growth rate of the Chinese economy as a whole has slowed to 7.4%, but manufacturing activity in areas such as Guangdong is actually contracting with consequential strikes against worker lay-offs, cuts in working hours, replacement of full-time staff with temporary workers, failure of factory owners to have in place statutory redundancy schemes to compensate workers, workers finding out that pension payments have not been made (sometimes for decades), and so on. As a result, workers of all ages and backgrounds are united against the threat of unemployment or pension poverty, and are prepared to take action for what they see as their legal rights.

ii. The available data shows a zero increase in the number of workers in the core age group available and wanting work in the SEZs, which means a stronger bargaining position of those on the shop floor.

iii. Workers better understand their rights and are becoming better organised. NGOs such as the China Labour Bulletin operate hotlines, drop-in centres and other outreach activities to raise workers' awareness of their legal rights to minimum wage rates, to limits on overtime hours, the requirement of the employer to pay pension contributions, health and welfare contributions, and even housing support. These organisations have long been the subject of government harassment but continue to give advice on how the workers can self-organise, and how to use the ACFTU to maximum advantage.

v. The first time police break the picket line and arrest strike leaders it is a major trauma for the workers involved, but the second time round the workers are prepared and the shock effect is substantially reduced. The brutality of the police and the ACFTU thugs is a diminishing asset to the state.

As the economic situation in China deteriorates, workers' struggles will inevitably become more intense. One solution could be to make repression more severe and such a trend has been observed in the *de facto* criminalisation of strike actions by the increasing frequency of striking workers being charged with criminal rather than civil offences. However, the recent response of the government has been to launch a raft of measures to head-off worker militancy and divert it into channels safe for the regime rather than embark on open confrontation. The first step was a move by the government to take the wind out of the sails of pay demands by approving an increase in minimum pay rates, up 19% in Guangdong the most militant area in China. The government obviously believes that as long as the workers feel they are making gains under the present system they will not radicalise.

More importantly for the future are the changes being made to industrial relations and the role of the ACFTU. This body, with 260 million members and nearly one million officers, is widely seen by workers as, at best, ineffective and all recent strikes (bar the one at Walmart) have been initiated from outside the ACFTU. New regulations issued by the People's Congress of Guangdong set out a new framework for collective bargaining and dispute resolution in which the ACFTU is expected to take more and firmer control of employee demands and collective bargaining. Given the importance of Guangdong to the national economy these proposals must have originated in Beijing.

The new regulations provide a structure which seeks to give an additional layer of control over the workers. First, and by far the most important, these new regulations (Article 24) make strike action, and incitement to strike action, unlawful during any "collective consultations". During such times the workers must act "peacefully and rationally". The obligation on the workers not to strike means there can be no immediate, effective response by the workers to remedy unilateral actions by the employers – an arbitrary reduction in piece rates, cutting ten minutes off the lunch break, etc.

The new Guangdong regulations show clear signs of having been drafted based on the experience of anti-trade union legislation in force elsewhere. Only demands which have the support of at least 50% of the workforce can be submitted, must be channelled through a branch of the ACFTU, and must be "reasonable".[47] Any demands for higher pay must be in accord with agreed performance criteria and based on the profits of the enterprise. The 50% figure is designed to appear reasonable but, in reality, to limit the activities of militants. The extended period allowed for negotiation will permit the enterprise to either wear down the workers or organise to transfer its facilities elsewhere, The Economist summed up: "The regulations effectively shut the door to the kind of spontaneously-formed groups of workers that have often taken the lead in Guangdong's strikes."[48]

The largest single cause of strikes in the Guangdong SEZs is factory owners attempting to move their enterprises to a new location surreptitiously to avoid paying wages owed, to avoid paying pension and other contributions, and to avoid paying compensation for redundancy, etc. Here, more than in any other element, the new regulations show their class bias. The regulations spell out that workers in dispute over a factory closure may not obstruct the removal of equipment and materials, nor may a worker who learns of such a plan convey that information to his/her colleagues because that would be construed as breach of Article 22, as engaging in actions that "intensify conflict".

The only fig leaf is the supposed protection for the workers' negotiators who may not be sacked while the negotiations are proceeding, unless the employer informs the class-collaborationist ACFTU and listens to any objections the ACFTU might make.

Importantly, the regulations seek to divide the workers by not providing cover for the temporary workers who comprise such a large proportion of the workforce in the SEZs. This is a deliberate attempt to subvert worker solidarity, precisely because in a number of important recent strikes there has been a noticeable level of mutual support between migrants and resident workers.

Those with experience of trade union negotiations know full well that employers invariably try to protract negotiations in an attempt to erode and break worker solidarity and facilitate the transfer of its facilities to a new site. The new regulations allow the employer to drag out the negotiations for at least ninety days after which the dispute goes to mediation – a process which might take further months, during which time the workers must continue with the wages and conditions previously existing.[47]

In the major strikes that have occurred in 2015 since the Guangdong regulations were announced, the ACFTU, despite representations from the workers concerned, has unquestioningly continued its previous policy of openly supporting the employer against the workers. Two actions, in particular, were widely reported.

The most widely reported action was by workers at the Shenzhen factory of Artigas Clothing and Leatherware.[49] In December 2014, about 1,000 workers at Artigas struck for nine days in an effort to get the company to listen to their demands for unpaid overtime and unpaid social insurance. The workers' leaders requested the local trade ACFTU union to intervene on their behalf, but on the morning of 18 December hundreds of police descended on the factory to arrest the strike leaders and disperse the picket lines. The workers were forced to return to work.

In June 2015 the dispute escalated when Artigas management began to remove equipment and machines from the factory without notice or negotiation with workers. More than 900 Artigas workers struck and occupied the factory plants from 9 June to prevent management from secretly removing the remaining machinery from the premises.

Artigas hoped that by formally offering to retain staff, even though the move would make it very difficult for the workers to actually transfer, it could avoid paying workers the severance and other social insurance payments they were entitled to under current regulations. By shutting down with no notice, the company hoped to complete the move before the workers could respond, and because few if any workers, would or could transfer, such a move would end the ongoing disputes over arrears in the payment of social security contributions and overtime.

These actions were taking place under the new regulations so a key issue was the refusal of management to enter collective negotiation with the workers concerning the closure and the resettlement scheme. An interim meeting was held between management and workers' representatives at the start of July, but the workers' request for collective negotiation was rejected. Subsequently, the management unilaterally terminated any further negotiation and announced that they would only communicate with the workers individually, a well-known divide-and-conquer technique for breaking the solidarity of the workers and preventing them from using their collective power.

Artigas workers travelled to Guangzhou, the capital city of Guangdong province, to present a petition to the Provincial Government, but the group was treated as an illegal gathering and sent back to Shenzhen in a bus escorted by police cars. On arrival the delegation were all arrested and detained overnight!

As part of their strategy, the management attempted to buy off a leading representative of the workers, Wu Weihua, offering her 150,000 Yuan (about UK£15,000 or US$20,000). She refused this bribe and was sacked. On the first day of the strike the police removed more than ten workers, including Wu Weihua. All were released later the same day except Wu. According to the police, she was "seized by the factory", meaning that the management had told the police to detain her. Importantly, the police did not follow their normal procedure of charging a striker with a civil offence, but instead charged Wu with the criminal offence of 'obstructing public administration'. This meant she could spend a month or more in jail before being brought to court.

Soon the police returned to the factory and detained five more workers and then told them that if they ended the strike and accepted 500-1,000 RMB per person as compensation, they would be released. Reluctantly, the workers agreed. The five detained workers walked free, but Wu remained in jail facing trial.[50]

This example demonstrates certain historical characteristics of workers' struggles across China. The workers involved tend to use the organisations at hand and the efforts by many Chinese workers to gain the support of the ACFTU in the struggle against their employers is confirmation. The new regulations recognise this and attempt to use it to the advantage of the Chinese bourgeois. The ACFTU will come under intense and contradictory pressures to make the occasional militant noise and lead the negotiation of pay and conditions for groups of workers, while simultaneously they will have to tell the workers that they can take no collective actions to help their demands. This process is just beginning and events thus far show that it will be a highly contradictory and convulsive one, with the lumbering, bureaucratic machinery of the ACFTU struggling to cope with the changes to be made.

The CCP wishes the ACFTU to head off worker militancy by taking control of negotiations on pay and conditions but the process will not be helped by the large number of important posts within the union held by senior managers of capitalist enterprises. They will oppose any change that impacts adversely on profitability. That the government will hold responsibility for the mediation procedures will involve it directly in industrial disputes which will open the door to the underlying political issues. The process may backfire badly because the tide of worker militancy is rising at a rate that may swamp any attempts by the ACFTU to contain it.

How militants can use the local ACFTU branch to aid their struggles is by no means clear. However, today the workers' movement has considerable experience of state-run unions, for example, in Stalin's Russia and Mussolini's Italy. In September 1934, the fascist regime in Italy passed a law ending the top-down appointment of all officials and giving a thin layer of elected officers the responsibility for negotiating minor elements such as toilet facilities. Militants who stand for such posts should ensure that the elections involve the greatest number of union members and are discussed at branch meetings, not only so that activists get to know each other but members discuss union democracy and the role of shop stewards. The new Guangdong regulations state (Article 13): "Negotiations representatives for the employees shall either be selected by the trade union or by a democratic election by the staff and workers that is organised by the trade union." If this loophole remains open then it should be used by militants to campaign on pay, conditions and union democracy.

16.7 The Growth of Inequality: Woman After the "Reforms"

The last thirty years has seen the creation of many millions of jobs, mostly in the private sector, and mostly taken by peasants moving from the countryside to better their living conditions. This engendered tremendous support for the regime, but now things are different. The migrant workers are no longer grateful for being given a job, any job; they are demanding decent wages and conditions. At the same time there is tremendous resentment in those areas which houses the giant SOEs and where living and working conditions are much worse than ever before. These developments have been accompanied by an enormous and growing polarisation between the classes. Huge social disparities are evident: in a generation, the top richest 10% have acquired 85% of the nation's assets.[51] Of course, there is no inheritance tax.

Incomes are similarly skewed. The top 5% pay themselves 23% of China's total household income but the bottom 5% receive a miserly 0.1%.[52] A new wealthy bourgeois class is being created but there are many millions unemployed or under-employed, particularly in the so-called rust belt. It is now a common sight, even in Beijing, to see poor locals clamouring to wash the windows of the Rolls Royces of dollar millionaires.[53] These glaring social inequalities are a major source of discontent, as is the obvious corruption of state and Party officials.

The Gini coefficient is an internationally recognised measure of how a nation's income is distributed amongst its citizens. A Gini coefficient of zero represents a society in which all citizens have equal income. A Gini coefficient of 100 is where one single citizen receives all the income and every other citizen receives nothing. The OECD, United Nations and other international bodies claim that a Gini coefficient of greater than about 40 represents a society with an unacceptably skewed income distribution and potentially destabilising social inequality.

China has not made its Gini coefficient public since 2000, when the figure was 41. Unofficially, Chinese media reported that it stood at 47.4 in 2012. At that level China is more unequal than Indonesia at 34.3, India at 36.8, and the US at 40.8 The urban Gini has remained between 47 and 49 for the past decade, indicating that China has become one of the most unequal societies in the world.[54]

Giant luxury skyscrapers sprout but are surrounded by immense areas of urban poverty. This growing social divide is symbolised by the fact that far fewer Chinese have access to clean water than to a cell phone. This alone would be enough to provoke class struggles in China, where the manners and practices of the newly rich are increasingly reminiscent of the behaviour of pre-revolutionary landlords resulting in the Xinhua agency claiming: "If the trend goes unchecked, ... the widening gap may trigger social unrest."[55]

For women overall, participation in the workforce increased from about 30% during the early years of the reform, to 40% in the 1990s and to about 45% today. However, when the SOEs were preparing for privatisation it was policy to sack women before men, thus the employment rate for urban female labour declined from 75% in 2000 to 61% in 2010, the lowest for thirty years.

At the same time relative pay has decreased. In 1988, the average woman worker earned 55% of the wage of an average male worker, by 1994 this figure had declined to 42%, and today, on average, is about one third. The government has a policy of equal pay for equal work, but even where men and women do the same work, the pay of a Chinese woman is typically only about two-thirds that of the man. The proportion of women in work is rising but their wage rates are falling, relatively. The explanation is that under the reforms women are increasingly being employed in unskilled, low-paid jobs while, simultaneously, pay differentials have risen sharply.[56]

Market forces are exacerbating gender earnings inequality. Cross-sector analyses show that the gender earnings gap is smallest in government and public institutions and largest in the private sector. Increasingly, women are employed on a production line, in a service industry or clerical job with lower income and fewer fringe benefits. As would be expected, few of these women are CCP members.[57]

At a time when the Chinese government is bewailing a shortage of skilled workers, women receive significantly less education than men, on average 7.5 years as against 8.5 years. Universities blatantly enforce gender discriminatory entry policies. Because women now regularly score better marks in China's all-important college entrance exams, universities and colleges raise the admissions standards for women leaving women with higher marks than male entrants without a place.[58] Many university courses regularly refuse female applicants; no women are allowed on many engineering degrees which guarantee a senior job after graduation.

That discrimination is increasing, is important. Practices which put the man on a pedestal simply because he is male show how centuries-old discrimination can resurface in the 21st Century if social conditions are right. The drive towards capitalism has strengthened and encouraged practices from the imperial era that even the Stalinist regime of Mao considered abominations.

Since about 2007 the government, with the active support of the All China Women's Federation (ACWF, staffed by Party bureaucrats), has been waging a widespread, raucous and misogynistic campaign against those women who dare to choose not to marry. The reason given is that unmarried males are turning to activities which "endanger the social order,including, gambling, rioting, stealing and gang fighting."[59] China has one of the highest male to female ratios in the world, about 120:100. For comparison, India has a ratio of about 115:100. Both imbalances are due primarily to sex-selective abortions. This implies that in some rural areas of China as many as one in ten foetuses which would have been born a girl are aborted. This is an astounding number. The practice remains illegal but the figures show that while the law was largely enforced in the workers' state, the capitalist regime closes its eyes to the matter.

Long gone are the days when members of the ACWF would publicly confront a violent husband and teach him the error of his ways. Instead, China is in the middle of an epidemic of violence against women. There is no law in China specifically concerned with domestic violence and police officers attend an incident as enforcers of social stability, not to protect the victim. Yes, China classifies intentional injury as a criminal offence but in domestic cases only long-term and repeated violence, supported by independent evidence is sufficient for a judgement on behalf of the wife. Even then, the husband is likely to be awarded the family home![60]

In considering birth defects, it is notable to observe that as China's pollution levels increase there has been a sharp rise in the number of babies born with a deformity. The link between the two has been the subject of numerous scientific, even government, publications.[61] However, the official line is to place the blame for these defects on the behaviour of the mothers, marrying later in life or neglecting their health during pregnancy.[62]

The anti-woman attitude of the Deng administration showed itself early on with the enforced retirement of many leading women in the Party and state hierarchies and their replacement by men. In 2012 the Party's Organisation Department published figures to show that, at Minister level or above, 11% of officials were female, though more than 40% of Party members are women. There is no woman on the Standing Committee of the Politburo (7 members) and only two, Liu Yandong and Sun Chunlan, on the Politburo itself (25 members). Of these two, Liu Yandong is an established member of the 'Prince Party', the closed circle of senior officials who carve up money and influence in China between them. Her father was Liu Ruilong, a former Vice-Minister of Agriculture. She has taken care never to voice a political point of view in public.[63]

16.8 Summary

China has returned to capitalism. The three key indicators of this – the monopoly of foreign trade, a planned economy, and nationalisation of key industries have been reversed and replaced by a market economy with each enterprise striving to maximise its profits. The transition was initiated and overseen by a Stalinist bureaucracy greedy to retain its privileges and which saw capitalism as a safer bet than a worker's democracy.

In assessing the role of the CCP and its leaders, we must consider how well they have achieved their goals. Whatever their roots, this group has dismantled the planned economy and privatised state assets, and in so doing they have, almost without exception, acquired vast private fortunes which are invested not only in China but around the world. Their greed knows no bounds, while still raking off enormous salaries and perks as Party tops they have their villas in the south of France, their apartments in Beverley Hills and their houses in London. Their children go to the world's top private schools and, under current laws, will inherit their parent's huge fortunes. Re-reading Lenin on the British Labour Party:

> "... whether or not a party is really a political party of the workers does not depend solely upon a membership of workers but also upon the men that lead it, and the content of its actions and its political tactics. Only this latter determines whether we really have before us a political party of the proletariat. Regarded from this, the only correct, point of view, the Labour Party is a thoroughly bourgeois party, because, although made up of workers, it is led by reactionaries, and the worst kind of reactionaries at that, who act quite in the spirit of the bourgeoisie"[64]

It is unambiguously clear that the CCP is a bourgeois party.

Social inequality is growing fast, class differentiation is a fact; despite the state retaining a significant degree of control over industry and over such factors as exchange rates, an economic downturn was clearly seen in 2008. Today state control is much less and the threat of a world crisis of overproduction is growing fast. China produces as much steel as the rest of the world combined and overproduction has meant the price of steel price in China is now less per tonne than cabbage.

Monopoly capital, of which Foxconn is an extreme example, is creating gigantic global-scale factories that dominate the lives of Chinese workers. Foxconn and its fellows have been enabled by an economic transformation at a national level in which the leadership of the CCP has chosen to ally itself with and become part of big business in the belief that this will allow it to continue running China. What Foxconn provides is living proof of Trotsky's analysis made near the end of his life that modern monopoly capitalism does not rest on competition and free private initiative but on centralised command. There is an identity of outlook and interests between capitalist cliques at the head of these giant companies, banking consortia, etc., and those holding state power. They collaborate at every step and neither can allow free trade unions.[65] This has been taken to extremes in China where the same group (CCP members) are in control of government, trade unions, and many of the most important industrial enterprises and banks.

The alliance extends from local governments reducing relocation costs, maintaining minimum wages at artificially low levels, acting as the recruiting sergeants for incoming factories, to labour laws which effectively outlaw strikes. We have seen that to maximise profit from these factories the bourgeoisie has restructured the form of the relationship between bourgeois and proletarian. These forms, including residence permits and dormitory-labour schemes, are subjecting workers to more intense exploitation and great hardship and suffering. Contradictions between capital and labour are accumulating at the point of production and, notwithstanding an alliance of state, unions and employers, are resulting in increasing levels of struggle by the Chinese proletariat.

Chapter 17
Workers in Struggle

17.1 Introduction

The new working class in China has had to struggle against both capital and state every step of the way from its very inception. It struggles against the state in the form of the ACFTU and the police, both of whom actively support the employers and strike break. Migrant workers also struggle against the state for the democratic right to settle in industrial cities and towns of their choice. In respect of their struggle against capital, these predominantly women workers must look for ways of organising outside the official trade unions but also in ways that also counteracted the discipline of the dormitory-labour regime.[1]

Chinese workers increasingly self-organise within their individual workplaces to press for higher wages, on-time payment of wages and social security benefits. It is claimed that, in Guangdong alone, there is now at least one strike a day involving over 1,000 workers, with many smaller strikes occurring. So far, these individual strikes have not coalesced into a broader, co-ordinated movement, which would, almost certainly, incur a speedy government crackdown.

17.2 Recent Workers Struggles

One of the great strengths of the workers in factories feeding multi-national enterprises was demonstrated on 17 May 2010 when Tan Guocheng (a second generation migrant worker) pressed the emergency stop button on his assembly line at the Honda transmission factory in Foshan, and exhorted 1,900 of his co-workers mostly in their late teens and early twenties to follow him on a strike for a doubling of the basic rate. The managers, moved quickly and promised to meet the workers' demands but immediately fired Guocheng and another leader. The workers' response was to shut down the plant in a strike that lasted two weeks, this time taking care not to identify their leaders.[2,3]

Local government, the ACFTU, and the employers combined to bring the strike to an end. Representatives from the local technical schools were brought in to threaten trainees that they would not get their diplomas if they continued the strike. The ACFTU trucked in a gang of about 100 thugs (in yellow ACFTU caps) to bully the workers back to work, but the sight of their fellow workers being beaten to the ground made other groups of workers in the plant threaten to stop work and the thugs were withdrawn.

Appreciating that solidarity is the great strength of striking workers, the ACFTU and the management met each worker separately in a joint effort break the strike. The company promised they would not retaliate or dismiss any worker and would give a substantial pay increase, but whilst a few workers capitulated, the great majority said no.[4]

Honda, like most multinationals relies on a long and complex supply chain and in two weeks, the strike at the Foshan transmission plant had paralysed Honda's operations in the whole of China. Finally, Honda offered pay rises of between 30% and 50% and added a housing subsidy of 50 yuan per month. This split the strikers who returned to work on 31 May, but it was not a complete victory, as the two sacked leaders were not reinstated.

The Honda strike was not an isolated incident. There had been a significant level of industrial strife in China over the preceding period, the most violent being two major incidents at SOEs about to be privatised. In the second week of August 2009, thousands of workers organised a protest successfully opposing privatisation of the state-owned Linzhou Steel Corporation, in Anyang City, Henan province. This action involved the workers kidnapping the state official sent to oversee the takeover. Many of these workers were to lose their jobs, but all were to lose their pensions, medical care and housing allowances. Fengbao Iron and Steel, the private group to which Linzhou Steel was going to be sold at less than half its estimated value is owned by Li Guangyuan, who started his business empire by taking over a TVE using his position as village Party secretary to secure a good deal.[5] Protests were all the more forceful because Fengbao has a poor record of social insurance payments, unpaid wages and the illegal seizure of farmland.[6]

Around the same time there was a serious strike and riots at the state-owned Tonghua Iron & Steel Corporation, in Jilin province. The Corporation was to be sold to a private company, the Beijing-based Jianlong Heavy Machinery Group, and the workforce reduced from about 30,000 to approximately 5,000. With this announcement, a spontaneous stoppage of work and a mass demonstration including local residents and workers from other plants occurred. The local authorities responded by mobilising thousands of police who engaged in street battles to break up the protest, during which the new general manager appointed by Jianlong, Chen Guojon, was killed. The regional government was forced to cancel the privatisation of the company and bring it back under state ownership.[7]

Irrespective of China's heavy censorship of Facebook, Twitter, and the internet generally, word of such events circulates and one incident will influence and even spark another.[8] During April and May 2014, thanks to chatrooms, blogging and text messages, a strike of previously unknown magnitude and length broke out in six factories in Dongguang owned by the Taiwanese multinational Yue Yuen. On 14 April as many as 48,000 workers downed tools over severance pay, wage arrears and non-payment of medical insurance, pension contributions, injury compensation, housing allowance, and other so-called fringe benefits. The public activities of both strikers and the police were immediately reported on the internet for all to see.

In terms of the new capitalist China this was an historic event. Police were called in to break the strike and the internet carried videos of strikers being beaten. Almost immediately, pickets were thrown up around stores selling Yue Yuen products (such as Adidas, Nike, and Timberland) in Los Angeles, Manchester, Melbourne, New York, Oxford, San Francisco and Taiwan.[9] The outcry had an effect and in an unprecedented step the government ordered the factory to increase wages and pay its social security contributions. Simultaneously two independent militants, Zhang Zhiru and Lin Dong, arrested and held in jail for two days for assisting the strikers, were released.

Public sympathy and media attention have also made the authorities less quick to arrest and haul workers away.[10] Some companies, such as Honda, have international reputations to protect and their sales would suffer if they were seen to endorse the use of force to repress striking workers, especially where those strikers are women.

Unofficial strikes (those not organised by or approved by the ACFTU) have hit a number of multinational firms in the manufacturing sector, from Foxconn to IBM, Honda, Cooper Tire and Rubber, Walmart, and Microsoft. According to the Hong Kong-based China Labour Bulletin,[11] the number of "collective actions" from July to September 2014 was nearly double compared with the same period the previous year and in the first quarter of 2105 the figures for strikes rose by another 15%. Importantly, "collective actions" are spreading beyond China's manufacturing centre of Guangdong, where the number of strikes has remained more or less constant, to inland China and major cities such as Wuhan and Chengdu. These movements are an important indication of what is to come.[12]

Mining is another industry where the regime has destroyed any basis of support amongst the workers. Coal supplies almost three-quarters China's energy needs and the coal industry was one of the first to be privatised when, at the end of the last century, the central government closed down or contracted out to private entrepreneurs most small and middle-sized state-owned coal mines. Soon after, many large-scale state-owned mines were also contracted out to private operators.

For decades the leaders of China have pleaded with China's coal miners to increase production as a service to the country, This culminated in 2008 with President Hu Jintao's visit to the coal fields of Datong in Shanxi Province, the heart of China's coal country, where he pleaded with miners to ensure essential supplies to guarantee the steady and rapid development of the economy. At the time energy shortages and rising coal prices made coal mining very lucrative. The apparently insatiable demand for coal in China attracted unscrupulous business people eager for profit and unconcerned with the lives of others, so that mine outputs greatly exceeding safe production levels.[13]

The workers and the ACFTU responded with enthusiasm, and in a spirit of co-operation agreed to accept the government line that privatisation would increase production. The new operators and subcontractors were allowed to hire inexperienced rural migrants to work in the mines. The result was an increase in production and profitability, but a simultaneous drop in wage rates and a catastrophic collapse in safety standards. According to government figures over 50,000 miners have died in accidents since the turn of the century, peaking at 7,000 in 2002. These are the reported data, the real figures are much higher. Local authorities conceal accidents or under-report fatalities to the higher authorities, especially in cases of accidents involving fewer than 10 deaths when mine operators have been known to move the corpses to other locations and pay the victims' families compensation if they promise to keep quiet.

The government's mine privatisation programme and its licensing and approval procedures are an open invitation to corruption. Collusion between mine owners, operators and local government officials to cover up accidents and evade punishment is now widespread and blatant, so that mine operators brazenly flout of the law. Li Tieying, Vice chairman of the Standing Committee of the National People's Congress (NPC), acknowledged that: "... corruption was behind almost every accident that caused exceptional loss of life." Under the present system the safety interests of miners are either ignored or openly violated. Militants are already arguing that the only effective way to protect the lives and rights of miners is to develop democratically elected and truly representative workers' organisations that can stand up to the currently overwhelming power of management and safeguard working conditions at the coalface.

However, the coal industry has been hard hit by the slowdown in China's industrial expansion, output dropped by nearly 5% in the first three months of 2015 alone, with many companies now posting losses rather than profits. The consequences for coal-face miners followed the now established pattern of non-payment of wages, wage cuts, unpaid wage arrears, lay-offs, failure to make the statutory compensation payments, etc.[14]

Workers from China's coal mines are doubly angry; at being fooled by the government, and having to shoulder the results of the economic slowdown. There have been protest strikes and mass demonstrations, but the industry continues to contract because the cause is overproduction on an international scale, with a consequent drop in the price of coal. Redcar lost its steel plant and some 2,500 jobs, but the Longmei Group, a state-owned Chinese coal company in north-eastern China's Heilongjiang province, announced in April 2015 it would lay-off half its workforce of 240,000, the single biggest job cut in China for years. Immediately several thousand protesting coal miners took to the streets in the city of Qitaihe. Scuffles with the police broke out when workers refused to disperse. The protest reportedly continued sporadically for at least one week.[15]

17.3 Women Lead and Students Join In

A sanitation workers strike in the Autumn of 2014 at the Guangzhou Higher Education Mega Center (GHEMC) – a complex of some 200,000 students – has demonstrated an important new stage in trade union struggles in China. While the ACFTU was noticeable by its absence there appeared a new factor, student support for, and participation in, the strike.

The GHMEC was cost-cutting by outsourcing and privatising local government services by contracting work to the lowest bidder. In late August 2014 an attempt was made to introduce a sub-contractor, Sui Cheng Property and Resources Development Company, which threatened the jobs of more than two hundred sanitation workers. The resulting strike, during which garbage piled up in the streets of Guangzhou's premier higher education site, sets a promising precedent for solidarity between locals and migrants, for women workers' leadership, and for student-worker collaboration.[16]

Workers were faced with signing up with the new company and accepting pay cuts, loss of benefits, loss of seniority and increased workloads, or finding a new job. Leaked documents revealed that the local government had originally budgeted for 426 sanitation workers but employed just 212, with the result that between US$11 and 16 million remains unaccounted for.

Adequate sanitation is essential for an urban environment, waste cannot be moved to other areas, and thus provides a strategic arena for labour struggles. Moreover, sanitation workers tend to be older, and the workforce is generally more stable than in light manufacturing or commercial service industries. Hence, they are more likely to stick to their jobs and fight to retain existing conditions. Additionally, they have a strong basis for holding together as the great majority of them were locals who had worked at the Center since it opened a decade previously. That said, the strike demonstrated impressive solidarity between local and migrant workers who formed about 10% of the workforce, were especially active, during the strike and comprised half the workers' representatives at the negotiating table.

The two groups, locals and migrants stood together in their demands. Early in the strike, the workers demanded that migrants be paid their lawfully due social security payments which the company had been paying to local workers, but denying migrants. This was among the demands won. Workers also demonstrated unity at the end of the strike when the new contractor offered locals immediate work for a 30-day "assessment period", while migrants were told they would have to wait. The workers refused to be split in this way, and returned to work on 12 September, only after the company retracted its earlier statements and promised all workers they would be rehired.

It is now common to see women on strike in China, but it is rare to see such a strong and visible female leadership. The GHEMC's sanitation workers are 80% female, and of the male employees, many are married to women who also work there. Initially all the elected representatives were women, but it was agreed that in the interests of sexual equality one man should join the negotiators. It was noticeable that women took the leadership role without hesitation.

A small group of students were actively engaged, attending workers' meetings and demonstrations, reporting the struggle on the internet and generally boosting morale. Hundreds, even thousands, of students, locally and at other universities expressed support for the strike. Although only a tiny proportion of the 200,000 students at GHEMC were involved, their actions set a precedent for student-worker collaboration in future struggles. This is especially important because China is experiencing sharply declining post-graduation prospects. Being a student no longer sets one apart from the working class, and these two important groups are starting to merge in their discontents. Students are increasingly experiencing the same kinds of discrimination as other migrant workers. Early in 2015, for example, Beijing denied permanent residence to graduate students not in a job or without a Masters degree or PhD![17]

The results of this strike are an important victory. But the precise gains are not as important as the experience of worker self-organisation and collaboration between locals and non-locals, and between students and workers.[18]

17.4 Overproduction and Recession

Some are arguing that the call for a 'harmonious society' by the present regime is the first stage in recognising that the provision of workers' rights such as the right to organise, to bargain collectively, will decrease strike actions. That leaders in democratic countries grant labour rights not out of altruism or a sense of fairness, but out of an acknowledgement that collective bargaining can markedly reduce the occurrence of strikes and level class conflict, is readily observable.[19]

The Chinese economy is now governed by the laws of capitalism. There has been massive investment based on the hope of an ever-growing world market. But such a scenario cannot be sustained indefinitely, and at a certain stage China will face a major economic and social crisis. It is not possible to say precisely when this will happen, or in what form, but when it comes it will be part of a world crisis of overproduction and the consequences will be an explosion of the class struggle.

This situation has been glimpsed twice already. In the period after the massive layoffs in SOEs at the end of the 1990s, Chinese capitalism experienced its first general overproduction crisis, marking a clear transition from the old bureaucratically-planned economy to the new capitalist economy of surplus production, meaning abundance for the few and cruel shortages for the many.[20]

In 2008, even before the global financial crisis had fully hit, over half of China's toy manufacturers – more than 3,600 mainly small and mid-size light engineering companies – had to temporarily shut down or went out of business completely.[21] Indeed, by October 2008 about 8,500 enterprises in Guangdong province alone had shut their doors, leaving hundreds of thousands of workers from export-oriented manufacturing industries jobless.[22] Not only were there lay-offs but, in addition, local minimal wage increases were suspended all over China and there was a significant cut in real wages of those still employed.[23]

Yet, after an initial small hic-cup, China as a whole appeared to escape relatively unscathed, largely because the government injected the equivalent of US$586 billion into the economy. This included quantitative easing to the tune of an extraordinary US$81 billion, and large state investments in infrastructure projects. These measures did protect the economy from a sharp fall in exports and did enable continued economic expansion but there were major long-term consequences, the most important being the build-up of massive overcapacity across the economy, especially in construction and heavy industry. In China, the utilisation of productive capacity is only 70-75%, compared with 79% in the US. The stimulus package failed to increase the rate of economic expansion. True the economy did continue to expand, but at a rate which, by 2014, had fallen to the lowest for a generation. Such figures herald the beginning of the end for China's 'miraculous' boom, as the reality of capitalist crisis impinges on the world's largest exporting economy.[24]

The Chinese economy now relies more heavily than in the 1990s on the world market, but the latter "is not in good shape", with the biggest threat, by far, coming from the Eurozone which produces almost a fifth of world output but is presently leading the planet into economic stagnation.[25] With its consumer spending stubbornly stuck at about 36-37% of GDP since 2010, possibly the lowest of the major economies, there is no way China could avoid suffering a substantial downturn were a slump to occur in its customer countries.

The attacks on corruption by state and Party officials must be also seen in this light. Indeed highly publicised corruption trials are for show, attempts to assuage the anger of ordinary Chinese, and distract attention from the ongoing corruption all around them. But can such moves neutralise the class struggle in China and the impact of a global recession? None of these measures are going to solve the main problem of overproduction on a world scale which threatens a sharp cut-back in Chinese industry.

China is facing a very special scissors crisis – either its annual growth rate will continue to be artificially enhanced by government funding in which case it will face even greater problems of overproduction than it does today because the world market is unable to consume the goods produced, or there will be a serious decline in the rate of economic growth with a level of industrial strife that makes today's actions look like a picnic in the park. Carrying on as before and hoping for the best is the third possible option. Government stimuli can postpone a crisis, but only at the risk of deepening it further once it comes. Such moves will only defer the day of reckoning, and the longer it is postponed the harder will be the crash.

China's annual growth rate is now in the process of inevitable and unavoidable decline. In the meantime militant actions by workers have forced wage rates up, a process not entirely unwelcome to the state because it has meant more money for consumers, boosting the internal market which they hope will make up – to an extent – for the loss in exports. The government has promised to increase pensions and minimum wage rates in an attempt to increase the home market and reduce dependence on exports, but such moves are coming late in the day. The Chinese bureaucracy is beginning to feel the constraints of the world economic crisis which is forcibly setting the agenda for its policies.

Workers in the coal-mining and steel industries, two of the sectors most affected by excess capacity, already realise the precarious nature of their employment as the government begins to rationalise what is deemed "wasteful production". These jobs, which had little to offer save security of employment, have been sustained by cheap loans from the big four state banks. The state now wants to end that remaining benefit by a concerted programme of privatisation which has forced groups of workers to engage in strike action and take their protests onto the streets, in some cases successfully. This cannot continue and the state intends to defeat this opposition, if necessary through police action.

Any decrease in the rate of expansion of China's economy will have a major knock-on effect on other national economies, and the world economy as a whole. Australia, South Africa, and particularly Latin America will all see their raw material exports hit by China's lowered growth projections. For example, China currently buys 40% of Chile's copper, and copper prices fell by 11% after the IMF published its lowered projections for China's growth. The fall in oil prices 2014-2015 was also closely related to the slowdown of the Chinese economy.

The *New York Times* of 16 December 2013, explained that China's hunger for Latin America's raw materials had fuelled the region's most prosperous decade for a generation, filling government coffers and helping halve the region's poverty rate. That era is rapidly drawing to an end. The IMF's conference in Santiago in December 2014 saw China's slowdown as the biggest challenge to Latin America's 'prosperity'. This slowdown in China's rate of expansion will turn it into a major contributing factor to a world crisis of capitalism.

A key indicator of a capitalist system is the appearance of speculative bubbles, especially property bubbles which are a clear signal of over-capacity in industry. At the time, in 2008, when the Chinese government began its quantitative easing and other measures to boost the economy, Marxists predicted that the programme would only give temporary relief, and that at the expense of gigantic speculative and inflationary bubbles.

However, the Chinese state sustained the process, generating one of the most spectacular property bubbles ever. This began in 2008 and accelerated at such a rate that by end of 2013 the area of land equivalent to that occupied by the imperial palace in Beijing was worth more, on paper, than the whole of California, including San Francisco and Los Angeles.[26] The result has been a building boom and massive oversupply with the amount of unsold commercial and residential property hitting an all-time record in 2014. This boom is staggering towards its end but the fear is that a downturn in property prices could dash hopes for a recovery of China's economy.[27]

The Chinese Government in a decision reminiscent of Margaret Thatcher's crusade for popular capitalism – to be achieved through the privatisation of the nationalised industries – decided that small investors should be allowed to borrow money from the state banks to invest in industry. Previously, government regulations had banned such activities (known as margin trading) as a form of gambling, but now the government was attempting to resuscitate the economy with the end of the housing bubble, and this was one way of injecting money into private businesses and, simultaneously, convincing millions of Chinese that they had a stake in capitalism.

After falling steadily for four years, Chinese stocks finally began to rise in the summer of 2014. Initial investors appeared to be making a handsome return with little or no effort. Soon hundreds of thousands of people were borrowing heavily in order to buy stocks and shares. As government policy fed through there was a burst of frenzied speculation and the Chinese stock market rose by 150% during 2014-2015. China's stock market, unlike those in New York, London or Hong Kong is dominated by individual Chinese investors and not institutions. In a scenario that had strong similarities with the 'Roaring Twenties' and the 1929 crash, hundreds of thousands of people borrowed heavily in order to buy shares; grandparents, migrant workers and college students were all pouring money into buying stocks and shares.[28]

But soon the price of the shares bore no relation to the values of the companies which issued them or to the profitability of those companies. For a while, China's stock market became detached from reality, the result being, despite government efforts, a collapse which left millions who had jumped on the bandwagon facing substantial personal losses. To stop the fall continuing the Chinese government effectively closed the stock market to allow the situation to cool down, to no avail. This crash undermined the authority of the Beijing government which had taken the decision to relax the rules on margin trading. It also demonstrated the dangers of capitalism and the security and relative stability of the public sector.

The simple fact is that Chinese productive capacity exceeds the limits of a capitalist world market. At the end of 2014, the official urban jobless rate was 4.6% but this figure excludes the many millions of migrant workers because when these lose their jobs they are supposed to return to their home village, and so are not included in these statistics. Unofficial estimates put the figure closer to 20%.

The problem of unemployment is not secondary, for at least twenty-five years, the bureaucracy has been determined to create sufficient jobs for a rapidly expanding workforce in an attempt to guarantee social stability and control. Should this end, the state will soon discover the consequences of depriving industrial workers of their livelihoods.

17.5 Revolution and the Question of Leadership

The policy of Party and union leaders clashes headlong with the growing mood of anger and frustration that is building up in the factories, steel plants, construction industry, mines and elsewhere. However, the growing crisis of overproduction on a world scale means there is little or no hope in conciliation between the new bourgeoisie, whose interests demand driving down living standards and, ultimately, the destruction of any free trade unions with the right to strike.

What are the tasks of Marxists and revolutionaries in this situation? Obviously, the immediate one is to analyse what is happening, to present an explanation that corresponds to the real situation in order to enter into a meaningful dialogue with workers, students, and honest CCP members. Thus, it is necessary to study the Chinese economy, society, and politics. It would be a serious error to try to deal with a complex, contradictory and historically unprecedented process on the basis of ready-made formulae which do not correspond to what the Chinese people are living through.

The CCP being both the party of government and state apparatus will be subject to all the centrifugal forces that in Western democracies are represented by a whole range of parties and other organisations. Depending on the relative strengths of those forces there could be serious divisions between the tops in the bureaucracy who are already billionaires and an integral part of big business, and those in the front line (usually men) who have to face a roomful of angry strikers (often women) and explain why nothing can be done.

It would be expected that those Party members who are union officials and thus closest to the workers' struggles, many of whom will have benefitted least from the transition to capitalism, will see their material interests best served by taking the leadership of those struggles. There will also be rank and file elements within the CCP who look with horror on the transition to capitalism in China and the inequalities it has brought. Both currents are confirmed by letters and articles that have appeared in the Chinese press. Many hark back to Maoist China. But in the present context those who seek a way out through a 'return to Mao' would find themselves forced to confront the question of workers' power and soviet democracy. The closer to the rank and file these people are the more readily they will accept such ideas. Chinese workers will not willingly accept a move back to Stalinism; they want to move forward to real workers' power, towards genuine socialism.

At the moment we are seeing a growing strike movement which, so far, in its actions has pushed the official unions to one side. If the ACFTU is to take the lead it must utilise its remaining strengths. The first is that the unions have played a significant role in the field of health, social security and the like, and so have a basis of support amongst less militant workers. Secondly, the most militant groups of workers are migrant women and due to the contract system many are transients moving from one factory to another, even from one city to another, but the local union offices and staff remain in place and, with the new regulations, a few officials are changing their strategy from outright opposition to any actions against employers, to one of listening to workers with grievances and, in rare cases, supporting them.

The official unions have the enormous advantage that when the working class begins to move, it invariably expresses itself through its traditional mass organisations, although these can be in surprising and unanticipated ways. Even today the first step taken by many workers who, for the first time, find themselves in conflict with management, is to visit the local union branch office to get advice and support. It is absolutely necessary for genuine Marxists to find a way to the rank and file of the Chinese trade union movement.

As Russia returned to capitalism the Communist Party fractured, but that has not happened in China, instead the CCP has remained in control and successfully transformed itself into a mass bourgeois party. We can correctly observe that the CCP has many millions of members and that as the class war in China heats up it will be reflected in the Party. To what degree and to what extent cannot be predicted. However, in the event of an open struggle between a wing of the CCP and the new bourgeoisie, Marxists would fight for the defeat of the main enemy, the bourgeoisie, while patiently explaining that only the transfer of power to the working class can solve the problems facing China.

The aim would be to mobilise the masses but not to defend the privileged positions of bureaucrats. While supporting opposition within the CCP (or any break away section) to the new bourgeois, Marxists would explain to the workers the need to take the power into their hands through, for example, workers' councils or factory committees, initially as organs of struggle and then as Soviet organs of workers' power. It should never be forgotten that Soviets were not an invention of the Bolsheviks or any other party, but rather the spontaneous invention of the working class. Chinese workers will want to move forward to real workers' power, towards genuine socialism.

An important consideration is that in China there has never been any Bolshevik tradition. For decades, the dominant ideology was authoritarian – Stalinist; whatever Mao said must be correct, and whatever Mao proposed must be adopted. However, since 1980, Mao's ideas have been thrown overboard. Indeed, it was no mere oversight that the Mao era was omitted from the historical review presented at the Beijing Olympic ceremony. No reminder was permitted of a non-capitalist alternative. However, Maoism is not the only tradition. There is also the important tradition of Chen Duxiu (1879-1942), and it is positive that in the recent period students and others have established Chen Duxiu societies and Marxist circles specifically to study his works. This is symptomatic of a real desire amongst many activists to discover the true ideas of Marxism.

Young workers, particularly migrant women workers, peasants, and students now have experience of the new Chinese capitalist state and growing numbers are turning against it. The great weakness of these Chinese leftists is that their struggles tend to be isolated, but this is gradually being overcome as they link-up using the internet, risking severe penalties.

A revolutionary or even workers' party is lacking but it was Chen Duxiu who first recognised the necessity of founding a revolutionary party to transform China into a workers' state. It is as true now as it was then, that Marxists and revolutionaries must take the first steps in the building of a democratic centralist Party which strives for Soviet power.

Nevertheless, proletarian consciousness is rising, and there is a sense amongst many that the left is on the verge of a leap forward. But this will only occur if workers, peasants and intellectuals find issues that unite the forces of opposition. Socialists will, of course, fight for immediate demands but pose them in a way that links day-to-day problems to the socialist transformation of society. Such demands, transitional demands as Trotsky referred to them, act as a bridge between actions taken in the struggle for bettering the condition of the masses and the idea of the socialist revolution.

The 'partial', 'minimal' demands of the masses must be supported, as every successful struggle raises the combativity of the workers involved. It might be necessary to start with small demands that are relatively easy to win in order to build up a dynamic, the speed of progress is not critical, but when workers are in struggle events tend to unfold fast. As the international capitalist system becomes ever more degrading and decadent the most advanced workers should advance a platform of transitional demands, the essence of which is that they are directed against the very foundations of the bourgeois regime. In their totality, the transitional demands seek to systematically mobilise the masses for the proletarian revolution.[29]

The socialist revolution would be unthinkable without the day-to-day struggle for advances under capitalism. Only in, and through, such struggles can the working class acquire the necessary experience and organization to challenge the capitalist system. However, any protesters must prepare to face a state apparatus which is the fusion of a monstrous Stalinist regime with the most repulsive features of capitalism.

A campaign for transitional/democratic demands could provide the basis for a powerful mobilisation of workers and peasants. In the context of a rigid, bureaucratic regime such demands would be based on a class struggle policy based on the workers' rights to act in their own interests, and almost certainly include:

- the right to make one's voice heard through public demonstrations, leaflets, newspapers and websites;
- freedom of association whether a trade union or political party;
- freedom to bargain collectively and to take industrial action on such issues as unemployment, low pay, health and safety;

- freedom to form picket lines and self-defence squads to protect them;
- a return to a national health service and free schooling;
- greater equality for all forms of labour, against social inequality, disclosure of the assets of the Party tops.

The precise demands, the way they are posed and the means by which they realised are extremely important so they have to be determined by those directly involved. Clearly, a governmental slogan will be required to bind these demands into a coherent programme. In Russia this was given substance in "All Power to the Soviets", and this may be one path for the Chinese revolution. Such a slogan would have to be built on freedom to form action committees in every factory, workplace, college, street, army barracks, and village, and for aggregates of such committees to form the cores of a new generation of democratic Soviets.

The workers would demand the renationalisation of all the main sectors of the economy and could immediately begin to take over the administration of industry, society and the state and move in the direction of socialism in the real sense of the word, not the bureaucratic caricature of Stalinism. Such a programme of popular democratic and transitional demands would be the antithesis of Stalinism. Under such conditions it would be impossible to re-impose a Stalinist totalitarian regime.

In their struggles, the workers need mass organizations and these will be, in the early stages, trade unions. It is necessary for revolutionaries in China to be active in the ACFTU, because in the structure of the CPC state, it is there that class relations are expressed most directly and immediately. Every attempt to subordinate the union to the capitalist enterprise must be opposed: instead workers must demand it supports their claims.

In China, at least initially, it will not be possible to replace the leadership of the ACFTU at the top, regional or even local level because these leaders are not elected. Additionally, the overwhelming majority of branch officers are senior managers in the enterprise which may give demands for representation on the branch committee a particularly sharp form. However, it is quite possible to militate in the factories and local union branches for the election of shop stewards and factory committees to represent the workers, and to argue that the "good practice" of co-opting strike leaders onto local branch committees is made universal.

The factory committee gives the demands of the workers an organised expression. Elected by all the factory employees, the factory committee immediately creates a counterweight to the administration. The prime significance of the factory committee lies in the fact that it becomes a kind of military HQ for layers of the working class. When, as often happens in China, there is a temporary seizure of the factory or part of it that raises in a practical manner the question of who is boss of the factory – the capitalist or the workers – and at such times the factory committee takes on special significance.

17.6 Summary

The totalitarian nature of the state and the relative inexperience of the Chinese bourgeoisie mean that a revolutionary explosion could take place with little warning. The cavalier manner in which the state has behaved towards the traditionally more important sections of the working class means the bourgeoisie in China do not have an established labour aristocracy to stand in the way of the growth of revolutionary consciousness. The previous chapter described how every stratum of workers in heavy industry suffered severely, millions of jobs lost, cuts in pay, worse working conditions, loss of sick pay, housing and pension schemes. In heavy industry there is no privileged section of workers willing to protect the regime.

The adverse effects of capitalist restoration experienced by Chinese workers have occurred while the economy has been expanding relatively rapidly. Chinese capitalism currently finds stability in its dynamism, like a cyclist it maintains her/himself because s/he is moving forward. But the world economy has its brake on and is entering a crisis of overproduction to which Chinese dynamism is making a sizeable contribution. A worldwide crisis of over production would hit China hard, the worst effects of capitalist restoration are yet to come. But a crisis-ridden world market would block the tried-and-tested safety valve for Chinese capitalism – rapid industrial expansion and an increase in exports.

Chapter 18
Uninterrupted Revolution or Permanent Revolution?

18.1 Introduction

This chapter draws together the arguments on whether the Maoist theory of stages or Trotsky's theory of the permanent revolution more accurately described the processes of the Third Chinese Revolution. It explains why it was possible for a deformed workers' state to revert to capitalism in a so-called cold process, without a revolution. Finally, it addresses whether the return to capitalism in China challenges the theory of the permanent revolution and asks whether the theory of permanent revolution remains relevant in the China of today.

The acid test of any theory is how well it measures up to reality. Has Mao's Stalinist theory of stages been proven correct by the Third Chinese Revolution, and permanent revolution proven wrong? Hardline Stalinists such as Carlos Rafael Rodríguez, Cuban Minister responsible for agrarian reform (1962–1965)[1], have continued to argue for the theory of stages. These people are now supported in their view by former Trotskyists such as the leadership of the American Socialist Workers Party who grew tired and impatient with the slow and arduous work of building a revolutionary party and chose, at the cost of basic theory, to become uncritical cheer-leaders for the Castro regime in the false hope that this would accelerate the growth of their organisation. The old Cuban leaders were primarily activists not theoreticians, and to get Russian aid and break the American blockade were willing to endorse such Stalinist concepts as the theory of stages, and there being no need for proletarian democracy or Soviets. The American SWP chose to compromise not with the best elements of the Castroist regime but the worst.

There is a parallel phenomenon that must be addressed here, one that appeared amongst the radical students who fought on the barricades in Paris in 1968, and their fellows who demonstrated on the streets of London, Rome and Berlin, and gained popularity as news of the Cultural Revolution spread. It was accepted that the theory of permanent revolution was correct and, because Mao had come to power in a semi-colonial country he must, somehow, be an 'unconscious Trotskyist' and his interpretation of the theory of stages could have no substantial differences with the theory of the permanent revolution. This view infected a number of revolutionary Marxists; people who should have known better opened the doors of their organisations to self-professed anti-Trotskyists with disastrous consequences.

Though the conclusions of the two arguments appear to be opposites, the opportunist method that gave rise to them is the same: impatience, looking for short cuts to building the revolutionary party.

18.2 New Democracy – a Necessary Stage?

Mao's *New Democracy* asserts that the bourgeois stage is necessary, that it is not possible to achieve socialism without passing through such a stage and the quickest and most efficient way of doing this is to join the national bourgeoisie in a bloc of four classes. Mao, of course, had the right to believe in any scheme he wished, but it is the responsibility of a political leader to test his/her ideas against reality. Unfortunately, just as Stalinism entered its death throes this argument has been revived by those who label Mao's theory as the two-stage, uninterrupted revolution.[2]

The essence of this argument is that there was a clear and definite bourgeois-democratic stage in the Third Chinese Revolution (and the October Revolution), and that this is an indispensable pre-requisite in all socialist revolutions. This stage, it is argued, is necessary in order to carry through, for example, the agrarian revolution which has to precede the socialist. This is a shadow of Kamenev's argument of April 1917, that because the agrarian revolution had hardly begun in Russia, therefore the bourgeois revolution had not been completed and thus a socialist revolution was premature. It is, of course, quite the opposite of Lenin, who argued consistently that the inability of the bourgeoisie to complete the agrarian revolution to the satisfaction of the peasants was the very reason a socialist revolution was possible, and that the bourgeois-democratic agrarian revolution in Russia took place only because it was preceded by the proletarian revolution.[3] Both Trotsky and Lenin (and Stalin, incidentally) agreed that the October Revolution was a socialist revolution which resulted in a workers' and peasants' government resting on the dictatorship of the proletariat.

In China it is obvious that such an intermediate, New Democratic, stage was not necessary at all. This is confirmed by six clear and undeniable facts:

- The CCP and the PLA assumed power in China without any need for an alliance with other forces. The CCP was the only party in the PRC with any real authority and the PLA was the power of the new state right from the start.
- On seizing bureaucratic capital, the properties of those at the top of the KMT, the PRC owned so much of industry and the banking system that it was in *de facto* control of the national economy. It could (and should) have had to hand, and immediately introduced, a pre-prepared national economic plan that included monopolising foreign trade and wholesale food distribution. If the CCP had proactively carried through these rational measures instead of waiting until they were forced to do so by inflation, sabotage, the US embargo and the needs of the Korean War, the regime would have been a workers' state from 1949 and the Chinese people would not have had to undergo unnecessary privation and hardship.
- The specific weight of the national bourgeoisie that remained in China after 1949 was minimal, its growth and strength was artificial, enhanced by the advantages showered on it by the PRC. When the CCP withdrew its support the national bourgeoisie was rapidly, easily and almost entirely peacefully swept from the scene. This was because the balance of forces was so strongly in favour of the CCP/PLA, which demonstrated clearly that any base the bourgeoisie had in post-revolution China was more illusion than reality.
- The policy of "Land to the Tiller" was carried through, but artificially delayed while the CCP tried to build the 'rich peasant economy' instead of paying attention to the wishes of the vast majority of the peasants – the poor and middle peasants. The agrarian revolution could and should have been carried out more rapidly, more efficiently and more thoroughly. The *New Democracy* actually delayed land reform but, as in Russia, the transition to a workers' state preceded the completion of land distribution.
- The duration of the bourgeois stage of the New Democracy could hardly have been any shorter. There was no time for the national

> bourgeoisie to significantly advance the economy before they were discarded and what they did achieve was largely due to their special treatment by the regime.

The contribution of the national bourgeoisie was, essentially, negative and corrosive. Its drive for profit made it ready to disrupt the government's economic plans and its greed meant it bribed state officials on a grand scale. Because it was working with a Stalinist bureaucracy which saw perks as its right, and which pandered to the national bourgeoisie this corruption was all-pervasive. The most significant contribution of the national bourgeoisie to the New Democracy was the level of sleaze, bribery and dishonesty it generated.

However, the most irrefutable argument for the unnatural nature of the New Democracy is obvious when one recalls that the new Chinese state had a long border with the Soviet Union. Only the Stalinist nature of the two regimes and the false creeds of socialism in one country and the theory of stages prevented a union of the two states and the immediate progression of China to a workers' state.

In both Russia and China the overthrow of the bourgeois regime took place before the agrarian revolution was finished. That both workers' states existed with a substantial private sector in agriculture should not be surprising since ownership of the land is not a deciding factor in determining the class character of a regime. The Russian dictatorship of the proletariat, first with Lenin as leader and then bureaucratically deformed, continued until 1929 based on private farming. Without Stalin's premature and forced collectivisation the situation could have continued. In China the 1st FYP which inaugurated the workers' state rested to a large extent on private farmers.

The theory of the permanent revolution readily accepts the importance of democratic demands for the mobilisation of the urban and peasant masses. However, it argues that the common interests of the reactionary elements (e.g. compradors, landlords, big bourgeoisie) in so-called backward countries and their intimate links with imperialism, means the national bourgeoisie as a whole will oppose the carrying through of the bourgeois democratic revolution. To overcome this opposition, to implement popular democratic demands (e.g. achieving national independence, overcoming hunger and famine, equality for women, control of inflation, land to the peasant, planning to overcome natural and man-made disasters, etc.), it is necessary for the oppressed sectors of society to take governmental power. With this action the natural flow of events is inevitably in the direction of the overthrow of capitalist property relations, for the establishment of a workers' state and the first steps towards socialism.

To appreciate such an analysis, and plan accordingly, was to develop a political line best matched to the actual forces that existed in China after WWII. Such an analysis is certainly not ultra-left as Stalinists have traditionally claimed. For example, handicraft workers and family shops would not have been dragooned into state controlled co-operatives, and the peasants would not have been forcibly collectivised. With Soviet democracy and workers' control of production it would have been possible, if so desired, to incorporate a privately-owned light industry into a national plan.

The belief in the necessity of a bourgeois phase caused the defeat of the 1925-27 Chinese Revolution because it limited the mobilisation of the oppressed masses to demands acceptable to the landlord families of the officers in the NRA. But even after 1949, the disadvantages of this unnecessary stage were many, including: restraining the self-organisation of the working class, denying the poor and middle peasants the right to seize land, restrictions on women's rights, waste of time, effort and money in pandering to the national bourgeoisie, and facilitating the development of widespread corruption throughout the Party and government.

History is littered with leaders such as Oliver Cromwell who held to one programme at first but carried out another under the pressure of events, Mao is another such. After 1949 Mao assessed the strength of the forces competing for a place in government, saw which way the wind was blowing and tacked accordingly. This is not surprising, it is characteristic of the petty-bourgeoisie.

Today, in late capitalism, surrendering a major gain of Marxist theory and retreating to the pre-Leninist argument that a socialist revolution must be preceded by the completion of the bourgeois-democratic stage, is openly and unambiguously counter-revolutionary. The irony is that the American SWP renounced permanent revolution in favour of uninterrupted revolution just prior to the collapse of the Stalinist regimes of Eastern Europe and Russia. Just as these bureaucratic regimes tottered and began to implode the SWP declared itself in favour of one of the basic features of Stalinism. But one cannot compartmentalise political degeneration, sacrificing permanent revolution in favour of Stalinist ideology naturally led to political decay generally in the organisation. The latest development along this trajectory was the SWP leadership's decision, during Israel's slaughter in Gaza in the summer of 2014, to embrace Zionism.[4]

18.3 Mao and Uninterrupted Revolution

Mao's uninterrupted revolution (the name was ripped from Lenin's article *Social-Democracy's Attitude Towards the Peasant Movement,* 1 September 1905)[5] contained the key assumption that the Chinese Revolution would pass through two stages. In the first stage, the bourgeois democratic revolution would be carried out by a 'united front of all revolutionary classes', including the national bourgeoisie, to overthrow the imperialists, feudal rulers and reactionary traitors. During this stage national independence would be achieved and agrarian reform implemented. Subsequently, after Chinese capitalism had developed separately from international imperialism to a degree that made the transition to socialism possible, the capitalists would peacefully (it was hoped) step aside and allow the revolution to move to a second stage in which the CCP would lead China to socialism. Finally, the new workers' state would adopt the policy of Peaceful Coexistence, thus allowing the CCP to preserve its own narrow national power base.

The CCP always argued that the ultimate goal of the Chinese Revolution was to achieve socialism, and this would require the prior development of capitalism 'to a certain degree'. It was supposed that during the New Democracy the social weight of the proletariat would grow, while remaining under CCP guidance and control, and this would allow China to carry through its bourgeois-democratic revolution while steering clear of imperialism and heading towards the realisation of socialism.

At the time he wrote *On New Democracy* in 1940, Mao hoped for a united front against the Japanese armies and a post-war coalition government with Chiang Kai-shek. It was expected that national bourgeois and petty-bourgeois parties supporting capitalism would be an integral part of the revolutionary forces, since the tasks of the bourgeois-democratic revolution would be achieved without challenging the principle of capitalist property relations. In underdeveloped countries such as China, the second stage, the proletarian revolution, would arrive at some time in the future in a quite separate transformation. The two stages were carefully compartmentalised and separated by 'scores of years' with the socialist revolution 'a thing of the rather far future'.

Mao was not wedded to historical accuracy so when *On New Democracy* and *The Chinese Revolution and the Chinese Communist Party* were re-published in 1951, having been tested against reality, the unity with "other classes" was downplayed by editing out offending phrases and inserting expressions such as "under the leadership of the proletariat" into the text.

The reason for these editorial additions is obvious. The stagist theory of *New Democracy* had been found wanting. During WWII the united front with the KMT was at best partial and temporary; after the war, instead of inviting the Communists to join him in government, Chiang launched an all-out military assault on them. The national bourgeoisie noticeably failed to rally to the united front and by the end of the civil war it was found that the national bourgeois elements that had remained in China had little substance. One of the main planks of the *New Democracy* was noticeable by its absence. On the other hand the hunger, poverty, unemployment, inflation and other problems facing the Chinese masses demanded solutions that were socialist in principle.

However, even as he confronted the fact that the national bourgeoisie in China after 1949 was, at best, economically weak, Mao continued to assert that China had to pass through all the necessary stages of a democratic bourgeois republic in order to achieve socialism. Just as Stalin would say one thing while doing the opposite, in 1958 at the 8th National Congress of the CCP, Mao reviewed his analysis:

> "I advocate the theory of uninterrupted revolution. You must not think that this is Trotsky's theory of uninterrupted revolution. In making revolution, it should be like striking the iron while it is hot, one revolution to follow another ... Trotsky advocated that socialist revolution be undertaken even before the democratic revolution was accomplished. We do not proceed like that."[6]

In fact, Trotsky said the socialist revolution would begin before the democratic revolution was finished and become entwined with it.

Mao was determined to show how his theory of uninterrupted revolution differed from Trotsky's permanent revolution. Despite the experience of China 1949-1953 which saw the interpenetration of different stages of economic development, particularly the introduction of a national plan and wholesale nationalisation of industries to solve the crises the nation faced, Mao continued to assert that the different stages of development of the uninterrupted revolution were separate and should not be confused, the democratic revolution would be accomplished before the socialist:

> "The democratic revolution will undergo several stages of development, all under the slogan of a democratic republic, not that of a soviet regime. ... We stand for

> going through all the necessary stages of a democratic republic in order to arrive at socialism."[7]

The historic current within which Mao has a leading position, Stalinism, has, ever since Stalin published Foundations of Leninism in April 1924[8], consciously and unswervingly counter-posed uninterrupted revolution to Trotsky's theory of the permanent revolution. However, Pierre Rousset (a leading member of the United Secretariat of the Fourth International, with responsibility for developing its strategy for the 21st century) has claimed the differences between Mao's theory of uninterrupted revolution and Trotsky's theory of permanent revolution are more apparent than real due to "lack of precision in the theoretical formulas."[9]

It is not surprising, then, that Mao's theory of uninterrupted revolution is still being touted as a strategy for victory in colonial and semi-colonial countries. The lessons of the October 1965 slaughter of one million Communists in Indonesia when the Indonesian Communist Party attempted to apply 'uninterrupted revolution' have not been assimilated, and Maoism continues to surface in different guises, as in the guerrilla movement in Nepal.[10]

18.4 Permanent Revolution

The theory of the permanent revolution presents a model in which completing the tasks of the bourgeois-democratic revolution in so-called backward countries flows naturally into the socialist revolution because the common interests of feudalists, landlords, and national capitalists with the imperialists are far greater than any common interest with the poor peasants, middle peasants or proletarians.

On 29 August, 1917, Lenin wrote *From a Publicist's Diary* in which he publicly endorsed Trotsky's analysis:

> "You do not have to give these demands (seizure of the landlords' land and its division amongst the peasants) a lot of thought to see that it is absolutely impossible to realise them *in alliance* with the capitalists, without breaking completely with them, without waging the most determined and ruthless struggle against the capitalist class, without overthrowing its rule."[11]

Lenin also concluded that the presence of the Soviet Union meant that colonial and semi-colonial countries, certainly those in Asia, did not need to pass through a capitalist phase. This was endorsed by the Baku Congress of the Peoples' of the East held in September 1920 which declared most definitely that the poor peasants of the East did not have to proceed via bourgeois democracy; did not have to pass through a phase of capitalist development before they could go over to a Soviet system.[12] The Congress also accepted that the Russian experience had demonstrated that middle peasants would support socialist revolution if the resulting regime approved the seizure of the landed estates and their distribution to the peasants by the peasants.

This analysis is, of course, quite the opposite of the 'bloc of four classes' proposed by Mao and Stalin. At the time it assumed governmental power in 1949, the CCP already had control over those sectors of the economy most important for a socialist transition; heavy industry and banking. The big estates and landlordism had to be eradicated and the land distributed amongst the peasants, preferably by the peasants themselves, and this should and could have been done quickly. The artificial delay in the move to a workers' state was based on erroneous ideological concepts.

Of course the theory of the permanent revolution in no way precludes the development of pre-capitalist, colonial countries into capitalist countries as happened with India. It argues that the struggle for national democratic demands opens the possibility of direct transition to a workers' state as happened in Russia 1917-1918, and was brilliantly confirmed in China in 1949-1953. The theory also provides a guide to the limits that will be imposed on the struggle for national independence if the national bourgeoisie retain the leadership. In countries such as India the struggle ended with the conquest of political independence, but the completion of the democratic tasks was only partial, as the position of women and the poor peasants only too clearly demonstrate. Nor does the theory reject the possibility that certain *external* factors could intervene to generate the bourgeois revolution and the capitalist mode of production. In certain specific circumstances it might be in the interests of a section of the imperialists to force through a capitalist transformation in a relatively backward country. This is what began in Japan, in 1852, when Commodore Perry used gunboat diplomacy to force Japanese ports to open to American trade, and continued after WWII when the US administration feared Japan could be lost to Communism if its economic foundations were not restructured and strengthened.

18.5 Capitalist Restoration and Permanent Revolution

Does China's return to capitalism contradict the theory of permanent revolution? Does the theory of permanent revolution offer any insight into the coming Chinese socialist revolution?

To answer the first question we must place the theory of the permanent revolution in context as the application of the general law of combined and uneven development to the specific circumstances of the democratic revolution in so-called backward countries during late capitalism, and must conclude it is not directly applicable to capitalist restoration. At the same time, we note that the question is somewhat artificial as it could equally have been addressed to the former Soviet Union and Eastern Europe. We also note that Trotsky's analysis of the Russian Soviet regime[13] did accurately predict that if a hardened bureaucratic caste remained in power there was every likelihood of capitalist restoration (see Chapter 15).

The second question is valid, but only to the extent that the theory of the permanent revolution analyses the coming Chinese revolution as a classical, proletarian, socialist revolution from the outset; the urban population of China is in the majority and China is a modern state with an advanced and extensive industrial base. The method contained within the theory teaches us that inevitably the first goals of the revolution will include democratic demands and the fight of the revolutionary forces to genuinely implement these demands will win them the support of the urban and peasant petty-bourgeois masses. Enacting the democratic demands will, necessarily, take place in parallel with taking the first steps towards socialism. Permanent revolution rejects completely the need for any alliance with the national bourgeoisie, perceiving it as fully integrated into world imperialism.

Strike figures show a new proletariat numbering nearly three hundred million is being tempered on the anvil of the struggles taking place in China's workshops. No amount of state repression has been or will be able to stop the rise of this objective process. At the same time, the integration of China's industries into the world market means it cannot avoid capitalist crises of overproduction, and these will inevitably generate revolutionary movements. The driving force of the revolution will be the working class which will lead the peasantry, and the main methods of the revolution will be mass strikes supported by peasant uprisings.

The bourgeoisie in China is the ruling class and overlaps substantially with the CCP (and, thus, also the state apparatus) because it was this organisation that was responsible for re-launching capitalism in China and providing the owners and managers of many important enterprises. This gives the bourgeoisie a very high degree of state support in, for example, dealing with strikes. But there is an important corollary, the very integration that has been so helpful to the growth of capitalism will mean the bourgeois state will find it very difficult to accommodate the just and democratic demands of the masses. The material interests and innate conservatism of this block will mean it will fiercely oppose the development of free expression, particularly any free trade union movement.

However, the lack of an established labour aristocracy and the inexperience of the Chinese bourgeoisie means that a revolutionary explosion could take place with little warning. This would be in the context of a crisis-ridden world market that would block the tried-and-tested safety valve for Chinese capitalism – rapid industrial expansion and an increase in exports.

The socialist revolution would be unthinkable without the day-to-day struggle for advances under capitalism. Only in, and through, such struggles can the working class acquire the necessary experience and organization to challenge the capitalist system. However, any protesters will face a state apparatus which is the fusion of a monstrous Stalinist regime with the most repulsive features of capitalism.

A revolutionary or even workers' party is lacking but, nevertheless, proletarian consciousness is rising, and there is a sense amongst many that the left is on the verge of a leap forward. But this will only occur if workers, peasants and intellectuals find issues that unite the forces of opposition. Socialists will, of course, fight for immediate demands but pose them in a way that links day-to-day problems to the socialist transformation of society. Such demands, transitional demands as Trotsky referred to them, act as a bridge between actions taken in the struggle for bettering the condition of the masses and the idea of the socialist revolution.

18.6 Summary

The Third Chinese Revolution was a magnificent historic achievement despite the best efforts of the Stalinists to side-track it into the dead end of class-collaboration, first with the KMT and when this proved impossible, with the remnants of the national bourgeoisie who had not fled to Taiwan with Chiang.

It is blindingly obvious that the *New Democracy* was neither a natural nor a necessary stage in the Third Chinese Revolution. It was imposed on the revolution in a most unnatural and artificial manner by the CCP itself in order that the revolutionary process would appear to follow the path pre-scribed by Stalin and Mao. To achieve this, the agrarian programme was limited and the proletariat constrained. But the revolution refused to be confined in this way and it burst through.

The apparent successes of the national bourgeoisie during the New Democracy was achieved because of government-provided resources and careful tending, only to be repaid by economic sabotage and corruption of Party and state on a fantastic scale. In a war with American imperialism, facing a damaging embargo on trade, the bureaucratic state acted swiftly to preserve itself and within four years of its launch, the *New Democracy* was dead in the water, and the PRC was consciously moving in the direction of a centrally planned economy (though without workers' democracy).

Stalinist regimes may have varied from country to country and era to era but all had certain qualities in common. The CCP met all the necessary criteria; its ideological basis was socialism in one country at home and peaceful co-existence abroad, it had a privileged bureaucratic caste (after 1953 this rested on the property foundations of a workers' state), it repressed workers' democracy, it was a monolithic, totalitarian regime both within Party and government, its policies zigged and zagged between ultra-leftism and open class collaboration according to the short-term needs of the bureaucracy. In the special circumstances that existed in China, a Stalinist party was forced to go further than it wished in breaking with the bourgeoisie, but did not become a genuinely revolutionary workers' party.

Marxism is concrete so it is important to observe the actual events in China, to see how and why the class-collaborationist perspective of the *New Democracy* and the theory of stages collapsed so completely and so quickly. But it is also necessary to place these events within a correct overall perspective. The necessity of taking measures which were objectively socialist to solve the problems of the democratic revolution was clearly spelled out by Lenin in 1917 and repeated many times thereafter. The permanent revolution is a tendency for revolutions in backward countries to transcend the bourgeois-democratic phase and turn into socialist revolutions.[14] China was living proof of this.

Stalinist regimes have always acted as a brake on economic progress, but following the utter chaos of the KMT and by putting state plans and other socialist forms into place, it initially took the Chinese economy forward at a rapid pace. However, as the economy became increasingly complex, a centralised bureaucratic system that attempted to control every aspect of economic life could no longer cope and became an absolute impediment to progress. To counter this the Party adopted a Chinese New Economic Policy which was initially successful in greatly increasing agricultural production and convincing many in the CCP that a market economy was the route to rapid industrial expansion.

Escalating social unrest caused by dissatisfaction with aspects of the regime's policies climaxed in the Tien An Men Square events. The outcome was that the hard-liners took control of the Party and determined that a full market economy was necessary to generate the economic growth necessary to save their skins; that the best way to ensure their benefits continued and could be handed down to their children was for China to move to a capitalist system with themselves as owners of property. The most common forms were for CCP officials who were the managers of TVEs and small/medium SOEs to buy such enterprises at give-away prices and for senior local government bureaucrats to purchase properties and shares using the monies received from bribes. At no time did the bureaucracy consider workers' democracy as a means of governing the economy to eliminate waste and corruption. That would have meant the end of their privileges.

Step by step the CCP dumped the measures necessary for a workers' state. Each step in the process was justified as necessary for maintaining the dynamism of the economy and expanding employment prospects for those flooding into the cities from the countryside. The first to go was the monopoly of foreign trade, then central planning was replaced by the profit motive and commodity production, and next was the privatisation of small, medium and large SOEs. Today, only a small number of certain strategic industries (e.g. telecommunications for control of the media), hopelessly unprofitable industries (e.g. industries of the rust belt), and the Big Four banks (each with massive debts) remain in state hands. China is now a fully-fledged capitalist country though its capitalist class lacks both experience and refinement.

China's emergence as a major capitalist power temporarily provided world capitalism with a much needed boost, but soon it was serving to sharpen all the old contradictions and raise them to a new level. The massive investment in Chinese industry expressed itself as an avalanche of cheap commodities which soon saturated many sectors of the world's economy. Now there is increasing overcapacity in the Chinese economy itself.

The combination of a capitalist restoration and the consequent opening of the economy to a huge influx of capital investment often subsidised by the state, combined with a vast supply of cheap labour from the countryside, has enabled China to rapidly develop a powerful modern industrial base. That period of explosive growth is nearing its limit. Now China finds itself faced with the same problems that afflict every capitalist economy.

The successes of China's economy have been based on the labour of Chinese workers. However, with the development of capitalism came enormous class differentiation, and China has become one of the most unequal and corrupt societies in the world. The flaunting of the obscene wealth of the ruling elite and their children (the "Princelings") is bitterly resented by the population. That said, the base of the Chinese capitalist class is very narrow. China is run by a tiny elite of super-rich oligarchs who have enriched themselves by plundering the state and brutally exploiting the labour of the Chinese workers. It is true that beneath them there are layers of factory managers, directors, bureaucrats, and officials in state and Party institutions. Together with their families, these form part of the establishment. But even after taking them into account, the overwhelming majority of the population is excluded from economic wealth and the power bestowed by it.

It is possible, given the colossal accumulation of discontent, that attempts to rationalise the big factories of heavy industry in the North-East will provoke fierce defensive struggles which might, under certain conditions, become transformed into offensive actions. The world working class is entering an epoch of permanent and increasing austerity which will require class battles to retain the gains remaining from the relative boom of the post WWII years, such as the UK National Health Service. One thing is clear, workers are beginning to look for ways of fighting back. There will be many false starts such as Syriza in Greece. But once the class begins to move, the whole attitude of the workers will change, the entire political atmosphere will be transformed and what might seem impossible today will be realised. Jeremy Corbyn's election to leader of the UK Labour Party, is especially important as he in now leader of the traditional party of the British working class. His victory has opened up enormous possibilities for British workers and if the momentum that gained him that victory can be maintained then a real threat to the British ruling class will appear.

The history of the last hundred years has demonstrated that a healthy socialist revolution needs a revolutionary leadership armed with correct theory based on the collective experience of the revolutionary movement on a world scale. Without Lenin, the October Revolution would never have taken place. In the absence of this subjective factor, all kinds of aberrations can occur as China is witness. In the absence of such a revolutionary leadership, there will be extreme confusion and disorientation of the workers and it is possible that the movement will be defeated. The problem facing the Chinese working class today can be summed up in one word – *leadership*.

Capitalism in China may continue for some time on a very unstable basis. But something more than just favourable objective conditions, numerical strength or even the willingness of the masses to fight is necessary for a socialist revolution. *The subjective factor is also indispensable.*

The Chinese leadership know this and that is why it monitors the internet so vigorously. It is no accident that since 2013 the Chinese state has been spending more on internal security than on defence, the budget for 2015 is US$24.6 billion, up 11% on 2014.[15] However, the new generation of young workers is not prepared to put up with the low wages and bad conditions that their grandparents, former peasants recently arrived from dirt-poor villages were willing to accept. So it is also not surprising, that the CCP has given the ACFTU a more active role in controlling workers' discontent and supressing workers' self-organisation.

The growing mood of discontent in Chinese society is expressed by the rising number of street demonstrations, strikes and other actions in the factories. In a totalitarian society, where discontent is forcibly suppressed and there are few legal safety valves, explosions can occur suddenly and without warning. The workers in the older heavy industries were loyal to the regime because it provided them with secure employment and reasonable living conditions, but now they are faced with large scale unemployment coupled with worse conditions and cuts in pay. They are well and truly disillusioned with the regime and are starting the fight back. The workers in the new electronic factories in the SEZs began as inexperienced peasants grateful to get out of their village, now the third generation is arriving in the factories and demanding better pay and work conditions. Until now these two groups of workers were at different stages of development in their fight with the regime. Now their interests are coinciding and a new stage of the struggle has been reached.

The Chinese working class is destined to play a key role in world history in the coming period. Napoleon is reported as having said that, "China is like a sleeping giant. And when she awakes, she shall astonish the world." Paraphrasing Napoleon we can say that today that sleeping giant is the Chinese proletariat. When it rises no force on the planet will be able to stop it and it will transform the whole world.

References

TCQ - The China Quarterly
MIA - Marxist Internet Archive
U.P. - University Press
w.m.org - www.marxists.org
w.m.com - www.marxist.com
CLB - China Labour Bulletin

Chapter 1

The First Chinese Revolution: Early Years of the Chinese Communist Party

[1] Hinton, W. *Fanshen*, Pelican, 1972.

[2] Chen Han-sheng, *The Burdens of the Chinese Peasantry*, Pacific Affairs, 1929 2(10)644-658.

[3] Pearce, B. *Marxism and the Asiatic Mode of Production*, Rev. Hist. 2002 Vol 8 No 2.

[4] Mandel, E. *Ten Theses on the Social and Economic Laws Governing the Society Transitional Between Capitalism and Socialism*, 1973, w.m.org.

[5] Marx, K. *British Rule in India*, New York Daily Tribune, June 25, 1853.

[6] Harrison, J. *The Communists and Chinese Peasant Rebellions,* Victor Gollanz, 1970.

[7] Pantsov, A. *The Bolsheviks and the Chinese Revolution 1919-1927*, Curzon. 2000.

[8] Marx, K. 7 July 1882, CW 19:213-216.

[9] Chesneaux, J. *Peasant Revolt in China 1840-1949*, Thames and Hudson, 1973.

[10] McColl, R. *The Oyuwan Soviet Area*, Jnl of Asian Studies, 1961, 27(1) 41-60.

[11] Morley, D. *90 Years of the Chinese Communist Party*. 2011, w.m.com.

[12] Tawney, R. *Land and Labour in China*, Allen & Unwin, 1932.

[13] Pantsov, A. and Levine, S. *Mao*, Simon & Schuster, 2012, p17.

[14] Tawney, Op. cit.

[15] Chen Han-seng, *The Present Agrarian Problem in China*, , 5th Biennial Conference of the Institute of Pacific Relations, Banff, Canada, August 14 to 28, 1933.

[16] Fairbank, Op. cit.

[17] Endicott, M. *Five Stars Over China*, Toronto, 1953.

[18] Mandel, E. *The Third Chinese Revolution*, May 1950. www.marxists.org.

[19] Tawney, Op. cit.

[20] Buck, J. *Land Utilization in China,* Paragon, 1964.

[21] Chen Han-seng, Op. cit.

[22] Allen, R., et al., *Wages, Prices and Living Standards in China 1795-1925*, http://cei.ier.hit-u.ac.jp.

[23] Slee, C. *Peoples' Republic of China at 60*, Green Left Weekly #811, September 23, 2009.

[24] Belden, J. *China Shakes the World*, Gollancz, 1951, p151.

[25] Wittfogel, K. *Results and Problems of the Study of Oriental Despotism*, Jnl of Asian Studies, 1969, 28(2)357-365.

[26] Marx, K., and Engels, F. *The Holy Family*, w.m.org.

[27] Samyorup, *Women in the Chinese Revolution (1921-1950)* New Vistas Publications.

[28] Belden. Op. cit. p311.

[29] Belden. Op. cit. p310.

[30] Franke, W. *A Century of Chinese Revolution, 1851-1949*, 1970, Blackwell, p95-99.

[31] Ho Kan-chih, *A History of the Modern Chinese Revolution*. 1960, PFLP, p12-15.

[32] Saich, T. *The Origins of the First United Front in China*, Brill, 1991, p116-117, p87.

[33] Conway, F. *Women in the Chinese Revolution*, Fourth International, 1951, 12(4)109-113).

[34] Basin, A. *The Failure of the Chinese Communist Party 1921-27*, MA Thesis. Montreal University, 1973.

[35] Morley, Op cit.

[36] Fairbank, Op. cit.

[37] North, R. *Moscow and the Chinese Communists*, Stanford U.P., 1963.

[38] Serge, V. *The Class Struggle in the Chinese Revolution*, 1927, Rev. Hist. 5(3)83.

[39] Jacobs, D. *Recent Russian Material on Soviet Advisers in China: 1923-1927*. The China Quarterly, No. 41, 1970, p103-112.

[40] Pantsov, *The Bolsheviks* ... Op. cit.

[41] Lenin, V. *Left-Wing Communism: An Infantile Disorder*, May 1920 CW 31:17-118.

[42] Riddell, J. *The Comintern in Lenin's Time*, Socialist Voice Pamphlet, 2008.

[43] Brooks, M. *The Kapp Putsch: the United Front in Action*, 2010, w.m.org.

[44] *A Militant Agreement for the Uprising*, 1905, CW8:158-166.

[45] Woods, A. *Bolshevism the Road to Revolution*, 1999, w.m.com.

[46] Lenin, V. *Remarks on the Draft Theses on Tactics* ... , June 1921, CW 42:319.

[47] Broue, P, *The German Revolution* 1917-1923. Brill, 2004, p473.

[48] Vatlin, A. *International Communism and the Communist International 1919-43*, MUP 1998, p120.

[49] Cliff, T. *Lenin Vol. 3*, Bookmarks, London, 1987.

[50] Lenin, V. *Speech in Defence of the Tactics of the Communist International*, July 1920, CW 32:470-473.

[51] Trotsky, L. *First Five Years of the Communist International*, New Park, p328.

[52] Chattopadhyay, K. *The Marxism of Leon Trotsky*, Progressive Publishers, India, 2006.

[53] Lenin, V. *Report of the Commission on the National and Colonial Questions*, July 1920 CW31:240-245.

[54] Lenin, V. *Address to 2nd Congress of Communist Organisations of the East*, Nov 1919, CW 30:161.

[55] Lenin, V. *Preliminary Draft Thesis on the Agrarian Question*, July 1920, CW 31:152-164.

[56] Lenin, V. *From a Publicist's Diary*, Aug. 1917, CW 25:278-286.

[57] Lenin, V. *Revision of the Party Programme*, June 1917, CW 24:469.

[58] Lenin, V. *Report on the Commission* ... Op. Cit. p244.

[59] Ibid, p243.

[60] Lenin, V. *Draft Theses on National and Colonial Question,* June 1920, CW31:149-150.

[61] *Supplementary Theses on the National and Colonial Question*, 2nd Congress CI, w.m.org.

[62] Riddell, Op. cit.

[63] Report of 6th Session, Baku Congress of the Peoples of the East, September 1920, www.marxists.org.

[64] Lewis, J. *Peasant Rebellion & Communist Revolution in Asia,* Stanford U.P. 1974.

[65] Chow Tse-tung, *The May Fourth Movement*, Harvard U.P. 1960.

[66] Dirlik, *The Origins of Chinese Communism* O.U.P. 1989, p57 and 63.

[67] Morley, Op. cit.

[68] Alexander, R. *International Trotskyism 1929-1985,* 1991, Duke U.P. rosswolfe.files.wordpress.com.

[69] Dirlik, Op. cit. p153 et seq.

[70] Fairbank, Op. cit. p250.

[71] Dirlik, Op. cit. p149-150.

[72] Peng Shuzhi, *Introduction to Leon Trotsky on China,* 1976, Monad.

[73] Saich, T. *The Origins* ... Op. cit., p116-117.

[74] Dov Bing, *Sneevliet and the Early Years of the CCP,* The China Quarterly, 1971, No. 48, p677-697.

[75] Saich, T. *The Rise to Power of the Chinese Communist Party*, Sharpe, 1996 p11.

[76] Chang Kuo t'ao, *The Rise of the Chinese Communist Party 192l-27*, Lawrence, 1971, p136-152.

[77] Dov Bing, Op. cit.

[78] Pantsov and Levine, *Mao,* Op. cit. p121.

[79] Benton G. *Bolshevising China: From Lenin to Stalin to Mao, 1921–1944.* Leeds Univ., East Asia Papers No. 22, 1966.

[80] Pantsov and Levine, *Mao*, Op. cit.

Chapter 2

The Communist International, the Kuomintang and the CCP

[1] Alexander, R. *International Trotskyism 1929-1985,* 1991, Duke U.P. rosswolfe.files.wordpress.com.

[2] Dov Bing, *Sneevliet and the Early Years of the CCP,* The China Quarterly, 1971, No. 48, p677-697.

[3] Mao Tse-tung, Footnote 21 to *Analysis of the Classes in Chinese Society*, Selected Works FLP, 1926, Vol1 p13-21.

[4] Brandt, C. *Stalin's Failure in China*, 1924-27, Harvard U.P. 1959, p47.

[5] Saich, T. *The Origins of the First United Front in China*, Brill, 1991, p116-117, p 84.

[6] Isaacs, H. *Documents on the Comintern and the Chinese Revolution*. The China Quarterly, 1971, No. 45, p100-115.

[7] Chen Duxiu *The Immediate Tactics of the CCP*, November 1922. Henk Sneevliet papers, socialhistory.org.

[8] North, R. *Moscow and the Chinese Communists*, Stanford U.P., 1963.

[9] Alexander, Op. cit.

[10] Lescot, P. *Before Mao,* Collins, 2004, p40.

[11] Ho Kan-chih, *A History of the Modern Chinese Revolution*, PFLP, 1959, p40.

[12] *Manifesto of the 2nd Congress of the CCP* Brandt et al, in *A Documentary History of Chinese Communism*, Allen & Unwin, 1952, p65.

[13] Lenin, V. *Draft Theses on the National and Colonial Question* June 1920, CW31: 144-151.

[14] Lenin, V. *Speech on Affiliation to the British Labour Party*, May 1920, CW 31: 257-263.

[15] Dov Bing, Op. cit.

[16] *Bolshevik Leadership Correspondence 1912–1927*, Rosspen, 1996.

[17] Chen Duxiu *Appeal to All the Comrades of the Chinese Communist Party* December 10, 1929, w.m.org.

[18] Alexander, Op. cit.

[19] Sneevliet papers, Op. cit.

[20] Brandt et al., *A Documentary* .... Op. cit. p67.

[21] 4th Congress of the Communist International, *Theses on the Eastern Question*, 5 December 1922, w.m.org.

[22] *Theses on the Eastern Question*, Op. cit.

[23] Trotsky, L. *The Challenge of the Left Opposition (1928-29)* New York 1981, p202-3.

[24] Sneevliet papers Op. cit.

[25] Mao Zedong, *Analysis of the Classes in Chinese Society*, Footnote 13, 1926 w.m.org.

[26] Dorland, A. *The Concept and Function of "China" in Trotsky* MA thesis, Mc Gill Univ., Montreal, Canada. 1971.

[27] Schram, S. *Mao's Road to Power* Sharpe, 1992, Vol 2 p157.

[28] Degras, J. *The Communist International, Selected Documents*, 1965, OUP, Vol 2 p25-26.

[29] Jacobs, D. *Borodin: Stalin's Man in China*. Harvard U.P., 1981.

[30] Lenin, V. From a Publicist's Diary, Sept. 1917, CW 25:278-286.

[31] Borkenau, F. *Communist International, 1919-1945,* Faber and Faber, Ltd., p278 and 343.

[32] Pantsov, A., and Levine, S. *Mao*, Simon & Schuster, 2012, p123.

[33] Brandt et al, *A Documentary* ... Op. cit. p71-2.

[34] Mao Zedong, *Peking Coup d'Etat and the Merchants*, 11 July 1923, w.m.org.

[35] Pantsov and Levine, Op. cit. p129-133.

[36] Jacobs, Op. cit.

[37] Peng Shu-tse, Introduction to *Leon Trotsky on China*, Pathfinder, 1976, p42-44.

[38] Lescot, Op. cit.

[39] Jacobs, Op. cit.

[40] Chen Duxiu, *Appeal*... Op. cit.

[41] Alexander, Op. cit.

[42] Benton G. *Bolshevising China: From Lenin to Stalin to Mao, 1921–1944*. Leeds Univ., East Asia Papers No. 22, 1966.

[43] Benton, Ibid.

[44] Alexander, Op. cit.

[45] Peng, Op. cit. p47-48.

[46] Alexander, Op. cit.

[47] Schram, Op. cit. p237.

[48] Dorland, Op. cit.

[49] Isaacs, H. *The Tragedy of the Chinese Revolution,* w.m.org.

[50] Millward, L. *Workers in the Chinese revolution of 1926-7,* Workers' Liberty 12-13, August 1989.

[51] James, C.L.R. *The World Revolution*, w.m.org.

[52] Marx, K. and Engels, F. *Address to the Central Committee Communist League*, March 1850, MESW, 1:107.

[53] Lescot, Op. cit.

[54] James, Op. cit.

[55] James, Op. cit.

[56] Chen Duxiu *Appeal* ... Op. cit.

[57] Dorland, Op. cit.

[58] Broue, P. *Chen Duxiu and the Fourth International*, Rev. Hist. Vol 2 No 4 1990.

[59] Lenin, V. *Preliminary Draft Theses on the National and Colonial Questions*, June 1920, CW31 p144-151.

[60] Pantsov and Levine, Op. cit. p143 et seq.

[61] Stalin, J. *Speech Delivered at a Meeting of Students of the Communist University of the Toilers of the East*, May 18, 1925 Vol 7 p135 – 155.

[62] Broue, *Chen Duxiu* ... Op. cit.

[63] Isaacs, *Tragedy* ..., Op. cit.

[64] Peng Shuzi, *The Causes of the Victory of the Chinese Communist Party over Chiang Kai-Shek*, February, 1952 w.m.org.

[65] Pantsov, A. *The Bolsheviks and the Chinese Revolution 1919-1927*, Curtzon. 2000, p106.

[66] (Note: the Russian Communist Party changed its name twice during the period covered by this book. In 1918 it had adopted the name Russian Communist Party (Bolshevik) (RCP(B)), between 1925 and 1952 it was the All-Russian Communist Party (Bolsheviks) (AUCP(B)), and after 1952 it was known as Communist Party of the Soviet Union (CPSU)).

[67] Degras, J. (ed), *The Communist International 1919 – 1943, Documents,* OUP, 1956, Vol 2, p275 et seq.

Chapter 3

Stalin sets the Pattern for the Chinese Revolution

[1] Segal, R. *The Tragedy of Leon Trotsky*, Peregrine Books, 1983, p232/3.

[2] Souvarine, B. *Stalin, a Critical Survey of Bolshevism.* 1939, w.m.org.

[3] Daniels, R.V. *The Conscience of the Revolution*, Harvard U. P., 1965, p424.

[4] Podsheldolkin, A. *The Origins of the Stalinist Bureaucracy – Some New Historical Facts* 1990, w.m.org.

[5] Lenin, V. *Our Tasks in the Soviet of Workers' Deputies*, 1905, CW10:26 and 28.

[6] Lenin, V. *Two Tactics of Social Democracy...*, July 1905, CW9:15-140.

[7] Bunyan, J and Fisher, H. *The Bolshevik Revolution 1917-1918: Documents and Materials*, Stanford U.P., 1961, p220.

[8] Cliff, T. *Lenin* 2:191, Bookmarks, London, 1987.

[9] Schapiro, L. *The Communist Party of the Soviet Union*, Methuen, 1960, p243.

[10] Podsheldolkin, Op. cit.

[11] Sakwa, R. *The Communist Party and War Communism in Moscow, 1918-1921*, PhD Thesis, Univ. of Birmingham, 1984, www.history.ac.uk.

[12] Cliff, T. *Lenin*, 3:139-142.

[13] Wright, J. *The Truth about Kronstadt,* February 1938, w.m.org.

[14] Cliff, T. *Trotsky,* Pluto Press, 3:182.

[15] Pirani, S. *The Russian Revolution in Retreat 1920-1924*, Routledge, 2008, p19-20.

[16] Carr, E. *History of Soviet Russia*, Pelican, 1966, 4:14.

[17] Woods, A. *Lenin's Last Struggle,* Wellred Books, 2009.

[18] Pirani, S. *The Communists' Dilemma*. www.solidarity-us.org/atc 2008.

[19] Medvedev, R. *On Socialist Democracy*, Spokesman Books, 1977, p221.

[20] Murphy, K. *Class Struggle in a Moscow Metal Factory*, Berghan Books, 2005, p83.

[21] Murphy, Op. cit. p87.

[22] Allen, N. *The Challenge of the Left Opposition (1923-25)*, Pathfinder Press, 1975, p50.

[23] Murphy, Op. cit. p102 et seq.

[24] Pirani, S. *The Russian workers and the Bolshevik Party in power*, 2006, www.revolutioninretreat.com.

[25] Murphy, Op. cit. p89.

[26] Liebman, M. *Leninism Under Lenin*, Merlin Press, 1975, p307.

[27] Schapiro, Op. cit., p231 et seq.

[28] Pirani, *The Russian workers …* Op. cit.

[29] Rigby, T. *Communist Party Membership in the USSR 1917-1967*. Princeton U.P., 1968, p241-242.

[30] Trotsky, L. *Stalin,* Hollis and Carter, 1947, p384-5.

[31] Pirani, S. *The Party Elite, Industrial Managers, Specialists and Workers, 1922-23*. 2006, www.revolutioninretreat.com.

[32] Schapiro, Op. cit. p234/6.

[33] Daniels, Op. cit. p201.

[34] Lenin, V. *Speech Closing the 4th Congress*, April, 1920, CW30:485.

[35] Murphy, Op. cit. p164.

[36] Lenin, V. *Preliminary Draft Resolution of the 10th Party Congress of the CPU on Party Unity*, CW32:241.

[37] Lenin, V. *Resolution on Party Unity*, March 1921, CW32:261.

[38] Liebman, Op. cit. p292/300.

[39] Serge, V. *Year One of the Russian Revolution*, Pluto Press, 1992 p118/9. Serge, V. *Memoirs of a Revolutionary 1901-1942*, O.U.P.,

[40] Krupskaya, N. *Memories of Lenin*, Panther History, 1970, p124-5.

[41] Daniels, Op. cit. p163.

[42] Segal, Op. cit. p253.

[43] Daniels, Op. cit., p170.

[44] Cliff, *Lenin*, Op. cit. 3:365.

[45] Podsheldolkin, Op. cit.

[46] Deutscher, I. *Stalin* Pelican Books, London, 1984 p259.

[47] Schapiro, Op. cit. p256 et seq.

[48] Pirani, S. *The Party Elite ….* Op. cit.

[49] Serge, Op. cit. p79.
[50] Lenin, V. *Letter to Molotov*, CW33:257.
[51] Pirani, *The Party Elite…* Op. cit.
[52] Carr, Op. cit. 4:40.
[53] Deutscher, Op. cit. Chapter 7.
[54] Podsheldolkin, Op. cit.
[55] Degras, J. (ed), *The Communist International 1919 – 1943, Documents,* OUP, 1956,1:26.
[56] Riddell, J. *Comintern – Revolutionary Internationalism in Lenin's Time*, A Socialist Voice Pamphlet, 2008.
[57] Broue, P, *Revolution in Germany (1917-1923)*, Brill, Ch37.
[58] Sewell, R. *Germany: from Revolution to Counter-Revolution*, Wellred, 2012.
[59] Broue, Op. cit. P, *Revolution in …*, p806-808.
[60] Broue, P. *History of the Bolshevik Party (CP) of the USSR* w.m.org.
[61] Grant, T. *Russia: From Revolution and Counter Revolution*, Wellred, 1997 p122-123.
[62] Stalin, J. *Foundations of Leninism*, April 1924, CW6:17-196.
[63] Segal, Op. cit. p288/9.
[64] Lenin, V. *Third All-Russian Congress of Soviets*, January, 1918, CW26:470.
[65] Lenin, V. *Speech on the International Situation*, November, 1918. CW28:151.
[66] Deutscher, Op. cit. p283/6.
[67] Stalin, J. *October Revolution and the Tactics of Russian Communists* December 17 1924 6:394.
[68] Carr, Op. cit. 2:43.
[69] Stalin, J, *Foundations …* Op. cit.
[70] Segal, Op. cit. p288/9.
[71] Deutscher, Op. cit. p293.
[72] Daniels, Op. cit. p282/3.
[73] Lenin, V. *Speech on the International Situation*, November, 1918. CW28:151.
[74] Woods, A. and Grant, T. *Lenin and Trotsky What They Really Stood For*, 1969, w.m.org.
[75] Lenin, V. *Can the Bolsheviks Retain State Power?*, October 1917, CW26:87-136.
[76] Hiroaki Kuromiya, *Stalin's Industrial Revolution*, CUP 1988.
[77] Chattopadhyay, K. *The Marxism of Leon Trotsky*, Progressive Publishers, India, 2006, p393.
[78] Stalin, J. *New Tasks in Economic Construction*, June 23, 1931, CW13: 53-82.
[79] Riddell, J. *Comintern: Revolutionary Internationalism in Lenin's Time*, Socialist Voice, 2008.
[80] Atkinson, D. *Women in Russia,* Stanford, U.P., 1977, p122.
[81] Riddell, Op. cit.
[82] Trotsky, L. *The Revolution Betrayed*, Pathfinder Press, 1972. p153-154.
[83] Cliff, T. *Class Struggle and Women's Liberation*, Bookmarks, 1984, p148-149.
[84] Trotsky, *The Revolution Betrayed*, Op. cit. p152.
[85] Ibid p145-147.
[86] Cliff, *Class Struggle …* Op. cit. p150-151.
[87] Grant, Op. cit. p301-303.

[88] Rogovin, V. *1937 Stalin's Year of Terror.* Mehring Books 1998, p140-141.

[89] Cohen, Op. cit. A. *The Communism of Mao Tse-Tung.* Univ. of Chicago Press, 1966.

[90] Stalin, J. *The Results of the First Five-Year Plan, Report Delivered to the Joint Plenum of CC and CCC on January 7, 1933.* 13:215-216.

[91] Degras, Op. cit. 3:359.

[92] Stalin, J. *Constitution (Fundamental law) of the Union of Soviet Socialist Republics* 5 December 1936 w.m.org.

[93] Weaver, S. *The New Soviet Constitution*, w.m.org.

[94] Souvarine, B. *Stalin, a Critical Survey of Bolshevism.* 1939, w.m.org.

[95] Zhou Enlai, *Report on the Work of the Third National Congress of the People's Republic of China*, Peking, 1965, p26.

[96] Stalin, J, *Report to the 17th Party Congress on the Work of the Central Committee of the C.P.S.U.(B.)* 1934, CW13:374.

[97] Pantsov, A. *Chinese Students at the International Lenin School, in Moscow 1926-1938*, Capital University.

[98] Saich, T. *The Chinese Communist Party during the Era of the Comintern (1919-1943)*, www.hks.harvard.edu.

[99] Benton, G. *Bolshevising China: From Lenin to Stalin to Mao, 1921–1944.* Leeds University, East Asia Papers No 22.

[100] Yueh Sheng, *Sun Yat-sen University in Moscow and the Chinese Revolution: A Personal Account.* Univ. of Kansas, Center for East Asian Studies, East Asian Series, 1971, p1.

[101] Pantsov, A. *The Bolsheviks and the Chinese Revolution 1919-1927*, Curtzon. 2000. p114.

[102] Yueh, Op. cit. p116.

[103] Yueh, Op. cit. p81.

[104] Stalin, J. *Talk with Students at Sun Yat-sen University* May 13 1927, 9:243–273.

[105] Yueh, Op. cit.

[106] Pantsov, A, *Chinese Students …* Op. cit.

[107] Wang Fan-hsi. *Memoirs of a Chinese Revolutionary*, Columbia U.P., 1991.

[108] Trotsky, L, *The Challenge of the Left Opposition (1926-27)*, Pathfinder Press, 2003, p535.

[109] Deutscher, Op. cit. p312.

[110] Elleman, B. *Moscow and the Emergence of Communist Power in China* 1925-1931, Routledge 2010.

[111] Wang Fan-hsi. Op. cit.

[112] Pantsov, *The Bolsheviks ….* Op. cit.. p163-174.

[113] Pantsov, *The Bolsheviks …* Op. cit. p183.

[114] Pantsov, A, *Chinese Students …* Op. cit.

[115] Pantsov, A, *Chinese Students …* Op. cit.

[116] Yueh, Op. cit. p217.

[117] Boorman, H. and Howard, R. *Biographical Dictionary of Republican China*, Columbia U.P., 1967, Vol. 3.

[118] Chou En-Lai, *The Communist International and the Chinese Communist Party*, 1960 FLPH, Selected Works, 2:314.

[119] Lih, L. *Stalin's Letters to Molotov 1925-1936*, Yale U.P., 1995.

[120] Pantsov, *Chinese Students …* Op. cit.

[121] Yueh, Op. cit. p174 – 175.

[122] Yeung, Op. cit p180-182.

[123] Pantsov's interview with Wang Fanxi, Leeds 1992, p 187.

[124] Kegan, R. *The Comintern, the 28 Bolsheviks and the Alumni of Sun Yat-sen Unversity.* Int. Rev. of History and Political Science, Vol 11, p79-80, 1974.

[125] Yueh, Op. cit. p118.

Chapter 4

The Rise of the Second Chinese Revolution

[1] Roberts, J. *Lenin, Trotsky and the Theory of the Permanent Revolution,* Wellred, 2007.

[2] Saich, T. *The Rise to Power of the CCP*, Sharp, 1994, p240.

[3] Tien-Wei Wu. *Chiang Kai-shek's March Twentieth Coup d'Etat of 1926,* Jnl Asian Studies, 1968 27(3)585-602.

[4] Peng Pi-lan, *The Chinese Revolution,* Education for Socialists, SWP, 1972, p9.

[5] North, R. *Moscow and the Chinese Communists,* Stanford U.P., 1963.

[6] Tien-Wei Wu. Op. cit.

[7] North, Op. cit.

[8] Cliff, T. *Trotsky,* Pluto Press, 1991, Vol 3:197.

[9] Pantsov, A. *The Bolsheviks and the Chinese Revolution 1919-1927,* Curtzon. 2000, p131.

[10] Tien-Wei Wu. Op. cit.

[11] Alexander, R. *International Trotskyism 1929-1985: A Documented Analysis of the Movement.* 1991, Duke U.P., rosswolfe.files.wordpress.com.

[12] Cliff, *Trotsky,* Op. cit. Vol 3:201.

[13] Lescot, P. *Before Mao* Harper Collins 2004, p70.

[14] Elleman, B. *Moscow and the Emergence of Communist Power in China 1925-1931,* Routledge 2010, p24-25.

[15] Stalin, J. *International Press Correspondence* April 25 1927.

[16] Chen Duxiu *Appeal to All the Comrades of the Chinese Communist Party* 10 December, 1929, w.m.com.

[17] Dorland, A. *The Concept and Function of "China" in Trotsky* MA thesis McGill Univ., Montreal, Canada. 1971.

[18] McColl, R. *The Oyuwan Soviet,* Jnl of Asian Studies, 1967, 27(1)41-60.

[19] Alexander, R. Op. cit.

[20] North, Op. cit. p102.

[21] Wang Fan-hsi, *Memoirs of a Chinese Revolutionary,* Columbia U.P., New York, 1980, p25.

[22] Degras, J. *The Communist International, 1919-1943: Documents,* O.U.P. 1965, Vol 2:337.

[23] Cliff, *Trotsky,* Op. cit. Vol 3:187-224.

[24] Pantsov, A. & Levine, S. *Mao,* Simon & Schuster, 2012, p163.

[25] James, C.L.R. *The World Revolution,* w.m.org.

[26] North, R. and Xenia E. *M.N. Roy's Mission to China,* Univ. of California Press, 1963, p31.

[27] James, Op. cit.

[28] North and Xenia, Op. cit. p30-35.

[29] Saich, Op. cit. p219-228.

[30] Schram, S. *Mao's Road to Power* Sharpe, 1992, Vol 2 p421-422.

[31] Cliff, *Trotsky* Op. cit. Vol 3:203.

[32] James, Op. cit.

[33] (ibor, M. *The Chinese Revolution*, London, Thames and Hudson 1961, p73-79.

[34] Mao Zedong, *Report of an Investigation into the Peasant Movement in Hunan* March 1927 w.m.org.

[35] Wittfogel, K. *The Legend of Maoism*, The China Quarterly 1960 Vol 2: 72-86.

[36] Wittfogel, Op. cit.

[37] Cohen, A. *The Communism of Mao Tse-tung*. Univ. Chicago Press, 1966, p30 and 49.

[38] Wittfogel, Op. cit.

[39] Cohen, Op. cit. p37.

[40] Kwan, D. *Marxist Intellectuals and the Chinese Labour Movement*, Univ. of Washington Press, 1997, p249.

[41] Isaacs, H. *Tragedy of the Chinese Revolution*, Secker & Warburg, 1938 p143.

[42] Lescot, Op. cit. p75/7.

[43] Tawney, R. *Land and Labour in China*, Allen & Unwin, 1932.

[44] Isaacs, Op. cit. p235.

Chapter 5

The Defeat of the Second Chinese Revolution

[1] Wang Fan-hsi. *Memoirs of a Chinese Revolutionary*, Columbia U.P., 1991.

[2] Chen Duxiu *Appeal to All the Comrades of the Chinese Communist Party* December 10, 1929, w.m.org.

[3] Sukhanov, N. *The Russian Revolution 1917 A Personal Record*, OUP, London, 1955, p8-9 and 12.

[4] Nassonov, N. Fokine, N. and Albrecht, A. *The Letter from Shanghai*, March 17 1927, *Problems of the Chinese Revolution*, New Park, 1969.

[5] Isaacs, H. *The Tragedy of the Chinese Revolution*, w.m.org, p179.

[6] Pantsov, A., and Levine, S. *Mao*, Simon & Schuster, 2012, p178.

[7] Chen Duxiu *Appeal* ... Op. cit.

[8] Isaacs, Op. cit. p176.

[9] Trotsky, L. *To the Politburo of the AUCP(B) CC*. 31 March 1927. www.oocities.org.

[10] Chen Duxiu *Appeal* ... Op. cit.

[11] Trotsky, L. *Class Relations in the Chinese Revolution*, 3 April 1927, w.m.org.

[12] Isaacs, Op. cit. p185.

[13] CCP and KMT joint manifesto issued in Shanghai on 6 April, *International Press Correspondence*, 14 April, 1927.

[14] North, R. *Moscow and the Chinese Communists*, Stanford U.P., 1963. p92-94.

[15] Stranahan, P. *The Chinese Communist Party during the Third Period, 1927-34*, in *In Search of Revolution*, I.B. Tauris, 2004.

[16] Trotsky, L. *Stalin and the Chinese Revolution* w.m.org.

[17] McColl, R. *The Oyuwan Soviet*, Jnl of Asian Studies, 1967, 27(1)41-60.

[18] Trotsky, L. *Problems of the Chinese Revolution*, New Park, 1963, p231-232.

[19] Stalin, J. *Questions of the Chinese Revolution.* April 21 1927 CW9:224-234.

[20] North, Op. cit. p98/9.

[21] *Theses of Comrade Stalin for Propagandists*, Approved by the CC of the CPSU, International Press Correspondence, 28 April, 1927, p. 543.

[22] Isaacs, Op. cit. p224.

[23] Lenin, V. *Draft Theses on National and Colonial Questions*, June 1920, CW31:149.

[24] Stalin, J. *Questions of the Chinese Revolution*, April 21 1927, CW9:224-234.

[25] Chen Duxiu, *Pravda* of 15 May 1927 reprinted the speech of Chen Duxiu made just over a fortnight earlier on 29 April at the Convention of the Chinese Communist Party.

[26] Alexander, R. *International Trotskyism 1929-1985,* 1991, Duke U.P. rosswolfe.files.wordpress.com.

[27] North, Op. cit. p102.

[28] Isaacs, Op. cit. p256.

[29] Peng Shuzhi, Introduction *Trotsky on China*, Monad Press, 1976.

[30] Burnham, J. *The People's Front*, 1937, w.m.org.

[31] Cohen, A. *The Communism of Mao Tse-Tung*. Univ. of Chicago Press, 1966, p94 et seq.

[32] Isaacs, Op. cit. p145.

[33] Stalin, J. *Talk with Students of the Sun Yat-sen University*, May 13, 1927 CW9:243-73.

[34] North, Op. cit., p102.

[35] Trotsky, L. *Problems of the Chinese Revolution*. New Park, 1969.

[36] Stalin, J. *Concerning Questions of the Chinese Revolution* May 24, 1927 CW9:241.

[37] North, R., and Xenia E. *M.N. Roy's Mission to China*, Univ of California Press, p106-107.

[38] North and Xenia, Op. cit., p106.

[39] Chen Duxiu, *Appeal* ... Op. cit.

[40] Chen Duxiu *Appeal* ... Op. cit.

[41] North and Xenia, Op. cit., p108.

[42] Vishnayakova, V. *Two Years in Revolutionary China, 1925-27*, Harvard East Asian Monographs, 1971, p320.

[43] Tien-wei *Wu A Review of the Wuhan Debacle: The Kuomintang-Communist Split of 1927*, Jnl Asian Studies, 1969, 29(1)125-143.

[44] International Press Correspondence 16 June 1926, p737.

[45] Fan-hsi, Op. cit. p37.

[46] Chen Duxiu *Appeal* ... Op. cit.

[47] Roy, M. *Revolution and Counter-Revolution in China*, Renaissance Publishers, 1946, p 615.

[48] Wittfogel, K. *The Legend of "Maoism"*, TCQ, 1960, No 2, p16-34.

[49] Chen Po-ta. *Mao Tse-tung on the Chinese Revolution*, 1963 FLPH, Peking.

[50] Chen Duxiu *Appeal* ... Op. cit.

[51] Stalin, J. *Questions of the Chinese Revolution,* w.m.org.

[52] Chen Duxiu *Appeal* ... Op. cit.

[53] Alexander, Op. cit.

[54] Hsiao Tso-liang *Chinese Communism and the Canton Soviet of 1927*, The China Quarterly, 1967, No 30 p49-78.

[55] Hofheinz, R. *The Autumn Harvest Insurrection*, The China Quarterly, 1967, No. 32, p37.

[56] Pantsov AND Levine, *Mao,* Op. cit. p191-192.

[57] Roy, Op. cit., p405.

[58] Roy, Op. cit. p405.

[59] Thornton, R. *The Comintern and Chinese Communists 1928-31*, p102-105.

[60] Hsiao Tso-liang, Op. cit.

[61] Thornton, R. *Emergence of a New Comintern Strategy for China: 1928*, in International Communism and the Communist International 1919-43, MUP, 2004, p66-110.

[62] Stranahan, P. *The CCP During the Third Period, 1927-34*, in In Search of Revolution, Ed. Worsley, M. Tauris, 2004.

[63] North and Xenia, Op. cit., p112.

[64] Peng Pi-lan, *The Chinese Revolution,* Education for Socialists, SWP, 1972, p12.

[65] Strong, A. *China's Millions,* Univ. of Michigan, 2006, p242&251-2.

[66] Roy, M. T*he Lessons of the Chinese Revolution*, Labour Monthly, Nov., 1927, w.m.org.

Chapter 6

From the Canton "Commune" to the Jiangxi "Soviet"

[1] *Political Resolution of the November Plenum of the CC., CCP,* International Press Correspondence, January 26, 1928.

[2] Hofheinz, R. *The Autumn Harvest Insurrection*. The China Quarterly, No. 32 (Oct.-Dec., 1967), p37-87.

[3] Peng Pi-lan, *The Chinese Revolution*, Education for Socialists, SWP, 1972, p13.

[4] Deutscher, I. *Stalin* Pelican Books, London, 1984, p399/400.

[5] Hsiao Tso-Liang, *Chinese Communism and the Canton Soviet of 1927*, The China Quarterly. 1967 No 30 p49-78.

[6] Hofheinz, Op. cit.

[7] Guillermaz, J. *The Nanchang Uprising*, The China Quarterly, No. 11, 1962, p160-168.

[8] Schwartz, B. *Chinese Communism and the Rise of Mao*. Harper Torchbooks 1967 p92.

[9] Guillermaz, Op. cit.

[10] North, R. *Moscow and the Chinese Communists*, Stanford Univ. Press, 1963.

[11] Hofheinz, Op. cit.

[12] North, *Moscow* ... Op. cit. p113 et seq.

[13] Braun, O. *A Communist Agent in China 1932-1939*, C. Hurst & Co., 1982.

[14] Chen Duxiu *Appeal to All the Comrades of the Chinese Communist Party* December 10, 1929, w.m.org.

[15] Liu Shaoqi, *Letter to the Party Centre Concerning Past Work*... March 1937, in Saich, T. *The Rise to Power of the CCP*, Sharp, 1994, p779 – 782.

[16] Schwartz, Op. cit. p105.

[17] Elleman, B. *Moscow and the Emergence of Communist Power in China 1925-1931*, Routledge 2010.

[18] Blick, R. *Canton Commune*, Rev. Hist. 1991 Vol 3 No 4.

[19] Isaacs, H. *Tragedy of the Chinese Revolution*, Secker & Warberg, 1938, p372.

[20] Fox, R. *The Commune of Canton*, w.m.org.

[21] *Communist International,* February 25, 1927, p. 19, w.m.org.

[22] *Communist International,* June 29 1927, w.m.org.

[23] North, R. *The Rise of Mao Tse-Tung,* The Far Eastern Quarterly, 1952 11(2)137-145.

[24] Schwartz, Op. cit.

[25] Trotsky, L. *Problems of the Chinese Revolution*, New Park 1969, p120-184.

[26] Trotsky. L. *The Chinese Question After the 6th Congress,* w.m.org.

[27] Lescot, P. *Before Mao*, Harper Collins, 2004, p105-111.

[28] Thornton, R. *Emergence of a New Comintern Strategy for China: 1928,* in International Communism and the Communist International 1919-43, MUP, 2004, p66-110.

[29] Saich, T. *The Rise to Power of the Chinese Communist Party*, Sharpe, 1996, p358-368.

[30] Pantsov, A. and Levine, S. *Mao*, Simon & Schuster, 2012, p193.

[31] *The Red Armies in 1929-1930*: Rev Hist. 1990 2(4)22-25.

[32] Pantsov and Levine, Op. cit. p225-226.

[33] Perry, E. *Reclaiming the Chinese Revolution*, Jnl of Asian Studies, 2008, 67(4)1147-1164.

[34] Harrison, J. *The Li Li-san Line and the CCP in 1930 (Part 1)* The China Quarterly, No. 14, 1963, p178-194.

[35] Lescot, Op. cit. p120.

[36] Harrison, Op. cit. *(Part 1)*.

[37] Saich T. *The CCP during the era of the Comintern (1919-1943),* www.hks.harvard.edu.

[38] Sullivan, L. *Reconstruction and Rectification of the Communist Party in the Shanghai Underground: 1931-34*, The China Quarterly, No. 101, 1985, p78-97.

[39] Durand, D. *The Birth of the Chinese Left Opposition*, Rev. Hist. 1990, Vol 2, No 4.

[40] Wang Fan-hsi, *Memoirs of a Chinese Revolutionary*, Columbia U.P., 1980, p114/5.

[41] Stranahan, P. *The CCP During the Third Period, 1927-34*, in In Search of Revolution, I.B. Tauris, 2004.

[42] Lescot, Op. cit. p121/2.

[43] Lescot, Op. cit.

[44] Hofheinz, Op. cit.

[45] Saich, *The Rise* ... Op. cit. p428-439.

[46] Cohen, A. *The Communism of Mao Tse-tung.* Univ. of Chicago Press, 1966, p43.

[47] Thornton, R. *Comintern and the Chinese Communists 1928-31*, Univ. of Washington Press, 1969, p102-107.

[48] Mao Zedong *On Correcting Some Mistaken Ideas in the Party*, Dec 1929; *A Single Spark Can Start a Prairie Fire*, Jan 1930.

[49] Braun, O. *A Comintern Agent in China*, Hurst & Company, 1982, p55.

[50] Thornton, *The Comintern* ... Op. cit. p136.

[51] Saich *The Rise* ... Op. cit. p439-445.

[52] Hofheinz, Op. cit.

[53] *Inprecor*, Vol. 10, August 21, 1930, p777.

[54] Harrison, J. *The Li Li-san Line and the CCP in 1930 (Part 2)* The China Quarterly, No. 15, 1963, p140-159.

[55] Harrison, Op. cit. *(Part 2).*

[56] *Inprecor* 7 August 1930 p697-698.

[57] Harrison, Op. cit. *(Part 2).*

[58] Schwartz, Op. cit.

[59] North, *The Rise of* ... Op. cit.

[60] Harrison, Op. cit. *(Part 1).*

[61] Schwartz, Op. cit.

[62] Saich T. *The CCP during the era of the Comintern (1919-1943)* www.hks.harvard.edu.

[63] Pantsov, A. *How Stalin Helped Mao Zedong* ... Issues & Studies, 2005, 41(3)181-207.

[64] Lescot, Op. cit. p136.

[65] Harrison, Op. cit. *(Part 1).*

[66] Isaacs. Op. cit. p387-8.

[67] Liu Shaoqi, Op. cit.

[68] Harrison, Op. cit. *(Part 1).*

[69] Report to the Executive Committee of the All-China TU Federation, in Isaacs, H. Op. cit. p388.

[70] Lescot, Op. cit.

[71] Harrison, Op. cit. *(Part 1).*

[72] Benton G. *Bolshevising China: From Lenin to Stalin to Mao, 1921 – 1944*. Leeds Univ., East Asia Papers No 22, 1996.

[73] Benton Op. cit.

[74] Pantsov and Levine, Op. cit. p237-8.

[75] Schwartz, Op. cit.

[76] Kagan, R. *The Chinese Trotskyist Movement and Ch'en Tu-hsiu*, PhD, Univ. of Pennsylvania, p155.

[77] Peng Pi-lan, *The Chinese Revolution*, Education for Socialists, SWP, 1972, p13.

[78] Sullivan, Op. cit.

[79] Stranahan, Op. cit.

[80] *The Peasant War in China*, Rev. Hist., 1990 2(4)23.

[81] Saich, *The Rise* ... Op. cit. p440.

[82] Trotsky, *Problems* ... Op. cit. p71.

[83] McColl, R. *The Oyuwan Soviet Area*, J. Asian Studies 27(1)41-60, Nov. 1967.

[84] *Letter of the ECCI received 16 November 1930*, Degras, J. Vol 3 p135-140.

[85] Degras, J, *The Communist International, Selected Documents* , O.U.P., 1965. Vol 3:168.

[86] Isaacs, Op. cit p393.

[87] Sullivan, Op. cit.

[88] Chen Duxiu, *Appeal* ... Op. cit.

[89] *International Press Correspondence,* December 12, 1928.

Chapter 7

From the Jiangxi "Soviet" to Yenan

[1] Morley, D, *The CCP 1927-37*, 2014, www,marxist.com.

[2] *Resolution on Certain Questions in the History of our Party … 11th Central Committee of the CCP*, www.marxist.org.

[3] Braun, O. *A Communist Agent in China 1932-1939*, Hurst & Co., 1982, p15.

[4] *International Press Correspondence* 1 June 1932.

[5] Averill, S. *Transition from Urban to Rural in the Chinese Revolution*, The China Journal, No. 48, 2002, p87-121.

[6] Averill, *Transition* … Op. cit.

[7] Thornton, R. *Comintern and the Chinese Communists 1928-31*, Univ. of Washington Press, 1969, p130/131.

[8] Mao Zedong, *Report of the Chingkanshan Front Committee to the Central Committee,* Nov 1928, w.m.org.

[9] Guillermaz, J. *A History of the Chinese Communist Party 1921-1949*, Methuen, 1972, p208.

[10] Shao-Chuan Leng, *Pre-1949 Development of the Communist Chinese System of Justice*, The China Quarterly, No. 30, 1967, p93-114.

[11] Shao-Chuan Leng, Op. cit.

[12] Shao-Chuan Leng, Op. cit.

[13] Cheng, L. *Women and Class Analysis in the Chinese Land Revolution*, Berkeley Journal of Gender, Law and Justice, 2013, 4(1)62-93.

[14] Hinton, W. *Fanshen*, Pelican, 1972, p573.

[15] Saich, T. *The Rise to Power of the CCP*, Sharp, 1994, p355.

[16] Hinton, W. *Fanshen*, Pelican, 1972.

[17] Cheng, L. Op. cit.

[18] Averill, S. *Party, Society, and Local Elite in the Jiangxi Communist Movement*, Jnl. Asian Studies, 1987, 46(2)279-303.

[19] Averill, S. *Party,*… Op. cit.

[20] Saich, T. *The Rise … Op. cit.* p556.

[21] Tomlinson, B.R. *The Chinese Revolution and the Peasantry*, School of Oriental & African Studies, Univ. of London.

[22] Chi-hsi Hu, *The Sexual Revolution in the Kiangsi Soviet*, The China Quarterly, No. 59, 1974, p477-490.

[23] Chi-hsi Hu, Op cit.

[24] Hinton, Op. cit. p184-188 and 208.

[25] Deutscher, I. *Ironies of History*, OUP, 1966, p89.

[26] Johnson, K. *Women, the Family and Peasant Revolution in China*, Univ. of Chicago Press, 1983.

[27] Duncan, J and Li, P. *Women and Land Tenure in China*, 2001, Rural Development Institute.

[28] Kyung Ae Park, *Women and Revolution in China*, Korea and World Affairs, 1990 14(4)747-774.

[29] Johnson, K.A. *Women, the Family and Peasant Revolution in China*, Univ of Chicago Press, 1983.

[30] Cheng, OP. cit.

[31] *Letter from ECCI to CCP,* 29 Oct 1929, in Saich T. *The Rise* … Op. cit.

[32] Schwartz, B. *Chinese Communism and the Rise of Mao*, Harper Torchbooks 1967 p174 et seq.

[33] Braun, Op. cit. p57.

[34] Short, P. *Mao A Life,* John Murray, 2004, p265-267.

[35] Anon. *The Peasant War in China*, Rev. Hist., 1990, 2(4)22-25.

[36] Schwartz, Op. cit.

[37] Thornton, R. *The Emergence of a New Comintern Strategy for China: 1928*. In International Communism and the Communist International 1919-43, MUP, p104-110.

[38] Short, Op. cit. p268-271.

[39] Saich, *The Rise* … Op. cit. p509-524.

[40] Schwartz, Op. cit.

[41] Dorrill, W. *Origins of the Maoist Myth*, China Quarterly, Vol 36 1968, p45-60.

[42] Short, Op. cit.

[43] Selden, Op. cit. p79.

[44] Braun, Op. cit. p20.

[45] Barnouin, B., and Yu, C. *Zhou Enlai*, Chinese UP, 2006, p44-49.

[46] Saich, *The Rise* … Op. cit. p509-524.

[47] Brandt, C. *A Documentary History of Chinese Communism*, Allen & Unwin, 1952, p217.

[48] Shao-Chuan Leng, Op. cit.

[49] Isaacs, H. *Tragedy of the Chinese Revolution*, Secker & Warberg, 1938, p 421, www.marxists.org.

[50] Anon. *The Peasant War in China* Rev History, 1990, p24.

[51] Isaacs, Op. cit. p391.

[52] Saich, *The Rise* … Op. cit. p558.

[53] Dorrill, Op. cit.

[54] North, R. *Moscow and the Chinese Communists,* p160-167.

[55] Benton, G. *Zheng Chaolin* New Left Review 14-04-03.

[56] Kampen, T. *Mao Zedong, Zhou Enlai and the Evolution of the Chinese Communist Leadership*, Nordic Institute of Asian Studies, 2000, p60.

[57] North, Op. cit. p158.

[58] Pantsov, A. & Levine, S. *Mao*, Simon & Schuster, 2012, p265-6.

[59] Harrison, J. *The Li Li-san Line and the CCP in 1930 (Part 2*), The China Quarterly, No. 15, 1963, p140-159.

[60] Saich, *The Rise* … Op. cit. p509-524.

[61] Kampen, *Mao Zedong,…* Op. cit.

[62] Degras, J. *The Communist International, 1919-1943: Documents,* Vol 3:168.

[63] Isaacs, OP. cit. p418-419.

[64] Chi-Hsi Hu, *Hua Fu, the Fifth Encirclement Campaign and the Tsunyi Conference,* The China Quarterly, No. 43, 1970, p 31-46.

[65] Sheng, M. *Mao, Stalin, and the Formation of the Anti-Japanese United Front: 1935-37,* China Quarterly No. 129, 1992, p149-170.

[66] Saich, *The Rise* … Op. cit. p509-524.

[67] Wales, N. *Red Dust*, Stanford U.P., 1962, p3.

[68] Smedley, A. *The Great Road*, Monthly Review Press, 1956, p309.

[69] Sheng, Op. cit.

[70] Kampen, *Mao Zedong* ... Op. cit.

[71] Garavante, A. *The Long March*, The China Quarterly, No 22, 1965, p89-124.

[72] Yang, B. *The Zunyi Conference as One Step in Mao's Rise to Power*, The China Quarterly, No. 106, 1986, p235-271.

[73] Kampen, T. *The Zunyi Conference and Further Steps in Mao's Rise to Power* The China Quarterly, No. 117, 1989, p118-134.

[74] Peng Shuzi: *Some Comments on Mao Tse-tung* 1968; Peng Shuzi Internet Archive.

[75] Garavante, Op. cit.

[76] Garavante, Op. cit.

[77] Selden, M, *The Yenan Way*, Harvard U.P. 1971, p6.

[78] Goodman, D. *Revolutionary Women and Women in the Revolution*, The China Quarterly, No. 164, 2000, p915-942.

[79] Guillermaz, Op. cit. pp267 et seq.

[80] Sheng, Op. cit.

[81] Sheng, Op. cit.

[82] Gillin, D. *"Peasant Nationalism" in the History of Chinese Communism*, Jnl. Asian Studies, Feb 1964, Vol 23, pp269-289.

[83] Tomlinson, Op. cit.

[84] Duncan, J and Ping, L. *Women and Land Tenure in China*, 2001, Rural Development Institute.

Chapter 8

Yenan, the Second United Front, and the War Against Japan

[1] Shao-Chuan Leng, *Pre-1949 Development of the Communist Chinese System of Justice*, The China Quarterly, No. 30, 1967, p93-114.

[2] Cohen, A. *The Communism of Mao Tse-Tung*. Univ. of Chicago Press, 1966, p193.

[3] Degras, J. *The Communist International, 1919-1943*, OUP, 1956, Vol 3:353-355.

[4] Benton, G. *The "Second Wang Ming Line" (1935-38)*, The China Quarterly, No. 61, 1975, p61-94.

[5] Wang Ming, *Report to the 7th World Congress*, 1935. www6.svsu.edu/~jalewis2.

[6] Benton, *The Second...* Op. cit.

[7] Benton, *The Second...* Op. cit.

[8] Sheng, M. *Mao, Stalin, and the Formation of the Anti-Japanese United Front: 1935-37*, The China Quarterly No. 129, 1992, p149-170.

[9] Sheng, Op. cit.

[10] Sheng, Op. cit.

[11] Mao Zedong, *Open Cable Message for Armistice and Negotiations for Establishing an Alliance Against Japanese Aggression*, 5 May 1936, w.m.org.

[12] Dimitrov, G. *Speech on the Chinese Question*, 10 Aug 1937, w.m.org.

[13] Dimitrov, G. *Notes on the Chinese Question*, 11 Nov 1937, w.m.org.

[14] Benton, G. *The Second…* Op. cit.

[15] Wang Ming, *Revolutionary Movement* at www6.svsu.edu/~jalewis2/Communist%20 International/1935.

[16] Isaacs, Op. cit. p440.

[17] Sheng, Op. cit.

[18] Shum Kui Kwong, *The Second Wang Ming Line (1935-38)* The China Quarterly No 69, 1977, p136-154.

[19] Sheng, Op. cit.

[20] Mao Zedong – *Open letter from the CCP to the KMT*, 26 Aug 1936 w.m.org.

[21] Sheng, Op. cit.

[22] Benton, *The Second…* Op. cit.

[23] Wang Ming, Communist International, Oct. 1937, Vol.14, No.10.

[24] van Slyke, L. *The United Front in China,* Jnl. of Contemporary History, 1970, 5(3)119-135.

[25] Braun, O. *A Communist Agent in China 1932-1939*, Hurst & Co. Ltd., 1982, p187.

[26] Pantsov, A. *How Stalin Helped Mao Zedong …* Issues & Studies, 2005, 41(3)181-207.

[27] Snow, E. *Red Star Over China*, Gollanz, 1968, p231.

[28] Smedley, A. *Battle Hymn of China*, Da Capo Press, 1975.

[29] Li Fu-jen, *End of the Chinese Soviets*, New International, Jan 1938 pp16-20, MIA.

[30] Braun, Op. cit. p195-197.

[31] Wales, N. *Why the Chinese Communists Support the United Front: An Interview with Lo Fu*, Pacific Affairs, 1938, 11(3)311-322.

[32] Saich, T. *The Rise to Power of the CCP*, Sharp, 1994, p771-3.

[33] Trotsky, L. *Revolution and War in China* Jan 1938 w.m.com.

[34] Kampen, T. *Mao Zedong, Zhou Enlai and the Evolution of the Chinese Communist Leadership*, Nordic Institute of Asian Studies, 2000, p86-93.

[35] Pantsov, A. & Levine, S. *Mao*, Simon & Schuster, 2012, p323.

[36] Epstein, I. *My China Eye*, Long River Press, 2000.

[37] Shum Kui Kwong, Op. cit.

[38] Mao Zedong, T*alks with Messrs K'o Lo-man, Ya-Te, Fu Lu-te and Lei K'o-nan*, CW Vol 6 Part 1, 2 July 1938, w.m.org.

[39] Mao Zedong *The New Stage,* October 1938, www.marxists.org.

[40] Rousset, P. *The Maoist Project Tested in the Struggle for Power*, International Institute for Research and Education Number 3.

[41] Braun, Op. cit. p235.

[42] Belden J, *China Shakes the World*, Gollancz. 1951, p51 and 398.

[43] Ibid, p406.

[44] Mao Zedong, *On New Democracy*, January 1940, www.marxist.org.

[45] Pantsov, A. *How Stalin Helped Mao Zedong …* Issues & Studies, 2005, 41(3)181-207.

[46] Ibid.

[47] Wang Ming, Communist International, Vol.14, No.10, Oct. 1937.

[48] North, R. *Moscow and the Chinese Communists*, Stanford Univ. Press, 1963, p189/190.

[49] Li Fu-jen, *After the Fall of Wuhan*, January 1939, MIA.

[50] Belden, Op. cit. p71-78.

[51] Rosinger, L. *Politics and Strategy of China's Mobile War*, Pacific Affairs, 1939, 12(3)263-277.

[52] Braun, Op. cit. p17.

[53] North, Op. cit. p189/190.

[54] Ibid p204.

[55] Hu Chiao-mu, *Thirty Years of the CCP*, 1951, FLPH.

[56] Stranahan-Jackal, P. *Changes in Policy for Yenan Women, 1935-1947*: Modern China, 1981, 7(1)83-112.

[57] Belden. Op. cit. p122.

[58] Saich, *The Rise*, ... Op. cit. p935.

[59] Engels, F. *Origins of the Family, Private Property, and the State*, w.m.org.

[60] Stranahan, Op. cit.

[61] *Liberation Daily*, 2 and 3 July 1941, quoted in Stranahan, Op. cit.

[62] Saich, *The Rise*, ... Op. cit. p1016.

[63] Chi-hsi Hu, *The Sexual Revolution in the Kiangsi Soviet*, The China Quarterly, No. 59, 1974, p477-490.

[64] *Liberation Daily*, 26 Oct. 1941, quoted in Stranahan, Op. cit.

[65] Hua Chang-ming, *The feminine condition and the Chinese Communists in action: Yan'an, 1935-1946.* Paris: Centre de Recherches et de Documentation sur la Chine Contemporaine de l'Ecole des Hautes Etudes en Sciences Sociales, 4, 1981.

[66] Hu Chiao-mu, Op. cit.

[67] Johnson, C. *Peasant Nationalism and Communist Power*, Stanford U.P. 1962, p56.

[68] Selden, M. *The Yenan Way*, Harvard U.P. 1971, p188-189.

[69] Ibid, p111.

[70] North, Op. cit. p196.

[71] Ding Ling, *Thoughts on 8 March, libcom.org/library/thoughts-8-march-women%E2%80%99s-day.*

[72] Benton, G. *The Yenan Opposition*, NLR., 92. 1975, p93-106.

[73] Hua Chang-Ming, Op. cit.

[74] Manning, K. *Making a Great Leap Forward?*, Gender & History, 2006, 18(3)574-593.

[75] Wu, E. *The Secret Speeches of Chairman Mao*, 1989, Harvard U.P., 1989, p456.

[76] Cheek, T. *The Fading of Wild Lilies*, The Australian Journal of Chinese Affairs, No 11, 1984, p25-58.

[77] libcom.org/library/wild-lily.

[78] Cheek, Op. cit.

[79] libcom.org/library/wild-lily.

[80] Mao Zedong *Talks at the Yenan Forum on Literature and Art*, 2 May 1942, w.m.org.

[81] Benton G. *Bolshevising China: From Lenin to Stalin to Mao, 1921 – 1944.* Leeds Univ., East Asia Papers No 22, 1996.

[82] Chang, J. and Halliday, J. *Mao*, Vintage, 2007, p321-322.

[83] Fairbank, J. *The Great Chinese Revolution 1800-1985* Harper Perennial, 1987 p255 et seq.

[84] Shao-Chuan Leng, *Pre-1949 Development of the Communist Chinese System of Justice*, The China

Quarterly, No. 30, 1967, p93-114.

[85] Short, P. *Mao*, McMillan, 2001.

[86] Deutscher, I. *Stalin*, Pelican, 1949, p582-3.

[87] Goodman, D. *Revolutionary Women and Women in the Revolution*, The China Quarterly, No. 164, 2000, p915-942.

[88] Stranahan, Op. cit.

[89] Stranahan, Op. cit.

[90] Goodman, Op. cit.

[91] Hua Chang-Ming. Op. cit.

Chapter 9

The Final Collapse of the KMT: the CCP Assumes Power

[1] Woods, A. *The Chinese Revolution of 1949*, 1 October 2009, w.m.com.

[2] Sheng, M. *Mao, Stalin, and the Formation of the Anti-Japanese United Front: 1935-37*, The China Quarterly No. 129, 1992, p149-170.

[3] Peng Shuzi, *Some Comments on Mao Tse-tung*, 1968, w.m.org.

[4] Ibid.

[5] Hinton, W. *Fanshen*, Pelican, 1972, p378.

[6] Belden, J. *China Shakes the World*, Gollancz, 1951, p121.

[7] Pantsov, A. and Levine, S. *Mao*, Simon & Schuster, 2012, p340-342.

[8] Chen Po-ta, *Stalin and the Chinese Revolution*, 1953, FLPH.

[9] Ibid.

[10] Pantsov and Levine, Op. cit., p373.

[11] Schram, B. *Political Thought of Mao Tse-tung*, Praeger, 1963, p295.

[12] Pantsov and Levine, Op. cit. p345 and 392.

[13] Belden, Op. cit. p98.

[14] Glass, F. *China After World War II*, 1946, w.m.org.

[15] Pantsov and Levine, Op. cit. p347.

[16] Chang, J. and Halliday, J. *Mao*, Vintage, 2007, p149.

[17] North, R. *Moscow and the Chinese Communists*, Stanford Univ. Press, 1963, p205/240.

[18] Peng Shuzi, *The Causes of the Victory of the Chinese Communist Party over Chiang Kai-Shek*, Feb., 1952, w.m.org.

[19] Hinton, Op. cit. p182.

[20] Kerry, T. *Mao-Stalin Rift: Myth or Fact*, 1960, w.m.org.

[21] Mandel, E. *The Third Chinese Revolution*, May 1950. MIA.

[22] Wang Fanxi, *The Stalinist State in China*, 1951, Socialist Review.

[23] Hinton, Op. cit. p711.

[24] van Slyke, L. *The China White Paper*, 1967, Stanford, U.P.

[25] Kerry, *Mao-Stalin,* .... Op. cit.

[26] Cohen, A. *The Communism of Mao Tse-tung*. Univ. of Chicago Press, 1966, p94 et seq.

[27] Kerry, *Mao-Stalin* … Op. cit.
[28] North, *Moscow* … Op. cit p223.
[29] Mandel, E. *The Third Chinese Revolution*, May 1950] MIA.
[30] Peng Shuzi, Op. cit.
[31] Ibid.
[32] North, *Moscow* … Op. cit. p205 et seq.
[33] Chao Kuo-chun, *Agrarian Policy of the Chinese Communist Party* Asia Publishing House. 1960.
[34] Glass, *China* … Op. cit.
[35] Tanaka Kyoko, *The Civil War and Radicalization of the Chinese Communist Agrarian Policy, 1945-1947*, Papers on Far Eastern History, No. 8, 1973, p49-114.
[36] Sullivan, W. *Land Reform Plans in China*, Far Eastern Survey, 1950, 19(4)33-38.
[37] Hinton, Op. cit. p573.
[38] Mao Zedong, *On Policy*, 25 December 1940, SW II, p.446.
[39] Tanaka Kyoko, *Mao and Liu in the 1947 Land Reform*, The China Quarterly, No. 75, 1978, p566-593.
[40] Ibid.
[41] Hinton, Op. cit. p281-2.
[42] Hsieh Yueh, *Mao Tse-tung's "Revolution", Report on Chinese Stalinism*, 1949, w.m.org.
[43] Saich, T. *The Rise to Power of the CCP*, Sharpe, 1996, p1295-8.
[44] Hsieh Yueh, Op. cit.
[45] Glass, *China* … Op. cit.
[46] Mao Zedong, *New Democracy*, 1940, w.m.org.
[47] Shao-Chuan Leng, *Pre-1949 Development of the Communist Chinese System of Justice*, The China Quarterly, No. 30, 1967, p93-114.
[48] Wang Fanxi, Op cit.
[49] Hinton, Op. cit. p572-583.
[50] Shao-Chuan Leng, Op. cit..
[51] Wang Fanxi, Op. cit.
[52] Glass, *China* … Op. cit.
[53] Grant, T. *The Unbroken Thread*, Wellred Books, 1989, p282-288.
[54] Belden, Op. cit., p376.
[55] North, *Moscow* … Op. cit. p239.
[56] Peng Shuzi, *The Causes* … Op. cit.
[57] Ibid.
[58] CIA Report, *Developments in China* 1949, ORE 44-49.
[59] Schram, S. *Mao Tse-Tung*, Penguin Books, 1966, p242.
[60] CIA Report, … Op. cit.
[61] Thompson, T. *China's Nationalisation of Foreign Firms 1949-57*. University of Maryland, 1979.
[62] Shao-Chuan Leng, Op. cit.
[63] Lenin, V. *Report on the Tasks of the Soviet Power*, 25 October 1917, CW26:240.
[64] Sullivan, Op. cit.

[65] Lui, C. *An Aborted Revolution*, Fourth International, 1950 11(1)3-7.

[66] Ibid.

[67] North, *Moscow* … Op. cit. p205/240.

[68] Peng Shuzi, *The Causes* … Op. cit.

[69] Hsieh Yueh, Op. cit.

[70] Ibid.

[71] Ibid.

[72] Belden, Op. cit., p330 and 341.

Chapter 10

The New Democracy

[1] Roberts, J. *Lenin, Trotsky and the Theory of the Permanent Revolution*, Wellred, 2007, p138.

[2] Mao Zedong, *On New Democracy*, Jan 1940, w.m.org.

[3] collections.mun.ca/PDFs/radical/*MaoTseTungontheChineseRevolution*.pdf

[4] Mao Zedong, *On Coalition Government*, April 1945, w.m.org.

[5] Mao Zedong, *The Fight for a New China*, New Century Publishers, 1945.

[6] Mao Zedong, *On Coalition Government*, 1945, w.m.org.

[7] Liu Shaoqi, *Strengthen the Great Revolutionary Unity of the Chinese People*, Sept. 1949, w.m.org.

[8] Kerry, T. *The Mao Myth* Pathfinder Press, 1977, p129.

[9] Service, J. *Lost Chance in China*, Random House, 1975, p306-07.

[10] Groot, G. *The CCP and United Front Work*, 2004, Routledge, p48.

[11] Woods, A. *The Chinese Revolution of 1949*, 1 October 2009, w.m.com.

[12] Moorad, G. *Lost Peace in China*, E.P. Button & Co., 1949, p197-98.

[13] Mandel, E. *The Third Chinese Revolution*, 1950, w.m.org.

[14] Woods, Op. cit.

[15] Fairbank, J. *The Great Chinese Revolution 1800-1985*, Harper Perennial, 1987, p278.

[16] Twitchett, D. and Fairbank, J. (eds) Cambridge History of China, CUP, 1987, Vol.14, p74.

[17] Mandel, *The Third* … Op. cit.

[18] Peng Shuzi, *Report on the Chinese Situation*, Education for Socialists, SWP, 1952, p43-47.

[19] Kerry, *The Mao Myth*, …Op. cit.

[20] Roberts, Op. cit. p172-192.

[21] Grant, T. *The Unbroken Thread*, Wellred Books, 1989, p301-303.

[22] Chow Ching-wen, *Ten Years of Storm*, https://archive.org/details/*tenyearsofstorm*t013586mbp.

[23] Hsieh Yueh, *Mao Tse-tung's "Revolution", Report on Chinese Stalinism*, 1949, w.m.org.

[24] Peng Shuzi, *Report on* … Op. cit.

[25] CIA Report on Developments in China 1949, ORE 44-49.

[26] Mandel, *The Third*… Op. cit.

[27] Ladejinsky, W. *Carrot and Stick in Rural China*, Foreign Affairs, 1957, 36(1)91-104.

[28] Tomlinson, B. *The Chinese Revolution and the Peasantry*, School of Oriental & African Studies, Univ. of London.

[29] Kaple, D. *Dream of a Red Factory: The Legacy of High Stalinism in China*, OUP, 1994.

[30] Wang Fanxi, *The Stalinist State in China...* 1951, Socialist Review.

[31] Ibid.

[32] Anon. *Labor in Revolutionary China*, Fourth International, March-April 1953.

[33] Mao Zedong, *Fight for a Fundamental Turn*, June 1950, w.m.org.

[34] Peng Shuzi, *Report on* .... Op. cit.

[35] Fairbank, J. – *The Great Chinese Revolution 1800-1985* – Harper Perennial, 1987, p279.

[36] Belden, J. *China Shakes the World*, Gollancz, 1951, p109.

[37] Stranahan-Jackal, P. *Changes in Policy for Yenan Women, 1935-1947*: Modern China, 1981, 7(1) 83-112.

[38] Ibid.

[39] Sargeson, S. *Why Women Own Less,* China Perspectives [Online], 2012/4)

[40] Maitan, L. *Cuba, Military Reformism and Armed Struggle in Latin America*, Intercontinental Press, 20 April 1970, p360.

[41] Lowy, M. *Combined and Uneven Development*, Verso, 1981, p83.

[42] Ibid, p95.

[43] Birchall, I. 1980, w.m.org.

[44] Mao Zedong, *The Chinese Revolution and the Chinese Communist Party*, Dec. 1951, w.m.org.

[45] Lowy, Op. cit. p118.

[46] Lowy. Op. cit. p122.

[47] Peng Shuzi, *The Causes* ... Op. cit.

[48] Roux, A, *Le Casse-tête Chinois,* Editions Sociales, 1970, p. 83.

[49] Anon. *Labor in Revolutionary China,* Op. cit.

[50] Belden, Op. cit. p331.

[51] Peng Shuzi, *The Causes* ... Op. cit.

[52] Lenin, V. *Draft of a Revised Programme*, May 1917, CW 24:469.

Chapter 11

The Unexpectedly Short Life of the New Democracy

[1] Grant, T. *The Unbroken Thread,* Fortress Books, p282-288 and 345.

[2] Mao Zedong, *The Present Situation and our Tasks*, Dec. 1947, w.m.org.

[3] Harris, N. *The Mandate of Heaven*, 1978, Quartet Books.

[4] Zhaojin Ji, *A History of Modern Shanghai Banking*, East Gate Books, 2003, p243.

[5] Lee Tak, *Chinese Bankers ... the Case of Chen Guangfu*, Univ. of Hong Kong, jds.cass.cn.

[6] Mandel, E. *The Third Chinese Revolution Part II,* 1950, w.m.org.

[7] Hsieh Yueh, *Mao Tse-tung's "Revolution", Report on Chinese Stalinism*, 1949, www,marxists.org.

[8] Wales, N. *Why the Chinese Communists Support the United Front: An Interview with Lo Fu*, Pacific Affairs, 1938, 11(3)311-322.

[9] Mao Zedong, *The Chinese Revolution and the Chinese Communist Party*, 1951 edition, w.m.org.

[10] Thompson, T. *China's Nationalisation of Foreign Firms 1949-57*. Univ. of Maryland, 1979.

[11] *Labour Laws and Regulations of the People's Republic of China*, 1956, p65.

[12] Harris, Op. cit.

[13] Far Eastern Economic Review, 26 January 1950.

[14] Duncan, J. and Li, P. *Women and Land Tenure in China*, 2001, Rural Development Institute.

[15] Mao Zedong, *New Democracy*, 1940, w.m.org.

[16] Twitchett, D. and Fairbank, J. (eds) Cambridge History of China, CUP, 1987, Vol.14, p81.

[17] Ibid, p54.

[18] Kazuku Ono, *Chinese Women in a Century of Revolution*, Stanford, U.P., 1989, p179.

[19] Duncan, and Li, Op. cit.

[20] Leader, S, *The Emancipation of Chinese Women*, World Politics, 1973 26(1) 55-79.

[21] Kazuku Ono, Op. cit. p180.

[22] *People's Daily*, 16 May 1956, quoted in Manning, K. *Marxist Maternalism* … The China Review, 2005, 5(1) 81-108.

[23] Leader, Op. cit.

[24] People's Daily, editorial, *Mobilize all Women to Build up the Country and Manage Family Affairs by Industry and Thrift* September 9, 1957.

[25] Leader, Op. cit.

[26] Hao Yufan and Zhai Zhihai, *China's Decision to Enter the Korean War*, The China Quarterly, No. 121, 1990, p94-115.

[27] Ibid.

[28] Ibid.

[29] Whiting, A. *China Crosses The Yalu: The Decision to Enter the Korean War*. Macmillan, 1960.

[30] Kailai Huang, *American Business and the China trade Embargo in the 1950s*, 2001, Economic and Business History.

[31] Service, J. *Lost Chance in China*, Random House, 1975, p306-07.

[32] Thompson, Op. cit.

[33] Peng Shuzi, *Report on the Chinese Situation*, Education for Socialists, SWP, 1952.

[34] Twitchett and Fairbank, Op. cit. p94.

[35] Thompson, Op. cit.

[36] Fairbank, J. *The Great Chinese Revolution 1800-1985*, Harper Perennial, 1987, p277 et seq.

[37] Kwong, J. *The Political Economy of Corruption in China*, 1997, Sharpe, p6.

[38] Peng Shuzi, *The Causes of the Victory of the Chinese Communist Party over Chiang Kai-Shek*, Feb., 1952, w.m.org.

[39] Ibid.

[40] Peng Shuzi, *Report* … Op. cit.

[41] Mandel, E. *Report to 11th Plenum IEC of the FI*, May 1952, w.m.org.

[42] Harris, Op. cit.

[43] Cohen, A. *The Communism of Mao Tse-tung*. Univ. of Chicago Press, 1966, p113.

[44] Hansen, J. *The Problem of Eastern Europe*, w.m.org.

[45] Cohen, Op. cit.

[46] Mandel, *Report to 11th Plenum* … Op. cit.

[47] Chatham House, *From Land Reform to Communes in China*, The World Today, 1959, 15(3)124-133.
[48] Li, H. *Village China Under Socialism and Reform*, Stanford U.P., 2009, p24.
[49] Meisner, M. *Mao's China and After*, The Free Press, 1999, p108.
[50] Cohen, Op. cit. p116-121.
[51] Fairbank, Op. cit., p281.
[52] Rousset, P. *The Chinese Revolution*, International Institute for Research and Education Number 3.
[53] Grant, Op. cit. p279.
[54] Marx, K. *The Civil War in France*, Part III, 1871, w.m.org.
[55] Trotsky, L. *The Transitional Programme*, 1938, w.m.org.
[56] Trotsky, L. *In Defence of Marxism*, 1938, w.m.org.
[57] Trotsky, L. *The Permanent Revolution*, Red Letter Press, p289.

Chapter 12
Establishing the Chinese Workers' State

[1] Lardy, R. *Chinese Economic Planning*, Sharpe, Inc., 1978.
[2] Lardy, N. *Foreign Trade and Economic Reform in China*, Univ. of Cambridge, 1992, p16-17.
[3] Zhou Enlai, *Report of the Work of the Government*, 23 September, 1954, FLPH.
[4] Shabad, T. *Communist China's Five Year Plan*, Far Eastern Survey, Dec., 1955 24(12)189-191.
[5] Twitchett, D. and Fairbank, J. (eds) Cambridge History of China, CUP, 1987, Vol.14, p156.
[6] Ibid. p184.
[7] Kerry, T. *The Mao Myth* Pathfinder Press, 1977, p49.
[8] Lenin, V. *Speech in Favour of the Resolution on the Current Situation*, April 1917, CW 24:308.
[9] Peng Shu-tse, *The CCP in Power*, Monad Press, 1980, p162-166.
[10] Pantsov, A. and Levine, S. *Mao*, Simon & Schuster, 2012, p403-404.
[11] Mao Zedong, *Refute Right Deviationist Views*, 15 June 1953, w.m.org.
[12] Selden, M. *The Political Economy of Chinese Development*, East Gate Books, 1993, p127-130.
[13] Twitchett, and Fairbank, Op. cit. p166.
[14] Li, H. *Village China Under Socialism and Reform*, Stanford U.P., 2009, p25.
[15] Twitchett, and Fairbank, Op. cit. p162.
[16] Chatham House, *From Land Reform to Communes in China*, The World Today, 1959, 15(3)124-13.
[17] Mao Zedong, *On the Cooperative Transformation of Agriculture*, www.marxists.org.
[18] Twitchett, and Fairbank, Op. cit. p168.
[19] Pantsov and Levine, Op. cit., p418-420.
[20] Fairbank, J. *The Great Chinese Revolution 1800-1985,* Harper Perennial, 1987.
[21] Bernstein, T. *Mao Zedong and the Famine of 1959-1960*, The China Quarterly, No. 186, 2006, p421-445.
[22] Twitchett, and Fairbank, Op. cit., p366 & 379.
[23] Roberts, J. *Lenin, Trotsky and the Theory of the Permanent Revolution*, Wellred Books, 2007, p156-158.
[24] Trotsky, L. *Transitional Programme*, 1938, www.marxists.org.
[25] Ibid.

[26] Riddell, J. *The Comintern's Unknown Decision on Workers' Governments*, 14 Aug. 2011, John Riddell. wordpress.com.

[27] Trotsky, *Transitional Programme*, Op. cit.

[28] Hansen, J. *The Problem of Eastern Europe,* w.m.org.

[29] Trotsky, L. *History of the Russian Revolution*, Preface w.m.org.

[30] Woods, A. *The Chinese Revolution of 1949,* 1 Oct 2009, w.m.com.

[31] Peng Shuzi, *The Causes of the Victory of the CCP over Chiang Kai-shek*, Feb. 1952, w.m.org.

[32] Hinton, W. *Fanshen*, Pelican 1972, p210.

[33] Mao Zedong, *On New Democracy*, 1940, FLPH, p362, www.marxists.org.

[34] Grant, T. *The Unbroken Thread,* Fortress books, 1989, p282-289.

[35] Rousset, P. *The Chinese Revolution*, International Institute for Research and Education Number 3.

[36] Grant, Op. cit., 1989, p282-289.

[37] Hansen. J. *The Problem of Eastern Europe,* Feb. 1950, w.m.org.

[38] Trotsky, L. *The Revolution Betrayed*, w.m.org.

[39] Trotsky, *Transitional Programme*, Op. cit.

Chapter 13

China Under Mao: The Great Leap Forward

[1] Twitchett, D. and Fairbank, J. (eds) Cambridge History of China, CUP, 1987. Vol 14, p130.

[2] Peng Shuzi *An Appraisal of the Political Life of Mao*, Monad, 1980, 394-399.

[3] Twitchett and Fairbank, Op. cit. p256.

[4] Maitan, L. *Party, Army and Masses in China,* New Left Books, 1976, p48-49.

[5] Twitchett and Fairbank, Op. cit. p299 et seq.

[6] Bernstein, T. *Stalinism, Famine, and Chinese Peasants: Grain Procurements during the Great Leap Forward*, Theory and Society, 1984, 13(3) 339-377.

[7] Shue, V. *The Fate of the Commune,* Modern China, 1984, 10(3) 259-283.

[8] Mao Zedong, *Editor's Notes from Socialist Upsurge in China's Coutryside*, Sept. and Dec. 1955, Vol. 5.

[9] Twitchett and Fairbank, Op. cit. p95.

[10] Engels, F. *The Peasant Question in France and Germany*, 1894, Selected Works Marx and Engels, Vol. II, 1962, Moscow p433.

[11] Lenin, V. *Speech Delivered at the 1st Congress of Agricultural Communes*, 4 December 1919 CW 30:195.

[12] Lenin, V. *Report on Work in the Countryside*, 23 March 1919, CW 29:198-215.

[13] Lenin, V. *Preliminary Draft Theses on the Agricultural Question.* June 1920 CW 31:152-164.

[14] Trotsky, L. *Transitional Programme*, w.m.org.

[15] Bernstein, *Stalinism …* Op. cit.

[16] Stalin, J, (1934) *Report to the 17th Party Congress on the Work of the CC of the C.P.S.U.(B.)* w.m.org.

[17] Twitchett and Fairbank, Op. cit. p145.

[18] Red Flag, *The Advantages of the Communes,* No. 8, Sept., 1958.

[19] Peng Shuzi, *A Criticism of the Various Views Supporting the Chinese Rural People's Communes*, Aug 1959, w.m.org.

[20] Dutt, G. *Problems of China's Rural Communes*, The China Quarterly, No. 16, 1963, p112-136.

[21] Red Flag, Op. cit.

[22] Lippit, V. *The Commune in Chinese Development*, Modern China, 1977 3(2) 229-255.

[23] Wagner, D. *Background to the Great Leap Forward in Iron and Steel*, Curzon Press. 1997.

[24] Harris, N. *The Mandate of Heaven*, Quartet Books Limited 1978.

[25] Dutt, Op. cit.

[26] Crossman, R. New Stateman, 28 December 1958, p6.

[27] Harris, N. *The Mandate of Heaven*, Quartet Books Limited 1978.

[28] Dutt, Op. cit.

[29] Bernstein, T. *Mao Zedong and the Famine of 1959-1960*, The China Quarterly, No. 186, 2006, p421-445.

[30] Dutt, Op. cit.

[31] Ibid.

[32] Ibid.

[33] Bernstein, *Mao Zedong*… Op. cit.

[34] Dutt, Op. cit.

[35] Pantsov, A. and Levine, S. *Mao*, Simon & Schuster, 2012, p480.

[36] Duncan, J and Li, P. *Women and Land Tenure in China*, 2001, Rural Development Institute.

[37] Dutt, Op. cit.

[38] Bernstein, *Mao Zedong* … Op. cit.

[39] Ibid.

[40] Manning, K. *The Gendered Politics of Woman-Work: Rethinking Radicalism in the Great Leap Forward* Modern China, 2006, 32(3)349-384.

[41] Pantsov and Levine, Op, cit, p475.

[42] Bernstein, *Mao Zedong* … Op. cit.

[43] Bernstein, *Stalinism,* … Op. cit.

[44] Harris, Op. cit.

[45] Bernstein, *Mao Zedong* … Op. cit.

[46] Johnson, K. *Women, the Family and Peasant Revolution in China*, Univ. of Chicago Press, 1983.

[47] Crook, I. *First Years of Yangyi Commune*, International Library of Sociology, 1966, p244.

[48] Manning, *The Gendered* … Op. cit.

[49] Kyung Ae Park, *Women and Revolution in China*, Korea and World Affairs, 1990 14(4)747-774.

[50] Manning, *The Gendered* … Op. cit.

[51] Peng Shuzi, *A Criticism of the Various Views Supporting the Chinese Rural People's Communes*, Aug 1959, w.m.org.

[52] Borge, T. *Women in the Nicaraguan Revolution*, Pathfinder, 1982.

[53] Peng Shuzi, *A Criticism* … Op. cit.

[54] Manning, *The Gendered* … Op. cit.

[55] Leader, S.G. *The Emancipation of Chinese Women*, World Politics, 1973 26(1)55-79.

[56] Ibid.

[57] Fincher, L, *Leftover Women: The Resurgence of Gender Inequality in China*, Zed Books, 2014.

[58] Twitchett and Fairbank, Op. cit. p61.

[59] Peng Shuzi, *A Criticism* ... Op. cit.

[60] Manning, K. *Marxist maternalism, memory, and the mobilization of women in the Great Leap Forward*, The China Review, 2005 5(1)81-108)

[61] Shue, Op. cit.

[62] Rousset, P. *People's Republic of China at 60: Maoism and Popular Power, 1949–1969*, links.org.au.

[63] Weston, F. *China: Communist or Capitalist*, 2010, w.m.com.

Chapter 14

China Under Mao: The Great Proletarian Cultural Revolution

[1] MacFarquhar, R. *The Politics of China*, 1997, CUP, p226.

[2] Peng Shuzi *An Appraisal of the Political Life of Mao*, Monad, 1980, 394-399.

[3] Peng Shuzi, *The Chinese Communist Party in Power*, Monad Press, 1980, p270-275.

[4] Twitchett, D. and Fairbank, J. (eds) Cambridge History of China, CUP, 1987. Vol 14, p130.

[5] Ibid, p464 and 476.

[6] Peng Shuzi, *Two Interviews on the Cultural Revolution*, 1967, w.m.org.

[7] Rice, E. *Mao's Way*, Univ. of California Press, 1972, p208.

[8] Peng Shuzi, *Two Interviews* ... Op. cit.

[9] Peng Shuzi, *The Relationship and Differences Between Mao Zedong and Liu Shaoqi*, 1968, w.m.org.

[10] Peng Shuzi, *Two Interviews* ... Op. cit.

[11] Andreas, J. *Battling over Political and Cultural Power during the Chinese Cultural Revolution*, Theory and Society 31(4)463-519.

[12] Ibid.

[13] Ibid.

[14] Peking Review, Vol 33 No 33, *Decision of the Central Committee of the Chinese Communist Party Concerning the Great Proletarian Cultural Revolution*, www.massline.org.

[15] Yan Jaiqi and Gao Gao, *A Turbulent Decade*, 1996, Univ. of Hawaii, pp55 et seq.

[16] www.npr.org.

[17] Guo Jian, *Resisting Modernity in Contemporary China*, Modern China, 1999 25(3) 343-376.

[18] Hongsheng Jiang, *The Paris Commune in Shanghai*, PhD Thesis Duke University, 2010, p275. http://dukespace.lib.duke.edu.

[19] Hongsheng Jiang, Op. cit., p290.

[20] Peking Review, 13 Jan. 1967, www.massline.org.

[21] Hongsheng Jiang, Op. cit., p292)

[22] Peking Review, 13 Jan. 1967, www.massline.org.

[23] Peking Review, 20 Jan. 1967, www.massline.org.

[24] New China's News Agency, 12 Jan. 1967 *A Proposal of Setting up Shanghai Revolutionary Rebel Organizations' Liaison Post.*

[25] Tao Zhu's Speech at the China Medical University, in Jiang, Op. cit. p361.

[26] Hongsheng Jiang, Op. cit., p428.

[27] Ibid. p408.

[28] Guo Jian, Op. cit.

[29] Hongsheng Jiang, Op. cit., p417.

[30] Mao Zedong, *Talks at Three Meetings With Comrades Chang Ch'un-ch'iao And Yao Wen-yuan*, February 1967, w.m.org.

[31] Hongsheng Jiang, Op. cit., p478.

[32] Marcy, S. *China 1977: End of the Revolutionary Mao Era*, www.workers.org.

[33] Hongsheng Jiang, Op. cit., p490.

[34] Mobo, Gao. *The Battle for China's Past*, 2008. Pluto Press, p62.

[35] Hongsheng Jiang, Op. cit., p442.

[36] Hong Yung Lee, *The Politics of the Chinese Cultural Revolution*, 1980, Univ of California Press, p244 et seq.

[37] Hai Feng, *An Account of the Cultural Revolution in the Canton Area*, 1971, Union Research Institute, Hong Kong, p384.

[38] Qui Jin, *The Lin Biao Incident in the Cultural Revolution*, Stanford, U.P., 1999.

[39] Hong Yung Lee, Op. cit.

[40] Waldergrave, W. *Memoirs*, Constable, 2015.

[41] Trotsky, L. *The Class Nature of the Soviet State*, 1933, www.marxist.org.

[42] Trotsky, L. *The Revolution Betrayed*, w.m.org.

[43] Lafraniere, F., and Burns, J. *Washington Post*. 11 April 2012.

Chapter 15

China Marches Back to Capitalism

[1] Trotsky, L. *The Class Nature of the Soviet State*, October 1933.

[2] Rogovin, V. *1937 Stalin's Year of Terror*, Mehring Books, 1998; Rogovin, V. *Stalin's Terror of 1937-1938*, Mehring Books, 2009.

[3] Trotsky, L. *Revolution Betrayed*, Ch9, 1936, ww.marxists.org.

[4] Brook, D. *Modern Revolution*, U.P. of America. 2005.

[5] Suliman, O. *China's Transition to a Socialist Market Economy*, Quorum Books, 1998.

[6] Fan, Y. et al., *Chinese Village Entrepreneurs*, Durham University Business School, 1996.

[7] Ibid.

[8] Ibid.

[9] Hart-Landsberg, M., and Burkett, P. *China and Socialism*, Monthly Review Press, 2010.

[10] Wu Jinglian, *30 Years of Reform and Prospects for the Future*, Development Research Centre of the State Council of PRC. 2008.

[11] Suliman, Op. cit.

[12] At this time the European Union was coming to the end of a similar process of modernising small and medium enterprises to make them more efficient and profitable. It appears that the Chinese had studied the European initiative and were following a similar path.

[13] OECD, *State Owned Enterprises in China*, 2009.

[14] Jie Dong, *Mergers and Acquisitions*, PhD Thesis, Manchester University, 2006.

[15] Vogel, E. *Deng Xiaoping and the Transformation of China*. Harvard U.P. 2011.

[16] Jung Chang, *Wild Swans*, Flamingo, 1991.

[17] Kosuth, D. *Tiananmen Square ...*, International Socialism, Issue 66, 2010.

[18] Thompson, P. *Democracy and Popular Power in Beijing*, Radical America, 22(5)17-26 1990.

[19] Mandel, E. *For the Beijing Commune*, July 1989, http://www.ernestmandel.org; www.tsquare.tv/links/Walder.html.

[20] Thompson, Op. cit.

[21] China Labour Bulletin, 26 Nov 2014.

[22] Shambaugh, D. *China's Communist Party*, University of California Press, 2008.

[23] OECD, *FDI in Figures*, 2013, latest figures available at time of going to print.

[24] Reuters, Jan 2014.

[25] Wikipedia.

[26] Cheng, L. *China's Changing Political Landscape*, Brookings Institution Press, 2009.

[27] Chan, A., and Unger, J. *A Chinese State Enterprise under the Reforms*, China Journal, No. 62 (Jul., 2009), pp. 1-26.

[28] Garnaut, R., et al., *China's Ownership Transformation*, International Finance Corporation, World Bank, 2005.

[29] China's Foreign Trade, www.china-embassy.org/eng.

[30] Garnaut, Op. cit.

[31] Lardy, N. *The Rise of Private Business in China*. Institute for International Economics, 2014.

[32] Sweetman, A. and Zhang, J. *Economic Transitions with Chinese Characteristics*, McGill, 2009.

[33] Lardy, N. *Markets over Mao*, Peterson Institute, 2014.

[34] In Nicholas Lardy on *Markets over Mao*, www.youtube.com.

[35] Carpenter, T, and Dom, J. *China's Future: Constructive Partner or Emerging Threat?* Cato Institute, 2000.

[36] Economist Intelligence Unit, *Grappling with Leviathan*, 12 January, 2015.

[37] IMF, *Country Reports, China*, 2004; Hurst, W. *The Chinese Worker after Socialism*, CUP, 2009.

[38] Economist, 30 Aug 2014.

[39] Walker, R and Buck, D. *The Chinese Road*, New Left Review 46, July-Aug 2007.

[40] Lardy, *The Rise* ... Op. cit.

[41] Pringle, T, *Trade Unions in China*, Routledge, 2013.

[42] Becker, J and Elfstrom, M, *The Impact of China's Labour Contract Law on Workers*, International Labour Rights Forum May 12, 2010.

[43] The World Bank, http://data.worldbank.org.

[44] www.wto.org.

[45] Price Waterhouse Coopers, *Annual Survey of Foreign Banks in China*, January 2014.

[46] http://data.worldbank.org.

[47] Economist, 19 Feb 2013.

[48] United Nations, *Chinese Direct Investment in Latin America*, Nov. 2013.

[49] China Daily Mail, 8 Jan 2013.

[50] http://english.cpc.people.com.

[51] Hsu, S., Wu, Y., and Zhao, S. *In Search of China's Development Model*, Routledge 2011.

[52] Dickson, B. *Wealth into Power: The Communist Party's Embrace of China's Private Sector*, CUP, 2008.

[53] Hu, R. *China's Paradoxical Reforms*, Global Business and Economics Review, 2011, 8(3)11-21.

[54] BBC News 12 Oct. 2012.

[55] Chong-En Bai, et al., *Crony Capitalism with Chinese Characteristics* Tsinghua University, School of Economics and Management, May 2014.

[56] BBC News, 11 June 2015.

[57] BBC News, 11 November 2013.

[58] Morley, D and Congyue Da, *China: Growing Strikes, Corruption and Debt are Harbingers of Coming Revolution* , marxist.com, 23 October 2013.

[59] BBC News, 31 October 2014.

[60] BBC News, 13 October 2013.

[61] Guardian, 19 June 2014.

[62] Weil, R. *A House Divided: China after 30 Years of 'Reforms'*, Economic and Political Weekly, 43(52)61-69, Dec. 2008.

[63] China Labour Bulletin, 5 Aug 2015.

[64] U.S. National Bureau of Statistics, 2003.

[65] Hart-Landsberg, M and Burkett, P, *China and Socialism*, Monthly Review, 56(3) 2004.

[66] Chong-En Bai, et al., *Crony Capitalism with Chinese Characteristics*, Tsinghua University, School of Economics and Management, May 2014.

[67] Trotsky, L. *The Revolution Betrayed*, www.marxist.org.

[68] Trotsky, L. *In Defence of Marxism*, www.marxist.org.

[69] Jae Ho Chung and Tao-Chiu Lam, *China's "City System" in Flux*, The China Quarterly, No 180 (2004), pp945–64.

[70] Ibid.

Chapter 16

A New Chinese Working Class

[1] Chan, K. *China, Internal Migration*. Blackwell Publishing, 2013.

[2] The World Bank, http://data.worldbank.org.

[3] Li Shi, *Rising Income and Wealth Inequality in China*, Beijing University, 2011.

[4] Foreign and Commonwealth Office, *China: Labour Relations in Guangdong*, 30 Jan. 2015, ww.gov.uk.

[5] Reuters, *IMF sees China slowdown risks*, 7 Oct. 2015.

[6] Guardian, 20 January 2015.

[7] Thompson, E. *The Making of the English Working Class*, Victor Gollancz Ltd., 1963.

[8] Pringle, T. *Trade Unions in China*, Routledge, 2013.

[9] Engels, F. *Conditions of the Working Class in England*, 1887, www.marxists.org.

[10] Pun, N. and Smith C. *Putting Transnational Labour Process in its Place*, Work, Employment and Society 21(1)27-45, March 2007.

[11] CLB, *Wages in China*, clb.org.hk.

[12] Pun N. et al. *The Role of the State...*, Global Labour Journal, 1(1)132-151, 2010.

[13] Pun N. and Lu H. *A Culture of Violence*, The China Journal, No64, July 2010.

[14] Pun, N. *Women Workers* ... Gender & Development, 12(2)29-36 July 2004.

[15] BBC Panorama programme, 18th December, 2014.

[16] Pun, N., and Chan, J. *Global Capital, the State, and Chinese Workers: The Foxconn Experience*, Modern China: 38(4)383–410, 2012.

[17] Economic Observer, 4 May 2012.

[18] Mail Online, 26 June 2010.

[19] Pun, N. *Gender and Class*, International Labour and Working Class History, No81, pp178-181, Spring 2012.

[20] Pun, N., and Lu, H. *Unfinished Proletarianization* ..., Modern China, 36(5)493-519, Sept. 2010.

[21] Pun and Chan, *Global Capital*, … Op. cit.

[22] CLB, *The Workers' Movement in China 2011-2013*, clb.org.hk.

[23] *Dongguan Daily*, 2 Aug, 2011.

[24] Pun, *The Role of the State*... Op. cit.

[25] Yang Su and Xin He, *Street as Courtroom*, Law and Society Review, 44(1)157-184, March 2010.

[26] Burnett, J. *Women's Employment Rights in China*..., Indiana Journal of Global Legal Studies, 17(2)289-318, Summer 2010.

[27] Li Jinhua. Auditor-General of the National Audit Office PRC, Radio Free Asia, 30 September. 2006.

[28] CLB, *No Way Out*, clb.org.hk.

[29] Ibid.

[30] Ching Kwan Lee, *Against the Law: Labour Protest in China*, University of California Press, 2007.

[31] Pun, N. and Xu, Y. *Legal Activism or Class Action?*, China Perspectives, No 2011/2.

[32] Yang Su and Xin He, *Street as Courtroom*, … Op. cit.

[33] Weil, R. *A House Divided: China after 30 Years of 'Reforms'*, Economic and Political Weekly, 43(52)61-69, Dec. 2008.

[34] Ibid.

[35] Blecher, M. *Hegemony and Workers' Politics in China*, The China Quarterly, No. 170 (Jun., 2002), pp. 283-303.

[36] Howell, J. *All-China Federation of Trade Unions beyond Reform?*, The China Quarterly, No196, pp845-863, Dec. 2008.

[37] Ibid.

[38] Mingwei Liu, *Union Organisation in China*, Industrial and Labor Relations Review, 64(1)30-52, Oct 2010.

[39] Ching Kwan Lee, *From the Iron Rice Bowl to Informalization: Markets, State and Workers in a Changing China*. Cornell U.P., 2011.

[40] Mingwei Liu, Op. cit.

[41] Pun and Chan, *Global Capital*, …, Op. cit.

[42] CLB, 24 April 2014, clb.org.hk.

[43] In These Times, 25 June 2015.

[44] Reuters Business News, 7 April 2014.

[45] CLB, 27 July 2015, , clb.org.hk.

[46] Foreign and Commonwealth Office, Op. cit.

[47] Rhomberg, C. *A Turning Point for Chinese Workers?* 02 April 2015.

[48] Economist, *Guangdong Province Pioneers a New Approach to Keeping Workers Happy*, 31 Jan. 2015.

[49] Hong Kong Federation of Trade Unions, *Violence Against Workers in Artigas Factory*, en.hkctu.org.hk.

[50] Chuang, *The Criminalisation of Strikes*, http://chuangcn.org/2015.

[51] Li Liao, et al., *Family Finances in Urban China*, J. Family Economic Issues, Vol 31 pp259-279, 2010.

[52] New York Times, 19 July 2013.

[53] Forbes Magazine, January 2013 and March 2014.

[54] World Bank, *Challenge of High Inequality in China*, Aug 2013.

[55] http//news.xinhuanet.com/English.

[56] Burnett, Op. cit.

[57] Nie, L. et al. *Gender, Family, Socioeconomic Status, and Work Values in China*, Am. Int. J. Soc. Sci. Vol. 3 No. 2; March 2014.

[58] BBC News 17 Oct. 2013.

[59] *People's Daily*, June 2012, quoted in Fincher.

[60] Fincher, L. *Leftover Women*, Zed Books. 2014.

[61] Bienkowski, B. *China's Babies at Risk from Soot, Smog*. Environmental Health News, April 2014.

[62] Fincher, Op. cit.

[63] The Telegraph, 16 March 2013.

[64] Lenin, V. *Speech on Affiliation to the British Labour Party*, May 1920, CW 31: 257-263.

[65] Trotsky, L. *Marxism and Trade Unions*, Plough Press, 1968.

Chapter 17

Workers in Struggle

[1] Pun, N, *Gender and Class*, International Labor and Working Class History, No81, Spring 2012, pp178-181.

[2] Robertson, G and Teitlebaum, E. *Labor Protest in Developing Countries*, American Journal of Political Science, 55(3) 665-677, July 2011.

[3] Martin, J. w.m.com, 2010.

[4] Ibid.

[5] Ibid.

[6] China Daily, 15 August 2015.

[7] Ibid.

[8] CLB, 20 March 2013, clb.org.hk.

[9] The Guardian, 12 June 2014.

[10] Wenfang Tang and Qing Yang, *The Chinese Urban Caste System in Transition* The China Quarterly, No. 196, 2008, pp. 759-779.

[11] CLB, www.clb.hk.

[12] CLB 7 April 2015, clb.org.hk.

[13] Yi Xi, Labornotes, 16 October, 2014.

[14] CLB, 13 Feb, 2015, clb.org.hk.

[15] Yi Xi, Op. cit.

[16] Robertson and Teitlebaum, Op. cit.

[17] Walker, R and Buck, D. *The Chinese Road*, New Left Review 46 July Aug 2007.

[18] Weil, R. *A House Divided: China after 30 Years of 'Reforms'*, Economic and Political Weekly, 43(52)61-69, Dec. 2008.

[19] Ngai, P., et al., *The Role of the State ...* Global Labour Journal 1(1)132-152, 2010.

[20] Mingwei Liu, *Union Organizing in China*, Industrial and Labor Relations Review, 64(1)30-52 Oct. 2010.

[21] Kevin Bai, *China's Crude Steel Capacity and Utilisation Development* 03 June 2015.

[22] BBC News 7 January 2015.

[23] D. Telegraph, 2 May 2014.

[24] Time Magazine, 15 May 2014.

[25] Morley, D. *Chinese Stock Volatility*, 10 July 2015, w.m.com.

[26] Trotsky, L. *The Transitional Programme*, w.m.org.

[27] CLB Report: *Coal Industry in China*, clb.org.hk.

[28] CLB 29 April 2015, clb.org.hk.

[29] CLB 29 September 2015, clb.org.hk.

Chapter 18

Uninterrupted Revolution or Permanent Revolution?

[1] Rodriguez, C. *Lenin and the Colonial Question*, New International, 1(1)93-144, 1983.

[2] Lorimer, D. www.dsp.org.

[3] Roberts, J. *Lenin, Trotsky and the Theory of the Permanent Revolution*, Wellred, 2007, p172-192.

[4] Young, A. *Decline and fall: The US SWP's Final Embrace of Zionism*, Links International, 18 Sept. 2014.

[5] Roberts,Op. cit. p182-183.

[6] Star, J. *Conceptual Foundations of Mao Tse-Tung's Theory of Continuous Revolution*, Asian Survey, 11(6)610-662, June 1971.

[7] Schram, S. *Mao Tse-tung and the Theory of the Permanent Revolution*, The China Quarterly, No. 46 (Apr.-Jun., 1971), pp. 221-244.

[8] Stalin, J. *Foundations of Leninism*, April 1924, w.m.org.

[9] Rousset, P. *The Chinese Revolution*, International Institute for Research and Education, Number 3.

[10] Conlon, B and Hulaki, K. *Nepal: A Revolution Adrift*, 2013, w.m.com.

[11] Lenin, V. *From a Publicist's Diary., From a Publicist's Diary* Aug 1917, CW 25:278-286.

[12] Report of 6th Session, Baku Congress of the Peoples' of the East, September 1920, www.marxists.org.

[13] Trotsky, L. *Revolution Betrayed*, Ch9, w.m.org.

[14] Grant, T. *The Unbroken Thread*, Fortress Books, p282-288 and 345.

[15] Bloomberg News, 5 March 2015.

Index

More Titles

Bolshevism: The Road to Revolution

by Alan Woods

Ted Grant Writings: Volumes 1-2

by Ted Grant

Reason in Revolt

by Alan Woods and Ted Grant

Reformism and Revolution

by Alan Woods

Kashmir's Ordeal

by Lal Khan

Dialectics of Nature

by Frederick Engels

Coming Soon

Where Is Britain Going?

by Leon Trotsky

Ireland: Republicanism and Revolution

by Alan Woods

The Selected Works of James Connolly

by James Connolly

Stalin: An Appraisal of the Man and His Influence

by Leon Trotsky

Ted Grant Writings: Volume Three

by Ted Grant

Lightning Source UK Ltd.
Milton Keynes UK
UKOW06f2224220116

266955UK00001B/1/P